*Oracle Press*™

# Effective Oracle by Design

Oracle Press™

# Effective Oracle
# by Design

Thomas Kyte

**McGraw-Hill**/Osborne

New York  Chicago  San Francisco
Lisbon  London  Madrid  Mexico City
Milan  New Delhi  San Juan
Seoul  Singapore  Sydney  Toronto

*The McGraw·Hill Companies*

**McGraw-Hill**/Osborne
2100 Powell Street, 10th Floor
Emeryville, California 94608
U.S.A.

To arrange bulk purchase discounts for sales promotions, premiums, or fund-raisers, please contact **McGraw-Hill/Osborne** at the above address. For information on translations or book distributors outside the U.S.A., please see the International Contact Information page immediately following the index of this book.

## Effective Oracle by Design

890 DOC DOC 019

ISBN 0-07-223065-7

**Publisher**
   Brandon A. Nordin

**Vice President & Associate Publisher**
   Scott Rogers

**Acquisitions Editor**
   Lisa McClain

**Project Editor**
   Monika Faltiss

**Acquisitions Coordinator**
   Athena Honore

**Technical Editors**
   Anjo Kolk

   Jonathan Lewis

   Connor McDonald

   Mogens Nørgaard

   Mark A. Williams

**Copy Editor**
   Marilyn Smith

**Proofreader**
   Claire Splan

**Indexer**
   Irv Hershman

**Composition**
   Tabitha M. Cagan, Tara Davis

**Illustrators**
   Kathleen Edwards, Melinda Lytle, Lyssa Wald

**Series Design**
   Jani Beckwith, Peter F. Hancik

**Cover Series Design**
   Damore Johann Design, Inc.

This book was composed with Corel VENTURA™ Publisher.

# About the Author

Although I've been working for Oracle since version 7.0.9 (that's 1993 for people who don't mark time by Oracle versions), I've been working *with* Oracle since version 5.1.5c (a $99 single-user version for DOS that came on 360K floppy disks). Before starting at Oracle, I worked for over six years as a systems integrator building large-scale, heterogeneous databases and applications, mostly for military and government customers. These days, I spend a great deal of time working with the Oracle database and, more specifically, working with *people* who are working with the Oracle database. I interact directly with customers, specifying and building their systems or, more frequently, helping them rebuild (or tune) them. In addition, I am the Tom behind the "AskTom" column in *Oracle Magazine*, answering people's questions about the Oracle database and its tools. On a typical day, I receive and answer 30 to 40 questions at http://asktom.oracle.com/. Then, every two months, I publish a special "best of" installment in the magazine (all of the questions are available on the Web, and are stored, naturally enough, in an Oracle database). As I mentioned earlier, I'm also the author of *Expert One on One Oracle* (Wrox Press, 2001), a book about general use of the database and how to develop successful Oracle applications.

Basically, I spend a lot of time helping people be successful with the Oracle database. During free moments, I build applications and develop software within Oracle Corporation itself.

# About the Tech Editors

Connor McDonald has 11 years of Oracle expertise specializing in performance tuning ranging from Oracle 6 to Oracle 10. In 2002, he won the worldwide BMC SmartDBA competition, and was voted one of the best speakers at the annual U.K. Oracle conference. Like Tom, he is a member of the OakTable network—a collection of approximately 40 world professionals with a passion for getting the best out of the Oracle database.

Mogens Nørgaard was the first Oracle Support manager to standardize his group's performance optimization methods exclusively upon Oracle's response time statistics. He is one of the original founders of the OakTable Network, a founder of Miracle A/S, and is a frequent contributor to the Oracle-L list server.

Anjo Kolk, Chief Oracle Technologist, Precise Software Solutions, Inc., has over 16 years of Oracle experience. He has partnered with ISVs and customers all over the world to improve the implementation and performance of their systems. Drawing on this experience, Anjo developed a tuning methodology called YAPP (Yet Another Performance Profiling methodology) that is currently used by the oraperf.com web site.

Jonathan Lewis is known internationally as the author of *Practical Oracle 8i Building Efficient Databases* (Addison Wesley, 2001) and as the presenter of the seminar *Optimising Oracle – Performance by Design*. He is one of the leading independent specialists in the U.K., with more than 17 years experience designing, implementing, and troubleshooting Oracle-based systems.

Mark A. Williams is a production DBA in Indianapolis, where he lives with his wife Lynda and their two children, David and Elizabeth. He holds Oracle Certified Professional credentials as an Oracle Certified DBA for Oracle7, Oracle8, Oracle8i, and Oracle9i. He has been working with Oracle since release 7.0.1.16 of the database, and is an avid advocate of both Oracle the product and the company. He would like to thank Tom for providing such great material to work with.

# Contents

# Acknowledgments

I am indebted to many people for their help in completing this book. I work with the best and brightest at Oracle and each contributed to this project in one way or another.

First, I'd like to thank the book's technical reviewers—in particular, Jonathan Lewis, Connor McDonald, Mogens Nørgaard, Anjo Kolk, and Mark Williams. Their insightful and brutally honest comments made this a much better book.

I want to extend a thank you to my coworkers as well for their support during this book-writing ordeal. It took much more time and energy than I ever imagined, and I appreciate their flexibility.

I'd also like to acknowledge Oracle users everywhere. Much of what I wrote about here arose directly from their excellent queries. In the book, you'll see this clearly, as I've used many of their questions to frame particular discussions.

Lastly, but most importantly, I would like to acknowledge my family's continual support. Without the enthusiasm of my wife Lori, son Alan, and daughter Megan, I'm not sure I could have ever finished this book.

# Introduction

The target audience of this book is the Oracle development team—the group that has 100 percent control of the overall performance of the system. This team includes the data modelers, the developers, and the DBA staff. This is contrary to the popular myth that the DBA is responsible for every aspect of an application's performance and has complete control over it. The best way to understand the fallacies surrounding this old view is to use the analogy of a car race. The DBA is the pit-stop guy who changes the tires, makes sure the engine is gassed up, and that the car functions. If you give this pit-stop guy (DBA) a Lincoln Navigator (a truly huge truck) and tell him you want to race the Indy 500 with it, what will happen? The DBA can make sure the truck runs as fast as it can but he cannot affect the performance of the truck on a tight corner at 100+ miles per hour. There is really very little he can do once the car has been designed and built (short of throwing it out and starting over—the car is the application here).

The primary audience for this book is the Oracle development team that's not quite sure how to approach designing and building a scalable system using Oracle that performs. This is not a beginner's book. It's for the Oracle developer who already knows how to enter SQL statements, use SQL*Plus, and so on. It will not teach you SQL; it will teach you the things you need to know to write "good" SQL. It will not teach you how to code an application; it will teach you the things you need to know to write a "good" Oracle-based application.

I'll use yet another analogy to describe how this book will present information. Pretend for a moment that the developer is instead a physician and the application is the patient. There are many types of MDs:

- **The emergency room (ER) doctor**   These physicians do "triage," separating the hopeless patients from those that can be helped, performing quick-fixes along the way to keep patients alive as long as possible. They will take a heart-attack patient with a history of smoking, bad diet, and no exercise and stabilize their condition.

- **The operating room (OR) doctor**   The OR physician gets the patient after they've gone through triage and after the ER doctor has temporarily patched them up. The OR doctor strives for long-term fixes to keep the patient not only alive but functioning as well as possible. They perform the by-pass operation on the heart attack victim, attempting to clear the arteries.

- **The physical therapist (PT)**   The PT gets the patient when the OR doctor is through and begins the long and painful (not to mention expensive) process of rehabilitation.

- **The preventative medicine doctor** These physicians strive to avoid the preceding three doctors at all costs. They counsel the patient to quit smoking, eat a healthy diet, and exercise, developing a multistep program to get them in shape. If they do their job right, barring unfortunate incidents (like a car accident), the patient will never see the ER, OR, or PT doctors.

Now, the world needs all types of doctors—after all, accidents do happen. But perhaps the most important M.D. is that last one, the preventative medicine doctor, who attempts to keep his patient from needing the other three.

It is my belief (experience) that most people, and books, approach tuning with the mindset of the first three doctor types I mentioned. They believe strongly in the "hero" developer—the ER or OR doctor. Perhaps because of this, good design and implementation typically seems a thankless exercise. The ER and OR docs, meanwhile, get all the fame, snatching the patient from the brink of death (and thus saving the system by doing something miraculous). They get called in at the last moment; slave to keep the patient alive, and are handsomely paid as well. The physical therapists, on the other hand, are the unlucky souls who get the system after the ER/OR doctor has patched it up, and are thus tasked with the responsibility of keeping it going.

I'm well-equipped to speak from the ER perspective since I am, in fact, one of those "heroes" who are often called in to "lay hands on" systems and make them better. I could have written that book—indeed, I've been told I *should* write that book—but I didn't.

What *is* missing, however, is the comprehensive approach that includes the preventative medicine doctor training. There are some books out there that cover it though—my favorites being Guy Harrison's *Oracle SQL High Performance Tuning*, 2$^{nd}$ Edition (Prentice Hall, 2001) and Jonathan Lewis's *Practical Oracle 8i Building Efficient Databases* (Addison Wesley, 2001). These books, including my own, *Expert One on One Oracle*, (Wrox Press, 2001) work to remove the need for the hero. Remember, firefighters are heroes when they do their job—we all just hope *we* never need them personally!

Instead, this book acts as a mentor to the reader, providing an overall structure and approach to performance tuning that includes discussions about:

- Tuning before you start designing

- Designing with specific performance goals in mind and continuously testing towards them

- Trial and error (making sure each item works as advertised, and knowing your software; many performance issues are directly related to not understanding how the database software actually works)

- Real-life accidents. We'll also look at the ER/OR doctor roles, but this isn't one of the book's end-all goals. After all, the knowledge you learn as a preventative medicine doctor should help limit the roles of those more colorful M.D.s.

Whereas most books focus totally on being a hero, this one concentrates on becoming a solid producer of quality output. Rather than dwelling on fixing a broken system, it focuses on building systems that do not break. After all, over time, it's the person who does this (builds systems that don't break) who's seen as the real hero.

# CHAPTER
1

## The Right Approach to Building Applications

I n this chapter, we will look at some of the "softer" issues regarding Oracle best practices. These issues pertain to system design, development, testing, deployment, and maintenance. They are not really Oracle-specific, but they are approached from an Oracle perspective. Each of these items would be relevant in virtually every system, regardless of the software or even the goal (what you were trying to build).

This will be the least technical of all of the chapters in this book. Nevertheless, it may be the most important one. Time after time, the mistakes I see being made are more procedural than technical in nature. Here are a few examples:

- The tendency to put up walls between developers and database administrators (DBAs). I'll examine the potential consequences of this and offer advice to help make the relationship more productive for everyone involved.

- The decision that a testing environment is too costly. On the contrary, not having one is far more expensive in the long run.

- The failure to fully exploit what the database has to offer. This can be due to ignorance; or it can stem from a desire to remain database-independent; or it can be related to fear, uncertainty, and doubt what I call FUD. In any case, it often leads to applications that take longer than necessary to develop and that don't perform up to the developer's expectations.

These and related topics are the focus of this chapter.

# It's a Team Effort

Team effort really has nothing to do with technology or software. This is all about human interaction. Let's face it: Many of the issues we encounter during software development have more to do with politics than they have to do with technology. I cannot tell you how many times I've seen development efforts thwarted by policy, procedure, and politics, rather than stymied by some technical challenge.

Too often, the relationship between database development team members and the DBA staff members that support them is characterized by a heavy-duty "us versus them" mentality. In such an atmosphere, DBAs often feel a need to protect the database from the developer. On the other hand, developers feel that they must thwart the DBA in order to implement features in the way they desire. At times, trying to get these two groups to work together, I've felt more like a marriage counselor than an onsite database expert!

What we really must remember is that teamwork is a two-way street. Developers often feel that DBAs impose too much of a burden on them to prove why they need a certain privilege or why they need a certain feature enabled. In fact, this is often a reasonable request. The granting of database privileges should be done with care and thought. There is nothing wrong with a DBA requesting that a developer document why he needs, for example, the CREATE VIEW privilege granted directly to his development account (we'll take a deeper look at this in a moment). On the other hand, it is unreasonable for a DBA to assume *carte blanche* authority to outlaw certain database features, such as database views, stored procedures, or triggers.

Here is just one example of such attitudes in action (taken from my AskTom web site):

"Stored procedures—are they evil?

What are the drawbacks of using stored procedures? Is there any overhead? I am a novice Oracle DBA. I have been asked by one of the SQL programmers to authorize him with the CREATE PROCEDURE system privilege on an ORACLE user..."

In my answer, I explained the overwhelming benefits of stored procedures. I pointed out how they can help the DBA tune the applications (without having to dive into the application). I emphasized that stored procedures are a great security mechanism, a performance enhancement tool, and an awesome programming device. I advised the DBA to permit the use of stored procedures. I suggested that developers could do as much, if not more, damage by putting bad SQL in their client applications. Furthermore, I pointed out that if the SQL were in stored procedures, at least the DBA could reasonably inspect it and help to tune it and manage it.

The follow-up responses were extremely polarized, demonstrating the existence of a chasm between the development and DBA camps. The attitude of the DBAs was, "It's my job to protect the database." The attitude of the developers was, "It's my job to code, and it's their job to let me do that." One developer expressed the opinion that it's the DBA's job to review every line of code that goes into the database. A DBA rejected this, saying that it was, in fact, the developer's job to do that. And so the argument went on.

In reality, it would be impossible for the DBA to inspect and review each line of code going into the database, forgetting for the moment that a DBA isn't a developer in general and wouldn't necessarily understand what they were even looking at if they did review the source code.

Clearly, the DBA staff and the development staff often feel that they have totally different objectives, but this is not the case. The DBA doesn't work just to protect the database, but neither does the DBA work solely to serve the developer.

Much like an overprotective parent, a DBA who takes the "protect the database from the developers" mindset will not be productive. On the other hand, the developer isn't programmed to thwart the DBA (contrary to popular DBA lore). Developers have a job to do and are just trying to do it. Their shared objective is to build a functional database application that meets the end users' requirements, performs well, scales as required, is maintainable, and was developed in as cost-effective a manner as possible. Unless the two teams work together toward this common goal, the chances for success are severely curtailed. If there is a virtual wall, or even worse, a physical wall between the two teams, many of these goals cannot be realized.

## DBA and Developer Roles

Typically, the DBA knows more than the developer about the database and how it works, and the developer knows more than the DBA about software development. This is a natural outcome of their job descriptions.

DBAs are generally responsible for understanding the database architecture, how to patch the database, and how it works. They would not be able to craft a successful backup and recovery procedure (for example, if they did not have this knowledge) as an intimate understanding of the Oracle architecture is needed to accomplish that particular task. If the DBA didn't understand the architectural relationship between database control files, datafiles, and redo logs, they would invariably make mistakes during the backup and recovery process. The DBA lives to work with the database.

Developers are generally programmers/analysts who see the database as just another tool—something that must be used to achieve an end. In many cases, they spend much of their time doing "nondatabase" work, such as interface design.

What we need here is some cross-pollination. If the two teams can work together, then gradually, the developers will know more about how the database works, and the DBAs will be in a much better position to help facilitate their development processes.

I've drawn up two lists of do and don't advice—one list for DBAs and one for developers—that will be helpful in closing out this section. This advice addresses some of the more damaging attitudes that exist.

## DBA Dos and Don'ts

DBAs, do not consider that your primary job is to protect the database from the evil developers. The database is their tool, and you can and should counsel them on how best to use it, rather than attempt to protect it from them. Do not consider the developer your enemy.

Also, do not outlaw a feature or function without proper justification. Too often, these decisions are based on fear and uncertainty, or on that one bad experience. The following are some common restrictions:

- **No views allowed.** The reasoning behind this is usually that a DBA once experienced bad performance with a view and, therefore, views must be evil. If you applied such reasoning consistently, you would end up outlawing SQL when you came across a poorly performing query.

- **No stored procedures allowed.** This one really confuses me, since a DBA should optimally want everything in a stored procedure. If this were the case, they would know exactly what module depended on what database object. They would be able to easily tune a poorly performing module if the problem was SQL-based (just read the code from the data dictionary and play with the SQL). Try having a DBA tune a Java 2 Enterprise Edition (J2EE) application some day, since they are *not* developers, they do not program using J2EE, they would not know where to begin. If the database portion of the application is in the database, tuning the database access becomes easy.

- **No features added after version 6 allowed.** This is common among old-time DBAs, who are leery of anything new—PL/SQL, triggers, application contexts, fine-grained auditing, fine-grained access control, and so on. All they want is keyed reads into the database (if they could only outlaw joins!). My suspicion here is this is a DBA who wants as little responsibility for anything at all. If all the developers do are simple Data Manipulation Language (DML) statements, the DBA's job is trivial. But the company as a whole loses, since it paid a lot of money for this database stuff but cannot use it.

■   No adoption of new features for *N* releases. The idea behind this is to let everyone else deal with any problems with this feature; we'll use it in three or four years. The problem is that for those three or four years, you could be missing out on the greatest thing since sliced bread—a feature that could save you hours or days of effort (hence, money). Locally managed tablespaces (introduced in Oracle8i, Release 1) come to mind as the classic example. This good feature had many positive benefits, yet many DBAs outlawed it. The reasons were never technical; they were all FUD (fear, uncertainty, doubt)-based.

"I read about the advantages of locally managed tablespaces and asked my senior DBA if, for the new data warehouse initiative, we could change tablespaces to locally managed. He says that there are performance issues with locally managed tablespaces…"

The DBA was right, there are performance issues, but they are all *positive.* The tablespaces the DBA was using (dictionary-managed) are the ones that have negative performance issues. Lack of correct information leads to rejection of new features.

On the other hand, don't get sucked into "feature obsession," when a feature or function is deemed so unique and so cool that you feel compelled to use it. For example, consider Extensible Markup Language (XML) functionality in the database. Just because it is there doesn't mean everything should be stored in XML. It is just as easy to get carried away with a feature as it is to ignore it.

Here are some dos for DBAs:

■   Do consider the developer as someone you can teach and to whom you can pass on your database knowledge. You will find that, over time, that pesky developer actually wants to do the right thing. If you teach people the right way—better yet, teach them how to discover for themselves the right way—they will use it. People want to do the right thing, but they are starved for information. Spread your knowledge around.

■   Do evaluate and test new features as they come out. Do not dismiss them out of hand. Do not let one bad experience with a feature cause you to dismiss it entirely. Everything has a time and place; every feature is there for a reason. Perhaps (most likely) the bad experience was due to an inappropriate application of the technology. A hammer is a really good tool for nailing down things down, but it is horrible tool to use to screw in things.

■   Do back up your policy and procedures with factual evidence. Never be in the position of saying "I've heard they were slow," or "I've heard there were bugs." Hearsay isn't admissible in court, and it shouldn't be admissible here. This is just like believing all of those performance-tuning myths that abound, such as "If you have a 99.9% cache hit ratio, your job is done," or "A table should be in one extent." In this book, I will present factual evidence to back up my assertions. You should expect no less from anyone else (yourself included!)

### Developer Dos and Don'ts

To the developers, I say this:

- Do not try to work around the DBAs; work with them. If you present a factually correct and compelling argument, odds are they will listen. It is when you try to do whatever you want, without involving them, that they start locking you out entirely. You become that loose cannon—something to rightly fear.

- Do not assume that the DBAs are working against you. In most cases, the policies and procedures in place are there for a reason. Work to change the rules you don't agree with, but don't try to subvert them (loose cannon syndrome again).

- Do ask the DBAs to tell you why. If you suggested the use of locally managed tablespaces, but the senior DBA said no because of "performance issues," ask that senior DBA for those performance-related references. Explain that you want to learn why locally managed tablespaces have these bad performance characteristics (they don't, by the way).

- Do make sure you know what you are talking about. Otherwise, you'll instantly lose credibility. Use the scientific method: Start with a hypothesis. Construct a test to prove (or equally as often disprove) the hypothesis. Make sure the test is general enough (broad enough) to prove the point and is reproducible. Have others reproduce it. Prepare the results and have others critique it. In that fashion, you'll have a very solid leg to stand on when describing why your approach is correct.

In short, I believe the DBA and development team need to work together as a whole. They should sit together and converse, meeting on a regular basis. They should not be considered two independent divisions that just throw work to each other over a wall. The "them versus us" mentality will prohibit a fast, reliable, available system. Rather than have development teams and DBA teams in separate areas, it makes more sense to have a unified team of developers and DBAs who can take advantage of each other's specialized knowledge.

# Read the Documentation

The Oracle database comes with more than 100 manuals (108 with Oracle9i Release 2). There are over 46,000 pages of text. It can be quite intimidating trying to figure out where to begin. In fact, many people are so intimidated by so much documentation that they pretend it doesn't exist. In reality, it is really quite simple to figure out where to begin once you are told, and that is what this section is all about. First, we will go over the key pieces of documentation, and then I'll suggest just what should be considered mandatory reading.

"I have learned a lot from your site. One point that you constantly bring up that wasn't getting through my thick head though was READ THE CONCEPTS GUIDE. So, over the past couple of weeks, I put a copy of the PDF version on my laptop and worked my way through it. I am very glad that I did (a reread is coming soon)! Many things I didn't understand are clear now, and being a consultant who works with a lot of other developers and DBAs, I now know most all of you have not read this either."

That is the best testimonial I could ever have hoped for. I frequently get questions that start with, "Please don't point me to the documentation." This is a request that I almost always ignore, because often their question is elegantly answered in the documentation. I frequently begin an answer with, "Well, the handy-dandy *Concepts Guide* has this to say on the topic...." I have been known to say more than once that if you simply read the *Concepts Guide* from cover to cover and retain just 10% of what it contains, you'll already know 90% more than most people do about Oracle and how it works. And, in the future, when a problem comes up, you can say, "I remember something about that. Let's look in the *Concepts Guide* for a solution."

# A Guide to the Guides

Given that there are more than 100 pieces of documentation, the road maps I suggest after this guide to the guides are surprisingly terse. The guides summarized here are the ones you should hit from cover to cover (precisely which ones depends on whether you are a developer or a DBA). The remaining documentation can serve as reference material, depending on your needs and interests.

## The Concepts Guide

The *Concepts Guide* is the one piece of Oracle documentation that I make a point to read with each major release of the database. It contains a wealth of information on topics such as:

- **What is Oracle?** An introduction to the database, memory structures, distributed database, concurrency controls, data consistency, security, administration, and other topics.

- **Database structures** An in-depth look at how things are stored. The who, what, where, when, and why of database blocks, extents, segments, tablespaces, and more.

- **The Oracle instance** What an instance of Oracle is: startup, shutdown processing, how applications interact with an Oracle instance, what the memory and process architecture look like, and how database resources are managed.

- **Data** An overview of the entire set of schema objects (such as tables, views, indexes, and so on), all the options available with each type of object, and all the datatypes— both native and user-defined.

- **Data access** SQL, PL/SQL, and Java interactions with the database, how dependencies are managed and maintained between schema objects, and transaction management and triggers.

- **Parallel operations** The hows and whens of parallel operations including parallel query, parallel DML, parallel operations for administration, and so on.

- **Data protection** Perhaps one of the most important sections, it covers topics such as how concurrency and consistency work in Oracle, how and when is data integrity enforced, how security fits into all of this, and what is available to protect data. It also explains how to use privileges and roles, as well as how to audit what is happening.

One of the nice attributes of the *Concepts Guide* (besides being totally free) is that it acts as a readable "index" to the rest of the documentation. Frequently, topics end with "See Also" links that point to the other pieces of Oracle documentation for all of the gory details. The *Concepts Guide* is a high-level overview, the metadata document for the rest of the documentation. As you read through it, you will be naturally guided to the other relevant pieces of Oracle documentation. You will follow your interests and drill down over time.

## New Features Guide

If you don't know something exists, you'll never be able to use it, right? The *New Features Guide* is a comprehensive guide to the new features, by release, for the past couple of releases. For each feature, the guide includes a terse explanation, along with a pointer to where you can find more details. It also includes a list of "what's included" in each of the flavors of Oracle (Personal, Standard, and Enterprise). This matrix will save you much frustration if you are designing a system to run on the Standard Edition of Oracle, because the features available to you are clearly listed. In Oracle8i and before, this guide was titled *Getting to Know*.

Additionally, the beginning of most documents now contain a "What's New In" section as well. The *New Features Guide* presents most new features including administrative, development, performance, scalability, availability or whatever. The individual documents present a more focused list of "What's New." For example, the Administrators Guide will have a "What's New in Administration" section whereas the Application Developers Guide will have a "What's New in Application Development" section.

## Application Developers Guide

There are actually quite a few guides that start with *Application Developers Guide* for various Oracle features, such as Advanced Queuing (messaging software), LOBs (Large Objects), Object Relational Features, and Workspace Management. Recommended reading for all developers is the *Fundamentals* guide. This comprehensive guide takes you through topics such as the following:

- Understanding the various programmatic environments you can access

- Designing your database schemas

- Maintaining data integrity via constraints

- How to begin indexing your data—what to consider, how SQL statements are processed by the engine, using dynamic SQL, using PL/SQL, implementing security, and so on

Whereas the *Concepts Guide* explains the existence of these features, the *Application Developers Guide* explains how to exploit them.

## PL/SQL Users Guide and Reference

PL/SQL is one of the single most important languages developers have access to when developing against Oracle. A good understanding of what it can and cannot do for you is vital. The *PL/SQL Users Guide and Reference* covers the fundamentals of PL/SQL, error handling, syntax, packages/procedures, and many other PL/SQL-related topics.

## Performance Tuning Guide and Reference

One of my favorite and most frequently referenced guides on a day-to-day basis is the *Performance Tuning Guide and Reference* (called the *Designing and Tuning for Performance Guide* in Oracle8i and earlier). The first half is geared toward developers. It describes how the optimizer actually works, how to gather statistics correctly, how the different physical structures work and when they are best used (for example, when an index-organized table is a good thing). Most important, it fully documents the basic tools you need to use: Explain Plan, SQL_TRACE, TKPROF, Autotrace, and even Statspack!

While the first half of this book is relevant to DBAs as well as to developers, the second half of the book is all about the work of DBAs. It covers topics such as building a database for performance, memory configuration, understanding operating system interactions and resource usage, configuring shared servers and dedicated servers, how to gather statistics, how and when to use performance views, and how to use other performance tools. This is a must read—before you begin tuning and before you begin implementing. Even if you have been working with Oracle for 100 years, you will find something new and useful in here.

## Backup and Recovery Concepts

If there is one thing a DBA is not allowed to mess up *ever,* it is backup and recovery. Even if you are using a tool to automate backups, and even if you think you know it all, read the *Backup and Recovery Concepts Guide.* A solid, core understanding of how backup and recovery works will never be something you regret having.

Reading the RMAN guide isn't enough. I know this based on the number of questions I get from people who just read that and don't understand why they cannot fully recover after restoring last week's control files. They are missing that basic understanding of how the files work with each other and what needs to be restored given the current situation. Unless you want to cost your company thousands of dollars (or probably more), read the *Backup and Recovery Concepts Guide.* And if you don't understand something in it, read it again and again until you do. Then test it out; try out your knowledge. You don't want to discover the day of recovery that your knowledge isn't up to par with reality.

## Recovery Manager Reference

The *Recovery Manager Reference* talks about the tool you want to be using to back up your database. Forget the old scripts and lose `tar`, `cpio`, `dd`, and `ocopy`. RMAN is the bookkeeper you always wanted. Its features—block-level, in-place recovery, backup retention policies, hot backups, and more—make learning this tool 100% worth your while.

## Administrators Guide

Yes, I know DBAs are already administrators, but you will still learn something you didn't know by reading the *Administrators Guide.* This is where you might discover for the first time that there is a resource manager inside the database (new in 8i; enhanced in 9i). Or, you might learn about fine-grained auditing, new in Oracle9i. I bet that if you read this guide, you will learn something new.

Some new features of Oracle with regard to administering the database are to be found only in this document. These are the features deemed "not general enough" to make it into the *New Features Guide.* Additionally, all of the new features relevant to database administration are listed here, without being intermingled and obscured by other new features.

## Road Maps to Reading

Here, I present road maps—suggested sets of mandatory reading. I offer three sets: one for everyone, one for people who consider themselves DBAs, and one for people who consider themselves developers.

### Required Reading for Both Developers and DBAs

For both groups, to be read with each and every new release, we have:

- *Concepts Guide*
- *New Features Guide*

### Required Reading for Developers

For developers, continue your reading with:

- *Application Developers Guide (Fundamentals)*
- *PL/SQL Users Guide and Reference*
- *Performance Tuning Guide and Reference* (*Designing and Tuning for Performance Guide* in 8i and earlier)

As noted earlier, developers should be sure to read the first half of the *Performance Tuning Guide and Reference*, and look over the other sections at your leisure. As a prequel to this guide in Oracle9i and later, consider looking at the *Performance Method* (9i Release 1) or *Performance Planning* (9i Release 2) reference. This guide, weighing in at a very light 60 pages, describes the topics you need to understand in order to be successful, such as scalability, system architecture, application design principles, and so on.

### Required Reading for DBAs

After the *Concepts Guide* and *New Features Guide*, DBAs should continue with:

- *Backup and Recovery Concepts*
- *Recovery Manager Reference*
- *Backup and Recovery Concepts* (No, this isn't a typo. Yes, I put it in here twice. It really is that crucial. It is the one thing you are not allowed to get wrong. It is also the thing that DBAs get wrong the most. Just read it and understand it. You won't regret it.)
- *Administrators Guide*
- *Performance Tuning Guide and Reference* (with special attention to the second half)

### Recommended Reading

After reading the guides listed in the previous sections, it is a matter of what interests you.
Are you a developer with a need to do XML processing? Well, there are no fewer than three XML guides available. Are you interested in the Java capabilities? There are guides on this topic as well.

Are you a DBA who needs to understand how to set up and configure a failover environment? The manuals have that covered as well.

As you dive into and actually read the documentation, you'll find it is really pretty good. I'm not saying that just because I work for Oracle, rather I'm saying that because most of what I know about Oracle today comes from these very documents. I really do read that *Concepts Guide*. The way I put together things like a "new features seminar" is to dig into the *New Features Guide*. I encourage you to go to http://otn.oracle.com and click the documentation link. It's all there, just waiting to be read.

# Avoid the Black Box Syndrome

Without a fundamental knowledge of the Oracle database and how it works, it is very easy and common for developers to adopt an approach that is flawed or just plain wrong. Many times, people approach the database as if it were a black box—a commodity as interchangeable as a battery in a radio. According to this approach, you use the database, but you avoid, at all costs, doing anything that would make you database-dependent, as if that were a bad thing. In the name of database independence, you will refuse to use the features of the database, to exploit its capabilities. You actually choose to write off, to not use, most of the functionality that you or your customers have paid for. It means you have chosen to take the path of do-it-yourself— to write more code than you need to maintain and to take longer to get to market.

For a company that has decided to use a particular database, the decision to develop more code that must be maintained and to take longer to get to market must not be taken lightly. It costs money, both in real, measurable terms (you are taking longer to develop the same functionality, and they must pay you) and in softer terms of lost opportunity.

## Database Independence versus Database Dependence

Here is something that you might find controversial: Database dependence (regardless of the database you are using; this does not apply to just Oracle) should be your goal, not something you avoid. You want to maximize your investment in your database. You want to develop the best software in the least amount of time against that database. The only way to do that is to fully exploit what the database has to offer.

The truth is that, with the exception of trivial applications, achieving database independence is not only extremely hard, but it is also extremely costly and consumes a huge amount of resources. Yes, perhaps a simple report could be database-independent. But could this be the case with a scalable transaction system? No, not unless you take the approach of companies like PeopleSoft or SAP, and do it on the same scale as they do. Like the products of those companies, your application would not use SQL beyond simple "keyed reads" (sort of like a VSAM file on a mainframe would be used, a file read by a key only—no joins, no analysis, just keyed reads). You would not use any vendor extensions, nor most ANSI SQL functions, since not all vendors have implemented them. You would not be using the database for concurrency controls (since they all do it differently). You would not be using the database for analytics (again, because they all do it differently). In practice, you would end up writing your own database. In fact, SAP did just that: wrote its own database!

So, unless you are making a product that will actually ship on many different databases as off-the-shelf software, database independence isn't a goal you want to achieve. In reality, most software is built to run in-house against a corporate, standard database. The need for database independence is questionable at best in these circumstances. Getting applications built, getting them built quickly, and getting them built with as few lines of code as possible for maintenance—those are the goals you want to satisfy. Working to stay database-independent or, even worse, just ignoring (either purposely or due to lack of knowledge) the capabilities of your database, is not a laudable goal.

The best way to achieve some level of application portability across multiple databases would be to code all of the database components of your applications in stored procedures. Now that may sound counterintuitive. If we code in stored procedures, and every vendor has its own language, won't we be tied to that vendor? Yes and no. The visual component of your application is safe. The application logic—the logic that falls outside the data logic—is safe. The data logic is encoded in the way that is best for the database on which you are executing. Since it is hidden in a stored procedure, you can make use of—in fact, would almost be forced to make use of—every vendor extension and feature you could in order to have the best data layer. (We'll go over an example of this soon.)

Once developed and deployed, the application stays deployed on that database forever. If it is moved to another database, that move is typically done in combination with a rework of the application itself, as a major upgrade with new features and functions. It is not a simple port.

## Dangers of Black Box Syndrome

Here are the reasons why you should not treat the database as a generic black box:

- **Inability to get the correct answer**   Concurrency controls are major differentiators between the databases. Applications will get different results given the same exact inputs, in the same exact order, depending on the database it was run against.

- **Inability to perform**   Your performance will be a fraction of what it could and should be.

- **Inability to quickly deliver software**   You spend large amounts of time "doing it yourself."

- **Inability to maximize your investment**   You spent large amounts of money on this database software; use it. Ironically, the reason people sometimes change vendors is because one does not appear to perform well enough, but the reason for this poor performance is that they didn't use the vendor-specific features in the first place!

These are not listed in any order. Depending on who you are, different points will mean different things. Let's take a look at some examples.

### Inability to Perform

Suppose you were developing an application that had a requirement to show an employee hierarchy or a BOM (bill of material) hierarchy. In Oracle, showing almost any hierarchy is achieved via the CONNECT BY statement in SQL. The most efficient, effective way to accomplish this goal would be something similar to the following (using the standard Oracle SCOTT.EMP table):

```
scott@ORA920.US.ORACLE.COM> select rpad('*',2*level,'*') || ename ename
  2  from emp
  3  start with mgr is null
  4  connect by prior empno = mgr
  5  /
```

```
ENAME
-----------------------------
**KING
****JONES
******SCOTT
*******ADAMS
******FORD
********SMITH
****BLAKE
******ALLEN
******WARD
******MARTIN
******TURNER
******JAMES
****CLARK
******MILLER

14 rows selected.
```

CONNECT BY is not ubiquitous. Many databases do not support this syntax. With other databases, you might need to write some procedural logic and populate a temporary table with the results. You could do that in Oracle as well, but why? It would be slower, it would consume more resources, and it would be the wrong way to do it. Rather, you should do things the right way. In this case, use the CONNECT BY construct and "hide" it in a stored procedure. In this way, you can implement it differently in another database, such as Microsoft SQL Server, if and when the need ever arises (this is rare, in my experience).

Let's take this a step further. Suppose that you need to return a result set that displays employee information, including the employee name, department, and salary. You also want a running total of the salary by department and the percentage the employee salary represents by department and in total (for example, employee X in department Y makes 10% of the total salary in her department and 1% of the total salaries in the company). The right way to do this in Oracle is to use analytic functions, as follows:

```
scott@ORA920.US.ORACLE.COM> column pct_dept format 99.9
scott@ORA920.US.ORACLE.COM> column pct_overall format 99.9
scott@ORA920.US.ORACLE.COM> break on deptno skip 1

scott@ORA920.US.ORACLE.COM> select deptno,
  2          ename,
  3          sal,
  4          sum(sal) over (partition by deptno order by sal,ename) cum_sal,
  5          round(100*ratio_to_report(sal)
  6              over (partition by deptno), 1 ) pct_dept,
  7          round(100*ratio_to_report(sal) over () , 1 ) pct_overall
  8    from emp
  9   order by deptno, sal
 10   /
```

```
   DEPTNO ENAME           SAL    CUM_SAL PCT_DEPT PCT_OVERALL
---------- ---------- ---------- ---------- -------- -----------
       10 MILLER          1300       1300     14.9         4.5
          CLARK           2450       3750     28.0         8.4
          KING            5000       8750     57.1        17.2

       20 SMITH            800        800      7.4         2.8
          ADAMS           1100       1900     10.1         3.8
          JONES           2975       4875     27.4        10.2
          FORD            3000       7875     27.6        10.3
          SCOTT           3000      10875     27.6        10.3

       30 JAMES            950        950     10.1         3.3
          MARTIN          1250       2200     13.3         4.3
          WARD            1250       3450     13.3         4.3
          TURNER          1500       4950     16.0         5.2
          ALLEN           1600       6550     17.0         5.5
          BLAKE           2850       9400     30.3         9.8

14 rows selected.
```

However, these analytic functions are a feature that many relational databases do not have, so this is essentially a database-dependent technique. There is another way to do this that would work in most databases. This other approach involves the use of self-joins, views, and the like.

```
scott@ORA920.US.ORACLE.COM> select emp.deptno,
  2             emp.ename,
  3             emp.sal,
  4             sum(emp4.sal) cum_sal,
  5             round(100*emp.sal/emp2.sal_by_dept,1) pct_dept,
  6             round(100*emp.sal/emp3.sal_overall,1) pct_overall
  7    from emp,
  8         (select deptno, sum(sal) sal_by_dept
  9             from emp
 10          group by deptno ) emp2,
 11         (select sum(sal) sal_overall
 12             from emp ) emp3,
 13         emp emp4
 14    where emp.deptno = emp2.deptno
 15      and emp.deptno = emp4.deptno
 16      and (emp.sal > emp4.sal or
 17           (emp.sal = emp4.sal and emp.ename >= emp4.ename))
 18    group by emp.deptno, emp.ename, emp.sal,
 19            round(100*emp.sal/emp2.sal_by_dept,1),
 20            round(100*emp.sal/emp3.sal_overall,1)
 21    order by deptno, sal
 22  /
```

```
   DEPTNO ENAME              SAL   CUM_SAL PCT_DEPT PCT_OVERALL
---------- ---------- ---------- ---------- -------- -----------
       10 MILLER           1300       1300     14.9         4.5
          CLARK            2450       3750     28.0         8.4
          KING             5000       8750     57.1        17.2

       20 SMITH             800        800      7.4         2.8
          ADAMS            1100       1900     10.1         3.8
          JONES            2975       4875     27.4        10.2
          FORD             3000       7875     27.6        10.3
          SCOTT            3000      10875     27.6        10.3

       30 JAMES             950        950     10.1         3.3
          MARTIN           1250       2200     13.3         4.3
          WARD             1250       3450     13.3         4.3
          TURNER           1500       4950     16.0         5.2
          ALLEN            1600       6550     17.0         5.5
          BLAKE            2850       9400     30.3         9.8

14 rows selected.
```

This works and is more database-independent. However, not many companies that need this functionality have only 14 people in them; most have hundreds or thousands. Let's scale the example up and see what happens in terms of performance. When we run this against data sets of various sizes, we see this sort of performance:

| Rows in table | CPU/analytics | CPU/generic | Difference |
|---|---|---|---|
| 2000 | 0.05 | 2.13 | 42 times |
| 4000 | 0.09 | 8.57 | 95 times |
| 8000 | 0.19 | 35.88 | 188 times |

As the data scales up, the generic implementation gets progressively worse in exponential fashion. The correct implementation in an Oracle environment scales linearly as the data doubles, and so does the amount of time required to process the analysis. As we doubled the number of rows of data, the generic implementation fell apart.

Now, if I were the end user, I know which implementation I would prefer you to use, and it is not the generic one! This also illustrates why the analysis tools that feature on their packaging "we exploit your native database!" are much more desirable than those that boast "we run generically on 15 databases!" Tools and applications that exploit the database fully will perform better than generic solutions. About the only person who would be happy with the generic solution would be your hardware vendor. You obviously need to upgrade those CPUs.

There are other possible solutions to this problem. A common one would be to use temporary tables, placing the data in them a bit at a time. However, they all suffer from the same fundamental problems as described earlier: They are the wrong way to do it in Oracle (they might be the right way to do it in some other database), and they involve writing a lot more code, which can also be much harder to write.

As another example, I worked with a customer who refused to use a bitmap index. His thinking was, "Well, not everyone has them, so I cannot put it into my system, since that index created would be different in Oracle than everywhere else. I want a generic script that can run on all databases." Using a bitmap index, the query would go from running in hours to executing in less than a minute. But this customer chose to penalize all implementations because a few might not have a specific feature. I don't know about you, but I would rather have the bitmap index in Oracle than to have no index in all.

## Inability to Get the Correct Answer

As with the problem of being unable to perform, not being able to get the correct answer happens often when you think of the database as a black box. In the previous section, the results were clear, because the raw performance data immediately revealed the right and wrong approach. However, sometimes it is harder to see what you are doing is wrong.

Let's look at an example that concerns Oracle's consistency and concurrency controls (multiversioning, read consistency, locking, and so on), because this is where proponents of the black box ideology frequently come unstuck. Consider a simple transaction against a master/detail table. The goal here is to maintain an aggregation of a details table's rows in the parent table; for example, to maintain the sum of individual employee salaries in the department table. For illustrative purposes, we'll use these two simple tables:

```
ops$tkyte@ORA920> create table dept
  2  ( deptno          int primary key,
  3    sum_of_salary number
  4  );
Table created.

ops$tkyte@ORA920> create table emp
  2  ( empno      int primary key,
  3    deptno     references dept,
  4    salary     number
  5  );
Table created.

ops$tkyte@ORA920> insert into dept ( deptno ) values ( 1 );
1 row created.

ops$tkyte@ORA920> insert into dept ( deptno ) values ( 2 );
1 row created.
```

Now, when we perform transactions against the child table EMP, we'll include an UPDATE to the parent table DEPT in order to keep the SUM_OF_SALARY column in sync. For example, our transactions would include the UPDATE statement that appears last in this transaction:

```
ops$tkyte@ORA920> insert into emp ( empno, deptno, salary )
  2  values ( 100, 1, 55 );
1 row created.

ops$tkyte@ORA920> insert into emp ( empno, deptno, salary )
```

```
   2  values ( 101, 1, 50 );
1 row created.


ops$tkyte@ORA920> update dept
   2     set sum_of_salary =
   3     ( select sum(salary)
   4          from emp
   5             where emp.deptno = dept.deptno )
   6     where dept.deptno = 1;
1 row updated.

ops$tkyte@ORA920> commit;
Commit complete.
```

This seems straightforward—just insert a child record and update the parent record sum. Nothing so simple could be wrong, or could it? If we query our schema right now, it appears correct:

```
ops$tkyte@ORA920> select * from emp;

    EMPNO     DEPTNO     SALARY
---------- ---------- ----------
      100          1         55
      101          1         50

ops$tkyte@ORA920> select * from dept;

    DEPTNO SUM_OF_SALARY
---------- -------------
         1           105
         2
```

If we were to add rows to the child table for DEPTNO 1 or DEPTNO 2 and run that update, everything would be just fine, or so we might think. What we haven't considered is what happens during concurrent access to these tables. For example, let's see what happens when two users work on the child EMP table at the same time. One user will add a new employee to DEPTNO 2. The other user will transfer EMPNO 100 from DEPTNO 1 to DEPTNO 2. Consider what happens when these transactions execute simultaneously. Let's look at a specific sequence of events:

| Time | Session 1 Activity | Session 2 Activity |
|------|--------------------|--------------------|
| T1 | Insert into EMP (EMPNO, DEPTNO, SALARY) values (102, 2, 60); added new employee to DEPTNO 2 | |
| T2 | | Update EMP (set DEPTNO = 2 where EMPNO = 100); transferred employee across departments |

| Time | Session I Activity | Session 2 Activity |
|------|--------------------|--------------------|
| T3 | | Update DEPT for departments 1 and 2 since we modified a record in both departments |
| T4 | Update DEPT for department 2, the department we modified. This will BLOCK since Session 2 has the row locked. However, the query component of the UPDATE started so its result set is already decided. Oracle's consistent read mechanism will return to the UPDATE statement what is committed in the database as of time T4 | |
| T5 | | Commit transaction, Session 1 will become unblocked now. |
| T6 | Commit transaction | |

We can simulate this transactional sequence of events easily using two sessions and switching back and forth between them on screen.

Here is the example with two sessions. The SQLPlus prompt indicates which session we are using. You would open two SQLPlus windows in order to reproduce this example:

```
Session 1> insert into emp ( empno, deptno, salary )
  2   values ( 102, 2, 60 );
1 row created.

Session 2> update emp
  2      set deptno = 2
  3    where empno = 100;
1 row updated.

Session 2> update dept
  2      set sum_of_salary = ( select sum(salary)
  3                              from emp
  4                             where emp.deptno = dept.deptno )
  5    where dept.deptno in ( 1, 2 );
2 rows updated.

Session 1> update dept
  2      set sum_of_salary = (select sum(salary)
  3                             from emp
  4                            where emp.deptno = dept.deptno)
  5    where dept.deptno = 2;
```

Now, at this point, Session 1 will block. It is attempting to modify a row that Session 2 currently has locked. However, the read portion of the UPDATE statement (the query portion) is "as good as processed" already. Oracle has already frozen that result using a mechanism called a Consistent Read—we'll cover that topic in more detail in Chapter 5. In short, Session 2's update of the DEPT table will not see the row Session 1 inserted, and Session 1's update statement will not see Session 2's update of the EMP table. Continuing with the example:

```
Session 2> commit;
Commit complete.
```

At this point, Session 1 will become unblocked. You'll see the "1 row updated" message in Session 1's window immediately. Finishing up in Session 1 then:

```
Session 1> commit;
Commit complete.

Session 1> select * from dept;

    DEPTNO SUM_OF_SALARY
---------- -------------
         1            50
         2            60

Session 1> select deptno, sum(salary) from emp group by deptno;

    DEPTNO SUM(SALARY)
---------- -----------
         1          50
         2         115
```

It is obviously wrong. The value for DEPTNO 2 is incorrect. How could that be? If you run this in SQL Server, for example, the scenario would have been slightly different (things would have been forced to execute in a different order), but the numbers would add up. In SQL Server the sequence of events would be:

| Time | Session 1 Activity | Session 2 Activity |
| --- | --- | --- |
| T1 | Insert into EMP (EMPNO, DEPTNO, SALARY) values (102, 2, 60); added new employee to DEPTNO 2. | |
| T2 | | Update EMP (set DEPTNO = 2 where EMPNO = 100); transferred employee across departments. |

| Time | Session 1 Activity | Session 2 Activity |
|---|---|---|
| T3 |  | Update DEPT for departments 1 and 2 since we modified a record in both departments. This statement blocks on read of EMP. Row inserted at time T1 is locked, and SQL Server blocks waiting for that lock to be released. |
| T4 | Update DEPT for department 2 (department modified). This statement also blocks on read of row updated at time T2. |  |
| T5 | Server detects a deadlock condition, for both sessions 1 and 2. One is chosen as deadlock victim and rolled back—session 1 in this example. Forced rollback. | Statement becomes unblocked. |
| T6 |  | Commit transaction. |

Here, SQL Server, due to its locking and concurrency control mechanism, will not permit these transactions to execute concurrently. Only one of the transactions will execute; the other will be rolled back, and the answer will be "correct" in SQL Server. So, this must be a bug in Oracle, right? No, not at all.

Oracle has a feature called multiversioning and read consistency (a feature that sets Oracle apart from most other relational databases). The way it works is different from how SQL Server works (I would say superior, offering more highly concurrent, correct answers without the wait, but that's beside the point here). Due to Oracle's concurrency model, the documented way in which it treats data, the second session would not see (would not read) any data that was changed since its statement (the update) began. Hence, the update would never see that extra record that was inserted. If the interleaving of the transactions had been just a bit different, the results could have been different as well. (You can read about Oracle's multiversioning and read consistency feature in the *Concepts Guide*.)

The moral to this story is that the underlying fundamental concurrency and consistency models of the various relational databases are radically different. A sequence of statements in one database can, and sometimes will, result in a different outcome in a different database. It is the "sometimes" part of that statement that is troublesome. These sorts of data-integrity issues are hard to spot, unless you've actually mastered your database and read its documentation. And, they are even harder to debug after the fact. Reading a piece of code, it would not be intuitive that the condition described in this example may exist. If you implement your transactions for the target database and don't expect a transaction from one database to work exactly the same on another database, you'll be safe from issues like this.

If the Oracle development team members don't understand how Oracle implements its concurrency and consistency mechanism, or even worse, if they assume it works like the mechanism in SQL Server or DB2 works, the most likely outcome is corrupt data, incorrect analysis, and incorrect answers.

## Inability to Quickly Deliver Software

It takes less time to write a database application when you make full use of the database and its feature set. Take that earlier example of using analytic functions (in the "Inability to Perform" section). Not only did it perform in a fraction of the time of the generic example, it took a fraction of the time to develop it! Trying to answer the stated question without using the analytic functions was hard. If I had to use a temporary table to get the results bit by bit, that would have taken quite a bit of procedural code and a lot of time to write.

As another example, suppose you need to provide a feature in your application whereby all changes made are audited. The history of a row from start to finish must be maintained in the database. You have two choices:

- Design, write, debug, and then maintain your own implementation.

- Use a single database command to enable the same functionality.

How quickly do you think you could do the first choice? What if you need to do it for 50 different tables? You would need to type in all of the code to do it yourself. Then you would need to add in the time for testing, debugging, and maintaining it as well.

### NOTE
*The feature being described here is a generic solution that may work well for you—then again, its generic implementation may have certain performance characteristics that would preclude it from working in your system. As we'll stress throughout this book, you must test and benchmark this (and any) feature before just "turning it on."*

Using the second choice, it would take about a minute to implement auditing for all 50 tables:

```
ops$tkyte@ORA920> create table emp
  2  as
  3  select empno, ename, sal, comm
  4    from scott.emp;
Table created.

ops$tkyte@ORA920> alter table emp
  2  add constraint emp_pk
  3  primary key(empno);
Table altered.

ops$tkyte@ORA920>
ops$tkyte@ORA920> begin
  2      dbms_wm.EnableVersioning
  3      ( 'EMP', 'VIEW_WO_OVERWRITE' );
  4  end;
  5  /
PL/SQL procedure successfully completed.
```

That is it! One statement, part of the built-in Workspace Manager database feature, did it all. (See the Oracle *Application Developers Guide – Workspace Manager* for complete details on this database feature, which does a lot more than shown here.) Let's look at some transactions executed against the EMP table after executing this implementation:

```
ops$tkyte@ORA920> update emp set sal = 5000
  2    where ename = 'KING';
1 row updated.

ops$tkyte@ORA920> commit;
Commit complete.

ops$tkyte@ORA920> update emp set comm = 4000
  2    where ename = 'KING';
1 row updated.

ops$tkyte@ORA920> commit;
Commit complete.

ops$tkyte@ORA920> delete from emp
  2    where ename = 'KING';
1 row deleted.

ops$tkyte@ORA920> commit;
Commit complete.
```

And now we can review the end results. The Workspace Manager built a series of views, one of which is the EMP_HIST view that contains the row-level history of each record. Here, we can see the type of change (insert, update, or delete), as well as when the record was created and retired (either modified or deleted):

```
ops$tkyte@ORA920> select ename, sal, comm, user_name,
  2            type_of_change, createtime,
  3            retiretime
  4     from emp_hist
  5    where ename = 'KING'
  6    order by createtime;
```

| ENAME | SAL | COMM | USER_NAME | T | CREATETIM | RETIRETIM |
|-------|-----|------|-----------|---|-----------|-----------|
| KING  | 5000 |      | OPS$TKYTE | I | 08-JUN-03 | 08-JUN-03 |
| KING  | 5000 | 4000 | OPS$TKYTE | D | 08-JUN-03 |           |
| KING  | 5000 |      | OPS$TKYTE | U | 08-JUN-03 | 08-JUN-03 |
| KING  | 5000 | 4000 | OPS$TKYTE | U | 08-JUN-03 | 08-JUN-03 |

Querying from the EMP_HIST view that the Workspace Manager set up, you can see the history of each and every row in my table. There is another view, EMP, you could query that would appear to have only the current version of the row. I know you thought you had a table EMP, but the Workspace Manager actually renamed your table to EMP_LT and created a view EMP for you to use.

This view hides the additional structures the Workspace Manager added to version-enable your data. You could enable this versioning and auditing for an existing application, without changing the application or altering the way it works. And you can do it rapidly.

**CAUTION**
*As with any change, you must understand what is happening under the covers. You must understand the implications and limitations of the implementation. Workspace Manager has great functionality, but it imposes its own limitations and restrictions. Before turning on this feature for every database table in your application, make sure to read about it, understand it, and test it thoroughly!*

**NOTE**
*In order to drop the EMP table created in this example, you must disable versioning on the table first. That is accomplished via: "begin DBMS_WM.DisableVersioning ('EMP'); end;" in SQLPlus.*

### Inability to Maximize Your Investment
Our goals as an Oracle development team are to deliver fast, functional, scalable database applications to our users rapidly and for the lowest cost. To achieve these goals, you need to maximize the use of each and every piece of software you purchased, from the operating system on up. You'll need to avoid the black box syndrome to do that.

- You want fast applications, so use the database features like analytics.
- You want applications fast, so use the database features like Workspace Manager.
- You want applications for the least development cost, so use the appropriate database features to avoid doing it yourself.

# It's a Database, Not a Data Dump
This section is for everyone who feels that constraints should be verified in the client or middle tier, foreign keys just make the database slow, and primary keys are a nuisance.

"We have a City table, consisting of different cities where our client's offices are located. We have a VB form for inserting employee-related details. We have a foreign key on the City column in the Employee table, whose parent key is the City table. One of our consultants recommended that we discard this check for the validity of the city entered and suggested that we maintain all city validation checking through front-end coding. The reasons cited were that referential integrity checking at the back-end would be too time-consuming and would slow down the data-entry processing jobs. I wasn't truly convinced by his reasoning. Is his argument valid?"

My recommendation was to get rid of that consultant as fast as humanly possible.

# Use Primary and Foreign Keys

There are quite a few reasons why getting rid of foreign key and database validation checks is the worst approach in the world. Here are three questions to ask if someone suggests getting rid of them:

■ Is this the only application that will be accessing this data forever?

That is a rhetorical question. History proves time and time again that the answer is a resounding no. This data will be reused in many applications by many development teams (otherwise, it would be pretty useless data). If you hide all of the rules, especially fundamental ones like primary or foreign keys, deep inside the application, what happens in two years when someone else starts using this data? How will that application be prevented from corrupting your database? What happens to your existing applications when they start to query and join data and there is no matching primary key? Suddenly, your application breaks, their application is wrong, and the data is corrupt. The Internet revolution/evolution we all just went through should prove this point in spades. What were the last systems to get moved over to Internet-based ones in your company? Most likely, it was that set of applications that had 100% of the data logic embedded in the client.

■ How could doing this processing be faster on the client?

The front-end must make a round-trip to the database in order to do this. Also, if the front-end tries to cache this information, it will only succeed in logically corrupting the data! There may be something to be said for caching on the client *and* on the server, but not just on the client. The end users' experience may be nicer if, on tabbing out of a field, they were notified, "Sorry, missing or invalid foreign key." But that does not mean that you can permanently move this check from the database *to* the client. Sure, you can replicate it, but move it? Never.

■ Are the consultants who are advising getting rid of the keys paid by line of code?

This could be true—the more they write, the more they make, the more they have to maintain, and the more they have to debug. As the earlier example of auditing showed (in the "Inability to Quickly Deliver Software " section), sometimes you can do in one line of code that uses a database feature what might take dozens or hundreds of lines of code otherwise. If the database does something, odds are that it does it better, faster, and cheaper than you could do it yourself.

# Test the Overhead of Referential Integrity

To test the performance cost of using referential integrity, we can create a small CITIES table using the ALL_USERS data dictionary table for sample data. Include the requisite primary key constraint on this table. Then create two child tables, which are reliant on the data in the CITIES table. Table T1 includes the declarative foreign key. Oracle will not permit a row in this table unless a matching row exists in the parent CITIES table. The other table has no such constraint; it is up to the application to enforce data integrity.

```
ops$tkyte@ORA920> create table cities
  2  as
  3  select username city
  4    from all_users
  5   where rownum<=37;
```

```
Table created.

ops$tkyte@ORA920> alter table cities
  2   add constraint
  3   cities_pk primary key(city);
Table altered.

ops$tkyte@ORA920>
ops$tkyte@ORA920> create table with_ri
  2   ( x     char(80),
  3     city references cities
  4   );
Table created.

ops$tkyte@ORA920> create table without_ri
  2   ( x     char(80),
  3     city varchar2(30)
  4   );
Table created.
```

Now, we are ready to test. We'll use the built-in SQL_TRACE capability of the database and TKPROF to analyze the results.

**NOTE**

*TKPROF is part of a SQL Profiling tool built into Oracle. It is an invaluable performance tool. See Chapter 2 for more details on using SQL_TRACE and TKPROF if you are not familiar with them.*

The benchmark will test the efficiency of single-row inserts into both tables using a simple loop. We'll insert 37,000 rows into each table.

```
ops$tkyte@ORA920> alter session set sql_trace=true;
Session altered.

ops$tkyte@ORA920> declare
  2       type array is table of varchar2(30) index by binary_integer;
  3       l_data array;
  4   begin
  5       select * BULK COLLECT into l_data from cities;
  6       for i in 1 .. 1000
  7       loop
  8           for j in 1 .. l_data.count
  9           loop
 10               insert into with_ri
 11               values ('x', l_data(j) );
 12               insert into without_ri
 13               values ('x', l_data(j) );
 14           end loop;
```

```
15      end loop;
16  end;
17  /
```

PL/SQL procedure successfully completed.

Now, let's review the TKPROF report resulting from this:

INSERT into with_ri values ('x', :b1 )

| call | count | cpu | elpsed | disk | query | current | rows |
|------|-------|-----|--------|------|-------|---------|------|
| Parse | 1 | 0.00 | 0.02 | 0 | 2 | 0 | 0 |
| Execute | 37000 | 9.49 | 13.51 | 0 | 566 | 78873 | 37000 |
| Fetch | 0 | 0.00 | 0.00 | 0 | 0 | 0 | 0 |
| total | 37001 | 9.50 | 13.53 | 0 | 568 | 78873 | 37000 |

***********************************************************
INSERT into without_ri values ('x', :b1 )

| call | count | cpu | elpsed | disk | query | current | rows |
|------|-------|-----|--------|------|-------|---------|------|
| Parse | 1 | 0.00 | 0.03 | 0 | 0 | 0 | 0 |
| Execute | 37000 | 8.07 | 12.25 | 0 | 567 | 41882 | 37000 |
| Fetch | 0 | 0.00 | 0.00 | 0 | 0 | 0 | 0 |
| total | 37001 | 8.07 | 12.29 | 0 | 567 | 41882 | 37000 |

As we discovered, for 37,000 single row inserts, we used 0.000256 CPU seconds per row (9.50/37000) with referential integrity. Without referential integrity we used 0.000218 CPU seconds per row. Will your human being end users realize you have imposed this whopping 0.00004 CPU second penalty on them?

All told, the declarative referential integrity in the database added may be 10% to 15% overhead. For that, you get the peace of mind that lets you sleep at night knowing the integrity of your data is protected and you used the fastest way to develop the application. You know that no matter what new application is added to the system, it will encounter this rule and will not be able to violate it. This same principle works on a much grander scale, beyond simple primary and foreign keys.

## Middle Tier Checking Is Not a Panacea

Here is an idea I hear espoused often these days: Use the application's middle tier for doing work such as performing data verification and checking security. Using the middle tier might sound great. The benefits appear to be that it makes the application faster, more flexible, database–independent, and secure. But is it? Let's take a closer look at each of these claims.

"We have some consultants building an application for us. They will have an Oracle database that contains only tables, views, and indexes. Most of the work, such as constraint checking, will be in the middle tier. According to them, this makes the application faster.

Also, they say it makes the application more flexible, able to use different databases because most of the code is in the application. Last, the security checking is done at the application level (middle tier), and they have their own auditing feature that creates their own tables in the Oracle database."

In short, I would say these people will end up with an application that performs slower than it could, takes much longer to develop than it should, and has much more code to maintain than necessary. It will not be database-independent or flexible. In fact, it will be a way to lock the customer into using this consulting firm forever. To top it off, it will have security that is far too easy to get around.

### Is It Faster?

If all of the constraint checking is done in the middle tier, typically in Java, this will be faster, they say. Well, that means in order to load data, they must write a loader (one that can do constraint checking). Will their loader be faster than the native direct path load? Their constraints will be checked in Java. Will that be faster than native database code in C? (I would take them on in that race, for sure.) If they have a parent table with a million rows and a child table with ten million rows, and they need to enforce referential integrity, what will be faster: querying the database over the network to check and lock the parent row, or letting the database perform this check upon insertion? That's a rhetorical question, there will be no contest. Their application will be many times slower performing checks like that.

I would say their claim to faster would need to be backed up with real statistics, from real case studies. I've never seen one yet. However, I have seen a lot of cases where the converse has been shown: Doing it yourself is much slower than doing it in the database. Again, consider the auditing example described earlier (in the "Inability to Quickly Deliver Software" section).

### Is It More Flexible?

I don't know about you, but if I needed to alter a constraint—say $X$ in table T must be changed from between 25 and 100 to between 50 and 100—I would find doing it in the database a bit more flexible. I can do this in two commands: one to add a constraint and one to drop the old constraint. The database will verify the existing data for me, and even report exceptions so I can fix them. If you choose to do this in their middle tier, you must edit the procedural code in many cases and read all of the data out of the database to verify it, bringing it back over the network.

Even if you make this rule "table-driven" or "parameter-driven," it is no easier than updating a constraint in the database itself. You still need to validate the data. What if the data is known to be valid? Will the fact the constraint isn't done by the database make it more efficient to implement, since you don't need to check each row of data? Well, the database can do that as well. You can enable the constraint in the database without validating the underlying data, meaning the database doesn't need to check the existing data unless you want it to.

Doing constraint checking outside the database does not add flexibility. There is a ton of code to be written, but I don't see that as being flexible. This sounds more like the application designers don't know how to use the database.

In addition, this actually makes the entire database less flexible, less able to support the needs of this company over time. Why? Well, the only way to the database is through this application. Does this application accept ad-hoc SQL queries, or does it do only what the developers programmed it to do? Of course, it will not accept ad-hoc SQL. It will not be extensible by the customers; it will not be flexible as their needs change over time.

Take this argument back in time five or six years, and change *middle tier* to *client application*. Do you have a custom-developed piece of code written in 1996 that is client/server-based and has all of the business rules cleverly hidden inside it? If you do, you probably are still looking for ways to get out of that situation. Don't do it again with a new technology (application servers). Rest assured that in two years, some new, cool development paradigm will arise. If your data is locked up in some application, it won't be very useful or flexible at that point.

Another consideration is that if all of the security, relationships, caching, and so on are in the application, using third-party ad-hoc query tools cannot be permitted. The security (data filtering and access auditing) would be subverted if you accessed the data directly. The data integrity is in question (if the application caches). The data relationships are not known, so the query tool has no idea what goes with what in the database.

I've never seen a set of data that the business users are fully satisfied accessing *only* through the application. The set of questions they want to ask of the data is virtually infinite, and the developed application could not have anticipated all of those questions.

### Is It Database-Independent?

Let's look at the claim that using the middle tier makes the database independent. Is it a transactional system? If so, there are going to be issues with regards to concurrency controls and data consistency. If you didn't need subtly different code for different databases, why wouldn't PeopleSoft and SAP just use Open Database Connectivity (ODBC) or Java Database Connectivity (JDBC) to connect to everyone and be done with it?

Is it an application for a company, custom-coded to that organization? This company has a database, which cost real money. The company managers should not be paying someone else to rewrite the functionality of the database in a middle tier. That would be like getting taxed two times on the same paycheck.

### Is It More Secure?

As for the security, to say that the data is secured because the application has good security is really missing the point. The further from the data security lies, the less secure the data is. Consider auditing, for example. If you have a DBA access the data directly, will that be audited? No, absolutely not. If you used the database to audit, you could do things like:

- Detect the DBA doing malicious things.

- If the DBA disabled auditing, you would be able to detect that she did that (and get rid of her).

- If the DBA mucked with the audit trail (not possible if you use operating system auditing and don't give the DBA operating system privileges), you can detect that (and get rid of her).

In short, you can detect that your data has been compromised and take corrective action. If the auditing takes place at the application layer, it is far too easy to get around it.

# Build a Test Environment

I have had many conversations that went like this:

Them: "Our production application is behaving badly. It is doing <*something*>."

Me: "When you ran it in test, what was the outcome there?"

Them: "Test? What is 'test'?"

Me: "When you tested this process in your test environment, what happened there?"

Them: "Oh, we don't have a test environment."

Well, it just goes downhill from there. How many people are furiously mad at me personally because they did something in production I told them to try, without testing it first? I just assumed they would (I'm more careful about assumptions now). How many people have upgraded their database, for example, without testing it? How many people have upgraded their operating system without testing it?

If you do not have a test environment, you are just inviting disaster to lunch. There is a development environment, which most people have (although I have met some who do it on a production system, believe it or not). There is a production environment. There must also be a test environment. It is here that you will prove that your application works as advertised and that anything untoward is found before your end users are exposed to it. Specifically, you should use your test environment to do the following:

- ■   Benchmark your application. Test that it scales to the required load (number of users). Test it for performance (that it can handle the load within required response times). This is key.

- ■   Verify that your fixes actually work, especially in conjunction with the rest of the system, and that they do not cause more harm than good.

- ■   Assure yourself that the upgrade script you worked on in development actually works. Make sure that you can, in fact, upgrade production with your latest releases.

- ■   Make sure that major things like patch upgrades, major version releases, and operating system patches don't knock out your system.

One of the things I hear frequently is "We can't afford a test system." Personally, I fail to understand how anyone can afford *not* to have a test system. If you add up the cost of your production system being down for an afternoon—just one afternoon—I'm sure that would more than pay for a test system, regardless of the size of your organization. If your organization is small, your test system should likewise be small and inexpensive. If your organization is large, your system should be large and cost more. However, you have many more people who depend on it. Don't forget that cost is measured not only in financial terms, but also in terms of stress, customer anger, and your reputation (which may be irretrievably lost).

A realistic test system must be a fairly good mirror of your target system. Does it need to be exactly the same? No, but it should be as close as possible. The operating systems should be the same, at the same versions and patch levels. The databases should be exactly the same (well, the test systems database might run ahead since you'll *actually test* your upgrade there). The amount, type, and speed of storage should be the same, if at all possible.

Here are some points to bear in mind as you develop your test system:

- Use data that is representative of the data in your real system.

- Test with more than one user.

- Your test environment should be as close as possible to the actual environment in which your system will operate.

Let's take a closer look at each of these suggestions.

# Test Against Representative Data

Testing against representative data is crucial. If you want to get a realistic feel for how the system will perform, your test system must be loaded with as much data as your real system. The query that works great in a test system with a thousand rows might become your worst nightmare when executed against a million rows in production.

Some people adopt the strategy of importing the statistics from their production system into their test system. They think they can get the optimizer to generate the plans that will be used in production and test using that data. The theory is that they don't need to actually have one million rows in the table; they can just tell the optimizer that there are one million rows. That approach will work only if you can read a query plan and be 100% confident that the plan is good and will give subsecond response times. I've looked at many query plans in my life, and I don't feel like I could make such a judgment call. Most people are striving to get query plans that use indexes all of the time, without realizing that as you scale up, indexes may not always be the best solution. The only way to determine that your plans will perform as expected is to test them against representative data.

This is not to say that DBMS_STATS with its ability to export and import statistics is not very useful. Quite the contrary—I've seen people use (with great success) the ability to import/export statistics, but not to *tune in test*. Instead, they take the results of a statistics gathering done in test and import into production! Quite the reverse of what most people initially consider using DBMS_STATS for. These people will take a recent backup of their production system, restore it to test (for testing) and gather statistics there by using the test machines' extra capacity to perform work so that the production system does not have to. Also, using DBMS_STATS to set statistics is useful to see exactly when certain thresholds will cause query plans to change over time as a learning tool more than anything else.

## Consider Using Data Subsetting

Do you need to load 100% of production data into your test system? Not necessarily. Many times, you can load some horizontal "slice" of it. For example, if your online transaction processing

(OLTP) system is using partitioning and you've ensured that all queries make use of partition elimination (for example, you set up partitioning so that each query will hit a single partition of a segment), you can get away with loading and testing just one or two partitions of each table. This is because you are now testing the queries against the same amount of data as they will hit in production. Partition elimination is removing the other partitions from consideration, just as they will be excluded from the query in your production environment.

### Know the Optimizer Will Change Query Plans over Time

Using representative data will not ensure that your query plans in your production and test systems are identical, but you should not be expecting this anyway. Considerations such as the physical placement of data in the table affect how the optimizer develops query plans. For example, suppose we create two tables: one that is physically loaded in sorted order (so the rows are inserted into the table in order of the primary key values) and one that is randomly sorted. These two tables will contain the same data, but in different sorted order:

```
ops$tkyte@ORA920> create table clustered ( x int, data char(255) );
Table created.
ops$tkyte@ORA920> insert /*+ append */
  2    into clustered   (x, data)
  3   select rownum, dbms_random.random
  4     from all_objects;
29315 rows created.
ops$tkyte@ORA920> alter table clustered
  2   add constraint clustered_pk primary key (x);
Table altered.
ops$tkyte@ORA920> analyze table clustered compute statistics;
Table analyzed.
ops$tkyte@ORA920> create table non_clustered ( x int, data char(255) );
Table created.
ops$tkyte@ORA920> insert /*+ append */
  2    into non_clustered (x, data)
  3   select x, data
  4     from clustered
  5    ORDER BY data;
29315 rows created.
ops$tkyte@ORA920> alter table non_clustered
  2   add constraint non_clustered_pk primary key (x);
Table altered.
ops$tkyte@ORA920> analyze table non_clustered compute statistics;
Table analyzed.
```

Arguably, the CLUSTERED and NON_CLUSTERED tables are identical, except for the physical order of their rows on disk. One is sorted by its primary key, and the other is not. The optimizer is aware of this via the CLUSTERING_FACTOR:

```
ops$tkyte@ORA920> select index_name, clustering_factor
  2     from user_indexes
  3    where index_name like '%CLUSTERED_PK';
```

```
INDEX_NAME                        CLUSTERING_FACTOR
------------------------------    -----------------
CLUSTERED_PK                                   1106
NON_CLUSTERED_PK                              29291
ops$tkyte@ORA920> show parameter optimizer_index
NAME                                TYPE         VALUE
----------------------------------  ----------   -----------------------
optimizer_index_caching             integer      0
optimizer_index_cost_adj            integer      100
ops$tkyte@ORA920> set autotrace traceonly explain
ops$tkyte@ORA920> select * from clustered where x between 50 and 2750;
Execution Plan
-----------------------------------------------------------
   0      SELECT STATEMENT Optimizer=CHOOSE (Cost=109 Card=2702 …)
   1    0    TABLE ACCESS (BY INDEX ROWID) OF 'CLUSTERED' (Cost=109 Card=2702
   2    1      INDEX (RANGE SCAN) OF 'CLUSTERED_PK' (UNIQUE) (Cost=7 Card=2702)
ops$tkyte@ORA920> select * from non_clustered where x between 50 and 2750;
Execution Plan
-----------------------------------------------------------
   0      SELECT STATEMENT Optimizer=CHOOSE (Cost=109 Card=2702 …)
   1    0    TABLE ACCESS (FULL) OF 'NON_CLUSTERED' (Cost=109 Card=2702 …)
```

The point to take from this example is not that the optimizer made a mistake. Rather, realize that the optimizer can, and will, change query plans over time. That is part of its normal functioning— what it does by design. Here, the optimizer correctly chose a full-table scan when the data was scattered (when the table was not sorted by primary key). It is the correct plan. What might happen if you tested this example on a smaller database, one that was not scaled up? You might have forced the use of an index in the misguided belief that indexes are good and full-table scans are bad. It would work great on your tiny database but fail miserably in production against the live data. Here, if I were trying to tune against a small database and forced an index to avoid the evil full-table scan, I would have ruined performance in the production system.

**NOTE**
*If you run this example, you may well discover that the results are not exactly the same on your system. For example, you may discover both queries FULL SCAN the table or both use INDEXES. This will be a function of many variables (see Chapter 6). Individual settings such as the db_file_multiblock_read_count, db_block_size, and even the number of objects in your database that have OBJECT_ID values in the requested range, may affect your outcome. If you play with the range of values used in the predicate (50 and 2,750 in this example), you will be able to see the different plans.*

So, in short, you won't know all of the query plans perhaps, but you'll have peace of mind knowing that the code was tested fully against real, representative data. The probability of things going smoothly in production is greatly enhanced.

## Don't Test with a Single User

A common mistake is to incorrectly or improperly design applications in a transactional environment. Not understanding how the database works with regards to multiple users accessing data is a sure path to disaster.

"We are doing a stress test with our application developed in Java. The test hangs at the Oracle database. When I looked at the database, it seems one process is blocking another. For example, SID 55 was blocking 50. When I killed SID 55, SID 50 ran but blocked SID 35, and so on. Before the stress test, and when we ran the application by itself, it worked fine. That means SQL statements are committed properly. But somehow when multiple processes access the database resource, it breaks."

Fortunately, they caught this in their test environment! Unfortunately, they apparently didn't understand what they were observing, and their conclusion that SQL statements were being committed properly is 100% in conflict with the fact that they obviously have massive concurrency issues here. Their application, by design, is serializing (one after the other), and they are not performing the transactions correctly. They need to kill sessions to get the next one going, thus losing the work performed in the course of doing so.

You need to test your application under load, with many sessions concurrently accessing the data, the same way it will be in "real life". You need to test to scale. Another perspective on this point is to test with a realistic user base. A team of developers was working on a container-managed persistence (CMP)-based Java application. All of the code was generated from a tool, and they had no idea how it worked at the database level. Upon testing to scale, they quickly discovered that their generated application serialized immediately. They were doing exactly one transaction at a time, making for a very nonscalable system. It turned out that every user started by locking a single row in a single table, for instant serialization. A little application redesign with that in mind fixed the problem.

The point is that you want to catch things like this in the test system, not in production. If you want to lose credibility with your end users and customers, just roll code right from development into production. It will be the fastest way to accomplish that goal.

## Don't Test in a Dust-Free Lab

If your real system will have 50 other things going on when your application is running, make sure that you have either accounted for them in some fashion or that you have them running on your test system.

I worked on an implementation where the test system had all of the components of the actual production system, except for one. An interface to an external system was "stubbed" out on the test system. The team measured how long it would take to call this external system (about 0.1 to 0.5 second maximum), and the stubbed-out test function just waited that long and returned a valid but made-up response. Maybe you can guess what happened: When it went into production, the system screeched to an immediate halt. This was not a problem with the database (a popular culprit); in fact, there was very little happening on the database server.

After days of working backward through the stack, the development team discovered that the external system interface was—you guessed it—serializing requests. This would not have been too bad had this not been a public web site, with high volumes of transactions hitting it every day in an unpredictable order. Every day at lunch, boom! The site would collapse, as potential customers sat at their desks, trying to order something from this site.

Your test environment should mirror reality—every bit and every piece. You don't want to air your dirty laundry in public, and the surest way to do that is to roll out a system tested in pristine conditions.

# Design to Perform; Don't Tune to Perform

This heading is quite multifaceted—the "tune" could refer to a SQL query or to the data model. The true message of this section is that if your data model is poorly designed, all the SQL tuning in the world isn't going to help you. You will simply end up redesigning your schema for version 2. After reading this section, you might consider looking forward to Chapter 7, where we'll talk about the "physics" behind schema design.

## Don't Use Generic Data Models

Frequently, I see applications built on a generic data model for "maximum flexibility" or applications built in ways that prohibit performance. Many times, these are one and the same thing! For example, it is well known you can represent any object in a database using just four tables:

```
Create table objects ( oid int primary key, name varchar2(255) );
Create table attributes
( attrId int primary key, attrName varchar2(255),
datatype varchar2(25) );
Create table object_Attributes
( oid int, attrId int, value varchar2(4000),
primary key(oid,attrId) );
Create table Links ( oid1 int, oid2 int,
primary key (oid1, oid2) );
```

That's it. No more CREATE TABLE for me! I can fill the ATTRIBUTES table with rows like this:

```
insert into attributes values ( 1, 'DATE_OF_BIRTH', 'DATE' );
insert into attributes values ( 2, 'FIRST_NAME',    'STRING' );
insert into attributes values ( 3, 'LAST_NAME',     'STRING' );
commit;
```

And now I'm ready to create a PERSON record:

```
insert into objects values ( 1, 'PERSON' );
insert into object_Attributes values( 1, 1, '15-mar-1965' );
insert into object_Attributes values( 1, 2, 'Thomas' );
insert into object_Attributes values( 1, 3, 'Kyte' );
commit;
insert into objects values ( 2, 'PERSON' );
insert into object_Attributes values( 2, 1, '21-oct-1968' );
```

```
insert into object_Attributes values( 2, 2, 'John' );
insert into object_Attributes values( 2, 3, 'Smith' );
commit;
```

And since I'm good at SQL, I can even query this record to get the FIRST_NAME and LAST_NAME of all PERSON records:

```
ops$tkyte@ORA920> select
        max( decode(attrName, 'FIRST_NAME', value, null )) first_name,
  2     max( decode( attrName, 'LAST_NAME',  value, null ) ) last_name
  3       from objects, object_attributes, attributes
  4      where attributes.attrName in ( 'FIRST_NAME', 'LAST_NAME' )
  5        and object_attributes.attrId = attributes.attrId
  6        and object_attributes.oid = objects.oid
  7        and objects.name = 'PERSON'
  8      group by objects.oid
  9   /

FIRST_NAME           LAST_NAME
-------------------- --------------------
Thomas               Kyte
John                 Smith
```

Looks great, right? I don't need to create tables anymore, because I can add columns at the drop of a hat (with an insert into the ATTRIBUTES table). The developers can do whatever they want, and the DBA can't stop them. This is ultimate flexibility. I've seen people try to build entire systems based on this model.

But how does this model perform? Miserably, terribly, and horribly. A simple `select first_name, last_name` from `person` query is transformed into a three-table join with aggregates and all. Furthermore, if the attributes are NULLABLE—that is, there might not be a row in OBJECT_ATTRIBUTES for some attributes—you may need to use an outer join instead of just joining, which might remove more optimal query plans from consideration.

Writing queries with this model might look straightforward. For example, if I wanted to get everyone who was born in March or has the last name of Smith, I could simply take the query to get the FIRST_NAME and LAST_NAME of all PERSON records and wrap an inline view around it:

```
ops$tkyte@ORA920> select *
  2     from (
  3   select
       max(decode(attrName, 'FIRST_NAME', value, null)) first_name,
  4   max(decode(attrName, 'LAST_NAME',  value, null)) last_name,
  5   max(decode(attrName, 'DATE_OF_BIRTH',  value, null))
                                                  date_of_birth
  6       from objects, object_attributes, attributes
  7      where attributes.attrName in ( 'FIRST_NAME',
                                        'LAST_NAME', 'DATE_OF_BIRTH' )
  8        and object_attributes.attrId = attributes.attrId
  9        and object_attributes.oid = objects.oid
 10        and objects.name = 'PERSON'
```

```
11    group by objects.oid
12          )
13    where last_name = 'Smith'
14        or date_of_birth like '%-mar-%'
15    /
```

```
FIRST_NAME            LAST_NAME            DATE_OF_BIRTH
--------------------  -------------------  --------------------
Thomas                Kyte                 15-mar-1965
John                  Smith                21-oct-1968
```

So, it looks easy to query, but think about the performance! If you had a couple thousand OBJECT records and tens of thousands of OBJECT_ATTRIBUTES, Oracle would need to process the entire inner group by query first and then apply the WHERE clause.

This is not a made-up data model, one that I crafted just to make a point. This is an actual data model that I've seen people try to use. Their goal is ultimate flexibility. They don't know what OBJECTS they need, and they don't know what ATTRIBUTES they will have. Well, that is what the database was written for in the first place: Oracle implemented this thing called SQL to define OBJECTS and ATTRIBUTES and lets you use SQL to query them. People who use a data model like this are trying to put a generic layer on top of a generic layer, and it fails each and every time, except in the most trivial of applications.

"I have a table with a BLOB field, for example:

```
Create table trx (   trxId Number(18),
    trxType Varchar2(20),  objValue    Blob )
```

BLOB fields contain a Java-serialized object, different objects based on types, though all of them implement the same interface. We have always accessed this object through a J2EE container, so it works fine, so far. Now, users want to use reports using SQL*Plus, Crystal Reports, etc. So they want a solution to this BLOB issue."

This is an interesting problem. Here, the application developers have taken this generic model one step further than I had ever imagined! Instead of having objects with attributes, they just "BLOB" all of the object attributes into an unreadable string of binary bits and bytes. In Java, *serialization* means to take a data structure and put it into a "flat" format, one that could be written to a file and read back later to populate that Java data structure. The formal definition from Sun's Java Development Kit (JDK) is:

Object Serialization extends the core Java Input/Output classes with support for objects. Object Serialization supports the encoding of objects, and the objects reachable from them, into a stream of bytes; and it supports the complementary reconstruction of the object graph from the stream. Serialization is used for lightweight persistence and for communication via sockets or Remote Method Invocation (RMI). The default encoding of objects protects private and transient data, and supports the evolution of the classes. A class may implement its own external encoding and is then solely responsible for the external format.

So, here the Java developers have decided to use the database as a big data dump, a bit bucket. They are storing their data in a database, but they are not using the database. They didn't want to be bothered with things like data models and other formalities. They just want to write some code and store some stuff. And now, the end users are clamoring at their door for their data! These guys wanted to know how we could efficiently parse these BLOBs apart in order to support some SQL access to the data. The answer is that it's just not possible to do this in an efficient, high-performance manner.

To both of these groups of people, I have only one reply: You need to be more specific and less generic. Sure, generic is flexible, but generic has lower performance, is harder to query, and is harder to maintain. There is no data dictionary, and there is no metadata. The people who do generic are doing it to cut corners. The maintenance of this code is nightmarish. And just try to have someone who didn't build it fix or enhance it! This approach also removes value from the data itself, because the data is wholly locked up in the application.

# Design Your Data Model for Efficiency

You should design your data model to answer your most common queries as efficiently as possible. It should be clear by now that, unless you design your system to efficiently and effectively answer the questions your end users will be asking, your system will fail miserably.

"We have this query we need to run hundreds of times a minute and it takes forever, bringing our system to its knees, Please help!"

```
if type = 'A' join to tablea
if type = 'B' join to tableb
…
```

A query like this does conditional joining. (A similar problem is a query that needs to do `where exists` type processing four or five levels deep.) It is obvious that the data model was not set up to answer the question they ask hundreds of times per minute.

When I set about building a system, the first thing I want to figure out is how we can store the data in such a way that the most frequently executed, performance-critical, important queries are answered as fast as humanly possible. This takes place well before the tables are created, and then we create very specific tables to handle that requirement. We choose very specific indexing technologies. We design the system to perform from day one. Tuning will happen only because I made an incorrect assumption during the design and implementation, not because, "Well, you always tune after you deploy."

The tuning-after-deploying approach just doesn't work. Why? Because the system is already deployed. Can you change your physical structures *after* you've deployed the system? Not really. Can you change the fundamental architecture after you've deployed the system? No, not really. Those changes require another version of the product. They are certainly not things you are going to be able to fix overnight.

The requests I walk away from are those that start with, "We are in production. The code cannot be changed. You are not allowed to bring the system down. But make it go faster.

You know, wave a wand or something and set `fast=true init.ora` on." It just doesn't happen like that, ever.

As an example, consider an internal, web-based calendar system my team worked on recently. This application was to be used by between 10,000 to 20,000 users on a daily basis, 24 hours a day, 7 days a week. In addition to the web interface, it had to support a Palm Pilot synchronization. Another group had been working on this project for a while, but had yet to bring it to fruition. So we were asked to take a stab at it (more to get them going than anything else).

We looked at the problem and decided that this system was 90% read; more than 9 out of 10 requests would be of the form "show me my appointments." The other 10% of the access would be writes: "create this one-time appointment," "create this repeating appointment," and so on. The most important query was "show my appointments where appointment date is between START and STOP," where START and STOP would be dictated by the view of the data, which would be a single day, a week, or a month.

## Design for Writes or Reads?

So, how should this system be designed? To make writes super fast or to make reads super fast? The other team looked at the requirements and said, "We have to sync with a Palm Pilot. We'll just use their data model. It will make writing that sync routine easy."

We looked at them and said, "Geez, if we don't concentrate on a data model that supports more than 90% of our requests, it'll be really slow and not scale up very well. Besides, the Palm data model was built for a single-user device with a dedicated CPU and small amounts of RAM, which must also double as disk (persistent) storage. We are on a multiple-user device with tens of users per CPU and have virtually unlimited disk storage and gobs of RAM. Our design criteria are really different. We'll sync with the Palm, but we won't store data in our database in the same way the Palm would."

The problem we had with the Palm model was simple. In order to store a repeating appointment, it would store a single record. This record would have attributes like START_DATE, DESCRIPTION, REPEAT_TYPE (daily, weekly, or monthly), INTERVAL (for example, if repeat type were daily and interval were 2, it would repeat every OTHER day), and END_DATE. So, this single record would need to be procedurally "forecast out" each time a user wanted her calendar. For example, suppose that you had this entry:

```
Start date:   04-jan-2003
Description: Manager Meeting
Repeat_type: Weekly
Interval:    1
End date:     01-jan-2004
```

Then you asked to see your calendar for July 2003. The Palm would loop, starting from the START_DATE, adding one week while the result was less than July 2003. It would output the records for the month of July and stop when the result of adding a week took it past the end of July. It would then go to an EXCEPTIONS table to see if there were any exceptions for the month of July. For example, the 05-Jul-2003 meeting may have been canceled for the American Fourth of July holiday. It would be recorded as an exception and would be removed from the four meetings in July.

Now, that works fine for a Palm Pilot. When you are not using SQL as your query language, you own the CPU, and storage is at a premium, every byte you save is well worth your effort.

But, put that same record in a relational database and try to write a SQL query that will tell you that in July there are four meetings on the fifth, twelfth, nineteenth, and twenty-sixth, except that the meeting on the fifth was canceled. Although it can be done, it is extremely expensive and requires what I call "a trick." The relational database hates to make up data, and that is what we would need to trick it into doing here if we used the Palm model. There is only one row. We would need to multiply it out, to synthesize these other rows. It is hard, slow, and unscalable.

On the other hand, it would be rather easy during the creation of this event to loop and insert a row for each occurrence. True, we would put in 52 (or more, if the duration were longer) rows, but you know what? Databases were born to store data. It is what they do best. And we have tons of storage on the server (as opposed to the Palm, with its extremely limited storage). Also, we would query this event many, many times more than we insert it (read-intensive; nine out of ten or more requests are to read data). If the rows exist, I can easily report back events in a given month. If they do not exist, if we used the Palm model, I would need to fetch all of the repeating events and forecast them out, procedurally generating the data.

Consider also that a web calendar would be used to coordinate people's schedules for meetings and such. The end user asks a simple question like, "What time on Tuesday can Bob, Mary, George, and Sue get together?" If we used the Palm model (built and designed for single users, with extremely limited RAM and disk resources), we couldn't use the database to answer the query, because the data doesn't exist in the database. Only the information an application could use to generate the data exists. We would need to pull all the appointments for Bob, Mary, George, and Sue for that day, get all the repeating appointments, forecast them out, sort them, and then figure out what time period all of them had available.

On the other hand, if I had a table that just had start and stop times in it for each user, I could write a SQL query to tell me the available slots. This solution has every attribute we could want: It uses less code, requires less work for the database (it sends out less data, because it can run this query as efficiently as running the queries to return *all* of these users' data), and it is easier to maintain.

## Which Data Model Worked?

The other group decided to optimize writes at the expense of queries. They heard a rumor somewhere that writes are bad and slow, so they write as little as possible. They used the Palm model to simplify the development of a Palm sync module. They wrote a lot of procedural code in order to forecast out the schedules.

They felt we were wrong and should use what they called "a normalized schema, like the Palm." We felt they were really wrong and needed to study the database and how it works a little longer. Their major criticism of us, besides not using this standard Palm model, was that our database would be (they theorized) 9 terabytes (TB) in size. The fact is that no one ever made an appointment that repeated every day for ten years, let alone 1,000 of them.

Their solution didn't quite "fly," as they say. They found they could scale to about 6 to 12 concurrent users before they needed to add more application servers. Their approach to scaling was to throw more hardware at it. The database machine was feeding data to the application servers as fast as the servers could eat it, but there just weren't enough CPU cycles on the application servers to keep the pages going. If you have the physical design fundamentally wrong, no amount of hardware, tuning, or tweaks—short of a reimplementation—will solve your problem.

Our solution was to use a data model that answered the most frequently asked questions and kept the writes to a minimum. We didn't even order a separate application server machine. Instead, we used the single database server to host the database and the application server. On a fraction of the hardware, we served pages faster than the other team ever dreamed. The reason was because we designed for performance. We did not choose a design because the code would be easier (heck, they never got to write the Palm sync module, because they spent all of their time coding the middle tier and trying to get it to go faster). We chose a model that made our application perform and scale well.

The Palm sync module was written, and coordinating the two different models wasn't that hard after all. The sync was just a big "bump and grind." We basically could take the contents of the Palm Pilot (we know that they are small), dump them in the database, merge the two versions of reality (sync them), and then send the changes back to the Palm.

The system has been quite successful. In the end, our database was 12.5GB after a year of use with more than 28,000 users and more than 12 million appointments. As the number of appointments has gone up, response times have stayed perfectly flat (after all, we are just querying with a "between A and B"). That someone has 5,000 appointments in total is not relevant (it would be on the Palm model—just try that sometime). A user has only so many appointments in a given day, week, or month, and that's all the database considers when using its indexes.

The moral to this story is to make your data model fit your needs, not the other way around. If you want performance, design for it from day one. You won't try to (and won't need to) retrofit it in version 2.0.

# Define Your Performance Goals from the Start

When you set out to build an application, it is vital that, right from the very start, you are working with definite, clearly defined metrics that characterize precisely how your application is expected to perform and scale. These metrics include your expected user load, number of transactions per second, acceptable response times, and so on. You can then go about collecting the performance data that will categorically prove (or disprove) that your application is achieving its goals. Many of the difficult situations I encounter arise because people have simply not defined these metrics.

Here are some typical scenarios related to this issue:

- **Make it go faster!**   This is a result of not ever having set performance goals for the system. These people never laid down the law regarding how many users they were going to support, doing how many transactions per second, with response times in the $x$ to $y$ millisecond range. They just know their system is going too slow, but they have no idea what is fast enough.

- **Is my system tuned?**   The only way to know if a system is tuned is to have some metrics and a goal to achieve. If you are meeting or exceeding that goal, your system is tuned. If not, you have some work to do.

- **Everyone says we should do it.**   Some people do a particular maintenance operation on a scheduled basis; for example, they'll rebuild their indexes every week. When asked why, the response is, "Well, everyone knows you need to rebuild indexes, so we do." They've never measured to see if they are doing more harm than good, or even to see if they are doing any good at all. Odds are their work either has no impact or a negative impact more often than it has a positive impact. These sort of practices are able to perpetuate only because people generally do not set, collect, keep, or analyze hard numbers with regard to their system.

You must work to definite goals, and you must then collect the data that can give a definite measure of your success.

"I've got a question I would like to ask and am hoping you can answer or point me in the right direction. I need to generate some monthly reports for upper management to give them an indication of how the DBs are performing. I know there are loads of performance indicators that you can extract from Oracle. However, from my experience, upper-management people don't care about the technical details. They just want something that's pretty to look at and easy to understand. Which statistics do you think management need?"

This is a classic quandary. Upper management (whatever that is) just wants to be told everything is okay. They have no clearly defined goals or targets to meet. Their attitude is "just tell me my cache hit ratio is good or something," or "show me a pretty graph." In this context, such reports are useless in determining if you are meeting your goals.

## Work to Clear, Specific Metrics

I have a theory that a system can always go 1% faster. So, in theory, we should be able to make our databases infinitely fast. Unfortunately, we cannot do this. The reasons are twofold. The first is pure math: You never quite get to zero; As you slice 1% off, it is 1% of a smaller number; hence, the 1% is smaller each time (the 1% performance gain is less and less each time). The other reason is that each 1% is much harder to achieve than the previous 1%. The more you tune, the harder it is to tune more. Every 1% (which is getting smaller) costs more to achieve than the previous 1% did.

So, what you need from the very beginning—way back in development—are hard and fast metrics upon which to benchmark yourself. If you are told you must be able to support 1,000 users, 100 of whom will be active concurrently, with response times measuring 0.25 seconds given a well- known transaction, you can actually design and size a system to do that. You can set up simulations to prove that you are meeting those benchmarks. You can actually feel 99.9% confident the day that system is turned on that it will meet those goals. And if the system you constructed doesn't meet your requirements, you are also made painfully aware of that. But at least you know *before* you roll it out.

On the other hand, what if you are told you will have a lot of users, who will be doing some work (not sure what), and your system must be fast? Then you cannot possibly design, let alone size, a system. It is amazing how many people have "specs" like this, however. I've been on many a conference call in which the person on the other end wants to know why we cannot tell him how big a machine to buy given "a lot of users, want it fast, doing some transactions." My only response to that is, "How much money do you have? Buy the biggest machine you can afford and hope for the best."

## Collect and Log Metrics over Time

If you keep a long-term history of specific metrics, you can judge over time how things are going. Statspack (covered in Chapter 2 of this book and fully documented in the Oracle *Performance Tuning Guide and Reference*) is an excellent way to do this. If only every site I walked into had the past six months of Statspack information waiting to be reviewed. If only they did a 15-minute snapshot every day, once or twice during their peak times. Then we would be able to identify exactly when that query started performing badly (we would watch it rise up through the top SQL section of the report). Or we would be able to see not only when performance started to go down, but what wait event was causing it over time. Or we would see the effect that adding that new application had on our soft parse ratio, whether it was negative or positive.

Additionally, having some sample key transactions and their statistics recorded would be nice. If possible, you would set up a stored procedure, for example, that ran representative sample queries and even transactions that modified the data in the same way the end users did. You would run this job periodically throughout the day, taking a snapshot of performance over time. It would record the response times for these representative queries and transactions. Now, you could proactively monitor performance over time and even graph it. Not only would you have something to show "upper management," but you would also be able to pinpoint exactly when performance started to go down and by how much. A combination of the monitoring results and Statspack reports would be invaluable when you ask someone to "make it go faster."

## Don't Do It Because "Everyone Knows You Should"

More often than not, unquestioning acceptance of conventional wisdom does harm to a system as frequently as it helps it. The worst of all possible worlds has DBAs or developers doing something simply because "everyone knows you should."

"Why does rebuilding an index cause increased redo log generation *after* the index has been built? I have a table with 35 million rows and an index (nothing is partitioned). Transactions against this table are constant. It's always 500,000 rows per day. This generally creates 10 logs a day. Once a month, the indexes are rebuilt (alter index rebuild). On the day following the index rebuild, 50 logs are created. On the following days, 45 logs, then 40, 35, 30, 25, down to 10. At 10 logs, this remains constant. Mining the logs we see that we have increased INTERNAL INDEX UPDATES. Why does this happen? Is this always the case?"

It was interesting to me that the DBA identified the cause of a big performance issue and resource hog—the index rebuild—yet persisted in doing it! Like people, indexes have a certain size they tend to be. Some of us are chubby, some skinny, some tall, and some short. Sure, we can go on a diet, but we tend to gravitate back to the weight we were. The same is true for indexes. In this case, the index wanted to be wide and fat, and every month, the DBA rebuilt it (put it on a diet). It would spend the first half of the month getting fat again and generating gobs of redo due to the block splits it was undergoing to get there. In this case, rebuilding the index on the system had these effects:

- The system would generate five times the redo.
- The system would run slower.
- The system would consume more resources (CPU, I/O, latching, and so on).
- The system would not be able to handle the same user load.

These effects continued until the system got back to where it wanted to be. And then, the DBA would do it all over again! He would destroy the equilibrium that the system worked so hard to get to!

Here, the DBA luckily caught onto the extra redo log generation, and that concerned him enough to investigate further. Fortunately, the solution is rather straightforward: Stop rebuilding that index.

My favorite example is, "We rebuild indexes every week or month. Everyone knows you should do that on a regular basis." If only they actually measured what they did and checked what happened after they did it. It is the rare index that needs to be rebuilt. It is not a rule that indexes need to be rebuilt. It is rare that any operation like this would need to be done on a regular schedule. It is rare to need to reorganize a table, yet I see people do it just as a matter of standard operating procedure.

Of course, there are extreme cases, particularly with regard to bitmapped indexes after mass data loads, where rebuilding is suggested. But in the day-to-day operation of a transactional system, the need to rebuild indexes is so rare that I've never actually done it myself in 15 years, except to move an index from one physical location to another. And we don't even need to do that much today, because it's much easier to use logical volumes and move things around outside the database.

The bottom line here is that if you keep hard-and-fast metrics (that Statspack report, for example), you will be able to quantitatively prove that what you are doing is good; that it has a positive effect. If index rebuilding is beneficial, then the day after an index rebuild should have a much better Statspack report than the day before, right? The buffer get statistics for that top query that uses that index should be much lower (and if that index wasn't in the top queries, why was it so important to rebuild it anyway?), and the overall system performance should be measurably better. If the Statspack report shows nothing changed and your query response times are the same, the best you can say is that the rebuild was harmless. Or, you might find that the procedure is not harmless; it consumes resources, wastes time, and decreases performance until things get back to the way they were.

# Benchmark, Benchmark, Benchmark

Many people think of benchmarking as something very big, and sometimes it is. To me, benchmarking comes in all shapes and sizes. Most of my benchmarks are done on a very small scale. I benchmark an idea or an approach. Then there is the benchmark I will do in order to see if our application designed for 10,000 concurrent users will actually work. These benchmarks can incur a large amount of time and energy. Both benchmarks are necessary.

A third type of benchmark is to have specific metrics from the beginning of the project, as we covered in the previous section. This is the benchmark in the form of a Statspack report or a custom procedure that measures typical response times over the course of the day for standard and common transactions in your system. This activity benchmarks your ongoing performance to ensure that the system continues to meet or exceed its design specifications over time.

In practice, I find that most people ignore all of these types of benchmarks. They never test their approaches to see how, or even if, they will scale. They never test their system to see if, after all of the bits and pieces are put together, it will scale. Then when it fails, what do we hear? "Oh, the database is slow." Yes, the database does appear slow. But that is a symptom, not the problem. The cause is typically a poorly written program or a poorly architected system that was never tested.

It is important to understand that a benchmark must model *your* reality. A benchmark must be designed, tested, and implemented using your specifications. Running a TPC-C on your hardware will not tell you how your application will perform, unless, of course, your company is built around the limits of a TPC-C benchmark (doubtful). A benchmark is a personal thing, which is unique to you and your application.

**NOTE**
*For information on the Transaction Processing Council's standard suite of benchmarks, please see http://www.tpc.org/. The scope of the benchmark, as well as results, are available there.*

## Small-Time Benchmarking

In what I call "small-time benchmarking," the Oracle team is interested in deciding between two different approaches to a problem, or someone on the team is trying to prove that a certain technique is infinitely more scalable than some other technique. For this type of benchmarking, you are proving quantitatively that approach A is superior, inferior, or the same as approach B.

These tests are best done in isolation; that is, on a single-user database. You will be measuring statistics and latching (locking) activity that result from your approaches. You do not wish for other sessions to contribute to the system's load or latching while this is going on. A small test database is perfect for these sorts of tests. I frequently use my desktop PC or laptop, for example. I believe all developers should have a test database they control on which to try ideas, so they don't need to ask a DBA to do it.

### Use a Simple Test Harness

I perform small-time benchmarking so often that I have set up a test harness, which I call Runstats. It measures three things: wall clock (or elapsed) time, system statistics (such as parse calls, for example), and latching. The system statistics show, side by side, how many times each approach did something and the difference between the two. The latching information is the key output of this report.

*Latches* are a type of mutual exclusion, or locking mechanism. Mutual exclusion/locks are serialization devices. Serialization devices inhibit concurrency. Things that inhibit concurrency are less scalable, support less users, and require more resources. Our goal is to build scalable applications—ones that can service one user as well as 1,000 or 10,000 users. The less latching we incur in our approaches, the better off we are. I might choose an approach that takes marginally longer to run on the wall clock but that uses 10% of the latches. I know that the approach that uses fewer latches will scale much better than the approach that uses more latches.

So, what does Runstats entail? Well, I'll defer a detailed discussion of the guts of Runstats until Chapter 2, when we look at the tools we need to use. Here, I will show the end results of Runstats, so you can see how important it is to do these sorts of benchmarks.

As an example, suppose that we want to benchmark the difference between two different approaches to inserting data into a table. We have a requirement to load data into some database table, but we won't know which table until runtime (hence, static SQL is out of the question). One approach we take will use *bind variables*, which act as placeholders in a SQL statement and allow for the SQL statement to be used over and over again. The second approach we try will not use bind variables. For whatever reason, this second approach is widely used by many ODBC and JDBC developers. We'll compare the two methods and analyze the results. We'll start by creating a test table:

```
ops$tkyte@ORA920> create table t ( x varchar2(30) );
Table created.
```

We begin by coding two routines for our two approaches. One routine uses dynamic SQL with bind variables. The other routine uses dynamic SQL without any bind variables. It concatenates the character string literal to be inserted into the SQL statement itself.

```
ops$tkyte@ORA920> declare
  2          procedure method1( p_data in varchar2 )
  3          is
  4          begin
  5              execute immediate
  6              'insert into t(x) values(:x)'
  7              using p_data;
  8          end method1;
  9
 10          procedure method2( p_data in varchar2 )
 11          is
 12          begin
 13              execute immediate
 14              'insert into t(x) values( ''' ||
 15                replace( p_data,'''', '''''' ) || ''' )';
 16          end method2;
```

First, notice that it is actually harder to code without using bind variables! We must be careful of special characters like quotation marks (*quotes* for short). In fact, the goal of the REPLACE function call in method2 is to make sure the quotes are doubled up, as they must be.

Now, we are ready to test our two different methods. We do this in simple loops. And the last thing we do is print the elapsed timings and finish the PL/SQL block:

```
 17  begin
 18      runstats_pkg.rs_start;
 19      for i in 1 .. 10000
 20      loop
 21          method1( 'row ' || I );
 22      end loop;
 23      runstats_pkg.rs_middle;
 24      for i in 1 .. 10000
 25      loop
 26          method2( 'row ' || I );
 27      end loop;
 28      runstats_pkg.rs_stop;
 29  end;
 30  /
884 hsecs
```

```
2394 hsecs
run 1 ran in 36.93% of the time
```

Now, we can start to see concrete evidence of which approach is superior. Already, we see method1 with bind variables comes in at 37% of the time that method2 does. Going further and looking at the statistics and latches used, we find even more evidence:

| Name | Run1 | Run2 | Diff |
|---|---|---|---|
| ... | | | |
| LATCH.row cache enqueue latch | 72 | 40,096 | 40,024 |
| LATCH.row cache objects | 88 | 40,128 | 40,040 |
| LATCH.library cache pin | 60,166 | 108,563 | 48,397 |
| LATCH.library cache pin alloca | 116 | 78,490 | 78,374 |
| LATCH.child cursor hash table | 19 | 79,194 | 79,175 |
| LATCH.shared pool | 30,181 | 162,931 | 132,750 |
| LATCH.library cache | 60,363 | 249,568 | 189,205 |

```
PL/SQL procedure successfully completed.
```

As you can see, the method that didn't use bind variables used considerably more latches (remember that latches are locks of a type, and locks are scalability inhibitors). In fact, if you add them up, you will find that method1 used about 275,000 latches and method2 used about 884,000, for a difference of well over 600,000. That is huge! This conclusively proves that using bind variables is not only faster, but is also much more scalable. The more latching and locking going on in a system, the fewer users you have doing things concurrently. Latching issues cannot be fixed with more CPUs. Locking is not something you can fix with hardware. Rather, you need to remove the source of contention, and, in this case, we found it.

**TIP**
*If you would like to see more case studies using Runstats, just go to http://asktom.oracle.com/ and search for "run stats" (in quotes). As of the writing of this book, I had more than 101 such examples online.*

## Other Benchmarking Tools

The following are some other tools that you can use for small-time benchmarking:

- **TKPROF, TIMED_STATISTICS, and SQL_TRACE** Excellent methods to see exactly what your programs are doing and how well they are doing it.

- **DBMS_PROFILER** For fine-tuning PL/SQL code.

- **Explain Plan** To see what the query is going to do.

- **Autotrace** To see what the query actually did.

We will explore these tools in Chapter 2.

# Big-Time Benchmarking

By "big-time benchmarking," I mean that you are testing the system as a whole; you are testing to scale. There is no other way to know whether the system that works great with five users will work just as well with 1,000 users. There is no other way to know whether the system that works great with 5,000 rows will work just as well with 500,000 rows. Unless you want to look really bad on the opening day for your system, you will benchmark. You will simulate. You will do it realistically. You will spend the money, time, and energy for it (and it will cost some of each). It is not easy to do, but unless you really just want to throw something at the wall and see if it sticks, you will do big-time benchmarking.

This one step is key to success; it is crucial. And this is the one step the large preponderance of Oracle development teams skip entirely. Time after time, I see systems that are lacking because of situations like one of these:

- They have never been tested.

- They have been tested with unrealistic numbers of users. (Sure, we tested with ten users, and it works fine; turn it on for the 1,000 real ones now.)

- They have been tested with tiny databases. (It's really fast with one row, so you can ship it.)

## Test with Representative Amounts of Data

One example will clarify the need to test with a realistic amount of data. I was part of a team that was a beta test site for a product (that will remain nameless). We installed it, set it up, and turned it on. It was about the slowest thing on the planet. It took 30 to 45 seconds for the initial page to come up, and every page after that was the same. We did the old export/import of our database schema to their machines, and the developers could not reproduce the problem.

After a little TKPROF work on our own, we quickly discovered the problem. Our database had more than 40,000 named accounts in it, and their database contained ten accounts. The queries they had written against the data dictionary to check privileges worked great with ten users, but fell apart fast with 40,000 users. They had just never bothered to test with more than one user account on their system. So, while they benchmarked with "thousands of sessions," all of the sessions were running as the same user! Their benchmark tests were unrealistic; they did not match the real-world situations in which their application would be used. After the developers created a couple of thousand accounts, they found, and subsequently fixed, their performance issues.

## Test with Realistic Inputs

Another benchmark I was pulled into concerned a three-tier, Java-based application. The middle tier was code generated from a piece of software. The developers were disappointed in the performance they were receiving. The problem turned out not to be the database, or even the application itself ultimately. It was an ill-designed benchmark. It was easier to script with a single-user account, so that is what they did. They did not realize that the first line of SQL code in each container was:

```
SELECT * FROM USER_TABLE WHERE USERNAME = :X FOR UPDATE
```

The container was serializing transactions at the user level. They had one user using the system (heavily), so that user was waiting in a really long line to perform the transaction. This is similar to the issue described in the previous section, but instead of being a query performance issue, it was a performance issue inflicted due to concurrency controls gone awry. And they had gone awry because of an impossible real-world situation: a single user having hundreds of transactions going on concurrently!

By spending more time on the benchmarking aspect and setting up a realistic test, the developers achieved their goal. The scary part is that this particular example is a two-way street. Fortunately for this group, the benchmark returned disappointing results, so the developers looked deeper. As shown in the previous example of using a single user in the tests, however, it would be just as easy to feed the system unrealistic inputs that would cause it to run faster and scale better than it could in reality. It is important to ensure you are testing reality.

## Make Sure You Verify the Results

I was called onsite to help a customer resolve severe performance issues in a production system. The system hardly ran at all. It became the production system after a successful benchmark "proved" it could scale to more than 10,000 users. But now the production system was failing with fewer than 200 concurrent users. What happened?

As it turns out, the numbers the developers got back from the benchmark were wholly unrealistic. The response times reported by the tool they were using just didn't reflect numbers that were possible. Every screen, every web page, had 0.01 to 0.05 second response times. This system could scale infinitely according to the benchmark. They stopped at 10,000 users, but they could have gone higher.

What the developers didn't check was whether the benchmark process was working. Actually, every page was returning the infamous "404 – Not found" error. They didn't know this, because they never checked. They didn't record any metrics (so they had no idea if transactions were being performed). They didn't instrument their code (see the next section for more on that topic), so they didn't know it was not even really being run. They just thought, "What a fine system we built!"

When we fixed the benchmark, it became painfully obvious what was happening. Their system did not use bind variables! If you refer to the previous section about small benchmarks, you will understand what happened. As you add more users, you add more contention; more contention means more waiting; more waiting means slower response times. As they added users, the system spent most of its time keeping them in line, waiting to parse SQL. This was a really huge machine we were running on—a 48 CPU box. But no amount of additional CPUs would help them here. The problem was the long lines waiting to get into the shared pool. After two weeks of really long days finding and fixing code, the system was back up (up for the first time, actually).

The users had no confidence in the development team after this. They had totally lost any respect for them. For weeks, the end users were sitting staring at screens that didn't work. In this respect, it's worth noting that from a user perspective, performance is no different from functionality. A lot of developers will say "it works, but it's slow," whereas the user perspective (the only correct one after all) is that "it does not work, because it's slow." A mistake like this will take a long time to get over. For those in charge, it can be a career-changing event; that is, they may need to find a new one.

### Don't View Benchmarking as a Chore

Benchmarking is one of the most important steps in development, beyond getting the design right (designing for performance). This is the step were you get to prove that your design is sound (or to be shown otherwise). It is your chance to do this without incurring the wrath and scorn of the end users, your customers. I would much rather fail in a small room in front of a few people and have an opportunity to fix the problem than to fail in front of a crowd of hundreds (or thousands), and then scramble to try and patch it as quickly as possible.

If you develop real stuff, benchmark it. If you aren't benchmarking, ask your manager why the work you do isn't important enough to actually test. If you cannot afford to test it before inflicting it on your customers, is it really that important to them?

Not only will you avoid embarrassment by benchmarking, you'll save time and money as well. How is that? Doesn't it take time and money to conduct these tests? Certainly, it can take a lot of time and money actually, but consider the cost of having 1,000 people sitting on their hands for two weeks while you "fix" the system? How much time was that? What is the cost of not only those 1,000 people, but also the people they service? For example, if it's a system to order products, not only are 1,000 people prevented from working, but the work they are not doing is the way that the company made money in the first place. The cost is huge.

Do not let a tight schedule at the end of development force you to skip the benchmarking process. The pain of trying to fix a production system that was not tested to scale far outweighs the pain of pushing the deployment schedule back a week or two (or longer if the test fails!).

# Instrument the System

By "instrument the system," I mean that you should liberally and in great volume spread debug code throughout your application. To instrument the code means to embed in your systems the ability to generate copious amounts of trace information at will.

This will provide you the ability to do two things:

- **Debug the code without a debugger**   When you run into a problem with the database, the support technicians tell you to enable trace events that generate trace files containing tons of diagnostic information. This enables the support and development team to debug your problems, without ever touching your system. Imagine for a moment the impact of Oracle not having SQL_TRACE or the event system.

- **Identify where bad performance is in your system**   If you are building *N*-tier applications with many moving pieces, this is extremely vital. When the support desk calls you and says "it is going slow," how will you find out where your system is slowing down without the ability to have the code itself tell you what is taking a long time?

There are those that will say, "But this will add overhead. I really don't need to do this." Instrumentation is not overhead. Overhead is something you can remove without losing much benefit. Removing (or not having) instrumentation takes away considerable functionality. You wouldn't need to do this if your systems never break, never need diagnostics, and never suffer from performance issues. If that is true, you don't need to instrument your system (and send me your email address, because I have a job offer for you).

## Trace from asktom.oracle.com

To see instrumentation in action, go to asktom.oracle.com and click any article from the home page. You'll see a URL similar to:

```
http://asktom.oracle.com/pls/ask/f?p=…::NO::…
```

If you simply type over that URL and replace the word NO with YES, you'll see the same page, but with a lot of state and timing information dumped into it. (This example is not a functional URL; go to the asktom web site to get a real one to test this on.)

Every single application I work on has this feature—this tracing ability—in some form. If someone reports a slow page, I can easily and quickly determine which region of the page is causing the problem. If a certain query that paints part of the page is taking an inordinate amount of time, it will be obvious where that is.

In addition to this instrumentation inside the page, I audit each and every page access as well. That means that for each page accessed in my application—every page, every time—I insert an audit trail record containing whatever information I desire. On the asktom web site, I nominally capture the IP address, browser, time of request, duration of the request, what page in what application was requested, and other bits of data. This allows me to rapidly respond to questions like, "How many people use asktom?" and "How many pages (versus images and such) do you serve up every day?"

"Over the last 24 hours, I have observed that accessing your site and clicking on Ask Question, Read Question, Review Question, etc., all go slowly (taking around one to three minutes instead of a couple of seconds, as before). Are others facing the same problem?"

I just went to my statistics page, generated right from my audit trail as part of my system (clicked a button) and saw this:

|  | Last 24 hours | Last 60 minutes | Last 60 seconds |
| --- | --- | --- | --- |
| Page Views | 27,348 | 759 | 9 |
| Page Views/Sec | 0.317 | 0.211 | 0.150 |
| IP Addresses | 2,552 | 130 | 4 |
| Views per IP Address | 10.716 | 5.838 | 2.250 |
| Users | 2,986 | 147 | 6 |
| Views per User | 9.159 | 5.163 | 1.500 |
| Distinct Pages | 20 | 16 | 3 |
| Avg Elap/Page (secs) | 0.25 | 0.40 | 0.77 |
| Fastest Page (secs) | 0.13 | 0.1 | 0.28 |

I instantly saw that the access problem was not caused by the database. In fact, it probably wasn't a widespread problem at all (that is, this person was having an isolated experience).

I could tell it wasn't the database by the Avg Elap/Page value, which fell right into the norm (the database was generating pages as per normal). I could tell it wasn't a widespread problem because the number of page views fell well within my normal range. (I have another report I look at from time to time that tells me page views per day/week and so on.) Basically, I know that during the week I get between 25,000 and 35,000 page views a day on average, from 2,000 to 3,000 different IP addresses. The last 24 hours on asktom.oracle.com fell well within the norm. If pages had been taking two to three minutes to generate instead of well under a second, people would have stopped clicking them, and the hit counts would have been way down.

So, within a couple of seconds, I was able to rule out the database, the web server, and my front-end network as the causes for the visitor's slow responses. I also asked people coming to asktom.oracle.com to tell me how it was performing, and without exception, their answer was that its performance was normal, further confirming that this was an isolated incident.

Later, the poser of this question informed me that the problem was resolved. As he was somewhere deep in Australia, and I'm on the East Coast of the United States, I can only speculate that there was some nasty network issue that got corrected.

## Instrument for Remote Debugging

Another example of the benefits of instrumentation involves a piece of code I wrote a long time ago, when the Internet was just catching on. Many of you are familiar with mod_plsql, an Apache module Oracle provides that allows URLs to run PL/SQL stored procedures; this is the way asktom.oracle.com works, for example. The precursor to mod_plsql was called OWA, for the Oracle Web Agent. This was originally a CGI-BIN program that shipped with the Oracle Internet Server (OIS) version 1.0, which became the Oracle Web Server (OWS) version 2.0 and 2.1.

The OWA *cartridge*, as it was called, was fairly simple in its functionality: It ran stored procedures and that was about it. I reimplemented the same concept in 1996, but added support for file uploading and downloading, flexible argument passing, database authentication, an <ORACLE> tag (like PSPs, or PL/SQL Server Pages), compression, web-timed statistics, and so on—many features you now see in the mod_plsql module. (The success of my piece of software prompted the developers to include these features in the supported code.)

I called my piece of software OWAREPL and put it up on the Internet. It was downloaded thousands of times, and I still hear about people using it today. It is a piece of C code, about 3,500 lines of it, using OCI (the Oracle Call Interface) to interact with the database.

Since I do not write 100% bug-free code, and people used this software in ways I never anticipated (as people are known to do), I needed to be able to remotely debug this piece of code. Fortunately, I had the code fully instrumented and able to dump huge amounts of diagnostic information. Time after time, I was able to remotely diagnose and either fix or suggest a workaround for issues with this piece of software, all via email. All I had to do when someone hit a problem was send the following message:

Please set debugModules = all in the sv<webservername>.app configuration file. That will generate a trace file after you restart the web server. Run your application, reproduce the issue, and then email me the resulting trace file.

I never needed to physically log in to another machine outside Oracle in order to collect the diagnostic information. Not only that, but since this piece of code ran as a CGI-BIN or as a dynamically loaded cartridge under OWS/OAS, using a debugger was out of the question. If I didn't have this tracing ability, my only answer to questions about problems with the program would have been, "Gee, I don't know. Sorry."

By now, you realize how beneficial this technique is. The question remains, "How can I instrument my code?" There are many ways, and we'll explore them from the database on out to the typical application tiers (client server and *N*-tier applications).

## Use DBMS_APPLICATION_INFO Everywhere

DBMS_APPLICATION_INFO is one of the many database packages supplied with Oracle. It is also one of the most underutilized packages.

Did you know that if you execute a long-running command such as CREATE INDEX or UPDATE on a million rows in Oracle (*long-running* is defined as longer than three to five seconds), a dynamic performance view V$SESSION_LONGOPS will be populated with information? This view includes the following information:

- When the command started
- How far it has progressed
- Its estimated time to completion

DBMS_APPLICATION_INFO allows you to set values in the view V$SESSION_LONGOPS. This capability is useful for recording the progress of long-running jobs.

You may have wished that such a facility existed for your own long-running stored procedures and other operations. Well, you might be surprised to learn that, since version 8.0 of the database, DBMS_APPLICATION_INFO can help to answer all of these questions:

- What is the session doing, what form is it running, what code module is executing?
- How far along is that stored procedure?
- How far along is that batch job?
- What bind variable values were being used on that query?

DBMS_APPLICATION_INFO allows you to set up to three columns in your row of the V$SESSION table: the CLIENT_INFO, ACTION, and MODULE columns. It provides functions not only to set these values, but also to return them. Furthermore, there is a parameter to the built-in USERENV or SYS_CONTEXT function that will allow you to access the CLIENT_INFO column easily in any query. I can select userenv('CLIENT_INFO') from dual, for example, or use where some_column = sys_context( 'userenv', 'CLIENT_INFO') in my queries. The MODULE column should be the name of your major process, such as the package name. The ACTION column is suitable for storing the procedure name you are executing in a package.

**NOTE**
*The values you set in the V$ tables are immediately visible. You do not need to commit them to see them, making them very useful for communicating with the outside world.*

My general guidelines for using the DBMS_APPLICATION_INFO package are as follows:

- Use the SET_CLIENT_INFO call to store useful "state" information in V$SESSION. Use it for data you would like the DBAs or yourself to be able to see to gain some insight into what the program is doing. For example, you might consider putting the bind variable values in here before executing some long-running query. Then anyone with access to the V$ tables cannot only see your SQL, but also view the inputs to that SQL.

- Use the SET_MODULE/GET_MODULE call inside your PL/SQL routines as you enter and exit routines, at least the major routines. In this fashion, you can query V$SESSION and see what routine you are in currently. SET_MODULE allows you to set two components in V$SESSION: the MODULE and ACTION columns.

- Use the SET_SESSION_LONGOPS functionality for any routine that will take more than a couple of seconds, in general. This will allow you to monitor its progress, see exactly how far along it is, and estimate its time to completion.

If you are interested in more details on the DBMS_APPLICATION_INFO package, refer to the Oracle *Supplied Packages Guide*.

## Use DEBUG.F in PL/SQL

Another facility I use heavily is a custom-developed package I call DEBUG, with a function in it called simply F. It is a technique I have been using in my code for well over 16 years now. It started with a C implementation I modeled after `printf` (hence, the name DEBUG.F; in C the routine was called `debugf`). It is a package designed to allow you to add logging or trace statements to a PL/SQL application. It is simple to use. For example, you might code:

```
Create procedure p( p_owner in varchar2, p_object_name in varchar2)
As
     L_status number := 0;
Begin
     Debug.f( 'Entering procedure, inputs "%s", "%s"',
             P_owner, p_object_name );
     … some code …
     debug.f( 'Normal exit, status = %d', l_status );
end;
```

That would (if the debug package were told to generate debug trace files for this module via a call to DEBUG.INIT) generate a trace file message in the operating system that looked like this:

```
12062002 213953(P.PROCEDURE   5) Enter procedure inputs "A", "B"
12062002 213955(P.PROCEDURE 56) Normal exit, status = 0
```

This shows three bits of information:

- When procedure P was called (12062002 is the date in *MMDDYYYY* format, and 213953 is the time in *HH24MISS* format)

- If you print them, the inputs that were sent—any other DEBUG.F calls would have their output interspersed in this trace file

- That the routine was exited normally with a status of 0 two seconds later

From this sort of output, you can easily resolve debug issues, such as those that arise when someone calls you and says, "Hey, I'm getting an error from an end user running your code. What should we do?" The answer becomes, "In SQL*Plus, call DEBUG.INIT and tell it to debug (trace) procedure P for that user and that user only." After they reproduce the error, you generally have sufficient information in your trace file to debug that on your own now (for example, you have the inputs, or maybe the error is clear just from the generated trace and you can fix it).

Additionally, you have timestamps on processes. This is a very easy way to pinpoint where a slowdown is in a big, multiprocedure process. When you get the message, "Hey, your stuff is slow," you can enable tracing for a user and simply look at the timestamps to see what is slow (just like asktom.oracle.com, as described earlier). In a matter of seconds, you can track down where the performance issue is and zero in on it. You can review and download the DEBUG.F implementation from http://asktom.oracle.com/~tkyte/debugf.html.

# Turn on SQL_TRACE in Your Application

One of the most powerful tuning tools in the database is SQL_TRACE, which allows you to trace all SQL statements and PL/SQL blocks your application executes. It also includes information such as the number of I/O operations performed, how long the query ran (elapsed times), how many times the SQL was executed, and so on. Without a facility like SQL_TRACE, tuning a SQL application would be exceedingly difficult, at best. When you use SQL_TRACE, every piece of code that executes SQL in the database is already on its way to being partially instrumented. (For more information about SQL_TRACE, see the Oracle *Performance Tuning Guide and Reference*.)

So, why do so many systems that are implemented make it virtually impossible to use SQL_TRACE? The answer lies in the fact that most people don't think about tracing *until* after the system is having a performance issue (you know, after it is in production, without having been tested to scale). It is then that they discover the way they crafted their application makes it virtually impossible to trace using this vital facility.

"We have a web-based application where transactions are managed by MS-DTC (Microsoft Distributed Transaction Coordinator). All of the SQL to do select/insert/update/delete for all tables is in stored procedures, which are in packages. These stored procedures are called by COM+ components. The COM+ components use one username (app_user) to log in to the database and execute these packages. Connection pooling is managed by IIS, and depending on the users hitting the web site, I can see multiple app_user sessions connected to the database. In this scenario, how can I run TKPROF?"

Well, unfortunately for them, running TKPROF isn't going to happen very easily. The normal database methods of doing this, such as a SCHEMA LOGON trigger that enabled tracing for a session based on a single user, are useless. The use of a single username to log in to the database obviates that approach, and the connection pool further aggravates it. With a typical connection pool, a database session (the level at which we generally trace) is shared across multiple unrelated end-user sessions. Without a connection pool, the application would own a database connection, the level at which Oracle is built to "trace" at from start to finish.

With a connection pool, that one connection is shared by perhaps every end-user session in the system. We end up with a trace file that has not only the trace information we are interested in, but the trace information from any end-user session that used the connection (in short, a mess). The resulting trace files from such a thing would be meaningless (your SQL would be intermingled with my SQL, and with their SQL, and with everyone's SQL).

So, what they need to do in their application is

- Add the ability to set a flag as a property in a configuration file somewhere, so their COM components can be told "turn on tracing for GEORGE," or "turn on tracing for module X."

- When their COM component grabs a connection from the pool, it should issue `alter session set sql_trace=true` if appropriate.

- Immediately prior to returning the connection to the pool, if they enabled trace, they would need to issue `set sql_trace=false`.

Now, their application, which knows when GEORGE is running it or when module X is being executed, can enable and disable trace at will. They can selectively get the trace just for that user or that module. Now, the traces might all end up going into separate trace files on the server (since each time they grab a connection from the pool, they might get another session, and the trace files are session-based), but at least these files will contain only trace information for their user/module. They can run TKPROF on any one of the trace files and have meaningful information.

## Use Industry-Standard APIs

Even programming languages are getting into this "instrument-your-code" mode. For example, the web page at http://java.sun.com/j2se/1.4/docs/guide/util/logging/ describes a very sophisticated, extensible, logging Application Programming Interface (API) for J2EE-based applications. This API follows the same concepts I've been promoting here: Liberally sprinkle log messages throughout your code. This logger package generates log messages in XML, for example. Sun even has a nice Document Type Definition (DTD) for it, and you can code an XSL (Extensible Stylesheet Language) file to format the XML into a nice report. The log message might look something like this:

```xml
<?xml version="1.0" encoding="UTF-8" standalone="no"?>
<!DOCTYPE log SYSTEM "logger.dtd">
<log>
<record>
  <date>2002-12-06 23:21:05</date>
  <millis>967083665789</millis>
  <sequence>1234</sequence>
  <logger>demo.test.foo</logger>
  <level>INFO</level>
  <class>demo.test.LogTest</class>
  <method>writeLog</method>
  <thread>10</thread>
```

```
      <message>Entered routine, inputs = 5 and 'Hello'</message>
</record>
</log>
```

As you can see, this shows information that is similar to what the DEBUG.F routine (described earlier) generates. It outputs all of the information necessary to diagnose major performance issues (timestamps), and if you put enough diagnostic capabilities in there, it generates enough information to debug your applications without a debugger.

The logger package is new with J2EE 1.4, but there are many other solutions, such as the Log4J logging API or the Jakarta Common Logging Component. Search www.google.com for those keywords, and you'll find tons of information on them.

## Build Your Own Routines

If you are not using PL/SQL or Java J2EE, you can build your own DEBUG.F routines. I've done it for every language I've worked with. For example, earlier I described OWAREPL, a piece of software I wrote that many people downloaded and used over the years. I implemented debugf in C for that program. It works on the same principles as DEBUG.F in PL/SQL and the logger package in Java. If you are interested, you can download the source code (although it is now obsolete) from http://asktom.oracle.com/~tkyte/owarepl/doc/ and see it at work in startup.c and owarepl.h.

## Audit Is Not a Four-Letter Word

Many people are of the opinion that auditing is something to be avoided—unnecessary overhead. I find auditing to be extremely useful every day, in every way. I'm frequently asked, "How can we find out who dropped this table?" Well, after the fact, unless you had auditing enabled, you won't be able to do this easily. More important, an audit trail will show you useful information over time that allows you to pinpoint performance issues, usage patterns, and what's popular (and conversely what isn't). It allows you to see how people actually use your application or how they abuse it.

**NOTE**
*In Oracle9i with supplemental logging, you can use Log Miner to see who dropped a table. But an audit trail makes this easy and more efficient, because it can be selective. Redo is either generated for every drop operation or not at all.*

For example, on asktom.oracle.com, I noticed a sudden jump in hits on my site, from a normal of around 30,000 page views to more than 150,000. Wow, I thought, it has gotten really popular. Then I thought, or has it? That increase was too sudden and too large. In reviewing the audit trail, I detected a new browser—a web "whacker" if you will. Someone was crawling the asktom.oracle.com site and downloading the entire thing. Well, the problem was that every time that user hit the site with the web whacker, she got a new session ID in the URL, meaning that she downloaded the entire site *every* time.

The asktom.oracle.com site does not lend itself to incremental downloads. So, what did I do? I just added code to the header for asktom.oracle.com (the code that runs at the top of each page) that looked at the browser type. If it is a web whacker, the code returns a page that effectively says, "Please don't try to use download tools," with no links. Instantly, the page view totals on asktom.oracle.com went right back to their normal levels. Now, every time I see a spike in activity like that, my audit trail tells me what happened. It gives me the new browser type, and I filter that one out as well.

The funny thing about audit trails is that you don't realize that you need them until after you need them! Recently, I was asked (and I get this question about once a week—just replace *function* with *package, procedure, sequence, table, view* ...), "How do I get the following information from system tables? How do I identify the DDL actions performed in the last 24 hours? If a developer overwrites some function, how can I tell who did it?" The only way to know for sure is to have had auditing enabled—either basic auditing, using the built-in features of the database, or custom auditing, using system event triggers (BEFORE CREATE, BEFORE DROP, and so on).

In your application, you should audit activities as well, beyond the normal auditing that can take place in the database. You should audit into database tables. This is my preference because it's easy to mine the data in the database, but it's hard to mine data if it is in a file or XML document somewhere. Use a system like the one I have on asktom.oracle.com: every page view is an audit event, an insert into a table. Remember that databases were born to insert into; it is one of the things they do best. Don't be afraid to add an insert here and there to audit. The benefits far outweigh any perceived performance hit.

# Question Authority

Not long ago, a message came to me on asktom.oracle.com that began something like this:

I've recently read an article about performance on *<some web site>*, and I couldn't believe what I was reading about commits. I usually read your answers on this site, and I've read your book as well. You suggest avoiding frequent commits. Below is an extract of the article. Please let me know what you think about the author's suggestion regarding commits.

"Issue Frequent COMMIT Statements"

Whenever possible, issue frequent COMMIT statements in all your programs. By issuing frequent COMMIT statements, the performance of the program is enhanced and its resource requirements are minimized as COMMIT frees up the following resources: 1) Information held in the rollback segments to undo the transaction, if necessary 2) All locks acquired during statement processing 3) Space in the redo log buffer cache and 4) Overhead associated with any internal Oracle mechanisms to manage the resources in the previous three items."

Well, the funny thing was this performance article actually had more than 50 points in it— over 50 things to do to enhance performance. The problem was that, almost without exception, every item was either dead wrong (as this item on committing is) or totally misleading.

So, after debunking one item—this myth about commits (a very popular myth; for some reason, it seems many people have heard it and live by it)—the author of this paper got in touch with me. Concerned that this one item was wrong, he asked if I would review the rest and let him know if there were other issues. So I did. I wrote a point-by-point rebuttal for the first 25 items. Then, being really tired from all that typing, I just glanced at the rest and confirmed they were of the same quality. I sent the email off to the author, and he responded, "Thanks for pointing out all the errors. It's really surprising that the Tuning Book contained so many errors."

What's this? Turns out the 50-plus items he was attributing to himself weren't really his original ideas, but rather items he pulled from books on performance tuning. He never even tried the ideas to prove that they worked! He took verbatim as truth every word from those books.

## Beware of Universal "Bests"

Anything related to performance tuning can be proven (via benchmarking, for example). Not only can it be proven, but it should be proven. And even more important, the caveats must be pointed out as well. What works well in a certain set of circumstances may fail miserably in others.

For example, some people swear that you should never use IN (*subquery*); you should always use WHERE EXISTS (*correlated subquery*). There is another camp that believes the reverse. How could two groups come to such different—opposite, in fact—conclusions? Easily—they had different conditions under which they did their tuning. One group found that using IN for their set of queries with their data was really bad, and using WHERE EXISTS was really good. The other group with different data and different queries discovered the opposite. Neither group is correct; both are wrong, and both are right. Certain techniques are applicable in certain conditions. There are no rules of thumb in performance tuning that are universally applicable. This is why I avoid answering questions like these:

- What is the best way to analyze tables?
- What is the best kind of table?
- What is the best way to synchronize two databases?

If there were a universal best way, the software would provide only that way. Why bother with inferior methods?

## Suspect Ratios and Other Myths

You will hear unproven statements like, "Your cache hit ratio should be above 96% on a well-tuned system. Your goal is to adjust the buffer cache in order to achieve that." You should wonder why this is so. Did they prove it? Do others agree with it? For example, that buffer cache one is a popular myth. I have an "anti-myth" that contradicts it.

I have a theory that a system with a high cache hit ratio is a system in need of serious tuning! Why? Because you are doing too many logical I/Os. Logical I/Os require latches. Latches are locks. Locks are serialization devices, which inhibit scalability. A high cache hit ratio could be indicative of overusing and abusing indexes on your system. Consider this small example:

```
… Ok, here you go. So, joe (or josephine) SQL coder needs
to run the following query:
select t1.object_name, t2.object_name
  from t1, t2
 where t1.object_id = t2.object_id
   and t1.owner = 'WMSYS'
```

Here, T1 and T2 are huge tables, with more than 1.8 million rows each. Joe runs the query and uses SQL_TRACE on it to see how it is doing. This is the result:

| call | count | cpu | elapsed | disk | query | current | rows |
|------|-------|-----|---------|------|-------|---------|------|
| Parse | 1 | 0.00 | 0.00 | 0 | 0 | 0 | 0 |
| Execute | 1 | 0.00 | 0.00 | 0 | 0 | 0 | 0 |
| Fetch | 35227 | 5.63 | 9.32 | 23380 | 59350 | 0 | 528384 |
| total | 35229 | 5.63 | 9.33 | 23380 | 59350 | 0 | 528384 |

| Rows | Row Source Operation |
|------|----------------------|
| 528384 | HASH JOIN |
| 8256 | TABLE ACCESS FULL T1 |
| 1833856 | TABLE ACCESS FULL T2 |

"Stupid, stupid Cost Based Optimizer (CBO)," Joe says. "I have indexes. Why won't it use it? We all know that indexes mean fast! Not only that, but look at that cache hit for that query— about 50%. That's terrible! Totally unacceptable according to this book I read. Okay, let me use the faithful Rule Based Optimizer (RBO) and see what happens."

```
select /*+ RULE */ t1.object_name, t2.object_name
  from t1, t2
 where t1.object_id = t2.object_id
   and t1.owner = 'WMSYS'
```

So, Joe explains that, with these results:

```
Execution Plan
----------------------------------------------------------
   0        SELECT STATEMENT Optimizer=HINT: RULE
   1     0   TABLE ACCESS (BY INDEX ROWID) OF 'T2'
   2     1    NESTED LOOPS
   3     2     TABLE ACCESS (FULL) OF 'T1'
   4     2     INDEX (RANGE SCAN) OF 'T2_IDX' (NON-UNIQUE)
```

"Excellent," he says, "Look at that, it is finally using my index. I know indexes are good." Joe's problem is solved, until he runs the query, that is. TKPROF shows the true story:

| call | count | cpu | elapsed | disk | query | current | rows |
|------|-------|-----|---------|------|-------|---------|------|
| Parse | 1 | 0.00 | 0.00 | 0 | 0 | 0 | 0 |
| Execute | 1 | 0.00 | 0.00 | 0 | 0 | 0 | 0 |
| Fetch | 35227 | 912.07 | 3440.70 | 1154555 | 121367981 | 0 | 528384 |
| total | 35229 | 912.07 | 3440.70 | 1154555 | 121367981 | 0 | 528384 |

Be careful of what you ask for! Joe got his index used, but it was deadly. Yes, that is ten seconds versus one hour, and all because of indexes and good cache hit ratios. The DBA might be pleased now:

```
  1  SELECT phy.value,
  2         cur.value,
```

```
  3         con.value,
  4    1-((phy.value)/((cur.value)+(con.value))) "Cache hit ratio"
  5  FROM   v$sysstat cur, v$sysstat con, v$sysstat phy
  6  WHERE  cur.name='db block gets'
  7  AND    con.name='consistent gets'
  8* AND    phy.name='physical reads'
ops$tkyte@ORA920.US.ORACLE.COM> /

   VALUE      VALUE      VALUE Cache hit ratio
--------  ---------- ---------- ---------------
 1277377      58486  121661490       .989505609
```

A cache hit ratio of 98.9%—boy, did Joe do a good job or not! Obviously not, but many people would say "Well, that is a finely tuned system based on that cache hit. You know that a physical I/O is 10,000 times more expensive than a logical I/O is!" (that is said tongue in cheek of course, a physical I/O is not anywhere near 10,000 times as expensive as a cache read).

When you read generalizations like, "cache hit ratios of X% indicate you've tuned well," be suspicious. Remember that there are no universal rules that apply in all cases. In fact, if you read about ratios at all, be skeptical. It is not that ratios are useless; it is just that they are generally not useful all by themselves. They must be used in conjunction with other variables in order to make sense. The tools that show "green" lights when the cache hit ratio is 90% or more, versus red when it falls below, are somewhat misleading. A 99% cache hit ratio could be as indicative of a problem as it could be indicative of a well-run system.

**NOTE**
*I know of exactly one ratio that is meaningful all by itself, and even then, it doesn't apply to a data warehouse. This is the ratio of soft to hard parses, which should be near 100%. Bind variables that allow for soft parses are something you want to use. See the "Small-Time Benchmarking" section earlier in this chapter for proof.*

# Don't Look for Shortcuts

Don't look for shortcuts. Everyone is in search of the `fast=true init.ora` parameter. Let me bring you in on a secret: It doesn't exist (although there are some `slow=yes` ones out there!).

Frequently, I am asked about undocumented parameters or Oracle internals. My response is, "Have you read the *Concepts Guide* from cover to cover yet?" Invariably, they have not. They haven't mastered the basics yet, and they want "internals."

People believe there must be some hidden nugget—some magic thing—they can just turn on in their database, and it will go faster and run better. That way, they don't need to bother with learning about the database.

The real problem is that undocumented parameters have side effects that the uninitiated just cannot anticipate. They do not have enough knowledge of the basics to understand what ramifications setting some of these parameters might have. Lack of breadth of knowledge here, coupled with undocumented parameters, can lead to disaster.

Recently, we had a discussion on the Internet Usenet newsgroups about this. The thread on comp.databases.oracle.server was entitled, "Why are people so afraid of underscore parameters" (all Oracle database undocumented parameters start with an underscore character). Someone suggested, "Why not take _trace_files_public as an example? That may be technically the most harmless underscore parameter."

As its name implies, the _trace_files_public parameter makes the trace files generated by Oracle accessible to everyone. On a development instance, where the developers need to run a TKPROF report for tuning, this is very handy. On a production instance (where you should *not* be tuning anyway), turning on this parameter is a rather large security issue.

Sensitive information, such as passwords, can be generated in these trace files. There is an undocumented but well-known method to dump the library cache (a portion of the SGA, or shared global area), and this dump goes into a trace file. If a user has ALTER SESSION privileges and knowledge of this command, and _trace_files_public is set to true, you have a rather large security issue on your hands and you don't even realize it (you also have another security issue related to the ALTER SESSION privilege, but that is another story). Who can say what other unintended side effects will rear their ugly heads with the other "amazing" undocumented parameters.

In short, undocumented parameters on a production instance should be set only under the direction of Oracle support. No ifs, ands, or buts about it. This applies to even the most experienced Oracle teams. And, even when you are instructed to use an undocumented parameter, you need to reevaluate its usage when you upgrade your system. Typically, if you need to set an undocumented parameter, there is a reason, sometimes known as a *bug*. Bugs get fixed, and having the old, undocumented parameters set after an upgrade can be disastrous.

For example, for Oracle7.3, there was an undocumented way to enable bitmap indexes using an underscore parameter to set an event (before these indexes went into production in version 7.3.3). Word of this got around, and people started setting this parameter and training others to do it (if you search groups.google.com for "bitmap indexes 7.3 group:comp.databases.oracle.*", you'll find out how). Then they would upgrade to 7.3.3 and leave the event set. So, what happened? Well, the event caused the 7.3.3 code to run the old bitmap code, not the new production code (oops). As you can imagine, this caused some serious support issues, especially over time, as issues with the old code arose. In fact, some people left these events in all of the way up through Oracle8i, causing severe performance degradation of interMedia text searches, a special indexing technique for textual information in the database. That got filed as a bug—a performance bug, if you left that event on.

In my experience, I have not used internals knowledge nor undocumented magic incantations to make database applications perform faster, scale better, and achieve their goals. I used my knowledge of the basics—the knowledge I gained from the standard documentation, plus a lot of experience and common sense. As I stressed earlier in the chapter, to get the most out of your database, begin by reading the *Concepts Guide*. If you read 100% of that guide and retain even just 10% of it, you'll already know 90% more than most people. It is that basic knowledge that will make you successful, not some magic parameter.

# Keep It Simple

I follow the KISS principle (for keep it simple, silly; others have another word for the last *S*). I prefer the path of least resistance, or the course of action that is easiest to achieve without error.

## Consider Alternate Approaches

I frequently get questions that start with, "Without doing *X*, how can I do *Y*?" Time and time again, I see people opting for the hardest possible approach to a problem. They have a solution in mind, and they are going to use that solution regardless. They have precluded all other approaches.

For example, someone recently asked me about how to add a table column between existing columns, without dropping and re-creating the table. Her table (T) had the column order Code, Date, Status, and Actiondate, and she wanted to put a new column (New_Column) between the Status and Actiondate columns. I pointed out that the physical order of columns isn't something you should rely on. In order to achieve what she wants, she can take these simple steps:

- Rename <their table> to <their_table>_TABLE
- Alter the renamed table and add the new column
- Create view <their table> as `select code, date, status,` *`new_column,`* `actiondate from` `T_TABLE`

Her response was, "I want to add a column in the middle of the table, but I do not want to rebuild it and I don't want to use a view. Try again." Well, what could I say to that? She wanted to get from point A to point C and refused to go through point B, even though that is the only logical way to go. It would take all of five seconds to do this with a view; this is what views are all about. No application would be the wiser (unless the addition of this column broke it, of course). It is the smart, clean, and correct solution for the problem.

**NOTE**
*People have told me that views are slow. That is just not true. A view is nothing more then a stored query! If the stored query text is slow, sure the view (or queries against the view) will be slow. A view cannot be any slower than the query itself. When you use the specific query as defined by the view in straight SQL, you'll see the same performance.*

So, someone else comes along with this "great" idea (this was in version 8i, which does not have a rename column function, or else the steps would be shorter). Here T represents their original tablename and NEW_COLUMN is the column they wish to add:

- Alter table T and add NEW_COLUMN
- Alter table T and add ACTIONDATE_TEMP
- Update T and set ACTIONDATE_TEMP = ACTIONDATE
- Alter table T and drop column ACTIONDATE
- Alter table T and add ACTIONDATE
- Update T and set ACTIONDATE = ACTIONDATE_TEMP
- Alter table T and drop ACTIONDATE_TEMP

And voilà, you have "added" NEW_COLUMN in the middle. Let's see—she didn't want to rebuild the table, and she didn't want to use a view, but to this she says, "Thanks, that's my answer!" Never mind the fact that "her answer" rewrites the table over and over, most likely migrating many rows due to the updates and negatively impacting performance. Never mind that on a table of any size it would take many times longer than rebuilding the table. Never mind that no matter the size, it is infinitely complex when compared to using a view.

I am appalled that someone would think of this solution as viable and use it. It is the worst approach to a relatively simple problem. A rebuild would rewrite the table once. A view would be done with the change in five seconds. But she really wants to rewrite the table repeatedly. One false step, and the table would be destroyed as well (it is error prone).

## Let the Database Do What It Does Best

Another classic example of keeping it simple is to let the database do what it does best. Do not try to outsmart it.

As an example, I was recently asked my advice about outer joins. The DBA explained that he had a big CUSTOMERS table and seven or eight small tables referenced to CUSTOMERS columns (COUNTRY, STATE, CITY, CUSTOMER_GROUP, and so on). The data in the tables was language-sensitive, with the language depending on the web client language in parameter. In some cases, outer joins would be needed. He wanted to know the best way to handle this kind of query, and he had three ideas:

- Several outer joins and filtering with language in parameter

- Function-based column: fn_country(costumer.id_country,p_inlang)

- Only CUSTOMER columns in cursor, open it and apply fn_country on every fetch from ready and filtered customer data

I replied that his first idea, using outer joins, was the only really good choice, and there is more than one way to code it. Outer joins are not *evil*. When used appropriately, they are no faster or slower than a regular join. You can either code:

```
select t.*, t2.c1, t3.c2
  from t, t2, t3
 where t.key1 = t2.key1(+)
   and t.key2 = t3.key2(+)
```

or

```
select t.*, (select c1 from t2 where t2.key1 = t.key1) c1,
            (select c2 from t3 where t3.key2 = t.key2) c2
  from t;
```

The DBA's second idea, to use a function-based column, is an attempt to outsmart the database, essentially saying, "I can do an outer join faster than you can." Well, you cannot. The fn_country() approach would cause SQL to call PL/SQL, and that PL/SQL itself will call SQL again to either find a row or not. This is much less efficient than just letting SQL do its job in the first place. The third idea, applying fn_country on every fetch, is even worse, because it involves a client round-trip.

But this DBA was convinced that his second or third idea would work the best. He felt that the less burden on SQL, the faster it will go. After much back and forth, he finally called me on it. He said, "You demonstrate most of what you say with examples and numbers. I would appreciate it if you can show an example or two that can prove the above statements." Touché. If you refer back to the "Question Authority" section, you will see that he nailed it—it was time for me to put up or shut up.

I pulled out my trusty Runstats tool (described in the "Small-Time Benchmarking" section of this chapter). I started with two tables to compare outer joining versus trying to outsmart the engine:

```
create table t1 as select * from all_objects;
create table t2 as select * from all_objects where rownum <= 15000;

alter table t1 add constraint t1_pk primary key(object_id);
alter table t2 add constraint t2_pk primary key(object_id);

analyze table t1 compute statistics
for table for all indexes for all indexed columns;

analyze table t2 compute statistics
for table for all indexes for all indexed columns;
```

Then I created a function in the style the DBA suggested:

```
create or replace function get_data( p_object_id in number ) return varchar2
is
    l_object_name t2.object_name%type;
begin
    select object_name into l_object_name
      from t2
     where object_id = p_object_id;
    return l_object_name;
exception
    when no_data_found then
        return NULL;
end;
/
```

Now, I was ready to compare these two equivalent queries:

```
select a.object_id, a.object_name oname1, b.object_name oname2
  from t1 a, t2 b
 where a.object_id = b.object_id(+);

select object_id, object_name oname1, get_data(object_id) oname2
  from t1;
```

I fired up the Runstats test harness, and the results were incredible:

```
ops$tkyte@ORA920> begin
  2          runstats_pkg.rs_start;
  3          for x in ( select a.object_id,
  4                               a.object_name oname1,
  5                               b.object_name oname2
  6                       from t1 a, t2 b
  7                       where a.object_id = b.object_id(+) )
  8          loop
  9              null;
 10          end loop;
 11          runstats_pkg.rs_middle;
 12          for x in ( select object_id,
 13                               object_name oname1,
 14                               get_data(object_id) oname2
 15                       from t1 )
 16          loop
 17              null;
 18          end loop;
 19          runstats_pkg.rs_stop;
 20   end;
 21   /
84 hsecs
2803 hsecs
run 1 ran in 3% of the time
```

This ran in less than 5% of the runtime by the wall clock, simply by letting the database do what databases were born to do! Not only that, but look at the latching/statistic report generated by Runstats:

```
Name                               Run1        Run2        Diff
STAT...consistent gets - exami       21      78,155      78,134
STAT...session logical reads     15,553     109,775      94,222
STAT...consistent gets           15,524     109,747      94,223
LATCH.cache buffers chains       31,118     141,477     110,359
LATCH.library cache pin             167     126,460     126,293
LATCH.shared pool                   383     126,698     126,315
LATCH.library cache                 380     189,780     189,400
STAT...session pga memory max   196,608           0    -196,608
STAT...session uga memory max 1,767,880           0  -1,767,880
Run1 latches total versus runs -- difference and pct
33,264    590,820    557,556     5.63%

PL/SQL procedure successfully completed.
```

You can see there are 95,000 less logical I/O operations, for half million fewer latches (latches = locks, remember). Again, this was achieved by just letting the database do its thing.

By keeping it simple—not trying to outguess or outsmart the database—we achieved our goal. And this path was easier. It is so much easier to just outer join than it is to write a little function for each and every outer join we anticipate doing.

The point is that if there is an apparently easy way to do something and a convoluted, hard way to do the same thing, and they result in the same goal being met, by all means, be lazy like me and take the easy way. Not only is the easy way, well, easier, it is also usually the correct way as well.

# Use Supplied Functionality

Time and time again, I see people reinventing database functionality. Here are some of the top functions people refuse to use:

- **Auditing**   Rather than use the built-in AUDIT command of fine-grained auditing, some people are bent on doing it themselves via triggers. The most common reason is, "We've heard auditing is slow."

- **Replication**   Rather than use master-to-master replication, snapshot-based replication, or streams, some people do it themselves. The most common reason is, "We've heard the built-in stuff is complicated."

- **Message queuing**   Rather than use the advanced queuing (AQ) software in the database, some people look for undocumented features, tricky ways to have multiple processes read separate records from a "queue" table and process them efficiently. The most common reason is, "We just don't want to use AQ."

- **Maintaining a history of record changes**   Rather than use the Workspace Manager, which can do this automatically, some people write tons of code in triggers to attempt to do the same thing. The most common reason is, "We didn't know that functionality existed."

- **Sequences**   Rather than use a built-in sequence number, some people create their own approach using database tables. Then they want to know how to scale that up (which isn't possible, because if you use a table yourself, it will be a serial process, and serial means not scalable). The most common reason is, "Not every database has a sequence. We are developing for databases X and Y, and can use only features they both have."

The reasons for not using database functionality span from FUD (fear, uncertainty, doubt), to ignorance of what the database provides, to the quest for database independence. None of these are acceptable. We'll take a look at each reason in turn.

## We Heard Feature X Is Slow

This excuse has to do with the "fear" part of FUD. It seems to be a common perception that the built-in auditing facility in Oracle is slow. I believe this stems from the fact that if you have auditing turned on, the system runs slower than when auditing is not turned on (seems obvious). So, the mythology begins with:

- We didn't have auditing on, and things ran okay.

- We turned on auditing, and they ran slower.

- Therefore, auditing is really slow.

And that story is passed down from generation to generation of Oracle development staff. When I hear this, I ask these simple questions:

- Did you benchmark it?

- Do you have the hard and fast numbers?

- What exactly is the overhead?

- What are the numbers?

You probably can guess that no one has tried it; they just heard that it was slow.

What you will find out if you benchmark this is that built-in auditing has the following benefits over any other solution:

- It's faster, because it is internal. It is in the kernel; in C code that will be faster than the trigger you use to emulate its functionality.

- It's easier because it is a single command, rather than a design of an entire subsystem for your application, plus the code, plus the schema design, and so on.

- It's more secure because it is part of the database. It is evaluated to be "correct" by independent third parties. It is not a simple trigger someone can disable.

- It's more flexible because it is in the Oracle audit trail, or maybe better yet, it is in the operating system audit trail. There are hundreds of tools that know these schemas/formats. How many tools out there know your tables? You would have a very large do-it-yourself project, not only to capture but to report and make sense of the audit trail.

Let's look at a simple benchmark that you can try yourself. I wanted to audit inserts into a table. Here is one way (after making sure AUDIT_TRAIL was set in the init.ora parameter file):

```
create table t1 ( x int );
audit insert on t1 by access;
```

Here is another way:

```
create table t2 ( x int );
create table t2_audit
as
select sysdate dt, a.*
  from v$session a
 where 1=0;
create index t2_audit_idx on t2_audit(sid,serial#);

create trigger t2_audit
after insert on t2
begin
    insert into t2_audit
    select sysdate, a.*
      from v$session a
```

```
        where sid = (select sid
                       from v$mystat
                      where rownum=1);
end;
/
```

**NOTE**
*There are many ways to implement this "do it yourself" auditing. I chose a method that involved the least amount of code and used techniques I frequently see others implementing. Another valid approach would be to populate an application context upon logging into the system—removing the need to query the V$SESSION/V$MYSTAT table for every insert statement on T2. This will decrease the CPU used but you will lose some of the information that can change in V$SESSION during the course of your session.*

Now, it should be obvious which one was easier to develop and required less thought on my part, but which method performed better? Well, in order to answer this question, I set up a small procedure:

```
create table t1_times ( xstart timestamp, xstop timestamp );
create or replace procedure p1( n in number )
as
    l_rowid rowid;
begin
    insert into t1_times (xstart) values (systimestamp)
    returning rowid into l_rowid;
    for i in 1 .. n
    loop
        insert into t1 values (i);
        commit;
    end loop;
    update t1_times set xstop = systimestamp where rowid = l_rowid;
    commit;
end;
/
```

And did the same for T2. Then I ran this procedure five times in the background, each inserting 30,000 rows. Before and after doing this, I took a Statspack snapshot. Here are some of the relevant numbers:

| | TI with Native Auditing | T2 with DIY Auditing | Comment |
|---|---|---|---|
| **Transactions/Second** | 380 | 278 | 27% decrease in transactions/second |
| **CPU Time** | 302 | 443 | 146% of the CPU time |

Even for this simple example, the results are clear. It is easier, faster, and all around more efficient to use the native functionality. Again, do not accept word of mouth. Prove that a method is slower (or faster), or have it proven to you.

# We Heard Feature X Is Complicated

Just the other day, someone asked me how the MD5 function from the DBMS_OBFUSCATION_ TOOLKIT worked. When I asked why she was interested, she said she wanted to "optimize" a refresh of a slowly changing dimension in a data warehouse table. Her approach was to bring the primary key and a checksum of the rest of the data over a database link, and compute and compare the sent checksum to a checksum of the local data. If the checksums were different, they would go back and pull the entire row over the database link to update the row in the local database. If the row didn't exist, it would be inserted. After pulling changes and inserting new rows, she had to turn the problem around and send all of the primary keys over to the remote database to see if they still existed. If not, those keys had to be deleted locally.

My solution was to create a snapshot log on the remote table, create a snapshot locally with a refresh interval, and be done with it.

What happened here was she had heard that replication is complicated. Rather than investigate what it would take to accomplish her goal using that database feature, she set about doing it herself. Would her approach work? Well, she didn't consider some possibilities. What happens if someone modifies the remote table while making multiple passes on it and such (data-integrity issues)? What about the infrastructure you need to design and build to monitor such a solution? (There isn't a single systems management tool on the market that knows how to watch their process and page a DBA when it breaks). There were other things she hadn't yet considered, but would need to address in a production environment.

Yes, it's true that replication in general is complicated. It is not that the implementation in Oracle is complicated, but rather that the replication itself is hard stuff. It is not something you just throw into a system. There are many things to consider. But consider how hard it is to implement this feature yourself! For example, read-only snapshots, a feature available with Oracle since 1993 in version 7.0, completely satisfy the requirements of the preceding example. This feature is manageable and implemented in hundreds of locations. Doing it yourself, on the other hand, requires tons of design, code, and time.

Everything is complicated until you learn it. Driving a stick-shift car was complicated the first time I did it. Now, that I drive one every day, I don't even think about it.

# We Don't Want to

I have never been able to figure out why people go into the "I don't want to" mode with regard to database features. But, invariably, once they have this attitude, changing their minds is virtually impossible.

"Hey Tom, can you take a look at this SQL for me. I can get a much quicker result if I use `not in`, instead of `not exists`, but I would rather not.

```
[huge query cut out]

TKPROF REPORT:
call   cnt      cpu    elap     disk    query    rows
```

```
----- ---   --------   --------  -------  -------  ------
Parse   1      0.02       0.04         0        0       0
Execute 1      0.00       0.00         0        0       0
Ftch 1939  25772.65   25976.95    149793 29294754   29061
        ----   --------  ---------  -------  --------  -----
tot   1941  25772.67   25976.99    149793 29294754   29061
```

I tried using all the anti-join hints in the subquery without much success. (There are appropriate indexes on all tables and everything has been analyzed). If I were to modify it and say

```
AND a.x not in (select b.y from b WHERE b.a = 'X')
```

then it comes back in like five minutes as opposed to the almost eight hours for the original. What are your thoughts?"

My thoughts? My thoughts are that he knows the answer and knows exactly what to do. But, for whatever reason, he doesn't want to do it. My solution is that he should forget about what he would rather do and do what he knows he needs to do.

A technology that people commonly just "don't want to" use is the AQ software in the database. A common business problem is that applications will place messages into tables. These are records that represent work to be done (for example, process an order). The technical problem we need to solve here is how do we make it so that the following goals are met:

- Each message gets processed at most once.
- Each message gets processed at least once.
- Many messages must be worked on simultaneously by many background processes.

How can we have many users working concurrently on these rows while at the same time making sure each message gets processed at least, and at most, one time? We cannot just update a record and mark it in process. If we did that and did not commit, all of the other sessions trying to get a message would block on that row trying to update it (so the messages wouldn't be worked on simultaneously). If we update a record and mark it in process and commit it before actually processing it, the message won't be processed. If our process fails, the message is marked as processed (or in process). No one else would ever pick it up. In short, this is a very sticky problem in a relational database—we really want a multiple-consumer queue table. Fortunately, the database provides one for us. AQ does exactly this:

- It has simple routines to create a queue.
- It has simple stored procedures to enqueue a message, allowing a client to put a message in the queue.
- It has a simple stored procedure to dequeue a message, allowing a background process to retrieve a message. In fact, the dequeue is built to be highly concurrent. You could have two, three, or dozens of dequeue processes running concurrently against the same queue.

So, it just wouldn't make sense not to want to use AQ to solve our problem.

The only way I've succeeded in changing the "I don't want to" attitude is to apply peer pressure or pressure from management. A manager asking you, "Why are you writing hundreds of lines of code when you could just do this?" does seem to carry some weight.

# We Didn't Know

The worst reason not to use a database feature is because you didn't know about it. I will refer back to the "Read the Documentation" section earlier in this chapter, where I plead with you to read the manuals, or at least the *New Features Guide* and *Concepts Guide* (with each release).

What you don't know is costing you time, money, energy, and brain cells. The database incorporates a lot of functionality. Don't be penny wise but pound foolish here. Taking an afternoon to skim these manuals and discover what is out there will pay for itself in a week.

# We Want Database Independence

Another reason that people do things the hard way relates to the idea that one should strive for openness and database independence at all costs. The developers wish to avoid using closed, proprietary database features, even those as simple as stored procedures or sequences, because that will lock them into a database. But, in reality, the instant you develop a read/write application, you are already somewhat locked in.

You will find subtle (and sometimes not so subtle) differences between the databases as soon as you start running queries and modifications. For example, in one database (not Oracle!), you might find that your `select count(*) from T` deadlocks with a simple update of two rows. In Oracle, you'll find that the `select count(*)` never blocks for a writer. You'll find that, given the same exact transaction mix, reports come out with different answers in different databases because of fundamental implementation differences. It is a very rare application that can simply be picked up and moved from one database to another. There will always be differences in the way that the SQL is interpreted and processed.

As an example, consider a recent project to build a web-based product using Visual Basic (VB), ActiveX Controls, Internet Information Services (IIS) Server, and Oracle. The developers expressed concern that since the business logic had been written in PL/SQL, the product had become database-dependent. They wanted to know how to correct this. I was taken aback by this question. In looking at the list of chosen technologies, I could not figure out how being database-dependent was a bad thing:

- They had chosen a language that locked them into a single operating system and is supplied by a single vendor (they could have opted for Java).

- They had chosen a component technology that locked them into a single operating system and vendor (they could have opted for EJB or CORBA).

- They had chosen a web server that locked them into a single vendor and single platform (why not Apache?).

Every other technology choice they had made locked them into a very specific configuration. In fact, the only technology that offered them any choice as far as open systems went was the database. I had to assume that they were looking forward to utilizing the full potential of the other technologies, so why was the database an exception, especially when it was crucial to their success?

We can put a slightly different spin on this argument if we consider it from the perspective of "openness." You put all of your data into the database. The database is a very open tool. It supports data access via SQL, Enterprise JavaBeans (EJBs), Hypertext Transfer Protocol (HTTP), File Transfer Protocol (FTP), Server Message Block (SMB), and many other protocols and access mechanisms. Sounds great so far—the most open thing in the world.

Then you put all your application logic and security outside the database—perhaps in your beans that access the data, or in the Java Server Pages (JSPs) that access the data, or in your VB code running under Microsoft Transaction Server (MTS). The end result is that you have just closed off your database. No longer can people hook in existing technologies to make use of this data. They must use your access methods (or bypass security altogether).

This sounds all well and fine today, but remember that the "whiz bang" technology of today, such as EJBs, are yesterday's concepts and tomorrow's old, tired technology. What has persevered for over 20 years in the relational world (and probably most of the object implementations as well) is the database itself. The front-ends to the data change almost yearly, and as they do, the applications that have all of the security built inside themselves, not in the database, become obstacles, or road blocks to future progress.

Let's consider one Oracle-specific database feature called fine-grained access control (FGAC). In a nutshell, this technology allows the developer to embed procedures in the database that can modify queries as they are submitted to the database. This query modification is used to restrict the rows the client will receive or modify. The procedure can look at who is running the query, when they are running the query, what terminal they are running the query from, and so on, and can constrain access to the data as appropriate. With FGAC, you can enforce security such that, for example:

- Any query executed outside normal business hours by a certain class of users returned zero records.

- Any data could be returned to a terminal in a secure facility but only nonsensitive information would go to a remote client terminal.

Basically, it allows you to locate access control in the database, right next to the data. It no longer matters if the user comes at the data from an EJB, a JSP, a VB application using ODBC, or SQL*Plus—the same security protocols will be enforced. You are well situated for the next technology that comes along.

Now, which implementation is more open:

- The one that makes all access to the data possible only through calls to the VB code and ActiveX controls (replace VB with Java and ActiveX with EJB if you like; I'm not picking on a particular technology but on an implementation here)

- The solution that allows access from anything that can talk to the database, over protocols as diverse as Secure Sockets Layer (SSL), HTTP, and Net8 (and others) or using APIs such as ODBC, JDBC, OCI, and so on

I have yet to see an ad-hoc reporting tool that will query your VB code. However, I know of dozens that can do SQL.

The decision to strive for database independence and total openness is one that people are absolutely free to take, and many try, but I believe that it is the wrong decision. No matter what database you are using, you should exploit it fully; squeeze every last bit of functionality out of that product you can. You'll find yourself doing that in the tuning phase (which again always seems to happen right after deployment) anyway. It is amazing how quickly the database independence requirement can be dropped when you can make the application run five times faster just by exploiting the software's capabilities.

# Summary

In this chapter, we looked at many of the softer issues surrounding an Oracle database implementation. We've looked at the DBA/developer relationship and how that should work. We've looked into why it is important to understand the tool you have at your disposal—the Oracle database. I've stressed how it is more than just a bit bucket, a place to dump data. We've gone over what happens if you don't use a test environment, as well as covered many other issues.

I wanted to get across two very important messages. One is that it isn't true unless it can be proven to be true. And, if it can be proven to be true (or false) it should be. Remember your earlier education, when you were taught the scientific method: Formulate a test to fortify your hypothesis (or equally as likely, destroy it). Use this technique every day when developing your systems. Put simply, question authority.

The other main point to take away from this chapter is to exploit what you have. Exploit your operating system, your language, your middle tier, and your database. Use as much supplied functionality as possible. It is faster to develop, cheaper, and generally leaves you with a better product at the end of the day. Use the extra time you have to benchmark, instrument, and test!

In the next chapter, we'll take a look at the tools you can use not only to develop and tune your applications, but also to question authority and benchmark with. We've mentioned a few of them in passing in this chapter such as SQL_TRACE, TKPROF, and Runstats already. Now we are ready to go into greater detail.

# CHAPTER

## 2

# Your Performance
# Toolkit

n this chapter, we'll look at all of the tools I use on a recurring basis. These are the tools I use every day in order to test ideas, debug processes, tune algorithms, and so on. It is a fairly short list and incorporates only one graphical user interface (GUI) tool. All of the other tools are predominantly character mode, text-based tools.

In today's world, nearly everyone is using a GUI of some sort, be it the Macintosh, Linux, some Unix variant, or one of the many different Microsoft Windows versions. So, why is a tool like SQL*Plus, a command-line interface to the database, still relevant? For the same reason telnet (or more likely ssh, the secure shell) is useful. In a mobile environment, where you move from computer to computer, your networking capabilities and set of installed software do not remain constant. I've seen people sit down at someone else's computer and not be able to work because the editor they used wasn't installed, or the GUI tool they used to connect to the database wasn't there. But, in most cases, the standard command-line tools are there. If you can use them, you'll be able to work on almost any computer.

So, do I use any graphical tools for the database? The answer is very few. I use JDeveloper occasionally. I use Oracle Enterprise Manager (OEM) infrequently. But that is the extent of it. I would say that 99% of my interaction with Oracle in an ad-hoc fashion is via the good, old command-line SQL*Plus tool.

For application tuning, I use my favorite tools to make sure the application is as fast and as scalable as possible. First, I'll tune it in single-user mode, using EXPLAIN PLAN, AUTOTRACE, TKPROF, and/or Runstats. Then I'll tune the application in multiuser mode, using Statspack.

This chapter covers my tools of choice:

- SQL*Plus
- EXPLAIN PLAN
- AUTOTRACE
- TKPROF (hands down, my favorite)
- Runstats (a homegrown tool)
- Statspack
- DBMS_PROFILER
- JDeveloper (it's not just for Java anymore)

I'll describe the main uses of each tool, explain how to set it up, and offer tips for interpreting its output.

# SQL*Plus

SQL*Plus is ubiquitous, always available, and always the same. If you can operate SQL*Plus on your Windows machine, you can do it on Unix, Linux, and even the mainframe, without any training. I choose it as my primary means of "talking" to the database for the same reason I choose my editor of choice, vi: It is simple, powerful, and here. (Well, for Windows I need to carry a copy of vi in my pocket on a floppy disk, but at least it fits!)

Another major reason for using SQL*Plus as your tool of choice for testing is that it is reproducible. It is a known quantity and operates the same from release to release. If you want to prove a point, you cannot use TOAD (a common GUI), for example, for the simple reason that most people do not use TOAD. It's the same with virtually any other tool out there. Consider SQL*Plus your baseline tool, because it's something everyone has. If you use it constantly, you'll have the ability to sit down and be productive on anyone's workstation immediately.

These days, there is even iSQL*Plus. If you have a browser and can connect to the server hosting iSQL*Plus, you can interactively query and work with your database using just that. I make frequent use of iSQL*Plus from home to test on different versions of Oracle when answering questions submitted on the asktom web site. On my desktop machine at home, I have only the latest version of the database. When I want to test something on any earlier version (going all of the way back to version 7.0—ten releases), I need to connect to my servers at work. I use a broadband satellite connection, and as anyone who uses a satellite can tell you, doing client server (SQL*Net or telnet) operations over a satellite with a two-second turnaround time is painful (the satellite I use is about 22,000 miles from my house and every network request transmitted from my computer takes about two seconds to go up and come back to me). Using the web browser metaphor, whereby I submit a script in one message and receive all of the output in another message, turns a one-hour back-and-forth process that would have happened with client server techniques, into a two-second experience. So, over dial-up or other slow or high-latency connections, iSQL*Plus is a lifesaver. (And there is no way I could use a traditional client/server GUI tool in this environment.)

So, what do I use SQL*Plus for mainly?

- **AUTOTRACE**   This is a very simple method to get an execution plan for a query, to see statistics such as logical I/Os for a statement, and so on. (AUTOTRACE is covered in detail later in this chapter.)

- **As a scripting tool**   Some people use shell scripts to automate SQL*Plus; I use SQL*Plus to automate scripts. I can write a script in SQL*Plus to automate an export operation, for example, that can be used on *any* platform. I don't need to recode for Windows simply because I used Unix in the first place.

# Set Up SQL*Plus

The setup for SQL*Plus is amazingly easy. In fact, it should already be done. Every client software installation has it, and every server installation has it. That is why if you were to limit yourself to exactly one tool, SQL*Plus would be it. No matter where you go, it is there.

On Windows, there are two versions of SQL*Plus: a GUI one (the sqlplusw.exe program) and a DOS-based character-mode one (the sqlplus.exe program). The character-mode SQL*Plus is 100% compatible with SQL*Plus on every other platform on which Oracle is delivered. The GUI SQL*Plus, which offers no real functional benefit over the character mode—after all, it is a character-mode tool running in a window—is different enough to be confusing and isn't as flexible as the command-line version. Additionally, it is already officially deprecated in the next release of Oracle, so it won't be around for long. In the end, it is your choice, but you should give the character-mode sqlplus.exe a chance. Hey, at least you can pick the colors easily in a DOS window!

## Customize the SQL*Plus Environment

SQL*Plus has the ability to run a script automatically upon startup. This script can be used to customize your SQL*Plus environment and set up certain variables.

**NOTE**
*SQL*Plus can also run a glogin.sql (global login.sql) script, which can contain site-wide default settings. The use of the glogin.sql script is somewhat dated, however. It was more useful when dozens of people might share a single computer. Today, with most people having a desktop machine with SQL*Plus on it, the glogin.sql script's use is somewhat obviated.*

I'll share my login.sql script with you. This should give you a good idea of what you can do with such a script.

```
REM turn off the terminal output - make it so SQLPlus does not
REM print out anything when we log in
set termout off

REM default your editor here.  SQLPlus has many individual settings
REM This is one of the most important ones
define _editor=vi

REM serveroutput controls whether your DBMS_OUTPUT.PUT_LINE calls
REM go into the bit bucket (serveroutput off) or get displayed
REM on screen.  I always want serveroutput set on and as big
REM as possible - this does that.  The format wrapped elements
REM causes SQLPlus to preserve leading whitespace - very useful
set serveroutput on size 1000000 format wrapped

REM Here I set some default column widths for commonly queried
REM columns - columns I find myself setting frequently, day after day
column object_name format a30
column segment_name format a30
column file_name format a40
column name format a30
column file_name format a30
column what format a30 word_wrapped
column plan_plus_exp format a100

REM by default, a spool file is a fixed width file with lots of
REM trailing blanks.  Trimspool removes these trailing blanks
REM making the spool file significantly smaller
set trimspool on

REM LONG controls how much of a LONG or CLOB sqlplus displays
REM by default.  It defaults to 80 characters which in general
REM is far too small.  I use the first 5000 characters by default
```

```
Set long 5000

REM This sets the default width at which sqlplus wraps output.
REM I use a telnet client that can go up to 131 characters wide -
REM hence this is my preferred setting.
set linesize 131

REM sqlplus will print column headings every N lines of output
REM this defaults to 14 lines.  I find that they just clutter my
REM screen so this setting effectively disables them for all
REM intents and purposes - except for the first page of course
set pagesize 9999

REM here is how I set my signature prompt in sqlplus to
REM username@database>  I use the NEW_VALUE concept to format
REM a nice prompt string that defaults to IDLE (useful for those
REM of you that use sqlplus to start up their databases - the
REM prompt will default to idle> if your database isn't started)
define gname=idle
column global_name new_value gname
select lower(user) || '@' ||
substr( global_name, 1, decode( dot,
0, length(global_name),
dot-1) ) global_name
from (select global_name, instr(global_name,'.') dot
from global_name );
set sqlprompt '&gname> '

REM and lastly, we'll put termout back on so sqlplus prints
REM to the screen
set termout on
```

## Use @CONNECT

Once you start using the login.sql script, probably the first thing you'll discover is that SQL*Plus runs it *once,* on startup. If you reconnect, the prompt doesn't change, and some settings are reset. The setting I noticed right away was serveroutput. Consider the following:

```
$ sqlplus /

SQL*Plus: Release 9.2.0.1.0 - Production on Sun Dec 15 14:16:54 2002
Copyright (c) 1982, 2002, Oracle Corporation.  All rights reserved.
Connected to:
Oracle9i Enterprise Edition Release 9.2.0.1.0 - Production
With the Partitioning, OLAP and Oracle Data Mining options
JServer Release 9.2.0.1.0 - Production

ops$tkyte@ORA920> show serveroutput
serveroutput ON size 1000000 format WRAPPED
ops$tkyte@ORA920> connect /
Connected.
```

```
ops$tkyte@ORA920> show serveroutput
serveroutput OFF
ops$tkyte@ORA920>
```

Since I rely on the prompt being correct (so I know who I'm logged in as and what database I'm in) and on DBMS_OUTPUT output being shown, this is disappointing. My solution is to use @CONNECT, rather than CONNECT.

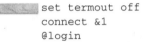
```
ops$tkyte@ORA920> @connect /
ops$tkyte@ORA920> show serveroutput
serveroutput ON size 1000000 format WRAPPED
ops$tkyte@ORA920>
```

@CONNECT is a very simple script that just reruns the login.sql script for me.

```
set termout off
connect &1
@login
```

> **NOTE**
> *In order to connect with SYSDBA, you will need to enter **@connect "/
> as sysdba"** with quotes to get the AS SYSDBA text part of the &1
> substitution variable.*

In this fashion, I always am working in the environment I expect to be in.

### Use SQLPATH

SQLPATH is the name of an environment variable you can set to tell SQL*Plus where to look for scripts. By using this environment variable, you can put your login.sql, connect.sql, and other scripts in a single directory, and SQL*Plus will find them for you. SQL*Plus will look in the current directory, and then it will look in the directory specified in the SQLPATH environment variable. This setting works on every platform that supports environment variables (such as Unix, Linux, Macintosh, and even Windows).

## Read the Documentation!

SQL*Plus is well-documented. All of the settings are available for you to see in the SQL*Plus documentation.

The most important chapter in the documentation, the one I refer to frequently, is the "SQL*Plus Command Reference" chapter. Here, you will learn about all of the SET options you have (there are *a lot* of them). It is amazing how many SQL*Plus questions I answer by supplying a URL for this particular chapter.

# EXPLAIN PLAN

EXPLAIN PLAN is the SQL command that you may use to get Oracle to tell you what the query plan for a given SQL query would be if you executed it *right now*. It's important to grasp the point that it is the plan that gets used if you were to execute the query in the current session, with the current settings.

EXPLAIN PLAN cannot tell you what plan was *actually* used to run a given query in the past, because that query execution could have taken place in a session with very different settings. For example, a query run in a session with a large sort area size may well use a different plan than the same query in a session with a small sort area size. (As you'll see in this chapter, Oracle9i does provide some ways to view the actual plan that was used for a query when it was executed.)

# Setup for EXPLAIN PLAN

Setup for EXPLAIN PLAN involves several scripts in $ORACLE_HOME/rdbms/admin:

- utlxplan.sql (for UTiLility eXplain PLAN table), which contains a CREATE TABLE statement for a table named PLAN_TABLE. This is the table in which EXPLAIN PLAN places the query plan.

- utlxplp.sql (for UTiLtility eXplain PLan Parallel), which displays the contents of the plan table, including information specific to parallel-query plans.

- utlxpls.sql (for UTiLity eXplain PLan Serial), which displays the contents of the plan table for normal, serial (nonparallel) plans.

In Oracle9i Release 2, you also need to be aware of an important package, named DBMS_XPLAN. This is a new supplied package that makes it very easy to query the plan table.

To set up for EXPLAIN PLAN, first create the plan table itself:

```
ops$tkyte@ORA920> @?/rdbms/admin/utlxplan
Table created.

ops$tkyte@ORA920> desc plan_table
 Name                                      Null?    Type
 ----------------------------------------- -------- --------------------
 STATEMENT_ID                                       VARCHAR2(30)
 TIMESTAMP                                          DATE
 REMARKS                                            VARCHAR2(80)
 OPERATION                                          VARCHAR2(30)
 … some columns removed …
 ACCESS_PREDICATES                                  VARCHAR2(4000)
 FILTER_PREDICATES                                  VARCHAR2(4000)
```

If you would like to make EXPLAIN PLAN available to the world out of the box, without setup, create a schema called UTILS or TOOLS. This schema would be granted CREATE SESSION and CREATE TABLE privileges. Create the plan table in this schema as a GLOBAL TEMPORARY TABLE with the "ON COMMIT PRESERVE ROWS" option and grant the ALL privilege on PLAN_TABLE to public. A DBA could then create a public synonym PLAN_TABLE for UTILS.PLAN_TABLE. Now, each developer can "share" the same plan table. All the developers would want to take care to issue a DELETE FROM PLAN_TABLE command or "TRUNCATE PLAN_TABLE" before using EXPLAIN PLAN. This will not cause concurrency issues; they will

not see other developers' plans; they will not see your plans; and there will be no blocking/
waiting issues.

# Use EXPLAIN PLAN

Now, you are ready to explain a query into your plan table. The format of the EXPLAIN PLAN
command is simply:

```
explain plan
    [set statement_id = 'text']
    [into [owner.]table_name]
for statement;
```

The text in brackets is optional, and we won't be using it in our examples. The statement_id
allows you to store multiple plans in the plan table. The owner.table_name, allows you to use
a table other then PLAN_TABLE if you prefer.

Here, we'll create a table to test with:

```
ops$tkyte@ORA920> CREATE TABLE t
    2  (
    3    collection_year int,
    4    data            varchar2(25)
    5  )
    6  PARTITION BY RANGE (COLLECTION_YEAR) (
    7    PARTITION PART_99 VALUES LESS THAN (2000),
    8    PARTITION PART_00 VALUES LESS THAN (2001),
    9    PARTITION PART_01 VALUES LESS THAN (2002),
   10    PARTITION PART_02 VALUES LESS THAN (2003),
   11    PARTITION the_rest VALUES LESS THAN (MAXVALUE)
   12  )
   13  ;
Table created.
```

This creates a very simple partitioned table. I have chosen a partitioned table to show why
EXPLAIN PLAN is still relevant, even though AUTOTRACE will seem to be much easier to use.
(Soon, we'll compare the EXPLAIN PLAN output to AUTOTRACE's output to demonstrate the
difference.)

We start with a delete operation against the plan table, to clear out any preexisting rows, and
then continue the EXPLAIN PLAN statement itself:

```
ops$tkyte@ORA920> delete from plan_table;
2 rows deleted.

ops$tkyte@ORA920> explain plan for
  2  select * from t where collection_year = 2002;
Explained.
```

That is it. Now, we are ready to run utlxpls (serial plan output). The results are as follows:

```
ops$tkyte@ORA920> @?/rdbms/admin/utlxpls
```

```
PLAN_TABLE_OUTPUT
-------------------------------------------------

-------------------------------------------------------------------
| Id  | Operation            |Name|Rows|Bytes|Cost|Pstart|Pstop|
-------------------------------------------------------------------
|   0 | SELECT STATEMENT     |    |  1 |  27 |  2 |      |     |
|*  1 |   TABLE ACCESS FULL  | T  |  1 |  27 |  2 |   4  |  4  |
-------------------------------------------------------------------

Predicate Information (identified by operation id):
---------------------------------------------------

   1 - filter("T"."COLLECTION_YEAR"=2002)

Note: cpu costing is off

14 rows selected.
```

That shows how Oracle will evaluate the plan. In a nutshell, a full-table scan will be performed on the table T. We can also see the cost of performing this step (COST=2), the expected number of rows to be returned, and how many bytes of output would be returned. The optimizer is "guessing" this information, since we did not analyze the table. We can also see that only one partition is being accessed, as shown in the Pstart and Pstop columns. So, while this is a full-table scan, partition elimination is making it possible for us to skip reading the bulk of the table.

Note that only Oracle9i Release 2 or later will have output exactly like what is shown here. In prior releases, you did not see the predicate information at the end of the report. This is new information printed by the DBMS_XPLAN supplied package, which is not available prior to Oracle9i Release 2. This additional information makes it easy to see exactly what portions of the predicate Oracle is applying at each step of the query plan.

### An AUTOTRACE Comparison

Even though we haven't talked about AUTOTRACE yet, we'll jump ahead a bit to make a point about the benefits of EXPLAIN PLAN. Let's compare the `utlxpls` output with the output provided by AUTOTRACE:

```
ops$tkyte@ORA920> set autotrace traceonly explain
ops$tkyte@ORA920> select * from t where collection_year = 2002;

Execution Plan
----------------------------------------------------------
   0      SELECT STATEMENT Optimizer=CHOOSE (Cost=2 Card=1 Bytes=27)
   1    0   TABLE ACCESS (FULL) OF 'T' (Cost=2 Card=1 Bytes=27)

ops$tkyte@ORA920> set autotrace off
```

Now, while getting AUTOTRACE to show us a plan is easy, we can see that a very important piece of information is missing here! The partition elimination information is not displayed. With the EXPLAIN PLAN scripts, we get that additional, important information (important when using partitioning, that is).

In summary, you should consider using EXPLAIN PLAN and DBMS_XPLAN in Oracle9i Release 2 to view query plans if the query plan is what you are interested in reviewing. Use AUTOTRACE to view statistics only. DBMS_XPLAN shows information relevant to the query, based on the query. AUTOTRACE always shows the same information, regardless of the query type.

## How to Read a Query Plan

Often, I am asked this question: "How exactly do we read a query plan?" Here, I will present my approach to reading the plan. We'll take a look at a query plan resulting from a query against the SCOTT/TIGER tables. Note that I have added primary keys to the EMP and DEPT tables, so they are indexed.

```
scott@ORA920> delete from plan_table;
7 rows deleted.

scott@ORA920> explain plan for
  2  select ename, dname, grade
  3    from emp, dept, salgrade
  4   where emp.deptno = dept.deptno
  5     and emp.sal between salgrade.losal and salgrade.hisal
  6  /
Explained.

scott@ORA920> @?/rdbms/admin/utlxpls

PLAN_TABLE_OUTPUT
---------------------------------------------------------------------
| Id  | Operation                     |Name     |Rows|Bytes|Cost |
---------------------------------------------------------------------
|   0 | SELECT STATEMENT              |         |    |     |     |
|   1 |  NESTED LOOPS                 |         |    |     |     |
|   2 |   NESTED LOOPS                |         |    |     |     |
|   3 |    TABLE ACCESS FULL          | SALGRADE|    |     |     |
|*  4 |    TABLE ACCESS FULL          | EMP     |    |     |     |
|   5 |    TABLE ACCESS BY INDEX ROWID| DEPT    |    |     |     |
|*  6 |     INDEX UNIQUE SCAN         | DEPT_PK |    |     |     |
---------------------------------------------------------------------

Predicate Information (identified by operation id):
---------------------------------------------------

   4 - filter("EMP"."SAL"<="SALGRADE"."HISAL" AND
           "EMP"."SAL">="SALGRADE"."LOSAL")
   6 - access("EMP"."DEPTNO"="DEPT"."DEPTNO")
```

```
Note: rule based optimization

21 rows selected.
```

How can we figure out what happens first, second, and so on? How does that plan actually get evaluated? First, I will show you the pseudo code for evaluation of the plan, and then we will discuss how I arrived at this conclusion.

```
For salgrade in (select * from salgrade)
Loop
    For emp in ( select * from emp )
    Loop
       If ( emp.sal between salgrade.losal and salgrade.hisal )
       Then
            Select * into dept_rec
              From dept
             Where dept.deptno = emp.deptno;

            OUTPUT RECORD with fields from salgrade,emp,dept
       End if;
    End loop;
End loop;
```

The way I read this plan is by turning it into a graph of sorts—an evaluation tree. In order to do this, you need to understand access paths. For detailed information on all of the access paths available to Oracle, see the Oracle *Performance and Tuning Guide*. There are quite a few access paths, and the descriptions in the guide are quite comprehensive.

To build the tree, we can start from the top, with step 1, which will be our root node in the tree. Next, we need to find the things that feed this root node. That will be accomplished in steps 2 and 5, which are at the same level of indentation, because they feed into step 1. Continuing, we can see that steps 3 and 4 feed step 2, and that step 6 feeds step 5. Putting it together iteratively, we can draw this evaluation tree:

Reading the tree, we see that in order to get step 1, we need steps 2 and 5; step 2 comes first. In order to get to step 2, we need steps 3 and 4; step 3 comes first. That is how we arrive at the pseudo code:

```
For salgrade in (select * from salgrade)
Loop
    For emp in ( select * from emp )
    Loop
```

The full scan of the SALGRADE table is step 3. The full scan of the EMP table is step 4. Step 2 is a nested loop, which is roughly equivalent to two FOR loops. Once we evaluate step 2 like that, we can look at step 5. Step 5 runs step 6 first. Step 6 is the index-scan step. We are taking the output of step 2 and using that to feed this part of the query plan. So, the output from step 2 is used to perform an index scan. Then that index scan output is used to access the DEPT table by ROWID. That result is the output of step 1, our result set.

Now, to make this interesting, we will run an equivalent query, but we will mix up the order of the tables in the FROM clause this time. Since I am using the rule-based optimizer (RBO), this will affect the generated query plan. (This is just one reason why you don't want to use the RBO; we will cover some more reasons in the "Understand the AUTOTRACE Output" section later in this chapter.) The RBO is sensitive to the order of tables in the FROM clause and will use the order in which we enter them to choose a "driving table" for the query if none of the predicates do so (in the event of a "tie," the RBO will look at the order the developer typed in table names to pick what table to use first)! We will use the same logic to build its query plan tree and evaluate how it processes the query.

```
scott@ORA920> delete from plan_table;
7 rows deleted.

scott@ORA920> explain plan for
  2  select ename, dname, grade
  3    from salgrade, dept, emp
  4   where emp.deptno = dept.deptno
  5     and emp.sal between salgrade.losal and salgrade.hisal
  6  /
Explained.

scott@ORA920> @?/rdbms/admin/utlxpls

PLAN_TABLE_OUTPUT
---------------------------------------------------------------
| Id  | Operation                       | Name      | Rows  | Bytes |
---------------------------------------------------------------
|   0 | SELECT STATEMENT                |           |       |       |
|   1 |  NESTED LOOPS                   |           |       |       |
|   2 |   NESTED LOOPS                  |           |       |       |
|   3 |    TABLE ACCESS FULL            | EMP       |       |       |
|   4 |    TABLE ACCESS BY INDEX ROWID| DEPT      |       |       |
|*  5 |     INDEX UNIQUE SCAN           | DEPT_PK   |       |       |
|*  6 |   TABLE ACCESS FULL             | SALGRADE  |       |       |
---------------------------------------------------------------
Predicate Information (identified by operation id):
---------------------------------------------------
   5 - access("EMP"."DEPTNO"="DEPT"."DEPTNO")
   6 - filter("EMP"."SAL"<="SALGRADE"."HISAL" AND
              "EMP"."SAL">="SALGRADE"."LOSAL")
Note: rule based optimization

21 rows selected.
```

Here, we see that steps 2 and 6 feed step 1, steps 3 and 4 feed step 2, and step 5 feeds step 4. The evaluation tree looks like this:

So, starting with steps 3 and 4, the pseudo code logic here is

```
For emp in ( select * from emp )
Loop
-- using the index
Select * from dept where dept.deptno = emp.deptno

    For salgrade in (select * from salgrade )
    Loop
        If ( emp.sal between salgrade.losal and salgrade.hisal )
        Then
            OUTPUT RECORD;
        End if;
    End loop;
End loop;
```

And that is it. If you draw a graphical tree, and then read it from the bottom up, left to right, you will get a good understanding of the flow of the data.

## Avoid the EXPLAIN PLAN Trap

EXPLAIN PLAN is a way to get the query plan for a given SQL query if you were to execute it *right now,* in your current environment. It will not show you necessarily what plan was used yesterday to run that query or what plan would be used if another session were to execute it in the future.

In releases prior to Oracle9i Release 1, capturing the actual plan was very hard to do if all you had was the query and wanted to see the plan (you needed to try to set up a session that was exactly the same as the session that ran the query). In Oracle9i, it is easy to see the actual plan for a query that has been executed. This information is in the new V$SQL_PLAN view.

**TIP**
*Using SQL_TRACE, you can capture the actual plan used at runtime. However, it requires that tracing was enabled when the query was executed. This technique is described in the section "TKPROF," later in this chapter.*

As an example, we will run the same query in different environments in such a way that the environmental settings would have a material effect on the query plan. To set up for this example, we'll create and index a table T:

```
ops$tkyte@ORA920> create table t
  2   as
  3   select * from all_objects;
Table created.

ops$tkyte@ORA920> alter table t add constraint t_pk primary key(object_id);
Table altered.

ops$tkyte@ORA920> begin
  2       dbms_stats.gather_table_stats
  3       ( user, 'T',
  4         method_opt => 'for all columns size AUTO',
  5             cascade => TRUE );
  6   end;
  7   /

PL/SQL procedure successfully completed.
```

**NOTE**
*The DBMS_STATS options I used are for Oracle9i Release 1 and up. They are roughly equivalent to* analyze table T compute statistics for table for all indexes for all indexed columns. *That command may be used in earlier releases of Oracle. It gathers the largest amount of statistics and is rather computationally expensive. Also, you may need to change* 32000 *in the following example to some smaller number if your ALL_OBJECTS table is smaller than mine is. My maximum OBJECT_ID is about 50,000. Adjust the values as needed to reproduce the effects shown.*

Now, in a session where the application has changed the `optimizer_index_cost_adj`, a setting that has a great influence on the optimizer and the plans it will choose, a user executed:

```
ops$tkyte@ORA920> alter session set optimizer_index_cost_adj = 10;
Session altered.

ops$tkyte@ORA920> select * from t t1 where object_id > 32000;
128 rows selected.
```

Suppose that we are interested in how that query executes for tuning purposes. So, we do an EXPLAIN PLAN on it in our *other* session, where this session setting was not made:

```
ops$tkyte@ORA920> delete from plan_table;
8 rows deleted.
```

```
ops$tkyte@ORA920> explain plan for
  2  select * from t t2 where object_id > 32000;
Explained.

ops$tkyte@ORA920> set echo off

PLAN_TABLE_OUTPUT
-----------------------------------------------------------------------
| Id  | Operation            | Name   | Rows  | Bytes  | Cost  |
-----------------------------------------------------------------------
|   0 | SELECT STATEMENT     |        |   235 | 22560  |    42 |
|*  1 |   TABLE ACCESS FULL  | T      |   235 | 22560  |    42 |
-----------------------------------------------------------------------

Predicate Information (identified by operation id):
--------------------------------------------------

   1 - filter("T2"."OBJECT_ID">32000)

Note: cpu costing is off

14 rows selected.
```

Apparently, that query is using a full-table scan. Or is it? Using the information from V$SQL_PLAN, we can tell for sure. Instead of using the EXPLAIN PLAN command, we'll just populate PLAN_TABLE with the information for this query right from the V$SQL_PLAN table:

```
ops$tkyte@ORA920> delete from plan_table
  2  /
2 rows deleted.

ops$tkyte@ORA920> insert into plan_table
  2  ( STATEMENT_ID, TIMESTAMP, REMARKS, OPERATION,
  3    OPTIONS, OBJECT_NODE, OBJECT_OWNER, OBJECT_NAME,
  4    OPTIMIZER, SEARCH_COLUMNS, ID, PARENT_ID,
  5    POSITION, COST, CARDINALITY, BYTES, OTHER_TAG,
  6    PARTITION_START, PARTITION_STOP, PARTITION_ID,
  7    OTHER, DISTRIBUTION, CPU_COST,
  8    IO_COST, TEMP_SPACE )
  9  select rawtohex(address)||'_'||child_number,
 10         sysdate, null, operation, options,
 11         object_node, object_owner, object_name,
 12         optimizer,  search_columns, id, parent_id,
 13         position, cost, cardinality, bytes, other_tag,
 14         partition_start, partition_stop, partition_id,
 15         other, distribution, cpu_cost, io_cost,
 16         temp_space
 17    from v$sql_plan
 18   where (address,child_number) in
 19         ( select address, child_number
```

```
20                  from v$sql
21                 where sql_text =
22                 'select * from t t1 where object_id > 32000'
23                  and child_number = 0 )
24   /
3 rows created.

ops$tkyte@ORA920> set echo off
@?/rdbms/admin/utlxpls

PLAN_TABLE_OUTPUT
------------------------------------------------------------------
| Id  | Operation                   | Name|Rows|Bytes |Cost(%CPU)|
------------------------------------------------------------------
|   0 | SELECT STATEMENT            |     |    |      |          |
|   1 |  TABLE ACCESS BY INDEX ROWID| T   | 235|22560 |  21   (5)|
|   2 |   INDEX RANGE SCAN          | T_PK| 235|      |   2   (0)|
------------------------------------------------------------------

8 rows selected.
```

Here, we see that the real plan was an index-range scan, not a full-table scan. It is not that EXPLAIN PLAN lied to us. Rather, it is that environmental differences can have a profound effect on a query plan. They could be as subtle as the simple change of a full-table scan to an index-range scan, like this, or as far-reaching as actually querying different objects (for example, table T is A.T when I query it, but it is B.T when you query it).

To be sure that you are looking at the real, live plan in Oracle9i, grab it from the V$SQL_PLAN dynamic view. Alternatively, if you have access to a SQL_TRACE trace file, you may find the actual plan used there, after using TKPROF to format it. That technique is discussed in the "TKPROF" section later in this chapter.

## Use DBMS_XPLAN and V$SQL_PLAN

If you edit the script utlxpls.sql in Oracle9i Release 2, you'll discover it is effectively one-line long:

```
select plan_table_output
from table( dbms_xplan.display( 'plan_table',null,'serial'))
```

If you edit that same script in Oracle9i Release 1 or earlier, you'll find a huge query. DBMS_XPLAN.DISPLAY is a better method for querying and displaying the plan output. It is a function that simply returns a collection, which is a procedurally formatted EXPLAIN PLAN output, including the supplemental information at the bottom of the report (new in Oracle9i Release 2). This is a side effect of using the new DBMS_XPLAN package.

So, if you do not have access to the utlxpls.sql script, the simple query shown here will perform the same function. In fact, the DBMS_XPLAN package is so good at adjusting its output based on the inputs that you do not even need to supply the inputs as utlxpls.sql does. This simple line suffices:

```
select * from table(dbms_xplan.display)
```

Using this feature coupled with the V$SQL_PLAN dynamic performance view, you can easily dump the query plans for already executed statements, directly from the database.

In the previous section, I demonstrated how you can use an INSERT into the PLAN_TABLE and then run utlxpls or utlxplp to see the plan. In Oracle9i Release 2, using DBMS_XPLAN and a view you can create, it becomes even easier. If you use a schema that has been granted SELECT privileges on SYS.V_$SQL_PLAN directly, you'll be able to create this view:

```
ops$tkyte@ORA920> create or replace view dynamic_plan_table
  2  as
  3  select
  4    rawtohex(address) || '_' || child_number statement_id,
  5    sysdate timestamp, operation, options, object_node,
  6    object_owner, object_name, 0 object_instance,
  7    optimizer,  search_columns, id, parent_id, position,
  8    cost, cardinality, bytes, other_tag, partition_start,
  9    partition_stop, partition_id, other, distribution,
 10    cpu_cost, io_cost, temp_space, access_predicates,
 11    filter_predicates
 12    from v$sql_plan;

View created.
```

Now, you can query any plan from the database with a single query:

```
ops$tkyte@ORA920> select plan_table_output
  2 from TABLE( dbms_xplan.display
  3            ( 'dynamic_plan_table',
  4              (select rawtohex(address)||'_'||child_number x
  5                 from v$sql
  6               where sql_text=
  7              'select * from t t1 where object_id > 32000' ),
  8              'serial' ) )
  9 /

PLAN_TABLE_OUTPUT
--------------------------------------------------------------
| Id  | Operation                   | Name|Rows| Bytes |Cst(%CPU)|
--------------------------------------------------------------
|   0 | SELECT STATEMENT            |     |    |       |         |
|   1 |  TABLE ACCESS BY INDEX ROWID| T   |291 | 27936 | 25   (0)|
|*  2 |   INDEX RANGE SCAN          | T_PK|291 |       | 2    (0)|
--------------------------------------------------------------
Predicate Information (identified by operation id):
--------------------------------------------------------------

   2 - access("OBJECT_ID">32000)

13 rows selected.
```

The emphasized text in the code is a query that gets the STATEMENT_ID. In this query, you can use whatever values you want to identify the exact query plan you wanted to review. The use of this technique, querying the V$ table rather then inserting the contents of V$SQL_PLAN into a "real table," is appropriate if you're generating the explain plan for this query once. Access to V$ tables can be quite expensive latch-wise on a busy system. So, if you plan on running the explain plan for a given statement many times over, copying the information to a temporary working table would be preferred.

# AUTOTRACE

A close cousin of the EXPLAIN PLAN is AUTOTRACE, which is a rather nifty feature of SQL*Plus. EXPLAIN PLAN shows you what the database will do when asked to run the query. AUTOTRACE gives you a look at how much work it actually took to perform your query, providing some important statistics regarding its actual execution. One of the nice things about AUTOTRACE is that it is fully accessible to each and every developer, all of the time. TKPROF (covered later in this chapter) is a great tool for tuning, but it relies on access to trace files, which may not be available in all environments.

I use AUTOTRACE as my first-line tuning tool. Given the query, representative inputs (binds) to the query, and access to AUTOTRACE, I generally have the tuning tools I need. Occasionally, I need to dig a little deeper with TKPROF, but most of the time, AUTOTRACE and SQL*Plus are sufficient.

"I have a poorly performing query. Can you help me?"

Give me the query in a SQL script, using bind variables where your application uses bind variables. Give me access to your database and make sure AUTOTRACE is on.

It is important when reviewing plans and tuning queries to emulate what your application does. I make sure to mention the bind variables, so that I'm not given the query select * from some_table where column = 55 to tune, when the application actually executes select * from some_table where column = :bind_variable. You cannot tune a query with literals and expect a query that contains bind variables to have the same performance characteristics.

## Set Up AUTOTRACE

AUTOTRACE's elegance is in its simplicity. Once the DBA sets up AUTOTRACE, anyone can use it. My preferred method for setting up AUTOTRACE is as follows:

1. Issue cd $ORACLE_HOME/rdbms/admin.

2. Log in to SQL*Plus as someone with CREATE TABLE and CREATE PUBLIC SYNONYM privileges (for example, as a DBA).

3. Make PLAN_TABLE universally available (as described earlier in the section about EXPLAIN PLAN).

4. Exit SQL*Plus and issue cd $ORACLE_HOME/sqlplus/admin.

5. Log in to SQL*Plus as SYSDBA (`sqlplus "/ as sysdba"`).

6. Run `SQL> @plustrce`.

7. Run `SQL> grant plustrace to public`.

By making it public, you let anyone trace using SQL*Plus. That way, everyone, without exception, can use AUTOTRACE. After all, we never want to give developers an excuse *not* to be tuning their code! (But if you want, you can replace public with some user.)

# Use AUTOTRACE

Now that the installation is complete, you are ready to start using AUTOTRACE. AUTOTRACE generates a report after any SQL DML statements (such as INSERT, UPDATE, DELETE, SELECT, and MERGE). You can control this report via the following SET commands in SQL*Plus:

- SET AUTOTRACE OFF   No AUTOTRACE report is generated. This is the default. Queries are run as normal.

- SET AUTOTRACE ON EXPLAIN   The query is run as normal, and the AUTOTRACE report shows only the optimizer execution path.

- SET AUTOTRACE ON STATISTICS   The query is run as normal, and the AUTOTRACE report shows only the SQL statement execution statistics.

- SET AUTOTRACE ON   The query execution takes place, and the AUTOTRACE report includes both the optimizer execution path and the SQL statement execution statistics.

- SET AUTOTRACE TRACEONLY   Like SET AUTOTRACE ON, but suppresses the printing of the user's query output, if any. This is useful for tuning a query that returns a large result set to the client. Rather then waiting for 1,000 rows of the output to be printed and scrolled on the screen (an operation that typically takes more time than actually executing the query itself), you can suppress this display.

- SET AUTOTRACE TRACEONLY STATISTICS   Like SET AUTOTRACE TRACEONLY, but suppresses the display of the query plan. It shows only the execution statistics.

- SET AUTOTRACE TRACEONLY EXPLAIN   Like SET AUTOTRACE TRACEONLY, but suppresses the display of the execution statistics, showing only the query plan. In addition, for SELECT statements, this setting does not actually *execute* the query. It only parses and explains the query. INSERT, UPDATE, DELETE, and MERGE statements *are* executed using this mode; only SELECT statements are handled differently.

These are just some of the options for the AUTOTRACE command. Refer to the SQL*Plus guide for information about all of the options.

# Format the AUTOTRACE Output

Now that AUTOTRACE is installed and you know how to enable it, let's look at the output it produces. We will display the plan and the runtime statistics. Since we don't care about seeing the data itself, we will suppress that. We will use the SCOTT/TIGER EMP and DEPT tables, and SET AUTOTRACE TRACEONLY in order to execute the query.

```
scott@ORA920> set autotrace traceonly
scott@ORA920> select *
  2      from emp FULL OUTER JOIN dept
  3            on (emp.deptno = dept.deptno)
  4   /
15 rows selected.

Execution Plan
------------------------------------------------------------
0   SELECT STATEMENT Optimizer=CHOOSE (Cost=10 Card=328 Bytes=38376)
1  0 VIEW (Cost=10 Card=328 Bytes=38376)
2  1   UNION-ALL
3  2     HASH JOIN (OUTER) (Cost=5 Card=327 Bytes=34335)
4  3       TABLE ACCESS (FULL) OF 'EMP' (Cost=2 Card=327 Bytes=28449)
5  3       TABLE ACCESS (FULL) OF 'DEPT' (Cost=2 Card=4 Bytes=72)
6  2     HASH JOIN (ANTI) (Cost=5 Card=1 Bytes=31)
7  6       TABLE ACCESS (FULL) OF 'DEPT' (Cost=2 Card=4 Bytes=72)
8  6       TABLE ACCESS (FULL) OF 'EMP' (Cost=2 Card=327 Bytes=4251)
```

This is probably my most-used format of the AUTOTRACE command, translating to "show me the statistics, but hold the data." So, what we can see is the query plan. We can see that a full outer join apparently takes a lot of work! It does an outer join of EMP to DEPT and then UNION ALLS that with an anti-join of DEPT to EMP. That is the definition of a full outer join: Give me every row from both tables, regardless of whether or not it has a match in the other table.

You do have some amount of control over the formatting of this report. The defaults (found in $ORACLE_HOME/sqlplus/admin/glogin.sql) are as follows:

```
COLUMN id_plus_exp FORMAT 990 HEADING i
COLUMN parent_id_plus_exp FORMAT 990 HEADING p
COLUMN plan_plus_exp FORMAT a60
COLUMN object_node_plus_exp FORMAT a8
COLUMN other_tag_plus_exp FORMAT a29
COLUMN other_plus_exp FORMAT a44
```

The ID_PLUS_EXP and PARENT_ID_PLUS_EXP columns are the first two numbers you see in the EXPLAIN PLAN output above. The PLAN_PLUS_EXP column is perhaps the most important one. It is the textual description of the plan step itself; for example, TABLE ACCESS (FULL) OF 'DEPT' (Cost=2 Card=4 Bytes=72). I find the default of 60 characters wide to be too small for most uses, so I set it to 100 in my login.sql file.

The last three settings control the output information displayed for parallel query plans. The easiest way to see which columns they affect is to run a parallel query with SET AUTOTRACE TRACEONLY EXPLAIN and turn them off, one by one. You'll clearly see what disappears from the report, so you'll know what they control. Here is a simple script to do that (assuming your system is set up to allow for parallel queries):

```
set echo on

set autotrace traceonly  explain
select /*+ parallel( emp 2 ) */ * from emp
```

```
/
COLUMN object_node_plus_exp NOPRINT
/
COLUMN other_tag_plus_exp NOPRINT
/
COLUMN other_plus_exp NOPRINT
/
set autotrace off
```

# Understand the AUTOTRACE Output

There are two possible parts to an AUTOTRACE output: the query plan report and the statistics. Looking first at the query plan, we see output like this:

```
Execution Plan
----------------------------------------------------------
0   SELECT STATEMENT Optimizer=CHOOSE (Cost=10 Card=328 Bytes=38376)
1 0   VIEW (Cost=10 Card=328 Bytes=38376)
2 1     UNION-ALL
3 2       HASH JOIN (OUTER) (Cost=5 Card=327 Bytes=34335)
4 3         TABLE ACCESS (FULL) OF 'EMP' (Cost=2 Card=327 Bytes=28449)
5 3         TABLE ACCESS (FULL) OF 'DEPT' (Cost=2 Card=4 Bytes=72)
6 2       HASH JOIN (ANTI) (Cost=5 Card=1 Bytes=31)
7 6         TABLE ACCESS (FULL) OF 'DEPT' (Cost=2 Card=4 Bytes=72)
8 6         TABLE ACCESS (FULL) OF 'EMP' (Cost=2 Card=327 Bytes=4251)
```

This shows the output of a query executed using the cost-based optimizer (CBO). You can tell that the CBO was used by the presence of the information at the end of the query plan steps in parentheses: the Cost, Card, and Bytes information. In this query plan output, the CBO information represents the following:

- **Cost**   The cost assigned to each step of the query plan by the CBO. The CBO works by generating many different execution paths/plans for the same query and assigns a cost to each and every one. The query plan with the lowest cost wins. In the full outer join example, we can see the total cost for this query is 10.

- **Card**   Card is short for *Cardinality*. It is the estimated number of rows that will flow out of a given query plan step. In the full outer join example, we can see the optimizer expects there to be 327 rows in EMP and 4 rows in DEPT.

- **Bytes**   The size in bytes of the data the CBO expects each step of the plan to return. This is dependent on the number of rows (Card) and the estimated width of the rows.

If the Cost, Card, and Bytes information is not present, that is a clear indicator the query was executed using the RBO. Here is an example that shows the difference between using the RBO and the CBO:

```
scott@ORA920> set autotrace traceonly explain
scott@ORA920> select * from dual;
```

```
Execution Plan
----------------------------------------------------------
   0      SELECT STATEMENT Optimizer=CHOOSE
   1    0   TABLE ACCESS (FULL) OF 'DUAL'


scott@ORA920> select /*+ FIRST_ROWS */ * from dual;

Execution Plan
----------------------------------------------------------
   0      SELECT STATEMENT Optimizer=HINT: FIRST_ROWS
                          (Cost=11 Card=8168 Bytes=16336)
   1    0   TABLE ACCESS (FULL) OF 'DUAL' (Cost=11 Card=8168 Bytes=16336)
```

We can see that the first query against DUAL used the RBO, because it does not show the Cost, Card, and Bytes information. The RBO uses a set of rules to optimize a query. It does not care about the size of objects (numbers of rows or amount of data in bytes). It only cares about the structures in the database (indexes, clusters, tables, and so on). Therefore, it does not use or report the Cost, Card, and Bytes information.

Continuing with the next section of the AUTOTRACE report, we see the runtime statistics:

```
Statistics
----------------------------------------------------------
        0   recursive calls
        0   db block gets
       13   consistent gets
        0   physical reads
        0   redo size
     1542   bytes sent via SQL*Net to client
      499   bytes received via SQL*Net from client
        2   SQL*Net roundtrips to/from client
        0   sorts (memory)
        0   sorts (disk)
       15   rows processed

scott@ORA920> set autotrace off
```

Table 2-1 briefly explains what each of these items means.

Now, let's look at these statistics in detail and see what they can tell us about our queries.

# What Are You Looking for in AUTOTRACE Output?

Now that you have seen how to get AUTOTRACE going, how to customize the look and feel of the report and what is reported, the question remains: What exactly are you looking for? Generally, you are looking at the statistics. Let's go over the statistics and the information they relay.

| Statistics Returned | Meaning |
|---|---|
| Recursive calls | Number of SQL statements executed in order to execute your SQL statement. |
| Db block gets | Total number of blocks read from the buffer cache in current mode. |
| Consistent gets | Number of times a consistent read was requested for a block in the buffer cache. Consistent reads may require read asides to the undo (rollback) information, and these reads to the undo will be counted here as well. |
| Physical reads | Number of physical reads from the datafiles into the buffer cache. |
| Redo size | Total amount of redo generated in bytes during the execution of this statement. |
| Bytes sent via SQL*Net to client | Total number of bytes sent to the client from the server. |
| Bytes received via SQL*Net from client | Total number of bytes received from the client. |
| SQL*Net roundtrips to/from client | Total number of SQL*Net messages sent to and received from the client. This includes round-trips for fetches from a multiple-row result set. |
| Sorts (memory) | Sorts done in the user's session memory (sort area). Controlled via the `sort_area_size` database parameter. |
| Sorts (disk) | Sorts that use the disk (temporary tablespace) because the sort exceeded the user's sort area size. |
| Rows processed | Rows processed by modifications or returned from a SELECT statement. |

**TABLE 2-1.** *AUTOTRACE Report Runtime Statistics*

## Recursive Calls

The recursive calls statistic refers to the SQL run on your behalf as a side effect of some other SQL statement. For example, if you execute an insert that fires a trigger that runs a query, that will be recursive SQL. You will see recursive SQL from many other operations, such as parsing a query, requesting additional space, working with temporary space, and so on.

A high number of recursive calls for repeated executions (to remove parsing and other first-time phenomena from consideration) is something to look at, to see if you can reduce or remove calls. If it can be avoided, it should be. It indicates additional work, perhaps unnecessary additional work, being done in the background. Here, we will look at some of the most frequent causes of a high number of recursive calls and some solutions.

**Hard Parses**    If the recursive calls number is initially high, I may run the query again and see if this statistic remains high. If it doesn't, that would indicate the recursive SQL was due to a hard parse. Consider the following example:

```
ops$tkyte@ORA920> alter system flush shared_pool;
System altered.

ops$tkyte@ORA920> set autotrace traceonly statistics;
ops$tkyte@ORA920> select * from scott.emp;
14 rows selected.

Statistics
----------------------------------------------------------
        531  recursive calls
          0  db block gets
         99  consistent gets
          2  physical reads
          0  redo size
       1315  bytes sent via SQL*Net to client
        499  bytes received via SQL*Net from client
          2  SQL*Net roundtrips to/from client
         11  sorts (memory)
          0  sorts (disk)
         14  rows processed

ops$tkyte@ORA920> select * from scott.emp;

14 rows selected.


Statistics
----------------------------------------------------------
          0  recursive calls
          0  db block gets
          4  consistent gets
          0  physical reads
          0  redo size
       1315  bytes sent via SQL*Net to client
        499  bytes received via SQL*Net from client
          2  SQL*Net roundtrips to/from client
          0  sorts (memory)
          0  sorts (disk)
         14  rows processed
```

```
ops$tkyte@ORA920> set autotrace off
```

As you can see, in this case, the recursive SQL was 100% due to parsing the query for the first time. Oracle needed to execute many queries (since we flushed the shared pool, its cache of this sort of information) in order to figure out the objects being accessed, permissions, and the like. The number of recursive SQL calls went from hundreds to zero, and the number of logical I/Os (consistent gets) dropped dramatically as well. This was all in reaction to not having to hard parse that query the second time around.

**PL/SQL Function Calls**     If the recursive SQL calls remain high, you need to dig deeper to determine why. One reason might be that you are calling a PL/SQL function from SQL, and this function executes many SQL statements itself, or refers to built-in functions such as USER that implicitly use SQL. All of the SQL executed in the PL/SQL function counts as recursive SQL. Here is an example:

```
ops$tkyte@ORA920> create or replace function some_function return number
  2  as
  3      l_user       varchar2(30) default user;
  4      l_cnt        number;
  5  begin
  6          select count(*) into l_cnt from dual;   7         return l_cnt;
  8  end;
  9  /
Function created.
```

The emphasized code will be counted as recursive SQL when we run this. The following is the output after running the query once (to get it parsed):

```
ops$tkyte@ORA920> set autotrace traceonly statistics;
ops$tkyte@ORA920> select ename, some_function
  2     from scott.emp
  3  /

14 rows selected.


Statistics
----------------------------------------------------------
          28   recursive calls
...
          14   rows processed

ops$tkyte@ORA920> set autotrace off
```

As you can see, there were 28 recursive calls, or 2 for each row queried.

A possible solution is to fold the PL/SQL routine right into the query itself; for example, by using a complex CASE statement or by selecting a SELECT. The previous query could have been written simply as:

```
ops$tkyte@ORA920> select ename, (select count(*) from dual)
  2  from scott.emp;
```

That will not incur any recursive SQL calls, and it performs the same operation.

As for the USER local variable, I would recommend setting that once per session (using a PL/SQL package), rather then referring to the USER pseudo column throughout the code. Every time you declare a variable and default it to USER, that will be a recursive SQL call. It's better to have a package global variable that is defaulted to USER and just reference that instead.

**Side Effects from Modifications**    Recursive calls may also occur when you are doing a modification and many side effects (triggers, function-based indexes, and so on) are happening. Take the following, for example:

```
ops$tkyte@ORA920> create table t ( x int );
Table created.

ops$tkyte@ORA920> create trigger t_trigger before insert on t for each row
  2  begin
  3      for x in ( select *
  4                    from dual
  5                   where :new.x > (select count(*) from emp))
  6      loop
  7          raise_application_error( -20001, 'check failed' );
  8      end loop;
  9  end;
 10  /
Trigger created.


ops$tkyte@ORA920> insert into t select 1 from all_users;
38 rows created.

ops$tkyte@ORA920> set autotrace traceonly statistics

ops$tkyte@ORA920> insert into t select 1 from all_users;
38 rows created.

Statistics
----------------------------------------------------------
         39  recursive calls
...
         38  rows processed

ops$tkyte@ORA920> set autotrace off
```

Here, firing the trigger, and then running that query for each row processed by the trigger, generated all of the recursive SQL calls. Generally, this is not something you can avoid (because you would need to remove the trigger entirely), but you can minimize it by writing an efficient trigger—avoiding as much recursive SQL as possible and moving SQL out of a trigger into a package (covered in detail in Chapter 5).

**Space Requests**     You may see large recursive SQL operations performed to satisfy requests for space, due to disk sorts or as the result of large modifications to a table that require it to extend. This is generally not a problem with locally managed tablespaces, where spaced is managed as bitmaps in the datafile headers. It can happen with dictionary-managed tablespaces, where space is managed in database tables much like your own data is managed.

Consider this example performed using a dictionary-managed tablespace. We'll start by creating a table with small extents (every extent will be 64KB).

```
ops$tkyte@ORA817DEV> create tablespace testing
  2   datafile '/tmp/testing.dbf' size 1m reuse
  3   autoextend on next 1m
  4   extent management dictionary
  5   /
Tablespace created.

ops$tkyte@ORA817DEV> create table t
  2   storage( initial 64k next 64k pctincrease 0 )
  3   tablespace testing
  4   as
  5   select * from all_objects where 1=0;
Table created.
```

Next, we'll insert a couple of rows into this table. The INSERT statement is carefully crafted using bind variables so that subsequent executes of that query will be soft parsed, so the recursive SQL we are attempting to measure will not include parse-related recursive statements. Consider this step a priming of the pump to get started, to warm up the engine:

```
ops$tkyte@ORA817DEV> variable n number;
ops$tkyte@ORA817DEV> exec :n := 5;
PL/SQL procedure successfully completed.
ops$tkyte@ORA817DEV> insert into t
  2 select * from all_objects where rownum < :n;
5 rows created.
```

And now we are ready to perform a mass insert into this table. Setting the bind variable to a large number and simply reexecuting that same SQL INSERT statement:

```
ops$tkyte@ORA817DEV> set autotrace traceonly statistics;

ops$tkyte@ORA817DEV> exec :n := 99999
PL/SQL procedure successfully completed.
```

```
ops$tkyte@ORA817DEV> insert into t
  2 select * from all_objects where rownum < :n;
23698 rows created.


Statistics
----------------------------------------------------------
      2910  recursive calls
      2441  db block gets
...
     23698  rows processed

ops$tkyte@ORA817DEV> set autotrace off
```

That is a lot of recursive SQL for that insert operation. No triggers or PL/SQL function calls are involved. This was all due to space management. So, can we decrease that easily? Sure, by using locally managed tablespaces:

```
ops$tkyte@ORA817DEV> create tablespace testing_lmt
  2 datafile '/tmp/testing_lmt.dbf' size 1m reuse
  3 autoextend on next 1m
  4 extent management local
  5 uniform size 64k
  6 /
Tablespace created.

ops$tkyte@ORA817DEV> drop table t;
Table dropped.

ops$tkyte@ORA817DEV> create table t
  2 tablespace testing_lmt
  3 as
  4 select * from all_objects where 1=0;
Table created.
```

That emulates our dictionary-managed table example exactly. The table T will have 64KB extents. Now, let's repeat the same insert test.

```
ops$tkyte@ORA817DEV> variable n number;
ops$tkyte@ORA817DEV> exec :n := 5;
PL/SQL procedure successfully completed.

ops$tkyte@ORA817DEV> insert into t
  2 select * from all_objects where rownum < :n;
4 rows created.

ops$tkyte@ORA817DEV> set autotrace traceonly statistics;
ops$tkyte@ORA817DEV> exec :n := 99999
PL/SQL procedure successfully completed.
```

```
ops$tkyte@ORA817DEV> insert into t
  2 select * from all_objects where rownum < :n;
23698 rows created.


Statistics
----------------------------------------------------------
      800   recursive calls
     2501   db block gets
...
    23698   rows processed

ops$tkyte@ORA817DEV> set autotrace off
```

This is much better. What are the 800 remaining recursive SQL queries? By using SQL_TRACE and TKPROF to analyze that (as explained in the section on TKPROF, later in this chapter), we would see that these were due to tablespace quota management—a series of SELECT and UPDATE statements to manage the quota information. This recursive SQL is truly unavoidable. Oracle will always be checking our quotas as we require more space. Still, we might be able to minimize the recursive SQL by using system-allocated extents or by using a larger uniform extent size to reduce the number of extents needed to hold this much data.

**NOTE**
*If you are testing this on 9iR2, you may discover that you cannot run this example. If your system tablespace was created as a locally managed tablespace, you cannot create any dictionary managed tablespaces at all. This is why my previous example was executed in my Oracle8i Release 3 (8.1.7) database, as noted in my SQL prompt!*

**Recursive SQL Wrap-Up**    Keep in mind that recursive SQL is something to be avoided *if possible,* but not anything to lose sleep over if it is not avoidable. Don't blindly try to get this to zero, because it is not possible or practical all of the time. If you see hundreds or thousands of recursive SQL calls, check it out. Find out what is causing it (SQL_TRACE will help greatly here), understand why it happens, and work on fixing the cause if possible.

### Db Block Gets and Consistent Gets
Blocks may be retrieved and used by Oracle in one of two ways: current or consistent. A current mode get is a retrieval of a block as it exists right now. You will see these most frequently during modification statements, which must update only the latest copy of the block. Consistent gets are the retrieval of blocks from the buffer cache in "read consistent" mode and may include read asides to UNDO (rollback segments). A query will generally perform "consistent gets."

These are the most important parts of the AUTOTRACE report. They represent your logical I/Os—the number of times you had to latch a buffer in order to inspect it. If you recall from Chapter 1, a *latch* is just another name for a lock; a latch is a serialization device. The less we latch, the better. In general, the less logical I/O we can do, the better.

**Query Tuning**    But how do we decrease the logical I/Os? In many cases, achieving this requires letting go of old myths, in particular, the myth that if your query isn't using indexes, the optimizer *must* be doing the wrong thing.

"I have created two tables:

```
create table I1(n number primary key, v varchar2(10));
create table I2(n number primary key, v varchar2(10));
and a map table
create table MAP
(n number primary key,
 i1 number referencing I1(n),
 i2 number referencing I2(n));
create unique index IDX_MAP on MAP(i1, i2)
```

Now, when I take the EXPLAIN PLAN for the query:

```
select *
  from i1, map, i2
 where  i1.n = map.i1
   and i2.n = map.i2
   and i1.v = 'x'
   and i2.v = 'y';
```

I see the plan as:

```
Execution Plan
----------------------------------------------------------
     0      SELECT STATEMENT Optimizer=CHOOSE
     1    0   NESTED LOOPS
     2    1     NESTED LOOPS
     3    2       TABLE ACCESS (FULL) OF 'MAP'
     4    2       TABLE ACCESS (BY INDEX ROWID) OF 'I2'
     5    4         INDEX (UNIQUE SCAN) OF 'SYS_C00683648' (UNIQUE)
     6    1     TABLE ACCESS (BY INDEX ROWID) OF 'I1'
     7    6       INDEX (UNIQUE SCAN) OF 'SYS_C00683647' (UNIQUE)
```

Is there any way to avoid the full-table scan on the MAP table? Whatever I try, one table is always going for a full scan. What should I do to avoid a full scan in such a case?"

My response was simple. I started with telling him to repeat the following:

Full scans are not always evil; indexes are not always good.

Say this over and over until he believed it. Then I asked him to look at his query and to tell me how a full scan could be avoided. Using the existing data structures, what plan could a human come up with that does not involve a full-table or index scan? I do not see any possible plan myself.

Additionally, given the existing structures, the indexes that are being used are actually deadly here. I can tell by the AUTOTRACE output that he is using the RBO (because there is no Cost, Card, and Bytes information). The plan the RBO came up with is a really bad plan in general. The CBO would be smarter and stop using the indexes. So, one solution is to simply analyze the tables and use a plan that avoids the indexes altogether!

Here, I'll show you a simple example. We'll join two tables together. Before we run the query, we'll use AUTOTRACE to see the plans that would be generated and try to outguess the optimizer with hints (in the erroneous belief that if the optimizer avoids an index, it has done the wrong thing).

```
ops$tkyte@ORA920> insert into i1
  2 select rownum, rpad('*',10,'*') from all_objects;
30020 rows created.

ops$tkyte@ORA920> insert into i2
  2 select rownum, rpad('*',10,'*') from all_objects;
30020 rows created.

ops$tkyte@ORA920> insert into map
  2 select rownum, rownum, rownum from all_objects;
30020 rows created.

ops$tkyte@ORA920> set autotrace traceonly

ops$tkyte@ORA920>  select *
  2    from
  3          i1,
  4          map,
  5          i2
  6   where      i1.n = map.i1
  7    and i2.n = map.i2
  8    and i1.v = 'x'
  9    and i2.v = 'y';

no rows selected


Execution Plan
----------------------------------------------------------
   0      SELECT STATEMENT Optimizer=CHOOSE
   1    0   NESTED LOOPS
   2    1     NESTED LOOPS
   3    2       TABLE ACCESS (FULL) OF 'MAP'
   4    2       TABLE ACCESS (BY INDEX ROWID) OF 'I2'
   5    4         INDEX (UNIQUE SCAN) OF 'SYS_C003755' (UNIQUE)
   6    1     TABLE ACCESS (BY INDEX ROWID) OF 'I1'
   7    6       INDEX (UNIQUE SCAN) OF 'SYS_C003754' (UNIQUE)
Statistics
----------------------------------------------------------
```

```
        0  recursive calls
        0  db block gets
    60127  consistent gets
        0  physical reads
       60  redo size
      513  bytes sent via SQL*Net to client
      368  bytes received via SQL*Net from client
        1  SQL*Net roundtrips to/from client
        0  sorts (memory)
        0  sorts (disk)
        0  rows processed
```

At this point, we can see that the performance of this query is poor, with more than 60,000 logical I/Os. For a query that ultimately returns no data, this is very high. Now, let's give the CBO an opportunity.

```
ops$tkyte@ORA920> analyze table i1 compute statistics;
Table analyzed.

ops$tkyte@ORA920> analyze table i2 compute statistics;
Table analyzed.

ops$tkyte@ORA920> analyze table map compute statistics;
Table analyzed.

ops$tkyte@ORA920>  select *
  2    from
  3            i1,
  4            map,
  5            i2
  6    where      i1.n = map.i1
  7    and i2.n = map.i2
  8    and i1.v = 'x'
  9    and i2.v = 'y';
no rows selected


Execution Plan
----------------------------------------------------------
    0      SELECT STATEMENT Optimizer=CHOOSE (Cost=21 Card=1 Bytes=40)
    1    0   NESTED LOOPS (Cost=21 Card=1 Bytes=40)
    2    1     HASH JOIN (Cost=20 Card=1 Bytes=26)
    3    2       TABLE ACCESS (FULL) OF 'I1' (Cost=10 Card=1 Bytes=14)
    4    2       TABLE ACCESS (FULL) OF 'MAP' (Cost=9 Card=30020 Bytes=360240)
    5    1     TABLE ACCESS (BY INDEX ROWID) OF 'I2' (Cost=1 Card=1 Bytes=14)
    6    5       INDEX (UNIQUE SCAN) OF 'SYS_C003755' (UNIQUE)

Statistics
----------------------------------------------------------
        0  recursive calls
```

```
      0  db block gets
     92  consistent gets
      0  physical reads
      0  redo size
    513  bytes sent via SQL*Net to client
    368  bytes received via SQL*Net from client
      1  SQL*Net roundtrips to/from client
      0  sorts (memory)
      0  sorts (disk)
      0  rows processed

ops$tkyte@ORA920> set autotrace off
```

As you can see, by avoiding the use of an index, we increased the performance and decreased the resource use of this query by many orders of magnitude. This is a great start.

Now, let's consider the predicates i1.v = value and i2.v =value. Perhaps creating an index on i1.v or i2.v would be helpful.

```
ops$tkyte@ORA920> create index i1_idx on i1(v);
Index created.

ops$tkyte@ORA920> analyze table i1 compute statistics;
Table analyzed.

ops$tkyte@ORA920> set autotrace traceonly

ops$tkyte@ORA920>  select *
  2  from
  3          i1,
  4          map,
  5          i2
  6  where     i1.n = map.i1
  7  and i2.n = map.i2
  8  and i1.v = 'x'
  9  and i2.v = 'y';

no rows selected


Execution Plan
----------------------------------------------------------
   0       SELECT STATEMENT Optimizer=CHOOSE (Cost=13 Card=1 Bytes=40)
   1    0    NESTED LOOPS (Cost=13 Card=1 Bytes=40)
   2    1      HASH JOIN (Cost=12 Card=1 Bytes=26)
   3    2        TABLE ACCESS (BY INDEX ROWID) OF 'I1'
                     (Cost=2 Card=1 Bytes=14)
   4    3          INDEX (RANGE SCAN) OF 'I1_IDX' (NON-UNIQUE)
                     (Cost=1 Card=1)
   5    2        TABLE ACCESS (FULL) OF 'MAP'
                     (Cost=9 Card=30020 Bytes=360240)
```

```
    6    1      TABLE ACCESS (BY INDEX ROWID) OF 'I2' (Cost=1 Card=1 Bytes=14)
    7    6        INDEX (UNIQUE SCAN) OF 'SYS_C003755' (UNIQUE)


Statistics
----------------------------------------------------------
        0  recursive calls
        0  db block gets
        2  consistent gets
        0  physical reads
        0  redo size
      513  bytes sent via SQL*Net to client
      368  bytes received via SQL*Net from client
        1  SQL*Net roundtrips to/from client
        0  sorts (memory)
        0  sorts (disk)
        0  rows processed

ops$tkyte@ORA920> set autotrace off
```

This just helps prove that indexes are not always best and full scans are not always to be avoided. The solution to this problem is to use the CBO and to properly index the data structures according to our data-retrieval needs.

In general, the major way to reduce db block gets and consistent gets is via query tuning. However, to be successful, you must keep an open mind and have a good understanding of the available access paths. You must have a good grasp of the SQL language, including the entire suite of functionality, so you can understand the difference between NOT IN and NOT EXISTS, when WHERE EXISTS would be appropriate, and when WHERE IN is a better choice. One of the best ways to discover all of this is through simple tests, such as the ones I've been demonstrating.

**Array Size Effects**    The array size is the number of rows fetched (or sent, in the case of inserts, updates, and deletes) by the server at a time. It can have a dramatic effect on performance.

To demonstrate the effects of array size, we'll run the same query a couple of times and look at just the consistent get differences between runs:

```
ops$tkyte@ORA920> create table t as select * from all_objects;
Table created.

ops$tkyte@ORA920> set autotrace traceonly statistics;

ops$tkyte@ORA920> set arraysize 2
ops$tkyte@ORA920> select * from t;
29352 rows selected.

Statistics
----------------------------------------------------------
    14889  consistent gets
```

Note how one half of 29,352 (rows fetched) is very close to 14,889, the number of consistent gets. Every row we fetched from the server actually caused it to send two rows back. So, for every two rows of data, we needed to do a logical I/O to get the data. Oracle got a block, took two rows from it, and sent it to SQL*Plus. Then SQL*Plus asked for the next two rows, and Oracle got that block again or got the next block, if we had already fetched the data, and returned the next two rows, and so on.

Next, let's increase the array size:

```
ops$tkyte@ORA920> set arraysize 5
ops$tkyte@ORA920> select * from t;
29352 rows selected.

Statistics
----------------------------------------------------------
       6173  consistent gets
...
```

Now, 29,352 divided by 5 is about 5,871, and that would be the least amount of consistent gets we would be able to achieve (the actual observed number of consistent gets is slightly higher). All that means is sometimes in order to get two rows, we needed to get two blocks: we got the last row from one block and the first row from the next block.

Let's increase the array size again:

```
ops$tkyte@ORA920> set arraysize 10
ops$tkyte@ORA920> select * from t;
29352 rows selected.

Statistics
----------------------------------------------------------
       3285  consistent gets
...

ops$tkyte@ORA920> set arraysize 15
ops$tkyte@ORA920> select * from t;
29352 rows selected.

Statistics
----------------------------------------------------------
       2333  consistent gets
...

ops$tkyte@ORA920> set arraysize 100
ops$tkyte@ORA920> select * from t;
29352 rows selected.

Statistics
----------------------------------------------------------
        693  consistent gets
```

```
...
ops$tkyte@ORA920> set arraysize 5000
ops$tkyte@ORA920> select * from t;
29352 rows selected.

Statistics
----------------------------------------------------------
      410  consistent gets
...
ops$tkyte@ORA920> set autotrace off
```

As you can see, as the array size goes up, the number of consistent gets goes down. So, does that mean you should set your array size to 5,000, as in this last test? Absolutely *not.*

If you notice, the overall number of consistent gets has not dropped dramatically between array sizes of 100 and 5,000. However, the amount of RAM needed on the client and server has gone up with the increased array size. The client must now be able to cache 5,000 rows. Not only that, but it makes our performance look choppy: The server works really hard and fast to get 5,000 rows, then the client works really hard and fast to process 5,000 rows, then the server, then the client, and so on. It would be better to have more of a stream of information flowing: Ask for 100 rows, get 100 rows, ask for 100, process 100, and so on. That way, both the client and server are more or less continuously processing data, rather than the processing occurring in small bursts.

> **NOTE**
> *A common criticism of PL/SQL is its slow performance. This is not a PL/SQL problem per se, but instead is due to the fact that people typically code PL/SQL in a very row-at-a-time oriented fashion. Given that even native dynamic SQL can now be bulk-based from Oracle9i, there is no longer any reason for this approach. We'll investigate this further in Chapter 9.*

I've found empirically that somewhere between 100 and 500 is a nice array size. Diminishing marginal returns kick in shortly after that range. Performance will actually decrease with larger array sizes.

Virtually every programming environment I've come across—from Pro*C, to OCI, to Java/ JDBC, and even VB/ODBC—allows you to tweak the array size. Refer to the documentation for your environment for specific instructions on handling array size.

### Physical Reads

The physical reads statistic is a measure of how much real I/O, or physical I/O, your query performed. A physical read of table or index data places the block into the buffer cache. Then we perform a logical I/O to retrieve the block. Hence, most physical reads are immediately followed by a logical I/O!

There are two major types of common physical I/Os:

- **Reading your data in from datafiles**  Doing I/O to the datafiles to retrieve index and table data. These operations will be followed immediately by a logical I/O to the cache.

■ **Direct reads from TEMP**   This is in response to a sort area or hash area not being large enough to support the entire sort/hash in memory. Oracle is forced to swap out some of the data to TEMP and read it back in later. These physical reads bypass the buffer cache and will not incur a logical I/O.

There is not a lot we can do about the first type of I/O, the reading of data in from disk. After all, if it is not in the buffer cache, it has to get there somehow. If you run a small query—a query that performs hundreds of logical I/Os (consistent gets)—and you repeatedly observe physical I/Os being performed, that could be an indication your buffer cache is on the small side (there isn't sufficient space to cache even the results of your small query with hundreds of logical I/Os). Generally, the number of physical reads should go down for most queries after you run the query once.

Many people think that they must flush the buffer cache before tuning, to emulate the real world. I feel quite the opposite. If you tune with logical I/Os (consistent gets) in mind, the physical I/Os will take care of themselves over time (assuming you ensure an even distribution of I/O across disks and such). Flushing the buffer cache during tuning is as artificial as running the query a couple of times and using the last results. Flushing the buffer cache gets rid of tons of information that rightly would be there in the real world when you run the query.

I suggest running the query twice. If the logical I/Os are small as a proportion of your buffer cache, yet you are still seeing physical reads, that most likely indicates direct reads from your temporary tablespace. We will take a look at fixing that problem here in this section. Later, when we talk about TKPROF and SQL_TRACE, we'll go into details about finding where physical I/Os are taking place.

To detect direct reads from TEMP, first disable automatic process global area (PGA) management by the server and physically set the sort area size and hash area size. If you are using Oracle9i and have WORKAREA_SIZE_POLICY = AUTO, the settings for the hash area size and sort area size, among others, are ignored (and this example won't work!). In this example, I've set the hash area size artificially low, in order to have the optimizer consistently choose a sort merge join to exercise the sort area size. I'll show the query plan for the first execution, but chop it out for the subsequent ones.

**NOTE**
*ALTER SESSION SET WORKAREA_SIZE_POLICY is a new feature of Oracle9i. This example will work in Oracle8i and earlier without issuing that command.*

```
ops$tkyte@ORA920> alter session set workarea_size_policy = manual;
Session altered.

ops$tkyte@ORA920> alter session set hash_area_size = 1024;
Session altered.

ops$tkyte@ORA920> create table t as select * from all_objects;
Table created.

ops$tkyte@ORA920> analyze table t compute statistics
  2 for table for columns object_id;
Table analyzed.
```

That sets up our test. Now, we'll try a big sort with 100KB, 1MB, and 10MB sort areas to see what happens in each case.

```
ops$tkyte@ORA920> set autotrace traceonly
ops$tkyte@ORA920> alter session set sort_area_size = 102400;
Session altered.

ops$tkyte@ORA920> select *
  2    from t t1, t t2
  3    where t1.object_id = t2.object_id
  4  /
29366 rows selected.

[results snipped out - second run after parsing and warming
 up the cache is relevant]

ops$tkyte@ORA920> /
29366 rows selected.


Execution Plan
----------------------------------------------------------
  0      SELECT STATEMENT Optimizer=CHOOSE (Cost=4264 Card=29366 Bytes=5638272)
  1    0   MERGE JOIN (Cost=4264 Card=29366 Bytes=5638272)
  2    1     SORT (JOIN) (Cost=2132 Card=29366 Bytes=2819136)
  3    2       TABLE ACCESS (FULL) OF 'T' (Cost=42 Card=29366 Bytes=2819136)
  4    1     SORT (JOIN) (Cost=2132 Card=29366 Bytes=2819136)
  5    4       TABLE ACCESS (FULL) OF 'T' (Cost=42 Card=29366 Bytes=2819136)


Statistics
----------------------------------------------------------
        0  recursive calls
      216  db block gets
      810  consistent gets
     4486  physical reads
        0  redo size
  2474401  bytes sent via SQL*Net to client
    22026  bytes received via SQL*Net from client
     1959  SQL*Net roundtrips to/from client
        0  sorts (memory)
        2  sorts (disk)
    29366  rows processed
```

Here, we can see that physical reads far exceed logical I/Os. That is one indicator that we had to swap to disk. The 2 sorts (disk) statistic helps back that up, but do not rely exclusively on that statistic to point this out. Other operations that use temporary space, such as a hash join, don't report sorts to disk, because they didn't sort! If the physical reads do not disappear on the second run, even though there are only hundreds of logical I/Os (you would expect that data to be in the cache), or the physical reads outnumber the logical I/Os, you should suspect that the allocated memory was exceeded.

So, what happens when we increase the sort area size for this process?

```
ops$tkyte@ORA920> alter session set sort_area_size = 1024000;
Session altered.

ops$tkyte@ORA920> select *
  2     from t t1, t t2
  3   where t1.object_id = t2.object_id
  4  /
29366 rows selected.

Statistics
----------------------------------------------------------
          0  recursive calls
         12  db block gets
        810  consistent gets
       1222  physical reads
          0  redo size
    2474401  bytes sent via SQL*Net to client
      22026  bytes received via SQL*Net from client
       1959  SQL*Net roundtrips to/from client
          0  sorts (memory)
          2  sorts (disk)
      29366  rows processed
```

The physical reads went down. We were able to store ten times the data in RAM. We did much less swapping in and out to TEMP.

Let's make the sort area bigger and see what happens.

```
ops$tkyte@ORA920> alter session set sort_area_size = 10240000;
Session altered.

ops$tkyte@ORA920> select *
  2     from t t1, t t2
  3   where t1.object_id = t2.object_id
  4  /
29366 rows selected.

Statistics
----------------------------------------------------------
          0  recursive calls
          0  db block gets
        810  consistent gets
          0  physical reads
          0  redo size
    2474401  bytes sent via SQL*Net to client
      22026  bytes received via SQL*Net from client
```

```
 1959  SQL*Net roundtrips to/from client
    2  sorts (memory)
    0  sorts (disk)
29366  rows processed
```

ops$tkyte@ORA920> set autotrace off

The need for physical reads went away entirely.

Some sites run with an absurdly small sort area size (hash area size and others). They do this out of the mistaken belief that, by setting the sort area size, they are permanently allocating that much memory per session. The sort area size settings control how much memory will be dynamically allocated at runtime in order to satisfy a sort request. After the sort is completed, this memory will be shrunk back to the sort area retained size. After the query result set is exhausted, this memory will be released entirely. The default settings are far too small, and even a modest increase would benefit many sites. Their overall performance may be enhanced simply by increasing this parameter. The optimizer will recognize the sort area size is larger and generate query plans that take advantage of it.

### NOTE
*This is not to say that you should rush and up your sort_area_size (refer back to Chapter 1 and test, test, test). Also note that in most cases you would be implicitly bumping up the hash area size as well.*

In Oracle9i and later, using the automated work area size policy, the sort area size is not an issue. Under this policy, the DBA tells Oracle how much dynamic memory it is allowed to use from the operating system for processing (separate from the SGA memory). Then Oracle will set sort areas, hash areas, and the like automatically, using 10MB when appropriate, 1MB when that is better, and 100KB when that makes sense. In fact, the amount used can vary from statement to statement in your session as the load goes up and down over time. The decision on the amount of memory to use is made dynamically for every single statement your session performs.

### Redo Size
The redo size statistic shows how much redo your statement generated when executed. This is most useful when judging the efficiency of large bulk operations. This comes into play most often with direct path inserts or CREATE TABLE AS SELECT (CTAS) statements. The amount of redo generated by MERGE, UPDATE, or DELETE statements will, in many cases, be outside of our control. If you perform these operations with as few indexes enabled as possible, you can reduce the amount of redo generated, but you will have to ultimately rebuild those disabled indexes. This is practical only in specialized environments when you are performing large data loads in general, such as a data warehouse.

**Bulk Loads**    Let's look at a common problem: How can you load a large number of rows into an existing table efficiently? If you are talking about a couple of thousand rows in a very large table, a straight insert is probably the right way to go. If you are talking about tens, or hundreds of thousands, or even millions of rows of data in a very large table, other methods will prevail.

"In development, our bulk inserts work very fast and generate very little redo. When we move into production, our INSERT /*+ append */ statements work much slower and generate many gigabytes of redo log, filling up our archive log destination. What is going wrong?"

It is not that anything is going wrong. It is that many people run the development and test machines in NOARCHIVELOG mode and production in ARCHIVELOG mode. This difference can be crucial, and is yet another reason why your test environment should mirror your production environment. You want to catch these differences in your testing and development phase, not in production!

Let's look at an example of a bulk load of data into a table. Since everyone has the ALL_OBJECTS view available, we'll use that for demonstration purposes. In real life, we would be loading from an external table (in Oracle9i and later), or we would be processing a file loaded by the SQLLDR tool (in Oracle8i and earlier). We'll begin by creating a table to load into:

```
ops$tkyte@ORA920> create table big_table
  2  as
  3  select *
  4    from all_objects
  5   where 1=0;
Table created.
```

That just created a table that is structurally the same as ALL_OBJECTS but has no data. So, let's fill it up:

```
ops$tkyte@ORA920> set autotrace on statistics;

ops$tkyte@ORA920> insert into big_table select * from all_objects;
29368 rows created.

Statistics
----------------------------------------------------------
...
3277944  redo size

ops$tkyte@ORA920> insert /*+ APPEND */ into big_table select * from
all_objects;
29368 rows created.

Statistics
----------------------------------------------------------
...
3328820  redo size

ops$tkyte@ORA920> commit;
Commit complete.
```

This is something that confuses many Oracle developers and DBAs. They think that second insert operation should not have generated any redo. We used the syntax for the direct-path insert (just like a direct-path load in SQLLDR), so it should bypass all of the redo generation. But that is not the case. A direct-path insert will only bypass redo generation in two cases:

- You are using a NOARCHIVELOG mode database (my database is in ARCHIVELOG mode).
- You are performing the operation on a table marked as NOLOGGING.

The insert /*+ APPEND */ will *minimize* redo generation in all cases, as it minimizes the amount of UNDO generated. The redo that would otherwise be generated for the UNDO information is not created, but ultimately the logging mode of the target table is what will dictate whether redo is generated for the table or not. So, let's put the table into NOLOGGING mode and retry the operation:

```
ops$tkyte@ORA920> alter table big_table nologging;
Table altered.

ops$tkyte@ORA920> insert into big_table
  2  select * from all_objects;
29368 rows created.

Statistics
----------------------------------------------------------
...
3239724   redo size

ops$tkyte@ORA920> insert /*+ APPEND */ into big_table
  2  select * from all_objects;
29368 rows created.

Statistics
----------------------------------------------------------
...
7536   redo size

ops$tkyte@ORA920> commit;
Commit complete.
```

Already, we can see how AUTOTRACE is useful in showing how similar commands might perform very differently. Using just a normal insert, we generated over 3.2MB of redo log. The second direct-path insert generated virtually no redo.

The fact that the normal insert generated redo is a point of some confusion as well. Just setting a table to NOLOGGING does not mean that all redo is prevented against this table. Only certain explicit, bulk operations such as this direct-path insert, will not be logged in the normal fashion. All other operations—such as insert, update, delete, and merge—will be logged as normal.

So, does that mean we should set all of our tables to NOLOGGING and use /*+ APPEND */ on all inserts? No, not a chance.

First, realize that this option works on only INSERT as SELECT statements (bulk inserts). It does *not* work with INSERT VALUES statements. I've seen many pieces of code with:

```
insert /*+ append */ into t values ( ... )
```

When I ask about it, the developer says, "Well, I didn't need that logged, so I turned it off." That just proves that the developer doesn't understand what this option does at all! So, using this on an INSERT with a VALUES clause only makes you look bad (it has no other effect!). By all means, if you can convert your code into SET AT A TIME logic and use /*+ APPEND */ on very large bulk operations, after coordinating with the DBA, do so. But don't even attempt to use it on a single row.

An important reason to avoid the NOLOGGING setting is its obvious result: This operation will not be logged. While that might sound excellent to some developers, that should send a shudder down a DBA's spine. You have this table loaded, and people start doing modifications against it. The next day, the disk crashes. "No problem," says the DBA, "I'll just restore from the backup two days ago." She rolls forward and finds this table you loaded yesterday wasn't recovered! All of the work of the last day is lost! Why? Because you prevented the redo from being generated. It is not in the archive logs, and it cannot be recovered. This underscores an important point: When using NOLOGGING operations, the development and DBA teams must be in close contact. The DBA needs to know to schedule a backup of the affected datafiles as soon as possible afterwards, to prevent data loss.

Here are a few other reasons not to set NOLOGGING and use /*+ APPEND */ on all inserts:

■ The direct-path insert writes data above the high-water mark for the table, ignoring any free space on the freelists, just as a direct-path load will. If you delete many of the rows in a table and then INSERT /*+ APPEND */ into it, you will not be reusing any of that space.

■ You must commit after a successful direct-path insert before reading from that table in that transaction. This could put commits into your transactions where they don't really belong.

■ Only one session at a time can direct-path insert into a table. All other modifications are blocked. This operation serializes (but you can do parallel direct-path inserts from a single session).

Again, this option should be used with care and thought. You need coordination among the people using it and the DBAs, so they can schedule that backup right after this occurs.

**Redo and Index Operations**     What happens if you are doing INSERT /*+ APPEND */ as SELECT, with the table set NOLOGGING, but you still have a lot of redo and archives? What could be wrong? The answer is that you have indexes on the table, and the indexes cannot just be appended to; they must be merged into. Since you need to merge data into them, you need redo in order to recover from instance failure (if your system crashed in the middle of the index operations, you would end up with a corrupt index structure). Hence, redo is generated for the index operations. We can see this readily by continuing on with this example:

```
ops$tkyte@ORA920> create index big_table_idx on
  2 big_table(owner,object_type,object_name);
Index created.
```

```
ops$tkyte@ORA920> insert /*+ APPEND */ into big_table
  2  select * from all_objects;
29369 rows created.

Statistics
-----------------------------------------------------------
...
18020324   redo size

ops$tkyte@ORA920> commit;
Commit complete.
```

Wow, what a difference an index can make! Indexes are complex data structures, so maintaining them can be expensive. Here, we know that the table data should generate about 3.2MB of redo, but this single index generated 18MB of redo!

If this were a bulk load into a data warehouse or data mart, I would do something similar to the following:

1. Set the indexes to the UNUSABLE state (not dropping them, just setting them as UNUSABLE for now).

2. Set the session to skip UNUSUABLE indexes and do the bulk load.

3. Re-enable the indexes.

Here are the steps you can take in SQL*Plus to see this (SQLLDR would be similar, but you would use the `skip_index_maintenance` parameter instead of the first two ALTER commands):

```
ops$tkyte@ORA920> alter index big_table_idx unusable;
Index altered.

ops$tkyte@ORA920> alter session set skip_unusable_indexes=true;
Session altered.

ops$tkyte@ORA920> insert /*+ APPEND */ into big_table
  2  select * from all_objects;
29369 rows created.

Statistics
-----------------------------------------------------------
...
      7588   redo size

ops$tkyte@ORA920> alter index big_table_idx rebuild nologging;
Index altered.
```

Now, all we need to do is schedule a backup of the affected datafiles, and we are finished with our load!

Why not just drop the indexes and re-create them? I've seen far too many systems where the DROP INDEX command worked, but the subsequent CREATE INDEX command failed for some reason. No one noticed they just lost an index, and performance went down the tubes.

**TIP**
*If nothing changed, but after your last data load, performance has been really bad, check that you aren't missing your index. If this is the case, just create the index, and your performance should return to normal.*

If you don't ever drop the index, but set it to UNUSABLE instead, you can never lose the index. If the command to re-enable the index fails, when the users run queries that need that index, they will get an error message, which, of course, they will report immediately. So, rather than having the system suffer from mysterious performance issues for hours or days, the DBA will get a call early on and fix the problem.

## SQL*Net Statistics
There are three pieces to the SQL*Net statistics:

- How much you sent to the server (bytes received via SQL*Net from client)
- How much the server sent to you (bytes sent via SQL*Net to client)
- How many round-trips where made (SQL*Net roundtrips to/from client)

The ones you have the most control over are the last two. You want to minimize the data sent to you. The way you control that is by selecting *only* the columns that are relevant to you. Frequently, I see people coding `select * from table`, and then using only one or two columns (out of thirty or forty column). Not only does this flood the network with a ton of unnecessary data, it consumes additional RAM, and it can radically affect the efficiency of your query plans. To avoid such a problem, select only those columns that are needed to solve your problem—no more, no less.

The number of round-trips is tunable when you are processing a SELECT command. To see this, let's reuse the earlier example that showed the effects of array size on the consistent gets statistics. By just providing the array size and number of round-trips, we can see the measurable impact the array size has on the SQL*Net roundtrips to/from client statistic:

```
ops$tkyte@ORA920> set arraysize 2
ops$tkyte@ORA920> select * from t;
29369 rows selected.
...
     14686  SQL*Net roundtrips to/from client

ops$tkyte@ORA920> set arraysize 5
...
      5875  SQL*Net roundtrips to/from client
```

```
ops$tkyte@ORA920> set arraysize 10
...
      2938  SQL*Net roundtrips to/from client

ops$tkyte@ORA920> set arraysize 15
...
      1959  SQL*Net roundtrips to/from client

ops$tkyte@ORA920> set arraysize 100
...
       295  SQL*Net roundtrips to/from client

ops$tkyte@ORA920> set arraysize 5000
...
         7  SQL*Net roundtrips to/from client
```

In general, the fewer round-trips, the better—to a point! Generally, an array fetch size of between 100 and 500 results in the best overall performance/memory usage.

### Sorts and Rows Processed

The final three statistics deal with sorts and row processing:

- Sorts (memory) shows how many sorts you did entirely in memory (no swapping to disks).

- Sorts (disk) shows how many sorts you did that required some temporary disk space.

- Rows processed shows how many rows were affected (either returned from a SELECT statement or modified due to an INSERT, UPDATE, DELETE, or MERGE statement).

Our goal is to reduce the number of sorts (disk). As demonstrated earlier in the section about the physical reads statistic, one method of accomplishing this is to set a sort area size that is more appropriate for what you are doing; that is, in practice, most sort area size settings are too small. Another method is plain, old-fashioned query tuning. Determine if there is an alternative yet equivalent method that you can use to reduce the size of the sort you need to perform, or even to remove the sort entirely.

Note however, that a "sorts to disk" of zero *does not mean you are bypassing TEMP altogether.* It is entirely possible for the sort to be done in memory but have the results of the sort written to disk. This will most commonly happen when the sort_area_retained_size (the amount of sorted data to retain in memory after sorting) is set smaller then the sort_area_size.

This completes the discussion of the AUTOTRACE statistics. As you've seen, AUTOTRACE is a fairly powerful tool. It is a large step above EXPLAIN PLAN, which can only show you what plan would be used, not what actually happens when you use that plan. However, it is a step below TKPROF, the tool we'll look at next.

# TKPROF

Oracle has the ability to turn on a fairly low-level tracing capability for us (generally done via the ALTER SESSION command). Once tracing is enabled, Oracle will record all of the SQL and top-level PL/SQL calls our application makes to a trace file on the server (the database server machine; never the client machine). This trace file will not only have our SQL and PL/SQL calls, but it will also contain our timing information, possibly information on wait events (what is slowing us down), how many logical I/Os and physical I/Os we performed, the CPU and wall clock (elapsed) timings, numbers of rows processed, query plans with row counts, and more. This trace file by itself is fairly hard to read. What we really want to do is generate a report from this trace file in a user-friendly format. That is TKPROF's only goal in life: to turn a trace file into something we can use easily.

As I've already mentioned several times, TKPROF is my favorite tuning tool. It's also one that seems to be widely overlooked by many people. Sometimes, this is out of ignorance—they didn't know it existed. Many times this is out of prevention—the DBA prevents developers from having access to this tool by preventing access to the necessary trace files. Here, I'll remove the ignorance and also provide a method to allow access to the trace files in a manner that might squelch the qualms of the DBA. First, we'll start with how to enable and run TKPROF.

**NOTE**
*You may occasionally need to go into a trace file and get a piece of detail that the TKPROF tool doesn't expose, but for the most part, you can ignore much of its contents. If you are interested in the guts of a trace file (what exactly is in there), see Chapter 10 of my book,* Expert One on One Oracle. *Also refer to the chapter on this utility in the* Oracle9i Performance Tuning Guide and Reference.

# Enable TKPROF

Before getting ready to run TKPROF, you need to understand how to enable it (methods for turning on SQL_TRACE). I keep a small script called trace.sql for this purpose. It simply consists of these two commands:

```
alter session set timed_statistics=true;
alter session set events '10046 trace name context forever, level 12';
```

In the event the system setting of timed statistics is not enabled, you will want to enable ALTER SESSION SET TIMED_STATISTICS=TRUE at the session level at the very least. Without timed statistics, a TKPROF report is virtually useless. You will not see CPU times, and you will not see elapsed times. In short, you won't be able to see where the bottlenecks are! Don't bother tracing unless you set this as well.

After setting timed statistics, you can enable tracing by using ALTER SESSION SET SQL_TRACE=
TRUE, or its close cousin ALTER SESSION SET EVENTS '10046 TRACE NAME CONTEXT FOREVER, LEVEL <N>, where <N> can be:

- 1 to enable the standard SQL_TRACE facility (same as SQL_TRACE=TRUE)

- 4 to enable SQL_TRACE and also capture bind variable values in the trace file

- 8 to enable SQL_TRACE and also capture wait events in the trace file

- 12 to enable standard SQL_TRACE and also capture bind variables and wait events

As you can see in my script, I use ALTER SESSION SET EVENTS '10046 TRACE NAME CONTEXT FOREVER, LEVEL 12'. This is especially valuable in Oracle9i, where the TKPROF utility includes wait events in the report (earlier releases did not). TKPROF won't show you bind variable values; for that, you need the trace file itself. Note that the inclusion of wait events in the trace file may significantly increase its overall size! You may have to check your max_dump_file_size init.ora parameter to ensure it is large enough to accommodate this additional information.

# Run TKPROF

To begin, we'll use a quick test to demonstrate what TKPROF provides and how to access the trace files on the server. We'll run the script to enable tracing, and then run some queries.

### Generate the Trace File
In this example, we'll use BIG_TABLE, a table created from ALL_OBJECTS and duplicated over and over to have quite a few rows. See the appendix for all details on the creation of this table.

```
ops$tkyte@ORA920> alter session set timed_statistics=true;
Session altered.

ops$tkyte@ORA920> alter session set events
  2 '10046 trace name context forever, level 12';
Session altered.

ops$tkyte@ORA920> select count(*) from big_table
  2  /

  COUNT(*)
----------
    176210

ops$tkyte@ORA920> select *
  2     from big_table
  3   where owner = 'SYS'
  4     and object_type = 'PACKAGE'
  5     and object_name like 'F%'
  6  /
...
6 rows selected.

ops$tkyte@ORA920>
```

Now that we've generated some activity and created a trace file, we are ready to run some queries to help us with running TKPROF.

### Get the Trace Filename
To run TKPROF, we need to know the name of the trace file. One of the following two queries will be useful in doing so. The first is for Windows, using the standard 8.3 filename convention found in Oracle8i and earlier. The second is for Unix and Windows in Oracle9i and later (they

fixed the filenames on that platform). It may need slight modifications for different Unix variants (this version works on Solaris and Linux).

```sql
select c.value || '\ORA' || to_char(a.spid,'fm00000') || '.trc'
  from v$process a, v$session b, v$parameter c
 where a.addr = b.paddr
   and b.audsid = sys_context('userenv','sessionid')
   and c.name = 'user_dump_dest'
/

select rtrim(c.value,'/') || '/' || d.instance_name ||
       '_ora_' || ltrim(to_char(a.spid)) || '.trc'
  from v$process a, v$session b, v$parameter c, v$instance d
 where a.addr = b.paddr
   and b.audsid = sys_context( 'userenv', 'sessionid')
   and c.name = 'user_dump_dest'
/
```

On my Linux server, for example, running that query before I exited SQL*Plus told me:

```
ops$tkyte@ORA920> select rtrim(c.value,'/') || '/' || d.instance_name ||
  2                        '_ora_' || ltrim(to_char(a.spid)) || '.trc'
  3    from v$process a, v$session b, v$parameter c, v$instance d
  4   where a.addr = b.paddr
  5     and b.audsid = sys_context( 'userenv', 'sessionid')
  6     and c.name = 'user_dump_dest'
  7  /

RTRIM(C.VALUE,'/')||'/'||D.INSTANCE_NAME||'_ORA_'||LTRIM(TO_CHAR
---------------------------------------------------------------
/usr/oracle/ora920/admin/ora920/udump/ora920_ora_14246.trc

ops$tkyte@ORA920> exit
Disconnected from Oracle9i Enterprise Edition Release 9.2.0.1.0 - Production
With the Partitioning, OLAP and Oracle Data Mining options
JServer Release 9.2.0.1.0 - Production
```

After running these queries, exit SQL*Plus (or whatever tool you are using). You need to do this to close the trace file completely and have all of the information available in the trace file.

### Create the TKPROF Report

Now that we have the name of the trace file, we are ready to run TKPROF. Issue the following command:

```
$ tkprof /usr/oracle/........./ora920/udump/ora920_ora_14246.trc tk.prf
```

This creates a text file, tk.prf, in our current working directory.

## Read a TKPROF Report

When we open the tk.prf text file, we find output similar to this:

```
select count(*) from big_table

call     count    cpu   elapsed    disk    query   current      rows
------- ------- ------ --------- ------- ------- --------- ----------
Parse        1   0.00      0.00       0       0         0          0
Execute      1   0.00      0.00       0       0         0          0
Fetch        2   0.22      0.52    2433    2442         0          1
------- ------- ------ --------- ------- ------- --------- ----------
total        4   0.22      0.52    2433    2442         0          1

Misses in library cache during parse: 0
Optimizer goal: CHOOSE
Parsing user id: 147

Rows     Row Source Operation
------- ------------------------------------------------------
      1  SORT AGGREGATE
 176210     TABLE ACCESS FULL BIG_TABLE
```

And in Oracle9i, we find this nice section included:

```
Elapsed times include waiting on following events:
  Event waited on                     Times   Max. Wait  Total Waited
  ---------------------------------   Waited  ---------  ------------
  SQL*Net message to client               2       0.00          0.00
  db file sequential read                 1       0.00          0.00
  db file scattered read                163       0.07          0.40
  SQL*Net message from client             2       0.00          0.00
********************************************************************
```

We'll take a look at this piece by piece, starting with the top.

### The Query and Execution Statistics

The report begins with the original text of the query that was processed by the database:

```
select count(*) from big_table
```

Next is a tabular report that shows vital execution statistics for each phase of the query itself. We see the three main phases of the query:

- **Parse** This phase is where Oracle finds the query in the shared pool (soft parse) or creates a new plan for the query (hard parse).

- **Execute** This phase is the work done by Oracle on the OPEN or EXECUTE statement of the query. For a SELECT statement, this will be empty in many cases. For an UPDATE statement, this will be where all of the work is done.

- **Fetch**   For a SELECT statement, this phase will be where most of the work is done and visible. For an UPDATE statement, it will show no work (you don't fetch from an update operation).

Every statement processed will have these three phases.
Across the top of the report, we find the headings:

- **Count**   How many times this phase of the query was performed. In a properly written application, all of your SQL will have a Parse count of 1 and an Execute count of 1 or more. You do not want to parse more than once, if at all possible.

- **CPU**   The amount of CPU time spent on this phase of the statement in thousands of seconds.

- **Elapsed**   The amount of wall-clock time spent on this phase. When the elapsed time is much larger than the CPU time, that means we spent some amount of time waiting for something. In Oracle9i with TKPROF, it is easy to see what that wait was for. At the bottom of the report, we see the wait was for "db file scattered read," which means we waited for physical I/O to complete.

- **Disk**   How many physical I/Os were performed during this phase of the query. In this example, when we fetched rows from the table, we performed 2,433 physical disk reads.

- **Query**   How many logical I/Os were performed to retrieve consistent mode blocks. Those are blocks that may have been reconstructed from the rollback segments, so we would see them as they existed when our query began. Generally, all physical I/Os result in a logical I/O. In most cases, you will find that your logical I/Os outnumber the physical I/Os. However, as we saw earlier in the AUTOTRACE section, direct reads and writes for temporary space violate that rule, and you may have physical I/Os that do not translate into logical I/Os.

- **Current**   How many logical I/Os were performed to retrieve blocks as of right now. You will most frequently see these during modification DML operations, such as updates and deletes. There, a block must be retrieved in current mode in order to process the modification, as opposed to when you query a table and Oracle retrieves the block as of the time the query began.

- **Rows**   The number of rows processed or affected by that phase. During a modification, you will see the Rows value in the Execute phase. During a SELECT query, this value appears in the Fetch phase.

A question that frequently comes up with regards to TKPROF and the report is, how could output such as the following be produced:

| call | count | cpu | elapsed | disk | query | current | rows |
|------|-------|-----|---------|------|-------|---------|------|
| Parse | 1 | 0.00 | 0.00 | 0 | 0 | 0 | 0 |
| Execute | 14755 | 12.77 | 12.60 | 4 | 29511 | 856828 | 14755 |
| Fetch | 0 | 0.00 | 0.00 | 0 | 0 | 0 | 0 |
| total | 14756 | 12.77 | 12.60 | 4 | 29511 | 856828 | 14755 |

How can CPU time be larger then elapsed time? This discrepancy is due to the way timings are collected and attempts to time very fast operations or lots of operations. For example, suppose you were using a stopwatch that measured only down to the second. You timed 50 events. Each event seemed to have taken two seconds according to the stopwatch. That means 100 seconds of time elapsed during these events right? Well, probably not. Suppose each event really took 2.99 seconds then you really had almost 150 seconds of time there.

Taking it a step further, suppose the stopwatch was continuously running. So, when the event started, you would look at the stopwatch and then when the event finished, you would look again and subtract the two numbers. This is closer to what happens with timing on a computer, you look at the system "watch," do something, and look again. The delta represents the timing of the event. Now, we'll perform the same timing test as mentioned previously. Again, each event appears to have taken 2 seconds, but they may have taken just 1.01! How so? Well, when the event started, the clock was really at 2.99, but you only saw "2" (the granularity of the stopwatch). When the event completed, the stopwatch reported 4 (and the real time was 4.00). The delta as you see it is 2, but the "real" delta is actually 1.01.

Over time, these discrepancies can accumulate in the aggregate total. The rule of averages would have them effectively cancel each other out more or less, but over time, a small error can creep in. That is the cause of the discrepancy—where the elapsed time is less then the CPU time. At the lowest level, Oracle is gathering statistics for timing at either the millisecond or microsecond level. And, further, it may time some events using one clock and other events using a different one—this is unavoidable as the timing information is gathered from the operating system, using its APIs. In this example, we executed a statement 14,755 times, meaning the average CPU time to execute that statement was 0.00865469 seconds. If we were to run this test over and over, we would find that the timings for CPU and elapsed are more or less the same. In general, this error is not so large as to send you looking down the wrong path, but it can be confusing the first time you see it.

### Query Environment

The next section of the TKPROF report tells us something about the environment the query ran in. In this case, we see:

```
Misses in library cache during parse: 0
Optimizer goal: CHOOSE
Parsing user id: 147
```

The misses in library cache of zero tells us this query was soft parsed—Oracle found the query in the shared pool already (I ran this query at least once before). The optimizer goal simply displays the setting of the optimizer goal when this query was parsed. In this case, it is CHOOSE, meaning either the RBO or CBO could be used. The parsing user ID shows the schema that was in effect when this query was parsed. If I query:

```
ops$tkyte@ORA920> select * from all_users where user_id = 147;

USERNAME                          USER_ID CREATED
------------------------------ ---------- ---------
OPS$TKYTE                             147 24-DEC-02
```

I can see that it was my account.

## The Query Plan

The next section of the TKPROF report is the query plan that was actually used when this query ran. This query plan is not generated by EXPLAIN PLAN or AUTOTRACE; rather, this query plan was written into the trace file at runtime. It is the "true" plan.

To show you why this information is relevant, I'll execute these SQL commands first:

```
ops$tkyte@ORA920> truncate table big_table;
Table truncated.

ops$tkyte@ORA920> alter table big_table add constraint big_table_pk
  2   primary key(object_id);
Table altered.

ops$tkyte@ORA920> analyze table big_table compute statistics;
Table analyzed.
```

Then I'll rerun TKPROF with another argument: the EXPLAIN argument.

```
$ tkprof ora920_ora_14246.trc /tmp/tk.prf explain=/

...
Rows     Row Source Operation
-------  ---------------------------------------------------
      1  SORT AGGREGATE
 176210    TABLE ACCESS FULL BIG_TABLE


Rows     Execution Plan
-------  ---------------------------------------------------
      0  SELECT STATEMENT    GOAL: CHOOSE
      1    SORT (AGGREGATE)
 176210      INDEX    GOAL: ANALYZED (FULL SCAN) OF 'BIG_TABLE_IDX'
                 (NON-UNIQUE)
```

That's strange—there are two query plans now. The first one is the true one, the one that was actually used. The second one is the plan that would be used if we ran the query right now. It's different because we added that primary key and analyzed the table. This is one reason why you might not want to use the EXPLAIN= option of TKPROF: It may not show you the actual plan that was used at runtime. Other settings that affect the optimizer, such as sort_area_size and db_file_multiblock_read_count, would have the same effect. If the session that ran the query had different settings from the default, EXPLAIN might show you the wrong information, as it did in this example.

The query plan TKPROF provides shows not only the query plan, but as an added bonus: the number of rows that flowed out of each step. Here, we can tell that 176,210 rows flowed out of the TABLE ACCESS FULL BIG_TABLE step into the SORT AGGREGATE, and that 1 row flowed out of that step. When tuning a query, this information can be extremely useful. It can help you identify the problematic parts of a SQL statement that you might be able to tune.

As an added bonus to this section, if we are lucky enough to have Oracle9i version 9.2.0.2 or higher, we might see output like this:

```
Rows       Row Source Operation
-------    --------------------------------------------------
      1    SORT AGGREGATE (cr=2300 r=2209 w=0 time=1062862 us)
 176210       TABLE ACCESS FULL OBJ#(30635) (cr=2300 r=2209 w=0 time=361127 us)
```

Now, we see even more detail. Not only do we get the plan and the number of rows flowing through each step of the plan, but we also see logical I/O, physical I/O, and timing information. (This 9.2.0.2 example was performed on a different server, so these statistics are slightly different than the ones shown earlier.) These are represented as follows:

- `cr` is consistent mode reads, showing consistent gets (logical I/O)

- `r` is physical reads

- `w` is physical writes

- `time` is elapsed time in millionths of a second; `us` stands for microsecond

### Wait Events

The last portion of this TKPROF report shows the wait events. This information is available in Oracle9i Release 1 and later when you use the SET EVENT syntax to enable tracing. In this case, the report for our query was:

```
Event waited on               Times    Max. Wait  Total Waited
---------------------------   Waited   ---------  ------------
SQL*Net message to client        2        0.00         0.00
db file sequential read          1        0.00         0.00
db file scattered read         163        0.07         0.40
SQL*Net message from client      2        0.00         0.00
```

This report clearly identified the "big" wait event for us: 4/10 second was spent waiting for I/O (we waited 163 times for that).

You can use that information in order to help you tune your queries. For example, if this query were performing poorly, we would know to concentrate on reducing or speeding up the I/O here. One approach in this case would be to add that primary key, as I did, and analyze the table. The query plan (as shown earlier) would become a faster index full scan (faster because the index is much smaller then the table, so there is less I/O).

## TKPROF for the Masses

Now that you've seen TKPROF and what it can do, how can you make it available to everyone? You know that in order for TKPROF to work, you need access to the trace files. This is the sticky point in many cases. The trace files can contain sensitive information, so you might not want developer 1 looking at developer 2's trace file. In a production system, you don't want anyone looking at the trace files except for the DBA staff.

I would argue that in a production system, you would be tracing just to get a dump (in order to diagnose an issue) and that would be done with the help of a DBA. However, in a development and test environment, you need a more scalable solution. In other words, the developers should be able to access these trace files without needing to ask a DBA to get the files for them. They need the trace file now, they need it fast, and they need it often. In order to get access to the trace file, they typically also need physical access to the server (to access the user_dump_dest directory).

## Typical Access Methods

There are a few traditional approaches to providing access to trace files:

- You could use the undocumented init.ora parameter _TRACE_FILES_PUBLIC=TRUE.

Do not use this on a live production system, because it will make all trace files publicly accessible, which could be a security issue. On a test or development machine, this is generally acceptable. You have a limited universe of developers who access this machine and, in general, it is okay for them to see their trace files. This makes the trace files readable by the world (usually, only the Oracle account and the DBA group can read these trace files!). It does not solve the problem of physical access, however. The developers still need some sort of access to the file system, which can be a show-stopper. Solutions include exporting the user_dump_dest directory as a read-only file system and allowing developers to mount it, or allowing telnet access to the server itself.

- Set up a cron job to run every *N* minutes to move trace files to a public directory.

I see this one frequently, but have never figured out why it is popular. As compared to the first method, it is harder in that you need to script it, you still need access to the server's file system, and it adds no security or anything useful. It impairs the access to the files, since the developers must wait *N* minutes for their trace files. In short, while it works, it certainly isn't a method I would suggest using.

- Supply a `setuid` type program (Unix) that lets the developers copy trace files.

Again, for the same reasons as the previous method, this is an overly complicated solution to a simple problem. I do not recommend it.

## An Alternative Solution to Provide Worry-Free Access

I am going to offer another alternative to providing trace file access that will work nicely and that I've used with great success. You do not need to set any undocumented init.ora parameters. You can make it so the developers can access *only* their trace files. You can remove the need to provide access to the physical server file system. It accomplishes the goal of providing immediate access to the trace files, while at the same time removing many of the concerns of doing so. You can do all of this with a fairly simple PL/SQL set of routines.

What we will do involves many steps, it's like we are creating an "application" and in fact, we are. The first step will be to create a schema with the minimal set of privileges necessary. This schema will be used to allow users to view trace files as if they were database tables (they can select * from "tracefile" in effect). In order to do this, we'll write a little PL/SQL to read a trace file and make that PL/SQL callable from SQL. We'll also use a LOGOFF trigger in order to capture the trace files that are generated into a database table, along with the "owner" of that trace file so that developers will only see their trace files and not just any trace file. And lastly, we'll develop a SQLPlus script that makes invoking TKPROF against these "database tables that are trace files" as easy as possible.

**Create a Schema**    First, we'll create a schema that will be used to provide access to the trace files owned by that user, *as if each trace file were a database table.* The end user will be able to `select * from their_trace_file`. Using SPOOL in SQL*Plus, they can save this trace file locally and not need to have access to the server at all. The user we need will be created with at least these privileges:

```
create user trace_files identified by trace_files
default tablespace users quota unlimited on users;

grant create any directory, /* to read user dump dest */
create session ,   /* to log on in the first place */
create table ,     /* used to hold users -> trace files */
create view ,      /* used so users can see what traces they have */
create procedure , /* create the func that gets the trace data */
create trigger ,   /* to capture trace file names upon logoff */
create type ,    /* to create a type to be returned by function */
administer database trigger /* to create the logoff trigger */
to trace_files;

/* these are needed to find the trace file name */
grant select on v_$process to trace_files;
grant select on v_$session to trace_files;
grant select on v_$instance to trace_files;
```

**Create a View and Table**    Next, we'll create a view that returns the name of the trace file for the current session. As discussed in "Get the Trace Filename" earlier in this chapter, this view may need to be customized for your operating system:

```
create view session_trace_file_name
as
select d.instance_name || '_ora_' || ltrim(to_char(a.spid)) ||
       '.trc' filename
  from v$process a, v$session b, v$instance d
 where a.addr = b.paddr
   and b.audsid = sys_context( 'userenv', 'sessionid')
/
```

> **NOTE**
> *Oracle8i Release 2 (version 8.1.6) added a new init.ora parameter, TRACEFILE_IDENTIFIER, that is settable at the session level that may be used to more easily identify tracefiles. When set, the tracefile_identifier string will be appended to the tracefile name. For that reason, you might also consider joining to v$parameter in the earlier view to pick up that part of the name if you choose to use it.*

And then create a table to hold the mapping of usernames to filenames. We'll also keep a TIMESTAMP (use DATE in Oracle8i and earlier) to see when the trace file session ended. The view is what end users will use to see which trace files they have available:

```
create table avail_trace_files
( username   varchar2(30) default user,
  filename   varchar2(512),
  dt         timestamp default systimestamp,
  constraint avail_trace_files_pk primary key(username,filename)
)
organization index
/
create view user_avail_trace_files
as
select * from avail_trace_files where username = user
/
grant select on user_avail_trace_files to public
/
```

**Create a Trigger**    Now, we'll use a LOGOFF trigger to capture the name of the trace file and the current username, if a trace file actually exists. We'll use a BFILE to achieve this.

**NOTE**
*You will need to use the correct directory name for your udump_dir directory. The one in the example is mine. Yours may be different!*

```
create or replace directory UDUMP_DIR
as '/usr/oracle/ora920/OraHome1/admin/ora920/udump'
/

create or replace trigger capture_trace_files
before logoff on database
begin
    for x in ( select * from session_trace_file_name )
    loop
        if ( dbms_lob.fileexists(
                    bfilename('UDUMP_DIR', x.filename ) ) = 1 )
        then
            insert into avail_trace_files (filename)
            values (x.filename);
        end if;
    end loop;
end;
/
```

**Add the Function**    Next, we need the function that will read and stream the trace data back to the end user. For this, we will use a pipelined PL/SQL function. In order to do that, we'll need a simple collection type:

```
create or replace type vcArray as table of varchar2(4000)
/
```

And then we add the function itself. It begins by issuing a SELECT against USER_AVAIL_
TRACE_FILES to make sure that the requested file is available for the currently logged-in user.
That SELECT INTO will raise NO_DATA_FOUND, which when propagated back to the calling
SELECT will just appear as "No data found." If that query succeeds, we'll go on to read the trace
file a line at a time and return it to the caller.

```
create or replace
function trace_file_contents( p_filename in varchar2 )
return vcArray
pipelined
as
    l_bfile        bfile := bfilename('UDUMP_DIR',p_filename);
    l_last         number := 1;
    l_current      number;
begin
    select rownum into l_current
      from user_avail_trace_files
     where filename = p_filename;
    dbms_lob.fileopen( l_bfile );
    loop
        l_current := dbms_lob.instr( l_bfile, '0A', l_last, 1 );
        exit when (nvl(l_current,0) = 0);
        pipe row(
          utl_raw.cast_to_varchar2(
            dbms_lob.substr( l_bfile, l_current-l_last+1,
                                                l_last ) )
        );
        l_last := l_current+1;
    end loop;
    dbms_lob.fileclose(l_bfile);
    return;
end;
/
grant execute on vcArray to public
/
grant execute on trace_file_contents to public
/
```

**NOTE**
*The* `pipelined` *keyword is new with Oracle9i Release 1 and later.
In prior releases, you would not use* `pipelined` *and* `pipe row( )`*.
Instead, you would declare a local variable of type vcArray, populate
it element by element, and return that at the end of the routine. See
http://asktom.oracle.com/~tkyte/tkprof_forall.html for an Oracle8/8i-
specific solution. Beware, large tracefiles will consume large amounts
of UGA/PGA memory using this technique. The url (http://asktom
.oracle.com/~tkyte/tkprof_forall.html) discusses another alternative
implementation using global temporary tables instead (the procedure
fills a global temporary table instead of an in-memory table).*

That is it. Let's test this solution.

**Test the Access**     At this point, we'll create a minimally privileged developer account and see if this works.

```
trace_files@ORA920> @connect "/ as sysdba"

sys@ORA920> create user developer identified by developer;
User created.

sys@ORA920> grant create session,
  2        alter session
  3  to developer;
Grant succeeded.

sys@ORA920> @connect developer/developer

developer@ORA920> select * from trace_files.user_avail_trace_files;
no rows selected

developer@ORA920> @connect developer/developer

developer@ORA920> select * from trace_files.user_avail_trace_files;
no rows selected
```

That logoff (by reconnecting, we logged off and logged back in) put nothing in there. We did not generate a trace file in that session. Now, let's try this:

```
developer@ORA920> alter session set sql_trace=true;
Session altered.

developer@ORA920> @connect developer/developer

developer@ORA920> column filename new_val f
developer@ORA920> select * from trace_files.user_avail_trace_files;

USERNAME        FILENAME                DT
--------        --------------------    ----------------------------
DEVELOPER       ora920_ora_14973.trc    29-DEC-02 04.31.05.241607 PM
```

By simply generating a trace file, we have a row in there now. Let's continue:

```
developer@ORA920> select *
  2  from TABLE( trace_files.trace_file_contents( '&f' ) );

COLUMN_VALUE
------------------------------------------------------------
/usr/oracle/OraHome1/admin/ora920/udump/ora920_ora_14973.trc
Oracle9i Enterprise Edition Release 9.2.0.1.0 - Production
With the Partitioning, OLAP and Oracle Data Mining options
```

```
JServer Release 9.2.0.1.0 - Production
ORACLE_HOME = /usr/oracle/ora920/OraHome1
System name:    Linux
Node name:      tkyte-pc-isdn.us.oracle.com
Release:        2.4.18-14
Version:        #1 Wed Sep 4 13:35:50 EDT 2002
Machine:        i686
Instance name: ora920
Redo thread mounted by this instance: 1
Oracle process number: 14
Unix process pid: 14973, image: oracle@tkyte-pc-isdn.us.oracle.com

*** SESSION ID:(9.389) 2002-12-29 16:31:05.154
APPNAME mod='SQL*Plus' mh=3669949024 act='' ah=4029777240
====================
PARSING IN CURSOR #1 len=32 dep=0 uid=237 oct=42 lid=237 tim=1016794399565448
hv=1197935484 ad='5399abdc'
alter session set sql_trace=true
END OF STMT
EXEC #1:c=0,e=127,p=0,cr=0,cu=0,mis=0,r=0,dep=0,og=4,tim=1016794399564994
====================
… <snipped out for brevity> …
XCTEND rlbk=0, rd_only=1
STAT #12 id=1 cnt=0 pid=0 pos=1 obj=0 op='UPDATE   '
STAT #12 id=2 cnt=0 pid=1 pos=1 obj=5992 op='TABLE ACCESS FULL
WM$WORKSPACES_TABLE '
STAT #11 id=1 cnt=4 pid=0 pos=1 obj=222 op='TABLE ACCESS FULL DUAL '

128 rows selected.
```

Now, just to show that the security works, let's log in as another user and try to query the same trace file:

```
developer@ORA920> @connect /

ops$tkyte@ORA920> select *
  2 from TABLE( trace_files.trace_file_contents
  3            ( ' ora920_ora_14973.trc ' ) );

 no rows selected

ops$tkyte@ORA920>
```

**Automate the Access**    So, now that we have this capability to access trace files, how can we use it? We could use a simple script, like this (called tklast.sql perhaps):

```
column filename new_val f
select filename
  from trace_files.user_avail_trace_files
 where dt = ( select max(dt)
```

```
                from trace_files.user_avail_trace_files
            )
/
set termout off
set heading off
set feedback off
set embedded on
set linesize 4000
set trimspool on
set verify off
spool &f
select * from TABLE( trace_files.trace_file_contents( '&f' ) );
spool off
set verify on
set feedback on
set heading on
set termout on
host tkprof &f tk.prf
edit tk.prf
```

This is all you would need to automate this process. It would find the last trace file for your username, retrieve it, and run TKPROF against it to format it.

We've looked at some tools Oracle provides out of the box, now we'll take a look at a benchmarking tool I've developed in order to test alternative approaches to a given problem— to see which approach is better. This tool is Runstats.

# Runstats

Runstats is a tool I developed to compare methods and show which is superior. We used Runstats in several examples in Chapter 1, where I introduced it as a small-time benchmarking tool. You can download a copy today from otn.oracle.com.

Runstats simply measures three key things:

- **Wall clock or elapsed time**  This is useful to know, but not the most important piece of information.

- **System statistics**  This shows, side by side, how many times each approach did something (such as parse calls, for example) and the difference between the two.

- **Latching**  This is the key output of this report.

As I've noted previously, latches are a type of lightweight lock. Locks are serialization devices. Serialization devices inhibit concurrency. Things that inhibit concurrency are less scalable, can support fewer users, and require more resources. Our goal is always to build applications that have the potential to scale—ones that can service 1 user as well as 1,000 or 10,000. The less latching we incur in our approaches, the better off we are. I might choose an approach that takes longer to run on the wall clock but that uses 10% of the latches. I know that the approach that uses fewer latches will scale infinitely better than the approach that uses more latches.

Runstats is best used in isolation; that is, on a single-user database. We will be measuring statistics and latching (locking) activity that result from our approaches. We do not wish for other sessions to contribute to the systems load or latching while this is going on. A small test database is perfect for these sorts of tests. I frequently use my desktop PC or laptop for example.

**NOTE**
*I believe all developers should have a test bed database they control to try ideas on, without needing to ask a DBA to do something all of the time. Developers definitely should have a database on their desktop, given that the licensing for the personal developer version is simply "use it to develop and test with, do not deploy, and you can just have it." This way, there is nothing to lose! Also, I've taken some informal polls at conferences and seminars. Virtually every DBA out there started as a developer! The experience and training developers could get by having their own database—being able to see how it really works—pays for itself in the long run by the increased experience.*

## Set Up Runstats

In order to use Runstats, you need to set up access to several V$ tables, create a table to hold the statistics, and create a Runstats package.

### Create a View for V$ Table Access
You will need access to three V$ tables (those magic, dynamic performance tables): V$STATNAME, V$MYSTAT, and V$LATCH. Here is a view I use:

```
create or replace view stats
as select 'STAT...' || a.name name, b.value
     from v$statname a, v$mystat b
   where a.statistic# = b.statistic#
   union all
   select 'LATCH.' || name,  gets
     from v$latch;
```

You can either have SELECT on V$STATNAME, V$MYSTAT, and V$LATCH granted directly to you (that way you can create the view yourself) or you can have someone that does have SELECT on those objects create the view for you and grant SELECT privileges to you.

### Create a Temporary Table
Once you have that set up, all you need is a small table to collect the statistics:

```
create global temporary table run_stats
( runid varchar2(15),
  name varchar2(80),
  value int )
on commit preserve rows;
```

## Create a Runstats Package
Last, you need to create the package that is Runstats. It contains three simple API calls:

- RS_START (Runstats Start) to be called at the beginning of a Runstats test

- RS_MIDDLE to be called in the middle, as you might have guessed

- RS_STOP to finish off and print the report

The specification is as follows:

```
ops$tkyte@ORA920> create or replace package runstats_pkg
  2  as
  3      procedure rs_start;
  4      procedure rs_middle;
  5      procedure rs_stop( p_difference_threshold in number default 0 );
  6  end;
  7  /

Package created.
```

The parameter `p_difference_threshold` is used to control the amount of data printed at the end. Runstats collects statistics and latching information for each run, and then prints a report of how much of a resource each test (each approach) used and the difference between them. You can use this input parameter to see only the statistics and latches that had a difference greater than this number. By default, this is zero, and you see all of the outputs.

Next, we'll look at the package body procedure by procedure. The package begins with some global variables. These will we used to record the elapsed times for our runs:

```
ops$tkyte@ORA920> create or replace package body runstats_pkg
  2  as
  3
  4  g_start number;
  5  g_run1     number;
  6  g_run2     number;
  7
```

Next is the RS_START routine. This will simply clear out our statistics holding table and then populate it with the "before" statistics and latches. It will then capture the current timer value, a clock of sorts that we can use to compute elapsed times in hundredths of seconds:

```
  8  procedure rs_start
  9  is
 10  begin
 11      delete from run_stats;
 12
 13      insert into run_stats
 14      select 'before', stats.* from stats;
 15
```

```
16        g_start := dbms_utility.get_time;
17   end;
18
```

Next is the RS_MIDDLE routine. This procedure simply records the elapsed time for the first run of our test in G_RUN1. Then it inserts the current set of statistics and latches. If we were to subtract these values from the ones we saved previously in RS_START, we could discover how many latches the first method used, how many cursors (a statistic) it used, and so on.

Last, it records the start time for our next run:

```
19   procedure rs_middle
20   is
21   begin
22        g_run1 := (dbms_utility.get_time-g_start);
23
24        insert into run_stats
25        select 'after 1', stats.* from stats;
26        g_start := dbms_utility.get_time;
27
28   end;
29
30   procedure rs_stop(p_difference_threshold in number default 0)
31   is
32   begin
33        g_run2 := (dbms_utility.get_time-g_start);
34
35        dbms_output.put_line
36            ( 'Run1 ran in ' || g_run1 || ' hsecs' );
37        dbms_output.put_line
38            ( 'Run2 ran in ' || g_run2 || ' hsecs' );
39        dbms_output.put_line
40        ( 'run 1 ran in ' || round(g_run1/g_run2*100,2) ||
41          '% of the time' );
42            dbms_output.put_line( chr(9) );
43
44        insert into run_stats
45        select 'after 2', stats.* from stats;
46
47        dbms_output.put_line
48        ( rpad( 'Name', 30 ) || lpad( 'Run1', 10 ) ||
49          lpad( 'Run2', 10 ) || lpad( 'Diff', 10 ) );
50
51        for x in
52        ( select rpad( a.name, 30 ) ||
53                 to_char( b.value-a.value, '9,999,999' ) ||
54                 to_char( c.value-b.value, '9,999,999' ) ||
55                 to_char( ( (c.value-b.value)-(b.value-a.value)), '9,999,999' ) data
```

```
56              from run_stats a, run_stats b, run_stats c
57           where a.name = b.name
58             and b.name = c.name
59             and a.runid = 'before'
60             and b.runid = 'after 1'
61             and c.runid = 'after 2'
62             and (c.value-a.value) > 0
63             and abs( (c.value-b.value) - (b.value-a.value) )
64                   > p_difference_threshold
65           order by abs( (c.value-b.value)-(b.value-a.value))
66       ) loop
67           dbms_output.put_line( x.data );
68       end loop;
69
70           dbms_output.put_line( chr(9) );
71       dbms_output.put_line
72       ( 'Run1 latches total versus runs -- difference and pct' );
73       dbms_output.put_line
74       ( lpad( 'Run1', 10 ) || lpad( 'Run2', 10 ) ||
75         lpad( 'Diff', 10 ) || lpad( 'Pct', 8 ) );
76
77       for x in
78       ( select to_char( run1, '9,999,999' ) ||
79                to_char( run2, '9,999,999' ) ||
80                to_char( diff, '9,999,999' ) ||
81                to_char( round( run1/run2*100,2 ), '999.99' ) || '%' data
82         from ( select sum(b.value-a.value) run1, sum(c.value-b.value) run2,
83                      sum( (c.value-b.value)-(b.value-a.value)) diff
84                  from run_stats a, run_stats b, run_stats c
85                 where a.name = b.name
86                   and b.name = c.name
87                   and a.runid = 'before'
88                   and b.runid = 'after 1'
89                   and c.runid = 'after 2'
90                   and a.name like 'LATCH%'
91               )
92       ) loop
93           dbms_output.put_line( x.data );
94       end loop;
95   end;
96
97   end;
98   /
```

Package body created.

And now you are ready to use Runstats.

## Use Runstats

In order to see Runstats in action, we'll demonstrate what happens when applications overparse. I see this frequently with JDBC- and ODBC-style applications, in which the developer will code a routine in the following fashion and then call this routine dozens or hundreds or more times per connection.

```
Procedure do_insert
    Open cursor
    Parse statement
    Bind variables (hopefully they do this!)
    Execute statement
    Close cursor
```

When what they should be doing is more like this:

```
Procedure do_insert
    If (first time) the
        Open cursor
        Parse statement
        First time = FALSE
    End if
    Bind variables
    Execute statement
```

The developers should parse the statement *once* during their connection, and then bind and execute it over and over again. *Parsing* of a statement is really just another name for *compiling*. Just as you would never compile a routine, call it, and discard the compiled code, only to recompile the routine later, you don't want to lose the parsed cursor either!

We will use Runstats twice. The first time, we will show a quick fix to the code that is in production via a server setting—something to help us while the developers revise the code. The second will compare the quick-fix code to the real thing. So, we'll start with these two demonstration routines:

```
create or replace package demo_pkg
as
    procedure parse_bind_execute_close( p_input in varchar2 );
    procedure bind_execute( p_input in varchar2 );
end;
/
```

As its name implies, one will always parse, bind, execute, and close a cursor. The other will be the correctly coded routine that will simply parse once and then bind/execute repeatedly. We will use DBMS_SQL as the implementation. DBMS_SQL is similar in nature to JDBC and ODBC, as far as preparing and executing statements, so the analogy here is a good one.

```
create or replace package body demo_pkg
as

g_first_time boolean := TRUE;
g_cursor     number;

procedure parse_bind_execute_close( p_input in varchar2 )
as
    l_cursor    number;
    l_output    varchar2(4000);
    l_status    number;
begin
    l_cursor := dbms_sql.open_cursor;
    dbms_sql.parse( l_cursor,
                    'select * from dual where dummy = :x',
                     dbms_sql.native );
    dbms_sql.bind_variable( l_cursor, ':x', p_input );
    dbms_sql.define_column( l_cursor, 1, l_output, 4000 );
    l_status := dbms_sql.execute( l_cursor );
    if ( dbms_sql.fetch_rows( l_cursor ) <= 0 )
    then
        l_output := null;
    else
        dbms_sql.column_value( l_cursor, 1, l_output );
    end if;
    dbms_sql.close_cursor( l_cursor );
end parse_bind_execute_close;

procedure bind_execute( p_input in varchar2 )
as
    l_output    varchar2(4000);
    l_status    number;
begin
    if ( g_first_Time )
    then
        g_cursor := dbms_sql.open_cursor;
        dbms_sql.parse( g_cursor,
                        'select * from dual where dummy = :x',
                        dbms_sql.native );
        dbms_sql.define_column( g_cursor, 1, l_output, 4000 );
        g_first_time := FALSE;
    end if;

    dbms_sql.bind_variable( g_cursor, ':x', p_input );
    l_status := dbms_sql.execute( g_cursor );
    if ( dbms_sql.fetch_rows( g_cursor ) <= 0 )
```

```
then
    l_output := null;
else
    dbms_sql.column_value( g_cursor, 1, l_output );
end if;
end bind_execute;

end;
/
```

## The Quick Fix Test

Now, we are ready to measure our first hypothesis: If we use a quick fix, we may get some more scalability out of our system. The quick fix is SESSION_CACHED_CURSORS, a parameter that controls whether Oracle will silently cache cursors in the background, much as it does with static SQL in PL/SQL (a key reason why coding database applications in PL/SQL is an excellent idea: so much of the work is done for you). We'll run a statement 1,000 times without, and then with, cursor caching enabled.

```
ops$tkyte@ORA920> begin
   2       runstats_pkg.rs_start;
   3       execute immediate
   4       'alter session set session_cached_cursors=0';
   5       for i in 1 .. 1000
   6       loop
   7           demo_pkg.parse_bind_execute_close( 'Y' );
   8       end loop;
   9       runstats_pkg.rs_middle;
  10       execute immediate
  11       'alter session set session_cached_cursors=100';
  12       for i in 1 .. 1000
  13       loop
  14           demo_pkg.parse_bind_execute_close( 'Y' );
  15       end loop;
  16       runstats_pkg.rs_stop(500);
  17   end;
  18   /
Run1 ran in 160 hsecs
Run2 ran in 146 hsecs
run 1 ran in 109.59% of the time
```

Interestingly, the code that is executed with cursor caching is only marginally faster, although many people expect it to be blindingly fast. The really important facts to see from this are in the second part of the Runstats report. This contains the statistics and latching information:

```
STAT...session cursor cache hi          0       999       999
LATCH.library cache pin            18,022    16,016    -2,006
LATCH.shared pool                  11,031     9,003    -2,028
LATCH.library cache pin alloca     10,038     6,008    -4,030
LATCH.library cache                25,062    20,022    -5,040
```

```
STAT...session uga memory            65,464          0   -65,464
STAT...session pga memory            65,536          0   -65,536
STAT...session pga memory max             0     65,536    65,536

Run1 latches total versus runs -- difference and pct
Run1      Run2      Diff     Pct
73,393    60,428    -12,965 121.46%

PL/SQL procedure successfully completed.
```

Here, we removed 20% of the latching on the library cache and shared pool by simply flipping a switch. This may have a profound impact on your system though, consider:

"Tom, these are the top-five wait events from a Statspack report. What would you recommend?"

| Event | Waits | Wait (cs) | %Total |
|---|---|---|---|
| library cache load lock | 3,561 | 182,952 | 11.58 |
| db file sequential read | 168,481 | 154,051 | 9.75 |
| log file sync | 31,884 | 102,048 | 6.46 |
| log file parallel write | 54,402 | 59,165 | 3.75 |

Basically, I looked at this and discovered tons of parsing and reparsing going on. I suggested flipping this SESSION_CACHED_CURSORS switch.

"We set the SESSION_CACHED_CURSOR to 100 and repeated the same test (after shutdown/restart). Latch contention on the library cache is reduced (approximately 50%)."

## The Best Practice Test

Now, to complete our example, we need to compare the PARSE_BIND_EXECUTE_CLOSE routine to the BIND_EXECUTE routine. How does the code that was fixed with a temporary bandage fare when compared to the code that is implemented using best practices? With Runstats, we'll compare the two routines:

```
ops$tkyte@ORA920> begin
  2         execute immediate
  3         'alter session set session_cached_cursors=100';
  4         runstats_pkg.rs_start;
  5         for i in 1 .. 1000
  6         loop
  7             demo_pkg.parse_bind_execute_close( 'Y' );
  8         end loop;
  9         runstats_pkg.rs_middle;
 10         for i in 1 .. 1000
 11         loop
 12             demo_pkg.bind_execute( 'Y' );
```

```
13        end loop;
14         runstats_pkg.rs_stop(500);
15    end;
16    /
Run1 ran in 114 hsecs
Run2 ran in 75 hsecs
run 1 ran in 152% of the time
```

There, we can see the runtime difference is much more striking. However, the really good stuff is yet to come:

| Name | Run1 | Run2 | Diff |
|---|---|---|---|
| STAT...session cursor cache hi | 999 | 1 | -998 |
| STAT...opened cursors cumulati | 1,001 | 2 | -999 |
| STAT...parse count (total) | 1,001 | 2 | -999 |
| STAT...recursive calls | 6,002 | 3,004 | -2,998 |
| LATCH.library cache pin alloca | 6,012 | 10 | -6,002 |
| LATCH.shared pool | 9,001 | 1,010 | -7,991 |
| LATCH.library cache pin | 16,014 | 2,024 | -13,990 |
| LATCH.library cache | 20,028 | 2,032 | -17,996 |
| STAT...session uga memory | 65,464 | 0 | -65,464 |
| STAT...session pga memory | 65,536 | 0 | -65,536 |
| STAT...session pga memory max | 0 | 65,536 | 65,536 |

```
Run1 latches total versus runs -- difference and pct
Run1      Run2      Diff      Pct
60,254    14,472    -45,782   416.35%

PL/SQL procedure successfully completed.
```

You can see that the BIND_EXECUTE routine used one-fourth the amount of latching that the PARSE_BIND_EXECUTE_CLOSE routine used. That could very well be the difference between discovering your application scales and finding your application doesn't work.

# Statspack

Statspack is a tool that was first officially introduced with version 8.1.6 of the database. It is designed as a replacement for UTLBSTAT (begin stats) and UTLESTAT (end stats—generate a report). At the end of the day, Statspack is basically just a textual report that describes how your database instance has been performing. It has the ability to keep a long-running archive of these reports (actually the base data that can be used to generate a report, stored in database tables), as well as utilities to selectively purge old data or just remove all of it. Its primary use is for tuning the database after the application has been tuned.

**NOTE**
*Statspack could be made to work with versions 8.1.5 and 8.0.6 of the database with a little effort. See www.oracle.com/oramag/ oracle/00-Mar/index.html?o20tun.html for details on accomplishing that. That article also provides a good overview of this tool.*

# Set Up Statspack

Statspack is designed to be installed when connected as SYSDBA (connect *username*/*password* as sysdba). In order to install Statspack, you must be able to perform that operation. In many installations, this will be a task that must be done by a DBA or administrator.

Once you have the ability to connect as SYSDBA (or, in Oracle8i and earlier, connect internal), installing Statspack is trivial. You simply run statscre.sql in Oracle8.1.6 or spcreate.sql in Oracle8i Release 3 (8.1.7) and later. These scripts are found in $ORACLE_HOME/rdbms/admin. Also in that directory is a text file spdoc.txt that you might want to read through before installing Statspack. It contains any last-minute notes and describes new feature enhancements.

When you are connected as SYSDBA via SQL*Plus, a Statspack install looks something like this:

```
[tkyte@tkyte-pc-isdn admin]$ sqlplus "/ as sysdba"
SQL*Plus: Release 9.2.0.1.0 - Production on Sat Jan 11 13:37:23 2003
Copyright (c) 1982, 2002, Oracle Corporation.  All rights reserved.

Connected to:
Oracle9i Enterprise Edition Release 9.2.0.1.0 - Production
With the Partitioning, OLAP and Oracle Data Mining options
JServer Release 9.2.0.1.0 - Production

sys@ORA920> @spcreate
... Installing Required Packages
```

**NOTE**
*This install will run dbmspool.sql to create the DBMS_SHARED_POOL package and dbmsjob.sql to create the DBMS_JOB package. On most systems, DBMS_JOB is already installed, and on many systems, DBMS_SHARED_POOL is as well. If you are installing Statspack into a used system, you may not want these packages to be re-created, because people may be using them. You can edit spcusr.sql and comment out the installation of these two packages.*

You'll need to know three pieces of information before running the spcreate.sql script:

- The password you want to assign to the PERFSTAT user that will be created

- The default tablespace PERFSTAT will use to hold the statistics tables it created (you cannot use the SYSTEM table). You may want to consider creating a special tablespace just for statspack collection so you can more easily monitor and manage the storage used by this tool.

- The temporary tablespace PERFSTAT should use (again, this cannot be SYSTEM)

The script will prompt you for this information as it executes. In the event you make a mistake or inadvertently cancel the installation, you should use spdrop.sql (in Oracle8.1.7 and later) or statsdrp.sql (in Oracle8.1.6 and earlier) to remove the user and installed views, prior to attempting another installation of Statspack.

The Statspack installation will create some .lis files (you will see their names during the installation). You should review these for any possible errors that might have occurred. They should install cleanly, however, as long as you supplied valid tablespace names (and didn't already have a user PERFSTAT).

## Use Statspack

The Statspack report provides the following information:

- Instance information, such as the database ID and name, versions, operating system hostname, and the like

- Snapshot information, such as the beginning and end times and duration of the snapshot—the collection points—as it is now (the Statspack report)

- Database cache size information for the buffer cache, log buffer, and shared pool

- Overall load statistics, by second and by transaction, such as the amount of redo generated, number of transactions, statements executed, and so on

- Efficiency percentages, also known as hit ratios, such as library cache hits, buffer hits, soft parse percentages, and so on

- Shared pool utilization showing memory usage over the observed period of time

- Top five timed events, what you have been waiting for/waiting on (perhaps the most important part of the report!)

- A report of all wait events in the system during the observed period of time

- Various top-SQL reports, such as the SQL with the most buffer gets (those that do the most logical I/O), the SQL with the most physical reads, the most executed SQL, the most frequently parsed SQL, and so on

- A statistics report showing all of the various counters for the observed period of time, such as how many enqueue waits there were (locks that caused a wait), how many physical reads, how many disk sorts, and so on

- I/O reports by tablespace and file

- Buffer pool statistics and buffer pool advisor

- PGA advisor

- Undo information

- Latching information

- Detailed SGA breakdown and utilization report

- A listing of the init.ora parameters in use

Some of these reports are version dependent, for example, the PGA advisor is a new 9i feature that you won't see in 8i, the functionality just did not exist in that release. Additionally, the reports you see will be a function of the level of snapshot you take as well as the reporting options you use. But, as you can see, this is potentially a ton of information. A small report might be 20 printed pages long. Fortunately, as we'll see in a bit, there are a few vital points to review, and they might send you to look at details in some section, but it shouldn't take you more than a couple of minutes to skim and absorb the contents of a Statspack report.

## What People Do Wrong with Statspack

The single most common misuse of Statspack I see is the "more is better" approach. People have sent me Statspack reports that span hours or even days. The times between the snapshots (the collection points) should, in general, be measured in minutes, not hours and never days.

The Statspack reports I like are from 15-minute intervals during a busy or peak time, when the performance is at its worst. That provides a very focused look at what was going wrong at that exact moment in time. The problem with a very large Statspack snapshot window, where the time between the two snapshots is measured in hours, is that the events that caused serious performance issues for 20 minutes during peak processing don't look so bad when they're spread out over an 8-hour window. It would be like saying, "Hey, I hit 32 red lights on my last 8-hour car ride." That doesn't sound too bad—4 an hour; must be a lot of city driving. But if I told you, "Hey, I hit 6 red lights in 15 minutes during lunch," then we have identified a serious bottleneck in your travels.

It's also true with Statspack that measuring things over too long of a period tends to level them out over time. Nothing will stand out and strike you as being wrong. So, when taking snapshots, schedule them about 15 to 30 minutes (maximum) apart. You might wait 3 or 4 hours between these *two* observations, but you should always do them in pairs and within minutes of each other.

Another common mistake with Statspack is to gather snapshots only when there is a problem. That is fine to a point, but how much better would it be to have a Statspack report from when things were going good to compare it with when things are bad. A simple Statspack report that shows a tremendous increase in physical I/O activity or table scans (long tables) could help you track down that missing index. Or, if you see your soft parse percentage value went from 99% to 70%, you know that someone introduced a new feature into the system that isn't using bind variables (and is killing you). Having a history of the good times is just as important as having a history of the bad; you need both.

"When looking through the Statspack report, I found that events direct path read and direct path write are always on the top two of the Top 5 Wait Events section, as follows:

```
Top 5 Wait Events
~~~~~~~~~~~~~~~~~~
Event                    Times    Wait(cs)   Wait%
direct path read           576         292   66.42
direct path write        2,314          61   13.86
log file parallel write     19          15    3.43
log file sync               16          13    3.09
```

What could be the problem? How can I fix it?"

Well, the observation period here was about 30 minutes. There were 2.92 seconds of wait on direct path reads. Big deal! In this case, it would not be worth his time and energy to pursue this one further. Realize that there will always be some wait events, somewhere. I remember in my physics class in college, we always did our calculations assuming a "frictionless surface" my freshman year. Trying to achieve zero waits is like trying to find that frictionless surface. It doesn't exist (as I was to find out in my second-year physics class, when it got a lot harder).

## Statspack at a Glance

What if you have this 20-page Statspack report and you want to figure out if everything is okay. Here, I'll review what I look for in the report, section by section. I'll use an actual Statspack report from one of my internal systems. We'll see if anything needs further investigation (turns out it did!).

### Statspack Report Header

This is the standard header for a Statspack report:

```
STATSPACK report for

DB Name        DB Id       Instance Inst Num Release      Cluster Host
-----------    -----------  -------- -------- -----------  ------- ----
ORA9I          2272536868  ora9i          1 9.2.0.1.0    NO      aria

               Snap Id     Snap Time      Sessions Curs/Sess Comment
               -------  ------------------  -------- --------- --------
Begin Snap:      1 30-Dec-02 09:58:58    67,254        3.0
  End Snap:      2 30-Dec-02 10:14:52    67,260        3.0
   Elapsed:                  15.90 (mins)

Cache Sizes (end)
~~~~~~~~~~~~~~~~~~
         Buffer Cache:        96M    Std Block Size:      8K
    Shared Pool Size:        112M       Log Buffer:    512K
```

Note that this section may appear slightly different depending on your version of Oracle. For example, the Curs/Sess column, which shows the number of open cursors per session, is new with Oracle9i (an 8i Statspack report would not show this data).

Here, the item I am most interested in is the elapsed time. I want that to be large enough to be meaningful, but small enough to be relevant. I am partial to numbers between 15 and 30 minutes; with longer times, we begin to lose the needle in the haystack, as noted in the previous section.

### Statspack Load Profile

Next, we see the load profile:

```
Load Profile
~~~~~~~~~~~~                    Per Second        Per Transaction
                            ---------------        ---------------
              Redo size:        75,733.92              20,737.70
          Logical reads:         1,535.11                 420.35
```

```
           Block changes:        449.56              123.10
          Physical reads:        562.99              154.16
         Physical writes:         62.53               17.12
              User calls:          8.04                2.20
                  Parses:         56.43               15.45
             Hard parses:          0.38                0.10
                   Sorts:         11.63                3.19
                  Logons:          0.30                0.08
                Executes:         94.21               25.80
            Transactions:          3.65


   % Blocks changed per Read:   29.29    Recursive Call %:     97.14
   Rollback per transaction %:   9.41      Rows per Sort:     752.04
```

Here, I'm interested in a variety of things, but if I'm looking at a "health check," three items are important: the Hard parses (we want very few of them), Executes (how many statements we are executing per second/transaction), and Transactions (how many transactions per second we process). This gives an overall view of the load on the server. In this case, we are looking at a very good hard parse number and a fairly light system load—just three to four transactions per second.

## Statspack Instance Efficiency Percentage

Next, we move onto the Instance Efficiency Percentages section, which includes perhaps the only ratios I look at in any detail:

```
Instance Efficiency Percentages (Target 100%)
~~~~~~~~~~~~~~~~~~~~~~~~~~~~~~~~~~~~~~~~~~~~~~~
            Buffer Nowait %:  100.00        Redo NoWait %:  100.00
            Buffer  Hit   %:   94.94     In-memory Sort %:   98.50
            Library Hit   %:   99.81         Soft Parse %:   99.33
         Execute to Parse %:   40.10         Latch Hit %:    99.91
  Parse CPU to Parse Elapsd %:  86.12     % Non-Parse CPU:    94.69


  Shared Pool Statistics      Begin    End
                              ------   ------
                Memory Usage %:  86.95   85.16
      % SQL with executions>1:  66.38   67.40
    % Memory for SQL w/exec>1:  67.28   69.68
```

The three in bold are the ones I zero in on right away: Library Hit, Soft Parse %, and Execute to Parse. All of these have to do with how well the shared pool is being utilized. Time after time, I find this to be the area of greatest payback, where we can achieve some real gains in performance. Here, in this report, I am quite pleased with the Library Hit and the Soft Parse % values. If the Library Hit ratio was low, it could be indicative of a shared pool that is too small, or just as likely, that the system did not make correct use of bind variables in the application. It would be an indicator to look at issues such as those.

The Soft Parse % value is one of the most important (if not the only important) ratio in the database. For your typical system, it should be as near to 100% as possible. You quite simply do not hard parse after the database has been up for a while in your typical transactional/general-purpose database. The way you achieve that is with bind variables!

In a data warehouse, we would like to generally see the Soft Parse ratio lower. We don't necessarily want to use bind variables in a data warehouse. This is because they typically use materialized views, histograms, and other things that are easily thwarted by bind variables. In a regular system like this, we are doing many executions per second, and hard parsing is something to be avoided. In a data warehouse, we may have many seconds between executions, so hard parsing is not evil; in fact, it is good in those environments.

Now, just so you know, the Soft Parse % is computed using this function:

```
round(100*(1-:hprs/:prse),2)
```

In this function, `:hprs` is the number of hard parses, and `:prse` is the total parse count. As you tune your system to reduce or eliminate hard parsing so that `:hprs` goes to zero, this ratio gets closer and closer to 100%. That is your goal in most cases.

The next ratio of interest is the Execute to Parse, which is computed using this function:

```
round(100*(1-:prse/:exe),2)
```

where `:prse` is the number of parses and `:exe` is the number of executions.

The number in this report, 40%, looks pretty bad. In this case, it is wholly unavoidable. The system we are looking at does only web-based applications using MOD_PLSQL exclusively. In such a system (this applies even to J2EE applications with a connection pool as well), it is not unusual to find a lower than optimal execute-to-parse ratio. This is due solely to the fact that each web page is an entire database session. The sessions are very short, so there is not much chance for reuse of cursors here. We don't generally have the same statement executing 1,000 times per page; hence, the execute-to-parse ratio will be low. Now, if this system were designed for serving web pages by day and batch processing by night, we would expect our execute-to-parse ratios to be excellent at night and bad during the day.

The moral to this story is to look at these ratios and look at how the system operates. Then, using that knowledge, determine if the ratio is okay given the conditions. If I just said that the execute-to-parse ratio for your system should be 95% or better, that would be unachievable in many web-based systems. That doesn't mean you shouldn't try! If you have a routine that will be executed many times to generate a page, you should definitely parse once per page and execute it over and over, closing the cursor if necessary before your connection is returned to the connection pool. (In MOD_PLSQL, this is all done automatically for you; you do not need to worry about caching the parsed statement, reusing it, and closing it.)

### Statspack Top 5 Timed Events

Moving on, we get to the Top 5 Timed Events section (in Oracle9i Release 2 and later) or Top 5 Wait Events (in Oracle9i Release 1 and earlier).

```
Top 5 Timed Events
~~~~~~~~~~~~~~~~~~~                                       % Total
Event                          Waits     Time (s) Ela Time
------------------------------ ----------- ----------- --------
CPU time                                       508      37.39
```

```
direct path write                      5,168        279     20.50
db file scattered read                38,554        270     19.85
log file sync                          2,610         88      6.50
direct path read                       2,702         86      6.29
        --------------------------------------------------------
```

This section is among the most important and relevant sections in the Statspack report. Here is where you find out what events (typically wait events) are consuming the most time.

In Oracle9i Release 2, this section is renamed and includes a new event: CPU time. CPU time is not really a wait event (hence, the new name), but rather the sum of the CPU used by this session, or the amount of CPU time used during the snapshot window. In a heavily loaded system, if the CPU time event is the biggest event, that could point to some CPU-intensive processing (for example, forcing the use of an index when a full scan should have been used), which could be the cause of the bottleneck. This example is from a four-CPU machine, so the fact that I used 508 out of 3,600 CPU seconds is okay (15 minutes × 60 seconds × 4 CPUs).

Next, we see the direct path write value, which isn't good. This wait event will be generated while waiting for writes to TEMP space generally (direct loads, Parallel DML (PDML) such as parallel updates, and uncached LOBs in version 8.1.6 and earlier (in 8.1.7 there is a separate wait event for lobs) will generate this as well). When I saw this, I dug a little further to see what was causing that number. As it turned out, our PGA_AGGREGATE_TARGET parameter was set far too low. We had it at 25MB instead of 250MB, which would be much more appropriate on our system. I reset it (online) and ran the Statspack report again. This time, the direct path write wait was virtually removed from the report. We had 120 waits for direct path writes, totaling three-thousandths of a second (as opposed to 279 seconds).

Next is the db file scattered read wait value, another high number is this example. That generally happens during a full scan of a table. I used the Statspack report to help me identify the query in question and fixed it. Then I regenerated the Statspack report, for the following updated Top 5 Timed Events report:

```
Top 5 Timed Events
~~~~~~~~~~~~~~~~~~                                        % Total
                                                         % Total
Event                       Waits      Time (s)   Ela Time
--------------------------  ---------  ---------  --------
CPU time                                   592      87.62
log file sync                3,607         31       4.62
log file parallel write      8,054         21       3.14
db file sequential read      2,844         10       1.51
control file parallel write    293          5        .79
```

The db file scattered read waits disappeared from the report. So far, so good.

## The Statspack Load Profile Revisited

Let's take a peek at the Load Profile section in the new Statspack report I ran for a 15-minute window after making just those two changes mentioned in the previous section.

```
       Load Profile
       ~~~~~~~~~~~              Per Second        Per Transaction
                               ---------------    ---------------
                Redo size:         9,564.85            1,367.28
            Logical reads:         1,025.17              146.55
            Block changes:            60.80                8.69
           Physical reads:             8.49                1.21
          Physical writes:             1.32                0.19
               User calls:            11.89                1.70
                  Parses:            122.11               17.46
             Hard parses:              0.52                0.07
                   Sorts:             23.46                3.35
                  Logons:              0.43                0.06
                Executes:            156.05               22.31
            Transactions:              7.00

  % Blocks changed per Read:    5.93    Recursive Call %:    97.77
  Rollback per transaction %:   0.00      Rows per Sort:      6.34
```

We were doing two times the transactions at this point, but we reduced the number of logical reads/transaction greatly (by fixing that one bad query). Physical reads are virtually nonexistent. We are doing two times the work, with a fraction of the waits.

I'm glad I went through this exercise now. Writing this section of the book actually paid off!

## Statspack Report Summary

The first page of the Statspack report told me almost everything I needed to know. Sure, I skipped ahead frequently. For example, when I saw the high number of direct path read waits, I went to the File I/O stats section of the Statspack to confirm my suspicion that TEMP was the culprit. Given the excessively high writes against my temporary tablespace during the period under observation, I was able to confirm that as the problem. Knowing that the major cause of that would be too small of a sort area, I skipped down to the init.ora section and found we were using the PGA_AGGREGATE_TARGET parameter, and that the setting of 25MB was far too small for my server. Increasing that to 250MB solved that problem. I changed that one thing, and then repeated the 15-minute Statspack report, using about the same load to confirm the fix.

Then I zeroed in on the high number of db file scattered reads. For that, I used the Top SQL reports to find the SQL with the most reads. I got lucky and spotted the query that was erroneously doing a full scan of a big table. Interestingly, the query had a hint in it (something I am very much against, see Chapter 6 on the CBO for details on that topic). The developers of the application built their system on a small database (they did not test to load; they violated one of my rules). The hinted query worked great on their toy system, but on my machine with well over 40,000 named accounts—well, let's just say it wasn't such a good idea. But those hints stayed in there and were obeyed, causing the query to do the wrong thing in production. Fixing that fixed the other major issue.

Now, I just need to look at how I can speed up my log disks, and I'm finished! That is how I distill a 20-page Statspack report down to something I can use from start to finish in a couple of minutes. Use the first page or two in depth, and then refer to the remaining material as needed.

# DBMS_PROFILER

I often speak to groups of people. On many occasions, I've taken impromptu polls, asking, "How many people have used the source code profiler built into the database?" Generally, no hands go up. "How many people were actually aware of the fact that there is a source code profiler in the database?" Again, zero, or close to it, hands go up.

A source code profiler like DBMS_PROFILER can, in minutes, pinpoint that section of code that deserves your undivided attention for an afternoon of tuning. Without it, you could spend a week trying to figure out where you begin to look. My goal here is not to teach you how to use DBMS_PROFILER, but rather to make you aware of its existence.

## Why You Want to Use the Profiler

Given my experience as a C programmer, I've found that a source code profiler is an invaluable tool for two main tasks:

- Testing your code, to ensure that you have 100% code coverage in your test cases

- Tuning your algorithms, by finding that "low-hanging fruit"—code that if tuned to death would give you the biggest payoff

I don't see how you can do this testing and tuning without using a profiler!

"Within a large loop, if we want to commit every 1,000 records (million or billion records), which is more efficient: using mod() then `commit`, or to set up a counter, such as `counter := counter + 1`, if count ... then `commit`; `counter := 0`;. For example, in the following:

```
1).....
   START LOOP
     ....
     cnt := cnt + 1;
     IF ( cnt%1000 ) = 0 THEN <= using mod() function
       commit;
     END IF;
     ....
   END LOOP;
   ....


2)....
   START LOOP
     ....
     cnt := cnt + 1;
```

```
              IF cnt = 1000 THEN <= no mod() function
                commit;
                cnt := 0;
              END IF;
              ....
           END LOOP;
           ....
```

Is 1 or 2 better?"

The fastest is to bite the bullet, configure sufficient rollback, and do the update in a single UPDATE statement. The second fastest is to bite the bullet, configure sufficient rollback, and do the transaction in a single loop without commits. The commit is what will slow you down. You'll have to consider how you'll restart this process as well. Watch out for the ora-01555, which will inevitably get you if you are updating the table you are reading as well.

DBMS_PROFILER is an easy way to determine the best procedural algorithm to use. As an example, I created the following procedures and ran them:

```
create or replace procedure do_mod
as
     cnt number := 0;
begin
     dbms_profiler.start_profiler( 'mod' );
     for i in 1 .. 500000
     loop
         cnt := cnt + 1;
         if ( mod(cnt,1000) = 0 )
         then
             commit;
         end if;
     end loop;
     dbms_profiler.stop_profiler;
end;
/

create or replace procedure no_mod
as
     cnt number := 0;
begin
     dbms_profiler.start_profiler( 'no mod' );
     for i in 1 .. 500000
     loop
         cnt := cnt + 1;
         if ( cnt = 1000 )
         then
```

```
            commit;
            cnt := 0;
        end if;
    end loop;
    dbms_profiler.stop_profiler;
end;
/

exec do_mod
exec no_mod
```

Now, after running DBMS_PROFILER, it reports:

```
====================
Total time

GRAND_TOTAL
-----------
      11.41


====================
Total time spent on each run

RUNID RUN_COMMENT    SECS
----- -----------  -------
    1 mod            8.18
    2 no mod         3.23


====================
Percentage of time in each module, for each run separately

RUNID RUN_COMMENT UNIT_OWNER  UNIT_NAME          SECS PERCEN
----- ----------- ----------- ---------------- ------- ------
    1 mod         OPS$TKYTE   DO_MOD            8.18  100.0
    2 no mod      OPS$TKYTE   NO_MOD            3.23  100.0
```

So already, this shows that the MOD function takes longer. Just to prove that it is MOD causing the difference, we can drill down further.

```
====================
Lines taking more than 1% of the total time, each run separate

RUNID    HSECS    PCT OWNER       UNIT_NA LIN TEXT
----- --------- ------ ----------- ------- --- --------------------
    1    550.06  48.2 OPS$TKYTE   DO_MOD    9 if ( mod(cnt,1000) =
                                               0 )
    1    135.22  11.9 OPS$TKYTE   DO_MOD    8 cnt := cnt + 1;
```

```
2      107.71    9.4  OPS$TKYTE     NO_MOD     8 cnt := cnt + 1;
2      104.34    9.1  OPS$TKYTE     NO_MOD     9 if ( cnt = 1000 )
1       67.95    6.0  OPS$TKYTE     DO_MOD     6 for i in 1 .. 500000
2       64.66    5.7  OPS$TKYTE     NO_MOD    12 cnt := 0;
1       64.64    5.7  OPS$TKYTE     DO_MOD    11 commit;
2       44.99    3.9  OPS$TKYTE     NO_MOD     6 for i in 1 .. 500000

8 rows selected.
```

That clinches it. Using MOD took about 5.5 seconds. Doing if ( cnt=1000 ) took 1 second, plus the time to do cnt := 0 gives a grand total of about 1.5 seconds. So, we are looking at 5.5 seconds for mod, and 1.5 seconds for cnt=1000; cnt:=0;.

## Profiler Resources

The following are some of the resources I recommend for getting information about setting up, installing, using, and interpreting the output of DBMS_PROFILER:

- *Expert One on One Oracle*, which has a section on setting up the profiler and using it in the appendix, "Necessary Supplied Packages."

- *Oracle Supplied Packages and Types Guide,* which has a section on how and why to use the profiler, documentation on the tables used to store the profiling information, security concerns/considerations, and documentation for each of the subprograms in the package.

- www.google.com, where you can search the Web for DBMS_PROFILER and find some articles. Also, search the Usenet news groups there as well. You'll find quite a few threads on it (many written by me.)

The source code profiler in Oracle is not much different from any source code profiler you might have used with a 3GL language. Well, that is only partially true. The one advantage this profiler has is that the data is stored in the database, in tables. This means that you can create your own custom reports above and beyond what is already there!

# JDeveloper (and Debugging)

It's not just for Java anymore. JDeveloper now supports a much broader range of functionality. For me, it has become the Java, PL/SQL, SQL, XML, HTML, and so on development tool of choice.

One of the coolest features of JDeveloper is the fact that it is now written entirely in Java. The same distribution you would run on a Macintosh is the one you would use on Linux, Solaris, HP/UX, or even Windows. That means that the day your application is ready on one platform, it is ready on all platforms.

**NOTE**
*In the past, there was a PL/SQL development tool called Procedure Builder, which was limited in scope and functionality. For example, trying to use it on Linux was pretty hard. Given that JDeveloper now runs the same on all platforms, I have the same functionality on the operating system I choose as you do on the one you want to use.*

The most exciting feature in JDeveloper in regard to PL/SQL support is its built-in capability to not only create, edit, and compile PL/SQL, but to interactively debug it as well. The same features one would expect from a C or Java debugger—breakpoints, watch variables, step over, step into, and so on—are fully available with PL/SQL running in an Oracle8i or later database. This is something that will save hours of development time. Not only do you get that nice syntax highlighting that immediately shows you the location of an unclosed quote that prevents your code from compiling, but you can debug it as well. Figure 2-1 shows an example of what you might expect to see.

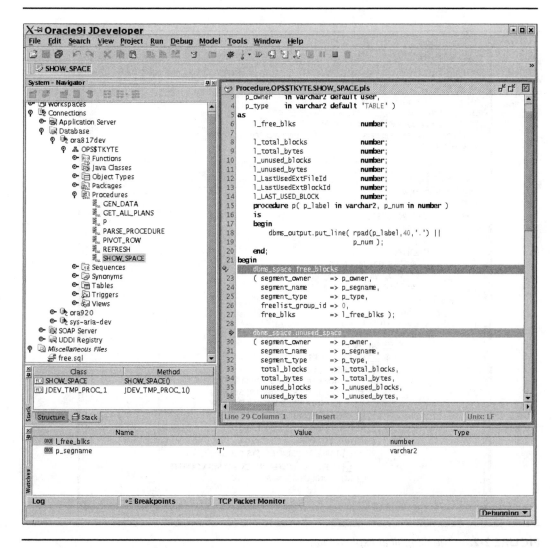

**FIGURE 2-1.** *The JDeveloper Main Screen*

In Figure 2-1, you can see the navigator on the left, which shows all of the database objects you can work with in JDeveloper now. Additionally, in this example, I'm in a debug session. I had a breakpoint set on the first line of a subroutine and am currently executing line 29 of the code, after stepping over the call to DBMS_SPACE.FREE_BLOCKS. At the very bottom of the screen, you can see some watch variables and their values, which change as the procedure modifies them. If I were to run this procedure to completion, any output it generates in the way of DBMS_OUTPUT calls would be displayed as well.

In this chapter, we've talked about using EXPLAIN PLAN, AUTOTRACE, and the like. JDeveloper has similar facilities built into it. Figure 2-2 shows an example of a very neat graphical query plan.

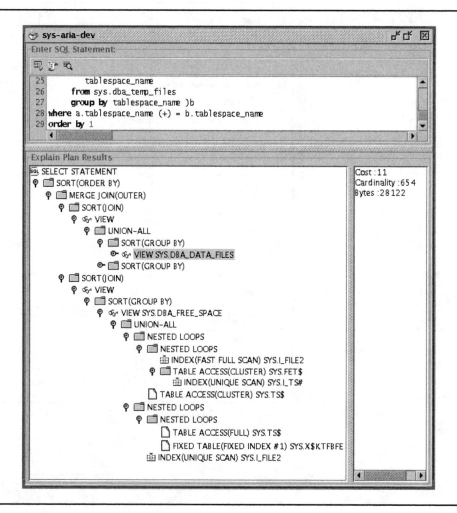

**FIGURE 2-2.** *The Graphical Explain Plan*

What is nice about this is that the information is collapsible, allowing you to easily read a multipage plan by expanding or collapsing entire nodes of the plan. In Figure 2-2, for example, the highlighted node is currently collapsed. If I were to expand it, that node would take up the entire screen. Off to the right side, you can see the details of each step of the plan.

In addition to niceties like the debugger, code-sensitive highlighting for PL/SQL, JDeveloper offers *code insight*. Using this feature, it pops up a list of available routines when you type in a package name or partial name, as shown in Figure 2-3, and you just select from that list.

You also get the SQL Worksheet, which is a nice GUI replacement for SQL*Plus, as shown in Figure 2-4. Although it is not as powerful as SQL*Plus, it does have some handy features, such as a spreadsheet widget to view results a page at a time, the ability to paginate up and down, SQL history recall, and so on.

So, if you have been ignoring JDeveloper for the last couple of years because it was a Java development environment, it is time to look again. This is a tool I find myself using more and more frequently when doing development, or even when I just need to run some queries, inspect table structures, and so on.

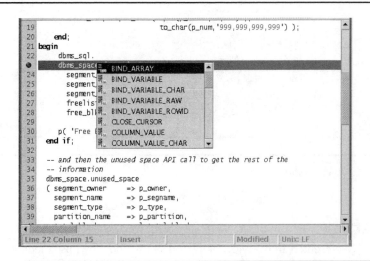

**FIGURE 2-3.**   *PL/SQL Code Insight*

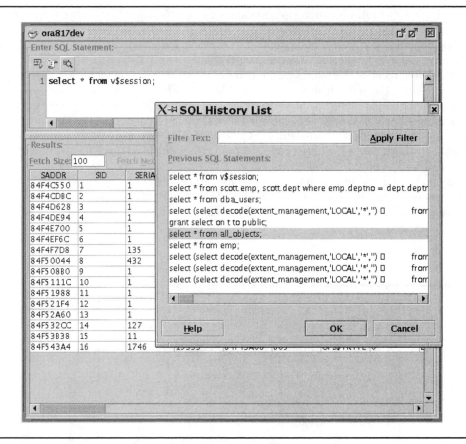

**FIGURE 2-4.** *SQL Worksheet*

# Summary

In this chapter, I've presented an overview of the tools I use and why I use them. Additionally, we explored how to use many of them. We've seen how to read AUTOTRACE and Statspack reports, for example. All of the tools, except for JDeveloper, come with the base database. This means that you have access to them, regardless of what version or flavor of Oracle you bought (Enterprise, Standard, or Personal).

Now that we've looked at some of the tools, let's take a look at the database architecture and how it will affect you. The next chapter covers some architectural topics regarding the database such as shared server versus dedicated server, clustering, partitioning, and the like. You'll see as we progress though this book that we'll constantly be coming back to the tools we just reviewed in this chapter over and over.

# CHAPTER
# 3

# Architectural
# Decisions

This chapter takes a look at some of the architectural (macro-level) decisions that can help (or hinder) you in achieving the sort of scalability and performance of which Oracle is capable. We will look at three main goals:

- **Achieving high concurrency**   Dedicated server versus shared server connections and clustering

- **Handling storage space effectively**   Locally managed tablespaces and partitioning

- **Taking advantage of parallel operations**   Parallel processing with Oracle's various options for parallel operations

I will not go into the details of the Oracle server process architecture and memory structures, or explain how to set up partitioning or parallel processing. (For that information, I will refer you to the relevant documentation.) Rather, I will focus on how and when to use these Oracle's features, and also attempt to dispel some myths about them.

# Understand Shared Server vs. Dedicated Server Connections

Using a dedicated server configuration is by far the most common method to connect to an Oracle database. It is the easiest to configure and offers many benefits when debugging or tracing a process. It is the connection option most people should be using day to day. A shared server configuration is more complex, but it can help you get more sessions connected using the same hardware (number of CPUs and memory).

**NOTE**
*Shared server configuration is also known as multithreaded server, or MTS, in earlier releases of Oracle. MTS and shared server are synonymous. This book uses the term "shared server".*

In this section, I'll briefly explain how the dedicated server and shared server connections work under the covers, and cover the pros and cons of each configuration. Then I'll deal with some common misconceptions with regard to the use of a shared server configuration.

"Should I be using the shared server configuration of Oracle?"

Unless you have more concurrent connections to your database than your operating system can handle, do not use shared server. Until the machine is so loaded with processes/threads that it cannot hold another one, use dedicated server. Then, when the machine hits that maximum threshold, where another connection is either not possible or adversely affects overall performance, that is the time to consider switching over to shared server. Fortunately, clients don't have control over this, so switching back and forth is trivial to accomplish and transparent to the application.

There are actually many reasons why dedicated server should be your first choice, but the main one is that on a system where dedicated server has not yet overloaded the system with processes/threads, *it will be faster.* So, unless dedicated server is the cause of your performance issues (system overload), shared server will not perform as well.

# How Do Dedicated Server Connections Work?

When you connect to an Oracle instance, in reality, you are connecting to a set of processes and shared memory. The Oracle database is a complex set of interacting processes that all work together in order to carry out requested operations.

### Dedicated Server Connection Steps

When you connect with a dedicated server over the network, the following steps take place:

1. Your client process connects over the network to a listener that is typically running on the database server. There are situations (see the "Take Advantage of Clustering" section later in this chapter for an example) where the listener will not be on the same machine as the database server instance.

2. The listener creates a new dedicated process (Unix) or requests the database to create a new dedicated thread (Windows) for your connection. The choice of whether a thread or process will be created is decided by the Oracle kernel developers on an operating system–by–operating system basis. They will choose the implementation that makes the most sense on that particular operating system.

3. The listener hands the connection off to the newly created process or thread.

4. Your client process sends requests to this dedicated server and it processes them, sending the results back.

Figure 3-1 shows how dedicated server configuration works. The Oracle instance will be a single process with threads on some platforms (Windows, for example) or each "bubble" will be a separate physical process (Unix, for example). In a dedicated server configuration, each client has its own process/thread associated with it.

The dedicated server will receive your SQL and execute it for you. It will read datafiles and place data in the cache, look in the database cache for data, perform your UPDATE statements, and run your PL/SQL code. Its only goal is to respond to the SQL calls that you submit to it.

So, in dedicated server mode, there is a one-to-one mapping between processes in the database and a client process. Every dedicated server connection has a dedicated server allocated solely to it. That does not mean every single session has a dedicated server, it is possible for a single application, using a single physical connection (dedicated server) to have many sessions concurrently active. In general however, when in dedicated server mode, there is a one-to-one relationship between a session and a dedicated server.

### Pros and Cons of Dedicated Server Connections

Here is a short list of the advantages of using a dedicated server connection to the database:

■ It is easy to set up. In fact, it requires almost no setup.

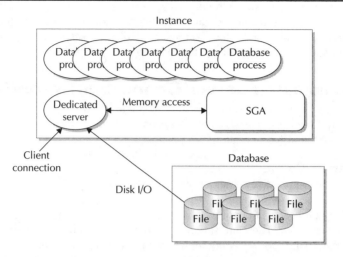

Instance

**FIGURE 3-1.** *The connection process in dedicated server configuration*

- It is the fastest mode for the database to operate in, using the shortest code path.

- Since trace files are tied to a process (a dedicated server, for example), facilities such as SQL_TRACE benefit from dedicated server mode. In fact, trying to use SQL_TRACE on a nondedicated server mode connection can sometimes be an exercise in futility.

- All administrative functions are available to you. (In shared server mode, certain administrative features—such as database startup, shutdown, and recovery features—are not available.)

- The memory for the user's user global area (UGA), which is session-specific memory, is allocated in the process global area (PGA) dynamically. It need not be configured in the shared global area (SGA).

Some of the disadvantages of using dedicated server connections are as follows:

- The client has a process/thread consuming resources (memory, CPU cycles for context switching, and so on) on the server from the time the session begins until it terminates.

- As the number of users increases, the operating system can become overloaded managing that many processes/threads.

- You have limited control over how many sessions can be active simultaneously, although Oracle9i has addressed this with the Resource Manager and the maximum active sessions per group rule.

- You cannot use this connection mode for database link concentration.

■ If you have a high rate of actual connects/disconnects to the data, the overhead of process and thread creation and destruction may be very large. A shared server connection would have an advantage here. Note that for most web-based applications, this is not an issue, because they typically perform some sort of connection pooling on their own.

As you can see from these lists, for most systems, the dedicated server benefits outweigh many of the disadvantages. On most conventional database servers today (typically, machines with two to four CPUs), you would need 200 to 400 concurrent connections before considering a different connection type. On larger machines, the limit is much higher.

There is no set limit at which a dedicated server configuration becomes infeasible. I've seen the need to stop using this configuration with 100 users. On the other hand, I've seen systems running with more than 1,000 users using dedicated server configuration without breaking a sweat. Your hardware and how you use the database will dictate your decision to switch to shared server connections. As long as you have the CPU and, to a lesser extent, the RAM, dedicated server configuration is the easiest and most functional approach.

# How Do Shared Server Connections Work?

The connection protocol for a shared server connection is very different from the one for a dedicated server configuration. In a shared server configuration, there is no one-to-one mapping between clients (sessions) and server processes/threads. Rather, there is a pool of aptly named *shared servers* that perform the same operations as a dedicated server, but they do it for multiple sessions as needed, instead of just one session.

Additionally, there are processes known as *dispatchers* that run when you are using a shared server connection. The clients will be connected to a dispatcher for the life of their session, and this dispatcher will facilitate the handing off of a client request to a shared server and getting the answer back to the client after the shared server is finished. These dispatchers running on the database are known to the listener process. As you connect, the listener will redirect you to an available dispatcher.

### Shared Server Connection Steps

When you connect via shared server connections, here is what typically happens:

1. Your client process connects over the network to a listener running on the database server. This listener will choose a dispatcher from the pool of available dispatchers for you to connect to.

2. The listener will send back to your client the address of the chosen dispatcher for you to connect to, or you may be redirected directly to the dispatcher (in some cases, the connection may be handed off directly). This happens at the TCP/IP-connection level and is operating-system dependent. If you were not directly handed off to the dispatcher, your client disconnects from the listener and your client connects to the dispatcher.

3. Your client process sends the request to this dispatcher.

Figure 3-2 illustrates the connection process in shared server mode.

So, as connection requests are received, first, the listener will choose a dispatcher process from the pool of available dispatchers. Next, the listener will send back to the client connection

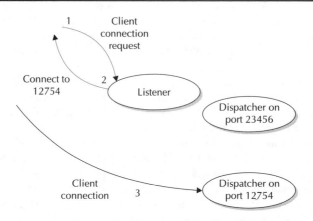

**FIGURE 3-2.** *The connection process in shared server configuration*

information describing how the client can connect to the dispatcher process. This must be done because the listener is running on a well-known hostname and port on that host, but the dispatchers will be accepting connections on randomly assigned ports on that server. The listener is aware of these random port assignments and picks a dispatcher for you. The client then disconnects from the listener and connects directly to the dispatcher. Finally, you have a physical connection to the database.

### Shared Server Command Processing

Now that you are connected, the next step is to process commands. With a dedicated server, you would just send the request (`select * from emp`, for example) directly to the dedicated server for processing. With shared server connections, this is a tad more complex. You don't have a single dedicated server anymore. There needs to be another way of getting the request to a process that can handle it. The steps undertaken at this point are as follows:

1. The dispatcher places the request in a common (shared by all dispatchers) queue in the SGA.

2. The first shared server that is available will pick up and process this request.

3. The shared server will place the answer to the request in a response queue private to the queuing dispatcher in the SGA.

4. The dispatcher you are connected to will pick up this response and send it back to you.

Figure 3-3 illustrates this process.

It is interesting to note that these steps are performed for each call to the database. Therefore, the request to parse a query may be processed by shared server 1, the request to fetch the first row from the query may be processed by shared server 2, the next row by shared server 3, and, finally, shared server 4 might be the one that gets to close the result set.

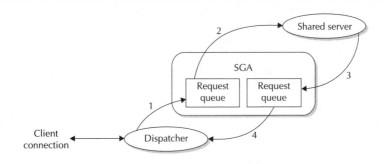

**FIGURE 3-3.**   *Processing a request in shared server configuration*

As you can see, the code path from the client submitting the request (some SQL) to getting an answer is a long and winding one. However, this architecture works well if you need to scale up your system. With dedicated server connections, every session is a new process. With shared server connections, the number of processes is fixed (or at least set within a hard-and-fast range) and controllable. In order to get the $N+1$ connection, all you need is available memory in the SGA for that session's UGA (memory used by the session for state variables, cursors, and other objects).

### Pros and Cons of Shared Server Connections
Here are some of the advantages of using a shared server connection to the database:

- It is more scalable as you need to scale up. On a machine that could physically handle 100 dedicated server connections, you might be able to handle 1,000 or more shared server connections, depending on the application. If you have a traditional client/server type of application where the vast majority of the connected sessions are inactive (for example, out of 1,000 connects, maybe only 50 to 100 are concurrently active, and the rest are experiencing "user think time"), then shared server configuration can be useful in scaling up your application. Note that this scaling refers to CPU scaling only—you still need sufficient memory for these 1,000 connections.

- It allows fine-grained control over how many sessions may be active concurrently; it imposes a hard limit on the number of overall active sessions.

- It uses marginally less memory than dedicated server configuration. The difference in memory usage is discussed in the section, "Shared Server Uses Significantly Less Memory" later in this chapter.

- It lets you get that $N+1$ user logged on when dedicated server configuration would fail.

- If you have a high rate of connects/disconnects, using shared server configuration may prove faster than dedicated server. The process and thread creation and destruction process is very expensive, and it may outweigh the overhead of the longer code path.

Some of the disadvantages of shared server configuration are as follows:

- It is more complex to set up than dedicated server configuration, although the GUI tools provided with the database generally hide that complexity today. Most of the setup problems I see people encountering are when they try to edit the configuration files by hand, instead of using the tools.

- On a system where dedicated server connections will work fine, shared server connections will be slower. A shared server's code path is, by definition, longer than a dedicated server's code path.

- Some features of the database are not available when connected via shared server. You *must* connect to the database in dedicated server mode for these features. For example, using shared server connections you cannot shut down or start an instance, perform media recovery, or use Log Miner.

- The memory for the sum of all of the concurrently connected sessions UGA must be computed and configured as part of the LARGE_POOL init.ora file setting. You need to understand the maximum degree of connectivity and size appropriately. In Oracle9i Release 2, with the ability to dynamically resize the LARGE_POOL setting online, this is less of a concern as you can monitor your memory use and alter it (but this is a manual change, not automatic).

- Tracing (using SQL_TRACE) is currently something I would deem as not feasible when using a shared server connection. The trace files are specific to a process, and in shared server mode, a process is not specific to a session. Not only will your SQL statements be written to many different trace files, other session's SQL statements will be written to these same trace files. You cannot ascertain which statements are yours and which are theirs.

- There is a potential for artificial deadlocks. These occur because once a shared server starts processing a request, it will not return until it is finished with it. Hence, if the shared server is sent an UPDATE request and the row is already locked, that shared server will block. Suppose the blocking session was idle for a period of time (not doing any work in the database so it doesn't have a shared server allocated to it) and all of the other shared servers get blocked as well by this idle session (or any other session), then when the session holding the lock attempts to commit or rollback (which would release the locks), it will hang because there are no more free shared servers. This is an artificial deadlock situation, where the blocker cannot free the blockees, since the blockees have all of the shared servers tied up.

- There is a potential for shared server monopolization. This occurs for the same reason as the artificial deadlocks. If you use shared server with long-running transactions, your sessions will monopolize a shared resource, preventing others from using it. If you have too many of these long-running transactions, your system's performance will appear abysmal, because short transactions must wait for long transactions to complete.

As you can see, for most general-purpose uses, shared server configuration is not worth it. Only when your database cannot physically handle the load should you consider using a shared server configuration.

# Common Misconceptions about Shared Server Connections

Through the asktom web site and Usenet newsgroup exchanges, I've become aware of some common misconceptions about shared server configuration. These misconceptions are being passed down from generation to generation of Oracle developers, and I would like to stop them in their tracks.

### Shared Server Uses Significantly Less Memory

This is one of the most highly touted reasons for using shared server: It reduces the amount of memory. I've seen people enable shared server, change their tnsnames.ora file to request shared connections, and change nothing else (configure no extra memory in the SGA). These systems immediately fall over as the SGA runs out of memory. These DBAs forgot that the UGA will still be 100% allocated, but now it will be allocated in the SGA instead of in local process memory. So, while the amount of memory used by operating system processes will be significantly reduced, this is offset in most part by the increase in the size of your SGA.

When you enable shared server, you must be able to somewhat accurately determine your expected UGA memory needs and allocate that memory in the SGA via the LARGE_POOL setting. So, the SGA requirements for the shared server configuration typically are very large. This memory must be preallocated, and thus, it can be used only by the database. It is true that in Oracle9i Release 2, you can dynamically resize the LARGE_POOL setting online, but for all intents and purposes, this must be preset. Compare this with dedicated server configuration, where anyone can use any memory not allocated to the SGA.

So, if the SGA is much larger due to the UGA being located in it, where do the memory savings come from? They come from having that many fewer PGAs allocated. Each dedicated/shared server has a PGA for process information (sort areas, hash areas, and other process-related structures). It is this memory requirement that you are removing from the system by using shared server mode. If you go from using 5,000 dedicated servers to 100 shared servers, it is the cumulative sizes of the 4,900 PGAs you no longer need that you are saving with shared servers. However, even this is questionable, since all modern operating systems employ sophisticated paging mechanisms that would effectively page out the memory not currently in use by the 4,900 PGAs.

So, shared server configuration can save some memory, but not nearly as much as some people expect (before actually doing it and discovering the hard way!).

### You Should Always Use Shared Server Configuration with Application Servers

Only if you have a large application server farm, where each application server has a large connection pool all connecting to a single database instance, should you consider using shared server configuration. Here, you have the same considerations as with any other system (the application server makes no difference). If you have a large number of connections and you are overloading the database server, it would be time to use shared server connections to reduce the number of physical processes.

"We are using connection pooling in the middle tier and shared server on the database tier. It is slow. Why?"

Well, it is slow because you are, in effect, caching a cache. This is like using an operating system cache *and* the database cache. If one cache is good, two must be twice as good, right? Wrong. If you are using a connection pool at the middle tier, the odds are you want to be using a dedicated server for speed. A connection pool will allocate a fixed (controllable) number of persistent physical connections. In that case, you do not have a large number of sessions and you do not have fast connect/disconnect rates—that is the recipe for dedicated server!

### Shared Servers Are Only for Client/Server Applications

This is the converse of the application server misconception of the previous section. Here, the DBA would never consider shared server configuration for an application server, since the application server is doing pooling already. Well, the problem with that theory is that the application server is just the client. You still have clients (the application server connection pool) and a server (the database). From the database perspective, this whole paradigm shift from client/server to *N*-tier application models never happened! It is apparent to the developer that they are different, but to the database, this difference is not really visible.

You should look at the number of concurrent physical connections to the database. If that results in too many processes for your system to handle, shared server connections may be the solution for you.

### An Instance Runs in Shared Server Mode (or Not)

This is probably the most common misconception: A database instance is in shared server mode or dedicated server mode. Well, the fact is, it may be both. You can always connect via a dedicated server configuration. You can connect via a shared server configuration if the necessary setup (dispatchers and shared servers) was configured. You can connect in one session using dedicated server mode, and then in another session, connect to the same database using shared server mode.

The database does not run in shared server or dedicated server modes. They are connection types, and a database can support both simultaneously.

## Dedicated Server vs. Shared Server Wrap-Up

Unless your system is overloaded, or you need to use shared server configuration for a specific feature, a dedicated server configuration will probably serve you best. A dedicated server is simple to set up and easier to tune with. There are certain operations that must be done in a dedicated server mode, so every database will have either both dedicated and shared servers or just a dedicated server set up.

On the other hand, if you know you will be deploying with shared server due to a very large user community, I would urge you to *develop and test* with shared server connections. Your likelihood of failure will increase if you develop under just a dedicated server configuration and never test on a shared server configuration. Stress the system, benchmark it, and make sure that your application is well-behaved under the shared server configuration; that is, make sure it does not monopolize shared servers for too long. If you find that it does so during development, it is much easier to fix the problem there than it is during deployment. You can use features such as advanced queues (AQ) to turn a long-running process into an apparently short one, for example, but you must design that into your application. These sorts of things are best done when you are developing your application.

If you are already using a connection-pooling feature in your application (for example, you are using the J2EE connection pool), and you have sized your connection pool appropriately, using shared server connections will be a performance inhibitor in most cases. You already designed your connection pool to be the size you need concurrently at any point in time, so you want each of those connections to be a direct, dedicated server connection. Otherwise, you just have a connection-pooling feature connecting to yet another connection-pooling feature.

For details on dedicated server and shared server architecture, as well as the Oracle memory structures (the PGA, SGA, and UGA), see the Oracle *Concepts Guide.*

# Take Advantage of Clustering

For high availability and the ability to scale horizontally, there is nothing like clustering. In order for that sentence to make sense, we'll need to define a few of the terms first.

*Clustering* is a hardware configuration whereby multiple computers are physically connected together to permit them to cooperate to perform the same task against a single set of shared disks. Clustering is a well-established technology, pioneered by Digital Equipment Corporation (DEC) with its VAX/VMS machines in the 1980s. Today, clusters can range from high-end machines or just a bunch of laptops running Linux hooked together with FireWire. The machines in the cluster have their own private network for communication, also known as a *high-speed interconnect.* Its implementation varies by hardware vendor, from the proprietary high-end solutions to just the network on Linux. This private network allows the machines in the cluster to communicate very rapidly.

In the past, clustering was a technology that was beyond the reach of most people. You needed specialized hardware configurations that hardware vendors typically supported only on the high end of their configurations. Hence, the cost barriers for the hardware to support clustering were high. Now, the ability to cluster commodity, off-the-shelf machines (such as those provided by Dell or Hewlett-Packard/Compaq), with operating systems such as Linux, opens the world of clustering to the masses. For hardware costs of less than $10,000 to $20,000, you could have a fully functional four- to eight-CPU cluster up and running overnight. All it takes is two servers and a cable.

*Horizontal scaling* is the ability to add capacity to your system by adding more machines. In the past, we have scaled vertically by putting additional CPUs into a single box, adding RAM, and so on. Vertical scaling works well until you hit the limits of your machine. For example, a 32-bit operating system cannot make significant use of memory beyond 4GB. A conventional Unix machine cannot scale beyond about 64 to 128 CPUs. Horizontal scalability breaks those barriers. Each machine might have hard limits, but together in a cluster, they can surpass those limits. Horizontal scaling provides the ability to add computer resources over time as the need arises.

*High availability* is one of the salient features of clusters. They are, by definition, highly available platforms. As long as one computer remains running in the cluster, the resources of the cluster are available. No longer does the failure of a single computer prevent access to your database.

In this section, we will look at a configuration of Oracle called Real Application Clusters (RAC) and how it works on clusters. We will also explore how RAC provides horizontal scalability and high availability.

"We are building the biggest database of all time, with the most users ever. It will start with 100 users for the first year, growing to 500 in two years, and getting way up there in users over the long haul. But this year, the needs are rather modest. What's the best way to do this?"

There are two approaches you could take in this case:

- **Buy the biggest machine you can**   This will give you the capacity available two years from now. The downside is that you will spend a lot of money today for something that will be one-tenth the cost in two years.

- **Buy a machine that fits your needs today**   Then buy another one in a year for half the price at twice the speed, and buy another when you need it, and so on. The upside is that you buy only what you need today and get what you need later for less. The only caveat is that you need to make sure the hardware you buy today is, in fact, clusterable. That is a question for your hardware vendor, and the answer varies from vendor to vendor.

## How Does RAC Work?

A database may be mounted and opened by many instances simultaneously, and that is what RAC is all about. In order to understand how RAC works, we first need to clear up one of the more confusing topics in Oracle: the difference between an instance and a database.

### An Instance vs. Database Refresher

An *instance* is simply the set of processes and memory used by these processes (the SGA). An Oracle instance does not need to have a database associated with it at all. You can start an instance without any datafiles whatsoever. An instance is not very useful in that mode, but you can have one.

A *database* is the set of files—redo, control, data, and temporary files—that holds your data. A database has no processes or memory; it just has files.

Typically, an Oracle instance is started with the `startup` command, but I'll take you through the long way, so you can see when we have an instance and when we have an instance that has a database associated with it:

```
idle> startup nomount
ORACLE instance started.

Total System Global Area 303108296 bytes
Fixed Size       450760 bytes
Variable Size   134217728 bytes
Database Buffers  167772160 bytes
Redo Buffers      667648 bytes
idle>
```

So, here we have an Oracle instance. If you were to run `ps` at the operating-system level (or use the equivalent tool on Windows), you would see the Oracle processes are running—the SGA is allocated. Everything is started, except for a database! In fact, there are even some queries we can run:

```
idle> select * from dual;

ADDR     INDX INST_ID D
-------- ---------- ---------- -
0A62D1C0  0  1 X
```

```
idle> select * from v$datafile;
select * from v$datafile
                  *
ERROR at line 1:
ORA-01507: database not mounted
```

So, DUAL is there (but it looks a tad strange, since it has extra columns), but not many other tables are available. For example, we do not have V$DATAFILE yet, because no datafiles are associated with this instance.

**NOTE**
*This special DUAL table is there for applications that need DUAL but are expected to work against databases that are not yet opened, such as RMAN. As soon as you open the database, the regular DUAL reappears.*

So, the Oracle instance is up and running, but has yet to associate itself to a set of files and make them accessible. We'll do that now:

```
idle> alter database mount;
Database altered.
idle> select count(*) from v$datafile;

  COUNT(*)
----------
        23


idle> alter database open;
Database altered.

idle> @login
sys@ORA920>
```

And there we go. Now, the database is open and ready for access. The ALTER DATABASE MOUNT command used the control files (specified in the init.ora file) to locate the redo, data, and temporary files. The ALTER DATABASE OPEN command made the database available to anyone via this instance.

Note that an instance here is a transient thing. An instance is simply a set of processes and memory. Once you shut down that instance, it is *gone* forever. The database persists, but instances are fleeting. Another interesting thing to note is that an instance can mount and open at the most *one* database during its life. We can see this simply by issuing these commands:

```
sys@ORA920> alter database close;
Database altered.

sys@ORA920> alter database open;
alter database open
```

```
*
ERROR at line 1:
ORA-01531: a database already open by the instance

sys@ORA920> !oerr ora 1531
01531, 00000, " a database already open by the instance"
// *Cause: During ALTER DATABASE, an attempt was made to open
//  a database on an instance for which there is already
//  an open database.
// *Action: If you wish to open a new database on the instance,
//  first shutdown the instance and then startup the
//  instance and retry the operation.
```

The reason this is interesting is that the converse is not true. As noted at the beginning of this section, a database may be mounted and opened by *many* instances simultaneously. The rules for databases and instances in Oracle are as follows:

- An instance is transient. It exists only as long as the related set of processes and memory exists.

- A database is persistent. It exists as long as the files exist.

- An instance may mount and open a *single* database in its life.

- A database may be mounted and opened by many instances, either one after the other or by many simultaneously (that is RAC).

## Instances in RAC

In an RAC environment, you run an instance of Oracle on each machine (also known as a *node*) in the cluster. Each of these instances mount and open the same database, since clusters share disks. It is important to keep in mind that there is only one database. Each Oracle instance has full read/write access to every byte of data in the database.

Each instance is a peer of every other instance in the cluster. You can update the EMP table from node 1. You can update the EMP table from node 2. In fact, you can update the record where ename = `KING` on both node 1 and node 2, following the same rules you would if you used only a single instance of Oracle. The same locking and concurrency control mechanisms you are familiar with on a single instance of Oracle with a single database hold true for Oracle running RAC.

Figure 3-4 shows what an RAC might look like with a four-node (four-computer) cluster. Each node would be running its own instance of Oracle (the processes/memory). There is a single database image shared by all nodes in the cluster, each having full read/write access to every byte of data in that database.

The basic premise behind Oracle RAC is that you run many instances of Oracle. Each instance is a stand-alone entity—a peer of the other instances. There is no master instance, so there is no single point of failure. Each instance will mount and open the same database—the same files. The instances will work together keeping their caches consistent with each other, to avoid overwriting changes made by other instances and to avoid reading old/stale information. If one of them fails for any reason—due to a hardware failure or a software failure—one of the

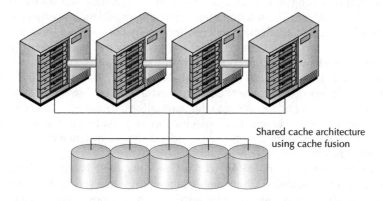

Shared cache architecture
using cache fusion

**FIGURE 3-4.** *RAC with a four-node cluster*

other remaining instances in the cluster will recover any work that the failed instance had in progress, and operations continue as before.

## A Service Refresher

There is one more term we need to define to understand how RAC works: *service*. You may have noticed that, starting in the Oracle8.0 days, it was recommended that a tnsnames.ora entry look like this:

```
ORA920.US.ORACLE.COM =
  (DESCRIPTION =
  (ADDRESS_LIST =
  (ADDRESS = (PROTOCOL = TCP)(HOST = tkyte-pc-isdn)
    (PORT = 1521))
  )
  (CONNECT_DATA =
  (SERVICE_NAME = ora920)
)
  )
```

Instead of this:

```
ORA920.US.ORACLE.COM =
  (DESCRIPTION =
  (ADDRESS_LIST =
  (ADDRESS = (PROTOCOL = TCP)(HOST = tkyte-pc-isdn)
    (PORT = 1521))
  )
  (CONNECT_DATA =
  (ORACLE_SID = ora920)
)
  )
```

That is, we stopped using an ORACLE_SID to identify a database and started using a more generalized SERVICE_NAME. The reason behind that recommendation was to pave the way for features like RAC. The client application will now optimally connect to a service. The service is a collection of instances, the most common of which is a collection of one. Whereas an SID identifies an instance, a service identifies a collection of one or more instances.

In this fashion, the client connects to the database, not to a particular instance, since each instance is a peer of every other instance. Using this extra level of abstraction allows for features like load-balancing (connecting the client to the least-utilized instance). It also creates a less error-prone connection. If you connect to a specific instance and that instance is not up, you will be made aware of it. If you connect to a service and at least one instance is up, you will not be made aware of the fact that the other N instances are down.

At a rather high level, that is how RAC works. Physically, there is one database with many instances. To the client applications that connect, there is just one service they connect to, and that service will get them connected to an instance, which provides full read/write access to the database. All of this happens without the application knowing a thing about what is going on behind the scenes. You can take your existing applications and point them at an RAC database, and they will run just as before. Any application that runs against Oracle9i will run unmodified on Oracle9i RAC in a cluster.

It is true that there are performance implications to consider under RAC as well. There are extreme cases where applications may run slower under RAC. For example, if you have a system that performs excessive parsing (due to lack of proper bind variable use), you'll rapidly discover that since library cache operations are globally coordinated in the cluster, the problem you had in a single instance is simply magnified in a cluster. I have seen people take the approach of "we will use clusters to hide our performance issues" only to discover that clustering in many cases will amplify an already poorly performing, poorly designed system. With RAC, you cannot fix issues such as:

- **Library Cache Contention**  If you had a problem with the library cache in a single instance, multiple instances will only amplify the problem.

- **Excessive IO**  Since IO is coordinated globally, an IO issue under a single instance configuration will likewise be amplified in a multi-instance configuration.

- **Locking (blocking)**  Especially concentrated locking issues of the type you might find in a system that uses a table with a counter to provide sequence numbers rather than using a sequence itself. This implementation causes contention in a single instance—contention that will be amplified in a clustered environment.

These design issues must be corrected using implementation techniques. For example, you will need to reduce library cache contention by proper use of bind variables and by parsing SQL statements only as often as you must (Chapter 5). You can reduce excessive IO by designing and implementing physical structures that are suitable for the way you use the data (Chapter 7). You can remove or reduce locking issues by using built-in database features such as sequences. Oracle9i RAC can scale, but it cannot fix an already broken system!

## What Are the Benefits of RAC?

So now that you know how RAC works, you can see how RAC is to databases what RAID is to disks. It provides a level of redundancy. If a disk fails in a RAID array, no problem; in most systems today, you can just hot-swap in a new disk. If an Oracle instance fails in RAC, no problem; the other instances will automatically take over. You can fix the failed instance, correcting the hardware or software problem that caused the failure.

RAC is a solution to make sure that once the database is up and running, nothing short of taking the entire data center out in a fire or other catastrophe will bring down your entire database. So, you can protect your disks with RAID or some other technology, networks with redundancy, and databases with redundant Oracle instances.

This is not something the company I work for just talks about, this is how we run our major systems ourselves. Internally, there is one email database for the company (yes, we store all of our email in Oracle). Now, the company is fairly large, with more than 40,000 users, all with email accounts. A single instance on the biggest hardware isn't big enough for us. As of the writing of this book, we have three instances of Oracle in a three-node RAC cluster, accessing this single database image. If you've ever interacted with Oracle (the company), you know it runs on email, and its email runs on RAC. We have failover scenarios using the Oracle9i Data Guard product as well, but to keep the email database up and running 24/7, we rely on RAC. The failover is only in the event the data center itself meets with some catastrophe.

Along with the benefit of high availability, the other main benefit of RAC is that it allows you to scale horizontally. As explained earlier, this means that rather than upgrading the existing machine, adding additional CPUs or whatnot, you can place another, small to medium-sized machine next to the existing hardware. Using RAC, you can buy what you need today and add capacity over time as you need it. That three-node RAC cluster we use at Oracle was a two-node RAC cluster at one point in time. We scaled it horizontally by adding another machine, not throwing out the existing hardware and getting bigger boxes.

# Clustering Wrap-Up

I really do envision RAC, and clustering technology in general, as being the current wave in computing. I remember back in the early 1990s, the contractor I worked for was very wary of a new technology that was coming out. It was called symmetric multiprocessing (SMP). In fact, that company was so wary of this technology that we got stuck with a bunch of single-CPU boxes. Well, today SMP is so prevalent that we just accept it as natural. Having a machine with two, four, eight, or more CPUs is normal.

I believe the same type of acceptance is happening now with clustering technology. The adoption rate is picking up. No longer do you need to buy large, expensive equipment to support a cluster. Today, you can get the benefits of it on small, commodity hardware. It is a very mature technology—the software has been in place for many years, and experience managing these systems in the real world exists. Clustering is no longer bleeding edge; it is becoming the norm.

If high availability and the ability to scale when you need to are what you want from your next system, or even your current system, consider clustering. The full concepts behind RAC are well-documented by Oracle. One guide in particular stands out—the *Real Applications Clusters Concepts Guide* (yes, another *Concepts Guide*). Here, you will find many of the details on the physical implementation of RAC, how the caches are kept consistent with each other (using a feature called *cache fusion*), and more. The *RAC Concepts Guide* has an entire section on nothing but scaling with RAC—a how-to guide if you will. For example, it describes how a parallel query might not only be parallelized on a single machine across all of the available CPUs, but also across all of the instances in an RAC cluster. The query may execute in parallel on each of the $N$ nodes in a cluster.

# Know When to Use Partitioning

*Partitioning* is the ability of the database to take very large tables or indexes and physically break them into smaller, more manageable pieces. Just as parallel processing can be useful to break a large process into smaller chunks that can be processed independently, partitioning can be used to physically break a very large table/index into several smaller chunks that can be *managed* independently.

In order to use partitioning as a tool to solve your problems, you need to have a solid understanding of how partitioning is physically implemented. Just as important, you must be able to state what it is you want to achieve via partitioning. How to best implement partitioning will vary based on your goals.

## Partitioning Concepts

Before we discuss when partitioning is useful, we need to review some of the basic partitioning concepts. These include the various types of partitioning schemes that Oracle uses for tables and indexes, and partition pruning.

### Partitioning Schemes

In a nutshell, there are four partitioning schemes Oracle employs for tables:

- **Range-based**   Data is separated into partitions using ranges of values. This is typically used on dates. For example, all data for "Q1 of the year" goes into this partition, and all data for "Q2 of the year" goes into another partition, and so on.

- **Hash-based**   A hash function is applied to a column(s) in the table. The more distinct this column is, the better; a primary key, for example, makes an excellent hash key. The hash function will return a number between 1 and $N$ that dictates in which of the $N$ partitions the data will be found. Due to the particular hashing algorithm Oracle uses internally, the hash function works best when N is a power of 2.

- **List-based**   You set up discrete lists of values to tell the database in which partition the data belongs. For example, you could use a CODE field and dictate that records with the codes A, X, and Y go into partition P1, while records with the codes B, C, and Z go into partition P2. List partitions are limited to single columns only as opposed to range or hash partitions that may work on multiple columns. What this means is that list partitioning can only look at a single column in a table in order to decide the partition to place the data in. This scheme is new with Oracle9i Release 1.

- **Composite**   This is a hybrid partitioning scheme. The data will be partitioned initially by range. Then each range partition may be further subpartitioned by either a hash or a list. So, you could set up four range partitions, one for each quarter of a year, and then have each of the quarterly partitions themselves partitioned by hash into eight partitions, resulting in a total of $4 \times 8 = 32$ partitions. Or, you might set up four range partitions, again by quarter, but then list each partition quarter by four regions, resulting in $4 \times 4 = 16$ partitions. Interestingly, with composite partitioning you don't need to have exactly the same number of subpartitions per primary partition. That is, one partition may consist of 4 subpartitions while another partition consists of 5 subpartitions.

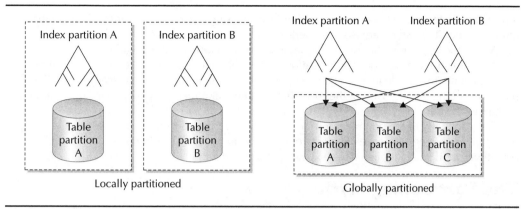

**FIGURE 3-5.** *The differences between locally partitioned and globally partitioned indexes*

There are two primary ways to partition indexes in Oracle, as illustrated in Figure 3-5:

- **Locally partitioned index**    For each and every table partition created, there will be an index partition. The data in each index partition points to data in exactly one table partition by definition. It is said that the table and index are *equipartitioned*. There is a one-to-one mapping between the table partition and index partition, so if the table has *N* partitions, the index has *N* partitions as well.

- **Globally partitioned index**    The index is partitioned by its own scheme. There is no parity between the index partitions and the table partitions. A single index partition may point to data in *any number of* table partitions, unlike the locally partitioned index. A globally partitioned index may only be range-partitioned. Indexes on partitioned tables are, by default, global indexes in a single partition (effectively, by default, they are not partitioned indexes at all).

That explains at a high level the physical storage mechanisms behind partitioning: We can partition a table by range, list, hash, or some combination of range and hash or list. Indexes can be locally or globally partitioned. The next concept we need to explore is partition elimination.

## Partition Pruning

*Partition elimination*, or *partition pruning*, is the ability of the optimizer to preclude from consideration certain partitions in the evaluation of a query. For example, suppose we have a table partitioned by the SALE_DATE column. Every month of data is in its own partition, and there is a locally partitioned index on this SALE_DATE column. Now, suppose we have this query:

```
select * from t where sale_date = :x
```

This query may use one of two query plans, depending on the values in the SALE_DATE column. Suppose the optimizer chose a full-table scan. Since the table is partitioned by SALE_DATE, the optimizer already knows that *N*–1 of the partitions that make up this table cannot have any data we need. By definition, only one of the partitions could possibly have our data. Hence, instead of fully scanning the entire table, Oracle will fully scan a single partition, significantly reducing the amount of I/O it would otherwise have performed.

Alternatively, assume the query plan included an index-range scan. Again, the optimizer would be able to remove from consideration $N–1$ of the index partitions. It knows that all of the rows of interest reside in a single index partition, so it would only range-scan a single index partition, getting the ROWIDs of the rows that matched, and then accessing that single partition to retrieve the data.

This capability of the optimizer to remove partitions from consideration is extremely powerful. From a performance perspective, it's the main reason for using partitioning. It is something we'll keep in mind as we explore partitioning further.

# The Partitioning Myth

Partitioning is not the proverbial `fast=true` setting (as I've stated before, there is *no* `fast=true`!). Partitioning is a very powerful tool that, when applied at the right time, solves a problem. Conversely, when inappropriately applied, partitioning only wastes resources, consumes additional time, and disappoints.

> "I'm really disappointed in partitioning. I took our largest OLTP table and put it into ten partitions. I thought everything should just go faster. That is what I was told. But what we've discovered is that everything, in fact, is running much slower than before. Our machine just cannot keep up. How could that be? Partitioning is supposed to speed everything up, isn't it? Partitioning adds too great of an overhead to be practical."

> In this case, they did not look at *how* partitioning worked under the covers; they did not understand what would happen to their queries at runtime. They heard partitioning should make things faster. They didn't really think about how it would affect their application by just turning it on, however. So, they took their biggest table, and not really having anything "logical" to partition it on, simply partitioned by hash on the primary key, which was a surrogate key populated by a sequence. They then proceeded to re-create all indexes as locally partitioned indexes. The problem was they did not always query the data by primary key; that is, the queries were *not* all of the form:

```
select * from t where primary_key=:x
```

> Rather they would query:

```
select * from t where some_column = :x
```

> A query against SOME_COLUMN would have to now inspect ten index partitions, so it would need to scan ten separate index structures!

> The solution is twofold. The technical solution is to globally partition the index on OWNER. The other part is to establish a reasonable goal for partitioning from the start. In a transactional system, partitioning generally *cannot* speed up queries. What it can do is reduce contention for the shared resource.

In order to demonstrate problems that can arise with partitioning, let's use the BIG_TABLE example once again. We'll take that 1.8 million-record table and hash-partition it:

```
create table big_table_hashed nologging
partition by hash(object_id) partitions 10
as
select * from big_table;
```

Next, we'll create a new record in BIG_TABLE and BIG_TABLE_HASHED. This will be the record of interest. We will use some column other than the column that the table was hashed on to pull up a record, the OWNER column:

```
insert into big_table ( owner, object_name, object_id,
                        last_ddl_time, created )
select 'SPECIAL_ROW' , object_name, object_id, last_ddl_time, created
 from big_table where rownum = 1;

insert into big_table_hashed ( owner, object_name, object_id,
                               last_ddl_time, created )
select 'SPECIAL_ROW' , object_name, object_id, last_ddl_time, created
 from big_table_hashed where rownum = 1;
```

We have no users named SPECIAL_ROW, so this insert operation created a record with a unique owner value in each table. Next, let's implement the index and analyze the tables:

```
create index big_idx1 on big_table(owner);
create index big_hash_idx1 on big_table_hashed(owner) LOCAL;

analyze table big_table for table for all indexes for all indexed columns;
analyze table big_table_hash
for table for all indexes for all indexed columns;
```

Consider the results of our first attempts:

```
big_table@ORA920> delete from plan_table;
4 rows deleted.

big_table@ORA920> explain plan for select * from big_table where owner = :x;
Explained.

big_table@ORA920> select * from table(dbms_xplan.display);
PLAN_TABLE_OUTPUT
```

| Id| Operation | Name | Rows | Bytes |Cost |
|---|---|---|---|---|---|
| 0 | SELECT STATEMENT | | 65493 | 5372K|169(1)|
| 1 | TABLE ACCESS BY INDEX ROWID| BIG_TABLE | 65493 | 5372K|169(1)|
|*2 | INDEX RANGE SCAN | BIG_TABLE_IDX | 65493 | |153(0)|

```
Predicate Information (identified by operation id):
---------------------------------------------------
   2 - access("BIG_TABLE"."OWNER"=:Z)
13 rows selected.
```

Now, using the default init.ora parameters more or less, we find:

```
big_table@ORA920> delete from plan_table;
3 rows deleted.

big_table@ORA920> explain plan for
  2 select * from big_table_hashed where owner = :x;
Explained.

big_table@ORA920> select * from table(dbms_xplan.display);

PLAN_TABLE_OUTPUT
-----------------------------------------------------------------------

-----------------------------------------------------------------------
|Id| Operation           | Name           |Rows |Bytes|Cost |PSTART|PSTOP|
-----------------------------------------------------------------------
| 0|SELECT STATEMENT     |                |18319|2289K|28(0)|      |      |
| 1| PARTITION HASH ALL|                  |     |     |     |   1  | 10   |
| 2|  TABLE ACCESS BY   |                  |     |     |     |      |      |
|  |  LOCAL INDEX ROWID| BIG_TABLE_HASHED|18319|2289K|28(0)|   1  | 10   |
|*3|   INDEX RANGE SCAN| BIG_HASH_IDX    | 7328|     |36(0)|   1  | 10   |
-----------------------------------------------------------------------

Predicate Information (identified by operation id):
---------------------------------------------------
   3 - access("BIG_TABLE_HASHED"."OWNER"=:Z)
14 rows selected.
```

At first, this looks reasonable—an index-range scan, just as before. But notice the partition start (PSTART) and stop (PSTOP) keys. It is scanning *every* index partition. It must do this, because every index partition could, in fact, contain any value of OWNER in it! The index is partitioned by OBJECT_ID, not by OWNER; hence, every index partition must be inspected. The results of this are dramatic. Just consider this query executed 1,000 times (we might be doing this many times per second).

```
select * from big_table where owner = :b1

call     count      cpu    elapsed   disk      query    current       rows
-------  ------  --------  --------- ------  ---------  ---------  ----------
Parse        1     0.00      0.00        0          0          0           0
Execute   1000     0.14      0.11        0          0          0           0
Fetch     1000     0.11      0.11        0       4000          0        1000
-------  ------  --------  --------- ------  ---------  ---------  ----------
total     2001     0.25      0.23        0       4000          0        1000
```

```
Rows      Row Source Operation
-------   ------------------------------------------------------------
  1000   TABLE ACCESS BY INDEX ROWID BIG_TABLE
  1000    INDEX RANGE SCAN BIG_TABLE_IDX

select * from big_table_hashed where owner = :b1

call      count      cpu    elapsed   disk     query    current      rows
-------   ------  --------  ---------  ------ ----------  ---------  ----------
Parse         1     0.00      0.00        0          0          0           0
Execute    1000     0.14      0.11        0          0          0           0
Fetch      1000     0.33      0.60       16      27000          0        1000
-------   ------  --------  ---------  ------ ----------  ---------  ----------
total      2001     0.47      0.72       16      27000          0        1000

Rows Row Source Operation
-------   ------------------------------------------------------------
  1000   PARTITION HASH ALL PARTITION: 1 10
  1000    TABLE ACCESS BY LOCAL INDEX ROWID BIG_TABLE_HASHED PARTITION: 1 10
  1000     INDEX RANGE SCAN BIG_HASH_IDX PARTITION: 1 10
```

That is a 675% increase in logical I/O. (Remember that a logical I/O implies a latch, a latch is a lock, and locks make an application less scalable.) It's also a 100% increase in CPU consumption. This simple operation has impacted performance in an extremely negative fashion. (Of course, this is something we should have caught during testing!)

**NOTE**
*Some might question, "Why 27,000 logical IOs versus 4,000?" Shouldn't it be 40,000 (ten times as much) or perhaps 30,000? Actually, on your system you might find that you see slightly different logical IO results. It all has to do with the height of the B\*Tree indexes. In this test, some of the index partitions had a height of two while others had a height of three, meaning sometimes it took two logical IOs to find "no data" and sometimes it took three. The single index in the non-partitioned example had a height of three, meaning every query read three index blocks and one table block (4 logical IOs per row). In the partitioned example, four of the index partitions had a height of two, and six had a height of three, giving us 1000\*((4\*2) + (6\*3) + 1) = 27,000 logical IOs.*

So, what technically could we do to fix the problem (short of unpartitioning the table, that is)? This is where the global index comes in. We could either partition the index by range into many partitions or simply use a single index partition. For the sake of demonstration, let's partition by range, splitting the index alphabetically into four, more or less even, ranges.

```
create index big_hash_idx1 on big_table_hashed(owner)
global partition by range (owner)
( partition values less than ( ' F' ),
 partition values less than ( ' M' ),
 partition values less than ( ' T' ),
 partition values less than ( MAXVALUE )
);
```

Now, the query plan for that same query is as follows:

```
-------------------------------------------------------------------------------
|Id| Operation                            | Name             | ...|Pstart|Pstop|
-------------------------------------------------------------------------------
| 0|SELECT STATEMENT                      |                  | ...|      |     |
| 1| PARTITION RANGE SINGLE               |                  | ...| KEY  | KEY |
| 2|  TABLE ACCESS BY GLOBAL INDEX ROWID  |BIG_TABLE_HASHED  | ...|ROWID |ROW L|
|*3|   INDEX RANGE SCAN                   |BIG_HASH_IDX      | ...| KEY  | KEY |
-------------------------------------------------------------------------------
Predicate Information (identified by operation id):
---------------------------------------------------
   3 - access("BIG_TABLE_HASHED"."OWNER"=:Z)
```

That is looking more like it. We can now see the index-range scan start and stop partitions are based on KEY. The optimizer will not hit all ten index partitions; it will hit only one. It will get the ROWID(s) for the matching rows, and then access a partition to get the row data for that ROWID. Now, let's try that same 1,000-query simulation.

```
select * from big_table_hashed where owner = :b1

call     count      cpu    elapsed    disk      query    current       rows
------- ------  -------- ----------- ------ ---------- ----------  ----------
Parse        1     0.00        0.00       0          0          0           0
Execute   1000     0.14        0.11       0          0          0           0
Fetch     1000     0.11        0.11       0       4000          0        1000
------- ------  -------- ----------- ------ ---------- ----------  ----------
total     2001     0.25        0.23       0       4000          0        1000

    1000   PARTITION RANGE SINGLE PARTITION: KEY KEY
    1000    TABLE ACCESS BY GLOBAL INDEX ROWID BIG_TABLE_HASHED PARTITION:
                                        ROW LOCATION ROW LOCATION
    1000     INDEX RANGE SCAN BIG_HASH_IDX PARTITION: KEY KEY
```

What a difference that makes! CPU time is now the same as in the nonpartitioned example. The logical I/Os are the same. But shouldn't we still be disappointed, because it is not any faster? No, because we would be looking in the wrong place for a performance increase. How much faster can a query that does four logical I/Os get?

The performance increase you may realize in this sample OLTP system comes from the fact that you now have four separate index structures and ten separate table structures. So, the next time you insert a record, you will experience perhaps 25% of the contention you would normally have on the index modification and 10% of the contention you would have on the table insert operation. This is also true with update and delete operations. You have more physical structures; you've spread contention for a shared resource out across many physical segments. Your queries might not run significantly faster, but your modifications may be accomplished much more quickly.

Consider the local unique index we'll maintain on the primary key in this example. In the past, there was one index structure and everyone was hitting the same "side" of it; that is, the users would insert 1, 2, 3, 4 ... *N* into this index in order. That is a lot of contention for the index blocks on the right side of the index, where the new values will go. Now, the index entry for primary key = 1 probably goes into a *different* index structure than primary key = 2, and so on. We are hashing these values and putting them into an index segment based on the hash values. We have just accomplished a very nice distribution of data across ten local index partitions, perhaps dramatically reducing contention for this shared resource.

Can partitioning speed up a query? Why, certainly it can, but typically *not in a transactional system*. A measurable reduction in query response time due to partitioning will be achieved when the original query takes a large amount of time to begin with. In a transactional system, you do not have those types of queries. However, in a data warehouse, you do have long-running queries.

# Why Use Partitioning?

There are three main reasons to use partitioning:

1. Increased availability

2. Easier administration

3. Increased performance

You might wonder why I listed them with numbers. I put them in order of achievability and immediate payback. Let's start with the easiest goal.

## Increased Availability

You get increased availability pretty much out of the box. The amount you achieve is a function of how much thought you put into your partitioning scheme, but you still instantly get more availability from partitioning. So, how does partitioning achieve the goal of higher availability? There are two main methods: partition elimination and divide-and-conquer.

For example, suppose we run a data warehouse, and a datafile goes bad (becomes media corrupt for whatever reason). We need to go to our backup and restore it. Meanwhile, our end users are still using this database. Since we used partitioning and have placed our partitions in separate tablespaces, only one partition in one tablespace is actually affected. We take that tablespace offline and recover it. In the end-user world, anyone who attempts to run a query that accesses that tablespace would be affected. However, a large population of our end users is *not affected* by this recovery, and they use the same table(s) and the same queries. It is just that their queries know that they do not need to access this data; it is removed from consideration, and the queries keep on going. As far as these end users are concerned, we never had a failure. Our system is more available from that perspective.

With partitioning, the system is also more available because you are managing things in smaller chunks. You might have a 2GB partition to restore, one out of fifty other partitions perhaps. You do not have a 100GB problem to deal with, just a little 2GB problem (or however big you make your partitions). Every administrative task that takes an object offline (makes it unavailable) is now affecting a much smaller object, so the operation runs faster. Suppose you need to rebuild a bitmap index after a couple of months of incremental loading (bitmap indexes do not respond well to incremental updates; they need to be rebuilt on a recurring basis). Would you like to rebuild the entire bitmap index in one big statement, requiring significant resources (you'll have two bitmaps for a while), or would you rather rebuild one-fiftieth of a bitmap index at a time?

## Easier Administration

Performing operations on small objects is inherently easier, faster, and less resource-intensive than performing the same operation on a large object. For example, if you discover that 50% of the rows in your table are migrated rows, and you would like to fix this, having a partitioned table will facilitate the operation. In order to fix migrated rows, you must typically rebuild the object, in this case, a table. If you have one 100GB table, you will need to perform this operation in one very large chunk, serially using ALTER TABLE MOVE. On the other hand, if you have 50 2GB partitions, you can rebuild each partition one by one. Alternatively, if you are doing this during off-hours, you can even do the ALTER TABLE MOVE PARTITION statements in parallel, in separate sessions, potentially reducing the amount of time the operation takes. If you are using locally partitioned indexes on this partitioned table, the index-rebuild operations will take significantly less time as well. Virtually everything you can do to a nonpartitioned object, you can do to an individual partition of a partitioned object.

**NOTE**
*There is a rather neat package, DBMS_PCLXUTIL, documented in the Supplied PL/SQL Packages and Types Reference that automates a parallel build of local indexes as well.*

Another factor that comes into play with partitioning and administration is a concept called a *sliding window*. This is applied in data warehousing and in some transactional systems, especially to audit trails whereby the system must keep *N* years of audit information online. Here, we have time-based information—a load into a warehouse of last month's sales, or an audit trail where each record is timestamped. Every month we would like to take the oldest month's data, purge it, and slide in the newest month's data. Using a conventional table, this would be a huge DELETE of the old data, followed by a huge INSERT of the new data. The continuous purge via DELETE and load via INSERT processing would consume a great deal of resources (both generate significant redo and undo information). They would tend to break down the indexes and table itself, with the delete operations leaving holes that may or may not be reused over time, introducing the possibility of fragmentation and wasting space.

With partitioning, the purge of the old data becomes trivial. It becomes a simple ALTER TABLE command that drops the oldest data partition. To slide the new data in, you would typically load and index a separate table, and then add that table to the existing partitioned table via an ALTER TABLE ... EXCHANGE PARTITION command, which swaps a table with a partition. In this case, you would swap a full table with an empty partition, just adding the data to the table. The downtime for the end users can be very near zero here, especially if care is taken to avoid constraint validation, which is entirely possible.

### Increased Performance

As you saw in the example in the previous section, partitioning for increased performance is a two-edged sword. Getting additional, measurable performance out of partitioning is the hardest (not hard, just the hardest) goal to achieve from partitioning because it requires the most thought.

Partitioning must be applied in such a way as to solve a real problem you are having. Just applying partitioning without some planning will more often than not slow you down. Think of partitioning like medicine. Medicine can make sick people healthier, stronger, and faster. Medicine can make healthy people die when administered improperly. Partitioning will do the same thing to your database. Before applying it, you need to elucidate what your goals in using partitioning are. Do you want to use partitioning to ease administrative overhead? Do you want to use partitioning to increase availability? Is your goal to increase performance (after identifying a performance issue, of course)?

## Partitioning Wrap-Up

Partitioning can be a great thing. Breaking a huge problem down into many smaller problems (the divide-and-conquer approach) can, in some cases, dramatically reduce the processing time. Partitioning can also be a terrible thing. When inappropriately applied, it can dramatically increase processing time.

Partitioning, in order to be properly used, must be properly understood. It is vital that you have a goal you want to achieve with partitioning. Don't use it until you do!

In many cases, the three things you can achieve with partitioning could be thought of as points on a triangle, like this:

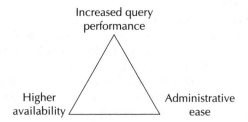

You can get to any point on or inside the triangle, but that might mean that the closer you get to any one point, the further you travel from the others. You need to, first and foremost, figure out why you want to use partitioning, and then with that goal in mind, design your physical schemas. For that, you will need to use your knowledge of the "physics" behind partitioning, what the database is able to do under the covers for you. Remember, this is an analogy. How big that triangle is, and thus how far away from any given point, is entirely a matter of implementation and need. In some cases, the triangle is very small meaning you can achieve all three. In other cases, you may find that due to your needs, you have to trade off one capability at the favor of another.

There are several Oracle manuals that provide details on partitioning: the Oracle *Concepts Guide*, *Data Warehousing Guide*, and *Administrators Guide*.

# Know When to Use Parallel Operations

Parallelism is something we apply to large jobs all of the time in real life. You never see a single person build a building. You see a large team of people build a building, all working simultaneously.

Oracle supports a wide variety of parallel operations:

- **Parallel query**   The ability to take a single SQL statement, break it into a series of operations that can be performed at the same time by different processes/threads, and executing them concurrently.

- **Parallel DML (modifications)**   Similar to parallel query, but for INSERT, UPDATE, and DELETE statements.

- **Parallel DDL**   For administrators, the ability to execute a wide variety of statements such as CREATE INDEX in a parallel fashion, not by running 15 CREATE INDEX statements at the same time (Oracle can, of course, do that), but rather by using $N$ processes to create a single index in parallel.

- **Parallel DIY**   Do It Yourself parallelism, which isn't really traditional Oracle parallelism. Oracle isn't divvying up the work, you are. This is one of the more overlooked opportunities for tuning! Oracle is great at supporting multiuser situations, taking advantage of that in your batch processing is another thing entirely.

Here, we will explore when and why you might use each of these options (and when and why you might not). But first, we will look at a couple other topics: the myth that all parallel operations are quicker than serial operations, and parallel administration, where I personally find parallelism to be most useful in day-to-day work.

## The Parallel Myth

Parallelism can be a great thing. Breaking a huge problem down into many smaller problems (the divide-and-conquer approach) can, in some cases, dramatically reduce the processing time.

Parallelism can be a terrible thing. Applying parallel processing to many classes of problems makes them run slower (or not any faster) but with much greater resource consumption. Parallelism, when inappropriately applied, can dramatically increase processing time. Like partitioning—and everything else—parallelism is just a tool. It works well when used correctly and can have disastrous results when used incorrectly.

"I'm trying to test the parallel query option. We have a two-CPU machine and enough disk controllers to support the disk. We've created a partitioned parallel table. It's partitioned by MONTH and looks like ALL_OBJECTS. We put 1,471,488 records in there via: insert /*+ append */ into tb_part_par select * from dba_objects. Then we created a nonpartitioned table TBL_NO_PAR as select * from tb_part_par. Next, we use AUTOTRACE and timing to see the difference:

```
SQL> set timing on
SQL> set autotrace on
SQL> select count(1) from tb_part_par;

COUNT(1)
----------
 1471488
```

```
Elapsed: 00:00:07.43

Execution Plan
-----------------------------------------------------------
  0 SELECT STATEMENT Optimizer=CHOOSE (Cost=1064 Card=1)
  1 0 SORT (AGGREGATE)
  2 1 SORT* (AGGREGATE)          :Q115000
  3 2  PARTITION RANGE* (ALL)     :Q115000
  4 3   TABLE ACCESS* (FULL) OF ' TB_PART_PAR'
         (Cost=1064 Card=1471488)  :Q115000

  2 PARALLEL_TO_SERIAL SELECT /*+ PIV_SSF */ SYS_OP_MSR(COUNT(*))
       FROM (SELECT /*+ NO_EXPAND ROWID(A2)

  3 PARALLEL_COMBINED_WITH_PARENT
  4 PARALLEL_COMBINED_WITH_PARENT
```

That is the parallel plan and results. In serial mode, we see:

```
SQL> select count(1) from tbl_no_par;

  COUNT(1)
----------
  1471488

Elapsed: 00:00:06.18

Execution Plan
-----------------------------------------------------------
  0 SELECT STATEMENT Optimizer=CHOOSE
  1 0 SORT (AGGREGATE)
  2 1 TABLE ACCESS (FULL) OF ' TBL_NO_PAR'
```

So, how come the time is almost the same? The table that has parallel should be faster, right (we have four disk controllers and two CPUs)?"

There are two things wrong here: assuming "parallel means faster" and using a flawed test. In short, there is overhead with a parallel query operation that makes itself very evident in things that run fast. *Fast* is a relative term. Setting up for a parallel query and the additional coordination that a parallel query must do can add seconds to a query's runtime. For a query that ran in hours and now runs in minutes, those seconds aren't meaningful. But, for a query that runs in less than ten seconds, this overhead is very noticeable. There is a high startup cost for a parallel query, meaning the query you want to make go faster needs to be really slow to begin with (and six to seven seconds just isn't slow enough).

The other problem with their test was that all of the I/O was going against a single tablespace that probably had a single file (they didn't really spread anything out; all of the partitions were in the same tablespace). Making the problem even worse is that they will find most of their objects in DBA_OBJECTS created on exactly the same day, and that is what they partitioned by; hence, a single partition here contained most of the data. So, even if the partitions were on different devices, in different tablespaces, this setup would not have affected the I/O distribution!

```
ops$tkyte@ORA920> select trunc(created,' mm' ), count(*) from
dba_objects
  2 group by trunc(created,' mm' );

TRUNC(CRE COUNT(*)
--------- ----------
01-MAY-02     29680
01-AUG-02         9
01-SEP-02         7
01-OCT-02        29
01-NOV-02        91
```

The day you installed or the day the sample datafiles used to seed your database was stamped out will be the most popular date by far in DBA_OBJECTS.

Forget about the disk layout for a moment, assuming that they used striped disks so there was an even I/O distribution. Why would this query run the same or marginally slower using parallel query? The reason is the overhead of parallel query. The sample set of data is only about 100MB to 125MB, and it is fully scanned serially in six seconds. The query just isn't big enough.

## Parallel Processing Overhead

To get an understanding of the overhead entailed for parallel processing, think of it like this: You are a manager, and you have a dozen people that work for you. Your boss asks you to write a one-page summary of a meeting. You can either:

- Write it yourself
- Have a dozen people do it
  - Call a meeting
  - Get the 12 people together
  - Assign someone to write the first paragraph (this takes time, because you need to explain what you want and divvy up the work)
  - Repeat the paragraph assignments for the remaining 11 people
  - Collect all of their subresults
  - Put them together into a single paper
  - Deliver the results

For this one-page summary, it would be infinitely more efficient to do the job in serial mode, by yourself. You just sit down and write the report from start to finish. You can do it much faster than getting everyone together (starting the parallel query slaves), coordinating their work (playing the query coordinator), collecting and merging their pieces of the answer, and returning the result.

Now, later your boss asks you to write a book that is 12 chapters long. Each chapter is relatively independent of the other chapters. They could be written in isolation, but there will be some coordination necessary to build the table of contents, the index, and such at the end. Now you can either:

- Write the book yourself (at about one hour per finished page)
- Do it in parallel
  - Divvy up the 12 chapters among your 12 employees
  - As they finish each chapter, review and edit it
  - Assemble the book

Now, doing it in parallel would not take one-twelfth the time of doing it yourself, because you would have the overhead required to coordinate 12 people. However, it would be much faster than writing it yourself; maybe you could get it done in one-tenth the time.

Parallel query operations are the same way. They are for taking massively hard, long things and making them faster. If you have a short problem (seconds), parallel query operations will not make it faster; in fact, they may make it much slower. If you have a long problem (minutes, hours, days) and *all other* tuning processes have been exhausted, using parallel query may be the saving grace.

### Parallel Processing Scalability

The other thing people get wrong with parallel query is its scalability. Parallel query is not a scalable solution! Parallel query was initially designed so that a single user in a data warehouse could completely and totally consume 100% of the resources on that machine. So, if you had a 16-CPU big box with gobs of RAM and tons of disk space, you could write a single query that would be able to make use of the entire machine. Well, if you have two people doing that, they will both be competing for the same resources—they will both try to consume 100% of the machine. Take that up to 100 users, and you can easily see the problem.

This is one of the reasons I like the parallel automatic tuning with the adaptive multiuser routines. If I am the only one on the machine, I can fully consume all of the resources. If, on the other hand, I run the same query when there are 50 other users logged in and running queries, I will most likely get far fewer resources (parallel threads) than I did when I was the sole user of the machine. The degree of parallelism is not fixed. It adapts to the current workload, making parallel query a more scalable solution than before. Instead of killing the machine or having queries fail because they could not get sufficient resources, I can let the machine adjust its resource usage over time. This provides the best of both worlds *and* what end users expect from a system. They know that when it is busy, it will run slower.

## Parallel Administration

This is by far my favorite use of the parallel operations. It is probably the most underutilized and overlooked feature as well. Here, the DBA is able to use parallel operations to speed up statements such as ALTER INDEX REBUILD (after a mass load), ALTER TABLE MOVE, or CREATE INDEX. It also works for database recovery, loading, collecting statistics, and so on. This is a use of parallel operation that benefits all system types—OLTP, data warehousing, or mixed workload. The faster the DBAs can complete their administrative functions, the more uptime the end users get. If you have an eight-CPU machine but only use one of them to create an index, you are missing the boat big time.

"Why shouldn't I just use ANALYZE TABLE? It's so easy. So what if my analyze window is three hours long now and tends to interfere with my hot backups (I/O contention)?"

The fact is a simple ANALYZE cannot be parallelized. DBMS_STATS, a better, more powerful way to collect statistics, can be parallelized. You can analyze a table in parallel using DBMS_STATS, you cannot with ANALYZE. Well, you can apply DIY parallelism in order to parallelize an ANALYZE. The individual ANALYZE commands will execute serially, but there is nothing stopping you from running many of them simultaneously. That is another perfectly valid approach.

The next time you execute any of the following operations, stop for a moment and ask yourself, "Would I benefit from parallelizing this operation—letting Oracle use the entire machine?"

- CREATE TABLE AS SELECT (CTAS)
- CREATE INDEX
- ALTER INDEX REBUILD
- ALTER TABLE MOVE
- ALTER TABLE SPLIT PARTITION
- ALTER INDEX COALESCE
- Statistics collection

In most cases, the answer would be a resounding, yes. The operation will run faster since these operations are generally done on big objects and would benefit from parallel operations.

For example, consider the case of what is known as a parallel direct-path load. This is perhaps the fastest way to load large amounts of data into the database. Suppose we want to load a table T using a parallel direct-path load. In order to accomplish this in the past, we would have needed to do this:

- Create a control file.
- Create a table, setting to NOLOGGING if necessary.
- Decide what the optimum degree of parallelism should be (say *N*).
- Split the input file into *N* files, one to be fed into each of the SQLLDR processes.
- Write a script to startup *N* copies of SQLLDR, each with different log filenames, bad filenames, discard filenames, and so on.

■ Run and monitor the script.

Furthermore, if it were determined that a different degree of parallelism were to be used, all of these steps would need to be redone.

In Oracle9i, we only need to issue the following commands to achieve this same parallel direct-path load:

■ `create external_table` (the ability to use SELECT on flat files, to use a file as if it were a database table)

■ `create table T nologging parallel as select * from external_table`

Here, the degree of parallelism could be chosen by Oracle itself based on available resources (you could choose to override this, if you like). The file, as long as it is a fixed-length file format (fairly common in large bulk loads), is split dynamically by Oracle based on the chosen degree of parallelism. A CTAS statement is a direct-path operation. There is no script to write—no muss, no fuss.

I recently used this method to load a data warehouse for a benchmark I was working on. What used to take a day to set up and test—with all of the scripting, file splitting, and so on—took literally minutes. Set up the external tables, and away we go. We just fired off a couple of these at a time, let the machine go to 100%, and then submitted some more. It was the easiest load I had ever done (oh, and it was fast, too).

# Parallel Query

Parallel query is suitable for a certain class of large problems: very large problems that have no other solution. Parallel query is my last path of action for solving a performance problem; it's never my first course of action.

## Parallel Query Settings

I will not discuss the physical setup of parallel query operations. That topic is well covered in both the Oracle *Concepts Guide* and *Data Warehousing Guide*. As I mentioned earlier, my current favorite way to set up parallelism in Oracle is using the automatic tuning option first introduced in Oracle8i Release 2 (version 8.1.6): PARALLEL_AUTOMATIC_TUNING = TRUE. With this setting, the other parallel settings are automatically set. Now, all I need to do is set the PARALLEL option on the table (not PARALLEL <N>, just PARALLEL) and Oracle will, when appropriate, parallelize certain operations on that table for me. The degree of parallelism (how many processes/threads will be thrown at a problem) will be decided for me and vary over time as the load on the system varies. I have found that, for most cases, this achieves my desired goal, which is usually to get the best performance, with the least amount of work, in a manner that is most manageable. Setting a single parameter is a great way to get there.

For the novice user wanting to play with parallel query for the first time, parallel automatic tuning is a good way to get started. As you develop an understanding of what parallel query does and how it does it, try tweaking some of the other parallel settings:

■ **PARALLEL_ADAPTIVE_MULTI_USER**  Controls whether the degree of parallelism should vary over time as the load on the system does; should the algorithm for assigning resources "adapt" to the increase in load.

- **PARALLEL_EXECUTION_MESSAGE_SIZE** Sets the size of the message buffers used to pass information back and forth between the processes executing the parallel query.

- **PARALLEL_INSTANCE_GROUP** Applies only to Oracle RAC configurations (Oracle Parallel Server, OPS, in Oracle8i and earlier). Allows you to restrict the number of instances that will be used to perform a parallel operation (as opposed to the number of processes an instance will use).

- **PARALLEL_MAX_SERVERS** Sets the maximum number of parallel query slaves (like dedicated servers but for parallel operations) your instance will ever have.

- **PARALLEL_MIN_PERCENT** Useful if you would like to receive an error message when you request a specific degree of parallelism but insufficient resources exist to satisfy that request. You might use this to ensure that a process that takes days unless it gets what it wants doesn't run unless it gets what it wants.

- **PARALLEL_MIN_SERVERS** Sets the number of servers to start when the instance starts and to keep started permanently. Otherwise, you may need to start the parallel processes in response to a query.

- **PARALLEL_THREADS_PER_CPU** Determines the default degree of parallelism and contributes to the adaptive parallelism algorithms, to determine when to back off on the amount of parallel resources.

- **RECOVERY_PARALLELISM** For crash recovery, sets how many parallel threads should be used. This setting can be used to speed up the recovery from an instance crash.

- **FAST_START_PARALLEL_ROLLBACK** Sets how many processes would be available to perform a parallel rollback after the recovery takes place. This would be useful on systems where many long-running transactions are constantly processing (which would need correspondingly long rollback times in the event of an instance crash).

### When Are Parallel Queries Useful?

A parallel query means the problem is really big. I find, most times, the problem shouldn't be that big. For example, you are full-scanning a huge table because the predicate on the table involves a low-cardinality column (you are probably thinking that I'm going to suggest a bitmap index here). Well, you should probably be full-scanning a small partition, because the table should have been partitioned by that value (or it could be that a bitmap index does come into play). In any case, look at all of the advanced features of the database for data warehousing before using parallel queries—maybe a materialized view, rebuilt in parallel, is the answer; maybe a bitmap join index does it.

Many problems are solvable via other database technologies. Parallel query is just one of the tools. Think of it as a power tool you might rent for a special project at home, not something you want to use casually.

Parallel query is something that I find no use for in a transactional system—just forget about it there. In a transactional system, you generally have a lot of users, running many concurrent sessions. Parallel query, which creates a lot of sessions to answer a question, just doesn't scale there. It does not make sense to let one user run a parallel operation when you have dozens of other users competing for the same resources.

But nothing is ever black and white—don't discount parallel query immediately after someone puts a "transactional" tag on your system. Most systems suffer from multiple-personality disorder. They are one thing by day, and another by night. It may well be that from midnight to

6:00 A.M., parallel query is a feature that is vital, but from 6:01 A.M. to 11:59 P.M., it is a tool that just doesn't make sense to use.

Parallel query is a feature I find useful in data warehouses where the concurrent user count is low (so there are plenty of resources to go around). If you have a 500 concurrent user data warehouse with 64 CPUs, parallel query probably is not going to apply. If you have a 5 concurrent user data warehouse with 64 CPUs, parallel query is going to be the coolest thing since sliced bread. It is all a matter of how many spare cycles you typically have when not using parallel query. If you have some, parallel query will help you use them up, which is a good thing—you want your system to be 100% utilized.

**NOTE**
*I frequently hear from people who are concerned that their systems are peaking at 100% utilization from time to time. I ask them, "Well, if it were running at 90%, would you be able to put that 10% in the bank for later?" No, you cannot. It's best to use it now while you can.*

So, my advice for parallel query is fairly easy and straightforward:

- Just set relevant tables to PARALLEL; do not specify a degree of parallelism.
- Use parallel automatic tuning.
- Look for opportunities to not have to use parallel query.

# Parallel DML

Parallel DML (PDML) is really just an administrative feature similar to CREATE TABLE, CREATE INDEX, or loading. It is something you would use infrequently, to perform a large bulk UPDATE or DELETE one time to fix some legacy data. You may be using a parallel MERGE command to refresh data monthly (or weekly) in a data warehouse. However, since there are many caveats regarding PDML, I address it separately from the standard administrative functions I covered earlier in the "Parallel Administration" section.

It used to be that in order to make use of PDML in Oracle, you needed to have tables themselves partitioned, and the degree of parallelism was set to the number of underlying partitions. In Oracle9i Release 2 and up, this is no longer true, but that probably isn't relevant. The reason I say that is because, like parallel query, you would use PDML against very large objects, and very large objects will be partitioned (at least, they would be if they were my large objects). So, even though you may modify in parallel objects that are not partitioned, it is not really that exciting.

The tables we want to use PDML on are so large that if we are not using partitioning, we should probably be adding it to our schema at this point. For example, instead of updating a billion-row table, you would CTAS in parallel a newly partitioned table that included the updated data in the SELECT statement itself.

There are many restrictions regarding PDML. The following are the major ones to consider:

- There can be no triggers on the tables being modified. In a data warehouse, this is generally okay. In a transactional system, if you attempt to use PDML to perform a mass fix of data, you must be aware of this.

- PDML cannot be replicated (since that is done via triggers).

- There are restrictions on the types of integrity constraints that are supported with PDML. For example, self-referencing constraints cannot be in place, since the table is being modified in parallel by many "sessions," and the sessions cannot see other sessions' changes.

- You cannot use database links (distributed transactions) with PDML.

- Clustered tables (B*Tree clusters and hash clusters) are not supported with PDML.

If you attempt a PDML operation and any of these rules are violated, you will not receive an error message. Rather, the statement will execute serially. You will want to monitor the parallel processing of your statement with the dynamic performance views, such as V$PX_PROCESS.

# DIY Parallelism

With DIY parallelism, we are asking not what Oracle can do for us, but rather what we can do with Oracle.

"I've been trying to resolve an issue whereby a PL/SQL procedure in a package takes a weekend to process 26,000 rows. It processes each of those 26,000 rows with reference to a specific period of time (one month), and for that it performs up to 40 calculations. Each of these calculations can involve a number of sums. So we have 26,000 rows, 40 calculations, each for every month from January 1999 to October 2002. It can take up to three hours to run one month, and that is perceived as a problem. We have a multi-CPU machine, but it only seems to be using one of them. Shouldn't the machine be 100% used by this process? We have plenty of spare CPU and plenty of RAM. We just don't seem to be able to use it.

I've spent lots of time over several days looking at Statspack reports, SQL_TRACE reports, and used DBMS_PROFILER, as you suggested. I've looked at init.ora parameters and modified some of those, also looking at the NT Performance Monitor. This time is the result of that tuning; it used to take longer! Statspack reports shows the biggest number of waits in a ten-minute period as 496 waits for log file parallel write, with a wait time of 22 cs. This doesn't seem a big deal. There is spare memory, spare CPU capacity, and it doesn't seem to be massively waiting on disk. So what IS taking the time?"

Well, what we have is the classic serial batch process. Here, parallel query, PDML, or whatever isn't going to do anything. They have a linear piece of code that processes 40 calculations a row at a time. They have 26,000 rows times 40 calculations. That is 1,040,000 calculations. In three hours, that is an average of 96 PL/SQL calculations per second. Coupled with the fact that this includes retrieving who knows how much data and doing some modifications to the database, this doesn't sound too bad. Remember that this is not 96 machine instructions per second (that would be really slow); this is 96 complex PL/SQL calculations that request data from the database and everything else.

Now, since there are no significant wait events, it must be the algorithm. It is the algorithm that is the issue here, not the ability of the database to process in parallel. No amount of parallel query will make this go faster (maybe slower, but not faster). The machine has not reached its limit; it has plenty of capacity. They need to change the algorithm to allow it to take advantage of this. My suggestion is to parallelize the problem. They have 26,000 rows. Divvy that up based on some predicate and run four or five copies of the stored procedure at the same time. They have plenty of extra CPU they aren't even using. Parallelize this operation over four "threads" and see what happens.

In many cases, when you see a batch process that looks like this pseudo code:

```
Create procedure batch_process
As
Begin
 For x in ( select * from T )
 Loop
  Process…
  Update T for that row or Insert that row
   Elsewhere…
 End loop
End;
```

And you cannot just make it a single SQL statement due to the complexity of the process, my suggestion to make it faster is to have more processes working on it. Even in a single-CPU machine, there are frequently spare CPU cycles while you are processing. You spend some amount of time waiting for I/O. Let another process make use of that. In this case, the solution to speed this up over three times is as follows:

```
Create procedure batch_process(start_id in number, stop_id number)
As
Begin
 For x in ( select *
    from T
    where id > start_id and id <= stop_id)
 Loop
  Process…
  Update T for that row or Insert that row
   Elsewhere…
 End loop
End;
```

And to run this procedure in *N* different sessions, feeding each session a different, nonoverlapping set of IDs. Generally, this parallelization can be done with little to no modification of the existing algorithms, short of adding these parameters and predicate.

All that is left now is to generate *N* sets of IDs to do this in parallel. Using the new PERCENTILE_
DISC function in Oracle9i, we can do this easily. PERCENTILE_DISC is a statistical function that
will return a discrete (hence the DISC) value from a set. You pass the percentile function a
percentage *X*, and it will return a value such that X% of the rows in the table have a value less
than that value.

For example, we have a table for testing called BIG_TABLE. It has 1.8 million rows in it.
Suppose we want to run the preceding process against it. We need four ranges. We can get them
right from the table itself using this technique:

```
big_table@ORA920> column c0 new_val c0
big_table@ORA920> column c1 new_val c1
big_table@ORA920> column c2 new_val c2
big_table@ORA920> column c3 new_val c3
big_table@ORA920> column c4 new_val c4
big_table@ORA920>
big_table@ORA920> SELECT min(object_id)-1 c0,
  2 PERCENTILE_DISC(0.25) WITHIN GROUP (ORDER BY object_id) c1,
  3 PERCENTILE_DISC(0.50) WITHIN GROUP (ORDER BY object_id) c2,
  4 PERCENTILE_DISC(0.75) WITHIN GROUP (ORDER BY object_id) c3,
  5 max(object_id) c4
  6 FROM big_table
  7 /

        C0         C1         C2         C3         C4
---------- ---------- ---------- ---------- ----------
         0     458464     916928    1375392    1833855
```

And then this query using those values shows we've covered the entire range of values in the
table. We can use c0 through c4 as inputs into a procedure to divvy up the table to be processed
in parallel:

```
big_table@ORA920> select
  2 sum( case when object_id > &c0 and object_id <= &c1
  3  then 1 else 0 end ) range1,
  4 sum( case when object_id > &c1 and object_id <= &c2
  5  then 1 else 0 end ) range2,
  6 sum( case when object_id > &c2 and object_id <= &c3
  7  then 1 else 0 end ) range3,
  8 sum( case when object_id > &c3 and object_id <= &c4
  9  then 1 else 0 end ) range4,
 10 count(*)
 11 from big_table
 12 /

    RANGE1     RANGE2     RANGE3     RANGE4   COUNT(*)
---------- ---------- ---------- ---------- ----------
    458464     458464     458464     458464    1833856
```

In this case, we were able to achieve between a 250% and 300% increase in throughput, without doing much work at all. In Chapter 8, we'll take another look at do-it-yourself parallelism. You'll see that we can accomplish the same goal using ROWID ranges which are even more efficient than the index key approach just shown here.

Now, bear in mind, you may not be able to immediately apply this to your process. It does depend on the underlying logic of the PL/SQL, C, Java, or other language routines. The point is that you should not overlook this approach. In fact, the best time to look at this approach is well in advance of tuning an application. This approach works best when designed in from the very beginning.

## Parallel Processing Wrap-Up

Parallel query is not a fix to a bad design; a good design is a fix for a bad design. If a physical redesign would obviate the need for parallel query, by all means, that would be the method to take. For example, it could well be that introducing partitioning in a manner that allows partition elimination to remove 90% of the data from consideration would obviate the need to run a parallel query. Look at the question and justify parallel operations on it, not the other way around.

In the early days of data warehousing, we saw a lot of large databases with a small number of users. Parallel query was a huge deal back then: small number of users + big machine = excess capacity. Today, warehouses are so mainstream, so functional, that many times, we have as many users connected to them as we do to our transactional systems. The abilities of parallelism may well be limited to administrative features at that point. There just won't be sufficient capacity to do otherwise.

The best sources for more information about parallel processing are the Oracle documentation once again. Here, I will point out a couple of more obscure pieces that you might want to look at in addition to the standard fare:

- *Oracle Concepts Guide*   But, of course, I recommend this guide. It includes a very good chapter on parallel processing in general and parallel features in Oracle.

- *Data Warehousing Guide*   Here, you will find two chapters on parallelism. They cover when to use it to how to use it in your data warehouse.

- *Supplied Packages Guide*   A hidden nugget is the DBMS_PCLXTUIL package. This package implements a "more parallel" local index create operation.

- *Supplied Packages Guide*   The DBMS_STATS package allows you to gather statistics on a table in parallel.

- *Administrators Guide*   This provides information about managing processes for parallel execution, parallelizing table creation, index creation, PDML, and so on.

# Summary

In this chapter, we took a look at how the architecture of Oracle can affect your application. It answered questions from simply, "How should I connect to the database?" to "Will partitioning make my database operations faster?"

Many of these topics could be books unto themselves. Much of the point here is that you need a good understanding of how these tools—these architectural implementations Oracle provides—work in order to be successful. For example, what if you just turn on parallel query to fix a performance problem? That isn't the answer. You will not accomplish your goal. Use parallel query wisely, in appropriate places, with a firm understanding of how it works and what it does, and you can reap incredible benefits.

Much like the old saying, "When all you have is a hammer, everything looks like a nail," these architectural implementations of Oracle's are simply a wide variety of tools in your toolbox. When used correctly, they work well. When used improperly, or with insufficient training, testing, or knowledge, they can be deadly

# CHAPTER
## 4

## Effective
## Administration

I n this chapter, we will explore some of the features I find useful in easing the burden of database administration. As with most things in life, there are hard ways to do things and there are easier ways. Correspondingly, there are tradeoffs to be made as well between the two. Sometimes the hard way is the only way because it gives you a degree of control you really need. Other times, the hard way is just that—the hard way.

So, for example, if you are running a 2TB database warehouse, a feature like Oracle Managed Files may not be an administrative ease to you, because you *need* the ability to control each and every individual file location, therefore, having all of the files appear in one directory simply won't be feasible or manageable. On the other hand, if you are building a small to medium-sized application to be deployed in one or two tablespaces on a striped disk array, using Oracle Managed Files makes all the sense in the world.

What I will do here is present some of my "most appreciated" administrative-easing features. These are features that are frequently underutilized. I'll explain how they work and when they are useful. In the end, you must decide whether or not a particular feature will help in your particular situation.

# Use SPFILEs to Start Your Database

In order to start an Oracle database, you need to have a parameter file. A parameter file contains important settings, such as the location of the control files for the database (which, in turn, point to where all other files are), what the DB_NAME is, and the other settable parameters. Oracle8i and earlier use a parameter file, a PFILE, which is a plain text (ASCII) file that resides on the machine. Oracle9i and later use a stored parameter file, an SPFILE, to start the database.

## The Problems with PFILEs

Using a PFILE meant that if you started a database running on Unix from your Windows PC, the parameter file for the database needed to be accessible on the PC. For some people, this was not a big deal. They would simply telnet into the database server itself and start it up or shut it down. The drawback to this was that everyone needed to physically access the server in order to ensure the correct init.ora file was being used to start the database (so everyone needed the ability to physically access the server).

Also, if you used system management tools to start and stop the database, the PFILEs needed to be physically wherever the system management tool was, and this generally was *not* the machine where your database ran (since the purpose of a system management tool is to manage multiple databases in your environment). If you used Oracle Enterprise Manager (OEM), for example, the PFILE for your database had to be physically stored on the machine that was running the Oracle Management Server (OMS). In a pinch, it may not be possible to simply log on to your database server and start up the database, because the necessary PFILE would not be there! This led to great confusion and "missing parameters" from time to time. If you simply started the database from a different machine, an entirely different set of parameters could be used, since a different PFILE would be used.

Another problem was that as changes were made to the instance via the ALTER SYSTEM command, you would need to remember to update each and every copy of the PFILE out there in order to have that new setting take effect after the next restart of the database. If you forgot, the system would run fine until someone restarted the database, and then you would discover that the new settings you made were no longer there. With multiple parameter files possibly strewn throughout your network, tracking down and updating each one could be a formidable task.

Enter the SPFILE with Oracle9i and later. This new facility ends the confusion over what is really used to start a database instance and solves the problem of propagating updates made with the ALTER SYSTEM command.

## How SPFILEs Work

An SPFILE is stored in a binary format on the server itself. You no longer need to have a local copy to start the database remotely. The binary file format serves two purposes:

- Changes made via the ALTER SYSTEM command may now persist across server restarts. It is no longer necessary to update the init.ora text file with every little change. You can use SQL to maintain your parameter settings.

- It prevents us (humans) from being tempted to edit the file using any sort of editor. It provides SQL to manipulate it and prohibits us from editing it directly. However, if you do want to edit the file, there are techniques you can employ to accomplish that. We'll look at those next in the section "Help, My SPFILE Is Broken and I Cannot Start."

The SPFILE is stored on the server in the location specified by the initialization parameter SPFILE:

```
ops$tkyte@ORA920> show parameter spfile

NAME                                  TYPE         VALUE
------------------------------------- ------------ ------------------
spfile                                string       ?/dbs/spfile@.ora
```

You can (but shouldn't unless you have some compelling reason to) change this location from the default. It would actually involve using a PFILE to set the SPFILE location since you couldn't know the location of the SPFILE until it was loaded (a chicken and egg type of problem).

## Convert a Database to Use SPFILE

If you create a new Oracle9i database, it will use an SPFILE by default. If you have an existing database, you can easily convert it over to using an SPFILE via this command:

```
create spfile from pfile  <='pfilename'>;
```

The next time you start up the database, it will use the SPFILE that was created in the default location, with the default name.

Conversely, you can create a textual version of this binary parameter file using the CREATE PFILE command:

```
create pfile <= 'filename'> from spfile <= 'filename'>;
```

This will always create the text parameter file on the server (not on the client that executed this command). You might use this technique to export all parameters, make many changes to them, and then create a new SPFILE using this PFILE.

If both the SPFILE and the PFILE exist, the SPFILE will override the PFILE and be used. You can always force Oracle to use a PFILE instead of the SPFILE by using the following command instead of just startup:

```
SQL> startup pfile=filename
```

## Save System Parameter Changes

With an SPFILE, when you make changes to system parameters, you can save them persistently as well. You now have an extended syntax of the ALTER SYSTEM command to set parameters:

```
ALTER SYSTEM set parameter = value SCOPE = MEMORY | SPFILE | BOTH;
```

With the SCOPE clause, you can set a system parameter as one of the following:

- **MEMORY**  Affects the database right now, but will not be in place after a restart. MEMORY is the default if you started the database with a PFILE (and is the only scope available with PFILEs).

- **SPFILE**  Does not change the current setting of the parameter, but will modify the SPFILE so that upon a restart, this parameter will take effect.

- **BOTH**  Changes the current instance's setting as well as updates the SPFILE. BOTH is the default if you started the database with an SPFILE.

## Are PFILEs Obsolete?

PFILEs can still be useful occasionally. Suppose that the SPFILE becomes unreadable or otherwise inaccessible. It might be nice to have a PFILE around to start with. Suppose you want to make a mass update to many variables. For example, you might be configuring shared server connections and have five or six MTS parameters you would like to set based on what someone emailed you. In this case, it may be easier to edit a PFILE instead of issuing the ALTER SYSTEM commands.

PFILEs can also serve as backups. I occasionally back up my SPFILE to a PFILE by using the CREATE PFILE FROM SPFILE command. I do this for the same reason I use the ALTER DATABASE BACKUP CONTROLFILE TO TRACE command as part of my backups. It is good to have the textual backup of these important binary files. Without control files, my database won't start. Without a PFILE or SPFILE, I cannot even *find* my control files, let alone think about bringing up my database! In short, having a PFILE backup of my SPFILE lets me sleep better at night.

**TIP**
*RMAN in Oracle9i Release 2 and later will consider parameter files as part of a backup set for the first time. Now RMAN gets every file you really need. In the past, it left them out, so you needed to back up your parameter files separately.*

# Help, My SPFILE Is Broken and I Cannot Start

Suppose we made a system parameter change, such as the following:

```
sys@ORA920.US.ORACLE.COM> alter system set processes=5000 scope=spfile;
System altered.

sys@ORA920.US.ORACLE.COM> shutdown
Database closed.
Database dismounted.
ORACLE instance shut down.

...
Connected to an idle instance.

idle> startup
ORA-00064: object is too large to allocate on this O/S (1,4720000)
idle> Disconnected
```

We're in a bad way now. We've set a system setting far too large for the way our system is configured, and our SPFILE is broken. We cannot do an ALTER SYSTEM, since we cannot start up the database. The SPFILE is a binary file, so we cannot edit it directly. What can we do?

We can rely on the fact that Oracle uses the *last specified* value for a parameter that it finds. Suppose that we list this in a parameter file:

```
Processes=1000
Processes=100
```

Oracle will use the last value of 100, not the value of 1000. So, we can simply create a PFILE that includes a reference to the "bad" SPFILE, and then override any individual parameters we desire:

```
spfile= /usr/oracle/ora920/OraHome1/dbs/spfileora920.ora
processes = 150
```

That basically says to include the SPFILE but use this value for processes instead of the one you find in there. Now, we issue the following command:

```
idle> startup pfile=temp.ora
ORACLE instance started.

Total System Global Area    143725064 bytes
Fixed Size                     451080 bytes
Variable Size               109051904 bytes
Database Buffers             33554432 bytes
Redo Buffers                   667648 bytes
Database mounted.
Database opened.
idle> show parameter processes
```

```
NAME                                   TYPE        VALUE
-------------------------------------- ----------- ---------------
...
processes                              integer     150
idle> alter system set processes=150 scope=spfile;
System altered.
```

We're back in business, and our SPFILE is now corrected for the next time we start up. An alternative method would have been to follow these steps:

1. Issue a CREATE PFILE FROM SPFILE command when the startup failed.

2. Edit the generated PFILE to correct the error.

3. Issue a CREATE SPFILE FROM PFILE command to regenerate the SPFILE with the correct settings.

4. Startup force the database.

Which method you use is up to you. The first method has fewer steps, but now your database is up and running on a PFILE instead of an SPFILE until you restart it again. The second method involves more steps, but when you bring the database back up, it will be running on the SPFILE, not a PFILE.

**TIP**
*On Unix, you can use the* strings *command to create a PFILE from an SPFILE without using SQL. The command* strings spfile$ORACLE_SID.ora > init$ORACLE_SID.ora *will extract the parameters from the SPFILE and put them in the PFILE for you.*

"How can I, at a glance, tell if I used an SPFILE or a PFILE to start up the database?"

Well, you can use V$SPPARAMETER to see this. Consider the following:

```
sys@ORA920> select isspecified, count(*)
  2 from v$spparameter
  3 group by isspecified;

ISSPEC    COUNT(*)
------    ----------
FALSE         221
TRUE           39
```

The fact that ISSPECIFIED is TRUE for some settings would indicate that you are using an SPFILE. These settings were specified in the SPFILE.

Suppose you start up with a PFILE, like this:

```
sys@ORA920> shutdown
Database closed.
Database dismounted.
ORACLE instance shut down.
sys@ORA920> startup pfile = initora920.ora
ORACLE instance started.

Total System Global Area  143725064 bytes
Fixed Size                   451080 bytes
Variable Size             109051904 bytes
Database Buffers           33554432 bytes
Redo Buffers                 667648 bytes
Database mounted.
Database opened.
sys@ORA920> select isspecified, count(*)
  2 from v$spparameter
  3 group by isspecified;

ISSPEC   COUNT(*)
------ ----------
FALSE        258
```

Then no parameter "is specified" in the SPFILE, which means they all come from the PFILE. So, after restarting with an SPFILE, you can just use this query:

```
sys@ORA920> select decode(count(*), 1, 'spfile', 'pfile' )
  2    from v$spparameter
  3   where rownum=1
  4     and isspecified='TRUE'
  5 /

DECODE
------
spfile
```

It would be easy enough to use that query as the text for a view so you can just query `select * from parameter_file_type`.

## SPFILE Wrap-Up

The old-style parameter files, PFILEs, can cause confusion by creating an environment with multiple parameter files strewn throughout the network. Having a single authoritative source for initialization parameter values for the database, regardless of what tool you use to start the database or where this tool exists in the network, is the biggest benefit of using SPFILEs. The ability to have your ALTER SYSTEM changes persist reduces the possibility that the parameter value you really need to have set disappears on the next database restart. SPFILEs also offer the ability to have parameter values "sanity checked." That is, if you try to `alter system set processes=no scope= spfile`, you'll get an "ORA-02017: Integer Value Required" error message immediately (and the change will not be made). The probability that your database won't restart next time due to an invalid parameter setting is reduced (but not eliminated, since you can still set processes to an integer that your system can't support). If a bad value does gets into an SPFILE (as demonstrated with the processes init.ora parameter value example you saw earlier in this section), it can be difficult to recover unless you know how. But you can fix this by using a PFILE that you either create by hand or via the CREATE PFILE command. Judicious use of the CREATE PFILE from SPFILE command as part of your backup plan will alleviate this issue as well.

Keep in mind that the SPFILE is a binary file. It is not a text file you can edit and comment, as you could with a PFILE. You must document your changes to the SPFILE in a system log elsewhere if you want to track why you changed a value over time.

# Let Oracle Manage Your Datafiles

In the past (roughly five to ten years ago), much effort was given to micro-managing datafiles and their placement on disk. We would place specific files on very specific devices, attempting to reduce or eliminate I/O contention. With small sets of tables, small databases, and small disks, this was sometimes achievable (but difficult). As the size of our databases increased and the number of database objects that would need placement ballooned over time—applications often have hundreds of tables and indexes—the ability to micromanage object placement successfully has been reduced. Fortunately, storage vendors invented techniques to help us achieve evenly distributed I/O at the logical disk level, instead of fine-tuning where specific tables or files were placed.

Storage features like logical volumes, RAID arrays, storage area networks (SANs), and network-attached storage (NAS) came into play. These days, most systems have a single, or few, mount points, huge logical devices that underneath are physically tens or hundreds of striped disks. Placing a file on a specific device isn't as meaningful here. Also, we have many more files today than we did ten years ago. Our databases have gone from hundreds of megabytes to hundreds of gigabytes or more. Trying to micromanage our datafiles can rapidly get out of control.

If you are in an environment where you have one or two large logical volumes for your database, or you just have a small database with one disk (one mount point), the ability to let Oracle "manage" your files—to use Oracle Managed Files (OMF)—is very appealing. Basically, with OMF, Oracle handles the following tasks:

- Create and name your datafiles
- Size your datafiles
- Extend your datafiles as needed
- Delete your datafiles if necessary

## When Is OMF Useful?

In this day and age, where a single file system or mount point is not a single physical disk anymore, but rather some striped, RAID array consisting of many disks, the need to place files in separate directories and/or disks is lessened. In many cases, using a single directory for application files is acceptable.

For developers, OMF is useful when you've developed an application that will create a tablespace, but you do not want to hard-code the physical location (filename) into your installation scripts, because that is not portable. All you need to do now is say, "You must have the DB_CREATE_FILE_DEST init.ora parameter set and make sure X megabytes of disk space is available." The DBA takes care of the rest, and your script just runs. In the event your application is removed, a simple DROP TABLESPACE gets rid of it, not only in the data dictionary but also in the operating system itself. So, you no longer need to put `c:\oradata\foo.dbf` or `/oradata/foo.dbf` into an installation script. You can just create a tablespace without any filenames whatsoever.

On a development or testing database, this is the way to go when creating tests to try out new ideas. No longer do you need to remember to clean up the operating system files when you drop a tablespace. Now the database can do that.

**TIP**
*You can use the DROP TABLESPACE tablespacename INCLUDING CONTENTS AND DATAFILES command to have Oracle clean up the datafiles when you drop a tablespace even when not using Oracle Managed Files.*

On the other hand, there are times when you need to use explicit datafile names and paths. In a large data warehouse, for example, where you have hundreds of gigabytes or even a terabyte or more of disk storage that is spread across many directories/mount points, you will want to use explicit datafile names.

If you install the Oracle database itself as part of your application installation, another capability of OMF might prove useful. The managed file concept may be carried a step further to include other types of Oracle files, not just datafiles. The DB_CREATE_ONLINE_LOG_DEST_N (where N is an integer between 1 and 5) init.ora parameter allows you to tell Oracle where to place newly created online redo log files as well as newly created control files. As part of your application installation process, you could simply request three directories in order to create the database: one for the data itself and two for the copies of the online redo log and control files. Of course, you would need to point out that the directories for the redo logs/control files should be on separate disks, since you are mirroring this information for protection from media failure, and using a single disk would be self-defeating.

For a typical database-creation process, the log and control files are usually specified during the initial creation using the Database Configuration Assistant (DBCA). Then we just explicitly name the redo/control files using that tool (actually, it names them for us). And, since we do not tend to drop control or log files, whether or not this is managed by Oracle doesn't affect us too much.

## How OMF Works

When you use OMF, you don't need to name the files, and you don't even need to know how big to make them. It is all taken care of for you. With OMF, creating a tablespace is as easy as this:

```
ops$tkyte@ORA920> create tablespace new_tablespace;
Tablespace created.
```

You've seen that syntax in the examples in this book. Let's see what Oracle did for us:

```
ops$tkyte@ORA920> begin
  2  print_table( 'select *
  3             from dba_data_files
  4            where tablespace_name = ''NEW_TABLESPACE'' ' );
  5  end;
  6  /
FILE_NAME                        : /../o1_mf_new_tabl_z2mgrv6c_.dbf
FILE_ID                          : 13
TABLESPACE_NAME                  : NEW_TABLESPACE
BYTES                            : 104857600
BLOCKS                           : 12800
STATUS                           : AVAILABLE
RELATIVE_FNO                     : 13
AUTOEXTENSIBLE                   : YES
MAXBYTES                         : 34359721984
MAXBLOCKS                        : 4194302
INCREMENT_BY                     : 1
USER_BYTES                       : 104792064
USER_BLOCKS                      : 12792
-----------------

PL/SQL procedure successfully completed.
```

**NOTE**
*This example uses my utility stored procedure PRINT_TABLE. It prints the results of a query "down the page" in SQL\*Plus. See the setup section in the Appendix for more information on this utility.*

We can see that Oracle created a datafile with the following characteristics:

- It has the unique (but strange) name o1_mf_new_tabl_z2mgrv6c_.dbf.

- Its size is 100MB.

- It is autoextensible and will autoextend one block at a time but that is really "an extent" at a time since the minimum the file will actually extend will be the extent size itself.

- It can grow to a maximum size of 32GB (if there is sufficient space on the file system).

**NOTE**
*It would be advisable to set the MAXSIZE parameter for your files to prevent them from attempting to grow larger than you want them to, or larger than your file system would support.*

As you can see, when Oracle names your files, they are not named intuitively. However, since the datafile names are easily retrieved via the data dictionary (DBA_DATAFILES) and all

backup scripts would be using this view to list the files to back up, this is not too much of
an issue.

"When we use OMF, how does it know where to put the file? And can we control how big the
file can be as well as all of the other attributes?"

The answer to the first question is that the file storage destination is defined by the
DB_FILE_CREATE_DEST parameter:

```
ops$tkyte@ORA920> show parameter db_create_file_dest

NAME                         TYPE         VALUE
---------------------------- ------------ ------------------------------
db_create_file_dest          string       /usr/oracle/ora920/OraHome1/or
                                           adata/ora920
```

If that area of disk fills up, the DBA can issue an ALTER SYSTEM command to point it at
another location.

The answer to the second question is that all of the attributes of the datafile can be controlled.
Suppose we wanted the file to autoextend 1MB at a time and have a maximum size of 2GB.
The following will accomplish that:

```
ops$tkyte@ORA920> create tablespace new_tablespace datafile
  2  autoextend on next 1m maxsize 2048m
  3  /
Tablespace created.
```

# OMF Wrap-Up

There are two major benefits of OMF:

- **Operational simplicity**   On a system with only one, or few, mount points (directories),
  installation of applications can be simplified using OMF. Hard-coded paths would not
  be part of the installation scripts.

- **Self-cleaning**   As tablespaces come and go, so do their datafiles. While it is true that
  the DROP TABLESPACE command can do that for you as well, OMF just "makes it so."

A possible problem is that all files tend to go into one mount point, until the DBA changes
the DB_CREATE_FILE_DEST parameter. If you are not careful, this could lead to hot spots, or
uneven I/O patterns on your disks. If this does occur, you can move the OMF datafile to another
device using operating system commands, and then use the ALTER DATABASE command to
rename the datafile, to let Oracle know where you put it. It's important to note that this would
be a semi-offline operation. The data in these files would not be available for writing while this
operation is taking place. You would have to either take the tablespace offline (no read or write)
or make the tablespace READ ONLY before copying the file (no writes allowed).

I use a mixture of OMF datafiles and explicitly named files (you can use both). For small applications with modest IO/disk needs, I use OMF. For applications that require many tablespaces and are I/O-intensive, I tend to fall back on explicitly named files that are spread out across multiple mount points. In other words, the more simple the application, the more simple my approach. I'll spend my time on the big applications and take the easy route on the small ones.

# Bulletproof Your Recovery

Recovery rank is a DBA's single most important responsibility. It does not matter what else you may or may not know; if you don't have a sound recovery plan, you haven't done your job. Who cares how fast you can make a query run after you just lost all of your data?

Recently, I was called into a customer site where the database had been down for almost ten days, ever since they had a media failure that necessitated restoring from backups. They had a multiterabyte instance and hadn't really tested the backups. In the interest of saving on cost, they had only one backup set (they overwrote the prior backups each time). When they tried to recover, they discovered that their backup scripts forgot to put the tablespaces into backup mode before starting the file copies. The scripts fired off both commands at that same time, and the copy started before the tablespaces were in the right mode. SYSTEM, the single most important tablespace, was not recoverable.

They spent many hours attempting to recover the database using magical undocumented methods, but all to no avail. In the end, they had to rebuild much of this instance. Fortunately, it was a data warehouse and rebuilding was an option for them. Had this been a transactional system, the failure could have been the end of that business. They would have been able to "scrape" much of the data out of the remaining datafiles and piece the database back together, but by then, it may have been too late. The point is that this situation was entirely avoidable.

## Backup Guidelines

Many failed database restorations are due to human error. Due to improper backup techniques, inadequate backup techniques, or simple lack of testing, the problems with the backup-and-restore process were not detected until the backups were needed. At that point, it is obviously too late to fix any problems. Here are a few examples of backup problems:

- Forgetting (or not knowing) that tablespaces needed to be in hot backup mode when performing user managed backups

- Backing up and restoring online redo logs (wiping out the current online redo logs, thus making full recovery impossible)

- Thinking that backing up rollback segments is a waste of time

That is not to say the hardware is never to blame or that the software is perfect. It's possible that the tape drive was writing the data improperly, but not returning any errors. Or, perhaps the Unix command-line tool "DD" (or whatever tool you used) introduced a subtle corruption into the data stream it was copying. However, even though these types of problems are not directly caused by the DBA, they are things the DBA should have detected by proactive testing.

My philosophy on database backups boils down to a couple of key points. They are summarized in the following sections.

## Use ARCHIVELOG Mode

Production systems must be in ARCHIVELOG mode, even many conventional data warehouses, although they are one of the glaring examples where this rule might not hold true. In a transactional system, where the loss of committed data is deemed unacceptable, ARCHIVELOG mode is absolutely necessary. Running a system in NOARCHIVELOG mode means you *will* (not might) lose your day's work at some point. For many companies, the loss of a day's work could mean they are out of business.

Even when your system is in ARCHIVELOG mode, beware of and monitor for nonlogged operations, such as a direct-path load or insert into a nonlogged table, an unrecoverable index build, and so on.

■ **Detect that nonlogging operations are happening.**   V$DATAFILE will tell you if a datafile has had a nonlogged operation performed on it. The UNRECOVERABLE_CHANGE# and UNRECOVERABLE_TIME columns will tell you when a file last had a nonlogged operation performed on it. Back up any file that has experienced a nonlogged operation as soon as possible to ensure that you can recover it.

■ **Determine if nonlogging operations should be permitted to continue.**   If so, you need to make sure you can *anticipate* when these nonlogged operations will occur, so you can schedule the backup appropriately to compensate for it. If not, you need to stop it from happening. In Oracle9i Release 2, you can even disable nonlogged operations in your database via the ALTER DATABASE command.

You do not want to find out the day you need to restore a tablespace that you do not have the necessary log information!

## Store Archive Logs Off the Source System

As soon as possible, either move or copy archive logs to another physical location (in another building, if possible). In the event of a catastrophic failure on the source system, you need to have the archived transaction information elsewhere. If you have all of your eggs in one basket, you will lose all of your eggs someday.

Your backups and archived redo logs must be stored on a storage device separate and distinct from your primary server (on another machine with its own storage, on tape drives, or some other container). You must ensure that the total loss of the primary server the data is on (along with all of its storage) does not preclude you from recovering the database elsewhere. What if there is a fire in the data center, and the building is burnt to the ground? Will you be able to recover from that?

### Maintain Multiple Backup Copies

You must keep at least two, if not more, copies of your backups. The reasons for this are at least twofold:

- **Disk failures**   If you overwrite your backups each time you take them, what happens when the disk fails during a backup? Don't laugh. This has happened far more often than once or twice in real life: During the day's backup, the disk being copied failed. Unfortunately, yesterday's backup no longer existed (it was being overwritten), and today's backup did not finish.

- **Corrupted data blocks**   Suppose that you back up your system, without realizing that it has a corrupted data block. When you do detect that corruption, if you have only the last backup, you have only a copy of the already corrupt block. The more backups you have from past points in time, the higher the probability of you being able to recover from a damaged block that you did not detect right away.

**NOTE**
*There are tools supplied with Oracle that can validate your backed-up datafiles such as DBV (database verify). It is beneficial to utilize this tool or other techniques to proactively look for issues such as block corruption. A technique that I've used in addition to DBV is to use the export tool (EXP) on modestly sized databases. EXP exercises the database, would find table level block issues, and it exercises the data dictionary as well, giving it the ability to detect logical corruptions. If you utilize RMAN, it will detect block level corruption during back up as well.*

In many cases, the overall size of the database will dictate how many backups you can reasonably keep; the larger the database, the fewer copies you can keep, of course. For example, I consider my asktom database as irreplaceable, so I have five of the last backups of this database tucked safely away.

### Test the Physical Backups

You must test your physical backups constantly, as part of your standard operating procedures. Just because a piece of hardware was working fine last month does not mean it is working fine this month. Only by periodically testing your backups and actually restoring them will you discover errors.

You do not need to restore the entire database. Pick part of it and restore just that component to a test system. Pick different components over time. Not only will this test the validity of your backups, but it will also give you the confidence that your procedures are accurate.

### Practice Your Restore Procedures

To ensure that you know how to restore your database in the event of a failure, practice. Then when the time comes, you will be ready, because you will have done it over and over.

I know of DBAs who have never performed a restoration. They have read about it, but they have never actually done it. Practice, in this case, does make perfect. You do not want to learn that you misunderstood something when you are under pressure to get the database back in running order. If you have the practical experience and fundamentals down, you'll be a lot more confident and proficient when you need to actually do the restore procedure. Additionally, when the time to restore comes, you'll be able to answer that nagging question everyone will be asking you, "How long will this take?" If you've already done it many times, you'll know how long the entire process will take from end to end.

You need to practice many different failure conditions. Shut down your test database, wipe out your control files, and then recover from that. Then lose a datafile. Then break something else.

If you are part of a DBA team, set up a challenge. Split into two teams. Have one team damage an Oracle database in some fashion. Challenge the other team to fix it. Learn from, and document, the steps to recover from each challenge.

## Use Tools to Reduce the Chances of Error

My number one recommendation is to stop using manual backups (simple file copies) immediately and to start using the supplied functionality in the Recovery Manager (RMAN). Let the software take over. A big advantage of using RMAN is that it makes it harder to create a backup that cannot be used. Not only that, it also plays bookkeeper for you. RMAN remembers where everything is, how current it is, where it would need to go in order to restore it, and so on. At the very moment you need someone cool-headed and confident (when you actually start to restore your database), RMAN is a tool you want to have.

If you haven't looked at RMAN recently, look again. It is the tool you want to use to back up, recover, and manage all of that information. The amount of time and energy you can save by learning and using RMAN will pay for itself in days. RMAN has hooks for every major backup/recovery vendor out there: Tivoli, Legato, CA, and so on. So even if you are using some high-end backup solution, RMAN plays an integral part. If you recall in Chapter 1, one of my required reading assignments for DBAs is the *Recovery Manager Reference*. That is where you need to get started.

## Consider Data Guard

If your data is vital—if you cannot afford to lose a single committed transaction, even as a result of an earthquake, fire, or some other disaster—consider Data Guard. This feature, also known as a standby database, could be an integral part of your backup and recovery solution. Using Data Guard, you automatically get many of the guidelines I've recommended implemented by force:

- Data Guard works only in ARCHIVELOG mode, so you know your system will be in that mode.

- As it is generated, redo information is moved off of the primary system, so you know the archives are being copied (in fact, the online redo logs are copied in real time).

- The physical backups will be tested. Data Guard works, in effect, by performing a restoration.

Data Guard is a tool that gives you a fully functioning backup. In the event of a catastrophic failure, that backup is at your disposal. It has additional benefits as well. The standby database can be used as a reporting system, and it can be used to back up the production instance. You can back up the standby to tape *instead of* the production instance, therefore, decreasing the I/O load in the production server. For details on using Data Guard, refer to the *Data Guard Concepts and Administration Guide*, which is available online at http://otn.oracle.com.

## Backup and Recovery Wrap-Up

As I said in the beginning of this section, recovery ranks as a DBA's single most important responsibility. This is where you need to be perfect. You can become perfect by adhering to the following:

- Use ARCHIVELOG mode.

- Move archive logs as soon as possible.

- Make multiple backup copies.

- Test your physical backups.

- Practice your restore routine.

- Use RMAN, rather than manual backups.

- Consider Data Guard for full protection.

Following these guidelines will not ensure that you can recover from everything. However, they will significantly decrease the number of failures you encounter.

Remember that, ultimately, you will be judged by how well (or not) you did your job during a database recovery situation. It is only a matter of time before you will be in this situation. Keep in mind the only document I repeated twice in the reading list in Chapter 1 was the *Backup and Recovery Concepts* Guide—yes, it's that important. Make sure you are not the cause of any failures. The software isn't perfect, but you can try to be, at least in this one special area.

# Use Locally Managed Tablespaces

In this section, we'll take a look at how Oracle manages data on disk. Since Oracle8i release 1, Oracle has supported two types of tablespaces: dictionary-managed tablespaces (DMTs) and locally managed tablespaces (LMTs). My recommendation regarding the use of DMTs versus LMTs is straightforward: Pretend DMTs do not exist; use only LMTs.

For databases that have existing DMTs, work on moving the objects out of them into newly created LMTs as the opportunity arises. You don't need to run out and move everything tomorrow, but over time, if you do reorganize an object, put it in an LMT. Don't simply convert existing DMTs into LMTs. Instead, move the objects and then drop the old tablespace. Using DBMS_SPACE_ADMIN.TABLESPACE_MIGRATE_TO_LOCAL will convert a DMT into a user-managed LMT, but will not achieve one of the major benefits of LMTs—uniformly sized extents. The odd-sized extents the DMT had before the migration will still exist.

There are actually two kinds of LMTs: system-managed LMTs and LMTs that allow you to set uniform extent sizes. Here, I'll explain why you should use LMTs and when to use each type of LMT.

## Why Are DMTs Obsolete?

With DMTs, space in datafiles is managed in data dictionary tables: SYS.UET$ for used extents and SYS.FET$ for free extents. Every time you need an extent added to a table or you free extents for reuse via a DROP or TRUNCATE command, Oracle will perform recursive SQL to insert or delete from these tables. This is very slow in many cases.

With DMTs, there are also issues with coalescing (joining together) contiguous free extents. In a DMT, free extents are stored as a row in the FET$ table. If you drop a table with two 5MB extents, Oracle will record them using a row apiece. Now, suppose those two extents were actually contiguous (right next to each other). Until some process (SMON) actually combines them into a single record, Oracle does not recognize them as representing 10MB of free space; rather, it sees them as two separate extents of 5MB apiece. An allocation request for 10MB of storage would ignore these extents until they were coalesced. Additionally, with DMTs, you need to take care to avoid having too many extents, because that situation has a big negative impact on the performance of many administrative functions, such as rebuilding, moving, truncating, and dropping objects.

Oracle handles LMTs quite differently. With this type of tablespace, datafile space is managed via a bitmap in the header of the datafiles themselves. Rather than having a row per used extent in SYS.UET$ and a row per free available extent in SYS.FET$, the datafile headers just have a series of zeros and ones. When you need a new extent, Oracle will go to the datafile header and scan the bitmap looking for free space. When you free an extent, Oracle just zeros out the corresponding bit(s). There are no issues with regard to coalescing free space. A set of contiguous zeros in the bitmap means all of this space is free and contiguous. You do not need to worry about avoiding thousands of extents in an object, because the space-management features are exceedingly fast compared with those for DMTs.

One of my favorite new features in Oracle9i Release 2 is the fact that if you create the default database using the Database Configuration Assistant (DBCA), SYSTEM will be installed as an LMT. Once that happens, *it is impossible to create a DMT.* This catches some people by surprise, but it should be a pleasant surprise. DMTs are obsolete; you should not be using them anymore. If you use the CREATE DATABASE command manually, you should specify "EXTENT MANAGEMENT LOCAL" in order to have your SYSTEM tablespace locally managed.

There has been a lot of FUD (fear, uncertainty, doubt) about LMTs. There are DBAs out there who refuse to use them still. Maybe it is because it makes this aspect of the database so much easier. I mean, what happens if you don't have tablespace fragmentation and you don't have considerations about INITIAL, NEXT, PCTINCREASE, and MAXEXTENTS? Aren't you just making the job of the DBA go away? Well, if that is all the DBA is doing, maybe so. But it is my experience that this is an aspect of database administration that most DBAs wish would disappear; they are tired of micromanaging the space allocation for each and every object.

Given that LMTs preclude fragmentation, are faster, are easier to use, and have not a single identifiable downside when compared to DMTs should be reason enough to start using them. The fact that in Oracle9i Release 2, by default, LMTs are the *only* kind of tablespace says a lot about where Oracle Corporation is going with this feature.

## Use System-Managed LMTs When You Do Not Know How Big Your Objects Will Become

With a *system-managed LMT*, the system figures out exactly what the extent sizes will be for a table. Oracle will use an internal, undocumented algorithm to allocate space for every object in the tablespace. With this method, the first couple of extents will be small (64KB), and then the extents will get larger and larger over time. They will all be multiples of each other. That fact precludes free space fragmentation in these tablespaces, because every chunk of free space is potentially usable by any other object. This is in contrast to a DMT, where an object will request arbitrary extent sizes, and if there is not a contiguous free extent large enough to satisfy the request, the request will fail. It is true that in a system-managed LMT, since there is more than one extent size, a request for space may fail even if there is existing free space. However, it is many times less likely due mostly to the fact that there is a very limited number of extent sizes. It would be rare to have free space that is not usable in a system-managed LMT and, in general, the space will be very small.

In the beginning, I was a little cautious about using this type of tablespace. It just didn't feel right. I was always taught that we should size our objects, watch their space usage like a hawk—micromanage the tablespace. Maybe I'm getting lazy, but I would prefer not to work that way if I can avoid it. With system-managed LMTs. I'm not kept awake at night wondering if a PCTINCREASE is going to go crazy on me or if my tablespace will be fragmented like Swiss cheese, with a lot of different-sized holes in it. Objects grow in a sensible fashion, without a lot of watching or handholding.

To see how space might be allocated in such a tablespace, let's use BIG_TABLE again (as noted in the Appendix, this is a table created from ALL_OBJECTS and duplicated over and over to have quite a few rows). For this demonstration, I made a copy of this table in an auto-allocate LMT.

**NOTE**
*Another feature I'm rather fond of is Oracle-managed files, which I'm using here. I do not need to specify the datafile information in the CREATE TABLESPACE command. I previously set up the DB_CREATE_FILE_DEST init.ora parameter, and Oracle will name, create, and manage the operating system files for me.*

```
big_table@ORA920> create tablespace SYSTEM_MANAGED
  2 extent management local;

Tablespace created.

big_table@ORA920> create table big_table_copy
  2 tablespace SYSTEM_MANAGED
  3 as
  4 select * from big_table;

Table created.

big_table@ORA920> select tablespace_name, extent_id, bytes/1024, blocks
  2 from user_extents
  3 where segment_name = ' BIG_TABLE_COPY'
  4 /

TABLESPACE_NAME      EXTENT_ID BYTES/1024 BLOCKS
-------------------------- ---------- ---------- ----------
SYSTEM_MANAGED        0   64   8
SYSTEM_MANAGED        1   64   8
...
SYSTEM_MANAGED       14   64   8
SYSTEM_MANAGED       15   64   8
```

```
SYSTEM_MANAGED        16   1024   128
SYSTEM_MANAGED        17   1024   128
...
SYSTEM_MANAGED        77   1024   128
SYSTEM_MANAGED        78   1024   128
SYSTEM_MANAGED        79   8192   1024
SYSTEM_MANAGED        80   8192   1024
...
SYSTEM_MANAGED        91   8192   1024
SYSTEM_MANAGED        92   8192   1024

93 rows selected.
```

As you can see in this example, the first 16 extents each are 64KB (but don't be surprised if you see something slightly different). The next 63 are each 1MB, and the remaining 14 are 8MB. As the object grew, the extents grew as well. That is a total of about 180MB of space in 93 extents, which is perfectly acceptable. For those who believe you must have your objects in one extent, I hope that this Oracle-supported algorithm, which promotes and encourages multiple extents, puts that notion to rest.

In this example, when we quadrupled the size of the BIG_TABLE_COPY to about 650MB, Oracle added another 64 extents, each 8MB, for a total of 512MB more. That table was just taking care of its space needs.

When you do not know how big your objects will become, system-managed LMTs are the way to go. This type of space management is most useful when you are creating objects for an application, and depending on how the people using the application configure it, some tables might be empty, some might be 100MB, and some might be 2GB. On another installation, the tables that were 2GB were empty, the tables that were empty are 100MB, and the tables that were 100MB tables are 2GB. In other words, you have no idea how big these tables are going to be in the real world. Here, having each object start at 64KB and stay that way for the first couple of extents lets the tables that are nearly empty stay very small. The tables that are going to get large will get large fast.

If you are using Oracle9i Release 2 with an LMT, you'll find that it uses system-managed extent sizing for the SYSTEM tablespace. For the SYSTEM tablespace, this extent-sizing strategy is the best thing ever. It will prevent dictionary tables from growing exponentially (as PCTINCREASE would have them doing after a while; even a small PCTINCREASE would cause a table to grow by huge amounts after a short period of time) and keep the number of extents at a reasonable maximum. Consider that if you install Oracle and use a ton of PL/SQL, your SYS.SOURCE$ table and the tables that hold the compiled PL/SQL will be huge. On the other hand, your friend may install Oracle and not write any lines of PL/SQL code. With the system-managed approach, Oracle will let the database figure out how big the extents should be.

System-managed LMTs work well, as long as the objects are destined to be 10GB or less. At 10GB, you would be using about 300 extents for the object in this type of tablespace, which is fine. Segments that exceed 10GB are fairly rare. If you are using partitioning, the individual partitions are the segments; 10GB partitions or smaller would be a good size. For tables and indexes that are getting into the 10GB size range, consider partitioning them into smaller, more manageable segments. For segments larger than 10GB, or for those that you prefer to size yourself for some reason, consider using LMTs with uniform extent sizes.

## Use Uniform Extent Sizes When You Know the Ultimate Size of an Object

The other type of LMT is one that supports uniformly sized extents. Using this strategy, each and every extent in the tablespace will be exactly the same size as every other extent in that tablespace. To see how this works, let's use the same example we did in the previous section with BIG_TABLE, but with a 5MB uniform extent size.

```
big_table@ORA920> create tablespace uniform_size
  2 extent management local
  3 uniform size 5m
  4 /
Tablespace created.

big_table@ORA920> create table big_table_copy
  2 tablespace uniform_size
  3 as
  4 select * from big_table
  5 /
Table created.

big_table@ORA920> select tablespace_name, extent_id, bytes/1024, blocks
  2 from user_extents
  3 where segment_name = ' BIG_TABLE_COPY'
  4 /

TABLESPACE_NAME      EXTENT_ID BYTES/1024 BLOCKS
----------------------------- ---------- ---------- ----------
UNIFORM_SIZE         0  5120  640
UNIFORM_SIZE         1  5120  640
...
UNIFORM_SIZE         34  5120  640

35 rows selected.
```

As expected, every extent that was and will ever be allocated in that tablespace will be 5MB—not a byte more, not a byte less.

So, when is this type of tablespace useful? It works well when you know the ultimate size of the object. For example, when you are loading a data warehouse, you have a good idea of what size the objects will be. You know that table will have 50 5GB partitions.

The trick here is to pick an extent size that will hold your object with the least amount of waste. If this segment is 5GB + 1 byte, it will need to extend one more time for that last byte, effectively wasting 4.99999GB of storage. In a large data warehouse, that is a drop in the bucket, but every bit (or byte) counts. You might be willing to set a target of 500 extents, which allows you to use a 10MB extent and waste, at most, 10MB of space.

Another factor to consider when deciding on an extent size is the desired monitoring granularity. An extent size that implies a new extent each month makes abnormal growth easy to spot. If you were to size the extents so that they grow by dozens every day, this spot check would be more difficult.

# Some LMT Caveats

Here, I will point out some caveats I've discovered along the way using LMTs. None of these issues are earth-shattering; none would make me stop using LMTs. I just wanted to make sure you are aware of these points.

## The Magic Number for Uniformly Sized Extents Is 64KB

There was a common myth when LMTs first came out that an LMT with a uniform extent size would waste its first extent for the bitmap used to manage the file; that is, if you used a 1MB uniform extent size, the first 1MB of the tablespace would be taken over by Oracle. People thought, "Oh my gosh, if I use a 100MB uniform size, I'll waste 100MB of data!" Well, there is overhead, but it is only 64KB, not the size of the extent.

The problem was that most people were creating their datafiles as an integral multiple of the uniform extent size. For example, if they used a 5MB extent size, they would use 100MB as a datafile size ($20 \times 5 = 100$). Oracle would look at this 100MB that was just given to it, take away 64KB for itself, divide what was left by 5MB, and truncate the result (no partial extents here). Thus, there were only 19 extents available in this tablespace right after creation! Here is a simple example showing the issue and then how to fix it. We'll start by creating a tablespace with uniform extent sizes of 5MB and a datafile of 100MB.

```
ops$tkyte@ORA920> create tablespace five_meg
  2    datafile size 100m
  3    uniform size 5m
  4  /

Tablespace created.
```

Now, we will query how much free space is available in this newly created tablespace.

```
ops$tkyte@ORA920> select sum(bytes/1024/1024) free_space
  2  from dba_free_space
  3  where tablespace_name = ' FIVE_MEG'
  4  /

FREE_SPACE
----------
        95
```

So, it would appear that 5MB of overhead was taken, but this is not really the case. Let's increase that file by a measly 64KB.

```
ops$tkyte@ORA920> column file_name new_val f
ops$tkyte@ORA920> select file_name from dba_data_files
  2    where tablespace_name = 'FIVE_MEG';

FILE_NAME
------------------------------
/usr/oracle/ora920/OraHome1/or
adata/ora920/o1_mf_five_meg_zc
54bj51_.dbf
```

```
ops$tkyte@ORA920> alter database
  2  datafile '&f' resize 102464k;
old   2: datafile '&f' resize 102464k
new   2: datafile
'/usr/oracle/ora920/OraHome1/oradata/ora920/o1_mf_five_meg_zc54bj5l_.dbf'
 resize 102464k

Database altered.

ops$tkyte@ORA920> select sum(bytes/1024/1024) free_space
  2  from dba_free_space
  3  where tablespace_name = 'FIVE_MEG';

FREE_SPACE
----------
       100
```

And there you go. We have all of our space. I'm not sure how many DBAs this feature scared off, but I hope they will come around after seeing this!

Note that this 64KB rule need not apply to system-managed extents! If you ran the above test without the `uniform size 5m` clause, you would find that there is initially 99.9375MB of available free space, and all but 64KB of it would be usable.

## System-Managed LMT Allocates from Files Differently

"How can you achieve 'poor-man's striping' of a table? That is, without using striping software at the operating-system level and without using partitioning, how would you stripe a table across multiple devices?"

To accomplish this, create a tablespace with many datafiles. Use an LMT, of course. Use a uniform extent size that will cause the table to go into 100 or so extents. Create the table in that tablespace. Allocate extents for it in a round-robin fashion, spreading the data out.

I had tested this in the past using a DMT, and Oracle always tended to go round-robin when allocating space. I had also tested this with an LMT using uniform extent sizes, and it worked the same. However, when the user tried to apply this technique, he used system-managed extents! The results were quite different than what I had experienced. But, after further testing, it seems that the round-robin technique will still kick in when the object gets large enough to mandate striping.

To see how the different types of LMT allocate from files, we will consider a small example. We will start by creating two tablespaces, each with four datafiles that are 64KB larger than 2MB (the extra 64KB you need for the bitmap). One will use 64KB uniform extents; the other will be system-managed.

```
ops$tkyte@ORA920> create tablespace uniform_extents
  2  datafile size 2112k, size 2112k, size 2112k, size 2112k
```

```
  3  uniform size 64k
  4  /

Tablespace created.

ops$tkyte@ORA920>
ops$tkyte@ORA920> create tablespace system_managed
  2  datafile size 2112k, size 2112k, size 2112k, size 2112k
  3  /

Tablespace created.
```

Next, we'll create a table in each tablespace.

```
ops$tkyte@ORA920> create table uniform_size ( x int, y char(2000) )
  2  tablespace uniform_extents;

Table created.

ops$tkyte@ORA920>
ops$tkyte@ORA920> create table system_size ( x int, y char(2000) )
  2  tablespace system_managed;

Table created.
```

Now, we'll fill each table to capacity using a loop. Note that the following is an example to illustrate a particular point: how the LMTs will allocate space from multiple files. The goal is to cause the table to extend and grow to fill all available space. In order to accomplish that, we use simple row-at-a-time inserts, followed by a commit. Real production code would use bulk inserts and commit only after all of the inserts were performed, of course. Unfortunately, in order to demonstrate a point, we need to use two extremely bad practices.

```
ops$tkyte@ORA920> begin
  2    loop
  3      insert into uniform_size values( 1, 'x' );
  4      commit;
  5    end loop;
  6  end;
  7  /
begin
*
ERROR at line 1:
ORA-01653: unable to extend table OPS$TKYTE.UNIFORM_SIZE
          by 8 in tablespace UNIFORM_EXTENTS
ORA-06512: at line 3


ops$tkyte@ORA920>
ops$tkyte@ORA920> begin
```

```
  2   loop
  3     insert into system_size values( 1, 'x' );
  4     commit;
  5   end loop;
  6  end;
  7  /
begin
*
ERROR at line 1:
ORA-01653: unable to extend table OPS$TKYTE.SYSTEM_SIZE
           by 128 in tablespace SYSTEM_MANAGED
ORA-06512: at line
```

Now, when we inspect how the extents were allocated, we'll see something very different in the algorithm:

```
ops$tkyte@ORA920> select segment_name, extent_id, blocks, file_id
  2  from dba_extents
  3  where segment_name in ( 'UNIFORM_SIZE' , 'SYSTEM_SIZE' )
  4  and owner = user
  5  order by segment_name, extent_id
  6  /

SEGMENT_NAME                       EXTENT_ID     BLOCKS     FILE_ID
------------------------------    ----------  ----------  ----------
SYSTEM_SIZE                               0           8          22
SYSTEM_SIZE                               1           8          22
SYSTEM_SIZE                               2           8          22
...note extent_id 3..14 were all in FILE_ID 22...
SYSTEM_SIZE                              15           8          22
SYSTEM_SIZE                              16         128          23
SYSTEM_SIZE                              17         128          24
SYSTEM_SIZE                              18         128          21
SYSTEM_SIZE                              19         128          22
SYSTEM_SIZE                              20         128          23
SYSTEM_SIZE                              21         128          24
SYSTEM_SIZE                              22         128          21
```

The output shows the first 16 extents for the system-allocated tablespace all came from the same file (FILE_ID 22 in this case). Oracle did this in order to keep all of the small extents together, to avoid allocating a lot of small extents in many different files in an attempt to reduce any potential fragmentation that might occur if we dropped an object from this tablespace. Only when the extents jumped from 8 blocks (64KB) to 128 blocks (1MB) did the round-robin algorithm come into play. Once we hit 1MB extents, the allocation went to file 23, 24, 21, 22, 23, and so on.

However, with the uniformly sized extents, fragmentation is not a concern, so this method uses round-robin allocation from the start.

```
UNIFORM_SIZE                              0           8          18
UNIFORM_SIZE                              1           8          19
UNIFORM_SIZE                              2           8          20
```

| | | | |
|---|---|---|---|
| UNIFORM_SIZE | 3 | 8 | 17 |
| UNIFORM_SIZE | 4 | 8 | 18 |
| UNIFORM_SIZE | 5 | 8 | 19 |
| UNIFORM_SIZE | 6 | 8 | 20 |
| UNIFORM_SIZE | 7 | 8 | 17 |
| UNIFORM_SIZE | 8 | 8 | 18 |
| ... | | | |
| UNIFORM_SIZE | 122 | 8 | 20 |
| UNIFORM_SIZE | 123 | 8 | 17 |
| UNIFORM_SIZE | 124 | 8 | 18 |
| UNIFORM_SIZE | 125 | 8 | 19 |
| UNIFORM_SIZE | 126 | 8 | 20 |
| UNIFORM_SIZE | 127 | 8 | 17 |

```
151 rows selected.
```

Most of the time, this difference in allocation doesn't really matter. The round-robin technique will kick in when the object gets large enough to mandate striping. I point it out mostly to show that the round-robin allocation will happen, but a simple test might not make that clear to you. If you allocate fewer than 16 extents in a test, you might be under the impression that it will never round-robin. (In fact, I was under that impression myself; it was only when making a larger test that I discovered the truth.)

### How to Autoextend Datafiles

This is not a caveat so much as a recommendation. Some people like autoextensible datafiles (I do). Some people hate them. If you are among those who use autoextensible datafiles, you should follow these guidelines when using them with LMTs:

■ With uniformly sized extents, set the next size equal to the extent size. Make sure to add that extra 64KB kicker we discussed. Set MAXSIZE to $N *$ extent_size + 64KB, if you set MAXSIZE at all (recommended—I always set MAXSIZE).

■ With system-managed extents, things get trickier. You don't know if the file wants to grow by 64KB, 1MB, or 8MB. I suggest you grow it 8MB at a time. Start the file at whatever size (the 64KB kicker doesn't come into play), but let it grow in 8MB intervals. Use the assumption that the larger segments are the ones that cause the file to autoextend.

### Beware of Legacy Storage Clauses!

This is a common point of confusion: Some people think that STORAGE clauses are meaningless with LMTs. This is true after the initial CREATE TABLE statement. However, during the CREATE statement, the STORAGE clauses are fully in effect, and you must be cautious of their side effects. Oracle will calculate how much storage would have been allocated using a DMT, and then allocate *at least* that much space in the LMT.

For example, suppose that you had this STORAGE clause:

```
storage ( initial 1m next 5m minextents 3 )
```

Oracle would allocate at least 1MB + 5MB + 5MB = 11MB of space in the LMT—1MB for the initial extent, and then two more 5MB extents to satisfy the MINEXTENTS clause. Now, suppose you did that CREATE statement in a tablespace with uniform extent sizes of 10MB. You would have

20MB allocated initially. After the CREATE statement, however, the INITIAL, NEXT, PCTINCREASE, MINEXTENTS, and MAXEXTENTS settings are ignored. The LMT takes over from there.

So, beware of statements bearing STORAGE clauses. They could allocate a lot more than you think! Be especially careful with the EXP (database export) tool. By default, that tool uses the option COMPRESS=Y, which causes it to sum up the *currently* allocated extent sizes and generates a STORAGE clause with an initial extent allocation of that size. That is not desirable.

## LMT and DMT Wrap-Up

In summary, my advice for tablespaces and LMT versus DMT is pretty clear. Never use a DMT again. Use only LMTs. Here are the reasons:

- You cannot have a fragmented LMT. Fragmentation of the sort you would get easily in a DMT cannot happen in a LMT.

- The number of extents in an object is not relevant. You need not be concerned with objects that have many extents. In the past, you *may* have had a reason to be concerned, not because of query performance but because of DDL performance, such as DROP or TRUNCATE.

- LMTs perform in a superior fashion to DMTs. The recursive SQL overhead is virtually entirely gone.

- LMTs require less thought. You do not need to try to figure out what the optimal INITIAL, NEXT, PCTINCREASE, and MAXEXTENTS are. They are not relevant (well, if you use them, they are relevant and usually disastrous).

Furthermore, for most general-purpose uses, LMTs with system-managed extent sizes are fine. It is the "supersize" case that needs fine-tuning these days—the data warehouse-sized objects.

Setting storage parameters is a thing of the past. Remove the STORAGE clause from your CREATE statements—at least the INITIAL, NEXT, MAXEXTENTS, MINEXTENTS, and PCTINCREASE clauses. It really is getting easier!

For details on DMTs and LMTs, see the trusty Oracle *Concepts Guide*, Part II Database Structures.

# Let Oracle Manage Your Segment Space

Do you know exactly how many freelists to set on your tables and indexes? Do you know how many freelist groups would give you optimal performance? Do you know exactly the right PCTUSED value to set on a segment? If you answered no to any of these questions, Automatic Segment Space Management (ASSM) might be for you.

Most people do not deviate from the default single freelist on a segment. It's even more rare for someone to modify the default PCTUSED setting of 40. Yet, in a transactional system, I frequently see freelist contention as a large contributor to performance woes and the PCTUSED setting leading to wasted space. Before we get into ASSM, let's review freelists and the PCTUSED setting, so you'll know just what ASSM does.

# Understand Freelists and Freelist Groups

A *freelist* is where Oracle keeps tracks of blocks under the high-water mark for an object. Each object will have at least one freelist associated with it. As blocks are used, they will be placed on or taken off the freelist as needed. It is important to note that only blocks under the high-water mark of an object will be found on the freelist. The blocks that remain above the high-water mark will be used only when the freelists are empty. In this fashion, Oracle postpones increasing the high-water mark for an object until it must.

## Multiple Freelists for an Object

An object may have more than one freelist. If you anticipate heavy insert or update activity on an object by many concurrent users, configuring more than one freelist can make a major positive impact on performance (at the cost of possible additional storage). Individual sessions will be assigned to different freelists, and when they need space, they will not contend with each other. The cost for the multiple freelists may be additional storage, because a given session will use only one freelist for a segment for its entire session. If an object has many freelists and each freelist has some blocks on it, a single session doing a large insert operation will ignore all but one of the freelists. When it exhausts the blocks on the freelist it is using, it will advance the high-water mark for the table and not use the other free blocks.

In order to see the differences between a segment with, and without, multiple freelists in a highly concurrent environment, let's set up a test. We start by creating a table T. We'll have five sessions inserting into this table concurrently. We will set up the table with a fixed-width column of 255 bytes, so that in an 8KB-block database, we would get about 26 rows per block. This means that every 26 inserts into this table would request a block from the freelist (the table will grow fast). The table and procedure to insert into this table are as follows:

```
create tablespace manual;

create table t
( x date, y char(255) default 'x' )
storage ( freelists &1 )
tablespace manual;

create or replace procedure do_insert
as
    l_stop  date default sysdate+5/24/60;
    l_date  date default sysdate;
begin
    while ( l_date < l_stop )
    loop
        insert into t (x)
        values (sysdate)
        returning x into l_date;
        commit;
    end loop;
end;
/
```

We use OMF to create the tablespace MANUAL, the default tablespace type. Also, notice that the number of freelists is a parameter to be passed in at runtime to this script (`freelists &1`).

We can then run this test with one freelist and then with five freelists to compare the performance. The procedure simply inserts data into the table T for a five-minute period. The L_STOP variable is set to five minutes in the future, and we just keep inserting SYSDATE in that table until SYSDATE exceeds that future time. Since the column Y is defaulted to X and is a CHAR(255) type, it always takes 255 characters, making our rows wide, so we get the desired 26 or so rows per block. We can run the tests using the following script on a RedHat Linux system with a single CPU running Oracle 9.2.0.3. I mention it because the latching will vary significantly from version to version, and operating system to operating system. It will even vary based on the number of CPUs. While you might not be able to exactly replicate my findings here, you will see analogous results:

```
exec perfstat.statspack.snap

declare
    l_job number;
begin
    for i in 1 .. 5
    loop
        dbms_job.submit( l_job, 'do_insert;' );
    end loop;
    commit;
end;
/

host sleep 400

exec perfstat.statspack.snap
```

**NOTE**
*In this example, we use DBMS_JOB to run five concurrent DO_INSERT routines, so you must ensure that JOB_QUEUE_PROCESSES is set to at least 5. Additionally, the Windows platform does not have a* `sleep` *command. On Windows systems, replace* `the host sleep 400` *with pause and just wait six minutes to hit the Enter key. Do not use DBMS_LOCK.SLEEP, because that will show up as a six-minute wait event in the Statspack report! That will skew the data we are trying to analyze.*

Now, we run the Statspack report for the single freelist example:

```
Load Profile
~~~~~~~~~~~~                                Per Second        Per Transaction
                                        ---------------    ---------------
...
```

```
                Executes:            1,483.23                    2.00
            Transactions:              740.47

Top 5 Timed Events
~~~~~~~~~~~~~~~~~~                                               % Total
Event                                 Waits     Time (s) Ela Time
------------------------------------  ------------ ----------- --------
buffer busy waits                     1,626          328     45.77
CPU time                                             219     30.61
latch free                              481           73     10.13
enqueue                                 121           52      7.31
free buffer waits                        23           16      2.18
```

In short, this shows we were performing 740 transactions per second (740 single row inserts per second) and our major wait event was a buffer busy wait. There are a couple of things that could cause a buffer busy wait event, but, in this case, it is due to the single freelist. We are doing one thing in this database—inserting five sessions into table T—so table T is the point of contention here.

When we rerun this test using five freelists, we observe this Statspack report:

```
Load Profile
~~~~~~~~~~~~                        Per Second        Per Transaction
                                   ---------------    ---------------
...
                Executes:            1,767.61                    2.01
            Transactions:              880.91
...
Top 5 Timed Events
~~~~~~~~~~~~~~~~~~                                               % Total
Event                                 Waits     Time (s) Ela Time
------------------------------------  ------------ ----------- --------
CPU time                                             258     44.61
latch free                              801          159     27.44
LGWR wait for redo copy              73,195           57      9.90
write complete waits                     38           34      5.82
free buffer waits                        35           23      3.95
```

We increased our transactions-per-second rate from 740 to 880 (for about a 20% increase) and reduced the buffer busy wait events from 1,626 to 11 (we need to look in the details to find that statistic, since it didn't make the top five list). The total time waited went from 328 seconds for the five sessions to 3 seconds. That is a fairly dramatic change. But realize that it represents a best-case scenario. Here, we got lucky—each of the five sessions appears (based on the fantastic results) to have been assigned to its own freelist. In the real world, we would probably not be so fortunate. We would definitely have increased concurrency by adding more freelists, but we would not have removed all waits.

## Multiple Freelist Groups

A *freelist group* is a collection of freelists. You may choose to create a table with two freelist groups of five freelists each. This is typically used in a Real Application Cluster (RAC) or Oracle

Parallel Server (OPS) environment in order to give each instance its own set of freelists to manage, and avoid cross-instance contention.

Freelist groups also can be useful for increasing concurrency in single-instance configurations. The reason for this has to do with the way free space is managed when there are multiple freelists. When a session modifies a block so that the block will be placed onto a freelist, it goes onto a *master freelist* for the segment. As space is needed, the blocks are moved in small amounts from the master freelist onto the individual freelists for the segment, called process freelists. This master freelist itself can be a point of contention if sessions are consuming free blocks at a high rate of speed. Now, if you have multiple freelist groups, you'll spread the points of contention out over many master freelists.

As an analogy, suppose you have a water cooler and a room full of thirsty people. The water cooler represents the single freelist, and the people in the room represent sessions that want to insert into a table. With a single water cooler from which to dispense water (free space), everyone will need to get in line and wait for the people in front of them to get their water. That is, there will be a line, or contention, for this single resource, as illustrated in Figure 4-1.

So, you add more water coolers to the room, say ten of them. Now, people can get in one of ten lines in order to get a drink, so things go much faster. This is analogous to having multiple freelists. But there is still a bottleneck in this system. As the water coolers are used, they run out of water and must be refilled. At this point, you have only one person capable of refilling the water coolers. This single person represents your single freelist group. Now, this one person cannot refill more than one water cooler at a time, so whenever more than one watercooler needs refilling, people need to wait. This is where the multiple freelist groups come into play. You could create the segment with ten freelists in two freelist groups, as illustrated in Figure 4-2. Now, you have two people who can refill any one of their five assigned water coolers. Those thirsty people get their drinks faster than ever before.

One thing to consider with freelist groups, however, is that space usage can be a real concern here. With a single freelist group and multiple freelists, there can be some small amount of wasted space, but with freelist groups, the amount of wasted space may appear to be huge, depending on how the table is used.

Consider a table where one process is continually inserting into the table and another process is continually processing and deleting rows from that same table (sort of like a queue). It is very easy to get into a situation where the table appears to grow and never reuse space. This is because the process that is inserting data may pull blocks from one freelist group, whereas the other process

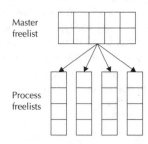

Master
freelist

Process
freelists

**FIGURE 4-1.** *Multiple freelists with one freelist group*

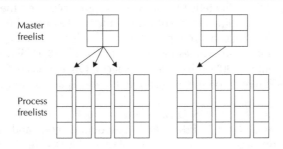

**FIGURE 4-2.**   *Multiple freelist groups*

that is deleting and freeing space places these blocks onto a separate freelist group. Hence, the session freeing space will never make a block available for the session requesting space. This is generally an atypical situation in regular single-instance Oracle, since it can happen with only truly long-running processes that get assigned to separate freelists in different freelist groups. Normally, if the processes come and go, they will tend to balance out over time.

In an environment with multiple Oracle instances, such as you find with OPS or RAC, the amount of wasted space associated with multiple freelist groups can be a problem. If a process inserts into a table on one instance and another instance is responsible for processing the row and deleting it, you may find that table grows without bounds. This is because the freelist groups will be assigned to each instance, and the space freed by instance A will not be usable by instance B. We'll discuss in a moment how ASSM can alleviate this issue in an RAC environment.

## How PCTFREE and PCTUSED Control Freelists

It might be interesting, before reading this section, to run a query and see the results:

```
select pct_free, pct_used, count(*)
  from dba_tables
 group by pct_free, pct_used
/
```

If you are like most people, the vast preponderance of your tables will have the default values. The PCTFREE and PCTUSED settings control when blocks will be put on and taken off the freelists. When used with a table, PCTFREE tells Oracle how much space should be reserved on a block for future updates. By default, this is 10%. That means that if we use an 8KB-block size, as soon as the addition of a new row onto a block causes the free space on the block to drop below about 800 bytes, Oracle would remove that block from the freelist and would use a new block instead. This 10% of the data space on the block is set aside for updates to the rows on that block. If we were to update these rows, the block should still be able to hold the updated row. PCTFREE tells Oracle when to take a block off the freelist, making it no longer a candidate for insertion in a heap organized table. More complex structures such as INDEXES and Index Organized Tables (IOTs) do not use the PCTFREE setting except during their initial creation or rebuild. That is because, in these objects, a row must be placed wherever that row belongs. The discussion of PCTFREE and PCTUSED in this section applies to normal heap-based tables only.

On the other hand, PCTUSED tells Oracle when to put a block on the freelist again. If PCTUSED is set to 40 (the default), and the block hits the PCTFREE level (it is not on the freelist currently), 61% of the block must be free space before Oracle will put the block back on the freelist. If you are using the default values for PCTFREE (10) and PCTUSED (40), a block will remain on the freelist until it is 90% full (10% free space). Once it hits 90%, it will be taken off the freelist, and it will remain off the freelist until the free space on the block exceeds 60% of the block.

Using the wrong setting for PCTUSED can waste space. For example, suppose you fill a table up with the default value of 10 for PCTFREE. You subsequently go in and delete about half the rows in every block during a purge routine. Now, all of the blocks are about 45% to 50% free space. You go to insert data again, and the table only grows. None of the existing free space is used, since the utilization of the existing blocks never falls below the 40 PCTUSED setting. The blocks are about 50% free, but they must become 61% free.

# The Case for ASSM

So, now that we understand freelists, freelist groups, and PCTUSED, we need to determine if we want to manually set them or if we want the database to do it for us.

Take the case of a transactional system, where we cannot tell with 100% certainty how many concurrent modifications of a table or index we might have. We do not know how empty the blocks might become in order to set PCTUSED properly, so space gets reused over time. Here, ASSM is most appropriate. When you use ASSM, the freelist, freelist groups, and PCTUSED settings will receive the tuning they have been missing.

To test this, let's create two tablespaces in Oracle9i Release 2: one with ASSM and one without it.

```
create tablespace auto_tbs datafile
size 64m autoextend on next 8m extent management local autoallocate
segment space management AUTO;

create tablespace manual_tbs datafile
size 64m autoextend on next 8m extent management local autoallocate
segment space management MANUAL;
```

We will set up a table in each as select rownum r, a.* from all_objects a where 1=0. Then we will create ten simultaneous sessions, each inserting into the AUTO table, and let them run for 15 minutes. We will do the same for the MANUAL table. Additionally, let's have some deletions take place as well, to see how space would (or would not) be reused.

The block of code for the test goes into an infinite loop (we'll kill it from another session when we want to stop) and inserts 25 rows at a time, and then inserts a single row and grabs the ROWID. That ROWID will be used in a DELETE every time we have saved up 100 of them. So, we'll insert 2,600 rows, delete 100, insert 2,600, delete 100, and so on. The code looks like this (just substitute MANUAL/AUTO in this code where you see ${type}):

```
declare
    cursor c
    is select rownum r, a.* from all_objects a;
    type c_rec is table of
        ${type}_table%rowtype index by binary_integer;
```

```
    type rowidArray is table of rowid index by binary_integer;
    l_rec   c_rec;
    l_rids  rowidArray;
    l_empty rowidArray;
    n       number      := 25;
begin
    loop
        open c;
        loop
            fetch c bulk collect into l_rec limit N;
            exit when l_rec.count = 0;
            forall i in 1 .. l_rec.count
                insert into ${type}_table values l_rec(i);
            insert into ${type}_table values l_rec(1)
            returning rowid into l_rids(l_rids.count+1);
            commit;
            if ( l_rids.count = 100 )
            then
                forall i in 1 .. l_rids.count
                    delete from ${type}_table
                      where rowid = l_rids(i);
                commit;
                l_rids := l_empty;
            end if;
        end loop;
        close c;
    end loop;
end;
/
```

Before and after running these tests, we take Statspack snapshots. The results are quite revealing:

**AUTO SEGEMENT SPACE MANAGEMENT**
```
Top 5 Timed Events
~~~~~~~~~~~~~~~~~~~                                  % Total
Event                       Waits    Time (s) Ela Time
------------------------ ------------ ----------- --------
enqueue                      4,626      2,541    65.27
db file parallel write         932        721    18.52
db file sequential read        212        201     5.17
```
**buffer busy waits           2,640        112     2.89**
```
latch free                   1,376        102     2.63
```

**MANUAL SPACE MANAGEMENT**
```
Top 5 Timed Events
~~~~~~~~~~~~~~~~~~~                                  % Total
Event                       Waits    Time (s) Ela Time
------------------------ ------------ ----------- --------
enqueue                      4,999      2,496    57.30
```

```
db file parallel write          748       710    16.29
buffer busy waits            20,953       678    15.56
db file sequential read         459       175     4.02
latch free                    1,727       111     2.55
```

The events we are most interested in here are the buffer busy waits. In this heavy insert operation example, these waits are induced by freelist contention. When we use ASSM, this contention is dramatically reduced, and to achieve this performance, we didn't need to fine-tune anything.

In this test case, both objects use the same amount of space. On my system with an 8KB block, each table averaged 67 to 68 rows per block.

Now, we run the same test using ASSM as we did with manual freelist tuning. The results here are as follows:

```
Load Profile
~~~~~~~~~~~~~                        Per Second        Per Transaction
                                  ---------------      ---------------
                    Executes:        1,805.20                    2.00
                 Transactions:         901.43


Top 5 Timed Events
~~~~~~~~~~~~~~~~~~~~~                                          % Total
Event                             Waits    Time (s) Ela Time
--------------------------------- ------------ ----------- --------
CPU time                                          266        40.65
latch free                          921           147        22.41
buffer busy waits                   508           128        19.63
LGWR wait for redo copy          62,846            49         7.56
free buffer waits                    42            22         3.43
```

This rate of 901 transactions per second is a marginal improvement over the rate of about 880 we saw when using multiple freelists. We do have more buffer busy wait events than we did in the prior run, up from 3 seconds to 128 seconds total wait time, but down from 328 seconds.

This test demonstrates that ASSM gives you many of the benefits of a finely tuned system, without requiring you to finely tune it.

# ASSM Wrap-Up

You would never be able to set the perfect number of freelists in the real world, nor would you even be able to get the perfect distribution over those freelists. Trying to find the segment that is in need of additional freelists—another aspect of segment management—is not something that you want to do. These are things you can leave to ASSM.

The performance boost you may observe, due to decreased buffer busy waits, may make ASSM a good choice for your system. You will, however, need to test this. There are cases where the space used by ASSM is significantly more then manual allocations (for example, with bitmap indexes). These space allocation anomalies are rare, but if you hit them, you will notice right away.

# Let Oracle Manage Your Rollback Segments

One of the mysteries of Oracle administration has centered around rollback segments. In the past, the DBA would need to determine things such as:

- How many rollback segments should I have in order to reduce undo segment header contention?

- How many extents should each rollback segment have?

- How big should each extent be?

- How fast do they tend to wrap around—to reuse their space?

**NOTE**
*Undo segment header contention is a function of the number of concurrent transactions in a system. Undo segment header contention arises from the fact that these headers are a point of low-level serialization (like latching a block would be), and if too many transactions are simultaneously using a single rollback segment, you'll have contention for these headers, just as you would have contention for a single freelist in a heavily inserted table.*

Oracle9i removes the need to make these decisions. Now, all you need to do is figure out how long you want to keep undo information. You just need to determine the duration of the longest running query you need to support in our system. Oracle will automatically manage the undo segments (rollback segments) from that point on. This makes it much easier to set up the database.

The database will create undo segments as concurrency increases on your system. In fact, when running the ASSM simulations described in the previous section, I saw this message in my alert logs:

```
Sun Jan 19 10:50:42 2003
Created Undo Segment _SYSSMU11$
Undo Segment 11 Onlined
Sun Jan 19 10:51:09 2003
```

That was Oracle determining I needed another undo segment in order to best support the degree of concurrency that was hitting my system at that point in time. I didn't need to run the test, find out I needed some more rollback segments, correct the situation, and rerun the test. The database did it for me on-the-fly.

All the DBA needs to do is set the UNDO_RETENTION init.ora parameter to the number of seconds undo data should be retained and monitor space usage by the UNDO tablespace itself (to ensure there is sufficient disk space). The remaining administrative details we used to worry about are handled for us.

The interesting thing about using the UNDO tablespace instead of configuring your own rollback segments is that under the covers, the same technology is at work. An UNDO tablespace is nothing more than a tablespace whereby Oracle creates and sizes rollback segments *for you*. They are still rollback segments. They work the same as manually configured rollback segments would work. It is just that Oracle is responsible for making sure there are enough rollback segments and that they are the right size.

# Set UNDO_RETENTION

The UNDO_RETENTION parameter specifies how long Oracle should attempt to retain undo information on disk before reusing it. You do not want your rollback segments to wrap around faster than the time it takes for your longest running query to execute. Otherwise, you will be subject to repeated and frequent ORA-01555 "Snapshot Too Old" errors on your queries.

Along with avoiding the infamous ORA-01555 error, the UNDO_RETENTION setting allows you to retain undo information to support the Flashback Query facility. For example, if you need to allow users to flashback up to three hours, this is the setting you would use.

Now the question might arise, is the undo retention period you set here a mandate or a suggestion? It's a suggestion. If Oracle has sufficient space or Oracle can extend the undo segment to have sufficient space, Oracle will not reuse the undo information until it has expired. On the other hand, Oracle will not fail a transaction just because insufficient space to satisfy the retention period was not available; that is, Oracle will prematurely expire undo information that was generated by committed transactions if it must. We can see this via a simple test.

We'll set up two UNDO tablespaces: UNDO_BIG and UNDO_SMALL. UNDO_BIG will start at 1MB and grow to 2GB. UNDO_SMALL will start at 1MB and remain at that size. We'll process transactions in each of these UNDO tablespaces and note their ending size. We'll use an UNDO_RETENTION setting of 10,800 (three hours).

```
SQL> create undo tablespace
  2  UNDO_BIG datafile
  3  size 1m autoextend on next 1m
  4  maxsize 2048m;
Tablespace created.

SQL> create undo tablespace
  2  UNDO_SMALL datafile
  3  size 1m autoextend off;
Tablespace created.

SQL> show parameter undo_retention

NAME             VALUE
---------------- -----
undo_retention   10800

SQL> alter system
  2  set undo_tablespace = UNDO_BIG
  3  scope = memory;
```

```
System altered.

SQL> drop table t;
Table dropped.

SQL> create table t
  2  ( x char(2000),
  3    y char(2000),
  4    z char(2000)
  5  );
Table created.

SQL> insert into t values('x','x','x');
1 row created.

SQL> begin
  2  for i in 1 .. 500
  3  loop
  4     update t set x=i,y=i,z=i;
  5     commit;
  6  end loop;
  7  end;
  8  /
PL/SQL procedure successfully completed.

SQL> select bytes,maxbytes
  2    from dba_data_files
  3   where tablespace_name = 'UNDO_BIG';

    BYTES   MAXBYTES
---------- ----------
  5242880 2147483648
```

This shows that we generated about 5MB of undo data. We know that because the UNDO_BIG tablespace, created with an initial size of 1MB, now has 5MB. Oracle enlarged it in order to retain our undo data for the three-hour suggested timeframe. We also know that the datafile could have extended to 2GB, but did not; therefore, 5MB is the amount of undo storage it required.

Now, we'll use a small UNDO tablespace and try again:

```
SQL> alter system
  2  set undo_tablespace = UNDO_SMALL
  3  scope = memory;
System altered.

SQL> show parameter undo_t

NAME                 VALUE
```

```
------------------  ----------
undo_tablespace     UNDO_SMALL
```

Say that we ran the same DROP TABLE, CREATE TABLE, and INSERT INTO TABLE commands that we did with the big UNDO tablespace, and updated it 500 times. This time, we see this:

```
SQL> select bytes,maxbytes
  2    from dba_data_files
  3    where tablespace_name = 'UNDO_SMALL';

    BYTES    MAXBYTES
---------- ----------
   1048576           0
```

Oracle did not expand our datafile (it was not allowed to), but yet it did not fail our transactions either. Instead, it prematurely expired undo information that was not needed to actually roll back with anymore. This may lead to the dreaded ORA-01555 and would be an indication that your UNDO tablespace is just too small for the work you do.

You can use the UNXPBLKREUCNT column of V$UNDOSTAT (a dynamic performance view) to see how many unexpired blocks where cycled out of the UNDO tablespace prematurely. In this case, that view shows that 413 blocks had been cycled out for the UNDO_SMALL tablespace test (a total of 3.3MB on my system).

**WARNING**
*If you create your UNDO tablespace without a MAXSIZE setting and set your undo retention period to a very large number, you will find that your UNDO tablespace will grow accordingly. Use MAXSIZE on the DATAFILE clause when using UNDO tablespaces to preclude them from growing larger than your system can support.*

## An UNDO Tablespace Caveat

UNDO tablespaces are very limiting as to what you may specify for physical storage allocation. You are limited to the following:

- You can specify the ultimate size of the UNDO tablespace by limiting the maximum size of the datafiles or disabling the autoextend attribute of the datafiles.

- You can specify the name of the datafile(s) used in support of the UNDO tablespace.

UNDO tablespaces use locally managed extents exclusively (that is a good thing). However, they use system-managed extent allocation only.

You may not specify a uniform size for the extents. The sizing and managing of the space in the UNDO tablespace is totally outside your control. You cannot force a big rollback segment in an UNDO tablespace to shrink. You cannot control when extents will be allocated for UNDO tablespaces.

For example, the current UNDO tablespace segment extend algorithm will enlarge a rollback segment before trying to reuse expired extents of other segments. If you use an UNDO tablespace with autoextensible datafiles, the tablespace may continue to grow, even when it technically does not need to grow. For this reason, using autoextend datafiles with UNDO tablespaces in a production environment is not recommended.

Currently, it is not possible to realistically shrink an UNDO tablespace that has grown large in response to a one-time, large transaction. Since UNDO *must* be backed up, this will affect the size of all future backups as well. If it were truly a one-time large operation, then the amount of UNDO allocated on disk would be artificially large. In this case, the easiest solution is

- Create a new UNDO tablespace, for example "create undo tablespace undo_new datafile size <n>".

- Start using this UNDO tablespace, for example "alter system set undo_tablespace=undo_ new scope=both".

- Drop the old UNDO tablespace. You may well encounter the message "ORA-30013: undo tablespace is currently in use." That just means there is a transaction still in need of this UNDO tablespace (still actively using it). In this case, you must wait some period of time before performing the drop.

As this operation could be impeded by concurrent transactions (preventing you from dropping the large UNDO tablespace) and could lead to ORA-1555 errors for long-running queries, it would be advisable to perform this sort of maintenance during a period of low activity in the database.

## UNDO Tablespace Wrap-Up

For operational simplicity, and for the needs of most systems, the UNDO tablespace cannot be beat. However, for some systems—high-end, high-throughput systems—the manual sizing you can achieve with rollback segments may be beneficial. It might be telling that when Oracle developers run a TPC-C benchmark (mixed workload, emphasis on OLTP), they use 1,000 hand-configured rollback segments. When they run a TPC-H (data warehouse benchmark), they use an UNDO tablespace.

Determining the proper number of rollback segments, as well as sizing them properly, is something that can typically be done on only the most predictable systems, such as transaction-oriented systems. Most implementations will not materially benefit from the fine-tuning of rollback segments and should generally use the UNDO tablespace. It will be the exception, not the rule, that uses rollback segments manually. Since you can easily move back and forth between the two styles of undo management (albeit with a database restart), it is a decision that is easy to make and unmake.

# Summary

Over the many years that I've used Oracle, I've seen it become easier to manage. The mundane tasks that consumed much of our time are becoming things of the past. For example, "defragmenting" our fragmented tablespaces could have been a large part of a DBA's job. Today with locally managed tablespaces and uniform extent sizes, fragmentation of a tablespace is a thing of the past. It used to be that the DBA had to figure out "how many rollback segments do I need?"

and "how large should each one be to avoid ORA-1555 snapshot-too-old errors?" Now, using UNDO tablespaces, they need to decide only "how long should undo be retained?"

One point I would like to drive home is that all DBAs need to read and reread the "Bulletproof Your Backups" section of this chapter. It is 100% true that you can make every other mistake known to man in your day-to-day work, but if you mess up the backup and recovery of the database, that will be the unforgivable sin. Make my data slow; we can fix that. Make my data disappear; we have nothing. The one thing a DBA cannot get wrong is backup and recovery. Become expert in that, and you'll have some level of job security for a long time to come. Information assurance—a large part of which is data protection—relies on that.

Lastly, I would like to point out that there exists a vast network of resources to bounce ideas off of and get advice from. This book, for example, is just one data point and there are thousands of discussion forums, written pieces of documentation, white papers, examples and so on. Two of my favorites are

- **http://groups.google.com/** Free access to the usenet discussion forums. Here you will find the groups comp.databases.oracle.*. Ask a question there and you might get an answer from halfway around the world in minutes. You might even find yourself answering some questions after a while (I know I did starting in about 1994).

- **http://otn.oracle.com/** The Oracle Technology Network, also known as "technet" discussion forums, white papers, documentation, software, utilities, examples, and much more.

Remember from Chapter 1, nothing is ever black and white—absolutes are rare. Keep in mind, not every feature is useful in every circumstance. Understanding how they work and where they are appropriate is as important as knowing they exist.

# CHAPTER
## 5

# Statement Processing

t is crucial to have a good understanding of exactly what happens when you submit a SQL statement to Oracle. With this knowledge, you'll have a deeper appreciation of why you want to use bind variables, why you sometimes might not want to use bind variables, and why your goal is to parse a statement once per session, not once per execution per session.

In this chapter, we'll investigate the complex actions that take place in order to execute a simple statement such as SELECT * FROM EMP or a more complex UPDATE statement. We'll see what database processes are involved, what memory structures are used, and the general process Oracle goes through to execute each and every statement you submit. Then we'll cover how to avoid bad practices by using bind variables correctly. Finally, we'll look at how to reduce parsing to achieve the best performance.

# Understand the Types of SQL Statements

Before we begin to look at how statements are executed, we'll discuss the types of statements that Oracle processes. Technically speaking, there are only two types of statements:

- **DDL (Data Definition Language)**   Statements you execute in order to modify the Oracle data dictionary. These are the statements that create tables, add users, drop columns from tables, create triggers, and so on.

- **DML (Data Manipulation Language)**   Statements you execute in order to access and or modify data in the database. These include SELECT, INSERT, MERGE, UPDATE, and DELETE commands.

Conceptually, we can add another type of SQL statement to this list: *queries*, which are just a special case of DML statements. So, the three types of statements could loosely be considered to be DDL to create objects, DML to modify data, and queries (SELECT statements) to retrieve data.

These three classifications of statements are very dependent on each other. For example, DDL performs many DML operations under the covers in order to do its job; a single DDL statement may perform hundreds of queries and modification statements. Similarly, a modification statement such as UPDATE performs a query (to find the data to update), and then a modification (to actually change the data).

In this chapter, we'll look at DDL (with separate sections on queries and modification statements) and DML processing in detail to discover how they each work. But first, we'll review the general steps involved in statement processing.

# How Are Statements Executed?

Oracle may go through four steps to execute statements from start to finish:

- **Parsing**   Perform a syntax and semantic check on the submitted statement to validate it.

- **Optimization**   Generate an optimal plan that can be used to execute the statement in the database.

- **Row-source generation**   Take the optimized plan and set up an execution plan, a tree to be executed, for your session.

- **Statement execution**   Execute the output of the row-source generation step to actually perform the query. In the case of DDL or modification DML statements, this step is the end. For a query statement, this step is the beginning of the fetch phase, whereby the client application may retrieve data.

Some of these steps may be omitted at runtime. For example, the optimization of a SQL statement is omitted the vast majority of times. This step can be skipped because Oracle saves the results of query optimizations in an area of memory called the *shared pool*. When Oracle detects that you are trying to run a statement that someone else already ran, and it can find that statement in this shared pool, it will skip the expensive process of query optimization, which greatly increases the efficiency of the system overall. We'll explore the benefits of this "shared SQL" in the "Use Bind Variables" section later in this chapter.

Even the parsing phase of statement execution may be omitted in a well-designed application that reuses statements. We'll explore the benefits of this in the "Parse as Little as Possible" section later in this chapter.

# Parsing

*Parsing* is generally the first step in statement execution. It is the act of breaking down the query into its component parts, separating the pieces of the statement in a data structure that can be processed by other routines. Oracle will determine the class of SQL statement (DDL or DML) and proceed based on that information. DDL statements do not go through the same set of steps as do DML statements. For example, DDL is never cached in Oracle's shared pool; hence, the shared pool check described here does not apply to it.

The parsing process starts with two steps:

- **Syntactical analysis**   Is the query valid SQL?

- **Semantic analysis**   Given that the query is valid SQL (follows all of the rules for well-formed SQL), does it make sense? Is it accessing objects you have access to? Are the columns you are selecting in the table you are accessing? Are there ambiguities that need to be resolved? For example, if you issue SELECT DEPTNO FROM DEPT, EMP, which DEPTNO column are you referring to: the one in EMP or the one in DEPT?

And then for DML statements, there is a third step:

- **Shared pool check**   Was this statement already parsed by some other user and can Oracle reuse the work that was already performed? If so, Oracle performs what is generally known as a *soft parse*. It is able to skip much of the arduous work of fully processing a statement to the point where we are ready to execute it. If not, Oracle performs what is known as a *hard parse*. All steps will be executed from start to end. DDL is always hard parsed and never reused.

### Syntax and Semantic Checks

Syntax and semantic checks perform different functions, but it is hard to see the difference between them. In short, a statement that breaks a rule for well-formed SQL will fail the syntax check, as in this example:

```
ops$tkyte@ORA920> select * form dual;
select * form dual
             *
ERROR at line 1:
ORA-00923: FROM keyword not found where expected
```

This is an example of a syntax error I make about 100 times a day—I inverted the *O* and *R* in *FROM*. The SQL parsing engine rejected this query for syntax reasons.

On the other hand, this query is rejected for semantic reasons:

```
ops$tkyte@ORA920> select x from dual;
select x from dual
         *
ERROR at line 1:
ORA-00904: "X": invalid identifier
```

The query is valid SQL according to the *SQL Reference Manual*. However, column X does not actually exist in the DUAL table. So, this is a semantic error, not a syntax error.

In the end, the difference between the two is not generally relevant to us. If the query failed due to a syntax error, we must correct the typo we have in the query. If the query failed due to a semantic error, we must figure out the real column name or get access to some object. Either way, the statement failed the parse, and we must fix it.

If the statement is found to be a DDL statement at this point, Oracle will go to the next phases of statement execution and develop a "plan" to execute the DDL (see the "DDL Processing" section later in this chapter). If the statement is found to be a DML statement, Oracle will now perform a shared pool check to see if it can reuse a previously optimized statement.

### Shared Pool Check

The shared pool concept is a key component of Oracle's architecture. The shared pool is a chunk of memory in Oracle's shared global area (SGA), where previously executed SQL statements, PL/SQL code, dictionary cache information, and many other items are cached for reuse by any and all sessions in the database. Proper use of the shared pool is crucial for building scalable solutions in Oracle. If you abuse the shared pool, you may find your application performs *very* poorly. When you make efficient use of the shared pool, you may find your application scales incredibly well.

Technically, Oracle has two parse classes:

■ **Hard parse** The statement goes through each and every step in the statement-execution phase: from parsing, to optimization, to row-source generation, to execution.

■ **Soft parse** The statement goes through some, but not all, of the steps. In particular, the optimization step (the most expensive step) is skipped. As you will see in the "Use Bind Variables" section later in this chapter, soft parsing greatly increases scalability.

A third type of parse I add to this list is a *softer soft parse*. We achieve a softer soft parse by using the SESSION_CACHED_CURSORS init.ora setting (added in Oracle8i). Here, a soft parse is made even more efficient under the covers, without modifying the behavior or code of an application. We'll explore the benefits of this in the "The Cost of Parsing" section later in this chapter.

There are two steps Oracle undertakes in order to perform a soft parse. First, Oracle must verify that we have a semantic match—that the statement we submitted to the database for processing is, in fact, the same as an already parsed statement. Second, it will perform an environment match—making sure the environment under which the statement is to be executed is the same. For example, if you submit a query using the OPTIMIZER_GOAL init.ora setting set to RULE, and someone else submitted the query with the OPTIMIZER_GOAL set to FIRST_ROWS, those two environments are incompatible; thus, the query plans cannot be shared, and you would have a hard parse.

In order to begin this process, Oracle must look for the statement in the shared pool. To accomplish this efficiently, Oracle will *hash* the SQL statement. *Hashing* is a mathematical technique whereby an infinite set of values (such as the set of all possible SQL queries in this case) is processed through a function that returns a number in a certain range of values. In short, hashing takes an infinite set of values and maps them to a finite set of values. Hashing is a common technique to perform fast lookups.

Once the hash has been generated, Oracle will search the shared pool for all statements that have the same hash value. It will then compare the SQL_TEXT it finds to the SQL you submitted to make sure that the text in the shared pool is exactly the same. This comparison step is important, since one of the properties of a hash function is that two different strings can hash to the same number.

People perform an analogous hashing process all of the time. For example, your kitchen probably has many drawers. You keep knives in one drawer, silverware in another, junk in a third, and so on. When you want a fork, you don't need to consider the other drawers, because you know that fork must be in the silverware drawer. You've hashed your kitchen items into bins so you can easily and effectively retrieve them. You still might need to sort through the spoons and butter knives to find a fork, but you can skip the other drawers.

Once a statement is found, Oracle will perform the semantic and environment checks. We'll take a look at each process in the following sections.

**Checking for a Semantic Match**     Oracle must verify that the statement you submit to the database, when matched to an existing SQL statement, is the *same* statement. But why is this necessary? If the statements are the same, they are a match, right? Well, this might not be true. Consider this simple SQL query:

```
SQL> select * from emp;
```

If user A were to submit that statement and user A owned a table named EMP, the optimized query plan would be one that referenced that user's table A. Now, user B submits that same statement, but user B also has a table EMP in her schema. Now, there must be a new plan generated, one that accesses B.EMP rather than A.EMP (it would be a bug otherwise). So, then we have two query plans generated. Later, user C submits the same query to the database. User C does not have a table named EMP, but there is a PUBLIC SYNONYM EMP that points to D.EMP, and user C has access to that object. This will result in yet a third query plan being generated. Now, there are three SELECT * FROM EMP statements in the shared pool. They all look the same—syntactically, they are identical—but they differ greatly in their semantic meanings. This is the crux of the semantic match: Not only must the queries appear to be the same, they also *must mean the same exact thing.*

If we follow through on the logical progression with users A, B, and C and add a SELECT * FROM EMP performed by user D, we will still end up with three copies of the SQL statement in the shared pool. Even though user D's query was against the D.EMP table directly and user C's query was against the public synonym EMP that pointed to D.EMP, Oracle is smart enough to know they are the same. We can prove that with a small test case.

We simply set up the four users A, B, C, and D. We grant CREATE SESSION and CREATE TABLE privileges to users A, B, and D, and grant just CREATE SESSION to C. Then we run the following script:

```
create public synonym emp for d.emp;
alter system flush shared_pool;

connect a/a
create table emp ( x int );
select * from emp;

connect b/b
create table emp ( x int );
select * from emp;

connect d/d
create table emp ( x int );
grant select on emp to c;
select * from emp;

connect c/c
select * from emp;
```

Now, let's take a quick peek at V$SQL, which shows all of the currently cached SQL statements.

```
ops$tkyte@ORA920> select address, executions, sql_text
  2      from v$sql
  3      where upper(sql_text) like 'SELECT * FROM EMP%';

ADDRESS    EXECUTIONS  SQL_TEXT
--------   ----------  ------------------------------
58DBD9CC            1  select * from emp
58DBD9CC            1  select * from emp
58DBD9CC            2  select * from emp
```

We can see that there are three versions of the query in the shared pool and that one of the versions was used two times—that is the query submitted by users C and D.

We can also query V$SQL_SHARED_CURSOR to determine exactly *why* Oracle developed three query plans, to discover the root cause for the mismatch here. This view has many columns that can be used to determine why a plan in the shared pool was not shared. For example, the ROW_LEVEL_SEC_MISMATCH column would be flagged for two queries that appear to be the same but differed at runtime based on the security predicate returned by Oracle's Virtual Private Database (VPD) feature. The OUTLINE_MISMATCH column would be flagged if one query used a query outline and the other did not. Other columns in this view provide similar mismatch information. In this example, we can see this information regarding our queries:

```
ops$tkyte@ORA920> select kglhdpar, address,
  2              auth_check_mismatch, translation_mismatch
  3    from v$sql_shared_cursor
  4   where kglhdpar in
  5   ( select address
  6       from v$sql
  7      where upper(sql_text) like 'SELECT * FROM EMP%' )
  8  /

KGLHDPAR ADDRESS   AUTH_CHECK_MISMATCH TRANSLATION_MISMATCH
-------- --------  ------------------- --------------------
58DBD9CC 59D4C9C8 N                    N
58DBD9CC 59E54EB0 Y                    Y
58DBD9CC 5898D42C Y                    Y
```

In this case, Oracle flagged two columns: AUTH_CHECK_MISMATCH, meaning the authorization/translation check failed for the existing cursor (query plan), and TRANSLATION_MISMATCH, meaning the base objects of the child cursor (query plan) do not match. This shows us exactly why there are three queries plans (child cursors): The base objects referenced were different.

Now that we understand the semantic match checking that takes place, let's look at environment matching.

**Checking for an Environment Match**    The environment is considered to be all of the session settings that can affect query plan generation, such as the WORKAREA_SIZE_POLICY or OPTIMIZER_MODE settings. The WORKAREA_SIZE_POLICY setting, for example, tells Oracle how it is to manage memory for operations such as a sort. The query plan for automatic work area sizing may be different from the query plan generated using a fixed sort area size of 64KB.

For example, let's consider a very simple SELECT COUNT(*) query against some table. We'll execute this exact query two times using different optimizer environments: one with WORKAREA_SIZE_POLICY = AUTO and the other with it set to MANUAL.

```
big_table@ORA920> show parameter workarea_size_policy;

NAME                    TYPE     VALUE
----------------------- -------  ------
workarea_size_policy    string   AUTO

big_table@ORA920> alter system flush shared_pool;
System altered.

big_table@ORA920> select count(*) from big_table;
  COUNT(*)
----------
```

```
    1833792

big_table@ORA920> alter session set workarea_size_policy = manual;
Session altered.

big_table@ORA920> select count(*) from big_table;
  COUNT(*)
----------
    1833792

big_table@ORA920> select sql_text, child_number, hash_value, address
  2    from v$sql
  3   where upper(sql_text) = 'SELECT COUNT(*) FROM BIG_TABLE'
  4  /

SQL_TEXT                                  CHILD_NUMBER HASH_VALUE ADDRESS
---------------------------------------- ------------ ---------- --------
select count(*) from big_table                      0 4059798264 58EF6C48
select count(*) from big_table                      1 4059798264 58EF6C48
```

This shows there are currently two versions of that query in the shared pool, due to the changes in some optimizer-related parameter in this case. We can verify this by looking at the dynamic performance view V$SQL_SHARED_CURSOR, as we did in the previous example.

```
big_table@ORA920> select optimizer_mismatch
  2    from v$sql_shared_cursor
  3   where kglhdpar in
  4   ( select address
  5       from v$sql
  6      where upper(sql_text) = 'SELECT COUNT(*) FROM BIG_TABLE' );

OPTIMIZER_MISMATCH
------------------
N
Y
```

Here, the column OPTIMIZER_MISMATCH is flagged with a Y for the child cursor, showing us there was some difference between the optimizer environments for the two queries.

Finally, at this point, when Oracle has finished all of this work and found a match, it can return from the parse process and report that a soft parse has been done. The queries (cursors, really, at this point) are addressable by their ADDRESS, a RAW column in the data dictionary that is actually a pointer value into Oracle's SGA.

**Parsing Wrap-Up**    To summarize where we are at this point in the parsing process, Oracle has taken the following steps:

■ Parsed (tokenized) the query

■ Checked the syntax

- Verified the semantics
- Computed the hash value

Additionally, Oracle may also have done this:

- Found a match
- Verified there is a query exactly the same as ours (it references the same objects)
- Validated that we have the necessary privileges to access all of the referenced objects
- Verified the statements were executed in the same environment

If Oracle found a match and succeeded in validating it, the next step in statement execution is skipped, to our great advantage. Otherwise, the next step in the process will be statement optimization and row-source generation.

# Optimization and Row-Source Generation

All DML statements are optimized at least once in their lives, when they are first submitted to Oracle. That takes place during a hard parse. Subsequent executions of that same statement that are found to be exactly the same syntactically and semantically, and that were executed in the same environment, may reuse the work of a prior hard parse. They would be soft parsed in that case.

The hard parse includes the step of query optimization. This is an arduous, CPU-intensive process that may take longer to perform than the actual statement execution! We can see how this works using TKPROF in an example. Consider this block of code:

```
drop table t;
create table t ( x int );
alter session set sql_trace=true;
begin
    for i in 1 .. 1000
    loop
        execute immediate 'insert into t values ( ' || i || ')';
    end loop;
end;
/
```

TKPROF will show that we spent three times as much CPU power on parsing the statement as we spent actually executing it!

```
OVERALL TOTALS FOR ALL RECURSIVE STATEMENTS

call      count       cpu    elapsed  disk     query   current      rows
-------  ------  --------  ---------- -----  -------- ----------  --------
Parse      1001      0.91        0.92     0         0          0         0
Execute    1001      0.31        0.39     0      1001       3040      1000
Fetch         1      0.00        0.00     0         1          0         0
-------  ------  --------  ---------- -----  -------- ----------  --------
total      2003      1.22        1.31     0      1002       3040      1000

Misses in library cache during parse: 1000
```

On the other hand, suppose that we use a bind variable by running this EXECUTE IMMEDIATE statement instead.

```
execute immediate 'insert into t values ( :x )' using i;
```

TKPROF would show that we spent about one-sixth of our total runtime parsing:

OVERALL TOTALS FOR ALL RECURSIVE STATEMENTS

| call | count | cpu | elapsed | disk | query | current | rows |
|---|---|---|---|---|---|---|---|
| Parse | 1001 | 0.05 | 0.04 | 0 | 0 | 0 | 0 |
| Execute | 1001 | 0.32 | 0.37 | 0 | 1001 | 3038 | 1000 |
| Fetch | 1 | 0.00 | 0.00 | 0 | 1 | 0 | 0 |
| total | 2003 | 0.37 | 0.42 | 0 | 1002 | 3038 | 1000 |

Misses in library cache during parse: 1

In addition to consuming CPU cycles, the act of hard parsing incurs high latch rates on the shared pool (a shared data structure that must be protected from concurrent modifications). As you'll see later in this chapter in the "Use Bind Variables" section, we want to skip this step as often as possible.

The job of query optimization is to find the best possible plan by which to execute your DML statements. Oracle currently supports two optimizer modes:

- **Rule-based optimizer (RBO)** With this optimizer, the query plan is developed based on a well-known set of rules. The size of objects, cardinality of columns, distribution of data, sizes of sort areas, and other elements are never considered when using the RBO. Only the codified rules are available for query optimization. This optimization technique should be considered obsolete.

- **Cost-based optimizer (CBO)** With this optimizer, queries are optimized based on statistics collected about the actual data being accessed. It will use the number of rows, the size of the data set, and many other pieces of information when deciding on the optimum plan. The CBO will generate many (perhaps thousands) of possible query plans—alternate approaches to solving your query—and assign a numeric cost to each query plan. The query plan with the lowest cost is the one that will be used.

These days, all applications should use the CBO. The RBO, used with Oracle since the very first releases, is considered the legacy approach to query optimization, and many new features are simply not available with it. In fact, Oracle Corporation is officially removing support for the RBO in the release of Oracle after Oracle9i Release 2. We'll discuss the optimizers in more detail in Chapter 6.

After optimization comes the row-source generator. The row-source generator is the piece of software within Oracle that receives the output from the optimizer and formats it into the actual execution plan. For example, when you use the AUTOTRACE facility within SQL*Plus, it prints a query plan. That tree-structured plan is the output of the row-source generator. The optimizer develops the plan, and the row-source generator turns it into a data structure that the rest of the Oracle system can use.

# Execution

The last step in statement execution takes the output of the row-source generator and actually executes the statement. It is the only mandatory step in the execution of DML. We can skip the parse, optimize, and row-source generation steps, and just execute the statement over and over. Because this is by far the most efficient method, you want to develop applications to use the rule "parse once, execute many" whenever possible. It significantly reduces the amount of CPU processing and latching performed by the system.

Recall the small example we used in the previous section:

```
execute immediate 'insert into t values ( :x )' using i;
```

What happens if we replace that with some static SQL?

```
insert into t values ( i );
```

TKPROF will now show us that we spent *no measurable amount of time parsing* and achieved the same goal!

OVERALL TOTALS FOR ALL RECURSIVE STATEMENTS

| call | count | cpu | elapsed | disk | query | current | rows |
|---|---|---|---|---|---|---|---|
| Parse | 13 | 0.00 | 0.00 | 0 | 0 | 0 | 0 |
| Execute | 1014 | 0.33 | 0.38 | 0 | 8 | 1060 | 1007 |
| Fetch | 8 | 0.00 | 0.00 | 0 | 14 | 0 | 1 |
| total | 1035 | 0.33 | 0.38 | 0 | 22 | 1060 | 1008 |

Misses in library cache during parse: 1

We can go one step further with this example and skip some of the executions. Well, we don't really skip them, but we do "bulk" them. Using bulk operations, we can execute a statement *N* times in a single execution. For example, this block of PL/SQL code accomplishes the same goal of inserting 1,000 rows:

```
declare
    l_data    dbms_sql.number_table;
    l_empty   dbms_sql.number_table;
begin
    for i in 1 .. 1000
    loop
        l_data(mod(i,100)) := i;
        if ( mod(i,100) = 0 )
        then
            forall j in 0 .. l_data.count-1
```

```
            insert into t values ( l_data(j) );
        l_data := l_empty;
    end if;
  end loop;
end;
/
```

TKPROF shows these results:

OVERALL TOTALS FOR ALL RECURSIVE STATEMENTS

| call | count | cpu | elapsed | disk | query | current | rows |
|------|-------|-----|---------|------|-------|---------|------|
| Parse | 13 | 0.00 | 0.00 | 0 | 0 | 0 | 0 |
| Execute | 24 | 0.01 | 0.01 | 0 | 8 | 60 | 1007 |
| Fetch | 8 | 0.00 | 0.00 | 0 | 14 | 0 | 1 |
| total | 45 | 0.01 | 0.02 | 0 | 22 | 60 | 1008 |

Misses in library cache during parse: 1

This shows that we can reduce our CPU times considerably. In the "Use PL/SQL to Reduce Parses" section later in this chapter, you'll see how this not only affected our CPU utilization, but our latching as well.

## Statement Execution Wrap-Up

In this section on statement execution, we covered the four stages that statements you submit to Oracle will undergo in order to be processed. Figure 5-1 illustrates the statement-processing steps.

When a SQL statement is submitted to Oracle, the parser will determine if it needs to be hard parsed or soft parsed. If the statement is soft parsed, Oracle can go straight to the SQL execution step and get our output. If the statement must be hard parsed, Oracle sends it to the optimizer.

Oracle will use either the RBO or the CBO to process the query. Once the optimizer has generated what it believes to be the optimal plan, it will forward the plan onto the row-source generator.

The row-source generator will convert the optimizer output into a format the rest of the Oracle system can process, namely an iterative plan that can be stored in the shared pool and executed. This plan is then used by the SQL engine to process the query and generate the answer (that is, the output).

# Queries from Start to Finish

In this section, we'll look at two queries to observe some of the ways in which Oracle accomplishes the processing of a query. These two queries are both very simple, but they are handled differently:

- One query can start returning rows long before it ever gets near the last row.

- The other query must wait until many (or all) rows have been processed before returning a single record.

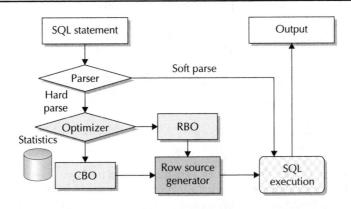

**FIGURE 5-1.** *Statement-processing steps*

Both queries use BIG_TABLE, a table in which we have well over a million rows. We'll query it twice—once without an ORDER BY and again with an ORDER BY—and compare the results.

"How many rows of data will come back from my query?"

In general, Oracle doesn't know until you actually fetch the last row of data how many rows will be returned. Oracle can guess (the AUTOTRACE facility shows us that guess), but it is nothing more than that.

# A Quick-Return Query

In this case, we will submit a rather simple block of PL/SQL code. It simply declares a cursor, opens it, fetches the first row, and closes that cursor.

```
alter session set sql_trace=true;
declare
    cursor c is select * from big_table;
    l_rec  big_table%rowtype;
begin
    open c;
    fetch c into l_rec;
    close c;
end;
/
```

Reviewing the TKPROF report from that execution, we would see something similar to this:

```
SELECT * from big_table
```

```
call       count      cpu    elapsed  disk       query   current    rows
-------    ------  --------  ---------- -----  ----------  ---------- ------
Parse          1    0.00      0.00     0           0          0         0
Execute        1    0.00      0.00     0         196          4         0
Fetch          1    0.00      0.10     4           4          0         1
-------    ------  --------  ---------- -----  ----------  ---------- ------
total          3    0.00      0.11     4         200          4         1

Rows     Row Source Operation
-------  ------------------------------------------------------------
      1  TABLE ACCESS FULL BIG_TABLE
```

As you can see, we got our first row back very quickly and performed very little I/O in doing so. It should be obvious from the report that Oracle doesn't know yet how many rows we might be returning, as it could not have possibly looked at all of them. Here, Oracle is getting the data in response to our fetch calls; the more rows we read, the more work it does. We can see that by fetching more than just the first row.

Let's use a modified block that executes five separate queries but fetches 1,000, 2,000, 3,000, 4,000, and then 5,000 rows.

```
declare
    c sys_refcursor;
    type array is table of  big_table%rowtype index by binary_integer;
    l_rec array;
begin
    for i in 1 .. 5
    loop
        open c for select * from big_table;
        fetch c bulk collect into l_rec limit i*1000;
        close c;
    end loop;
end;
/
```

TKPROF shows us the amount of work performed by each fetch (note that I used aggregate=NO on the TKPROF command line to get the separate FETCH results):

```
call       count      cpu    elapsed  disk   query current      rows
-------    ------  --------  ---------- -----  ------- -------  ----------
Fetch          1    0.01      0.01     1        14       0        1000
Fetch          1    0.03      0.03    15        25       0        2000
Fetch          1    0.05      0.06    24        35       0        3000
Fetch          1    0.06      0.06    41        47       0        4000
Fetch          1    0.08      0.08    47        58       0        5000
```

**NOTE**
*The use of the ref cursor was intentional in this example. My goal was
to see the amount of work performed by five separate queries. If I had
used standard static SQL in PL/SQL, PL/SQL would have cached my
cursor for me, making it impossible for TKPROF to separate the
statistics. Using this technique, I was able to use AGGREGATE = NO
on the TKPROF command line in order to have TKPROF give me five
sets of statistics.*

So, the more data we asked for, the more work Oracle does. Unless, and until, we ask Oracle
for the "last row" in our query, Oracle has no idea how many rows will be returned.

## A Slow-Return Query

Next, we'll execute a query with an ORDER BY in it. We'll simply add ORDER BY OWNER to
the original example:

```
declare
    c sys_refcursor;
    type array is table of  big_table%rowtype index by binary_integer;
    l_rec array;
begin
    for i in 1 .. 5
    loop
        open c for select * from big_table ORDER BY OWNER;
        fetch c bulk collect into l_rec limit i*1000;
        close c;
    end loop;
end;
```

TKPROF now shows us the following:

```
SELECT * from big_table order by owner
```

| call | count | cpu | elapsed | disk | query | current | rows |
|------|-------|------|---------|------|-------|---------|------|
| Fetch | 1 | 12.51 | 29.40 | 21858 | 22004 | 42 | 1000 |
| Fetch | 1 | 12.40 | 25.95 | 21851 | 22002 | 42 | 2000 |
| Fetch | 1 | 12.32 | 25.32 | 21859 | 22002 | 42 | 3000 |
| Fetch | 1 | 12.34 | 23.23 | 21866 | 22002 | 42 | 4000 |
| Fetch | 1 | 12.40 | 25.57 | 21859 | 22002 | 42 | 5000 |

This is very different from the other query. Here, Oracle read the entire table, sorted it, and
then gave us the first rows back. We waited over 25 seconds to see that single, first row, as
opposed to the instantaneous response we got with the previous version. The amount of work,
(CPU time and query mode block gets) performed by this query was more or less constant even
as the number of rows retrieved increased. This is as opposed to the prior example where the
amount of CPU time and query mode gets increased as the amount of data fetched increased.
This second case is an example of a query where Oracle answered the entire question, and then
started returning the results, rather than just returning results. There are many cases where this

will be true. For example, with aggregation, Oracle often answers the entire question and then returns the results. However, if Oracle can use an index to efficiently perform the aggregation without sorting, for example, you may find you can get the first row before Oracle generates the entire result set.

In this particular case, I did have an index on the OWNER column in the database. So, you might wonder why Oracle didn't use that index. In this case, it is because Oracle had no idea we were interested in *only* the first rows; we didn't tell Oracle that fact. We could let Oracle in on that particular detail, using a session setting or a hint in the query (see Chapter 6 for details on hints and when hinting might be an appropriate development technique).

```
declare
    cursor c is select /*+ FIRST_ROWS(1) */ * from big_table order by owner;
    l_rec  big_table%rowtype;
begin
    open c;
    fetch c into l_rec;
    close c;
end;
/
```

TKPROF now shows this report:

```
SELECT /*+ FIRST_ROWS */ * from big_table order by owner

call     count      cpu     elapsed  disk query     current   rows
-------  ------  --------  ----------  ----- -----  ----------  -----
Parse        1     0.00        0.00      0     0           0       0
Execute      1     0.00        0.00      0     0           0       0
Fetch        1     0.00        0.00      0     4           0       1
-------  ------  --------  ----------  ----- -----  ----------  -----
total        3     0.00        0.00      0     4           0       1

Rows     Row Source Operation
-------  -----------------------------------------------------
      1    TABLE ACCESS BY INDEX ROWID BIG_TABLE
      1     INDEX FULL SCAN BIG_TABLE_IDX
```

You can see we are back to the case where Oracle did not process the entire result set. However, before you got into the mindset that Oracle should have used the index, you would need to investigate what would happen in the case where you fetched *all* of the rows from the result set (a sensible assumption; you would typically fetch all of the data, not just a first row). When we do that, running both queries and exhausting their result sets, we discover this:

```
SELECT /*+ FIRST_ROWS(1) */ * from big_table order by owner

call     count      cpu     elapsed    disk    query current       rows
-------  ------  ------  ----------  -------  ---------- -------  --------
Parse        1    0.00        0.00        0           0       0         0
Execute      1    0.00        0.00        0           0       0         0
```

```
Fetch  1833793  80.41  101.78  44386  3667790      0  1833792
------ -------  ------ -------- ------- ---------- ------- --------
total  1833795  80.41  101.78  44386  3667790      0  1833792
```

```
Rows      Row Source Operation
-------   -------------------------------------------------
1833792   TABLE ACCESS BY INDEX ROWID BIG_TABLE
1833792     INDEX FULL SCAN BIG_TABLE_IDX
```

**SELECT * from big_table order by owner**

```
call    count    cpu elapsed   disk  query current    rows
------- ------  ------ ------- ------- ------- ------- --------
Parse       1   0.00   0.00       0       0       0       0
Execute     1   0.00   0.00       0     196       4       0
Fetch 1833793  60.77  81.26   40861   22002      31 1833792
------- ------  ------ ------- ------- ------- ------- --------
total 1833795  60.77  81.27   40861   22198      35 1833792
```

```
Rows      Row Source Operation
-------   -------------------------------------------------
1833792   SORT ORDER BY
1833792     TABLE ACCESS FULL BIG_TABLE
```

Oracle did the right thing, in general.

# Consistent Reads

All SELECT statements in Oracle operate in a mode known as *consistent read*. All of the blocks viewed by a given query are consistent with respect to each at some known point in time. Consider that select * from big_table order by owner query in the previous section. It took more than 81 seconds to finish executing. During that period of time, what would happen if other sessions were modifying the data? For example, what if after we read the first block of data, but before we read the last block of data, some other transaction came along and modified data in the first and last block of the table? Should we read data from the last block of that table that is from a different point in time than the data in the first block? Oracle believes strongly that the answer to that is no, you should not.

Consider what would happen if our BIG_TABLE was really a table of bank accounts. You issue a simple query to find out how much money is in the bank: select sum(balance) from big_table. What would happen if this timeline were true:

| Time | Action | Comments |
| --- | --- | --- |
| T1 | You issue select sum(balance) from big_table. | Your query begins to process. You read the first block of the table. Assume on this block, you find the checking account for account number 1234. This account has $500.00 in it. |

| Time | Action | Comments |
|---|---|---|
| T2 | The account holder for account 1234 approaches an ATM (automatic teller machine) and begins a transaction. | The account holder wants to transfer $200 from savings to checking. |
| T3 | Your query is still running; it is a large table. | You have moved off block 1 but are not near the "last" block in the table yet. |
| T4 | The account holder causes these two updates to execute: `update big_table set balance = balance+200 where account = 1234 and type = 'Checking';` and `update big_table set balance = balance-200 where account = 1234 and type = 'Savings'; commit;`. | The account holder has moved $200 from her savings account to her checking account. Remember that you already read the checking account record in step 1. |
| T5 | Your query gets to the last block in the table. In this block, you discover the row for savings account 1234. | Oracle detects this block changed, because it was modified after your query began. Oracle will use the undo data stored in an UNDO tablespace or manually configured rollback segment and return the block image that existed when your query began (or when the transaction began, with ISOLATION level SERIALIZABLE or READ ONLY). |

So, when you get your SUM(BALANCE) back from the database, it will be the SUM(BALANCE) that existed when your *query* began. It could alternatively be the answer that existed when your *transaction* began, if you use ISOLATION level SERIALIZABLE or READ ONLY. These ISOLATION levels make all queries you execute consistent with respect to each other as of the point in time your transaction began.

Even though Oracle may not have processed a single row, the query result set to be returned is already defined and fixed as of the point in time the query or transaction began. Consider what would happen if Oracle did not do this. For example, at time T5 in our example's timeline, if Oracle just read any data that happened to be there, the SUM(BALANCE) you got back would be off by $200! Oracle would see the update to account 1234's savings account but not the update to the checking account. You would get a sum that *never existed in the database at any point in time*. That's not a very good answer, but it's the one that most other databases would return.

We can see this consistent-read mechanism at work easily with a simple test. We will copy the SCOTT.EMP table and open three cursors against it. Two of the cursors will fetch the same row—the row for BLAKE. The third will go against a different row, that of SMITH.

```
ops$tkyte@ORA920> create table emp as select * from scott.emp;
Table created.

ops$tkyte@ORA920> variable a refcursor
ops$tkyte@ORA920> variable b refcursor
```

```
ops$tkyte@ORA920> variable c refcursor
ops$tkyte@ORA920> alter session set sql_trace=true;
ops$tkyte@ORA920> begin
  2      open :a for select empno from emp q1 where ename = 'BLAKE';
  3      open :b for select empno from emp q2 where ename = 'BLAKE';
  4      open :c for select empno from emp q3 where ename = 'SMITH';
  5  end;
  6  /
PL/SQL procedure successfully completed.
```

There is nothing earth-shattering about this yet, but what happens next will be interesting. We'll start by fetching and exhausting A's result set:

```
ops$tkyte@ORA920> print a

     EMPNO
----------
      7698
```

Then we'll update the row that A and B fetch 1,000 times, simulating other users modifying the data we are processing. Remember that Oracle has not materialized B's result set anywhere as yet. It is being processed as a fast-return query. Lastly, we'll delete the row that C's cursor is to return. All of this activity will be committed to the database.

```
ops$tkyte@ORA920> begin
  2      for i in 1 .. 1000
  3      loop
  4          update emp
  5              set sal = sal
  6            where ename = 'BLAKE';
  7          commit;
  8      end loop;
  9      delete from emp
 10       where ename = 'SMITH';
 11      commit;
 12  end;
 13  /
PL/SQL procedure successfully completed.
```

Now, we'll print the results of B and C.

```
ops$tkyte@ORA920> print b

     EMPNO
----------
      7698

ops$tkyte@ORA920> print c
```

```
EMPNO
----------
      7369
```

The first interesting thing is that C had anything to print at all. The row was deleted, and Oracle did not copy the data when we opened the cursor. In this case, when Oracle went to get the row for SMITH, it discovered the block that contained the SMITH row was modified. Oracle then reconstructed that block as it existed and used that information to report back the EMPNO.

Also interesting is B's result set processing as compared to A's. When we look at the TKPROF output, we see something like this (remember the first query is the result for ref cursor A, the result set we retrieved prior to modifying the data):

```
SELECT empno from emp q1 where ename = 'BLAKE'

call      count        cpu      elapsed   disk     query     current      rows
-------   ------   --------   ----------   -----   -------   ----------   -------
Parse          1      0.00        0.00        0         0            0         0
Execute        1      0.00        0.00        0         0            0         0
Fetch          1      0.00        0.00        1         3            0         1
-------   ------   --------   ----------   -----   -------   ----------   -------
total          3      0.00        0.00        1         3            0         1

Rows      Row Source Operation
-------   -------------------------------------------------------
      1   TABLE ACCESS FULL EMP (cr=3 r=1 w=0 time=329 us)


SELECT empno from emp q2 where ename = 'BLAKE'

call      count        cpu      elapsed   disk     query     current      rows
-------   ------   --------   ----------   -----   -------   ----------   -------
Parse          1      0.00        0.00        0         0            0         0
Execute        1      0.00        0.00        0         0            0         0
Fetch          1      0.00        0.00        0       999            0         1
-------   ------   --------   ----------   -----   -------   ----------   -------
total          3      0.00        0.00        0       999            0         1

Rows      Row Source Operation
-------   -------------------------------------------------------
      1   TABLE ACCESS FULL EMP (cr=999 r=0 w=0 time=4294 us)
```

Look at the differences there. The first query performed three query mode block gets (logical I/Os) in order to retrieve the data; the second performed almost 1,000 (close to the number of updates). These extra logical I/Os where due to Oracle reading the undo information to, in effect, roll back the block so we would get BLAKE's information *as of the point in time the query was opened.* TKPROF is showing us this work take place.

This consistent-read mechanism is one of the major features of Oracle. It is my personal favorite, even more so than row-level locking. Row-level locking is great. It increases concurrency. However, without consistent reads to accompany it, it is solving only half of the problem. The consistent-read mechanism does two things for us:

- **Gets us the correct, consistent answer** This happens transparently, and there are no ways to *not* get a consistent read in Oracle.

- **Gets us the correct, consistent answer without blocking or being blocked** Other database systems will permit you a consistent read, but at the expense of concurrency. They will employ shared read locks and other mechanisms, in effect, preventing concurrent modifications and reads of the same data. Oracle does not do that.

I recommend that you read Chapter 20, "Data Concurrency and Consistency," in the Oracle9i *Concepts Guide* (my favorite piece of Oracle documentation) to gain a thorough understanding of this mechanism.

# Modification DML from Start to Finish

Now, we'll look at how the modification DML statements—such as INSERT, UPDATE, DELETE, and MERGE—are processed by Oracle. In general, these statements have a query component. For example, an UPDATE, DELETE, or MERGE statement searches the table for rows to modify and then modifies them. An INSERT statement may or may not have this query component. For example, insert into t values (5) does not have a query component, but insert into t select empno from emp does have a query component.

In general, a modification statement will find the data it needs to update using the consistent-read mechanism described in the previous section. Then it will get that information again in current (as of right now) mode in order to modify it.

We'll start with a simple example in which we'll update every row in the SCOTT.EMP table.

```
update emp set sal = sal * 1.1
```

| call | count | cpu | elapsed | disk | query | current | rows |
|---|---|---|---|---|---|---|---|
| Parse | 1 | 0.00 | 0.00 | 0 | 0 | 0 | 0 |
| Execute | 1 | 0.00 | 0.01 | 1 | 3 | 15 | 14 |
| Fetch | 0 | 0.00 | 0.00 | 0 | 0 | 0 | 0 |
| total | 2 | 0.00 | 0.01 | 1 | 3 | 15 | 14 |

Here, the EMP table is an unindexed table with 14 rows. As you can see, we did 15 current mode gets, which is about the number of rows we modified. In fact, if we scaled this table up by adding more rows to it, we would find the current mode gets go up as well. For every row we modify, we got that block in current mode, performed the modification, and gave it back.

Now, suppose that we add an index on the SAL column.

```
ops$tkyte@ORA920> create index sal_idx on emp(sal);
Index created.

ops$tkyte@ORA920> alter session set sql_trace=true;
Session altered.

ops$tkyte@ORA920> update emp set sal = sal*1.1;
14 rows updated.
```

We would discover that our current mode gets go up as well.

| call | count | cpu | elapsed | disk | query | current | rows |
|------|-------|-----|---------|------|-------|---------|------|
| Parse | 1 | 0.00 | 0.00 | 0 | 0 | 0 | 0 |
| Execute | 1 | 0.00 | 0.00 | 0 | 3 | 71 | 14 |
| Fetch | 0 | 0.00 | 0.00 | 0 | 0 | 0 | 0 |
| total | 2 | 0.00 | 0.00 | 0 | 3 | 71 | 14 |

That is due to the extra index maintenance we must now perform. We must get that data in current mode as well.

So, in general, your modifications will do all of the work of a query. These DML statements will search and find the data they should update, which is only the data that matched your search criteria when the modification began. Then, once they find that matching data, they will get that row of data as it exists right now to make the modification to the data block.

DML does other work as well, such as redo generation so the modifications can be recovered in the event of a failure, undo generation so the modifications can be undone in the event you decide to roll back the transaction, and so on. Chapter 16, "Transaction Management," of the Oracle9i *Concepts Guide* goes into those subjects in more detail, and it also covers statement-level atomicity and other relevant topics.

# DDL Processing

DDL is interesting in that it is SQL, but it is not processed in the same manner as the most common SQL is processed. A CREATE statement is processed very differently from a SELECT or INSERT statement. DDL is more like a command to Oracle, whereas a SELECT statement is more like a program to be compiled and executed. When you issue `create table t ( x int )`, Oracle will not optimize that statement as it would a `select * from t` statement. Instead, Oracle will parse it, recognize it as DDL, and then do whatever that command says needs to be done.

DDL is the way in which you and I modify the data dictionary. Imagine how hard table creation would be if you needed to actually insert all of the data into the required tables. One way to think about DDL might be to consider it as a stored procedure of sorts. You might code an EMPLOYEE package with procedures HIRE_EMP, TRANSFER_EMP, and so on. Other users would invoke EMPLOYEE.HIRE_EMP( ... ) and pass you relevant data. Your procedure would perform all of the DML necessary to validate the information and modify the necessary tables. For example, it could take 50 SQL statements to hire that employee (add the new employee to your database). A table CREATE statement is no different. You give Oracle `create table t ( x int )`, and Oracle might need to run 50 SQL statements in order to verify that you have the privilege to create a table, what tablespace it belongs in, that you have not exceeded your quota on that tablespace, that you don't already have an object named T, and so on. Then it might execute many more statements to insert rows into SYS.OBJ$, SYS.COL$, and so on to make the table actually exist.

You can use SQL_TRACE and TKPROF to see this SQL executed on your behalf. This SQL, known as *sys recursive SQL*, is the SQL Oracle executes to make your command happen. If we execute the following SQL statements, we'll see the maximum amount of sys recursive SQL in the trace file that's possible for the CREATE TABLE command. For this example, we flush the shared pool in order to cause Oracle to need to reload the dictionary caches it might otherwise use to process the command. This enables us to see the most SQL done on our behalf.

```
ops$tkyte@ORA920> alter system flush shared_pool;
System altered.

ops$tkyte@ORA920> alter session set sql_trace=true;
Session altered.

ops$tkyte@ORA920> create table t ( x int );
Table created.
```

Now, if we run TKPROF on the resulting trace file, we see the following at the bottom of the report:

OVERALL TOTALS FOR ALL RECURSIVE STATEMENTS

| call | count | cpu | elapsed | disk | query | current | rows |
|------|-------|-----|---------|------|-------|---------|------|
| Parse | 142 | 0.23 | 0.18 | 0 | 788 | 0 | 0 |
| Execute | 327 | 0.08 | 0.09 | 0 | 107 | 30 | 8 |
| Fetch | 698 | 0.07 | 0.11 | 0 | 1441 | 0 | 498 |
| total | 1167 | 0.39 | 0.40 | 0 | 2336 | 30 | 506 |

That shows that Oracle parsed 142 SQL statements on our behalf and executed them 327 times. Some of the statements were SELECTs (we executed some fetches), and some were modifications (by editing the TKPROF report, you can verify that; you can see the actual DML statements in their entirety). When I dropped and created this table again, without flushing the shared pool, I found it took only 13 recursive SQL calls. This is because many of the calls to determine my privileges and such were cached the second time around.

**NOTE**
*I would be surprised if you get exactly the same number of parsed SQL statements, executions, and so on as shown in the example here. The results are tied to which features and functions you have enabled in your database. Features like Oracle label security, auditing, fine-grained access control, and change data capture will impact these numbers greatly.*

An important thing to realize about DDL is that there is an implicit COMMIT immediately before the statement is executed and a COMMIT or ROLLBACK right after. Conceptually, DDL is processed as follows:

```
Begin
    Commit;
    Parse the DDL - verify privileges and syntax
    Begin
```

```
        Do_the_ddl;
        Commit;
    Exception
        When others then
            Rollback;
    End;
End;
```

Therefore, DDL will always commit any outstanding work that was in progress before it begins. This means that if the DDL command fails, in many cases, you will *still* have committed your transaction. The exceptions to this are if the statement does not pass the parse phase or it failed the syntax or semantic check; then the commit would not have happened.

So, now that we have seen how statements are processed by Oracle, let's explore how to use that knowledge to efficiently use statements against Oracle. We'll do this by exploring bind variables and their usage, and then we'll look at how to reduce or eliminate the overhead of parsing in your applications.

# Use Bind Variables

The use of bind variables in DML (modifications as well as queries) is a topic that I've been known to expound on in some detail, since it is one of the most crucial design decisions you will make when building your application. If you do it right, you clear your way to achieving a high-performance, scalable system. Unfortunately, I see it done wrong time after time.

Bind variables allow you to write a SQL statement that is generic. Your statement accepts inputs or parameters at runtime. This allows Oracle to hard parse the statement—go through the entire parse/optimize step—once, and then soft parse it forever after that.

In the following code, we run a simple query, first without, and then with a bind variable:

```
scott@ORA920> select ename from emp where empno = 7369;
ENAME
----------
SMITH


scott@ORA920> select ename from emp where empno = 7521;
ENAME
----------
WARD


scott@ORA920> variable empno number
scott@ORA920> exec :empno := 7369;
PL/SQL procedure successfully completed.

scott@ORA920> select ename from emp where empno = :empno;
ENAME
----------
SMITH


scott@ORA920> exec :empno := 7521
PL/SQL procedure successfully completed.
```

```
scott@ORA920> select ename from emp where empno = :empno;
ENAME
----------
WARD
```

That, in a nutshell, is what bind variables are all about. We take the literals in a query—those values that can change from execution to execution—and replace them with a placeholder, the value of which can be supplied at runtime. Consider bind variables as you would parameters to a method or subroutine in your procedural code.

**NOTE**
*The 'execute :empno:= 123' type of code is just another example of a cursor with a literal. I am only using it to demonstrate the bind variable in the SQL statement, this type of rewrite is not what you do in real systems. In a real application written in Visual Basic, Java, C, you would have host variables that you assign values to and bind. You would not execute an anonymous PL/SQL block as I did to demonstrate the concept.*

# What Are the Advantages of Using Bind Variables?

So, what is the benefit of using bind variables? In plain terms, *they are the difference between having a successful system and having a system that will not function under load.* That sounds quite dramatic, maybe even overdone. After all, how can a simple little thing like a bind variable make such a vast difference?

In fact, it was this bind variable advice, and the need to prove its veracity to a sometimes-skeptical audience, that led me to develop the Runstats tool. In Chapter 1, I introduced Runstats with just such a test (in the "Small-Time Benchmarking" section). Here, I will employ it again to prove how crucial it is to use bind variables in your code. (See Chapter 2 for details on obtaining and running Runstats.)

## Without Bind Variables, Performance Suffers

Recall from the discussion of how Oracle processes statements, earlier in this chapter, that as Oracle parses a query, it looks in the SGA—specifically, in the shared pool—to see if this query has already been parsed and optimized. If it has, Oracle will skip the intensive process of query optimization and get right down to executing your statement. If it cannot find your query in the shared pool, it will perform a hard parse, going through the optimization steps. This is a very CPU-intensive operation.

Let's take a look at this with Runstats. We'll test the difference in the time required to execute a simple SELECT statement 5,000 times, first without bind variables:

```
'select x
   from t
  where x = ' || to_char(i);
```

And then using a bind variable:

```
'select x
   from t
 where x = :x' using i;
```

To perform the test, we first need to set up an empty table:

```
ops$tkyte@ORA920> create table t ( x varchar2(5) );
Table created.
```

Then we use Runstats to test the efficiency of these two methods of querying the data:

```
ops$tkyte@ORA920> exec runstats_pkg.rs_start

PL/SQL procedure successfully completed.

ops$tkyte@ORA920>
ops$tkyte@ORA920> declare
  2      type rc is ref cursor;
  3      l_cursor rc;
  4  begin
  5      for i in 1 .. 5000
  6      loop
  7          open l_cursor for
  8          'select x
  9             from t
 10            where x = ' || to_char(i);
 11          close l_cursor;
 12      end loop;
 13  end;
 14  /
PL/SQL procedure successfully completed.

 ops$tkyte@ORA920> exec runstats_pkg.rs_middle
PL/SQL procedure successfully completed.

 ops$tkyte@ORA920> declare
  2      type rc is ref cursor;
  3      l_cursor rc;
  4  begin
  5      for i in 1 .. 5000
  6      loop
  7          open l_cursor for
  8          'select x
  9             from t
 10            where x = :x' using i;
 11          close l_cursor;
 12      end loop;
 13  end;
```

```
 14  /
PL/SQL procedure successfully completed.

 ops$tkyte@ORA920> exec runstats_pkg.rs_stop(500)
Run1 ran in 949 hsecs
Run2 ran in 380 hsecs
run 1 ran in 249.74% of the time
```

So, it is clear that using a bind variable runs much faster in terms of elapsed wall clock time. The elapsed time to hard parse what is effectively the same statement over and over is more than four times longer without bind variables than it is with bind variables.

But could we have penalized the nonbind variable statement by doing it first? Let's switch the methods and see what happens:

```
Run1 ran in 376 hsecs
Run2 ran in 1032 hsecs
run 1 ran in 36.43% of the time
```

As you can see, the results are effectively the same.

## Without Bind Variables, Your System Does Not Scale

Not only is hard parsing a CPU-intensive operation, it is also a nonscalable operation. Parsing and optimizing of queries is something that cannot be done concurrently with many other operations. Oracle must control access to shared data structures—common metadata—in the SGA. Letting someone modify a data structure our session needs to read would ultimately lead to a system crash. Imagine someone modifying a linked list of cached dictionary information in the shared pool just as we were starting to use that list! So Oracle employs latches (lightweight serialization devices) to protect these shared structures.

In order to access the various components of the SGA, we must "latch" onto them. When we have them latched, concurrent operations in the database are affected. The more people you have parsing simultaneously, the more contention you have for these latches that protect the shared pool, and the less concurrent work you have going on.

Let's continue with our example and take a look at the rest of the Runstats report, with the statistics and latching results. Here, we find something like this:

```
Name                             Run1       Run2      Diff
STAT...parse time cpu             462         36      -426
STAT...parse time elapsed         485         35      -450
STAT...recursive cpu usage        559        107      -452
STAT...CPU used by this sessio    629        145      -484
STAT...CPU used when call star    629        145      -484
STAT...parse count (hard)       5,000          1    -4,999
LATCH.library cache pin        45,056     30,057   -14,999
LATCH.library cache pin alloca 40,020     20,022   -19,998
LATCH.row cache enqueue latch  20,008          4   -20,004
LATCH.row cache objects        20,008          4   -20,004
LATCH.shared pool              59,627     20,064   -39,563
LATCH.child cursor hash table  40,000         11   -39,989
LATCH.library cache           100,080     45,089   -54,991
```

There are some huge differences to be observed here. The statistics for parse time are obvious: more than an order of magnitude increase in CPU time for the hard parses versus the soft parses. But the most interesting differences are in the amount of latching taking place. Remember that latches are serialization devices—features to make it safe for many sessions to access and modify shared data structures, at a price. The more latches you use, the fewer concurrent operations you can achieve. The latching done by the hard parse is huge compared to the soft parse latch numbers. Runstats shows us the aggregate latching difference:

```
Run1 latches total versus runs -- difference and pct
Run1      Run2     Diff      Pct
328,496   118,614  -209,882 276.95%
```

The hard parse used more than double the number of latches! What this means is the elapsed time for parsing will go up as more and more users access the system. This single-user hard parsing took six to seven seconds. Given the amount of latching (which implies waits for latches as we have more concurrent users), we can easily anticipate the elapsed times increasing greatly as users attempt to gain the same latches concurrently.

In order to drive this point home, I took this example a step further. Earlier, we saw how many latches were taken. Now, we'll look at the effect this has on performance and scalability. In order to do this, we'll use DBMS_JOB to schedule concurrently executing background processes and use STATSPACK to analyze how well things perform. The two jobs we will execute are fairly straightforward. Each job will read a parameter table to determine what table they are to insert into and how many rows they should insert. At the end of their run, they will simply remove their row from this parameter table and exit. The first procedure "DONT_BIND" will execute the insert using hard-coded literal values, whereas the second routine "BIND" will use bind variables. The setup for that code is as follows:

```
create table job_parameters
( jobid number primary key,
  iterations number,
  table_idx number );
```

This is the table we'll use to pass parameters to our background jobs, we'll also be able to use that to determine when all of the jobs that were scheduled have completed execution. Next for the DONT_BIND routine:

```
create or replace procedure dont_bind( p_job in number )
as
    l_rec job_parameters%rowtype;
begin
    select * into l_rec from job_parameters where jobid = p_job;
    for i in 1 .. l_rec.iterations
    loop
        execute immediate
        'insert into t' || l_rec.table_idx || '
        values ( ' || i || ' )';
        commit;
    end loop;
```

```
    delete from job_parameters where jobid = p_job;
end;
/
```

As you can see, that procedure simply inserts into some table, Tn. It does not use bind variables but rather generates unique insert statements for each row. In this example, I am committing each row but only to simulate many transactions. If this were a real job loading hundreds of rows, the commit would not be in the loop but only after all of the inserts were done. It is only there to simulate many users performing small transactions concurrently. We'll have many copies of this job running simultaneously. Next, for the BIND routine:

```
create or replace procedure bind( p_job in number )
as
    l_rec job_parameters%rowtype;
begin
    select * into l_rec from job_parameters where jobid = p_job;
    for i in 1 .. l_rec.iterations
    loop
        execute immediate
        'insert into t' || l_rec.table_idx || ' values ( :x )' using i;
        commit;
    end loop;
    delete from job_parameters where jobid = p_job;
end;
/
```

Once these routines are in place, we just need a test driver. I used the following routine SIMULATE to perform that. Its job is

- ■ Create N tables for the simulation—one each for the DONT_BIND or BIND routines. I used separate tables for each routine in order to reduce contention as much as possible—we want to test binding and its effect on performance—removing other points of contention will help us zero in on that.

- ■ Submit N jobs and set up their parameters in the parameter table.

- ■ Take a STATSPACK snapshot and commit the job queue submissions. This will release the jobs for execution.

- ■ Periodically poll the JOB_PARAMETERS table to see if the jobs are still running, exit the polling loop and take another ending snapshot.

That was coded as follows:

```
create or replace procedure simulation
( p_procedure in varchar2, p_jobs in number, p_iters in number )
authid current_user
as
    l_job number;
    l_cnt number;
```

```
begin
    for i in 1 .. p_jobs
    loop
        begin
            execute immediate 'drop table t' || i;
        exception
            when others then null;
        end;
        execute immediate 'create table t' || i || ' ( x int )';
    end loop;

    for i in 1 .. p_jobs
    loop
        dbms_job.submit( l_job, p_procedure || '(JOB);' );
        insert into job_parameters
        ( jobid, iterations, table_idx )
        values ( l_job, p_iters, i );
    end loop;

    statspack.snap;
    commit;
    loop
        dbms_lock.sleep(30);
        select count(*) into l_cnt from job_parameters;
        exit when (l_cnt = 0);
    end loop;
    statspack.snap;
end;
```

Two more notes on that piece of code, the AUTHID CURRENT_USER was utilized in order to have ROLES in place while this procedure executed. That gave me easy access to STATSPACK since it is granted by default to the DBA role I had. Additionally, you must be granted EXECUTE on DBMS_LOCK directly or have execute on that package via some role. By default, it's not granted to any user or role.

I then ran this code using five users (five concurrently executing background jobs) inserting 50,000 rows apiece. I did this on two different machines:

- **aria-dev**   Sun UltraEnterprise 450 server, 2 UltraSPARC-II CPUs 400Mhz, 1536MB of physical memory

- **bosshog**   Dell PowerEdge 2650 server, 2 Xeon CPUs 2.8GHz, 512K Cache, 6GB of physical memory

And the results were very telling. Some of the statspack statistics were:

|  | Bosshog | | Aria-Dev | |
| --- | --- | --- | --- | --- |
|  | DON'T_BIND | BIND | DONT_BIND | BIND |
| Parses/second | 1,037 | 2,004 | 736 | 1,603 |

|  | Bosshog | | Aria-Dev | |
|---|---|---|---|---|
|  | DON'T_BIND | BIND | DONT_BIND | BIND |
| Hard Parses/second | 1,019 | 0.11 | 735 | 0.08 |
| Executions/second | 2,070 | 4,005 | 1,474 | 3,207 |
| Transactions/second | 1,016 | 2,000 | 735 | 1,602 |
| Soft Parse% | 1.71% | 99.99% | 0.08 | 99.99 |
| Non-Parse CPU% | 48% | 90% | 33% | 89% |
| CPU Time | 554 | 266 | 603 | 206 |
| Latch free waits | 263 seconds | 12 seconds | 439 seconds | 8 seconds |

These results were reproducible time after time. Not using bind variables consistently doubled or tripled our CPU time, added hundreds of seconds of wait time for "Latch Free," and the Latch report showed that it was the "shared pool" and "library cache" latches that were in contention. In this simple example, not using bind variables cut our transaction rates roughly in half.

Hard parsing is a scalability *killer*. If you need to do hundreds or thousands of queries per minute or even per second and you do not use bind variables, *your system will fail*. You cannot add more CPUs to fix this problem. You cannot scale with clusters. You have a system that no amount of hardware can fix, because it is not a problem of insufficient hardware. The problem arises when that other session has your data structure and you must wait for it. The only way to fix this problem is to use bind variables from the very beginning.

### Without Bind Variables, Code Is Harder to Write

Let's return to a section of our example:

```
'select x
    from t
  where x = ' || to_char(i);
```

Now, suppose, instead of X being a number, X was a character string. Our code would have to then be:

```
'select x
    from t
  where x = ''' ||  replace( inputs, '''', '''''  ) || ''';
```

What is the meaning of all of those quotes?

The enclosing quotes are necessary because the column we are comparing to is a character string; we need the query to read "where x = 'something'." The replace() function is there because we don't know what is going to be supplied at runtime. We need to escape the quotes in a string.

For example, suppose this was a search routine on a web site. The user types in **Ben and Jerry's**. The query we need to submit must be:

```
select * from t where x = 'Ben and Jerry''s'
```

It needs to have two quotes, not just one. If we did not do the `replace()` trick, the string would have been as follows:

```
select * from t where x = 'Ben and Jerry's'
```

That would have failed when we opened the cursor.

This demonstrates the point that it is actually harder to code applications that work correctly without using bind variables. Every time you had a string to put into a query, you would need to do this escaping. In PL/SQL, this is not a big deal because you can use the `replace()` function. But in C, Java, or Visual Basic (VB), this is often overlooked. You would be amazed how many forms on the Internet today might fail if you entered a string that has a quotation mark.

### Without Bind Variables, Your Code Is Less Secure

Another concern when you don't use bind variables revolves around security, specifically the risk of *SQL injection.* To understand how it works, suppose that we have an application that asks a user for a username and password. We execute this query:

```
select count(*) from user_table where username = THAT_USER
and password = THAT_PASSWORD
```

This seems innocent enough, right? Well, let's use SQL*Plus to test that theory and see what happens with, and without, bind variables.

```
ops$tkyte@ORA920> create table user_table
  2  ( username varchar2(30), password varchar2(30) );
Table created.

ops$tkyte@ORA920> insert into user_table values
  2  ( 'tom', 'top_secret_password' );
1 row created.

ops$tkyte@ORA920> commit;
Commit complete.

ops$tkyte@ORA920> accept Uname prompt "Enter username: "
Enter username: tom
ops$tkyte@ORA920> accept Pword prompt "Enter password: "
Enter password: i_dont_know' or 'x' = 'x
```

Notice the password we just used. It incorporates a little SQL there, doesn't it? Since we are just gluing strings together, not binding, the end user can actually *type in arbitrary SQL and have it executed!* Our application takes this string now and continues on:

```
ops$tkyte@ORA920> select count(*)
  2      from user_table
  3   where username = '&Uname'
  4      and password = '&Pword'
  5  /
old   3:  where username = '&Uname'
```

```
new    3:   where username = 'tom'
old    4:      and password = '&Pword'
new    4:      and password = 'i_dont_know' or 'x' = 'x'

  COUNT(*)
----------
         1
```

Look at that. Apparently, the password `i_dont_know' or `x' = `x' is our password. But if we use bind variables instead and accept the exact input from the end user, we see this:

```
ops$tkyte@ORA920> variable uname varchar2(30);
ops$tkyte@ORA920> variable pword varchar2(30);
ops$tkyte@ORA920> exec :uname := 'tom';
ops$tkyte@ORA920> exec :pword := 'i_dont_know'' or ''x'' = ''x';

PL/SQL procedure successfully completed.

ops$tkyte@ORA920>
ops$tkyte@ORA920> select count(*)
  2    from user_table
  3   where username = :uname
  4     and password = :pword
  5  /

  COUNT(*)
----------
         0
```

We get the correct answer.

Think about this the next time you put an application out on the Internet. How many hidden vulnerabilities might you have lurking in there if you develop your application using string concatenation instead of bind variables? Think of the "neat" side effects someone could have on your system. Consider this password:

```
ops$tkyte@ORA920> accept Pword prompt "Enter password: "
Enter password: hr_pkg.fire_emp( 1234 )
```

Whoops, this person just executed a stored function as the user who is connected to the database. While he might not get logged on, he nonetheless got connected to your system and fired someone. Is this unbelievable? Absolutely not. Search www.google.com for *SQL Injection*, and you'll see results 1 through 10 of about 15,800. Just consider the implications.

If you don't believe the performance-related arguments for using bind variables in your system, maybe this last bit will be enough to persuade you. Bind variables add security.

## Use Bind Variables with Java and VB

Programmers who use Java with JDBC may wonder if the bind variables recommendation applies to them. Specifically, whether to use `PreparedStatement`, which allows you to use bind variables, or use `Statement`, which requires the string concatenation approach. This discussion applies equally to VB programmers using VB with ODBC, because the concept of Statement and PreparedStatement exists in ODBC in the same fashion.

> "Please briefly skim this link [*link omitted*] which gives an excerpt for JDBC performance. It says always use Statement (no bind variables allowed) instead of PreparedStatement because it performs better, without discussing the impact on the database, only in terms of a single app metrics. Is this accurate, or is this information just extremely shortsighted with regards to overall database impact?"

Look at the proof from my Runstats test—case closed. Using PreparedStatement with bind variables is absolutely the only way to do it. Later on, I got a follow-up.

> "For a moment, keep aside shared pool, hard parse, and soft parse and talk about PreparedStatement and Statement as they are the only way to execute statements from Java. I wrote this benchmark code that shows a Statement performs better than a PreparedStatement, unless you execute the same statement a whole lot of times. So, I reproduced the findings of the above link and prove that Statement is better than PreparedStatement."

Well, if we ignore shared pool, hard parse, and soft parse, we totally miss the boat on this topic, because they are the only things to consider. The facts are that hard parsing incurs many latches, latches are serialization devices, and serialization is not a scalable thing. Therefore, as you add users, the system that uses Statement instead of PreparedStatement with bind variables will fail. But, even though I quite simply could not observe this request to put aside the shared pool and hard/soft parse, I had to explore it further.

So, starting with their benchmark code, which simply inserted into a database table, I made it a multiuser benchmark to demonstrate the fact that if you expand this simple, single-user benchmark out to a real-world example with multiple users, you will see clearly what the issue is and why you need to avoid Statement. But, an interesting thing happened. I could not reproduce their findings! Running their code, I found that a single statement, executed using either Statement or PreparedStatement, took the same amount of time initially, and after executing the SQL over and over, PreparedStatement was always much faster. This conflicted with their observations totally. The problem was a flaw in their test. It failed to do an initial load of the PreparedStatement class.

### An Initial Java Test

To demonstrate the use of Statement versus PreparedStatement, as well as how a seemingly simple, convincing test can be the most misleading thing in the world, we'll walk through a simple benchmark. We'll use the single table TESTXXXPERF, which was created using the script perftest.sql, as follows:

```
scott@ORA920> drop table testxxxperf;
Table dropped.
```

```
scott@ORA920> create table testxxxperf
  2  ( id number,
  3    code varchar2(25),
  4    descr varchar2(25),
  5    insert_user varchar2(30),
  6    insert_date date );
Table created.

scott@ORA920> exit
```

The main Java code consists of basically three subroutines: a `main` routine that connects to the database and then calls a routine to insert into that table using `Statement`, and then calls a routine to do the same with `PreparedStatement`. Here is the `main` routine:

```java
import java.sql.*;
import oracle.jdbc.OracleDriver;
import java.util.Date;
public class perftest
{
  public static void main (String arr[]) throws Exception
  {
    Connection con = null;
    DriverManager.registerDriver(new oracle.jdbc.OracleDriver());
    con = DriverManager.getConnection
    ("jdbc:oracle:thin:@aria-dev:1521:ora920", "scott", "tiger");
    con.setAutoCommit(false);
    Integer iters = new Integer(arr[0]);
    doStatement (con, iters.intValue() );
    doPreparedStatement(con, iters.intValue() );
    con.commit();
    con.close();
  }
```

This routine simply connects to my Oracle9i Release 2 instance as SCOTT/TIGER and disables the autocommit JDBC uses by default. Next, it invokes the subroutine to execute a `Statement` *N* times and then a `PreparedStatement` *N* times. I set it up to allow us to pass *N* into the Java routine so we can run multiple simulations.

Next, look at the `doStatement` routine:

```java
static void doStatement(Connection con, int count)
throws Exception
{
  long start = new Date().getTime();
  Statement st = con.createStatement();

  for (int i = 0; i < count; i++)
  {
    st.executeUpdate
    ("insert into testxxxperf " +
     "(id, code, descr, insert_user, insert_date)" +
```

```
        " values (" + i  + ", 'ST - code" + i + "'" +
        ", 'St - descr" + i + "'" + ", user, sysdate ) ");
    }
    long end = new Date().getTime();
    st.close();
    con.commit();
    System.out.println
    ("statement " + count + " times in " +
       (end - start) + " milli seconds");
}
```

This routine simply creates a `statement` object and then loops `count` times and builds a unique (never before seen) INSERT statement and executes it. It is somewhat scaled back from reality, in that it is not checking for quotes in strings and fixing them, but we'll let that go for now. Also note that it retrieves the time before and after executing the `Statement` and prints the results.

The third routine is `doPreparedStatement`:

```
static void doPreparedStatement (Connection con, int count)
throws Exception
{
    long start = new Date().getTime();
    PreparedStatement ps =
        con.prepareStatement
        ("insert into testxxxperf " +
         "(id, code, descr, insert_user, insert_date)"
         + " values (?,?,?, user, sysdate)");

    for (int i = 0; i < count; i++)
    {
      ps.setInt(1,i);
      ps.setString(2,"PS - code" + i);
      ps.setString(3,"PS - desc" + i);
      ps.executeUpdate();
    }
    long end = new Date().getTime();
    con.commit();
    System.out.println
    ("pstatement " + count + " times in " +
       (end - start) + " milli seconds");
    }
}
```

This is basically the same as the `doStatement` routine, but it uses `PreparedStatement` to insert `count` rows instead of `Statement`.

Lastly, we use a shell script to execute this code:

```
!#/bin/csh -f
sqlplus scott/tiger @perftest
java perftest $1
```

A CMD file for Windows might look like:

```
sqlplus scott/tiger @perftest
java perftest %1
```

Now, we run this with inputs of 1 (do one `Statement`/`PreparedStatement`), 10, 100, and 1,000. We get the following results:

| Rows to Insert | Statement | PreparedStatement |
|---|---|---|
| 1 | 0.05 second | 0.92 second |
| 10 | 0.34 second | 1.03 seconds |
| 100 | 2.69 seconds | 2.35 seconds |
| 1,000 | 26.68 seconds | 15.74 seconds |

From these results, we might conclude that if we are not going to execute the same statement over and over—about 100 times—we would best be served by using `Statement`. The problem is there is a flaw in our test! Let's find out why.

## A Multiuser Test

To test the code for a multiuser setup, we need to do a bit of rewriting. In a multiuser test, using `System.out.println` is not a very scalable testing tool, because it is hard to collect and analyze the results. So, let's set up a database table to hold the timing results. The slightly modified Java code has an extra subroutine named `saveTimes` to save the timing information into the database.

```java
static PreparedStatement saveTimesPs;
static void saveTimes( Connection con,
                       String which,
                       long elap ) throws Exception
{
  if ( saveTimesPs == null )
      saveTimesPs = con.prepareStatement
                      ("insert into timings " +
                       "( which, elap ) values "+
                       "( ?, ? )" );

  saveTimesPs.setString(1,which);
  saveTimesPs.setLong(2,elap);
  saveTimesPs.executeUpdate();
}
```

Then we modify the `doStatement` routine like this:

```java
static void doStatement (Connection con,
                         int count) throws Exception
{
  long start = new Date().getTime();
  Statement st = con.createStatement();
```

```
    for (int i = 0; i < count; i++)
    {
      st.executeUpdate
      ("insert into testxxxperf " +
       "(id, code, descr, insert_user, insert_date)" +
       " values (" + i  +
       ", 'ST - code" + i + "'" +
       ", 'St - descr" + i + "'" +
       ", user, sysdate ) ");
    }
    st.close();
    con.commit();
    long end = new Date().getTime();
//System.out.println( "STMT" + " (" + (end-start) + ")" );
saveTimes( con, "STMT", end-start );
    }
```

We modify the doPreparedStatement routine in the same way. This would simply save the times in a database table.

```
create table timings ( which varchar2(10), elap number );
```

This way, we can run a query to get average, minimum, and maximum times for multiple users.

After just commenting out the System.out.println lines and adding a routine to record the time, when we run this test in single-user mode, we get the following results:

| Rows to Insert | Statement | PreparedStatement |
| --- | --- | --- |
| 1 | 0.05 second | 0.05 second |
| 10 | 0.30 second | 0.18 second |
| 100 | 2.69 seconds | 1.44 seconds |
| 1,000 | 28.25 seconds | 15.25 seconds |

Here, we see that there is not only no penalty ever for using a PreparedStatement, but it quickly benefits us, even in single-user mode. That's very different from what the first test showed. What could be the cause of this surprising difference?

## What Changed?

In this example, the code being timed was no different—*not a single byte of code was changed.* Sure, we commented out System.out.println and added a call to saveTimes, but that code was never timed before. So, what did change?

It turns out the saveTimes routine is the culprit here. That code uses a PreparedStatement, which "warms up" the PreparedStatement class. It paid a one-time penalty to load that class (Java dynamically loads classes as you use them). The simple act of connecting did that for the Statement class (it is used during the connection to Oracle). Once the timing of the initial load of the PreparedStatement class was factored out, the tests show that a PreparedStatement is no more expensive to execute than a Statement is in JDBC.

The entire premise of a `Statement` being lighter weight and more efficient for small numbers of statements is wrong. If you use a single `PreparedStatement` anywhere in your code, you have paid this load penalty for *all* `PreparedStatement` uses.

The basic test itself was flawed because we were timing an unrelated "thing." Since most nontrivial Java JDBC programs are going to use a `PreparedStatement` somewhere, they all pay this load penalty. Not only that, but this load penalty isn't a penalty at all; it's simply the price of admission to building a scalable application on Oracle. If you don't use `PreparedStatement`—if you insist on using `Statement` and "gluing in the values," you are not only opening yourself up to the SQL injection security risk and buggy code, but you will also find that your application will not scale as you add users. There is no maybe here; there is no might not scale. Your application *will not* scale, period.

# There Are Exceptions to Every Rule

In this section, we've seen mathematical, scientific, reproducible proof that as a general rule, you should use bind variables:

- Bind variables are a sound method to reduce the number of latches (read that word as *locks*) your application will use when parsing queries.

- Soft parsing uses significantly less CPU time than hard parsing, and bind variables are the way to achieve soft parsing.

- Stringing literals into your SQL statements, rather than using bind variables, opens your system to the SQL injection security bug.

- Stringing literals into your SQL statements can cause the statement to fail if the user inputs some unanticipated characters such as quotation marks.

- No matter what environment you are using—PL/SQL, Java and JDBC, or some other language—using bind variables is not only at least as fast, if not faster, than not using bind variables, but the code is also easier to write.

In short, if you need to execute hundreds or thousands or more SQL statements per minute or second, use bind variables in place of literals that change in the SQL. The effect of not using them can be quite dramatic. All it takes is one bad query in your system that fails to use a bind variable, but is executed frequently, differing only in the literal values, to bring it to its knees.

Does that mean you should always use bind variables in every circumstance? No, those kinds of rules of thumb are dumb. For every rule of thumb out there, there are cases where they do not hold true. In some cases, on systems that measure queries per second (which we've been focusing on in the examples here), you don't want use bind variables. On a system where you are measuring seconds per query (a data warehouse, for example), rather than per second, bind variables are something you may actually want to avoid using.

## Queries-per-Second Systems

As you've seen, in a typical system, where a Statspack report tells you that you execute tens of queries or more per second on average, you should use bind variables. But I have seen binding taken to an extreme, when developers seek and destroy all occurrences of literals in queries wherever they exist (this is also an unfortunate side effect of `cursor_sharing=-FORCE`, a session or init.ora setting). The problem with this approach is that you could be removing from the optimizer crucial information that it would have used to generate an optimal plan at runtime.

For example, suppose we have a table that has a STATUS column with the value Y (to indicate the record was processed) or N (to indicate the record was not processed). Most of the records in such a table would be in the processed state, with a small percentage not processed. We have an application that must pick off the unprocessed (N) records, process them, and update their status. Therefore, we have the following simple query in our code:

```
select * from records_to_be_processed where status = 'N';
```

Now, suppose that someone imposed the rule that bind variables are mandatory, so we must change that 'N' into a bind variable. The problem we discover after doing so is that performance of our application just went down the tubes; what used to take seconds now takes minutes. The reason is simple: our query stopped using an index and is now full-scanning a rather large table. Consider this simple simulation:

```
ops$tkyte@ORA920> create table records_to_be_processed
  2  as
  3  select decode( mod(rownum,100), 0, 'N', 'Y' ) processed, a.*
  4     from all_objects a;
Table created.

ops$tkyte@ORA920> create index processed_idx on records_to_be_processed(processed);
Index created.

ops$tkyte@ORA920> analyze table records_to_be_processed compute statistics
  2  for table
  3  for all indexes
  4  for all indexed columns
  5  /
Table analyzed.

ops$tkyte@ORA920> variable processed varchar2(1);
ops$tkyte@ORA920> exec :processed := 'N'
PL/SQL procedure successfully completed.

ops$tkyte@ORA920> set autotrace traceonly explain
ops$tkyte@ORA920> select *
  2     from records_to_be_processed
  3   where processed = 'N';

Execution Plan
----------------------------------------------------------
   0      SELECT STATEMENT Optimizer=CHOOSE (Cost=2 Card=1 Bytes=97)
   1    0   TABLE ACCESS (BY INDEX ROWID) OF 'RECORDS_TO_BE_PROCESSED'
                                          (Cost=2 Card=1 Bytes=97)
   2    1     INDEX (RANGE SCAN) OF 'PROCESSED_IDX' (NON-UNIQUE)
                                          (Cost=1 Card=1)

ops$tkyte@ORA920> select *
  2     from records_to_be_processed
```

```
3   where processed = :processed;

Execution Plan
----------------------------------------------------------
   0       SELECT STATEMENT Optimizer=CHOOSE
                              (Cost=46 Card=16220 Bytes=1573340)
   1    0    TABLE ACCESS (FULL) OF 'RECORDS_TO_BE_PROCESSED'
                              (Cost=46 Card=16220 Bytes=1573340)
```

When we remove the fact that `processed = 'N'` from the query and just generically say where `processed = :`*some value*, the optimizer must make some assumptions. Here, it assumes that half of the table, on average, will be returned, since the statistics indicate there are only two values. In this case, the index should be avoided. In general, it did the right thing, but specifically, it did the wrong thing. It should be noted however, that there is a possibility that *autotrace is lying to us here!* There is a chance, due to bind variable peeking, that the optimizer will rethink that plan when asked to really execute the query and it would use an index. We'll visit that in more detail in the section on Bind Variable Peeking.

But, in this case, the only correct solution here is to put the literal back. No matter how many times we execute that query in our application, and no matter how many copies of our application we invoke, the query will *always* be where `processed = 'N'`. The value is a true constant that never changes.

If this query sometimes used `processed = 'N'`, sometimes used `processed = 'Y'`, and sometimes used `processed = 'Something else'`, using a bind variable would be the correct approach. In short, you need to use bind variables only when the value supplied to the query changes at runtime.

Another way to look at this is if you are using static SQL—SQL that is known fully at compile time—you do not need to use a bind variable; the values in the query can never change, no matter how many times you execute the query. On the other hand, if you are using truly dynamic SQL, whereby the query is dynamically constructed at runtime, you should use bind variables for those columns for which inputs change. For example, suppose you have some Java/JDBC code that looks like this:

```
PreparedStatement pstat =
conn.prepareStatement
("select ename, empno "+
   "from emp " +
  "where job = 'CLERK' " +
    "and ename like '" + ename_like + "'" );
```

That will result in a query like this being generated at runtime:

```
select ename, empno
  from emp
 where job = 'CLERK'
   and ename like '%A%'
```

At first glance, it might seem like you should bind both the literal `'CLERK'` and `'%A%'`. In fact, only `'%A%'` needs to be bound. No matter how many times that query is executed by that application, or how many times you run that application, the predicate where `job = 'CLERK'` is constant. Only the predicate against ENAME is variable, so only it needs to be bound. Here is the correct code in Java/JDBC:

```
PreparedStatement pstat =
conn.prepareStatement
("select ename, empno "+
    "from emp " +
    "where job = 'CLERK' " +
    "and ename like ?" );

pstat.setString( 1, ename_like );
```

It accomplishes the same goal, but properly uses bind variables where necessary.

The same concept applies in PL/SQL stored procedures as in any other language: If the literal in the query is invariant at runtime, it need not be bound. Consider this query:

```
for x in ( select *
              from emp
           where job = 'CLERK'
             and ename like p_ename ) ...
```

You do not want to replace the literal `CLERK` with a bind variable. Again, no matter how many times you run that query, the predicate will always be `where job = 'CLERK'`.

In PL/SQL, the only time you need to worry about bind variables is when you use dynamic SQL and build a query at runtime. In other languages that support only dynamic SQL, such as Java with JDBC and VB with ODBC, you need to take care to properly bind each query *when and where appropriate*. This is yet another reason to consider using stored procedures: They actually make it very hard to misuse or skip using bind variables! Bear in mind, the developers still must bind in their call to the stored procedure, they cannot skip it all together. But by using stored procedures, you will reduce the number of times they must bind. Typically, a single stored procedure call will execute many different SQL statements, each of which must be bound. They will bind once to the stored procedure and PL/SQL will take it from there.

### Seconds-per-Query Systems

In what I'll loosely refer to as *data warehouses*, instead of running say 1,000 statements per second, they do something like take an average of 100 seconds to run a single query. In these systems, the queries are few but big (they ask large questions). Here, the overhead of the parse time is a tiny fraction of the overall execution time. Even if you have thousands of users, they are not waiting behind each other to parse queries, but rather are waiting for the queries to finish getting the answer.

In these systems, using bind variables may be counterproductive. Here, the runtimes for the queries are lengthy—in seconds, minutes, hours, or more. The goal is to get the best query optimization plan possible to reduce the runtime, not to execute as many of OLTP, one-tenth-second queries as possible. Since the optimizer's goal is different, the rules change.

As explained in the previous section (considering the example with the `status = 'N'` query against the RECORDS_TO_BE_PROCESSED table), sometimes using a bind variable forces the optimizer to come up with the best generic plan, which actually might be the worst plan for the specific query. In a system where the queries take considerable time to execute, bind variables remove information the optimizer could have used to come up with a superior plan. In fact, some data warehouse-specific features are defeated by using bind variables. For example, Oracle supports a star transformation feature for data warehouses that can greatly reduce the time a query takes (this feature is discussed briefly in Chapter 6). However, one restriction that precludes star transformation is having queries that contain bind variables.

In general, when you are working with a seconds-per-query system, use of bind variables may well be the performance inhibitor!

# Bind Variable Peeking

A new feature of Oracle9iR1 is the capability of the optimizer to peek at bind variable values before hard parsing a query for the first time. What that means is the optimizer will look at the bind variable values and then optimize the query as if those values were literals in the query. If you remember from earlier, the difference between the following two queries

```
ops$tkyte@ORA920> select *
  2     from records_to_be_processed
  3    where processed = 'N';

ops$tkyte@ORA920> select *
  2     from records_to_be_processed
  3    where processed = :processed;
```

was the use of a bind variable. The optimizer, given that :processed could be supplied with *any* value at runtime, reported back that it would do a FULL TABLE SCAN for the second query whereas it was using an index for the first. In this case, that would be bad. The intent of this query was to get the non-processed records (of which there are few), and the index would be the best path. As noted, the correct solution to this issue would be to use the literal value 'N' in the query and don't bind in this case. However, the database is being a little tricky here. It is actually peeking at the bind variables supplied with the query the first time it is executed and using that information in order to optimize the query. Autotrace is misleading us here a little, but SQL_TRACE will tell us what is really going on. Suppose we have that same RECORDS_TO_BE_PROCESSED table setup and we execute:

```
Alter system flush shared_pool;
Alter session set sql_trace=true;
variable processed varchar2(1);
exec :processed := 'N';
select *
  from records_to_be_processed initially_N
 where processed = :processed;

exec :processed := 'Y';
select *
  from records_to_be_processed initially_N
 where processed = :processed;

exec :processed := 'Y';
select *
  from records_to_be_processed initially_Y
```

```
  where processed = :processed;

exec :processed := 'N';
select *
  from records_to_be_processed initially_Y
 where processed = :processed;
set autotrace off
```

That is, we execute the same query twice—once with N and then with Y as the inputs. Then we execute what is basically the same query, but since the correlation name is INITIALLY_Y instead of INITIALLY_N, the database will see them as two different queries and treat them as such. The trick here is the first pair of queries were executed with the inputs N and then Y, whereas the second set had Y and then N. If you asked autotrace to "traceonly explain" these queries, you would find that autotrace would report back FULL TABLE SCAN for each. TKPROF however tells a completely different story. The following extract is the result of running the previous four queries (in that order) using the TKPROF option of AGGREGATE=NO, so that each of the four executions would be reported separately in the report:

```
select * from records_to_be_processed initially_N where processed=:processed

call      count       cpu    elapsed   disk query    current        rows
-------  ------  --------  ---------- ----- -----  ----------  ----------
total        25      0.01       0.00     0   340           0         316
```

**Misses in library cache during parse: 1**

```
Rows      Row Source Operation
-------   --------------------------------------------------
   316    TABLE ACCESS BY INDEX ROWID RECORDS_TO_BE_PROCESSED
   316     INDEX RANGE SCAN PROCESSED_IDX
```

This is not what we expected. We expected a FULL TABLE SCAN, but apparently the optimizer went ahead and used the index range scan for us. This query was optimized *as if* it had the predicate "WHERE PROCESSED='N'". This is what bind variable peeking is all about. The first time the query is hard parsed, as evidenced by the `Misses in library cache during parse: 1`, the optimizer looked at the bind variables and optimized the query as if those literal values where placed in the predicate. Now, looking at our second execution, when we changed the bind variable value to Y:

```
select * from records_to_be_processed initially_N where processed=:processed

call      count       cpu    elapsed   disk query    current        rows
-------  ------  --------  ---------- ----- -----  ----------  ----------
total      2093      0.61       0.54     0  4644           0       31337
```

**Misses in library cache during parse: 0**

```
Rows       Row Source Operation
-------    ---------------------------------------------------
  31337    TABLE ACCESS BY INDEX ROWID RECORDS_TO_BE_PROCESSED
  31337     INDEX RANGE SCAN PROCESSED_IDX
```

Now we see the optimizer once again used the index, but only because this query was initially parsed with the bind variable set to N. The query plan is fixed at this point for any query that reuses this plan. This shows that a common misconception about bind variable peeking, that the optimizer looks at the bind variable values before each parse, is in fact not true. The optimizer peeks only when the optimizer is invoked! That is only during the hard parse of a query. Any query that reused this particular plan would use the index range scan.

Now, if we flip-flop the order of execution—hard parse with a bind variable value of Y and then soft parse with N—what do you think will happen? Well, here we would see that autotrace didn't really lie to us totally. We can still get a full table scan:

```
select * from records_to_be_processed initially_Y where processed=:processed

call       count      cpu      elapsed  disk query   current      rows
-------    ------     -------- --------- ----- -----  ----------   ----------
total       2093       0.40      0.38      0   2499         0        31337
```

**Misses in library cache during parse: 1**

```
Rows       Row Source Operation
-------    ---------------------------------------------------
  31337    TABLE ACCESS FULL RECORDS_TO_BE_PROCESSED
```

When the bind variable is initially set to Y, a full scan is preferred and will be used by all subsequent executions of this shared plan, as shown here:

```
select * from records_to_be_processed initially_Y where processed=:processed

call       count      cpu      elapsed  disk query   current      rows
-------    ------     -------- --------- ----- -----  ----------   ----------
total         25       0.01      0.01      0    464         0          316
```

**Misses in library cache during parse: 0**

```
Rows       Row Source Operation
-------    ---------------------------------------------------
    316    TABLE ACCESS FULL RECORDS_TO_BE_PROCESSED
```

When we looked at this example before (my solution to the "optimizer problem"), the optimizer choosing a full table scan does use a bind variable. In this case, that is correct. We should not bind this particular value since it never changes. We always query "where processed = 'N'". Bind variable peeking protects us. Autotrace might mislead us, but TKPROF would show us the optimizer does the right thing. So, in this case, it would be confusing, but not performance damaging in the long run.

Just think, you start up on Monday morning and the first query you submit uses a bind of :Processed := Y for some odd reason, full scan plan that week. You start up next Monday and the first query you submit using a bind of :processed := N index range scan plan that week.

Well, suppose you use LIKE a lot in a search system or something. Then this feature could be very beneficial. Suppose your application always uses LIKE without leading '%' meaning an index would be helpful generally. Left on its own, the optimizer will parse "select * from t where t like :x" as if :X could have a leading '%' so the predicate could in effect be "where t like '%'". An index on X would most likely be passed over in this case. But if your application always supplies some fairly selective string that does not begin with a %, you would be in a bad position. You want the index to be used for performance. You need to use bind variables for scalability and performance, but using a bind variable would hide the fact that your LIKE inputs are selective. Bind variable peeking to the rescue! Your first search after a reboot will supply the bind variable value that the optimizer will use to optimize that query. Assuming that an index *should be used for that value if it were a literal*, will be used. Consider this example where we'll simulate a table to search on:

```
create table t
as
select a.* from all_objects a;
create index t_idx on t(object_name);

analyze table t compute statistics
for table for all indexes for all indexed columns;

variable x varchar2(50)
alter session set sql_trace=true;
set termout off
exec :x := '%';
select * from t x_was_percent where object_name like :x;
exec :x := 'Y%';
select * from t x_was_NOT_PCT where object_name like :x;
exit
```

TKPROF shows us this time

```
select * from  t x_was_percent where object_name like :x

Rows     Row Source Operation
-------  --------------------------------------------------------
  30046  TABLE ACCESS FULL T

select * from  t x_was_NOT_PCT where object_name like :x

Rows     Row Source Operation
-------  --------------------------------------------------------
      0  TABLE ACCESS BY INDEX ROWID OBJ#(35635)
      0   INDEX RANGE SCAN OBJ#(35636)
```

but since you never parse with :x := '%' and the index should be used here, this bind variable peeking works to your advantage.

# Parse as Little as Possible

Earlier, we discussed how statements are processed as well as the difference between a hard parse and a soft parse. In this section, we'll take a look at hard parsing versus soft parsing, soft parsing versus softer parsing, and softer parsing versus the best parsing of all—no parsing. Then we'll explore some common methods for reducing the amount of parsing your application does.

## The Cost of Parsing

Consider the application that will insert frequently into a table. Here, the cost of parsing a statement over and over, even with soft parses, is very high. We can even quantify the difference between the two, as we did earlier in the "Without Bind Variables, Your System Does Not Scale" section. In the Runstats test we looked at in that section, we compared the number of latches used for hard parses (Run1) and soft parses (Run2):

```
Run1 latches total versus runs -- difference and pct
Run1       Run2       Diff      Pct
328,496    118,614    -209,882  276.95%
```

There, we saw quantitatively that soft parsing is better than hard parsing, but we can do better!

### Soft Parses vs. Softer Soft Parses

The SESSION_CACHED_CURSORS session or system setting allows Oracle to silently "cache" a cursor for an application. This is useful when the developed application is ill-behaved in its use of cursors. A well-behaved application would open a cursor to the database once per session and execute it many times over. An ill-behaved application tends to open a cursor once per execution, at great expense to database processing.

To compare the soft parse to what I call a "softer soft parse" (using session-cached cursors), we'll use Runstats to test a simulation, We'll set SESSION_CACHED_CURSORS to zero, run the soft parse loop, and then set SESSION_CACHED_CURSORS to 100 and run the same code.

**NOTE**
*I did not drop and re-create table T before this test. That would cause a hard parse to slip in there, something I wanted to avoid to make the test fair.*

```
ops$tkyte@ORA920> alter session set session_cached_cursors=0;
Session altered.

ops$tkyte@ORA920> exec runstats_pkg.rs_start
PL/SQL procedure successfully completed.

ops$tkyte@ORA920> declare
  2      type rc is ref cursor;
  3      l_cursor rc;
  4  begin
  5      for i in 1 .. 5000
  6      loop
```

```
 7              open l_cursor for
 8              'select x
 9                 from t
10                where x = :x' using i;
11              close l_cursor;
12         end loop;
13   end;
14   /
PL/SQL procedure successfully completed.

ops$tkyte@ORA920> exec runstats_pkg.rs_middle
PL/SQL procedure successfully completed.

ops$tkyte@ORA920> alter session set session_cached_cursors=100;
Session altered.
re-execute that same block of code


ops$tkyte@ORA920> exec runstats_pkg.rs_stop(100)
Run1 ran in 141 hsecs
Run2 ran in 108 hsecs
run 1 ran in 130.56% of the time
```

So, we can see here that session-cached cursors helped marginally with our execution time. The improvement is nothing like the difference between hard and soft parsing, but any gain is a good gain. The important numbers are the latching results:

```
Run1 latches total versus runs -- difference and pct
Run1        Run2        Diff     Pct
118,436     53,541     -64,895   221.21%
```

This shows that, in this case, session-cached cursors cut latching about in half. So, this softer soft parse can definitely increase the scalability of a system. However, it is not the long-term solution. The SESSION_CACHED_CURSORS setting is a godsend for an ailing system that overparses, but it is not the final answer. The real solution is to reduce the number of parse calls made by the application itself.

### Softer Soft Parses vs. No Parses

Many developers have a tendency to close statements as soon as they possibly can. Sometimes this is harmless because the statement would only be executed once per session anyway, but other times, this is a major performance inhibitor.

In this next example, we'll take advantage of the fact that PL/SQL, which is optimized for database access, will silently "cache statements" for us. When you say, "close cursor" in PL/SQL, PL/SQL says, "okay, it's closed," but in reality, it will keep the cursor open. PLSQL caches that statement in the hope that we'll use it again, but it caches it in a way that lets the server really close it later if necessary. For example, if our program needs to open another cursor but we would exceed the init.ora setting of OPEN_CURSORS, rather than failing your OPEN statement call, PL/SQL will give up one of the cached statements. PL/SQL can do this neat trick only with static SQL.

By using a ref cursor and a static cursor, we'll be able to clearly see the difference between a softer soft parse (using session-cached cursors) and no parse whatsoever. We'll compare 5,000 softer soft parses, versus one parse (we need to parse the cursor at least once during our session). Here is the modified code for that simulation:

```
ops$tkyte@ORA920> alter session set session_cached_cursors=100;
Session altered.

ops$tkyte@ORA920> exec runstats_pkg.rs_start
PL/SQL procedure successfully completed.

 ops$tkyte@ORA920> declare
  2        type rc is ref cursor;
  3        l_cursor rc;
  4   begin
  5        for i in 1 .. 5000
  6        loop
  7             open l_cursor for
  8             'select x
  9                from t
 10              where x = :x' using i;
 11            close l_cursor;
 12        end loop;
 13   end;
 14   /
PL/SQL procedure successfully completed.

ops$tkyte@ORA920> exec runstats_pkg.rs_middle
PL/SQL procedure successfully completed.

 ops$tkyte@ORA920> declare
  2            cursor c( p_input in varchar2)
  3            is
  4            select x
  5              from t
  6            where x = p_input;
  7   begin
  8        for i in 1 .. 5000
  9        loop
 10                    open c(i);
 11          close c;
 12        end loop;
 13   end;
 14   /
PL/SQL procedure successfully completed.

ops$tkyte@ORA920> exec runstats_pkg.rs_stop(100)
Run1 ran in 95 hsecs
Run2 ran in 40 hsecs
run 1 ran in 237.5% of the time
```

Already, we can see there is a high penalty for just soft parsing the query. Using the no parsing approach, we've cut the elapsed time more than in half to perform the same amount of work. Looking at the statistics and the latching differences, we see these results:

```
Name                            Run1     Run2       Diff
STAT...recursive calls         15,001   10,011    -4,990
STAT...opened cursors cumulati  5,004        6    -4,998
STAT...parse count (total)      5,004        6    -4,998
STAT...session cursor cache hi  5,001        3    -4,998
LATCH.shared pool              10,065    5,065    -5,000
LATCH.library cache            20,093   10,083   -10,010
LATCH.library cache pin        20,065   10,054   -10,011

Run1 latches total versus runs -- difference and pct
Run1      Run2      Diff     Pct
53,472    28,317   -25,155  188.83%

PL/SQL procedure successfully completed.
```

We can see that there is a large decrease in the number of latches—we've cut it almost in half yet again. The server statistics are showing us this very nice side effect PL/SQL has with its transparent caching abilities: We did 4,998 fewer parses, simply by letting PL/SQL do its job.

An expert in the field, Cary Millsap, has been known to say, "The best way to speed something up is to not do it at all." This truly applies to parsing.

## Use PL/SQL to Reduce Parses

By far, the easiest way to reduce the parses is to simply use PL/SQL. As demonstrated in the previous section, all static SQL found in PL/SQL is cached (kept open) for you. That way, the only places you need to worry about reducing the parsing would be calls to stored procedures. Instead of your application having hundreds of SQL statements that you would need to cache yourself, you can have instead just tens of stored procedure calls to handle. Each stored procedure would have many SQL statements in it, giving you a reduced number of PL/SQL statements in your application. Consider this example:

```
ops$tkyte@ORA920> create or replace procedure
  2  do_something( p_owner in varchar2 )
  3  as
  4  begin
  5      for x in ( select *
  6                    from all_objects
  7                   where owner = p_owner )
  8      loop
  9          exit;
 10          /* we would be processing these records here */
 11      end loop;
 12  end;
 13  /
Procedure created.
```

```
ops$tkyte@ORA920> alter session set sql_trace=true;
Session altered.

ops$tkyte@ORA920> declare
  2        l_cnt number := 0;
  3  begin
  4        for x in ( select * from all_users )
  5        loop
  6            do_something( x.username );
  7            l_cnt := l_cnt + 1;
  8        end loop;
  9        dbms_output.put_line( l_cnt || ' rows processed.' );
 10  end;
 11  /
44 rows processed.
PL/SQL procedure successfully completed.
```

How many times was the emphasized statement parsed: 1 time or 44 times (44 being the number of users in my ALL_USERS table when I ran this test)? Well, TKPROF (discussed in Chapter 2) will be useful in telling us exactly what happened here.

```
select * from all_objects where owner = :b1
```

| call | count | cpu | elapsed | disk | query | current | rows |
|------|-------|-----|---------|------|-------|---------|------|
| Parse | 1 | 0.00 | 0.00 | 0 | 0 | 0 | 0 |
| Execute | 44 | 0.01 | 0.01 | 0 | 0 | 0 | 0 |

The statement was parsed once and executed 44 times. PL/SQL cached that statement for us, but it is intelligent enough to give up the cursor handles when and if they are needed by the application.

There are some caveats even with PL/SQL, however. For example, the overuse of dynamic SQL will defeat this caching of SQL statements. PL/SQL cannot cache Oracle EXECUTE IMMEDIATE or OPEN REF_CURSOR FOR statements. Here, I'll present some alternatives that can help reduce parsing.

## EXECUTE IMMEDIATE Alternatives
EXECUTE IMMEDIATE takes this form:

```
Execute immediate some_plsql_string_that_contains_sql
```

Each and every time that piece of code executes, the statement could be totally different! Hence, caching that statement is not possible. When writing PL/SQL, however, we can use the DBMS_SQL package in order to cache the cursor, to avoid parsing and reparsing statements. We can also use a "bulk" processing technique.

**Use DBMS_SQL**    Using DBMS_SQL is a little more involved than using EXECUTE IMMEDIATE, but if you need to dynamically execute the same statement hundreds or thousands of times, it is worth the effort. Consider these routines to dynamically insert into a table that is not known until runtime:

```
ops$tkyte@ORA920> create or replace package dyn_insert
  2  as
  3      procedure dbms_sql_method( p_tname in varchar2,
  4                                 p_value in varchar2 );
  5
  6      procedure exec_imd_method( p_tname in varchar2,
  7                                 p_value in varchar2 );
  8  end;
  9  /
Package created.
```

They each take as inputs the name of the table to insert into and the value to be inserted. The DBMS_SQL_METHOD procedure will attempt to cache and reuse a parsed statement, whereas the EXEC_IMD_METHOD will simply use EXECUTE IMMEDIATE to run an INSERT statement from a string. The implementation of each is as follows:

```
ops$tkyte@ORA920> create or replace package body dyn_insert
  2  as
  3
  4  g_last_tname varchar2(30);
  5  g_cursor     number := dbms_sql.open_cursor;
```

Those global variables will be used by the DBMS_SQL_METHOD procedure. The G_LAST_TNAME variable will be used to remember the last table this procedure inserted into. If the table name does not change from call to call, it will simply reuse the last parsed insert; otherwise, it will parse a new statement. The G_CURSOR variable will simply hold a cursor handle for us for the life of the session. The implementation of this routine is:

```
  6
  7  procedure dbms_sql_method( p_tname in varchar2,
  8                             p_value in varchar2 )
  9  is
 10      l_rows number;
 11  begin
 12      if ( g_last_tname <> p_tname or g_last_tname is null )
 13      then
 14          dbms_sql.parse( g_cursor,
 15                          'insert into ' || p_tname ||
 16                          ' (x) values (:x)',
 17                          dbms_sql.native );
 18          g_last_tname := p_tname;
 19      end if;
 20      dbms_sql.bind_variable( g_cursor, ':x', p_value );
 21      l_rows := dbms_sql.execute( g_cursor );
 22  end;
```

Next, we have the EXEC_IMD_METHOD. The source code for this is much easier to implement. However, if the same statement is executed over and over, it will not perform as well.

```
23
24  procedure exec_imd_method( p_tname in varchar2,
25                             p_value in varchar2 )
26  is
27  begin
28      execute immediate
29      'insert into ' || p_tname || '(x) values (:x)'
30      using p_value;
31  end;
32
33  end;
34  /
Package body created.
```

Now, let's use Runstats to compare the methods.

```
ops$tkyte@ORA920> exec runstats_pkg.rs_start
PL/SQL procedure successfully completed.

ops$tkyte@ORA920> begin
  2      for i in 1 .. 5000
  3      loop
  4          dyn_insert.dbms_sql_method( 'T', i );
  5      end loop;
  6  end;
  7  /
PL/SQL procedure successfully completed.

ops$tkyte@ORA920> exec runstats_pkg.rs_middle
PL/SQL procedure successfully completed.

ops$tkyte@ORA920> begin
  2      for i in 1 .. 5000
  3      loop
  4          dyn_insert.exec_imd_method( 'T', i );
  5      end loop;
  6  end;
  7  /
PL/SQL procedure successfully completed.

ops$tkyte@ORA920> exec runstats_pkg.rs_stop(100)
Run1 ran in 240 hsecs
Run2 ran in 279 hsecs
run 1 ran in 86.02% of the time
```

Again, we see that parsing once is marginally better tan parsing over and over from and elapsed-time point of view. Now, let's look at the statistics and latching numbers:

```
Name                              Run1      Run2      Diff
STAT...recursive calls          10,021     5,029    -4,992
STAT...session cursor cache hi       3     5,001     4,998
STAT...opened cursors cumulati       6     5,007     5,001
STAT...parse count (total)           6     5,007     5,001
STAT...calls to get snapshot s   5,008    10,011     5,003
LATCH.shared pool               10,114    15,120     5,006
STAT...consistent gets              22     5,028     5,006
LATCH.library cache pin         20,081    30,093    10,012
LATCH.library cache             20,132    30,153    10,021
STAT...db block gets             5,687    15,711    10,024
STAT...session logical reads     5,709    20,739    15,030
LATCH.cache buffers chains      28,085    58,172    30,087

Run1 latches total versus runs -- difference and pct
Run1        Run2       Diff      Pct
84,943    140,045     55,102    60.65%

PL/SQL procedure successfully completed.
```

We can see the statistics and latching amounts for DBMS_SQL_METHOD are significantly less than that of EXECUTE IMMEDIATE. We did less than 40% of the latching by reusing that cursor over and over again.

There are other ways to achieve the same goal. Next, we'll look at how we can do this by using arrays and executing a single dynamic statement with many inputs.

**Use a Bulk Insert** Instead of dynamically inserting a row at a time as we just did, we can change the calling source code—the routines that invoke these procedures row by row—and have them set up an array of values to be inserted. In that fashion, we can use a single dynamically executed statement to insert 100 or 1,000 rows in bulk. That will remove the high cost of using EXECUTE IMMEDIATE (we will parse the statement only 5 to 50 times, not 5,000 times). However, it will also more heavily impact the calling code. But if you look at the payback, it may well be worth your time.

Here, we will compare the EXECUTE IMMEDIATE row-at-a-time processing with EXECUTE IMMEDIATE "bulk" processing. These results will be even more dramatic than those previous. We'll start by specifying a new package that incorporates our bulk processing, beginning with a collection type that will be used as input to our insert routine:

```
ops$tkyte@ORA920> create or replace type vcArray as table of varchar2(5)
  2  /
Type created.
```

Next is the new package, which we'll call DYN_INSERT2:

```
ops$tkyte@ORA920> create or replace package dyn_insert2
  2  as
```

```
  3          procedure exec_imd_method1( p_tname in varchar2,
  4                                      p_value in varchar2 );
  5          procedure exec_imd_method2( p_tname in varchar2,
  6                                      p_value in vcArray );
  7   end;
  8   /
Package created.
```

Here, we have a procedure that takes a row at a time—EXEC_IMD_METHOD1—and another routine that takes a collection or array of inputs to be inserted. Now for the package body:

```
ops$tkyte@ORA920> create or replace package body dyn_insert2
  2   as
  3
  4   procedure exec_imd_method1( p_tname in varchar2,
  5                               p_value in varchar2 )
  6   is
  7   begin
  8        execute immediate
  9        'insert into ' || p_tname || '(x) values (:x)'
 10        using p_value;
 11   end;
```

That routine is unchanged from our original implementation. Our new routine follows:

```
 12
 13   procedure exec_imd_method2( p_tname in varchar2,
 14                               p_value in vcArray )
 15   is
 16   begin
 17   /****
 18    **** This block of code can be used to emulate
 19    **** dynamic BULK inserts in Oracle8i
 20        execute immediate
 21        'begin
 22          forall i in 1 .. :n
 23             insert into ' || p_tname || '(x) values (:x(i));
 24         end;'
 25        using p_value.count, p_value;
 26    **** since the syntax that follows is new with Oracle9i
 27    ****/
 28
 29      forall i in 1 .. p_value.count
 30        execute immediate 'insert into ' || p_tname || '(x) values( :x )'
 31        using p_value(i);
 32
 33   end;
 34   end;
 35   /

Package body created.
```

Here, we are using the PL/SQL bulk FORALL syntax in a dynamically executed block of code. Now, we are ready to compare the two methods again. We'll run the bulk insert first:

```
ops$tkyte@ORA920> exec runstats_pkg.rs_start
PL/SQL procedure successfully completed.

ops$tkyte@ORA920> declare
  2      l_array vcArray := vcArray();
  3  begin
  4      for i in 1 .. 5000
  5      loop
  6          l_array.extend;
  7          l_array(l_array.count) := i;
  8          if ( mod(l_array.count,1000) = 0 or i = 5000 )
  9          then
 10              dyn_insert2.exec_imd_method2('T', l_array );
 11              l_array := vcArray();
 12          end if;
 13      end loop;
 14  end;
 15  /
PL/SQL procedure successfully completed.

 ops$tkyte@ORA920> exec runstats_pkg.rs_middle
PL/SQL procedure successfully completed.
```

As you can see, the calling code is a little more complex than in the previous version. The caller must collect together (batch) the rows it wants to insert. This is as compared to the row-at-a-time method:

```
ops$tkyte@ORA920> begin
  2      for i in 1 .. 5000
  3      loop
  4          dyn_insert2.exec_imd_method1('T',i );
  5      end loop;
  6  end;
  7  /
PL/SQL procedure successfully completed.

ops$tkyte@ORA920> exec runstats_pkg.rs_sto(500)p
Run1 ran in 8 hsecs
Run2 ran in 343 hsecs
run 1 ran in 2.33% of the time
```

But look at that difference: less than 3% of the runtime this time around, which is significantly better than just using DBMS_SQL. Looking at the statistics and latches information, we'll see why.

| Name | Run1 | Run2 | Diff |
|------|------|------|------|
| LATCH.simulator hash latch | 0 | 643 | 643 |
| STAT...redo entries | 559 | 5,553 | 4,994 |

```
STAT...session cursor cache hi          8       5,002       4,994
LATCH.redo allocation                 560       5,556       4,996
STAT...execute count                   11       5,011       5,000
STAT...opened cursors cumulati         10       5,010       5,000
STAT...parse count (total)             10       5,010       5,000
STAT...consistent gets                 27       5,030       5,003
STAT...recursive calls                 14       5,049       5,035
STAT...calls to get snapshot s         21      10,013       9,992
STAT...db block changes             1,105      11,117      10,012
LATCH.shared pool                     101      15,090      14,989
STAT...db block gets                  627      15,715      15,088
STAT...session logical reads          654      20,745      20,091
LATCH.library cache                   154      30,149      29,995
LATCH.library cache pin               102      30,104      30,002
LATCH.cache buffers chains          2,975      58,282      55,307
STAT...redo size                  141,076   1,230,880   1,089,804
```

Look at the difference in redo size! The bulk operations generate significantly less redo. In addition to being faster, they are much more efficient. Over all, the bulk operation used fewer physical resources, as shown by the statistics and the latches:

```
Run1 latches total versus runs -- difference and pct
Run1      Run2      Diff      Pct
3,984    140,440   136,456    2.84%

PL/SQL procedure successfully completed.
```

The results show less than 3% of the latching, which makes all of the difference in the world.

## Why Ref Cursors Cannot Be Cached

The ref cursor caveat may confuse you. Why can't a ref cursor be cached? Well, it has to do with the fact that not only can ref cursors be dynamically opened

```
open ref_cursor for some_query_in_a_string;
```

but that the same ref cursor may be opened many times before being closed! Consider this procedure:

```
ops$tkyte@ORA920> create or replace
  2  procedure p( p_cursor in out sys_refcursor )
  3  as
  4  begin
  5          open p_cursor for select * from dual;
  6  end;
  7  /

Procedure created.
```

**NOTE**
*In Oracle8i and before, you will need to create a package with a ref cursor type. The SYS_REFCURSOR datatype is new with Oracle9i Release 1 and later.*

Now, it would seem that PL/SQL should be able to cache that statement, as it does with "regular" cursors, but it cannot. The next part of this example demonstrates why this is so:

```
ops$tkyte@ORA920> variable x refcursor
ops$tkyte@ORA920> variable y refcursor

ops$tkyte@ORA920> exec p(:x);
PL/SQL procedure successfully completed.

ops$tkyte@ORA920> exec p(:y);
PL/SQL procedure successfully completed.

ops$tkyte@ORA920> print y
...
ops$tkyte@ORA920> print x
```

That single ref cursor is really *N* cursors, where *N* is not known until runtime. Here, we opened the same cursor two times in a row without closing it in between. Ref cursors are really like pointers to cursors; hence, PL/SQL cannot cache them as it can static SQL.

### PL/SQL for Parsing Reduction Wrap-Up
In summary, you should use PL/SQL to reduce the amount of parsing your system does. In PL/SQL, you should take the following approaches:

- Use static SQL in the form of implicit and explicit cursors whenever possible.

- Use DBMS_SQL over EXECUTE IMMEDIATE if you believe you will be executing the same dynamic statement over and over many times.

- In place of DBMS_SQL, consider using arrays and executing a single dynamic statement with many inputs. This can result in dramatic differences in runtime execution and greatly increased scalability, because the amount of resources needed decreases, and the number of latches necessary is significantly reduced.

## Move SQL Out of Triggers to Reduce Parsing
The use of SQL in triggers could be a cause of excessive parsing as well. Consider the following example. Our goal is to have a table of employees and a summary table of counts of employees by DEPTNO. We'll use a trigger after INSERT, UPDATE, or DELETE on the EMP table to maintain these counts:

```
ops$tkyte@ORA920> create table emp
  2  as
  3  select ename, empno, deptno
```

```
   4     from scott.emp;
Table created.

ops$tkyte@ORA920> create table emp_dept_cnt
   2  ( deptno primary key, cnt )
   3  organization index
   4  as
   5  select deptno, count(*)
   6    from emp
   7   group by deptno;
Table created.

ops$tkyte@ORA920> create trigger emp_dept_cnt_trigger
   2  after insert or update or delete on emp
   3  for each row
   4  begin
   5      if ( inserting or updating )
   6      then
   7          merge into emp_dept_cnt in_trigger
   8          using (select :new.deptno deptno from dual) n
   9             on ( in_trigger.deptno = n.deptno )
  10           when matched then
  11          update set cnt = cnt+1
  12            when not matched then
  13          insert (deptno,cnt) values (:new.deptno,1);
  14      end if;
  15      if ( updating or deleting )
  16      then
  17          update emp_dept_cnt in_trigger
  18             set cnt = cnt-1
  19           where deptno = :old.deptno;
  20      end if;
  21  end;
  22  /
Trigger created.
```

Now, if SQL statements were cached in triggers exactly like SQL statements in PL/SQL procedures were cached, what would happen after executing the following modifications?

```
ops$tkyte@ORA920> alter session set sql_trace=true;
Session altered.

ops$tkyte@ORA920> insert into emp (ename,empno,deptno)
  2 values ( 'tom',  123, 10 );
1 row created.

ops$tkyte@ORA920> insert into emp (ename,empno,deptno)
  2 values ( 'mary', 123, 10 );
1 row created.

ops$tkyte@ORA920> delete from emp;
16 rows deleted.
```

We would expect to see one parse on the MERGE statement and one parse on the UPDATE statement. However, TKPROF shows us that the MERGE statement was parsed twice: once for each of the insert operations. Furthermore, TKPROF shows us that the UPDATE statement was parsed once:

```
MERGE into emp_dept_cnt in_trigger
        using (select :b1        deptno from dual) n
          on ( in_trigger.deptno = n.deptno )
        when matched then
      update set cnt = cnt+1
        when not matched then
        insert (deptno,cnt) values (:b1        ,1)
```

| call | count | cpu | elapsed | disk | query | current | rows |
|------|-------|-----|---------|------|-------|---------|------|
| **Parse** | 2 | 0.00 | 0.00 | 0 | 0 | 0 | 0 |
| Execute | 2 | 0.00 | 0.00 | 0 | 8 | 2 | 2 |

```
UPDATE emp_dept_cnt in_trigger set cnt = cnt-1 where deptno = :b1
```

| call | count | cpu | elapsed | disk | query | current | rows |
|------|-------|-----|---------|------|-------|---------|------|
| **Parse** | 1 | 0.00 | 0.00 | 0 | 0 | 0 | 0 |
| Execute | 16 | 0.00 | 0.00 | 0 | 16 | 16 | 16 |

What we can ascertain from this example is that the SQL statements are cached only for the duration of the call to the server; that is, each discrete call we make to the server will result in the SQL statements used by the trigger being soft parsed once again. In order to avoid this, we will package our SQL and call the packaged SQL code from the trigger:

```
ops$tkyte@ORA920> create or replace package emp_dept_cnt_pkg
  2  as
  3      procedure insert_update( p_deptno in number );
  4      procedure update_delete( p_deptno in number );
  5  end;
  6  /
Package created.

ops$tkyte@ORA920> create or replace package body emp_dept_cnt_pkg
  2  as
  3
  4  procedure insert_update( p_deptno in number )
  5  as
  6  begin
  7      merge into emp_dept_cnt in_package
  8      using (select p_deptno deptno from dual) n
  9        on ( in_package.deptno = n.deptno )
 10      when matched then
 11    update set cnt = cnt+1
 12      when not matched then
 13      insert (deptno,cnt) values (p_deptno,1);
 14  end;
 15
```

```
16   procedure update_delete( p_deptno in number )
17   as
18   begin
19      update emp_dept_cnt in_package
20         set cnt = cnt-1
21       where deptno = p_deptno;
22   end;
23
24   end;
25   /
Package body created.
```

And then recode our trigger as follows:

```
ops$tkyte@ORA920> create or replace trigger emp_dept_cnt_trigger
  2   after insert or update or delete on emp
  3   for each row
  4   begin
  5      if ( inserting or updating )
  6      then
  7         emp_dept_cnt_pkg.insert_update( :new.deptno );
  8      end if;
  9      if ( updating or deleting )
 10      then
 11         emp_dept_cnt_pkg.update_delete( :old.deptno );
 12      end if;
 13   end;
 14   /
Trigger created.
```

TKPROF shows the following after executing the same sequence of insert/delete operations against the same data:

```
MERGE into emp_dept_cnt in_package
...
```

| call | count | cpu | elapsed | disk | query | current | rows |
|------|-------|-----|---------|------|-------|---------|------|
| Parse | 1 | 0.00 | 0.00 | 0 | 0 | 0 | 0 |
| Execute | 2 | 0.00 | 0.00 | 0 | 8 | 2 | 2 |

The parse count is down to one, where it will stay for the duration of our session.

# Prepare Once; Execute Many

This section applies to all 3GL languages and APIs such as Java/JDBC, C/OCI, or VB/ODBC. Here, your goal is to reduce parsing by reducing the number of times you parse! For example, in the earlier section on bind variables, I introduced a Java routine named saveTimes that looks like this:

```
static PreparedStatement saveTimesPs;

static void saveTimes( Connection con,
```

```
                         String which,
                         long elap ) throws Exception
{
  System.out.println( which + " (" + elap + ")" );
  if ( saveTimesPs == null )
      saveTimesPs = con.prepareStatement
                    ("insert into timings " +
                     "( which, elap ) values "+
                     "( ?, ? )" );

  saveTimesPs.setString(1,which);
  saveTimesPs.setLong(2,elap);
  saveTimesPs.executeUpdate();
}
```

Notice how this routine defined the `PreparedStatement` handle outside the Java method `saveTimes`, so it would be a persistent variable, available from call to call of `saveTimesPs`. Additionally, the code in `saveTimes` went out of its way to prepare that statement *once* during the life of that class. This permitted the Java code to prepare this statement once per session, instead of once per execution.

In all of your code, you should be looking for opportunities to parse once and reuse that statement as many times as possible. If you run your application with SQL_TRACE=TRUE and see high parse counts in the TKPROF report, you know you could be doing better.

# Summary

In this chapter, we covered how Oracle processes statements from beginning to end. We walked through the parsing, optimization, and execution of the major classes of statements: DDL and DML, including queries. We briefly touched on optimization but will cover that in more depth in the next chapter.

We then moved onto the vital topic of bind variables and their use. We discovered that by simply ignoring bind variables (by not using them), we could easily render our systems inoperable. Oracle would spend all of its time parsing and optimizing statements, instead of executing them. In addition to performance-related woes, we saw how not using bind variables opens our systems to SQL injection attacks. The system that does not use bind variables appropriately is not only less scalable, but it is also very insecure.

Finally, we talked about avoiding parsing whenever possible. Remember that the best way to speed something up is to *not do it at all*. That goal is especially true for parsing. We explored various methods to reduce parsing—from simply using PL/SQL, to being careful with dynamic SQL, to the bulk binding (also known as *array processing*) of many inputs to a single-statement execution.

Now, you have a fuller appreciation of the shared pool and how Oracle works hard to make sure that work done by one user is available for all users to share. You should have a good working knowledge of what really happens when statement processing takes place.

# CHAPTER
## 6

# Getting the Most Out of the Cost-Based Optimizer

or over a decade, Oracle has provided two optimizers: the rule-based optimizer (RBO) and the cost-based optimizer (CBO).

*With the RBO*, query plans are generated according to a predefined set of rules. It is possible to look at a query and, with knowledge of the tables and indexes in place, predict with 99.9% accuracy what the query plan will be. There are possible differences in query plans based on the order of index creation when two indexes "tie" with each other, meaning either index satisfies the rules. But in general, in a database, once you see the query plan for a rule-based optimized query, that query plan will persist. The query plan is generated by a very well-defined, rigid set of rules.

*With the CBO*, query plans are generated based on statistics and costs associated with performing certain operations. The optimizer generates most of the possible ways of processing a query, and each step in the generated query plan is assigned a cost. Ultimately, the query with the lowest cost "wins," and that will be the query plan chosen.

With the very next release of Oracle after version 9.2 (known at the time of writing as Oracle 10i), the RBO will be officially retired. Oracle will support just one optimizer, the CBO, and it will be all that we should use. For this reason, and many others, you should be looking at the CBO today. The RBO will still exist in the next release after Oracle after Oracle9i Release 2, but it will be an unsupported feature. No code changes will be made to RBO, and no bug fixes will be provided. (See the Oracle desupport notice for RBO at http://metalink.oracle.com/metalink/plsql/ml2_documents.showDocument?p_database_id=NOT&p_id=189702.1.)

The single biggest reason why some people have been reluctant to use the CBO is a lack of understanding of how it works and what it takes to make it do the right thing. A contributing factor to this reluctance may be found in history as well. The early releases of the CBO (prior to version 7.1.6 at least) quite simply did not work very well. However, the CBO is just a piece of software; it doesn't have a mind of its own. It makes all of its decisions based on inputs you give to it. After ten years of continual refinement, the decisions it makes are now, in general, quite sound. Once you know how to provide the right information, you'll get query plans that consistently perform as well as, or better than, the RBO. (The rules the RBO follows are fully documented in Chapter 8 of the Oracle9i *Performance Tuning Guide*, and Chapter 4 of the Oracle8i *Designing and Tuning for Performance Guide*.)

# Why the RBO Is Dead

Just to get you a little excited about the CBO and demonstrate its superiority to the RBO, let's start off with a small example. We'll use the same BIG_TABLE that we created in the setup section in the Appendix—the table that has more than one million rows of data. Suppose that we need to run a query such as the following:

```
select t1.object_name, t2.object_name
   from big_table t1, big_table t2
 where t1.object_id = t2.object_id
   and t1.owner = 'WMSYS'
```

**NOTE**
*In my examples, I use WMSYS. If you have no such schema, you'll
need to test with another schema name. WMSYS is a default schema
in Oracle9i, part of the workspace management feature.*

We use SET AUTOTRACE TRACEONLY EXPLAIN in SQL*Plus and discover that the CBO was about to use this plan:

```
Execution Plan
----------------------------------------------------------
   0      SELECT STATEMENT Optimizer=CHOOSE
          (Cost=4628 Card=8256 Bytes=404544)
   1    0   HASH JOIN
            (Cost=4628 Card=8256 Bytes=404544)
   2    1     TABLE ACCESS (FULL) OF 'BIG_TABLE'
              (Cost=2136 Card=8256 Bytes=222912)
   3    1     TABLE ACCESS (FULL) OF 'BIG_TABLE'
              (Cost=2136 Card=1833857 Bytes=40344854)
```

Well, *everyone knows* (conventional wisdom dictates) that indexes are the best way to do anything (that was *sarcasm* on my part; they are not always the best way). We know there is a perfectly good index on OBJECT_ID, so why isn't the CBO picking it? We discover through trial and error that if we use the RBO, it does what we think it should:

```
big_table@ORA920> select /*+ RULE */ t1.object_name, t2.object_name
  2    from big_table t1, big_table t2
  3   where t1.object_id = t2.object_id
  4     and t1.owner = 'WMSYS'
  5  /

Execution Plan
----------------------------------------------------------
   0      SELECT STATEMENT Optimizer=HINT: RULE
   1    0   TABLE ACCESS (BY INDEX ROWID) OF 'BIG_TABLE'
   2    1     NESTED LOOPS
   3    2       TABLE ACCESS (FULL) OF 'BIG_TABLE'
   4    2       INDEX (RANGE SCAN) OF 'OBJECT_ID_IDX' (NON-UNIQUE)
```

See that nice index-range scan. It is using our indexes, so this will be much faster, won't it? When we actually run the query, we discover to our dismay (using a TKPROF report):

```
select /*+ RULE */ t1.object_name, t2.object_name
  from big_table t1, big_table t2
 where t1.object_id = t2.object_id
   and t1.owner = 'WMSYS'
```

| call | count | cpu | elapsed | disk | query | cur | rows |
|------|-------|-----|---------|------|-------|-----|------|
| Parse | 1 | 0.00 | 0.00 | 0 | 0 | 0 | 0 |

```
Execute        1      0.00       0.00         0           0   0         0
Fetch      35227    912.07    3440.70   1154555   121367981   0    528384
-------   ------   -------- ----------   -------- ----------- --- ------
total      35229    912.07    3440.70   1154555   121367981   0    528384
```

The query took 15 CPU minutes and almost an hour of elapsed time to execute! Additionally, it performed over 121 million logical I/O operations!

Let's try the other plan, just to see what would happen:

```
select t1.object_name, t2.object_name
  from t t1, t t2
 where t1.object_id = t2.object_id
   and t1.owner = 'WMSYS'
```

```
call      count       cpu    elapsed      disk     query cur  rows
-------   ------   -------- ----------   -------- ---------- --- ------
Parse         1      0.00       0.00         0         0   0        0
Execute       1      0.00       0.00         0         0   0        0
Fetch     35227      5.63       9.32     23380     59350   0   528384
-------   ------   -------- ----------   -------- ---------- --- ------
total     35229      5.63       9.33     23380     59350   0   528384
```

Isn't that quite a bit different? When left to its own devices, the CBO's original plan with two full scans runs very fast indeed: 5.63 CPU seconds versus 912 CPU seconds, 10 seconds of elapsed time versus 1 hour, and fewer than 60,000 logical I/O operations versus more than 121 million. This is where some people might point out, "Ah, your buffer cache was too small, the large difference between 3,400 seconds of elapsed time and 912 CPU seconds shows that. It was because you did 1,154,555 physical IOs. You can tune this query by increasing your buffer cache." That would be one approach to making the RBO query go faster, however, that query will still take 912 CPU seconds to process, so while a larger buffer cache might be able to make it go three to four times faster, using the CBO will make it 344 or more times faster in this case.

In this case, the codified logic in the RBO that says "indexes are good so always use them" got us into serious trouble.

> **NOTE**
> *The RBO query would have done our cache hit ratio good! Look at the number of logical I/Os. That query experienced a 99% cache hit. The CBO query, on the other hand, came in at a miserable 70% cache hit. But tell me, which would you prefer?*

The CBO didn't ignore the index; it just realized that on the data of this volume, with this query, using an index would be the kiss of death. It appears that the CBO is much smarter than the RBO. That is sort of an unfair statement really. It is more accurate to say that the CBO has many more tools at its disposal than the RBO has available. For example, the RBO doesn't even know about hash joins. It is physically incapable of developing a plan that would incorporate one. The RBO will never "see" a bitmap index, cannot use a function-based index, and cannot be used to develop a plan against partitioned tables. Oracle can only use the CBO against certain table types such partitioned tables or index organized tables…. The list of what it cannot do is long and grows longer with each release of Oracle.

With its fuller toolkit of plans, the CBO has more opportunities to develop a well-performing query plan. Now, is the CBO perfect? No, it is a piece of software. It was written by humans, and humans make mistakes. Is the CBO the best-behaved piece of software right out of the box? Typically, no it is not. We need to set it up a bit. There are two very important parameters we must consider, depending on the type of system we are building. Also, we must gather some statistics. Then, and only then, the CBO will do its best. We will take a look at the two parameters and the statistics in the next section.

# Make the CBO Do Its Best

There are two very innocuous init.ora parameters that have default settings that are not right for many systems. First, we will look at those two parameters. Then, as an alternative to those parameters, we'll also investigate system statistics (statistics about the machine itself) available in Oracle9iR2 and later. With system statistics, the relative speed of the CPU and the speed of single-block and multiblock I/O are measured by Oracle, and more appropriate costs are assigned to these operations. That way, the CBO comes to the correct query plan based on your unique system characteristics.

> **NOTE**
> *It is unusual that default settings are incorrect for many systems. I have observed that Oracle development teams that do not look at and set these parameters are the teams that believe you must use hints and must always second-guess the optimizer. These are the teams that seem to struggle the most with the database, handcrafting each and every query, telling the database exactly how they would like to process it, instead of the other way around. Hopefully, after reading this section, those teams will come full circle, remove all of those hints, and let the optimizer do its job.*

## Adjust the OPTIMIZER_INDEX_CACHING and OPTIMIZER_INDEX_COST_ADJ Parameters

The OPTIMIZER_INDEX_CACHING and OPTIMIZER_INDEX_COST_ADJ parameters are the ones that have the most impact on the CBO and its correctness. In order to get the most out of the CBO, we will investigate these two parameters.

### Set OPTIMIZER_INDEX_CACHING

The Oracle CBO assigns costs to various steps in a query plan. It assigns these costs in large part based on the estimated amount of logical I/O (LIO) each step will perform. Let's see how this works with an example. We begin with two test tables:

```
ops$tkyte@ORA920> create table  t1
  2  as
  3  select mod(rownum,1000) id, rpad('x',300,'x') data
```

```
    4     from all_objects
    5   where rownum <= 5*1000;
Table created.

ops$tkyte@ORA920> create table  t2
    2   as
    3   select rownum id, rpad('x',300,'x') data
    4     from all_objects
    5   where rownum <= 1000;
Table created.

ops$tkyte@ORA920> create index t1_idx on t1(id);
Index created.

ops$tkyte@ORA920> create index t2_idx on t2(id);
Index created.

ops$tkyte@ORA920> begin
    2      dbms_stats.gather_table_stats
    3      ( user, 'T1', method_opt => 'for all indexed columns',
    4        cascade=>true );
    5      dbms_stats.gather_table_stats
    6      ( user, 'T2', method_opt => 'for all indexed columns',
    7        cascade=>true );
    8   end;
    9   /
PL/SQL procedure successfully completed.
```

We have two tables that have "nice" indexes in place, and everything is ready to go. We execute the following query and look at its query plan:

```
ops$tkyte@ORA920> set autotrace traceonly   explain

ops$tkyte@ORA920> select *
    2     from t1, t2
    3   where t1.id = t2.id
    4       and t2.id between 50 and 55;

Execution Plan
----------------------------------------------------------
    0      SELECT STATEMENT Optimizer=CHOOSE (Cost=28 Card=5 Bytes=1000)
    1    0   HASH JOIN (Cost=28 Card=5 Bytes=1000)
    2    1     TABLE ACCESS (BY INDEX ROWID) OF 'T2'
             (Cost=3 Card=5 Bytes=500)
    3    2       INDEX (RANGE SCAN) OF 'T2_IDX' (NON-UNIQUE) (Cost=2 Card=5)
    4    1     TABLE ACCESS (FULL) OF 'T1' (Cost=24 Card=26 Bytes=2600)
```

Wait a minute—why isn't the optimizer going after our index on T1 here? It has to do with the way that the optimizer calculates costs for index access. By default, it assumes every index access will incur physical I/O (PIO)—that the index data is not going to be found in the cache.

When calculating the cost of nested loops or in-list type operations, the optimizer is making the calculation with the belief that every index read will be a physical read from disk. Hence, operations that can do large multiblock I/O, such as that full scan of T2 in our example, may cost less than the presumed multiple physical I/Os we would do against the index structure. Here, Oracle is saying, "I would rather full-scan T1 using the predicate where t1.id between 50 and 55." It used the associative nature of T1.ID = T2.ID to realize that T1.ID must be between 50 and 55 if T2.ID is constrained to be between 50 and 55. We know it came to this conclusion in this case because of this information:

```
    4    1     TABLE ACCESS (FULL) OF 'T1' (Cost=24 Card=26 Bytes=2600)
```

This shows it is expecting 26 rows, not the 5,000 rows we put in there, so it must be filtering them.

Based on our knowledge of the system, we know that some (or most) of that index will, in fact, be in the buffer cache, or that at least we would presume it would be, since this is a heavily used table. We can use the OPTIMIZER_INDEX_CACHING parameter to tell Oracle the percentage of index blocks it could expect to find in the buffer cache on average. The default of zero causes Oracle to believe that the cache is devoid of index blocks. A maximum value of 100 causes Oracle to believe that the cache has all of the index blocks. The value you want to use is hard to pinpoint precisely, but it is somewhere between 0 and 100. You may want to start with something close to your cache hit ratio, and adjust up and down from there to see the effect on your system over time. For example, let's set it to 50 and try that same query:

```
ops$tkyte@ORA920> alter session set optimizer_index_caching = 50;
Session altered.

ops$tkyte@ORA920> select *
  2    from t1, t2
  3   where t1.id = t2.id
  4     and t2.id between 50 and 55;

Execution Plan
----------------------------------------------------------
   0      SELECT STATEMENT Optimizer=CHOOSE (Cost=28 Card=5 Bytes=1000)
   1    0   TABLE ACCESS (BY INDEX ROWID) OF 'T1' (Cost=5 Card=1 Bytes=100)
   2    1    NESTED LOOPS (Cost=28 Card=5 Bytes=1000)
   3    2     TABLE ACCESS (BY INDEX ROWID) OF 'T2'
                (Cost=3 Card=5 Bytes=500)
   4    3      INDEX (RANGE SCAN) OF 'T2_IDX' (NON-UNIQUE)
                (Cost=2 Card=5)
   5    2     INDEX (RANGE SCAN) OF 'T1_IDX' (NON-UNIQUE)
```

Now, the query plan shows that we do a completely different thing here. Gone is the full scan of BIG_TABLE. It is using a nested loops join to access the data. We have reduced the cost of the nested loops join to make it as appealing (apparently a bit more appealing) than the hash join from the previous version. Notice how the cost of the following step is missing:

```
   5    2        INDEX (RANGE SCAN) OF 'T1_IDX' (NON-UNIQUE)
```

That is a nuance of AUTOTRACE reporting; the query it uses has a decode function call that "hides" zero values. We actually made this step have a cost of zero, which affected the cost of higher-level steps, bringing down the estimated cost of this query plan.

**NOTE**
*The behavior of the optimizer may be version- and system-dependent. I used Oracle9i Release 2 version 9.2.0.3 in these examples. If you cannot replicate my findings exactly, don't worry. A different setting for WORKAREA_SIZE_POLICY, PGA_AGGREGATE_TARGET, SORT_AREA_SIZE, DB_CACHE_SIZE, and DB_FILE_MULTIBLOCK_READ_COUNT; different block sizes; different system loads; and so on may affect the cost estimates of a query.*

## Set OPTIMIZER_INDEX_COST_ADJ

If you think of the OPTIMIZER_INDEX_CACHING parameter as being used to tell Oracle the percentage of an index that is cached, you can think of the OPTIMIZER_INDEX_COST_ADJ parameter as telling Oracle how much of the table data will be cached. The lower the number, the less costly single-block table accesses become; conversely, the higher this number, the more costly. A way to think of this would be that this number reflects the cost of performing multiblock I/O (associated with full-table scans, for example) versus the cost of performing single-block I/O (associated with index reads). If you leave this parameter at the default setting of 100, these operations cost the same. Setting this value to 50 causes the optimizer to consider a single-block table access as half as expensive as multiblock I/O would be, effectively cutting in half the cost of table access (50/100).

If we were to set the OPTIMIZER_INDEX_CACHING parameter back to its default and use the OPTIMIZER_INDEX_COST_ADJ parameter in the example in the previous section, using the same data and indexes, we would discover this:

```
ops$tkyte@ORA920> alter session set optimizer_index_cost_adj = 50;
Session altered.

ops$tkyte@ORA920> alter session set optimizer_index_caching = 0;
Session altered.

ops$tkyte@ORA920> select *
  2    from t1, t2
  3   where t1.id = t2.id
  4     and t2.id between 50 and 55;

Execution Plan
----------------------------------------------------------
   0      SELECT STATEMENT Optimizer=CHOOSE (Cost=17 Card=5 Bytes=1000)
   1    0   TABLE ACCESS (BY INDEX ROWID) OF 'T1' (Cost=4 Card=1 Bytes=100)
   2    1     NESTED LOOPS (Cost=17 Card=5 Bytes=1000)
   3    2       TABLE ACCESS (BY INDEX ROWID) OF 'T2'
                  (Cost=2 Card=5 Bytes=500)
   4    3         INDEX (RANGE SCAN) OF 'T2_IDX' (NON-UNIQUE)
```

```
                       (Cost=2 Card=5)
   5    2            INDEX (RANGE SCAN) OF 'T1_IDX' (NON-UNIQUE) (Cost=1 Card=1)
```

We achieved the same plan, but it apparently is cheaper than the previous version! Will this plan run any faster than the other one with the same steps but different cost values? Of course not—all we've done is externally influenced the optimizer to cost things differently; it is the same plan as we achieved before.

### OPTIMIZER_INDEX_CACHING and OPTIMIZER_INDEX_COST_ADJ Wrap-Up

The setting of the OPTIMIZER_INDEX_CACHING and OPTIMIZER_INDEX_COST_ADJ parameters will not make the plans run faster. It just affects which plan is chosen. It is important to remember that setting these parameter values does not affect how much of the index is actually cached or how expensive a single-block I/O truly is in relation to multiblock I/O. Rather, this allows you to pass this information you have learned onto the CBO so it can make better decisions on your system. Also, it points out why just looking at the cost of a query plan in an attempt to determine which plan is going to be faster is an exercise in futility: Take two identical plans, with two different costs, which one is faster? Neither is.

The effect of adjusting these two parameters is that they have a profound and immediate impact on the CBO. They radically change the costing assigned to various steps. This, in turn, dramatically affects the plans generated. Therefore, you want to test thoroughly the effects of these parameters on your test system first! I've seen systems go from nonfunctional to blazingly fast simply by adjusting these two knobs. Out of all of the Oracle initialization parameters, these two are most likely to be defaulted inappropriately for your system. Adjusting them is likely to greatly change your opinion of the CBO's abilities.

You should consider setting these to nondefault values for many systems, or at least testing the two extremes:

- The default settings of OPTIMIZER_INDEX_CACHING = 0 and OPTIMIZER_INDEX_ COST_ADJ = 100. These are typically appropriate for many data warehouse/reporting systems.

- The settings of OPTIMIZER_INDEX_CACHING = 90 and OPTIMIZER_INDEX_COST_ ADJ = 25. These are typically appropriate for many transactional/OLTP systems.

## Use SYSTEM Statistics

Oracle9i introduced an alternative to OPTIMIZER_INDEX_COST_ADJ and OPTIMIZER_INDEX_ CACHING that is worth a serious look. The DBMS_STATS package was enhanced to collect a new type of statistic: system statistics. These statistics measure actual performance characteristics of your unique system. They measure your actual CPU and disk-performance characteristics using your actual workloads. They are not guesses. They are actual, measured observations of what has occurred in your system during the period of measurement. Depending on the type of work you actually perform, different costs will be associated with various operations, affecting the eventual query plans that result.

Every physical configuration will perform a little differently than any other configuration. That is why the perfect numbers for the OPTIMIZER_INDEX_* parameters cannot simply be stated. The best numbers rely on your system's fingerprint—its unique characteristics. Hence, the ability for us to measure, collect, and then use actual performance characteristics of our systems can reduce or remove the need to guess at these figures.

System statistics gathering works in one of two ways:

- You tell Oracle to start measuring now, and then after a while, you tell it to stop measuring.

- You tell Oracle to measure system statistics for the next *<some period of time>*, and Oracle will start and stop by itself.

In order to demonstrate how this works, we need to set up a simulation. For this example, we will use the explicit start/stop method. We need to simulate a typical load on our system as well, one that is representative of the load we would expect day to day. Normally, the DBA would simply gather these system statistics during normal loads on the system itself; no simulation is necessary.

## Workload Simulation Setup

We will simulate three different environments on a system, to see what kinds of costs Oracle would assign to various operations. We set up two routines: one to simulate classic OLTP operations using simple keyed reads, and the other to simulate a large report or data warehouse activity (a lot of full scans). Using DBMS_JOB to run them in the background, we will allow Oracle to measure three types of workloads:

- A pure OLTP workload

- A pure reporting or Decision Support System (DSS) workload

- A mixed workload, representing some concurrent OLTP and reporting activity

The procedure to simulate an OLTP-style workload is to have the routine iterate 10,000 times, generating a unique key to use to select from BIG_TABLE, fetch the entire result, and discard it. Using SQL_TRACE in a test run, we verify that this procedure does an INDEX UNIQUE scan on our primary key index, followed by a table access by ROWID to simulate the OLTP workload:

```
create or replace procedure oltp_style
as
    l_rec big_table%rowtype;
    l_n   number;
begin
    for i in 1 .. 10000
    loop
        l_n := trunc( dbms_random.value( 2, 1000000 ) );
        select * into l_rec from big_table where id = l_n;
    end loop;
end;
/
```

Next is the data warehouse or reporting style query. For that, we use the following procedure. Here, we use hints in order to achieve the plan we want: big full-table scans. The hints are not for performance, but rather to ensure the same plans are being measured for all three situations we are simulating.

```
create or replace procedure dw_style
as
    l_n number;
begin
    select count(*) into l_n
      from (
    select /*+ USE_HASH(t1,t2)
             FULL(t1) FULL(t2)
             NOPARALLEL(t1) NOPARALLEL(t2) */
          t1.data_object_id, t2.data_object_id
      from big_table t1, big_Table t2
    where t1.id = t2.id
          );
end;
/
```

## Run the Workload Simulations

Now, we set about to measure the three discrete workloads we want to simulate. Before we begin, we create a statistics table to hold the results of each operation. This allows us to run the three simulations, save their results, and then restore them at will for further analysis and testing. It also nicely demonstrates how the DBA would use this facility in the real world. You will find that your workload changes periodically. Maybe every day you go through cycles of OLTP during the day, reporting in the evening, and batch overnight. You might use three different sets of statistics over the course of a day (using DBMS_JOB to automatically put them in place at the times you designate). Or, you might be on a larger schedule, such as data warehouse during the week and loads/rebuilds on the weekend. Here, you might have two sets of system statistics: one for the week and another for the weekend.

Here are the steps to start this process:

```
exec dbms_stats.drop_stat_table( user, 'SYSTEM_STATS' );
exec dbms_stats.create_stat_table( user, 'SYSTEM_STATS' );
exec dbms_stats.delete_system_stats;
```

To run each simulation, the general process is as follows:

1. Run the stored procedure without gathering system statistics. This is just priming the pump—getting the shared pool warmed up.

2. Submit the procedure *N* times to the job queue, to permit it to run in the background.

3. Commit the DBMS_JOB calls so the job queue may see those jobs in the queue.

4. Begin gathering system statistics. We name each set of statistics: OLTP, DW for data warehousing, and MIXED for a mixed workload. These identifying tags are used to put in place the set of system statistics we want later.

5. Periodically, poll the job queues every five seconds until the jobs are finished running.

**6.** Finish gathering the system statistics.

For example, this PL/SQL block executed the OLTP workload:

```
declare
    n number;
begin
    oltp_style;
    dbms_job.submit( n, 'oltp_style;' );
    dbms_job.submit( n, 'oltp_style;' );
    dbms_job.submit( n, 'oltp_style;' );
    commit;

    dbms_stats.gather_system_stats( gathering_mode => 'START',
                                    stattab => 'SYSTEM_STATS',
                                    statid => 'OLTP' );

    select count(*) into n from user_jobs where what = 'oltp_style;';
    while ( n > 0 )
    loop
        dbms_lock.sleep(5);
        select count(*) into n from user_jobs where what = 'oltp_style;';
    end loop;

    dbms_stats.gather_system_stats( gathering_mode => 'STOP',
                                    stattab => 'SYSTEM_STATS',
                                    statid => 'OLTP' );
end;
/
```

For the data warehouse simulation, we use these DBMS_JOB.SUBMIT calls:

```
dw_style;
dbms_job.submit( n, 'dw_style;' );
dbms_job.submit( n, 'dw_style;' );
dbms_job.submit( n, 'dw_style;' );
dbms_job.submit( n, 'dw_style;' );
commit;
```

For the mixed workload simulation, use these DBMS_JOB.SUBMIT calls:

```
dbms_job.submit( n, 'dw_style;' );
dbms_job.submit( n, 'dw_style;' );
dbms_job.submit( n, 'dw_style;' );
dbms_job.submit( n, 'oltp_style;' );
dbms_job.submit( n, 'oltp_style;' );
dbms_job.submit( n, 'oltp_style;' );
commit;
```

## Review the Optimizer's Query Plans

Now, we want to review the plans that the optimizer would come up with for our sample query (the one used previously with OPTIMIZER_INDEX_COST_ADJ and OPTIMIZER_INDEX_CACHING). So, applying EXPLAIN PLAN on that query using AUTOTRACE, we see the following:

```
big_table@ORA920> alter system flush shared_pool;
System altered.

big_table@ORA920> alter session set optimizer_index_cost_adj=100;
Session altered.

big_table@ORA920> alter session set optimizer_index_caching=0;
Session altered.

big_table@ORA920> begin
  2       dbms_stats.import_system_stats
  3       ( stattab => 'SYSTEM_STATS', statid => 'OLTP', statown => user );
  3    end;
  4    /

PL/SQL procedure successfully completed.
big_table@ORA920> set autotrace traceonly explain
big_table@ORA920> select /* TAGGED OLTP */ *
  2       from t1, t2
  3     where t1.id = t2.id
  4       and t2.id between 50 and 55;

Execution Plan
----------------------------------------------------------
   0        SELECT STATEMENT Optimizer=CHOOSE (Cost=33 Card=5 Bytes=1000)
   1      0   HASH JOIN (Cost=33 Card=5 Bytes=1000)
   2      1     TABLE ACCESS (BY INDEX ROWID) OF 'T2'
                 (Cost=4 Card=5 Bytes=500)
   3      2       INDEX (RANGE SCAN) OF 'T2_IDX' (NON-UNIQUE) (Cost=3 Card=5)
   4      1     TABLE ACCESS (BY INDEX ROWID) OF 'T1'
                 (Cost=29 Card=26 Bytes=2600)
   5      4       INDEX (RANGE SCAN) OF 'T1_IDX' (NON-UNIQUE) (Cost=3 Card=1)
```

**NOTE**
*The comment /* TAGGED OLTP */ is not a hint; it is just a tag I added so that I could easily identify this query when running TKPROF or some other trace tool. Also, since system statistics do not invalidate any existing query plans when they are set, I needed to have unique SQL text in order to see the different plans for the same query using different system statistics.*

This is interesting. It is not the query plan generated using all default settings. It is not the query plan generated by setting or tweaking the OPTIMIZER_INDEX_COST_ADJ and

OPTIMIZER_INDEX_CACHING parameters. It is a different plan entirely, and it was achieved using all default parameters, without any tweaking or modifying on our part. But what drove the optimizer to avoid the full-table scan of T1 as it did in the default test earlier? Well, we can take a peek at the system statistics we just imported. They are now stored in the dictionary table SYS.AUX_STATS$:

```
big_table@ORA920> select * from sys.aux_stats$;

SNAME           PNAME        PVAL1   PVAL2
--------------  --------   ---------  --------------------
SYSSTATS_INFO   STATUS                COMPLETED
SYSSTATS_INFO   DSTART                05-18-2003 11:12
SYSSTATS_INFO   DSTOP                 05-18-2003 11:12
SYSSTATS_INFO   FLAGS            1
SYSSTATS_MAIN   SREADTIM     1.932
SYSSTATS_MAIN   MREADTIM      .554
SYSSTATS_MAIN   CPUSPEED       340
SYSSTATS_MAIN   MBRC            15
SYSSTATS_MAIN   MAXTHR          -1
SYSSTATS_MAIN   SLAVETHR        -1

10 rows selected.
```

This is the information Oracle used now to estimate the costs of various operations. The following statistics are shown:

| | |
|---|---|
| SREADTIM | Time to read single-block I/O, in milliseconds |
| MREADTIM | Time to read multiple blocks, in milliseconds |
| CPUSPEED | Available cycles per second, in millions (relative CPU speed) |
| MBRC | Average observed multiblock read count |
| MAXTHR | Maximum I/O system throughput in bytes/second |
| SLAVETHR | Average I/O Slave I/O throughput in bytes/second |

In this example, the I/O throughput numbers are both –1, indicating there was no observable value. Since this system did not perform very much actual physical I/O during this period of time, that makes sense. The other numbers were the observed response times for the various operations: 1.932 milliseconds response time for single-block I/O operations, 0.554 millisecond for multiblock I/O operations (of which we performed very little during this test), a relative CPU speed of 340 (which we'll see remains at a constant value across all of our tests), and a multiblock read count of 15 on average, for the few times we did multiblock I/O.

For comparison purposes, Table 6-1 shows the three sets of system statistics gathered and used in this particular test.

| Statistic | OLTP | DW | MIXED |
|---|---|---|---|
| SREADTIM | 1.932 | 0.595 | 7.225 |
| MREADTIM | 0.554 | 2.386 | 4.972 |
| CPUSPEED | 340 | 340 | 340 |
| MBRC | 15 | 7 | 9 |
| MAXTHR | *Na | 17,729,536 | 11,837,440 |
| SLAVETHR | *Na | Not available | Not available |

**TABLE 6-1.** *System Statistics Gathered for the OLTP, Data Warehouse, and Mixed Workload Simulation Tests*

**NOTE**
*You can use DBMS_STATS.SET_SYSTEM_STATS to set these statistics manually on your system to see the same results I observed. Any other method would be unlikely to exactly reproduce my results, for it is highly unlikely your system performs exactly as mine does.*

As you can see, each workload has its own characteristics here. The bottom line is that the optimizer now has very specific information about what it can expect from the system regarding CPU power and I/O processing under the various workloads. It has details never before available and, using these facts, it will be able to develop better query plans.

Looking at the query plan using the data warehousing style statistics, we observe the following:

```
big_table@ORA920> begin
  2      dbms_stats.import_system_stats
  3      ( stattab => 'SYSTEM_STATS', statid => 'DW', statown => user );
  4  end;
  5  /

PL/SQL procedure successfully completed.

big_table@ORA920> select /* TAGGED DW */ *
  2    from t1, t2
  3    where t1.id = t2.id
  4      and t2.id between 50 and 55;

Execution Plan
----------------------------------------------------------
   0      SELECT STATEMENT Optimizer=CHOOSE (Cost=34 Card=5 Bytes=1000)
   1    0   HASH JOIN (Cost=34 Card=5 Bytes=1000)
   2    1     TABLE ACCESS (BY INDEX ROWID) OF 'T2'
              (Cost=4 Card=5 Bytes=500)
   3    2       INDEX (RANGE SCAN) OF 'T2_IDX' (NON-UNIQUE) (Cost=3 Card=5)
```

```
   4    1       TABLE ACCESS (BY INDEX ROWID) OF 'T1'
                   (Cost=30 Card=26 Bytes=2600)
   5    4          INDEX (RANGE SCAN) OF 'T1_IDX' (NON-UNIQUE) (Cost=3 Card=1)
```

The plan is functionally the same, but the costs are a little higher. The cost of an index access is slightly higher, but not by much.

Progressing onto the mixed workload test, where we have the system very loaded with OLTP and data warehousing style work, we see a different story:

```
big_table@ORA920> begin
  2        dbms_stats.import_system_stats
  3        ( stattab => 'SYSTEM_STATS', statid => 'MIXED', statown => user );
  4    end;
  5    /
PL/SQL procedure successfully completed.

big_table@ORA920> select /* TAGGED MIXED */ *
  2     from t1, t2
  3    where t1.id = t2.id
  4      and t2.id between 50 and 55;

Execution Plan
----------------------------------------------------------
   0        SELECT STATEMENT Optimizer=CHOOSE (Cost=30 Card=5 Bytes=1000)
   1    0    HASH JOIN (Cost=30 Card=5 Bytes=1000)
   2    1     TABLE ACCESS (BY INDEX ROWID) OF 'T2'
                (Cost=4 Card=5 Bytes=500)
   3    2       INDEX (RANGE SCAN) OF 'T2_IDX' (NON-UNIQUE) (Cost=3 Card=5)
   4    1     TABLE ACCESS (FULL) OF 'T1' (Cost=26 Card=26 Bytes=2600)
```

Here, we are back to the original query plan we started with, by default. The costs are a little different, but it is the same full-table scan plan. In this case, it would be due to the extremely high single-block I/O access times versus the high, but much lower, multiblock I/O times. Apparently, under the load we put on our little system, single-block index access became very expensive and larger multiblock I/O less expensive. The optimizer used those facts in order to come up with the best plan under that working environment.

As one last observation, to see the different costs associated with certain operations, we explained the following two queries under each environment as well, to see how the costs of full-table scans and index accesses would be affected with each setting. The queries were simply:

```
select * from big_table OLTP;
select * from big_table OLTP where owner = 'ORDSYS';
```

The costing results under the OLTP system settings were, for example, as follows:

```
big_table@ORA920> select * from big_table OLTP;

Execution Plan
----------------------------------------------------------
   0        SELECT STATEMENT Optimizer=CHOOSE
```

```
          (Cost=3522 Card=1833792 Bytes=165041280)
   1    0    TABLE ACCESS (FULL) OF 'BIG_TABLE'
          (Cost=3522 Card=1833792 Bytes=165041280)



big_table@ORA920> select * from big_table OLTP where owner = 'ORDSYS';

Execution Plan
---------------------------------------------------------------
   0      SELECT STATEMENT Optimizer=CHOOSE
          (Cost=1665 Card=61952 Bytes=5575680)
   1    0    TABLE ACCESS (BY INDEX ROWID) OF 'BIG_TABLE'
          (Cost=1665 Card=61952 Bytes=5575680)
   2    1      INDEX (RANGE SCAN) OF 'BIG_TABLE_IDX' (NON-UNIQUE)
          (Cost=166 Card=61952)
```

In comparison, across all tests, we observe the costs shown in Table 6-2.

As you can see, the optimizer radically changed its relative cost of performing various operations given the different workloads. Remember that just because the cost changed it *does not imply that the operation is any faster or slower.* It only means that the optimizer has a better understanding of how your unique system will perform under a typical load and will assign a more correct cost to each phase of a query plan resulting in better performing query plans in your environment, under your load.

## System Statistics Wrap-Up

Using DBMS_STATS GATHER_SYSTEM_STATS, we are able to forgo fine-tuning the OPTIMIZER_ INDEX_CACHING and OPTIMIZER_INDEX_COST_ADJ parameters. The important consideration here, however, is that you must gather these system statistics when the system is running a *representative load.* If you do not, you may get the entirely wrong or misleading set of statistics loaded into the dictionary, and the CBO will make the wrong choice (the old "garbage in, garbage out" saying comes to mind here).

| Test | Full-Scan Cost | Range-Scan Cost | Table Access by Index ROWID Cost |
|---|---|---|---|
| OLTP | 3,522 | 166 | 1,665 |
| DW | 17,211 | 212 | 1,833 |
| MIXED | 2,507 | 151 | 1,610 |
| Default (no systems statistics and no OPTIMIZER_INDEX_* settings) | 2,136 | 145 | 1,590 |

**TABLE 6-2.** *Costs for the Workload Simulation Tests*

Furthermore, you will most likely want to have several sets of system statistics gathered on your system, each representing different load profiles. For example, you may be OLTP-heavy during the day, reporting/DSS-heavy in the evening, and batch-oriented at night. In this case, it would be wise to have three different sets of system statistics gathered that you import during the different periods of the day, each representing the different load and usage patterns in effect at that point in time. Since importing system statistics only affects plans generated from that time forward (it does not invalidate existing query plans in the shared pool), it *may* be necessary to flush the shared pool but only if you run the same exact queries during these different periods.

Lastly, you will want to make the gathering of system statistics a continual event, not something you just do once and forget about it. As your workload changes over time, so will these statistics. Consider that the numbers presented in the workload simulations here all came from the *same system*. These values will change radically as your workload changes over time. Additionally, just using this method will cause the observed system statistics to change over time! Using system statistics will affect future query plans. It is the effects of these query plans on your system that must then be measured. Perhaps the system stops doing full-table scans after analyzing your OLTP workload, so now the performance characteristics of your system are completely different and must be gathered again over time.

# Optimize the CBO

Now that we've seen the two most important init.ora parameters used with the CBO, we'll take a look at the rest. This section will cover the other important init.ora parameters that affect the behavior of the CBO in some way. The exception is the CURSOR_SHARING parameter, an important parameter introduced in Oracle8i Release 2 (version 8.1.6) that controls Oracle's behavior when parsing queries that contain literals. That parameter is covered in detail in Chapter 5 in the section, "Use Bind Variables."

## Set COMPATIBLE for Upgrades

The COMPATIBLE parameter dictates which features and functions are available to the database. If you attempt to use a feature that was introduced in version *Y* but COMPATIBLE is set to version *X*, you may find that you cannot use that feature.

In general, you would use COMPATIBLE during an upgrade process. You might decide to upgrade your Oracle9i Release 1 database to Oracle9i Release 2, but leave COMPATIBLE at 9.0.0. This will prevent the database from using new features that cannot be downgraded. Another way to think of this parameter is that by leaving it set to earlier releases, you are preventing the creation of new database (on-disk) structures and the features associated with them that did not exist in that earlier release.

After an upgrade is completed, you should consider testing it with COMPATIBLE set to your release level (notice that I said *test*, not just enable!) to permit the use of new features. Once you open the database with a higher COMPATIBLE setting, there is a good chance you will not be able to set it back down. This is because some features cause file format changes (different redo formats, different datafile writes, and so on) and cannot be downgraded.

For example, you might see the "ORA–00406" error:

```
$ oerr ora 406
00406, 00000, "COMPATIBLE parameter needs to be %s or greater"
```

```
// *Cause:  The COMPATIBLE initialization parameter is not high
//  enough to allow the operation. Allowing the command would make
//  the database incompatible with the release specified by the
//  current COMPATIBLE parameter.
// *Action: Shutdown and start up with a higher compatibility
//  setting.
```

If this happened, you would need to consider upgrading the COMPATIBLE init.ora parameter, realizing that you will no longer be able to downgrade the database. Before you make such a change, make sure to have a good backup from before the change handy, just in case of an unexpected side effect (as is always the case before making changes).

# Set DB_FILE_MULTIBLOCK_READ_COUNT to Reduce Full-Scan Costs

The DB_FILE_MULTIBLOCK_READ_COUNT parameter controls the number of blocks Oracle will read in a single I/O while doing a full scan or an index fast full scan. The higher this value, the lower the cost of a full scan.

Consider the following example:

```
big_table@ORA920> show parameter db_file_multi

NAME                                 TYPE        VALUE
------------------------------------ ----------- --------------------
db_file_multiblock_read_count        integer     16

big_table@ORA920> set autotrace traceonly explain
big_table@ORA920> select * from big_table;
Execution Plan
----------------------------------------------------------
   0      SELECT STATEMENT Optimizer=CHOOSE
          (Cost=2136 Card=1833857 Bytes=154043988)
   1    0   TABLE ACCESS (FULL) OF 'BIG_TABLE'
          (Cost=2136 Card=1833857 Bytes=154043988)

big_table@ORA920> alter session set db_file_multiblock_read_count = 32;
Session altered.

big_table@ORA920> select * from big_table;
Execution Plan
----------------------------------------------------------
   0      SELECT STATEMENT Optimizer=CHOOSE
          (Cost=1354 Card=1833857 Bytes=154043988)
   1    0   TABLE ACCESS (FULL) OF 'BIG_TABLE'
          (Cost=1354 Card=1833857 Bytes=154043988)

big_table@ORA920> alter session set db_file_multiblock_read_count = 64;
Session altered.

big_table@ORA920> select * from big_table;
```

```
Execution Plan
----------------------------------------------------------------
   0        SELECT STATEMENT Optimizer=CHOOSE
            (Cost=858 Card=1833857 Bytes=154043988)
   1    0    TABLE ACCESS (FULL) OF 'BIG_TABLE'
            (Cost=858 Card=1833857 Bytes=154043988)
```

As you can see, the higher DB_FILE_MULTIBLOCK_READ_COUNT is set, the lower the cost of a full scan. A full scan will become more appealing than an index access. This will bias a full scan over indexes as it increases.

The valid range of values for DB_FILE_MULTIBLOCK_READ_COUNT is highly operating system–dependent. Each operating system will have its true maximum on the size of an I/O. In this example, when we set our read count to 64, that was 64 × 8KB, or 0.5MB per I/O that we were requesting. Is our operating system able to accommodate that? We can consult our operating system tuning guide to find the maximum read size, or we can trick Oracle into giving us that information. To get the information from Oracle, we enable tracing like this (to capture wait events into the trace file) and set our DB_FILE_MULTIBLOCK_READ_COUNT very high:

```
big_table@ORA920> alter session set events
  2 '10046 trace name context forever, level 12';
Session altered.

big_table@ORA920> alter session set db_file_multiblock_read_count = 5000000;
Session altered.
```

Then we run a query that does a full scan, such as select /*+ noparallel(big_table) full(big_table) */ * from big_table. We'll undoubtedly see wait events on I/O, namely db file scattered read-wait events. Using the Unix utility grep to scan the trace file we generated, we find this:

```
$ grep scattered ora920_ora_31266.trc | more
WAIT #3: nam='db file scattered read' ela= 61870 p1=9 p2=33035 p3=126
WAIT #3: nam='db file scattered read' ela= 48985 p1=9 p2=33547 p3=126
WAIT #3: nam='db file scattered read' ela= 55994 p1=9 p2=33931 p3=126
WAIT #3: nam='db file scattered read' ela= 44090 p1=9 p2=34187 p3=126
WAIT #3: nam='db file scattered read' ela= 46638 p1=9 p2=34699 p3=126
WAIT #3: nam='db file scattered read' ela= 43463 p1=9 p2=35339 p3=126
WAIT #3: nam='db file scattered read' ela= 98053 p1=9 p2=35851 p3=126
WAIT #3: nam='db file scattered read' ela= 46462 p1=9 p2=36363 p3=126
```

The Oracle9i *Database Reference Guide* explains what the p1, p2, and p3 values represent, and it tells us p3 is the number of blocks we are requesting to read at one time. Apparently, on this operating system (Red Hat Linux), we can read just short of 1MB of data at a time. (On a Sun Solaris system, my maximum I/O size was 64 blocks, or 0.5MB, at a time.)

On a DSS or data warehouse system, you would want this set to the maximum I/O size your system permits. Not only does it affect query-plan generation, affecting the cost of a full-scan operation, but it also directly affects the performance of the query. The fewer I/O calls to the operating system, the faster a full scan will perform.

On a transactional system, where you do not anticipate doing full scans frequently, a smaller setting may be appropriate, to make full scans less appealing in those systems. You can always use the ALTER SESSION command in any batch jobs to permit them to use a larger multiblock read count.

In Oracle9i with support for multiple block size databases, it is interesting to note that this parameter is actually used to set the I/O size, not the number of blocks read! What that means is Oracle will take your db_file_multiblock_read_count and multiply it by your default blocksize (the blocksize of your SYSTEM tablespace). Oracle will use that as the I/O size on your system. If your default block size is 8K and you set this parameter to 16, you will only read eight blocks at a time in a 16K blocksize tablespace. It's not documented, but it was learned through testing.

"I have a 32K blocksize tablespace on a database where the "default" block size is 8K. Does the db_file_multiblock_read_count apply as a multiple of the 8K for all datafiles, or is it tablespace-dependant, for example, (32K*dfmrc) for 32K tablespace and (8K*dmfrc) for 8K tablespaces on the same instance?"

This was an interesting question so I set up a simulation to test with. I was using an 8K blocksize database by default and simply created a 16K tablespace to test with. In order to do this, I had to setup my 16K cache size first, I did that by sizing down my db_cache_size and then setting the db_16k_cache_size and creating a tablespace:

```
ops$tkyte@ORA920> show parameter db_cache_size;

NAME                                 TYPE        VALUE
db_cache_size                        big integer 67108864
ops$tkyte@ORA920> alter system set db_cache_size=32m;
System altered.

ops$tkyte@ORA920> alter system set db_16k_cache_size=32m;
System altered.

ops$tkyte@ORA920> create tablespace sixteen_k
  2   blocksize 16k
  3   extent management local
  4   uniform size 2m
  5   /
Tablespace created.
```

Then, I simply copied the BIG_TABLE into that tablespace:

```
ops$tkyte@ORA920> create table big_table_copy_16k
  2   TABLESPACE sixteen_k
  3   as
  4   select * from big_table.big_table;
```

```
Table created.

ops$tkyte@ORA920> analyze table big_table_copy_16k
  2 compute statistics for table;
Table analyzed.
```

Using the same technique just outlined, then setting the 10046 EVENT and inspecting the trace file after executing we get:

```
ops$tkyte@ORA920> select /*+ noparallel(b) full(b) */ count(*)
  2 from big_table_copy_16k b;

  COUNT(*)
----------
  1833792

ops$tkyte@ORA920> select /*+ noparallel(b) full(b) */ count(*)
  2 from big_table.big_table b;

  COUNT(*)
----------
  1833792
```

Upon inspecting the trace file, we discover:

```
select /*+ noparallel(b) full(b) */ count(*)
  from big_table_copy_16k b
END OF STMT
PARSE #1:c=1953,e=1728,p=1,cr=1,cu=0,mis=1,r=0,dep=0,og=4,
BINDS #1:
EXEC #1:c=0,e=132,p=0,cr=0,cu=0,mis=0,r=0,dep=0,og=4,
WAIT #1: nam='SQL*Net message to client' ela= 6 p1=1650815232 p2=1 p3=0
WAIT #1: nam='db file scattered read' ela= 88910 p1=13 p2=6 p3=8
WAIT #1: nam='db file scattered read' ela= 662 p1=13 p2=14 p3=8
WAIT #1: nam='db file scattered read' ela= 869 p1=13 p2=22 p3=8
  (repeated continuously)
 select /*+ noparallel(b) full(b) */ count(*)
  from big_table.big_table b
END OF STMT
PARSE #1:c=1953,e=1350,p=0,cr=0,cu=0,mis=1,r=0,dep=0,og=4,
BINDS #1:
EXEC #1:c=0,e=124,p=0,cr=0,cu=0,mis=0,r=0,dep=0,og=4,
WAIT #1: nam='db file scattered read' ela= 500 p1=9 p2=33035 p3=16
WAIT #1: nam='db file scattered read' ela= 501 p1=9 p2=33051 p3=16
WAIT #1: nam='db file scattered read' ela= 566 p1=9 p2=33067 p3=16
```

Now, my multiblock read count in this case was 16. When we queried the original BIG_TABLE that was in my default blocksize tablespace, we achieved a multiblock read count of 16 blocks at a time. The BIG_TABLE_COPY in the 16K blocksize tablespace was read eight blocks at a time—same size reads, just different block counts. Further, if you rerun the example but use a 4K blocksize tablespace you will discover:

```
select /*+ noparallel(b) full(b) */ count(*)
  from big_table_copy_4k b
END OF STMT
PARSE #1:c=1953,e=1781,p=1,cr=1,cu=0,mis=1,r=0,dep=0,og=4,
BINDS #1:
EXEC #1:c=0,e=130,p=0,cr=0,cu=0,mis=0,r=0,dep=0,og=4,
 WAIT #1: nam='db file scattered read' ela= 210816 p1=13 p2=18 p3=32
WAIT #1: nam='db file scattered read' ela= 26353 p1=13 p2=50 p3=32
WAIT #1: nam='db file scattered read' ela= 1145 p1=13 p2=82 p3=32
```

The 4K blocksize tablespace was read 32 blocks at a time—showing that Oracle in this case will read 16 (multiblock read count) * 8K = 128K at a time. This has an interesting side effect on the costing of full-table scans that you may want to be aware of. Given that we have three tables with the same exact data, using an IO size that is identical and sizes that are very near to each other (each table was within a few megabytes of one another), you would expect the cost of a full scan against each to be the same, but in fact:

```
ops$tkyte@ORA920> set autotrace traceonly explain
ops$tkyte@ORA920> select /*+ noparallel(b) full(b) */ count(*)
  2    from big_table_copy_4k b;

Execution Plan
----------------------------------------------------------
    0      SELECT STATEMENT Optimizer=CHOOSE (Cost=3273 Card=1)

ops$tkyte@ORA920> select /*+ noparallel(b) full(b) */ count(*)
  2    from big_table.big_table b;

Execution Plan
----------------------------------------------------------
    0      SELECT STATEMENT Optimizer=CHOOSE (Cost=2313 Card=1)

ops$tkyte@ORA920> select /*+ noparallel(b) full(b) */ count(*)
  2    from big_table_copy_16k b;

Execution Plan
----------------------------------------------------------
    0      SELECT STATEMENT Optimizer=CHOOSE (Cost=1857 Card=1)
```

Oracle is costing each query as if it would read radically differing amounts of data! See how the cost apparently decreased as the blocksize increased. This is something to be aware of when using tablespaces with different-sized blocks in the same database.

## Set HASH_JOIN_ENABLED to Control Hash Joins

The HASH_JOIN_ENABLED parameter is a fairly simple one to understand. It either enables (default) a hash join or disables this functionality. I recommend using the default setting of TRUE, to allow the optimizer to consider hash joins as a possible optimization technique.

Hash joins are brutally effective and efficient. However, they might not work as they should when an inappropriate HASH_AREA_SIZE setting inhibits the speed of the hash join itself. In Oracle9i, the use of the PGA_AGGREGATE_TARGET parameter removes this issue when using dedicated server configurations, because the system will do the right thing, given the amount of memory allocated to it. In Oracle8i and earlier, or when using a shared server in any release, setting HASH_AREA_SIZE (in fact, all of the *_AREA_SIZE parameters) and gathering appropriate statistics would be more appropriate than totally disabling this feature. The common reasons people turned off this feature—insufficiently sized HASH_AREA_SIZE and insufficient statistics.

## Set OPTIMIZER_DYNAMIC_SAMPLING to Gather Statistics Dynamically

The OPTIMIZER_DYNAMIC_SAMPLING parameter is new in Oracle9i Release 2 and will have a big effect on query plans under certain conditions. The CBO is reliant on having statistics gathered against all of the objects in a query; otherwise, it makes up default statistics for the objects that have none. These defaults are shown in Tables 6-3 and 6-4.

As you can see, these default statistics would not be very representative of many of your tables. In fact, *there are no default settings that would be representative of a typical system.* How many one-block tables do you have? Is your average row length really 100? On my 8KB

| Table Setting | Default Statistics |
| --- | --- |
| Cardinality | NUMBER_OF_BLOCKS * (block size minus overhead)/AVG_ROW_LEN |
| Average row length | 100 bytes |
| Number of blocks | 1 |
| Remote cardinality (distributed queries only) | 2,000 rows |
| Remote average row length | 100 bytes |
| Levels | 1 |
| Leaf blocks | 25 |
| Leaf blocks/key | 1 |
| Data blocks/key | 1 |
| Distinct keys | 100 |
| Clustering factor | 800 |

**TABLE 6-3.** *Default Statistics for Tables*

| Index Setting | Default Statistics |
|---|---|
| Levels | 1 |
| Leaf blocks | 25 |
| Leaf blocks/key | 1 |
| Data blocks/key | 1 |
| Distinct keys | 100 |
| Clustering factor | 800 |

**TABLE 6-4.**  *Default Statistics for Indexes*

blocksize database, all tables appear to have 82 rows in them if they are not analyzed. When a query mixes together objects that have statistics with objects that do not have them, using these defaults can be deadly. The optimizer just picks the wrong plan. It is the right plan given the information it has, but real-world performance would show it is the wrong plan to actually use.

This problem is particularly noticeable with temporary tables. There is simply no practical way to analyze them and gather statistics. You could use DBMS_STATS.SET_TABLE_STATS to put in representative statistics, but that would be problematic if you didn't know what the representative statistics should be, or if they changed from run to run. (In Oracle8i and earlier, this was your only option.) You can use DBMS_STATS in Oracle9i to gather statistics on them if you loaded them with representative data, but this suffers from the same issues. Also, the defaults for temporary tables are different from the defaults for regular tables. For example, consider the following:

```
big_table@ORA920> create global temporary table
  2  temp_table ( x int );
Table created.

big_table@ORA920> create table
  2  real_table ( x int );
Table created.

big_table@ORA920> alter session set optimizer_goal=first_rows;
Session altered.
```

Here, we have two tables that are arguably the same. We've forced the use of the CBO against these unanalyzed tables by setting OPTIMIZER_GOAL to FIRST_ROWS. Now, let's see what the optimizer thinks about each of these tables:

```
big_table@ORA920> set autotrace traceonly explain
big_table@ORA920> select * from temp_table;

Execution Plan
----------------------------------------------------------
   0      SELECT STATEMENT Optimizer=FIRST_ROWS
```

```
               (Cost=11 Card=8168 Bytes=106184)
   1    0    TABLE ACCESS (FULL) OF 'TEMP_TABLE'
               (Cost=11 Card=8168 Bytes=106184)

big_table@ORA920> select * from real_table;

Execution Plan
-----------------------------------------------------------
   0        SELECT STATEMENT Optimizer=FIRST_ROWS (Cost=2 Card=82 Bytes=1066)
   1    0    TABLE ACCESS (FULL) OF 'REAL_TABLE' (Cost=2 Card=82 Bytes=1066)
```

Interestingly, the temporary table appears to be much larger and the real table smaller. Enter dynamic sampling. Using this feature, the optimizer will, at query optimization time, dynamically gather just enough statistics on the referenced object to come up with a more meaningful, correct plan—in the most likely event that your temporary tables do not typically have 8,168 rows (if they do, you won't need this).

For the OPTIMIZER_DYNAMIC_SAMPLING parameter, the valid values are 0 through 10, with 0 meaning don't do any sample and 10 being the most aggressive. Level 1 is the default in Oracle9i Release 2 if the OPTIMIZER_FEATURES_ENABLED parameter is set to 9.2 or later. Otherwise, level 0 is the default. Table 6-5 describes each setting for this parameter.

| Setting | Description |
|---------|-------------|
| Level 0 | Do not dynamically sample the table(s). |
| Level 1 | Sample tables that have not been analyzed if there is more than one table in the query, the table in question has not been analyzed and it has no indexes, and the optimizer determines that the query plan would be affected based on the size of this object. |
| Level 2 | Sample all unanalyzed tables referenced in the query using default sampling amounts (small sample). |
| Level 3 | Same as level 2, but also include tables that use a guess for selecting some predicate. Use default sampling amounts. |
| Level 4 | Same as level 3, but include tables that have single-table predicates that reference two or more columns. Use default sampling amounts. |
| Level 5 | Same as level 3, but use 2 times the default sample size. |
| Level 6 | Same as level 3, but use 4 times the default sample size. |
| Level 7 | Same as level 3, but use 8 times the default sample size. |
| Level 8 | Same as level 3, but use 32 times the default sample size. |
| Level 9 | Same as level 3, but use 128 times the default sample size. |
| Level 10 | Same as level 3, but use all of the blocks in the table. |

**TABLE 6-5.** *Valid OPTIMIZER_DYNAMIC_SAMPLING Settings*

To show the effects of the OPTIMIZER_DYNAMIC_SAMPLING setting, let's look at a common example. Suppose that we have a global temporary table and we put some values in it at runtime—sometimes one value, sometimes a thousand values, and sometimes ten thousand values—and then we use that temporary table as an in-list in a query. The steps are as follows:

- Application puts 1, 10, 1000, 10,000, or some other number of rows into a temporary table.

- Submit a query in the form of `select * from my_table where column in (select column from temporary_table)`.

We discover that the query plan generally does not perform well. Oh, it performs adequately for large items in the in-list, but for small ones that should return quickly, it does not.

**NOTE**
*This example works only in Oracle9i Release 2 and later. Prior to that release, optimizer dynamic sampling did not exist.*

Dynamic sampling can help us here immensely. In order to see the dramatic effect of this on our query plans, we'll run a small simulation. In order to set up for this, we need a global temporary table that we'll use in our in-list test:

```
big_table@ORA920> create global temporary table t
  2  ( x int not null)
  3  on commit preserve rows;
Table created.

big_table@ORA920> create index t_idx on t(x);
Index created.

big_table@ORA920> insert into t
  2  select rownum
  3    from all_objects
  4  where rownum < 5;
4 rows created.
```

Now, we are ready to see what the optimizer does with this. We'll start by disabling the dynamic sampling.

```
big_table@ORA920> set autotrace traceonly
big_table@ORA920> alter session set optimizer_dynamic_sampling=0;
Session altered.

big_table@ORA920> select *
  2    from big_table
  3  where object_id in ( select x from t );

Execution Plan
----------------------------------------------------------
   0      SELECT STATEMENT Optimizer=CHOOSE
```

```
              (Cost=4818 Card=1833857 Bytes=177884129)
   1    0   HASH JOIN (SEMI) (Cost=4818 Card=1833857 Bytes=177884129)
   2    1     TABLE ACCESS (FULL) OF 'BIG_TABLE'
                (Cost=2136 Card=1833857 Bytes=154043988)
   3    1     INDEX (FAST FULL SCAN) OF 'T_IDX' (NON-UNIQUE)
                (Cost=4 Card=8168 Bytes=106184)


Statistics
----------------------------------------------------------
...
     22007  consistent gets
     21967  physical reads
...
         5  rows processed
```

**NOTE**
*See Chapter 8 for all of the details on hash joins. This hash semi-join
is processed very much like a hash outer join would be.*

In this case, it opted for a full-table scan of BIG_TABLE from which it would construct a
(hopefully in memory) hash table and then it would "probe" this hash table using the values
from the temporary table. Furthermore, it assumed it would see 8,168 rows in that index, and
that ultimately this query would return 1,833,857 rows! Well, we know that this is way off,
because the real result set was 5 rows. So, let's turn on dynamic sampling:

```
big_table@ORA920> alter session set optimizer_dynamic_sampling=1;
Session altered.

big_table@ORA920> select *
  2    from big_table
  3   where object_id in ( select x from t );

Execution Plan
----------------------------------------------------------
   0      SELECT STATEMENT Optimizer=CHOOSE
            (Cost=4818 Card=1833857 Bytes=177884129)
   1    0   HASH JOIN (SEMI) (Cost=4818 Card=1833857 Bytes=177884129)
   2    1     TABLE ACCESS (FULL) OF 'BIG_TABLE'
                (Cost=2136 Card=1833857 Bytes=154043988)
   3    1     INDEX (FAST FULL SCAN) OF 'T_IDX' (NON-UNIQUE)
                (Cost=4 Card=8168 Bytes=106184)


Statistics
----------------------------------------------------------
...
     22005  consistent gets
     21727  physical reads
...
         5  rows processed
```

Here, we observe the same bad performance. What's the reason for this? We put an index on the temporary table, and at the level 1 setting, the presence of an index will cause Oracle to skip dynamic sampling. So, let's take it up a level:

```
big_table@ORA920> alter session set optimizer_dynamic_sampling=2;
Session altered.

big_table@ORA920> select *
  2    from big_table
  3   where object_id in ( select x from t );

Execution Plan
----------------------------------------------------------
   0      SELECT STATEMENT Optimizer=CHOOSE (Cost=16 Card=4 Bytes=388)
   1    0   TABLE ACCESS (BY INDEX ROWID) OF 'BIG_TABLE'
            (Cost=3 Card=1 Bytes=84)
   2    1     NESTED LOOPS (Cost=16 Card=4 Bytes=388)
   3    2       SORT (UNIQUE)
   4    3         INDEX (FAST FULL SCAN) OF 'T_IDX' (NON-UNIQUE)
                  (Cost=4 Card=4 Bytes=52)
   5    2         INDEX (RANGE SCAN) OF 'OBJECT_ID_IDX' (NON-UNIQUE)
                  (Cost=2 Card=1)

Statistics
----------------------------------------------------------
...
         21  consistent gets
          0  physical reads

...
          5  rows processed
```

Wow! Here, the plan is totally different. Now, Oracle recognizes that if it starts with the tiny index and for every row it finds in there it does an index probe into the BIG_TABLE, things would be better for all. Notice how the cardinality is more or less accurate and, in particular, the consistent gets are 0.1% of the original plan! This is exactly what we were looking for on this query. But is this the correct query plan 100% of the time? No, it cannot be. It is the correct plan when there is a small amount of data in the temporary table, while larger amounts should use a different plan.

Let's see what happens when we load up that temporary table:

```
big_table@ORA920> set autotrace off
big_table@ORA920> delete from t;
4 rows deleted.

big_table@ORA920> insert into t
  2  select rownum
  3    from all_objects;
29577 rows created.
```

```
big_table@ORA920> set autotrace traceonly
big_table@ORA920> select *
  2    from big_table
  3    where object_id in ( select x from t );
29578 rows selected.


Execution Plan
----------------------------------------------------------
   0      SELECT STATEMENT Optimizer=CHOOSE
          (Cost=4206 Card=29578 Bytes=2869066)
   1    0   HASH JOIN (Cost=4206 Card=29578 Bytes=2869066)
   2    1     SORT (UNIQUE)
   3    2       INDEX (FAST FULL SCAN) OF 'T_IDX' (NON-UNIQUE)
              (Cost=4 Card=29577 Bytes=384501)
   4    1     TABLE ACCESS (FULL) OF 'BIG_TABLE'
              (Cost=2136 Card=1833857 Bytes=154043988)


Statistics
----------------------------------------------------------
...
     65565   consistent gets
         0   physical reads
...
     29578   rows processed
```

Now, that's a lot more consistent, but it also returns a ton more data. Can we prove that this is a better query plan? We can, if we can run a query that gets the same plan as when we had five rows in table T. So, let's tweak the query a bit, with some hints and a join instead of an IN and see what we get:

```
big_table@ORA920> select /*+ USE_NL(t big_table) */ *
  2    from big_table,
  3       (select /*+ INDEX_FFS(T T_IDX) */ distinct x from t ) t
  4    where object_id = x;

29578 rows selected.


Execution Plan
----------------------------------------------------------
   0      SELECT STATEMENT Optimizer=CHOOSE
          (Cost=59233 Card=29578 Bytes=2869066)
   1    0   TABLE ACCESS (BY INDEX ROWID) OF 'BIG_TABLE'
          (Cost=3 Card=1 Bytes=84)
   2    1     NESTED LOOPS (Cost=59233 Card=29578 Bytes=2869066)
   3    2       VIEW (Cost=142 Card=29577 Bytes=384501)
   4    3         SORT (UNIQUE) (Cost=142 Card=29577 Bytes=384501)
   5    4           INDEX (FAST FULL SCAN) OF 'T_IDX' (NON-UNIQUE)
                  (Cost=4 Card=29577 Bytes=384501)
```

```
6     2          INDEX (RANGE SCAN) OF 'OBJECT_ID_IDX' (NON-UNIQUE)
                 (Cost=2 Card=1)
```

```
Statistics
-----------------------------------------------------------
...
    67527   consistent gets
        0   physical reads
...
    29578   rows processed
```

This shows that the OPTIMIZER_DYNAMIC_SAMPLING setting deserves your attention if you make use of global temporary tables, especially indexed ones! You will want to use a setting of 2 or above, as the default level 1 setting is insufficient to have them dynamically sampled in that case. In general, OPTIMIZER_DYNAMIC_SAMPLING is something to look into if:

■ You execute queries against analyzed and unanalyzed objects.

■ You use features such as index-organized tables (IOTs) or partitioned tables that force the use of the CBO but do not gather statistics.

This can be set at the session level as demonstrated here, set at the database level in the init.ora file, or it can even be used as a hint in the query itself. I would consider this as one of the "less evil" hints, in the same class with FIRST_ROWS and ALL_ROWS, because its intention is to give the CBO more information with which to come to a conclusion, not to do the optimizer's job.

# Set OPTIMIZER_FEATURES_ENABLE to Control Feature Choices

The OPTIMIZER_FEATURES_ENABLE init.ora setting controls which features and functions the optimizer will consider when optimizing your query. It is designed to allow you to upgrade, but to keep the behavior of the optimizer as it was in the prior release, while you test. It does not guarantee the same plans will result in the new release as those that were chosen in the old release; the optimizer costing will change from release to release. However, it will prevent new functionality from being used.

For example, if you set OPTIMIZER_FEATURES_ENABLE to version 8.1.4, you will discover that your SQL that runs in PL/SQL (user-written recursive SQL) does not use the SESSION optimizer mode, but always uses CHOOSE. It was version 8.1.6 that added the enhancement whereby user-written recursive SQL would inherit the optimizer goal from the session. This sounds like a nice feature, but if you were not prepared, it could have dramatic effects on your query execution.

Normally, SQL in PL/SQL was optimized using the RBO or an ALL_ROWS approach. The thought behind ALL_ROWS type optimization was that the caller of the PL/SQL routine did not get the control back until the last row had been processed in the PL/SQL routine. Hence, an optimization goal of FIRST_ROWS would not make sense in a stored procedure. Who cares if the stored procedure gets the first row from a result set instantly if it takes five hours to get the last row, especially when the alternative is to wait ten seconds to get the first row and get the last row in 20 seconds. The end user waiting for the procedure to finish is the goal.

Consider this example in Oracle9i Release 2:

```
ops$tkyte@ORA920> create table t
  2  as
  3  select *
  4    from all_objects;
Table created.

ops$tkyte@ORA920> create or replace function get_row_cnt return number
  2  as
  3          l_cnt   number;
  4  begin
  5          select count(*)
  6          into l_cnt
  7          from t;
  8          return l_cnt;
  9  end;
 10  /
Function created.

ops$tkyte@ORA920> show parameter optimizer_features

NAME                                 TYPE        VALUE
------------------------------------ ----------- -----------
optimizer_features_enable            string      9.2.0

ops$tkyte@ORA920> alter session set sql_trace=true;
Session altered.

ops$tkyte@ORA920> alter session set optimizer_goal=first_rows;
Session altered.

ops$tkyte@ORA920> exec dbms_output.put_line( get_row_cnt );
29578

PL/SQL procedure successfully completed.
```

Now, the TKPROF utility shows us the following:

```
SELECT count(*) from t
...
Misses in library cache during parse: 1
Optimizer goal: FIRST_ROWS
Parsing user id: 241     (recursive depth: 1)
```

That query was optimized using our session settings. Well, that could be disastrous for an application upgrade from version 8.1.5 to 8.1.6 (or later), if you frequently set the optimizer goal to FIRST_ROWS in your session, but you counted on the CHOOSE method for your stored procedures to let them use the RBO or CBO as they saw fit. So, you could set OPTIMIZER_FEATURES_ENABLE as follows:

```
ops$tkyte@ORA920> alter system
  2 set optimizer_features_enable = '8.1.5' scope = spfile;
System altered.
```

Then restart the database, running the same example:

```
SELECT count(*)    from t
...
Misses in library cache during parse: 1
Optimizer goal: CHOOSE
Parsing user id: 241      (recursive depth: 1)
```

This shows that we have reverted to the old behavior.

The Oracle *Database Reference Guide* includes a table showing what behavior you can expect as far as query optimization goes with various settings of the OPTIMIZER_FEATURES_ENABLE parameter. I recommend that you use it only as a temporary stopgap after an upgrade, to revert to old behavior while you fix the underlying problem itself. Ultimately, you would like this parameter to be set to your current database version in order to take advantage of the new features and functions available.

# Set OPTIMIZER_MAX_PERMUTATIONS to Control Permutations

There are a number of ways to answer the same query, and a potentially huge number of plans may be generated for a query involving many joins. OPTIMIZER_MAX_PERMUTATIONS affects the number of join orders considered by the optimizer. The default used for the OPTIMIZER_MAX_PERMUTATIONS parameter varies depending on the OPTIMIZER_FEATURES_ENABLED setting. If that is set to less than 9.0.0, OPTIMIZER_MAX_PERMUTATIONS will default to 80,000; otherwise, it will default to 2,000. These are upper bounds and the optimizer may explore far fewer join orders—the order in which tables are actually joined to each other in the query plan. As each join order is considered by the optimizer, the cost of that join order is computed. That computed cost is compared to an internal (undocumented) function that uses the number of already considered joins as well as the number of non-single row tables (tables involved in the join that are not known to only return a single row). When the cost of a given join order is smaller then the number this function returns (and that number increases with each comparison as it is based on the number of already considered join orders), the optimizer will stop looking at other join orders. So, even when given ten tables to join, the optimizer could theoretically consider 10! (ten factorial) or 3,628,800 different join-order permutations, but it won't. It probably would not even consider 80,000 of them since the algorithms employed tend to stop it before it considers too many. Remember, the more plans considered, the longer it will take to parse a query.

> **NOTE**
> *You can use the 10053 trace event discussed next to see the number of join orders considered for a given query.*

The interesting thing about this parameter is that when it is set to any number less than 80,000, the optimizer uses different algorithms to generate initial join orders. The original join-order algorithm used by Oracle in earlier releases remained intact when this parameter was set to 80,000, presumably for backwards compatibility. Oracle changed the algorithms and in order to affect the least number of people unknowingly, they made the old algorithms the default (in versions 8i and before). By simply setting this parameter to 79,999, you may observe radically different results from optimizer. Some applications (such as Oracle Applications, for example) took advantage of this new algorithm and for many years have required the database to run with a value less than 80,000. Oracle9i for the first time defaults this parameter to a value less than 80,000, exposing these new join order algorithms for all.

So, how can we observe the differences here? A small test can be used to quickly demonstrate the difference between the setting of 80,000 and 79,999 and other values as well. We'll start with a table to test with:

```
ops$tkyte@ORA920> create table t
  2  as
  3  select mod(object_id,10) id, a.*
  4    from all_objects a;
Table created.

 ops$tkyte@ORA920> analyze table t compute statistics
  2  for table
  3  for columns id;
Table analyzed.
```

Next, we'll use an Oracle tracing facility, the 10053 trace (more details on that facility can be found in the "Use the 10053 Event to Trace CBO Choices" section later in this chapter) to explore how many join orders the optimizer considered. In order to do that, all we need to do is explain a query that uses our table and joins to itself a couple of times. We will create four explain plans for this query: one each with the optimizer max permutations set to 80000, 79999, 2000, and 100:

```
ops$tkyte@ORA920> alter system flush shared_pool;
System altered.

ops$tkyte@ORA920> alter session set events
  2  '10053 trace name context forever, level 1';
Session altered.

ops$tkyte@ORA920> alter session set optimizer_max_permutations=80000;
Session altered.

 ops$tkyte@ORA920> explain plan for
  2  select /* omp = 80000 */ count(*)
  3    from t t1, t t2, t t3, t t4, t t5, t t6
  4   where t1.id = t2.id
  5     and t1.id = t3.id
  6     and t1.id = t4.id
  7     and t1.id = t5.id
```

```
8      and t1.id = t6.id;
Explained.
```

Now, I did that for 79999, 2000, and 100 as well. Additionally, I ran the same tests using a 10 table join. Upon editing the generated trace file and looking for lines with "Join order" at the beginning of them, I was able to discover that the optimizer considered the following number of join orders for each setting:

| Optimizer_Max_Permutations | Join Orders Considered (6 tables) | Join Orders Considered (10 tables) |
| --- | --- | --- |
| 80000 | 240 | 80,000 |
| 79999 | 816 | 40,002 |
| 2000 | 816 | 1,003 |
| 100 | 63 | 63 |

As you can see, there was a huge difference between the setting of 80000 and 79999. It might seem strange that by lowering this parameter from 80000 to 79999 we actually increased the number of join orders compared once and decreased it another time, but that is entirely due to the different algorithms employed in each case and the reasoning behind making a smaller number the default in Oracle9i and later. The optimizer is using better heuristics when computing initial join orders and should be arriving at a better plan in this fashion.

Now, these extra comparisons did have a material affect on my parse time. In order to see that, I simply coded a PL/SQL block that incorporated these four queries and then set the optimizer_max_permutations setting before opening and closing each one. Using SQL_TRACE, I observed parse times of:

| Optimizer_Max_Permutations | Parse Time in CPU seconds (6 tables) | Parse Time in CPU seconds (10 tables) |
| --- | --- | --- |
| 80000 | 0.04 | 15.70 |
| 79999 | 0.15 | 7.93 |
| 2000 | 0.15 | 0.19 |
| 100 | 0.01 | 0.01 |

This makes sense because the amount of CPU time spent parsing is directly proportional to the number of join orders considered.

When would you consider using the OPTIMIZER_MAX_PERMUTATIONS setting? If, and only if, you have a query that is taking far too long to parse (for example, it is taking on the order of seconds to parse), you can consider trying this to reduce the parse time. In general, however, you would normally leave this parameter set to the default value. In Oracle8i, you might consider trying the 79999 or even 2000 value to enable the new algorithm in that release. You would, of course, want to try that on your *test system* first.

## Set OPTIMIZER_MODE to Pick a Mode

Basically, the OPTIMIZER_MODE setting tells Oracle two things:

- Which optimizer you wish to use when possible: RBO or CBO, or to choose between them based on which objects the query references

- How you would like queries to be optimized: to retrieve the last row as fast as possible (ALL_ROWS) or to retrieve the first row as fast as possible (FIRST_ROWS)

There are really four settings for this parameter, and the FIRST_ROWS setting also has five different levels. We'll take a look at each, starting with the value that you should be using at the database level.

### CHOOSE Mode

When OPTIMIZER_MODE is set to CHOOSE, Oracle will use either the CBO or RBO based on the objects the query references. Assuming the optimizer mode is set to the default of CHOOSE, Oracle will use the RBO by default if all of the following are true:

- No objects referenced in the query have statistics.

- No objects referenced in the query require the CBO; for example (not an inclusive list, bear in mind), IOTs, partitioned tables, and tables with nondefault degrees of parallelism require the CBO.

- Use no constructs that require the CBO; for example (again, not an inclusive list), domain indexes (Oracle Text, also known as interMedia), and certain ANSI join constructs require the CBO.

- The query contains no CBO hints. Any hints that specify an access path (full, hash, and so on), query transformations (merge, rewrite, and so on), join orders, join operations (nested loops, hash, and so on), or parallel execution is a CBO hint. The query may contain some hints, such as `/*+ rule */`, `/*+ append */`, and `/*+ cursor_sharing_exact */` and still use the RBO.

If any of the preceding is true, the CBO will be invoked to optimize the entire query. If none of the preceding is true, the RBO will be used.

You may wonder how you can tell which optimizer is being used. You can use AUTOTRACE to figure this out. Consider the following example. We'll start with two simple tables:

```
ops$tkyte@ORA920> create table iot( x int primary key ) organization index;
Table created.

ops$tkyte@ORA920> create table normal ( x int primary key );
Table created.
```

Now, we'll query the IOT table:

```
ops$tkyte@ORA920> alter session set optimizer_mode=choose;
Session altered.

ops$tkyte@ORA920> set autotrace traceonly explain

ops$tkyte@ORA920> select * from iot;

Execution Plan
----------------------------------------------------------
   0      SELECT STATEMENT Optimizer=CHOOSE (Cost=4 Card=1 Bytes=13)
   1    0    INDEX (FAST FULL SCAN) OF 'SYS_IOT_TOP_37843' (UNIQUE)
              (Cost=4 Card=1 Bytes=13)
```

Here, we can see that we are using the CBO because the COST=, CARD=, and BYTES= entries are in the query plan. This information is only available with the CBO and will appear whenever we are using it.

Next, we'll query NORMAL in the same fashion:

```
ops$tkyte@ORA920> select * from normal;

Execution Plan
----------------------------------------------------------
   0      SELECT STATEMENT Optimizer=CHOOSE
   1    0    TABLE ACCESS (FULL) OF 'NORMAL'
```

We can see we are using the RBO, because there are no COST=, CARD=, and BYTES= entries.

Now, let's look at a query against NORMAL that causes the CBO to be invoked:

```
ops$tkyte@ORA920> select n1.x, n2.x
   2 from normal n1 full outer join normal n2 on (n1.x = n2.x);

Execution Plan
----------------------------------------------------------
   0      SELECT STATEMENT Optimizer=CHOOSE (Cost=4 Card=83 Bytes=2158)
   1    0    VIEW (Cost=4 Card=83 Bytes=2158)
   2    1      UNION-ALL
   3    2        NESTED LOOPS (OUTER) (Cost=2 Card=82 Bytes=2132)
   4    3          TABLE ACCESS (FULL) OF 'NORMAL'
                    (Cost=2 Card=82 Bytes=1066)
   5    3          INDEX (UNIQUE SCAN) OF 'SYS_C006463' (UNIQUE)
   6    2        NESTED LOOPS (ANTI) (Cost=2 Card=1 Bytes=26)
   7    6          TABLE ACCESS (FULL) OF 'NORMAL'
                    (Cost=2 Card=82 Bytes=1066)
   8    6          INDEX (UNIQUE SCAN) OF 'SYS_C006463' (UNIQUE)
```

Apparently, the technique of a full outer join using the ANSI syntax caused the CBO to be invoked to optimize this query. The full outer join feature is one that is unknown to the RBO, so it cannot optimize a query containing that construct.

**NOTE**
*Many RBO users believe they are using the RBO when, in fact, they may be using the CBO, simply by using features that require it. This leads to excessively poor performance, since they typically have no statistics gathered on any object. This is yet another reason to use the CBO.*

Next, we'll add a valid CBO hint to the query:

```
ops$tkyte@ORA920> select /*+ ordered */ * from normal;

Execution Plan
----------------------------------------------------------
   0      SELECT STATEMENT Optimizer=CHOOSE (Cost=2 Card=82 Bytes=1066)
   1    0   TABLE ACCESS (FULL) OF 'NORMAL' (Cost=2 Card=82 Bytes=1066)
```

This invokes the CBO.

Now, let's combine the NORMAL table with the IOT table:

```
ops$tkyte@ORA920> select * from iot, normal;

Execution Plan
----------------------------------------------------------
   0      SELECT STATEMENT Optimizer=CHOOSE (Cost=6 Card=1 Bytes=26)
   1    0   MERGE JOIN (CARTESIAN) (Cost=6 Card=1 Bytes=26)
   2    1     INDEX (FAST FULL SCAN) OF 'SYS_IOT_TOP_37843' (UNIQUE)
              (Cost=4 Card=1 Bytes=13)
   3    1     BUFFER (SORT) (Cost=2 Card=82 Bytes=1066)
   4    3       TABLE ACCESS (FULL) OF 'NORMAL' (Cost=2 Card=82 Bytes=1066)
```

Finally, let's just analyze the table:

```
ops$tkyte@ORA920> analyze table normal compute statistics;
Table analyzed.

ops$tkyte@ORA920> select * from normal;

Execution Plan
----------------------------------------------------------
0      SELECT STATEMENT Optimizer=CHOOSE (Cost=1 Card=1 Bytes=13)
1    0   INDEX (FULL SCAN) OF 'SYS_C006463' (UNIQUE)
```

As you can see, the CBO is used in all of the cases except for the most simple, when you query unanalyzed objects that make no use of advanced or new features.

In general, all systems should be running with CHOOSE set at the database level up through Oracle9i Release 2. This lets the RBO be used when appropriate, and invokes the CBO when necessary. At the session level, you may choose to set your session to FIRST_ROWS or ALL_ROWS if desired, as we'll discuss shortly.

## RULE Mode

The RULE mode invokes the RBO when all of the following are true:

■   No objects referenced in the query require the CBO.

■   No constructs that require the CBO are used.

■   The query contains no CBO hints.

That is the same list that applies to the CHOOSE mode, with the exception of the first item. The only difference between RULE and CHOOSE is that the RBO will be used by default, even when statistics are present. The CBO still must be used in all of the other cases.

If we were to rerun the example from the previous section using the NORMAL and IOT tables, the only difference would be the last query, which would execute as follows:

```
ops$tkyte@ORA920> analyze table normal compute statistics;
Table analyzed.

ops$tkyte@ORA920> select * from normal;

Execution Plan
----------------------------------------------------------
   0        SELECT STATEMENT Optimizer=RULE
   1    0     TABLE ACCESS (FULL) OF 'NORMAL'
```

Here, the RBO was used even though statistics were present.

The only time I've recommended using the RULE mode was in an instance where only *some* of the tables had been analyzed. In this situation, the system's performance was going down the drain because most of the queries referenced both analyzed and unanalyzed tables. The conundrum was that they were using some features that required the CBO (IOTs and domain indexes, in particular); hence, the objects should have been analyzed. But they did not analyze the remaining objects, thinking they were just overhead. As a temporary workaround, we put the RULE mode into place so that unless a query needed to use the CBO (for example, it referenced the IOT or domain index), it would use the RBO. The immediate result was that status quo was restored; the system went back to performing as it had in the past. The long-term solution was to test with all objects analyzed, get moved over to the CBO 100%, and then set the optimizer mode back to CHOOSE. Here, we used RULE as a temporary stopgap to resolve a crisis.

## ALL_ROWS and FIRST_ROWS Modes

Both ALL_ROWS and FIRST_ROWS cause the CBO to be used for all queries, with the exception of a query that specifies the RULE hint directly. The difference between the two is how they optimize a query. The FIRST_ROWS optimization tells the optimizer that you would like the first row as fast as possible; this optimizes for initial response time. The ALL_ROWS optimization tells the optimizer that you would like the last row of the query as quickly as possible; this optimizes for total throughput.

You might use FIRST_ROWS in an interactive application where the end users (impatient humans) are waiting for some results on a screen. Here, the users may never get to the last row in the result set (they may never page down), and even if they do, the application is retrieving results in response to their pagination. Considering user interaction, the fact that it takes longer to get the last row using this mode than it does with the other optimization techniques isn't really relevant. The end-user experience is what matters; a good experience is getting immediate feedback page by page.

Note that FIRST_ROWS is a request, not an order, to the database. Certain operations, such as aggregation, sorting, and the like, may cause a FIRST_ROWS optimized query to use the same plan as an ALL_ROWS query. In cases such as aggregation, it is quite common that the last row must be retrieved before the first row can be returned.

Following my recommendation of using CHOOSE at the database level, using FIRST_ROWS should be handled at the application level. Applications can issue an ALTER SESSION statement to have FIRST_ROWS optimization enabled. This is easier than hinting each individual query, and preferred to setting it at the database level.

You might use ALL_ROWS in a batch or noninteractive application (a report), or in any application where getting the entire result set is key, rather than just getting the first row back as fast as possible. Here, the optimizer strives to generate a plan that gets the entire result set, including the very last row, as quickly as possible. That typically means it will do a lot of work up-front to get the first row, and then the rest of the rows come very quickly after that. Getting that first row might take 30 seconds, but the rest come in one second after that. Using FIRST_ROWS optimization with the same query might get the first row instantly, but take an hour to get the last row.

For example, we'll revisit the query we used at the beginning of the chapter (in the "Why the RBO Is Dead" section), which included the RULE hint in order to force the use of indexes:

```
select /*+ RULE */ t1.object_name, t2.object_name
  from t t1, t t2
 where t1.object_id = t2.object_id
   and t1.owner = 'WMSYS'
```

```
call      count       cpu    elapsed       disk       query cur     rows
-------   ------  --------  ---------  ---------  ---------- ---  -------
Parse          1     0.00       0.00          0           0   0        0
Execute        1     0.00       0.00          0           0   0        0
Fetch      35227   912.07    3440.70    1154555   121367981   0   528384
-------   ------  --------  ---------  ---------  ---------- ---  -------
total      35229   912.07    3440.70    1154555   121367981   0   528384
```

We know that if we run this query using the CBO, the entire result set is returned in ten seconds (versus the hour of runtime we observed here!). But would the CBO ever choose the same plan the RBO did, to use and abuse those indexes? The answer is yes. We can set the optimizer mode to ALL_ROWS and FIRST_ROWS and compare the plans:

```
big_table@ORA920> set autotrace traceonly explain

big_table@ORA920> alter session set optimizer_mode=all_rows;
Session altered.

big_table@ORA920> select t1.object_name, t2.object_name
  2    from big_table t1, big_table t2
```

```
  3    where t1.object_id = t2.object_id
  4      and t1.owner = 'WMSYS'
  5    /
Execution Plan
----------------------------------------------------------
  0        SELECT STATEMENT Optimizer=ALL_ROWS
           (Cost=4581 Card=8256 Bytes=404544)
  1    0    HASH JOIN (Cost=4581 Card=8256 Bytes=404544)
  2    1      TABLE ACCESS (FULL) OF 'BIG_TABLE'
        .      (Cost=2136 Card=8256 Bytes=222912)
  3    1      TABLE ACCESS (FULL) OF 'BIG_TABLE'
               (Cost=2136 Card=1833857 Bytes=40344854)

big_table@ORA920> alter session set optimizer_mode=first_rows;
Session altered.

big_table@ORA920> select t1.object_name, t2.object_name
  2    from big_table t1, big_table t2
  3    where t1.object_id = t2.object_id
  4      and t1.owner = 'WMSYS'
  5    /
Execution Plan
----------------------------------------------------------
  0        SELECT STATEMENT Optimizer=FIRST_ROWS
           (Cost=26904 Card=8256 Bytes=404544)
  1    0    TABLE ACCESS (BY INDEX ROWID) OF 'BIG_TABLE'
           (Cost=3 Card=1 Bytes=22)
  2    1      NESTED LOOPS (Cost=26904 Card=8256 Bytes=404544)
  3    2        TABLE ACCESS (FULL) OF 'BIG_TABLE'
                 (Cost=2136 Card=8256 Bytes=222912)
  4    2        INDEX (RANGE SCAN) OF 'OBJECT_ID_IDX' (NON-UNIQUE)
                 (Cost=2 Card=1)
```

Here, the CBO did choose the same plan that the RBO did when we first looked at this example. Is there an occasion when we would really want to use that second plan? Yes, there is.

Suppose that we have an interactive application, such as a search screen that presents the user with the first ten rows (hits) and includes a Page Down button to look at the next ten hits, and so on. Here, the FIRST_ROWS plan would be much more desirable. Consider this example, which runs this same query twice, but fetches only the first record from the result set:

```
big_table@ORA920> alter session set sql_trace=true;
Session altered.

big_table@ORA920> declare
  2      cursor all_rows is
  3      select /*+ ALL_ROWS */ t1.object_name a, t2.object_name b
  4        from big_table t1, big_table t2
  5      where t1.object_id = t2.object_id
  6        and t1.owner = 'WMSYS';
  7
```

```
 8      cursor first_rows is
 9      select /*+ FIRST_ROWS */ t1.object_name a, t2.object_name b
10        from big_table t1, big_table t2
11       where t1.object_id = t2.object_id
12         and t1.owner = 'WMSYS';
13
14      l_rec all_rows%rowtype;
15  begin
16      open all_rows;
17      fetch all_rows into l_rec;
18      close all_rows;
19
20      open first_rows;
21      fetch first_rows into l_rec;
22      close first_rows;
23  end;
24  /
PL/SQL procedure successfully completed.
```

The TKPROF report is quite startling this time (as startling as the first time we looked at this when we fetched the entire result set):

```
SELECT /*+ ALL_ROWS */ t1.object_name a, t2.object_name b
    from big_table t1, big_table t2
  where t1.object_id = t2.object_id
    and t1.owner = 'WMSYS'


call      count       cpu    elapsed       disk  query current rows
-------  ------  --------  ---------  ---------- ------ ------- ----
Parse         1     0.00       0.00          0      0       0    0
Execute       1     0.00       0.00          0      0       0    0
Fetch         1     1.27       6.75      13517  22113       4    1
-------  ------  --------  ---------  ---------- ------ ------- ----
total         3     1.27       6.76      13517  22113       4    1


Misses in library cache during parse: 1
Optimizer goal: ALL_ROWS
Parsing user id: 80      (recursive depth: 1)


Rows     Row Source Operation
-------  -------------------------------------------------
      1  HASH JOIN
   8256    TABLE ACCESS FULL BIG_TABLE
  10175    TABLE ACCESS FULL BIG_TABLE
```

That took 1.27 CPU seconds, but the end user waited almost 7 seconds to get the first row. It did 22,113 logical I/O operations, all for a single record. Let's compare that to the FIRST_ROWS optimization:

```
SELECT /*+ FIRST_ROWS */ t1.object_name a, t2.object_name b
       from big_table t1, big_table t2
      where t1.object_id = t2.object_id
        and t1.owner = 'WMSYS'

call      count       cpu    elapsed    disk    query  current    rows
-------  ------  --------  ---------- -------  ------- --------  ------
Parse         1      0.00        0.00       0        0        0       0
Execute       1      0.00        0.00       0        0        0       0
Fetch         1      0.00        0.00       3      115        0       1
-------  ------  --------  ---------- -------  ------- --------  ------
total         3      0.00        0.00       3      115        0       1

Misses in library cache during parse: 1
Optimizer goal: FIRST_ROWS
Parsing user id: 80      (recursive depth: 1)

Rows      Row Source Operation
-------   -------------------------------------------------------
      1   TABLE ACCESS BY INDEX ROWID BIG_TABLE
      2    NESTED LOOPS
      1     TABLE ACCESS FULL BIG_TABLE
      1     INDEX RANGE SCAN OBJECT_ID_IDX (object id 37090)
```

It is quite different. The runtime was immeasurably small, the response time was negligible, and the logical I/O number was quite small.

This FIRST_ROWS/ALL_ROWS difference is important in web-based applications where you do pagination. Suppose we have a query we need to execute frequently. The end user supplies the search criteria at runtime, and we need to efficiently allow them to page through the results. We need a query that allows us to get rows M through N of a result set. In Oracle that would be as follows:

```
Select *
  From ( select a.*, rownum r
           From ( YOUR_QUERY_GOES_HERE ) a
          Where rownum <= :max_row )
 Where r >= :min_row
```

All we need to do is wrap up our query and execute that with the proper maximum or minimum row values. Let's compare this approach with the previous example. We'll start by setting up a stored procedure that our application will use. It will take the following as input: a hint (for this demonstration only; in the real world, the hint would always be there, but we want to compare hint versus no hint), the owner to retrieve the objects for, and the MIN_ROW/MAX_ROW of the result set we are interested in:

```
big_table@ORA920> create or replace procedure
  2  get_result_set( p_hint      in varchar2,
  3                  p_owner in varchar2,
  4                  p_min_row in number,
```

```
 5                        p_max_row in number,
 6                        p_result_set in out sys_refcursor )
 7  as
 8  begin
 9      open p_result_set
10      for 'select *
11          from ( select ' || p_hint || ' a.*, rownum r
12                  from (select t1.object_name a,
13                              t2.object_name b
14                        from big_table t1, big_table t2
15                        where t1.object_id = t2.object_id
16                        and t1.owner = :p_owner ) a
17                  where rownum <= :p_max_row )
18          where r >= :p_min_row'
19          using p_owner, p_max_row, p_min_row;
20  end;
21  /
Procedure created.

big_table@ORA920> set timing on
big_table@ORA920> variable x refcursor
big_table@ORA920> set autoprint on
```

Now, assuming OPTIMIZER_MODE is set to the default of CHOOSE, we run this procedure in SQL*Plus and find this:

```
big_table@ORA920> exec get_result_set( null, 'WMSYS', 1, 3, :x )
PL/SQL procedure successfully completed.

A                   B                           R
------------------- ------------------- ----------
WM$LOCK_INFO_TYPE   WM$LOCK_INFO_TYPE            1
WM$LOCK_TABLE_TYPE  WM$LOCK_TABLE_TYPE           2
WM$RIC_TABLE        WM$RIC_TABLE                 3

Elapsed: 00:00:04.77
Elapsed: 00:00:04.79

big_table@ORA920> exec get_result_set( null, 'WMSYS', 30, 33, :x )
PL/SQL procedure successfully completed.

A                   B                           R
------------------- ------------------- ----------
WM$WORKSPACE_SAVEP  WM$WORKSPACE_SAVEP          30
OINTS_TABLE         OINTS_TABLE

WM$WORKSPACE_SAVEP  WM$WORKSPACE_SAVEP          31
OINTS_PK            OINTS_PK

WM$CONFLICT_PAYLOA  WM$CONFLICT_PAYLOA          32
```

```
D_TYPE                D_TYPE

WM$MODIFIED_TABLES WM$MODIFIED_TABLES        33
```

**Elapsed: 00:00:03.91**
**Elapsed: 00:00:03.92**

It is taking about four seconds to see a couple of rows consistently. In fact, no matter which row we ask for using the preceding technique, it will take about the same amount of time, because most of the work is done to get the first row.

Now, we'll try the same example with FIRST_ROWS optimization and see what happens:

```
big_table@ORA920> begin
  2  get_result_set( '/*+ FIRST_ROWS */' , 'WMSYS', 1, 3, :x );
  3  end;
  4  /
PL/SQL procedure successfully completed.

...
```

**Elapsed: 00:00:00.00**
**Elapsed: 00:00:00.02**

```
big_table@ORA920> begin
  2 get_result_set( '/*+ FIRST_ROWS */' , 'WMSYS', 30, 33, :x );
  3 end;
  4 /
PL/SQL procedure successfully completed.

...
```

**Elapsed: 00:00:00.01**
**Elapsed: 00:00:00.02**

```
big_table@ORA920> begin
  2 get_result_set( '/*+ FIRST_ROWS */' , 'WMSYS', 7300, 7302, :x );
  3 end;
  4 /

PL/SQL procedure successfully completed.
```

```
A                                B                                        R
------------------------------   ------------------------------   ----------
ALL_WORKSPACE_PRIVS              ALL_WORKSPACE_PRIVS                    7300
DBA_WORKSPACE_PRIVS              DBA_WORKSPACE_PRIVS                    7301
USER_WM_VERSIONED_TABLES         USER_WM_VERSIONED_TABLES               7302
```

**Elapsed: 00:00:00.13**
**Elapsed: 00:00:00.20**

The response time is immediate. But, as the user pages down through the result set, the return time for each page will get slower and slower using FIRST_ROWS. For ALL_ROWS, it remains more or less constant.

Keep in mind that people are impatient and have short attention spans. How many times have you gone past the tenth page on a search page on the Internet? When I do a Google (www.google.com) search that returns more hits than the number of hamburgers sold by McDonald's, I never go to the last page; in fact, I never get to page 11. By the time I've looked at the first five pages or so, I realize that I need to refine my search because this is too much data. Your end users will, believe it or not, do the same.

### Some Advice on Web-Based Searches with Pagination

My advice for handling web-based searches that you need to paginate through is to never provide an exact hit count. Use an estimate to tell the users about *N* hits. This is what I do on my asktom web site, for example. I use Oracle Text to index the content. Before I run a query, I ask Oracle Text for an estimate. You can do the same with your relational queries using EXPLAIN PLAN in Oracle8i and earlier, or by querying V$SQL_PLAN in Oracle9i and later.

You may want to tell the end users they got 1,032,231 hits, but the problem with that is twofold:

- It takes a long time to count that many hits. You need to run that ALL_ROWS type of query to the end to find that out! It is really slow.

- By the time you count the hits, in all probability (unless you are on a read-only database), the answer has already changed and you do not have that number of hits anymore!

My other advice for this type of application is to never provide a Last Page button or give the user more than ten pages at a time from which to choose. Look at the standard, www.google.com, and do what it does.

Follow those two pieces of advice, and your pagination worries are over.

# Rewrite Queries with QUERY_REWRITE_ENABLED and QUERY_REWRITE_INTEGRITY

The QUERY_REWRITE_ENABLED and QUERY_REWRITE_INTEGRITY parameters control a very interesting aspect of the Oracle database: its ability to rewrite your query into a totally different but equivalent query, using alternate objects in the database. This comes into use frequently in the area of materialized views, a data warehousing construct whereby the database maintains precomputed summaries, joins, and other costly operations. Using query rewrite, a query against a detail table can be automatically rewritten by the optimizer to use these summary tables, just as an index would be used to speed up the performance of an OLTP query.

### QUERY_REWRITE_ENABLED Settings

QUERY_REWRITE_ENABLED has three settings: TRUE, FALSE, and FORCE. When set to TRUE or FORCE, query rewrite is enabled. When set to FALSE, query rewrite is disabled. The default is FALSE, and since this parameter may be changed for the system dynamically, it is safe to leave it at the default. If you begin to use a feature that requires a value of TRUE, you can either use

ALTER SESSION to use it, or use ALTER SYSTEM to make it globally available without needing to shut down. QUERY_REWRITE_ENABLED must be TRUE or FORCE in order to do the following:

- Use function-based indexes. If you create an index on EMP(MY_FUNCTION(ENAME)), where MY_FUNCTION is some PL/SQL function you wrote, and want to actually use the index, you must have query rewrite enabled. In Oracle9i, query rewrite enabled is not necessary for built-in functions such as UPPER or LOWER, but in Oracle8i even those built-in functions necessitate query rewrite enabled.

- Allow for transparent use of materialized views. If you do not have QUERY_REWRITE_ ENABLED set to TRUE, a materialized view may be queried directly (opaquely), but queries will not be rewritten to take advantage of their existence.

## QUERY_REWRITE_INTEGRITY Settings

QUERY_REWRITE_INTEGRITY controls how Oracle rewrites queries. It may be set to one of these three values:

- **ENFORCED**   Queries will be rewritten using only constraints and rules that are enforced and guaranteed by Oracle. There are mechanisms by which we can tell Oracle about other inferred relationships using NOVALIDATE on a constraint, for example, and this would allow for more queries to be rewritten. But since Oracle does not enforce those relationships, it would not make use of those facts at this level.

- **TRUSTED**   Queries will be rewritten using the constraints that are enforced by Oracle, as well as the relationships we have told Oracle about that exist in the data but are not enforced by Oracle.

- **STALE_TOLERATED**   Queries will be rewritten to use materialized views, even if Oracle knows the data contained in the materialized view is stale (out of sync with the details). This might be useful in an environment where the summary tables are refreshed on a recurring basis, not on commit, and a slightly out-of-sync answer is acceptable.

## Query Rewrite Demonstration

To demonstrate the effect of these parameters, we'll use a small example that employs a materialized view and a function-based index as a case study. Suppose that we have very large EMP and DEPT tables in our data warehouse. We have a custom function written in PL/SQL that we've indexed on the DEPT table. We also have an index on an Oracle built-in function. In order to speed up the most frequently asked questions, we have a materialized view that prejoins EMP and DEPT together, computing a summary count of employees by department number. The setup for the two data warehouse tables is as follows:

```
ops$tkyte@ORA920> create table emp as select * from scott.emp;
Table created.

ops$tkyte@ORA920> create table dept as select * from scott.dept;
Table created.
```

Next, we'll create a function we'll want to apply frequently to a column in the DEPT table. Because we wish to create an index on this function, we must define it as a deterministic function. This function will return a predictable, constant result whenever it is given the same inputs; that is, the return value will not change over time for the same inputs. (See Chapter 5 of the Oracle9i Release 2 *Application Developers Guide* for all of the requirements for creating and using function-based indexes.)

```
ops$tkyte@ORA920> create or replace
  2  function my_function(p_str in varchar2) return varchar2
  3  deterministic
  4  as
  5  begin
  6          return initcap(p_str);
  7  end;
  8  /
Function created.
```

Next, we will create two indexes, one using a user-written function (the one we just coded) and one that uses the built-in function INITCAP directly. This will show a subtle difference between user-written functions and built-in functions with regard to these parameter settings.

```
ops$tkyte@ORA920> create index dept_idx_custom on dept(my_function(dname));
Index created.

ops$tkyte@ORA920> create index dept_idx_builtin on dept(initcap(dname));
Index created.
```

**NOTE**
*If you get an "ORA-1450 max key length exceeded" error when creating* dept_idx_custom, *the solution is to create the index using* substr(my_function(dname),1,30), *to shorten the length of the key. Note that you will need to use* substr(my_function(dname),1,30) *in your queries as well.*

Next, we'll create the materialized view on our data warehouse tables that prejoins and aggregates some data from EMP and DEPT:

```
ops$tkyte@ORA920> create materialized view emp_dept
  2  build immediate
  3  refresh on demand
  4  enable query rewrite
  5  as
  6  select dept.deptno, dept.dname, count (*)
  7    from emp, dept
  8   where emp.deptno = dept.deptno
  9   group by dept.deptno, dept.dname
 10  /
Materialized view created.
```

Lastly, we'll lie to the database to make it think these tables are really big. This is to simulate the data warehouse size these tables would be in real life:

```
ops$tkyte@ORA920> begin
  2  dbms_stats.set_table_stats( user, 'EMP', numrows => 100000 );
  3  dbms_stats.set_table_stats( user, 'DEPT', numrows =>  1000 );
  4  dbms_stats.set_table_stats( user, 'EMP_DEPT', numrows =>  1000 );
  5  end;
  6  /
PL/SQL procedure successfully completed.
```

The DBMS_STATS calls provide two things for us here:

■ In order to use QUERY_REWRITE, we must be using the CBO. Since we are running in CHOOSE mode, the very existence of the statistics we placed on these objects will cause the CBO to be invoked.

■ We've made the EMP and DEPT tables appear many times larger than they really are, so that the optimizer will use our materialized views (the source tables will appear less costly).

Now, we'll try some queries and see what happens:

```
ops$tkyte@ORA920> alter session set query_rewrite_enabled=true;
Session altered.

ops$tkyte@ORA920> alter session set query_rewrite_integrity=enforced;
Session altered.

ops$tkyte@ORA920> set autotrace traceonly explain
ops$tkyte@ORA920> select dept.deptno, dept.dname, count (*)
  2    from emp, dept
  3   where emp.deptno = dept.deptno
  4   group by dept.deptno, dept.dname
  5  /

Execution Plan
----------------------------------------------------------
   0      SELECT STATEMENT Optimizer=CHOOSE (Cost=11 Card=1000 Bytes=35000)
   1   0    TABLE ACCESS (FULL) OF 'EMP_DEPT'
              (Cost=11 Card=1000 Bytes=35000)
```

Here, we can see that Oracle did the query rewrite for us. The complex query we submitted that involved a join of two large tables and an aggregate was rewritten to simply full-scan the existing answer. That is the beauty of query rewrite and why I sometimes refer to materialized views as "the indexes of your data warehouse." Just as an index on EMP (EMPNO) would be used automatically by the optimizer to speed up an OLTP query, the EMP_DEPT materialized view is used automatically to speed up a data warehouse query.

Now, let's try some other queries:

```
ops$tkyte@ORA920> select count(*) from emp;

Execution Plan
----------------------------------------------------------
   0      SELECT STATEMENT Optimizer=CHOOSE (Cost=11 Card=1)
   1    0   SORT (AGGREGATE)
   2    1     TABLE ACCESS (FULL) OF 'EMP' (Cost=11 Card=100000)
```

Well, that's disappointing. We know we could have issued select sum ("count (*)") from emp_dept to answer that, but Oracle doesn't know that yet! This is because we have not told Oracle several things about the data:

- DEPTNO is the primary key of DEPT. That means that each EMP record will join to at most one DEPT record.

- DEPTNO in EMP is a foreign key to DEPTNO in DEPT. If the DEPTNO in EMP is not a null value, it will be joined to a row in DEPT (we won't lose any non-null EMP records during a join).

- DEPTNO in EMP is NOT NULL. This, coupled with the foreign-key constraint, tells us we won't lose any EMP records due to the join in the materialized view.

These three facts imply that if we join EMP to DEPT, each EMP row will be observed in the result set at least once, and at most once. Since we did not tell Oracle these facts, it was not able to make use of the materialized view. In a moment, we'll tell Oracle about those facts and see what, if any, difference they make. But first, let's see what happens with our function-based indexes using QUERY_REWRITE_INTEGRITY = ENFORCED:

```
ops$tkyte@ORA920> select * from dept where initcap(dname) = 'Sales';

Execution Plan
----------------------------------------------------------
   0      SELECT STATEMENT Optimizer=CHOOSE (Cost=2 Card=10 Bytes=300)
   1    0   TABLE ACCESS (BY INDEX ROWID) OF 'DEPT'
            (Cost=2 Card=10 Bytes=300)
   2    1     INDEX (RANGE SCAN) OF 'DEPT_IDX_BUILTIN' (NON-UNIQUE)
              (Cost=1 Card=4)

ops$tkyte@ORA920> select * from dept where my_function(dname) = 'Sales';

Execution Plan
----------------------------------------------------------
   0      SELECT STATEMENT Optimizer=CHOOSE (Cost=11 Card=10 Bytes=300)
   1    0   TABLE ACCESS (FULL) OF 'DEPT' (Cost=11 Card=10 Bytes=300)
```

Notice that Oracle used the function-based index on INITCAP, a built-in function, but ignored the existence of our index on MY_FUNCTION, custom code we wrote. This is due to the level of

QUERY_REWRITE_INTEGRITY. At the ENFORCED level, Oracle trusts only that which Oracle knows 100% to be true.

Oracle trusts that INITCAP is deterministic. Actually, it knows for a fact that INITCAP is a truly deterministic function—given an input *X*, the output will be constantly the same; the results from a specific input value will be deterministic, or constant.

Now, our function MY_FUNCTION purports to be deterministic, but Oracle doesn't know that for a fact. If our function turned out to be nondeterministic after all, the results from Oracle would appear to be wrong. To make the conscious decision to permit this function to be used, we need to go up a level in the query rewrite scale, which we'll do in the next step. But first, we'll tell Oracle about all of those constraints we have: the DEPT primary key, the foreign key from EMP to DEPT, and DEPTNO in EMP is NOT NULL.

Let's suppose that, for this humongous data warehouse, we scrubbed the data perfectly before loading, and we don't have the time to actually let Oracle revalidate these constraints. We'll just tell Oracle about their existence and not actually pay the penalty of checking that they are true row by row:

```
ops$tkyte@ORA920> set autotrace off

ops$tkyte@ORA920> alter table dept
  2  add constraint dept_pk primary key(deptno)
  3  RELY enable NOVALIDATE;
Table altered.

ops$tkyte@ORA920> alter table emp
  2  add constraint emp_fk_dept
  3  foreign key(deptno) references dept(deptno)
  4  RELY enable NOVALIDATE;
Table altered.

ops$tkyte@ORA920> alter table emp modify deptno not null NOVALIDATE;
Table altered.
```

Now, we'll run our query again:

```
ops$tkyte@ORA920> set autotrace traceonly explain
ops$tkyte@ORA920> select count(*) from emp;

Execution Plan
----------------------------------------------------------
   0      SELECT STATEMENT Optimizer=CHOOSE (Cost=11 Card=1)
   1    0   SORT (AGGREGATE)
   2    1     TABLE ACCESS (FULL) OF 'EMP' (Cost=11 Card=100000)
```

As you can see, we still have a full scan of EMP, without a shortcut to the EMP_DEPT table. This happens because we are still at the ENFORCED level of QUERY_REWRITE_INTEGRITY, and Oracle doesn't trust us yet. It does not trust our function MY_FUNCTION to be deterministic, and it does not trust that the three facts we've stated about EMP and DEPT are true, since it did not validate them itself. If Oracle had validated the constraints, that query would have rewritten itself to use the materialized view. So, we'll tell Oracle to trust us:

```
ops$tkyte@ORA920> alter session set query_rewrite_integrity=trusted;
Session altered.

ops$tkyte@ORA920> select count(*) from emp;

Execution Plan
----------------------------------------------------------
   0      SELECT STATEMENT Optimizer=CHOOSE (Cost=11 Card=1 Bytes=13)
   1    0   SORT (AGGREGATE)
   2    1     TABLE ACCESS (FULL) OF 'EMP_DEPT'
             (Cost=11 Card=1000 Bytes=13000)

ops$tkyte@ORA920> select * from dept where my_function(dname) = 'Sales';

Execution Plan
----------------------------------------------------------
   0      SELECT STATEMENT Optimizer=CHOOSE (Cost=2 Card=10 Bytes=300)
   1    0   TABLE ACCESS (BY INDEX ROWID) OF 'DEPT'
             (Cost=2 Card=10 Bytes=300)
   2    1     INDEX (RANGE SCAN) OF 'DEPT_IDX_CUSTOM' (NON-UNIQUE)
             (Cost=1 Card=4)
```

Now, our materialized view can be used in many more places than before, and our function-based index is usable for the first time.

Next, we'll take a look at the STALE_TOLERATED setting for QUERY_REWRITE_INTEGRITY. Here, we'll modify the base tables in our materialized view and see what happens to the query plans:

```
ops$tkyte@ORA920> set autotrace off

ops$tkyte@ORA920> insert into emp(empno,deptno) values ( 1,10 );
1 row created.

ops$tkyte@ORA920> commit;
Commit complete.

ops$tkyte@ORA920> set autotrace traceonly explain
ops$tkyte@ORA920> select count(*) from emp;

Execution Plan
----------------------------------------------------------
   0      SELECT STATEMENT Optimizer=CHOOSE (Cost=11 Card=1)
   1    0   SORT (AGGREGATE)
   2    1     TABLE ACCESS (FULL) OF 'EMP' (Cost=11 Card=100000)
```

Ah, it is back to its old tricks. We did nothing other than add a row to EMP, but Oracle knows immediately that our materialized view is stale—a query against it could return a different result than a query against the base tables. Hence, it avoids the query rewrite. However, in some circumstances, it would be acceptable to use the materialized view even though the answer is not 100% accurate (you will need to decide for yourself when this is the case). To use that stale view automatically, we do this:

```
ops$tkyte@ORA920> alter session set query_rewrite_integrity=stale_tolerated;
Session altered.

ops$tkyte@ORA920> select count(*) from emp;

Execution Plan
----------------------------------------------------------
   0        SELECT STATEMENT Optimizer=CHOOSE (Cost=11 Card=1 Bytes=13)
   1    0     SORT (AGGREGATE)
   2    1       TABLE ACCESS (FULL) OF 'EMP_DEPT'
                (Cost=11 Card=1000 Bytes=13000)
```

A setting of QUERY_REWRITE_INTEGRITY = TRUSTED would be safe for most systems out there. You must take care that the integrity constraints that you assert, but that Oracle does not actually validate, are 100% accurate and that your user-written functions really are deterministic; otherwise, you can expect suspect results. I would use STALE_TOLERATED at the session level only, and only at the request of the end user. Although STALE_TOLERATED may get your result faster, it may be the wrong result.

## Control PGA Memory with BITMAP_MERGE_AREA_ SIZE, SORT_AREA_SIZE, and HASH_AREA_SIZE

The BITMAP_MERGE_AREA_SIZE, SORT_AREA_SIZE, and HASH_AREA_SIZE parameters control the amount of process global area (PGA) memory that will be used to perform certain operations. The optimizer will look at their settings, and based on their respective sizes, may decide to prefer a sort-merge join over a hash join. For example, it may do a sort-merge join when the sort area size is very large and the hash area size is small.

As of Oracle9i, I personally consider these parameters *obsolete* when using dedicated server. You should be using WORKAREA_SIZE_POLICY = AUTO and PGA_AGGREGATE_TARGET settings instead, and forget about fine-tuning and tweaking these parameters. Hence, this discussion applies only to connections in Oracle9i using shared server and any connection to Oracle8i and earlier.

To see the difference these values can make in query plans, we'll look at what the optimizer decides to do given different values of SORT_AREA_SIZE and HASH_AREA_SIZE:

```
big_table@ORA817DEV> set autotrace traceonly explain

big_table@ORA817DEV> alter session set sort_area_size = 102400000;
Session altered.

big_table@ORA817DEV> alter session set hash_area_size = 204800000;
Session altered.

big_table@ORA817DEV> select a.object_type, b.object_name
  2    from big_table a, big_table b
  3    where a.last_ddl_time = b.last_ddl_time;
```

```
Execution Plan
----------------------------------------------------------
  0       SELECT STATEMENT Optimizer=CHOOSE
          (Cost=2021 Card=24843812209 Bytes=1142815361614)
  1    0   HASH JOIN (Cost=2021 Card=24843812209 Bytes=1142815361614)
  2    1    TABLE ACCESS (FULL) OF 'BIG_TABLE'
             (Cost=658 Card=1576192 Bytes=31523840)
  3    1    TABLE ACCESS (FULL) OF 'BIG_TABLE'
             (Cost=658 Card=1576192 Bytes=40980992)
```

So, given a 100MB sort area size and a 200MB hash area size, the choice was made to hash join the tables together.

Now, let's keep the 2:1 ratio, but downsize the sort area and hash area sizes to values that are commonly used:

```
big_table@ORA817DEV> alter session set sort_area_size = 65536;
Session altered.

big_table@ORA817DEV> alter session set hash_area_size = 131072;
Session altered.

big_table@ORA817DEV> select a.object_type, b.object_name
  2    from big_table a, big_table b
  3    where a.last_ddl_time = b.last_ddl_time;

Execution Plan
----------------------------------------------------------
  0       SELECT STATEMENT Optimizer=CHOOSE
          (Cost=72112 Card=24843812209 Bytes=1142815361614)
  1    0   MERGE JOIN (Cost=72112 Card=24843812209 Bytes=1142815361614)
  2    1    SORT (JOIN) (Cost=32569 Card=1576192 Bytes=31523840)
  3    2     TABLE ACCESS (FULL) OF 'BIG_TABLE'
              (Cost=658 Card=1576192 Bytes=31523840)
  4    1    SORT (JOIN) (Cost=39544 Card=1576192 Bytes=40980992)
  5    4     TABLE ACCESS (FULL) OF 'BIG_TABLE'
              (Cost=658 Card=1576192 Bytes=40980992)
```

We see that the optimizer is now opting for a sort-merge technique—sort the data, and then merge the two subresults together. The outcome of these two plans would be the same, but they would perform radically differently.

**NOTE**
*Most implementations simply leave SORT_AREA_SIZE and HASH_AREA_SIZE at the defaults, which is generally in the 64KB range. This is far too small in most cases. In general, a value of 512KB to 1MB should be considered. If you review a Statspack report and see many sorts to disk, reevaluate your sort area size.*

There is some amount of confusion over the SORT_AREA_SIZE parameter. Many people tend to keep it artificially low to save memory. They are concerned that sort area size bytes of RAM are allocated upon session startup and will be consumed for the life of the session. This is wrong. Sort area size is an upper-bound on the amount of memory that will be used to perform a sort. This size is dynamically allocated at the time of the sort, and it grows incrementally. For example, if you set it to 100MB but only use 512KB, only 512KB would ever be allocated. It is freed back to the PGA for reuse after the sort is complete. It is not dedicated to only sorting; it is used to sort and then given back for other things. Also, operating systems are developed to page out unused memory, so even if a process used 100MB of sort area size, and then didn't use it again, the pages of real memory backing that would be paged out over time naturally. This is what operating systems do; it is their job.

**NOTE**
*In Oracle9i, using WORKAREA_SIZE_POLICY = AUTO removes consideration about unused memory altogether. Work areas are dynamically allocated from the operating system in a special way that allows Oracle to give the memory directly back to the operating system when it is finished with that memory on operating systems that support this.*

To give you an idea of the impact a larger sort area size could have on your system, we'll run the same query over and over with 64KB, 640KB, and 6,400KB, and then compare the results. All three return the same answer; they just perform very differently. In the following, we encode the sort area size in the query itself, so the first query has `from big_table sa6553600` (6,400KB).

**NOTE**
*I used the ALTER SESSION SET SORT_AREA_SIZE=N command, where N was the size in bytes I wanted to use between each query execution. Additionally, in Oracle9i, you would need to ensure WORKAREA_SIZE_POLICY was set to MANUAL, or else SORT_AREA_SIZE would be ignored.*

```
select owner, object_name, object_type,
       sum(object_id), avg(object_id), min(object_id),
       max(object_id), stddev(object_id)
  from big_table sa6553600
 group by owner, object_name, object_type
```

| call | count | cpu | elapsed | disk | query | current | rows |
|------|-------|-----|---------|------|-------|---------|------|
| Parse | 1 | 0.00 | 0.00 | 0 | 0 | 0 | 0 |
| Execute | 1 | 0.00 | 0.00 | 0 | 0 | 0 | 0 |
| Fetch | 1643 | 37.39 | 63.79 | 22760 | 22861 | 117 | 24628 |
| total | 1645 | 37.39 | 63.79 | 22760 | 22861 | 117 | 24628 |

```
select owner, object_name, object_type,
       sum(object_id), avg(object_id), min(object_id),
       max(object_id), stddev(object_id)
  from big_table sa655360
 group by owner, object_name, object_type
```

| call | count | cpu | elapsed | disk | query | current | rows |
|------|-------|-----|---------|------|-------|---------|------|
| Parse | 1 | 0.00 | 0.01 | 0 | 0 | 0 | 0 |
| Execute | 1 | 0.00 | 0.00 | 0 | 0 | 0 | 0 |
| Fetch | 1643 | 48.20 | 711.00 | 84760 | 22861 | 387 | 24628 |
| total | 1645 | 48.20 | 711.01 | 84760 | 22861 | 387 | 24628 |

```
select owner, object_name, object_type,
       sum(object_id), avg(object_id), min(object_id),
       max(object_id), stddev(object_id)
  from big_table sa65536
 group by owner, object_name, object_type
```

| call | count | cpu | elapsed | disk | query | current | rows |
|------|-------|-----|---------|------|-------|---------|------|
| Parse | 1 | 0.00 | 0.00 | 0 | 0 | 0 | 0 |
| Execute | 1 | 0.00 | 0.00 | 0 | 0 | 0 | 0 |
| Fetch | 1643 | 73.31 | 1073.71 | 96864 | 22861 | 782 | 24628 |
| total | 1645 | 73.31 | 1073.71 | 96864 | 22861 | 782 | 24628 |

Notice the CPU time, elapsed time, and physical I/Os for each of the sort area sizes. There are some huge differences. In particular, note that the logical I/O is smaller then the physical I/O which might seem strange. The extra physical I/Os are direct reads from temporary space, since they bypass the buffer cache, they are not counted as logical I/Os in this case.

For reporting systems, data warehousing applications, or that occasional really big query, you should consider throwing a little extra RAM at the problem. Just going from 64KB to the "640KB should be big enough for anyone" step, we considerably cut down on physical I/Os (to TEMP space), as well as CPU and elapsed times. Going one step further reaped even larger gains. Remember that you cannot put RAM in the bank and save it up—you either use it or lose it.

SORT_AREA_SIZE and its cousins HASH_AREA_SIZE and BITMAP_MERGE_AREA_SIZE, should not be neglected in Oracle8i and earlier. Consider setting these values higher on a per-session basis when you know it can be extremely beneficial, if you do not set them higher at the database level itself. The payoff can be huge. On the other hand, do not go overboard and set these values to outrageously large values like 1024MB (one gigabyte). Not because you would run out of memory necessarily but because you would end up with plans that would want to take advantage of that much memory, and it is doubtful you really can allow everyone to have up to one gigabyte of memory.

# Use **STAR_TRANSFORMATION_ENABLED** for Star Queries

*Star queries* are typically found in data warehouses. The concept in a star data model is that you have a single large fact table that has many foreign keys to what are known as *dimension tables*.

For example, you might have a SALES table with a column SALES_DATE that is a foreign key to a dimension table CALENDAR. This dimension table CALENDAR would be used to convert the SALES_DATE into a FY_WEEK (FY stands for fiscal year), FY_MONTH, FY_QTR, FY_YEAR, and so on. This dimension table contains the rules for converting a SALES_DATE into a week, month, year, quarter, and so on. Additionally, the SALES table might have a foreign key CUST_ID to a CUSTOMER dimension table. The CUSTOMER dimension is able to turn a CUST_ID into a STATE, REGION, ZIP_CODE, or any other customer-related dimension. The reason this type of model is called a star data model should be clear now. When you envision this SALES table in the center with a lot of spokes coming out of it pointing to these individual dimensions, you end up with a picture that looks like a star.

A star query transformation in Oracle is a rewrite technique, similar to the materialized views and function-based indexes we discussed in the QUERY_REWRITE_ENABLED section. For example, suppose that we have a query in this form:

```
Select a.fy_qtr, b.state, sum(c.amount)
   From calendar a,
        Customers b,
        Sales c
 Where a.sale_date = c.sale_date
   And b.cust_id = c.cust_id
   And b.state = 'CA'
   And a.fy_qtr = '04-2004'
```

If each of the foreign keys from SALES to the other tables has bitmap indexes on it, this query rewrite will effectively rewrite the query in two stages. The first stage is as follows:

```
Select...
   From sales
 Where sales_date in ( select sales_date
                         from calendar
                        where fy_qtr = '04-2002' )
   and cust_id in ( select cust_id
                      from customers
                     where state = 'CA' )
```

This identifies the rows in the SALES table of interest rapidly, using the bitmap indexes. In stage two, it takes that much smaller subresult and joins that to the CALENDAR and CUSTOMERS tables. Since bitmap indexes can simply be AND'ed and OR'ed together, this allows Oracle to take many of these bitmap indexes, concatenate them into one index, and get the rows from the SALES table in one operation, rather than processing the query, index after index.

In general, if you are doing data warehousing and have met the prerequisites for star queries—you are using that data-modeling technique, you have the necessary bitmap indexes, and so on—you will want to set STAR_TRANSFORMATION_ENABLED = TRUE to allow this type of rewrite to take place. For a full discussion of star query data models and star query transformations, refer to the Oracle documentation. In particular, see the *Data Warehousing Guide*, which includes a few sections dedicated to this technique and data model.

## Set Others Parameters that Affect the Optimizer

In this section, we'll briefly revisit the other parameters that affect the CBO that we've seen from time to time in other chapters in this book:

- **PGA_AGGREGATE_TARGET**    This parameter controls the amount of RAM Oracle should use for PGA work areas. You use this instead of using SORT_AREA_SIZE, HASH_AREA_SIZE, and so on. This approach is recommended for use with Oracle9i and up. This parameter attempts to bound the amount of memory used for sorting and hashing of data, something that was not possible before. In Oracle8i (and earlier), the DBA would set a relatively fixed sort_area_size. Every sort could use up to that specified amount of memory. Suppose it was set to 10M. If there were 100 concurrent sorts, you could have as much as 1,000M of memory requested for sorting, which might easily be more then you have available on your system. Using the PGA_AGGREGATE_TARGET, you tell Oracle you are willing to use up to some amount of memory (say 500M) for sorting and hashing. Oracle would attempt to constrain the use of dynamic memory to 500M adjusting and readjusting how much memory each query would be able to use depending on the current load on the system. Hence, if the system is lightly loaded, larger sort areas would be used. Under heavy load, the work areas for sorting and hashing would be reduced. This allows you to use the memory when it is there, but not exceed the amount you have available when your system gets under load. It should be noted that this work area memory is for sorting and hashing and does not in any way limit the amount of memory your PL/SQL programs or Java-stored procedures may allocate.

- **WORKAREA_SIZE_POLICY**    This parameter goes with the PGA_AGGREGATE_TARGET parameter. It controls whether work areas, such as sort and hash areas, are manually sized by you or automatically sized by Oracle based on current resource usage. If this parameter is set to AUTO, then Oracle will use the PGA_AGGREGATE_TARGET to dynamically allocate sort and hash areas for sessions using dedicated server connections. If this parameter is set to MANUAL, then Oracle will look to the SORT_AREA_SIZE and HASH_AREA_SIZE parameters instead. In all cases, shared server connections continue to use SORT_AREA_SIZE and HASH_AREA_SIZE.

- **PARALLEL_***    This refers to the parallel parameters. We covered these in some detail in Chapter 3. I recommend setting the PARAMETER_AUTOMATIC_TUNING and PARALLEL_ADAPTIVE_MULTI_USER parameters if you intend on using parallel query, leaving the remaining parallel parameters for fine-tuning.

# Use the 10053 Event to Trace CBO Choices

Have you ever wondered why the CBO is making the choices it is making? It is not because it is arbitrary or capricious, rather the opposite. It is a piece of predicable software that comes to conclusions based on inputs. Given the same inputs, it will steadfastly give the same outputs (well, until you upgrade, that is). It appears arbitrary and capricious at times because what it does is among the most complex things Oracle itself does. Cost-based query optimization is a hard thing to do—truly computer science. The myriad facts, parameters, and choices that the CBO is faced with make it difficult for a human to predict what will happen.

When I'm faced with a query plan I just cannot explain, I use the 10053 trace event. I use this after I've tried all of the normal paths, such as using hints to get the query plan I felt I should have gotten in the first place. Most of the time, the COST/CARD output resulting from that exercise is sufficient to see where the plan went wrong and what statistics I might be missing.

Note that this trace event is undocumented, unsupported, and works only in certain circumstances. However, it is widely known outside Oracle Corporation. A simple Google search for event 10053 will return more than 1,500 documents on the Web and hundreds of hits on the newsgroups. There are even Oracle support notes on this topic available on metalink .oracle.com, the Oracle support web site, if you search for 10053.

I do not make a regular practice of reading these trace files. In fact, I most often use them in the filing of a Technical Assistance Request (TAR) with Oracle support. They provide information to the support analysts that can be useful in diagnosing optimizer-related issues. However, an example will show you what you might expect to see in the trace file generated by this event. In order to generate the CBO trace file, we need to set an event and then simply parse a query. One technique is as follows:

```
big_table@ORA920> ALTER SESSION SET EVENTS
  2 '10053 trace name context forever, level 1';
Session altered.

big_table@ORA920> explain plan for
  2 select * from big_table where object_id = 55;
Explained.
```

Now we are ready to inspect the trace file. You can use the same technique outlined in the "TKPROF" section of Chapter 2 to get a trace filename for your session (see that chapter for details if you do not know how to identify your session's trace file). Upon exiting SQL*Plus and editing the trace file, you will see something like this:

```
/usr/oracle/ora920/OraHome1/admin/ora920/udump/ora920_ora_23183.trc
Oracle9i Enterprise Edition Release 9.2.0.1.0 - Production
With the Partitioning, OLAP and Oracle Data Mining options
JServer Release 9.2.0.1.0 - Production
ORACLE_HOME = /usr/oracle/ora920/OraHome1
System name:    Linux
Node name: tkyte-pc-isdn.us.oracle.com
Release:    2.4.18-14
Version:    #1 Wed Sep 4 13:35:50 EDT 2002
Machine:    i686
```

```
Instance name: ora920
Redo thread mounted by this instance: 1
Oracle process number: 18
Unix process pid: 23183, image: oracle@tkyte-pc-isdn.us.oracle.com
```

This is just the standard trace file header. The interesting stuff comes next:

```
*** SESSION ID:(15.1158) 2003-01-26 16:54:53.834
QUERY
explain plan for select * from big_table where object_id = 55
*****************************************
PARAMETERS USED BY THE OPTIMIZER
*******************************
OPTIMIZER_FEATURES_ENABLE = 9.2.0
OPTIMIZER_MODE/GOAL = Choose
... lots chopped out here...
DB_FILE_MULTIBLOCK_READ_COUNT = 16
_NEW_SORT_COST_ESTIMATE = TRUE
_GS_ANTI_SEMI_JOIN_ALLOWED = TRUE
_CPU_TO_IO = 0
_PRED_MOVE_AROUND = TRUE
*******************************************
```

There, you will find the parameters that affect the CBO. The parameters that start with _ are undocumented parameters. Most of the other parameters are discussed in the previous sections. These are the parameters you have free access to modify as you see fit.

### CAUTION
*Never set _ parameters in a real system without the expressed guidance and consent of support. This is not just me "stating the company line" here; this is for real. Undocumented parameters have unanticipated side effects (they could be seriously damaging to your data, your security, and many other things). Undocumented parameters change in meaning from release to release. Every time you upgrade, you need to ask support, "Do I still need this undocumented parameter?" I will not discuss the meaning, range of values, or use of any of these undocumented parameters.*

Next in the trace file, you'll find the base statistical information used:

```
BASE STATISTICAL INFORMATION
***********************
Table stats    Table: BIG_TABLE    Alias: BIG_TABLE
  TOTAL :: CDN: 1833857  NBLKS:  22188  AVG_ROW_LEN:   84
-- Index stats
  INDEX NAME: OBJECT_ID_IDX  COL#: 4
    TOTAL :: LVLS: 2  #LB: 4202  #DK: 1833792  LB/K: 1  DB/K: 1  CLUF: 21921
  INDEX NAME: OBJECT_TYPE_IDX  COL#: 6
```

```
   TOTAL :: LVLS: 2  #LB: 5065  #DK: 27  LB/K: 187  DB/K: 2414  CLUF: 65187
_OPTIMIZER_PERCENT_PARALLEL = 0
```

You'll see this for all of the referenced objects in the query. This, in itself, can help you diagnose the problem right away. If you *know* that the cardinality of the table BIG_TABLE is really 1 and the number of blocks is 1, right here you can see what the problem is. The optimizer sees cardinality (CDN) of 1,833,857 rows and 22,188 blocks (NBLKS). So, the statistics would be out of date if there were really just one row. Here's a quick explanation of what the abbreviations mean:

| | |
|---|---|
| CDN | Cardinality, a count of rows |
| NBLKS | Number of blocks |
| AVG_ROW_LEN | The computed average row length |
| COL# | Column numbers in the table the index is on (select * from user_tab_columns where column_id = 4 and table_name = 'BIG_TABLE' would reveal the name of the column in this case) |
| LVLS | Number of levels in the B*Tree |
| #LB | Number of leaf blocks |
| #DK | Number of distinct keys |
| LB/K | Number of leaf blocks per key value on average |
| DB/K | Number of base table data blocks per key value; how many table accesses (logical I/Os) would be made using an equality predicate on this index. Directly related to the cluster factor that follows. |
| CLUF | Clustering factor of this index; a measure of how sorted a base table is with respect to this index. |

Many times, a quick scan of this information can pinpoint the problem right away. A smack to the forehead, followed by an ANALYZE of the table, and you've fixed the problem. If not, it starts to get more complex.

The next section shows the table-access cost, presenting the best access method for each table. Again, if the information appears incorrect to you, that would point to bad statistics or insufficient statistics (for example, no histograms, where histograms would have played an important role). In this example, you would see the following:

```
*****************************************
SINGLE TABLE ACCESS PATH
Column:  OBJECT_ID  Col#: 4      Table: BIG_TABLE   Alias: BIG_TABLE
    NDV: 1833792   NULLS: 0       DENS: 5.4534e-07
    HEIGHT BALANCED HISTOGRAM: #BKT: 75 #VAL: 76
  TABLE: BIG_TABLE      ORIG CDN: 1833857  ROUNDED CDN: 1  CMPTD CDN: 1
  Access path: tsc  Resc: 2136  Resp:  2136
  Access path: index (equal)
      Index: OBJECT_ID_IDX
  TABLE: BIG_TABLE
```

```
    RSC_CPU: 0   RSC_IO: 4
 IX_SEL:  0.0000e+00  TB_SEL:  5.4534e-07
 BEST_CST: 4.00  PATH: 4  Degree:  1
***************************************
```

Here, you can see more basic information and the costs associated with the various access paths into this table. This example shows two access paths:

- **Access Path: tsc**   A table scan, with a "serial" cost of 2136 (resc) and a parallel cost of 2136 (resp) in this case.

- **Access Path: index (equal)**   An index access based on an equality predicate. Other paths might be index-unique, no sta/sto keys–unbounded range scan (start/stop keys), index, and so on. This has a serial cost of 4 based on an estimated I/O (RSC_IO). Sometimes, it is not what is in the 10053 trace file that is interesting, sometimes it is what is *not* in the trace file. For example, consider this recent question I received.

"We have two fact tables in our data warehouse. One for transactions of type V, another for transactions of type M. Each table is partitioned by day and there are 90 days online. There are 145 million rows of type V, 133 million of type M. They are stuctured in exactly the same way (same partition key, same indexes, and so on). The only real difference is that the row size of the table of type V is larger (203 bytes) than the row size of the table of type M (141 bytes). We have a query to look for transactions of type V for customer X. Performance is good, and an identical query to look for transactions of type M for customer X. Performance is horrible. The difference between the two is the query against V is using an INDEX RANGE SCAN. The query against M will only use an INDEX FULL SCAN. What could be the reason?"

Well, we went back and forth on this, trying hints and spending time scratching our heads. Finally, I asked them to email me the 10053 trace files. What I discovered was the index was not only not being range scanned for the query against M, but it wasn't *even being considered*. That was a great clue. There was something that was precluding this index from being used in that fashion. I immediately asked for the CREATE TABLE and CREATE INDEX statements, something I should have asked for in the beginning. I was over analyzing the problem and didn't rule out the simple things first. When I got them, I discovered that the indexed column was a NUMBER(12) in the V table and a VARCHAR2(12) in the M table. It was a simple datatype conversion that was precluding the index from being used in a range scan! They were joining these V and M tables to some other table by this column. When it was a NUMBER, the index could be range scanned, when it was a VARCHAR2, it could not. In the end, what was assumed to be an optimizer problem turned out to be an implementation mistake. The column was supposed to be a NUMBER they implemented wrong. Fixing that issue solved the problem immediately. I'm not sure that if I had looked at the CREATE TABLES I would have caught it right away myself. It was something they overlooked easily enough and it was their data! The 10053 trace certainly helped here by showing that the access path was not even considered.

Now, continuing on in this trace file, you can also see the ORIG CDN, which is the original cardinality of the base table, as well as the CMPTD CDN, the computed cardinality—how many rows the optimizer expects to get back from this object (regardless of the access method).

Now, unfortunately, the interesting output of this is the PATH, which is a nebulous 4 in this case. The 4 just happens to mean index-range scan. We know that because the least-cost access path is the index (equal), and that it is really an index-range scan (it has to be). OBJECT_ID_IDX is a nonunique index, and the predicate was `where object_id = 55`.

Basically, in this section, you will be looking to see if the raw numbers even make sense, given your knowledge of the real situation. If not, it probably points to bad statistics, something you need to correct before assuming that something is wrong with the optimizer. Or, as noted, you'll be looking for what isn't there and then trying to figure out why.

The rest of this report, while interesting, is mostly useful only to Oracle support analysts and the optimizer developers themselves. It can be interesting to look at, to try and get a better understanding of the complexity of the software that is the optimizer. Here, you will see a review of all of the possible plans, including their costs and what they are doing. At the very bottom, you'll ultimately see the chosen plan and its cost.

Now, the trace file in this example is fairly small, concise, and easy to understand. If you take a nontrivial query, however, you'll see how complex this file can truly be. I did a 150-table join and traced it. The resulting trace file itself was almost 80,000 lines of text, simply due to the massive permutations by which the query could be processed after reordering the tables.

So, my recommendation with this 10053 trace event is that you use this only when you believe the optimizer to be very wrong. You would generate the trace file and look at the first few pages, eyeball the numbers and init.ora settings, and make sure that they are realistic. If not, you would start there by correcting the problem—adjusting the parameter you thought was already set, or fixing the statistics by updating out-of-date ones or doing a more comprehensive gather, to include histograms, for example.

Lastly, if all else fails, you have the trace file you need to open a TAR with Oracle support, to find out why a particular plan is being selected. At this point, it would be best if you actually have two traces: one for the original query and another for a hinted query that massively outperforms your existing one. This information will be more than enough for the support technicians to discover the scientific reason for the performance differences and probably to suggest a workaround to solve the problem.

# Summary

In this chapter, we discussed the two different optimizers in Oracle and why the CBO is the only one that deserves any serious consideration today, particularly in light of the fact that the RBO is officially no longer supported in the version after Oracle9i Release 2. That consideration, and the fact that the available set of access paths under the CBO is enormous when compared to the RBO, makes the CBO the obvious choice for all newly developed applications. I can say without hesitation that any data warehouse or reporting system that does not make use of the CBO is missing out on 90% of the functionality of Oracle.

We discussed the two extremely important parameters that most heavily influence the CBO: OPTIMIZER_INDEX_COST_ADJ and OPTIMIZER_INDEX_CACHING. We saw the effect that setting these parameters can have on the generated query plans. We also discussed how there might be two sets of settings for these parameters. One set is the default settings, which seem appropriate for many reporting/warehousing situations. The other set is where the settings are, in effect, opposite of their initial positions, giving the optimizer bias towards more single-block I/O, which seem appropriate for many transactional or OLTP systems. Most important, we have seen how gathering actual observed system statistics using DBMS_STATS in Oracle9i can permit the system to come to the right conclusions about which type of I/O to perform, without being nudged via parameter settings.

We also looked at many of the other parameters that influence the behavior of the CBO, with examples of many of the usages. Lastly, we looked at the 10053 trace event, a tool that can help us to understand *why* the optimizer did what it did.

# CHAPTER
# 7

# Effective
# Schema Design

our application will live and die based on its physical implementation. Choose the wrong data structures, and performance will be crippled and flexibility limited. Choose the correct data structures, and you could have great performance. In this chapter, we will look at some of the things you need to consider when designing your schema. Then we will focus on table types, some useful index types, and finally, compression.

# Fundamental Schema Design Principles

In this section, we'll consider some of the fundamental approaches that you should adopt when designing your schema. We'll cover integrity checking, datatype selection, and optimization for queries.

## Let the Database Enforce Data Integrity

We touched on this subject way back in the "It's a Database, Not a Data Dump" section in Chapter 1. There, I relayed the story of the consultant who wanted to remove all referential integrity from the database and do it in the application. I explained that this was a really bad idea, for the following reasons:

- Yours will not be the last application to want to use this data. If the rules governing the data integrity are hidden away in client applications, they will not be enforced uniformly, and they will be very hard to change.

- It is slower to manage data integrity on the client. It requires additional round-trips to the server, and it must be done on the server as well.

- It takes orders of magnitude more code to manage integrity on the client.

I have a theory as to why developers are sometimes inclined to do this on the client: It has to do with the DBA-versus-developer philosophy instead of the DBA-and-developers-working-together approach. If the integrity of the data is managed in the database, the developers feel they have lost control. If the integrity of the data is managed in the application, the developers feel they have regained that control. This is a shortsighted perspective. Neither the developer nor the DBA own the data. The data is the property of someone else: the end users. It is certainly not in the best interests of the end users to obfuscate the business rules and hide them in the client application.

### Why You Want to Keep Referential Integrity in the Database

Data-integrity rules must be placed into the database to ensure that they are consistently implemented and enforced. Application-specific rules—rules that apply only to the data in the context of the application's use of it—may be in the application.

Here are the reasons you want data integrity enforced by the database whenever possible:

- **Features such as query rewrite are thwarted.** These features are rendered less-than-useful if you do not tell the database about the relationships between objects, unless you declaratively spell out the rules regarding the data. In the section on QUERY_

REWRITE_ENABLED in Chapter 6, you saw an example of how a materialized view could not be used until the database was told about the relationship between the tables, the NOT NULL column, and the primary keys.

- ◼ **The data integrity will be compromised at some point in time.**   Virtually every developed system that chooses to enforce foreign key constraints outside the database has orphaned child rows (child rows without parents). If you have such a system, just run this query: select foreign_key_columns from child_table MINUS select primary_key_columns from parent. You may be surprised to find some in your own database! Run a couple of checks on your data, and you might find NULL values where none should be and data that does not conform to your business rules (out-of-range data, for example). These arise from an inconsistent application of the business rules.

- ◼ **Server-enforced integrity is blindingly fast.**   Is it slower than not using data integrity? Yes, of course it is. It adds an extra step, and it means that more code is executed in the server. Is it faster than you can code it yourself? Yes, it is. Is it applied consistently regardless of the application? Yes, it is.

- ◼ **The database provides more information.**   By keeping the integrity rules in the database, your system is infinitely more self-documenting. A simple query tells you what relates to what and how.

As a last reason for using server-enforced integrity, let's consider what happens when you try to do it yourself.

## The Problem with Do-It-Yourself Integrity Checks

Client-side enforcement of constraints is problematic at best, if you can do it at all. Here, we'll look at an example of the problems that can arise.

"I hope someone can help me and, therefore, thank you in advance if you can. I am using Oracle9 and the EMP table. I need to ensure that no department is to have more than eight employees and fewer than three, except when a transaction reduces the number of employees to 0."

Interestingly, this user posed this question to many individuals in different forums, and the most frequent response was something along the lines of the following trigger:

```
SQL> create or replace trigger xxx
  2  after delete or update or insert on emp
  3  declare
  4  begin
  5
  6    for irec in (select deptno, count(*) emps
  7             from emp
  8             group by deptno
  9             having count(*) <3
 10                 or count(*) >8)
```

```
11   loop
12       RAISE_APPLICATION_ERROR(-20000, 'Department '
13           ||irec.deptno || ' has '||irec.emps||' employees!');
14   end loop;
15   end;
16   /
```

In various forms, this trigger was implemented. Various optimizations were suggested, such as only checking the DEPTNO values that were inserted/updated/deleted (because the performance of the preceding trigger would be questionable if EMP were large), but the answers were pretty much uniform: Use a trigger and count.

The problem is that the trigger doesn't work! My solution to this problem was a bit more involved, but it would work in all situations. He needs to serialize access to employee records at the DEPTNO level during insert, delete, and update operations to the DEPTNO column, and use database check constraints. Then use a trigger to maintain that value.

When you need to enforce a simple rule, such as a department in the EMP table must have three to eight employees or zero employees, a trigger-and-count solution may seem like it should work. The trigger could just look for any DEPTNO in EMP that does not have a count of employees between 3 and 8. And indeed, when we perform a single-user test, such a trigger does appear to work:

```
ops$tkyte@ORA920> select deptno, count(*),
  2            case when count(*) NOT between 3 and 8 then '<<<===='
  3                else null
  4            end
  5      from emp
  6    group by deptno
  7    /

    DEPTNO   COUNT(*) CASEWHE
---------- ---------- -------
        10          3
        20          5
        30          6
```

Our initial data is valid; all of the aggregate counts fall within our required range. If we attempt to delete three employees from Department 20, our trigger kicks in and saves us:

```
SQL> delete from emp where empno in ( 7369, 7566, 7788 );
delete from emp where empno in ( 7369, 7566, 7788 )
*
ERROR at line 1:
ORA-20000: Department 20 has 2 employees!
```

Now, however, we'll simulate two simultaneous sessions modifying the table. We need to use two SQLPlus sessions in order to do this. I opened the first SQLPlus session and entered:

```
ops$tkyte@ORA920> delete from emp where empno in ( 7369, 7566 );
2 rows deleted.
```

Now, in the second session, I executed:

```
ops$tkyte@ORA920> delete from emp where empno = 7788;
1 row deleted.
ops$tkyte@ORA920> commit;
Commit complete.
```

Now, we have a pending deletion of two employees (7369 and 7566) and a committed deletion of a single employee (7788). All three of these employees work in Department 20. When we commit that first transaction, there will be only two people left in Department 20, which is in violation of our business logic. *Remember, our trigger has already fired and will not fire again.* The data has apparently been validated, but, actually, when we commit that first transaction, our data will be corrupted, our data integrity shattered. Return to that first session and enter:

```
ops$tkyte@ORA920> commit;
Commit complete.

ops$tkyte@ORA920> select deptno, count(*),
  2           case when count(*) NOT between 3 and 8 then '<<<===='
  3                else null
  4           end
  5    from emp
  6   group by deptno
  7  /

    DEPTNO   COUNT(*) CASEWHE
---------- ---------- -------
        10          3
        20          2 <<<====
        30          6
```

The reason the trigger fails to enforce our business logic as we expect is because this solution does not account for the fact that Oracle provides nonblocking reads, consistent queries, and multiversioning. (For details on the Oracle multiversioning model, see the Oracle9i Release 2 *Concepts Guide*, Chapter 20, "Data Concurrency and Consistency.") Even though our first transaction was still in progress (while it was not committed), the second transaction was not blocked from reading rows that were involved in that transaction. Our first transaction deleted two employees, which left three remaining, so all is well. Our second transaction was not aware of the uncommitted changes made by the first transaction, so the trigger saw four rows left in DEPTNO 20, and that was fine. When we committed, the data integrity was lost.

Note that in many other databases, this logic would appear to work. The reason is that the query against EMP in databases that do not provide nonblocking reads (Microsoft SQL Server and DB2, for example) would have blocked on the changed rows. In our example, the result would have been a self-deadlock, because the second delete would have hung on the read of the EMP table. This is yet another reason why database independence is something that is truly hard to achieve generically: The algorithms must be implemented for the database you are using.

To solve the problem, we can use serialization and server-enforced integrity. There are a couple of ways to do this. Here, we'll use the DEPT table, where we'll maintain an aggregate column EMP_COUNT. It looks like this:

```
ops$tkyte@ORA920> alter table dept
  2    add emp_count number
  3    constraint must_be_between_3_8
  4    check(emp_count between 3 and 8 OR emp_count = 0)
  5    deferrable initially deferred;
Table altered.

ops$tkyte@ORA920> update dept
  2      set emp_count = (select count(*)
  3                         from emp
  4                        where emp.deptno = dept.deptno )
  5  /
4 rows updated.

ops$tkyte@ORA920> alter table dept
  2    modify emp_count NOT NULL;
Table altered.
```

Now, we have an aggregate column in the DEPT table that we will use to maintain a count of employees. Additionally, this column has a declarative check constraint on it that verifies the count of employees is either 0 or between 3 and 8, as specified in the rule. Lastly, we made this constraint `deferrable initially deferred`, meaning it will not be validated until we commit by default. The reason for doing that is to permit multistatement transactions to execute without error. For example, we could update a row setting the DEPTNO from 20 to 30, reducing the number of employees in DEPTNO 20 to 2 but immediately follow that with an update of another row from DEPTNO 30 to 20, increasing the number of employees back to 3. If the constraint were validated after each and every statement, this sort of logic would fail.

Now, we need a trigger to maintain that value:

```
ops$tkyte@ORA920> create trigger emp_dept_cnt_trigger
  2    after insert or update or delete on emp
  3    for each row
  4    begin
  5        if ( updating and :old.deptno = :new.deptno )
  6        then
  7            return; -- no change
  8        end if;
  9        if ( inserting or updating )
 10        then
 11            update dept set emp_count = emp_count+1
 12             where deptno = :new.deptno;
 13        end if;
 14        if ( updating or deleting )
 15        then
```

```
16            update dept set emp_count = emp_count-1
17              where deptno = :old.deptno;
18         end if;
19   end;
20   /
Trigger created.
```

**NOTE**
*For ease of example, the SQL for the trigger is presented in-line. It would be advantageous to place the SQL into a stored procedure, especially in this case. Not only would we benefit from reducing the soft parsing our application performs, but we would also be able to get away with a single UPDATE statement.*

If we are updating and did not change the DEPTNO column, we just return; no changes need to be made. Otherwise, we update the DEPT table and increment or decrement the EMP_COUNT column as needed, since we are using foreign keys. We are assured that the UPDATE statements update at least and at most a single row in DEPT. (You cannot possibly have a child row in EMP with a DEPTNO that does not exist in DEPT, because the database is enforcing that for us.)

The update of the *single row* in DEPT also causes *serialization* at the DEPTNO level; that is, only one transaction can insert into DEPTNO=20 at any point in time. All other sessions trying to insert, delete, or transfer where DEPTNO=20 will block on that update. All of the other DEPTNO operations are available for modification; just not this one. We can still update other EMP rows in DEPTNO=20, as long as we do not change their DEPTNO. This serialization is what allows our constraint to be effective.

As another example, consider a primary key/foreign key relationship. The code you would write in order to use client-side enforcement of constraints would need to do the following:

| Action | Reaction |
|---|---|
| Insert into a child table or update a child table's foreign key value. | Lock the parent row for that foreign key (most people would simply select without locking). Note that this will serialize at the parent table row level. |
| Update the parent primary key or delete from parent table. | Lock the entire child table. Then look for child rows before you update or delete that parent row. That is your only recourse. You must lock the entire child table to prevent any rows that reference this primary key from being created. Oracle itself can bypass this child table lock and do it more efficiently, but only because it does it internally. |

Neither of these approaches is very good for concurrency. Oracle can do much better on its own. You will notice that many sessions can insert into a child table simultaneously if you use declarative integrity, and many sessions can modify the parent table using declarative integrity. If you do it yourself, *and you do it correctly,* you will be forced to serialize frequently, greatly decreasing concurrency and, hence, scalability in your database.

Don't believe anyone when they say, "Don't use integrity in the database. It is too slow." They either don't enforce data integrity at all or they have been doing it wrong (and, hence, have a false sense of security). If they did it right, their system is running many times slower than it should be! It is all about benchmarking and doing it right.

### Does that Mean that the Client Should Not Do Integrity Checking Itself?

It can be very useful for the client to do integrity checking for a variety of reasons. The important thing to remember, however, is that it must ultimately *still be performed in the database*. Client-side integrity is not a substitute for server-side integrity; it is a complementary addition. Here are some of the salient reasons for client-side integrity:

- **Better end-user experience**   Users can discover as they are typing that the data they entered doesn't stand a chance of being entered into the database. They do not need to wait until they select Save.

- **Reduced resource usage on the server**   By preempting bad data on the client, you do not make the server perform work that will ultimately need to be undone.

But, just as there are pros to most everything, there are cons as well. The major disadvantage with client-side integrity is that you now have two places where the rules are, and if they change over time, you must ensure they are changed in both locations. It would be frustrating for a client to not be able to input information the database should accept because the application is working from old rules. It would be equally as frustrating to work on a set of data and feel confident that it is valid, only to discover as you save the data from the application that the database will reject it. Good configuration management and software engineering principles will reduce the chances of having this happen.

## Use the Correct Datatype

Using the correct datatype seems like common sense, but virtually every system I look at does one of the following:

- Uses a string to store dates or times

- Uses a string to store numbers

- Uses VARCHAR2(4000) to store all strings.

- Uses CHAR(2000) to store all strings, wasting tons of space and forcing the use of a lot of `trim` function calls

- Puts text in a BLOB (raw) type

I have a very simple rule: Put dates in dates, numbers in numbers, and strings in strings. Never use a datatype to store something other than what it was designed for, and use the most specific type possible. Furthermore, only compare dates to dates, strings to strings, and numbers to numbers. When dates and numbers are stored in strings, or stored using inappropriate lengths, your system suffers:

- You lose the edit upon insertion to the database, verifying that your dates are actual dates and numbers are valid numbers.

- You lose performance.

- You potentially increase storage needs.

- You definitely decrease data integrity.

How many of you know what ORA-01722 or ORA-01858 errors are off the top of your head? I bet many of you do, because they are so prevalent in systems where numbers are stored in strings (ORA-01722: invalid number) and dates in strings (ORA-01858: a non-numeric character was found where a numeric was expected).

## How Data Integrity Decreases

Using an incorrect datatype is wrong for many reasons, but the first and foremost is *data integrity*. Systems that use strings for dates or numbers will have some records with dates that are not valid and numbers that are not numbers. It is just the nature of the game here. If you permit any string in your date field, at some point you will get dirty data in there.

Without data-integrity rules in place, the integrity of your data is questionable. I've needed to write the functions to convert strings to dates but return NULL when the date won't convert. I've also needed to try one of five date formats to see if I can get the date to convert. Can you look at 01/02/03 and tell what date that is? Is that *yy/mm/dd*, *dd/mm/yy*, or something else?

## How Performance Suffers

Beyond the obvious data-integrity issues associated with incorrect datatypes, there are other subtle issues. To demonstrate, we'll use an example of a table with two date columns. One will be stored in a string using YYYYMMDD and the other as a DATE type. We will index these values and analyze the tables completely.

```
ops$tkyte@ORA920> create table t
  2  as
  3  select to_char(to_date('01-jan-1995','dd-mon-yyyy')+rownum,'yyyymmdd') str_date,
  4         to_date('01-jan-1995','dd-mon-yyyy')+rownum date_date
  5    from all_objects
  6  /
Table created.

ops$tkyte@ORA920> create index t_str_date_idx on t(str_date);
Index created.

ops$tkyte@ORA920> create index t_date_date_idx on t(date_date);
Index created.

ops$tkyte@ORA920> analyze table t compute statistics
```

```
  2  for table
  3  for all indexes
  4  for all indexed columns;
Table analyzed.
```

Now, let's see what happens when we query this table using the string date column and the real date column. Pay close attention to the Cost and Card= component of the plan:

```
ops$tkyte@ORA920> set autotrace on explain
ops$tkyte@ORA920> select * from t
  2 where str_date between '20001231' and '20010101';

STR_DATE DATE_DATE
-------- ---------
20001231 31-DEC-00
20010101 01-JAN-01


Execution Plan
----------------------------------------------------------
   0      SELECT STATEMENT Optimizer=CHOOSE (Cost=5 Card=406 Bytes=6090)
   1    0   TABLE ACCESS (BY INDEX ROWID) OF 'T' (Cost=5 Card=406 Bytes=6090)
   2    1     INDEX (RANGE SCAN) OF 'T_STR_DATE_IDX' (NON-UNIQUE)
              (Cost=3 Card=406)

ops$tkyte@ORA920> select * from t where date_date between
to_date('20001231','yyyymmdd') and to_date('20010101','yyyymmdd');

STR_DATE DATE_DATE
-------- ---------
20001231 31-DEC-00
20010101 01-JAN-01


Execution Plan
----------------------------------------------------------
   0      SELECT STATEMENT Optimizer=CHOOSE (Cost=3 Card=1 Bytes=15)
   1    0   TABLE ACCESS (BY INDEX ROWID) OF 'T' (Cost=3 Card=1 Bytes=15)
   2    1     INDEX (RANGE SCAN) OF 'T_DATE_DATE_IDX' (NON-UNIQUE)
              (Cost=2 Card=1)
```

So, what happened there? Well, the optimizer understands VARCHAR2 types and it understands DATE types. The optimizer knows that between the two DATE items, December 31, 2000, and January 1, 2001, there is only one day. The optimizer also *thinks* that between the two string items, '20001231' and '20010101', there are a whole bunch of values. The cardinality is thrown off.

But, so what? What do we care if the cardinality is wrong? It won't affect our output—the answer. That is correct, but it could have some impact on our overall performance. Consider a different query against the same data, asking for effectively the same result set:

```
ops$tkyte@ORA920> select * from t
  2 where str_date between '20001231' and '20060101';

Execution Plan
----------------------------------------------------------
   0      SELECT STATEMENT Optimizer=CHOOSE (Cost=12 Card=2034 Bytes=30510)
   1    0    TABLE ACCESS (FULL) OF 'T' (Cost=12 Card=2034 Bytes=30510)

ops$tkyte@ORA920> select * from t where date_date between
to_date('20001231','yyyymmdd') and to_date('20060101','yyyymmdd');

Execution Plan
----------------------------------------------------------
   0      SELECT STATEMENT Optimizer=CHOOSE (Cost=12 Card=1823 Bytes=27345)
   1    0    TABLE ACCESS (BY INDEX ROWID) OF 'T' (Cost=12 Card=1823 Bytes=27345)
   2    1       INDEX (RANGE SCAN) OF 'T_DATE_DATE_IDX'
                 (NON-UNIQUE) (Cost=6 Card=1823)
```

**NOTE**
*As discussed in Chapter 6, different database parameter settings will*
*influence the cost of various operations. You may need to increase*
*the range of dates to see the same effect as shown in this example, but*
*it will happen at some threshold.*

This time, the fact that we hid a date in a string has a serious side effect. Our query plan has changed. We are now full-scanning for the string date but index-range scanning for the DATE type date. So, besides the fact that there is nothing stopping someone from inserting 20009950 as a date value into our field, the use of a string has withheld valuable information from the database. We lose all around.

## How You Might Increase Your Storage Requirements
In addition to using the proper base datatype such as number, date, or string, you should also use the most specific type you can. For example, use VARCHAR2(30) for a field that is up to 30 characters in length; do *not* use VARCHAR2(4000).

> "I work with a modelers group. My modeler would like to define every VARCHAR2 field with the maximum length, which means that a table with 20 VARCHAR2 fields will all be defined with a maximum of 2000 or 4000 bytes. I tried to talk to him about the reasons we identify data with correct lengths and names in order to understand what we have in our database. He told me that it doesn't matter, since Oracle just stores the length, etc., and there is no overhead. I don't believe this is true, but have been jumping between so many databases that I cannot find a document on the internals of Oracle storage. Can you help me out here with this question?"

My gut response was, "This is your data modeler, my goodness!" They are the ones who are supposed to be telling you that it is vital to use the appropriate length when defining fields! That is their *job*. Let's just forget about things like storage for a minute, why don't we ask him:

- What is going to happen when users pull this up in a query tool that formats each field based on the width of the column in the database? They'll see one column and need to scroll way over to see the second, the third, and so on.

- Say the code prepares a query that selects ten columns that are VARCHAR2. The developers, for performance, would like to array fetch (very important). They would like to array fetch say 100 rows (very typical). So, you have $4,000 \times 10 \times 100 =$ almost 4MB of RAM the developers must allocate! Now, consider if that were ten VARCHAR2(80) fields (it's probably much smaller than that). That's about 78KB. Ask the data modeler how much RAM he is willing to kick in for this system.

- Now, the developers start to build a data-entry screen to put data into the database. Wow, that code field can be 4,000 characters long and that first name can be 4,000 characters long. How the heck is anyone going to know what sort of data can really go in there?

Tell your data modeler group members that they need to consider the length as a constraint. Just as they use primary and foreign keys, they should use the proper and correct length on fields. You can always expand a field via a command like alter table t modify c varchar2(bigger_number). There is no reason to use the maximum length everywhere. It will hurt the applications you develop, because they will mistakenly allocate many megabytes of RAM. Just think of the array fetch example with an application server. Now, it's not just 4MB; it's 4MB × number of connections. You are talking some real memory here for a *single query*, and you'll be doing a lot of them at the same time.

A CHAR(2000) will consume 2,000 bytes of storage whether you put in the letter *a*, the string 'hello world', or 2,000 characters. A CHAR is always blank-padded. Additionally, are you thinking about using an occasional index in your system? If so, beware of storage-related problems. Consider the following:

```
tkyte@ORA817.US.ORACLE.COM> create table t ( a varchar2(4000), b varchar2(4000));
Table created.

tkyte@ORA817.US.ORACLE.COM> create index t_idx on t(a);
create index t_idx on t(a)
                       *
ERROR at line 1:
ORA-01450: maximum key length (3218) exceeded
```

**NOTE**
*In Oracle9i, the maximum key length is larger, but the restriction still exists. For example, an index on T(a,b) would raise: ORA-01450: maximum key length (6398) exceeded in Oracle9i with an 8KB blocksize.*

My system has an 8KB blocksize. I would need to use at least a 16KB blocksize to index a *single* column, but even then, if I tried to create a concatenated index on T(A,B), it would fail there!

The same holds true for your numbers and the new Oracle9i TIMESTAMP datatypes: When appropriate, use scales and precisions on those fields in order to better define your data integrity and to give applications that much more information about the data itself.

In short, never be tempted to use anything other than a DATE or TIMESTAMP datatype to hold a date value, and never be tempted to use a VARCHAR2 to hold a number. Use the appropriate and correct type for each to ensure maximum performance, and more important, to protect your data integrity.

## Optimize to Your Most Frequently Asked Questions

If you have a system you know will be executing some given query or set of queries hundreds of times per minute, or even per second, that system must be designed, optimized, and built around those queries.

For example, my workplace once had an internal system called Phone. You could telnet into any email machine (back when email was character mode), and on the command line, type phone *<search string>*. It would return data like this:

```
$ phone tkyte
TKYTE    Kyte, Tom     703/555 4567  Managing Technologies RESTON:
```

When the Web exploded in about 1995/1996, our group wrote a small web system that loaded this phone data into a table and let people search it. Now that it was in a database and had a little GUI to go with it, it started becoming the de-facto standard within the company for looking up information about people. Over time, we started adding more data and more fields to it. It really started to catch on.

At some point, we decided to add a lot more fields to the system and rebuild it with more features. The first thing we did, based on our knowledge of how people would use this simple little system, was to design the tables to hold this data. We had a read-only repository of data that people would be searching, and it needed to be fast. This system was growing in popularity every day and was threatening to consume our machine with its resources. We had a single 67-column, 75,000-row table upon which we wanted to perform a simple string search against various fields. So, if a user put in *ABC*, it would find *ABC* in the email address, or the first name, or the last name, or the middle name, and so on. Even worse, it would be interpreted as %ABC%, and the data was in mixed case.

There wasn't an index in the world that could help us here (we tried them all), so we built our own. Every night, as we refreshed the data from our human resources system (a complete refresh of data), we would also issue the following after we were finished:

```
CREATE TABLE FAST_EMPS
PCTFREE 0
CACHE
AS
SELECT upper(last_name)||'/'||upper(first_name)||'/' .... || '/' ||
               substr( phone, length(phone)-4) SEARCH_STRING,
       rowid row_id
  FROM EMPLOYEES
/
```

In effect, we built the most dense, compact table possible (PCTFREE 0) and asked that it be cached, if possible. Then we would query:

```
select *
  from employees
 where rowid in ( select row_id
                    from fast_emp
                   where search_string like :bv
                     and rownum <= 500 )
```

This query would always full-scan the FAST_EMP table, which is what we wanted, because that table was, in fact, our "index." Given the types of questions we were using, that was the only choice. Our goal from the outset was to minimize the amount of data that would be scanned, to limit the amount of data people would get back, and to make it as fast as possible. The query shown here accomplishes all three goals.

The FAST_EMP table is typically always in the buffer cache. It is small (less than 8% the size of the original table) and scans very fast. It has already done the work of the case-insensitive searching for us once (instead of once per query) by storing the data in uppercase. It limits the number of hits to 500 (if your search is broader than that, refine it; you'll *never* look at 500 hits). In effect, that table works a lot like an index, since it stores the ROWID in EMPLOYEES. There are no indexes employed on this system in order to do this search—just two tables.

Before settling on this design, we tried a couple of alternative approaches:

- We tried using a fast full scan on a function-based index (close, but not as fast).

- We tried interMedia text (not useful due to the %ABC% requirement).

- We tried having just an extra field in the base EMPLOYEES table (wiped out the buffer cache because it was too big to full-scan).

It may seem foolish to have spent so much time on this detail. However, this one query is executed between 150,000 and 250,000 times a day. This is two to three times a second, every second, all day long, assuming a constant flow of traffic (and we cannot assume that, since we frequently have spikes in activity, as most systems do). If this single query performed poorly, our entire system would fall apart, and it is just one of thousands of queries we need to do. By determining where our weak points would be—the lowest hanging fruit, so to say—and concentrating on them, we were able to build an application that scales very well. If we had tried the tuning-after-the-fact principle, we would have found ourselves rewriting after the fact.

The point is that when developing a system, you need to give a lot of thought to how people will actually use that system. Consider how physical organization can matter, and realize the impact a simple 100% increase in logical I/O might have on your system's performance.

## Overview of Table Types

Steve Adams (http://www.ixora.com.au/), a very bright guy who knows a lot about Oracle, has been known to say, "If a schema has no IOTs or clusters, that is a good indication that no thought has been given to the matter of optimizing data access." His point is that most systems use only two data structures in the Oracle database: heap-based tables (the kind you get from a simple `create table t ( x int)`) and B*Tree indexes (the kind you get from a simple `create index t_idx on t(x)`).

Oracle provides a wealth of other types of data structures you can use to store and access your data. In the following sections, we'll take a look at each of the different types, starting with tables and then moving onto indexes.

Let's define each type of table that we're going to consider before getting into the details.

- **Heap-organized table** This is a standard database table. Data is managed in a heap-like fashion. As data is added, the first free space found in the segment that can fit the data will be used. As data is removed from the table, it allows space to become available for reuse by subsequent insert and update operations. This is the origin of the name *heap* as it refers to tables like this. A *heap* is a bunch of space, and that space is used in a somewhat random fashion.

- **B*Tree Index Clustered table** Two things are achieved with this type of table. First, many tables may be stored physically joined together. Normally, one would expect data from only one table to be found on a database block. With clustered tables, data from many tables may be stored together on the same block. Second, all data that contains the same cluster key value will be physically stored together. The data is clustered around the cluster key value. A cluster key is built using a B*Tree index.

- **Hash-clustered table** This type is similar to a clustered table, but instead of using a B*Tree index to locate the data by cluster key, the hash cluster hashes the key to the cluster to determine the database block on which to store the data. In a hash cluster, the data is the index (metaphorically speaking). This would be appropriate for data that is read frequently via an equality comparison on the key. There are two types of hash-clustered tables: single-table and multiple-table hash clusters. We'll focus on single-table hash clusters here, because the clustered tables examples will show the use of multiple-table clusters.

- **Index-organized table (IOT)** Here, a table is stored in an index structure. This imposes physical order on the rows themselves. Unlike in a heap, where the data is stuffed wherever it might fit, in an IOT, the data is stored in sorted order according to the primary key.

- **External table** This is a new type with Oracle9i Release 1. As the name suggests, external tables give us the ability to store data in flat files outside the Oracle database. You cannot modify data in these table types; you can only query them. Also, they cannot be conventionally indexed.

For details about the basic Oracle table types, see the Oracle9i Release 2 *Concepts Guide*, Chapter 10, which has a "Tables" section.

We're not going to consider the heap-organized tables directly, as they are the standard table type that most people use all the time. However, we will use them in our benchmarks, to show the performance advantages that the other types can sometimes bring. Let's get started by considering clustered tables.

# B*Tree Index Clustered Tables

Clusters are segments in Oracle that do two things for us:

- They physically colocate data together by a common key. The data is not sorted; it's just physically stored together by key. If you have a cluster built on a number key, all of the data with the key value of 10 would be physically colocated together, optimally on the same database block, if it all fits.

- They allow us to store data from multiple database tables in the same physical database block. For example, the row for DEPTNO=10 from the DEPT table may be on the same block as the rows from the EMP table for that same DEPTNO. Consider this a method of prejoining data.

Immediately, we can see some potential advantages of using clusters. The physical colocation of data means that we can store rows from many tables on the same database block. The fact that all tables share one cluster key index means that we have a decreased need for indexes. (In fact, hash clusters remove the need for indexes completely, because the data is the index.)

In a nutshell, clusters allow us to limit the amount of I/O the system needs to perform in order to answer our queries. If we clump together data that is used together, the database will need to perform less-physical I/O and perhaps even less-logical I/O to answer our questions. However, you should be aware of two basic limitations of clusters:

- You cannot do direct-path loading into a cluster.
- You cannot partition clustered tables.

So, if you know you need to do either of the preceding with a table, a cluster is not the right choice.

**NOTE**
*I would argue that direct-path loading is something you seriously reconsider. Many times, people feel that using direct-path loading will speed up loading, when, in fact, the conventional-path load process would satisfy their needs. Then they would find that the advantages of using one of Oracle's more sophisticated storage devices would pay off thousands of times during the day as people access the data!*

You may not realize it, but you use clusters every day in Oracle, because the main tables in the data dictionary are stored in clusters (B*Tree clusters). To see them, use this query:

```
ops$tkyte@ORA920> select cluster_name, owner, table_name
  2    from dba_tables
  3    where cluster_name is not null
  4    order by cluster_name
  5    /
```

```
CLUSTER_NAME                         OWNER  TABLE_NAME
------------------------------       -----  ----------------------------
C_COBJ#                              SYS    CDEF$
                                     SYS    CCOL$

C_FILE#_BLOCK#                       SYS    SEG$
                                     SYS    UET$

C_MLOG#                              SYS    MLOG$
                                     SYS    SLOG$

C_OBJ#                               SYS    CLU$
                                     SYS    COL$
...
                                     SYS    LIBRARY$
                                     SYS    NTAB$
...
```

The C_OBJ# cluster itself has 16 tables in it. That means there could be rows from up to 16 tables stored on a single database block, all prejoined by their common key. When Oracle needs to find information about an object (a table, for example), it may need to do a single physical I/O to read in all of the information from 16 different tables!

In the remainder of this section, we'll walk through a cluster implementation. We'll discuss relevant considerations for the effective use of clusters, and we'll benchmark their performance against a more traditional implementation using conventional heap tables. As you will see as you read through this section, there are many situations where a cluster should be considered.

# Create Clusters

Oracle supports B*Tree clusters and hash clusters. The difference between these two types lies in *how* the data is accessed:

- The B*Tree cluster uses a conventional B*Tree index to store a key value and block address where the data can be found. So, much like using an index on a table, Oracle would look up the key value in the cluster index, find the database block address the data is on, and go there to find the data.

- The hash cluster uses a hashing algorithm to convert the key value into a database block address, thus bypassing all I/O except for the block read itself. With a hash cluster, the data is the index itself. Effectively, this means that there will optimally be one logical I/O used to perform a lookup.

We'll start with how to create a B*Tree cluster, and then discuss how to create a hash cluster.

## Create a B*Tree Cluster

Creating a B*Tree cluster object is fairly straightforward:

```
ops$tkyte@ORA920> create cluster user_objects_cluster_btree
  2  ( username varchar2(30) )
```

```
   3  size 1024
   4  /
Cluster created.
```

Normally, you expect a table to be the physical storage object (segment), but in this case, the cluster itself is the storage object. The cluster is the object that can have storage parameters; the tables created in a cluster cannot have storage parameters. The cluster is the object that specifies other parameters such as INITRANS, PCTFREE, PCTUSED, and so on.

The sample cluster we created will be "keyed" off a VARCHAR2(30) column called USERNAME. This implies that all the data in any table added to this cluster will be physically organized by some VARCHAR2(30) column, and that column will be a username or object owner. There is nothing to stop us from using *any* VARCHAR2(30) column as the key, but it would be bad practice to create a cluster on a key named USERNAME, and then later add tables to the cluster using something other than a username as the key.

The other interesting thing to note here is the SIZE parameter. This is used to tell Oracle that we expect about 1,024 bytes of data to be associated with each cluster key value. Oracle will use that to compute the maximum number of cluster keys that could fit per block. Given that I have an 8KB blocksize, Oracle will fit up to seven cluster keys per database block; that is, the data for up to seven distinct USERNAME key values would tend to go onto one block. As soon as I insert the eighth username, a new block will be used. That does not mean that the data is stored sorted by username here. It just means that all data relating to any given username will typically be found on the same block. As we'll see a little later, both the size of the data and the order in which the data is inserted will affect the number of keys we can store per block.

Next, we'll create our cluster key index:

```
ops$tkyte@ORA920> create index user_objects_idx
   2  on cluster user_objects_cluster_btree
   3  /
Index created.
```

This creates a B*Tree index that will contain an entry for each unique key value we put into the cluster and a pointer to the first block containing data for that key value. This index is not optional; it must be created in order to actually store data in the cluster. That is because the entire concept of the B*Tree cluster is predicated on storing like data together. In order to know where to put and where to get the rows in the cluster, Oracle needs this index. It tells Oracle that the data for KEY=X is on block Y.

The cluster index's job is to take a cluster key value and return the block address of the block that contains that key. It is a primary key, in effect, where each cluster key value points to a single block in the cluster itself. So, when you ask for the data for username SCOTT, Oracle will read the cluster key index, determine the block address for that, and then read the data.

## Create Hash Clusters

To create a hash cluster instead of a B*Tree cluster, add a HASHKEYS parameter and skip the creation of the cluster key index. Here is the example from the previous section created as a hash cluster:

```
ops$tkyte@ORA920> create cluster user_objects_cluster_hash
   2  ( username varchar2(30) )
```

```
3  hashkeys 100
4  size 3168
5  /
Cluster created.
```

In this CREATE CLUSTER statement, you see two key elements: HASHKEYS and SIZE.

HASHKEYS specifies the number of unique key values we expect over time. Here, we set it to 100. It does not limit us to only 100 distinct usernames; that is just the size of the hash table Oracle will set up. If we exceed that value, we will necessarily begin to get "collisions" in our hash table. This will not prevent us from working, but it will decrease the efficiency of our hash table.

SIZE has the same meaning as it did in our B*Tree cluster example. Here, since a hash cluster preallocates enough space to hold HASHKEYS/TRUNC(BLOCKSIZE/SIZE) bytes of data, we want to be more careful about the sizing. So, for example, if you set your SIZE to 1,500 bytes and you have a 4KB block size, Oracle will expect to store 2 keys per block. If you plan on having 1,000 hash keys, Oracle will allocate 500 blocks. In this case, since I have an 8KB blocksize, I more or less directed Oracle to allocate 50 blocks of storage (two keys per block).

### Create Tables in a Cluster

Let's move on and create two tables in our B*Tree cluster (the process is the same for the hash cluster). We will use a parent/child table built from the DBA_USERS/DBA_OBJECTS tables:

```
ops$tkyte@ORA920> create table user_info
  2  ( username, user_id, account_status,
  3    lock_date, expiry_date, default_tablespace,
  4    temporary_tablespace, created, profile )
  5  cluster user_objects_cluster_btree(username)
  6  as
  7  select username, user_id, account_status,
  8         lock_date, expiry_date,
  9         default_tablespace, temporary_tablespace,
 10         created, profile
 11    from dba_users
 12   where 1=0
 13  /
Table created.

ops$tkyte@ORA920> create table users_objects
  2  ( owner, object_name, object_id, object_type,
  3    created, last_ddl_time, timestamp, status )
  4  cluster user_objects_cluster_btree(owner)
  5  as
  6  select owner, object_name, object_id, object_type, created,
  7         last_ddl_time, timestamp, status
  8    from dba_objects
  9   where 1=0
 10  /
Table created.
```

So, here we've created two empty tables. The first, USER_INFO, will use its column named USERNAME to organize itself. The table USERS_OBJECTS will use its column OWNER. That means all of the data in the USER_INFO table with a USERNAME value of *X* will physically go in the database in about the same location as all of the data in the USERS_OBJECTS table when OWNER = *X*.

We could create the equivalent heap tables using the same CREATE TABLE AS SELECT statements without the CLUSTER clause. We are now ready to load data into our cluster tables.

# Use Clusters

Loading data into tables illustrates one of the key considerations in gauging the potential effectiveness of clusters in your application. Some of the other useful aspects of clusters we'll look at include reducing I/O, increasing buffer cache efficiency, eliminating index blocks, and creating read-only lookup tables.

### Control How the Data Is Loaded

We will use a multitable insert to populate both objects at the same time:

```
ops$tkyte@ORA920> insert
  2  when (r=1) then
  3  into user_info
  4  ( username, user_id, account_status, lock_date,
  5    expiry_date, default_tablespace, temporary_tablespace,
  6    created, profile )
  7  values
  8  ( username, user_id, account_status, lock_date,
  9    expiry_date, default_tablespace, temporary_tablespace,
 10    user_created, profile )
 11  when (1=1) then
 12  into users_objects
 13  ( owner, object_name, object_id, object_type, created,
 14    last_ddl_time, timestamp, status )
 15  values
 16  ( owner, object_name, object_id, object_type, obj_created, last_ddl_time,
 17    timestamp, status )
 18  select a.username, a.user_id, a.account_status, a.lock_date,
 19         a.expiry_date, a.default_tablespace,
 20         a.temporary_tablespace, a.created user_created, a.profile,
 21         b.owner, b.object_name, b.object_id, b.object_type,
 22         b.created obj_created,
 23         b.last_ddl_time, b.timestamp, b.status,
 24         row_number() over (partition by owner order by object_id) r
 25    from dba_users a, dba_objects b
 26   where a.username = b.owner
 27     and a.username <> 'SYS'
 28  /

4749 rows created.

ops$tkyte@ORA920> analyze cluster user_objects_cluster_btree compute statistics;
```

```
Cluster analyzed.

ops$tkyte@ORA920> analyze table user_info compute statistics
  2 for table for all indexes for all indexed columns;
Table analyzed.

ops$tkyte@ORA920> analyze table users_objects compute statistics
  2 for table for all indexes for all indexed columns;
Table analyzed.
```

You're probably wondering why we did the insert in this complicated fashion—with a join with ROW_NUMBER and such—rather than simply using two INSERT statements. While the latter option is indeed simpler, it may not achieve the goal of clustering data by key. Remember that when we created the B*Tree cluster we used this code:

```
ops$tkyte@ORA920> create cluster user_objects_cluster_btree
  2 ( username varchar2(30) )
3 size 1024
4 /
Cluster created.
```

That told Oracle, "There will be about 1KB of data associated with each key value, so go ahead and store up to seven username keys per block, or fewer if you need to." If we had inserted the data from DBA_USERS first into this table, there would be one row per user, with a small amount of data. We would easily get seven username keys per block. However, on my system, the DBA_OBJECTS data varied widely in size from 0.5KB to 139KB of data per key. So, when we inserted that data, the required clustering of data would not have been achieved. There is not enough room for seven keys per block every time. For some USERNAME values, there will be one key per block.

Our goal is to store this information together, and in order to do that, we need to load the data more or less together. This is an important thing to understand about clusters and why they work for something like the Oracle data dictionary so well. Consider how the data dictionary gets populated. You execute DDL such as:

```
create table t
( x int,
  y date,
  z varchar2,
  constraint check_cons check ( x > 0 ),
  constraint t_pk primary key(x,y) );

create index t_z_idx on t(z);
```

In the real data dictionary, there is a CLUSTER C_OBJ# object that contains tables such as CLU$ (cluster information), COL$ (column information), TAB$ (table information), IND$ (index information), ICOL$ (index column information), and so on. When you create a table and its related information, Oracle populates all of those objects *at about the same time*. In general, the amount of information (number of rows) does not go up or down very much, since you do not drop or add columns very often, the number of constraints is generally fixed, and so on. In this case, all of the information related to an object goes in once—on object creation—and tends to all go into the same block(s) together.

By loading all of the data for a given cluster key at the same time, we pack the blocks as tightly as possible and start a new block when we run out of room. Instead of Oracle putting up to seven cluster key values per block, it will put as many as will fit.

To see this in action, let's first look at the degree of colocation we achieved by loading the data at the same time. We'll do this by looking at the ROWIDs of the data and breaking down the rows by file and block. We'll quickly be able to see how the data is organized.

```
ops$tkyte@ORA920> break on owner skip 1
ops$tkyte@ORA920> select owner, arfno||'.'||ablock arowid,
                         brfno||'.'||bblock browid, count(*)
  2     from (
  3    select b.owner,
  4           dbms_rowid.rowid_relative_fno(a.rowid) arfno,
  5           dbms_rowid.rowid_block_number(a.rowid) ablock,
  6           dbms_rowid.rowid_relative_fno(b.rowid) brfno,
  7           dbms_rowid.rowid_block_number(b.rowid) bblock
  8      from user_info a, users_objects b
  9     where a.username = b.owner
 10           )
 11    group by owner, arfno, ablock, brfno, bblock
 12    order by owner, arfno, ablock, bblock
 13   /

OWNER        AROWID           BROWID            COUNT(*)
-----------  ---------------  ---------------   ----------
A            9.271            9.271                    1
```

This shows that for the OWNER = A, the row in USER_INFO is in file 9, block 271. Additionally, the row for USERNAME = A, the row in USERS_OBJECTS, is also in file 9, block 271. The individual rows from each table are physically colocated on the same database block. Continuing on:

```
AQ           9.271            9.271                   10

BIG_TABLE    9.271            9.271                   36

CSMIG        9.271            9.271                   14

CTXSYS       9.271            9.268                  101
             9.271            9.269                   34
             9.271            9.271                   31
             9.271            9.272                   97
```

This shows that for the OWNER = AQ data, the single row from USER_INFO is colocated on the same database block with ten rows from USERS_OBJECTS. The data is, in effect, prejoined.

We see the same thing with BIG_TABLE: The single row in USER_INFO is colocated with 36 rows from USERS_OBJECTS. This is also true for CSMIG. CTXSYS, however, is a bit different. CTXSYS has about 260 objects, and this many objects simply will not fit on a single block.

However, notice that the rows are still nicely clustered together, packed rather tightly on four blocks by the cluster key. So, even though they do not fit on a single block, the database took care to put them into as few blocks as possible.

Suppose we had instead loaded these tables in this less-thought-out fashion:

```
ops$tkyte@ORA920> insert
  2  into user_info
  3  ( username, user_id, account_status, lock_date,
  4    expiry_date, default_tablespace, temporary_tablespace,
  5    created, profile )
  6  select a.username, a.user_id, a.account_status, a.lock_date,
  7          a.expiry_date, a.default_tablespace,
          a.temporary_tablespace,
  8          a.created user_created, a.profile
  9    from dba_users a
 10   where a.username <> 'SYS'
 11  /
44 rows created.

ops$tkyte@ORA920> insert
  2  into users_objects
  3  ( owner, object_name, object_id, object_type, created,
  4    last_ddl_time, timestamp, status )
  5  select b.owner, b.object_name, b.object_id, b.object_type,
          b.created obj_created,
  6          b.last_ddl_time, b.timestamp, b.status
  7    from dba_users a, dba_objects b
  8   where a.username = b.owner
  9     and a.username <> 'SYS'
 10   order by object_type, object_name
 11  /
4717 rows created.
```

Arguably, we have the same data here, but the physical organization is quite different. Here, Oracle first received the USER_INFO data. This was quite small, so Oracle put seven key values per block on average. Then it received the USERS_OBJECTS data sorted in a fashion that ensured that the OWNER column was not coming in sorted order; this data was scrambled. Now, when we look at a sample of how colocated the data is, we find this:

```
OWNER         AROWID           BROWID           COUNT(*)
------------  ---------------  ---------------  ----------
A             9.269            9.377                     1
```

Already, we can see that the location of the data is not as orderly as before. Oracle inserted the single row for OWNER = A into block 269. Later on, when the USERS_OBJECTS row that corresponds to that entry came to be inserted, Oracle discovered that block was full; hence, it could not place the data from USERS_OBJECTS on that same block. The data from these two rows is now spread across two different blocks.

Continuing on, we can see the full extent of the damage:

| | | | |
|---|---|---|---|
| AQ | 9.268 | 9.268 | 8 |
| | 9.268 | 9.388 | 1 |
| | 9.268 | 9.532 | 1 |

The data for AQ is spread out on three discrete blocks now, instead of all ten rows on one block as before.

| | | | |
|---|---|---|---|
| BIG_TABLE | 9.272 | 9.272 | 8 |
| | 9.272 | 9.347 | 5 |
| | 9.272 | 9.372 | 1 |
| | 9.272 | 9.379 | 14 |
| | 9.272 | 9.381 | 7 |
| | 9.272 | 9.536 | 1 |

The data for BIG_TABLE is spread out over six blocks, as opposed to one.

| | | | |
|---|---|---|---|
| CSMIG | 9.269 | 9.384 | 8 |
| | 9.269 | 9.533 | 6 |
| CTXSYS | 9.269 | 9.269 | 53 |
| | 9.269 | 9.362 | 2 |
| | 9.269 | 9.363 | 2 |
| | 9.269 | 9.371 | 21 |
| | 9.269 | 9.372 | 54 |
| | 9.269 | 9.373 | 4 |
| | 9.269 | 9.374 | 23 |
| | 9.269 | 9.381 | 38 |
| | 9.269 | 9.386 | 4 |
| | 9.269 | 9.389 | 6 |
| | 9.269 | 9.390 | 7 |
| | 9.269 | 9.391 | 2 |
| | 9.269 | 9.534 | 47 |

And CTXSYS, which used to be nicely packed on 4 blocks, is now on 13!

What you should conclude from this example is that clusters will be most effective in environments where we can control how the data is loaded. For example, clusters are appropriate for warehousing-type operations where you reload from time to time and hence can control how the data is loaded to achieve maximum clustering. B*Tree clusters are also appropriate for update (transactional) systems if you tend to insert the parent and many (or most or all) of the child records at about the same time, similar to what happens when Oracle processes a CREATE TABLE statement. Most of the parent and child rows in the data dictionary are inserted at about the same time. B*Tree clusters are not as appropriate if the data arrives randomly, out of cluster key order, most of the time.

### B*Tree Clusters Can Reduce I/O and Increase Buffer Cache Efficiency
By buffer cache efficiency, I do not necessarily mean a cache hit ratio. Rather, by storing related information together, on the same blocks, we can increase the efficiency of our buffer cache. Instead of needing to manage 50 blocks in response to our query, the buffer cache may need to manage

only 1 or 2 blocks. It may not be evidenced as a better cache hit ratio (although it probably will be), and that is not the point really. A high cache hit ratio by itself doesn't mean the system is performing well. A reduced logical count and an SGA that needs less block buffer cache to achieve the same cache hit would indicate good performance.

Now, we are ready to test the efficiency of our B*Tree cluster. In order to do this, we'll assess the performance of our nicely packed cluster against the equivalent heap tables, using SQL_TRACE and TKPROF.

One of the things we want to observe is how much less, or more, physical I/O our cluster implementation will be compared to the heap table approach. So, the first thing to do is flush the buffer cache of all data related to the tablespace is which our cluster is stored. In order to do this, we simply take the tablespace offline, and then put it back online:

```
ops$tkyte@ORA920> alter tablespace users offline;
Tablespace altered.

ops$tkyte@ORA920> alter tablespace users online;
Tablespace altered.
```

Now for the benchmark code itself. We will retrieve all of the data from the two tables, cluster key by cluster key. We will do this ten times in all, just to have it run many times, over and over.

**NOTE**
*The /* CLUSTER */ in the query is not a hint. It is only there so that when we look at the TKPROF report, we can distinguish our two implementations easily.*

```
ops$tkyte@ORA920> alter session set sql_trace=true;
Session altered.

ops$tkyte@ORA920> begin
  2      for x in ( select username from all_users )
  3      loop
  4          for i in 1 .. 10
  5          loop
  6              for y in ( select a.username,
  7                                a.temporary_tablespace,
  8                                b.object_name ,
  9                                b.object_type /* CLUSTER */
 10                            from user_info a, users_objects b
 11                           where a.username = b.owner
 12                             and a.username = X.USERNAME )
 13              loop
 14                  null;
 15              end loop;
 16          end loop;
 17      end loop;
 18  end;
 19  /
```

```
PL/SQL procedure successfully completed.

ops$tkyte@ORA920> alter session set sql_trace=false;
Session altered.
```

Now that we have our report for the B*Tree cluster, we need to rebuild the tables as conventional heap tables. We use the same CREATE TABLE AS SELECT statements but remove the CLUSTER clause. Additionally, we add one index to each table.

```
ops$tkyte@ORA920> create index user_info_username_idx on user_info_heap(username);
Index created.

ops$tkyte@ORA920> create index user_objects_owner_idx on
  2  users_objects_heap(owner);
Index created.
```

On the heap tables, we use A.USERNAME = *bind_variable* and join by USERNAME to OWNER. We load these tables using the same multitable INSERT statement and run the same block of benchmark code, using /* HEAP */ in place of /* CLUSTER */ in the query. Now, in reviewing the TKPROF report, we see the following:

```
select a.username, a.temporary_tablespace,
       b.object_name , b.object_type /* CLUSTER */
  from user_info a, users_objects b
 where a.username = b.owner
   and a.username = :b1
```

| call | count | cpu | elapsed | disk | query | current | rows |
|---------|-------|------|---------|------|-------|---------|-------|
| Parse | 1 | 0.00 | 0.00 | 0 | 0 | 0 | 0 |
| Execute | 450 | 0.06 | 0.05 | 0 | 0 | 0 | 0 |
| Fetch | 47620 | 1.63 | 1.50 | 55 | 49730 | 0 | 47170 |
| total | 48071 | 1.69 | 1.56 | 55 | 49730 | 0 | 47170 |

```
Rows     Row Source Operation
-------  ---------------------------------------------------
  47170  MERGE JOIN CARTESIAN
  47170   TABLE ACCESS CLUSTER USERS_OBJECTS
    350    INDEX UNIQUE SCAN USER_OBJECTS_IDX
  47170   BUFFER SORT
    350    TABLE ACCESS CLUSTER USER_INFO
    350     INDEX UNIQUE SCAN USER_OBJECTS_IDX
*****************************************************************
select a.username,
       a.temporary_tablespace,
       b.object_name ,
       b.object_type /* HEAP */
  from user_info_heap a, users_objects_heap b
 where a.username = b.owner
```

```
    and a.username = :b1

call     count        cpu elapsed disk   query    current     rows
-------  ------   -------- ------- ----  -------  ---------- -------
Parse        1     0.00    0.00     0        0           0        0
Execute    450     0.06    0.06     0        0           0        0
Fetch    47620     2.32    2.10    74    95930           0    47170
-------  ------   -------- ------- ----  -------  ---------- -------
total    48071     2.39    2.17    74    95930           0    47170

Rows     Row Source Operation
-------  --------------------------------------------------------
  47170  MERGE JOIN CARTESIAN
  47170   TABLE ACCESS BY INDEX ROWID USERS_OBJECTS
  47170    INDEX RANGE SCAN USER_OBJECTS_OWNER_IDX
  47170   BUFFER SORT
    350    TABLE ACCESS BY INDEX ROWID USER_INFO
    350     INDEX RANGE SCAN USER_INFO_USERNAME_IDX
```

### NOTE
*You may be wondering how the CPU time could exceed the elapsed time. Here, it is because Oracle was timing a lot of very short events (47,620 fetches). Each fetch was timed individually. Any fetch that took less time to complete than the unit of measurement would appear to happen "instantly," in 0.00 seconds. Generally, this error is not relevant, but when you time many thousands of very short events, it will creep in and become visible, as it did here.*

The B*Tree cluster in this case did significantly less logical I/O (QUERY column) and less physical I/O. There were fewer blocks that needed to be read in from disk to accomplish the same task. If you scale this example up to hundreds of thousands or millions of records, you'll get the benefits of reduced physical I/O and increased buffer cache efficiency.

Instead of needing to read two or three index structures and blocks from multiple locations, you have one index structure (the cluster key index) to read. Also, in the best case, you have a single database block—one that contains all of the rows from all of the tables you need— to physically read into cache. You also have fewer index blocks and table blocks to cache. Whereas the conventional table query would have index blocks from two indexes (say three blocks at least per index) and table blocks from two tables (say one block at least for each table) for about eight blocks in cache, a cluster may have two or three index blocks plus one table block. You may be able to fit twice as much data into the cache, simply by having related data that is accessed together stored together.

## Hash Clusters Eliminate Index Blocks
If we run through the same example from the previous section using a hash cluster rather than a B*Tree cluster, the TKPROF report for the cluster query shows the following:

```
select a.username, a.temporary_tablespace,
       b.object_name , b.object_type /* CLUSTER */
```

```
     from user_info a, users_objects b
   where a.username = b.owner
     and a.username = :b1
```

| call | count | cpu | elapsed | disk | query | current | rows |
|------|-------|-----|---------|------|-------|---------|------|
| Parse | 1 | 0.00 | 0.00 | 0 | 0 | 0 | 0 |
| Execute | 450 | 0.05 | 0.05 | 0 | 4 | 0 | 0 |
| Fetch | 47610 | 1.67 | 1.46 | 61 | 49230 | 0 | 47160 |
| total | 48061 | 1.73 | 1.51 | 61 | 49234 | 0 | 47160 |

| Rows | Row Source Operation |
|------|---------------------|
| 47160 | MERGE JOIN CARTESIAN |
| 47160 | TABLE ACCESS HASH USERS_OBJECTS |
| 47160 | BUFFER SORT |
| 350 | TABLE ACCESS HASH USER_INFO |

If you recall, the totals for the B*Tree cluster and the conventional tables were, respectively:

| call | count | cpu | elapsed | disk | query | current | rows |
|------|-------|-----|---------|------|-------|---------|------|
| total | 48071 | 1.69 | 1.56 | 55 | 49730 | 0 | 47170 |
| total | 48071 | 2.39 | 2.17 | 74 | 95930 | 0 | 47170 |

So, that is on par with the B*Tree cluster. However, here, the data is, in effect, the index. Oracle did not scan any indexes to find the data. Rather, it would take the USERNAME value passed into the query via the :b1 bind variable, hash it to a block address, and go to that block.

If a B*Tree index can increase the buffer cache utilization by simply storing similar data together, a hash cluster goes one step further by eliminating the index blocks altogether. You can fit more relevant data in your buffer simply because you have less relevant data.

### Single-Table Hash Clusters Are Useful for Read-Only Lookup Tables

A *single-table hash cluster* is a special case of a cluster, whereby only one table may exist in the cluster at any point in time. Oracle is able to optimize the access to this table, since it knows that the blocks contain data from exactly one table. Therefore, it is easier to process these blocks, because Oracle no longer has the overhead of remembering which rows come from which table.

Where would a single-table hash cluster be useful? Almost anywhere you do a lookup (turn a code into a value). Normally, each lookup would involve two or three index accesses, followed by a table access by ROWID. With a single-table hash cluster, those three or four logical I/Os may be turned into a single logical I/O.

To demonstrate this use, we'll set up a small test case. We'll use DBA_OBJECTS again and, knowing that we'll want to put about 50,000 lookup items in our single-table hash cluster, we'll create the cluster as follows:

```
ops$tkyte@ORA920> create cluster object_id_lookup
  2  ( object_id number )
```

```
   3   single table
   4   hashkeys 50000
   5   size 100
   6   /
Cluster created.
```

Here, we used the keyword SINGLE TABLE to indicate to Oracle we want to use this special-case table. Additionally, we used HASHKEYS 50000 to indicate the desired size of our hash table. Lastly, we know the rows are about 100 bytes on average for the data we are going to load into this hash table, so we used SIZE 100.

Now, we are ready to create a single-table hash cluster table as well as a heap lookup table in order to see the difference between the two as far as I/O goes. To do this, we'll populate 50,000 rows into each, using DBA_OBJECTS two times with a UNION ALL. Since my DBA_OBJECTS view has about 35,000 rows in it, this gave me more than 50,000 rows, so I used ROWNUM to generate just the 50,000 rows I wanted to test with:

```
ops$tkyte@ORA920> create table single_table_hash_cluster
   2   ( owner, object_name, object_id,
   3     object_type, created, last_ddl_time,
   4     timestamp, status )
   5   cluster object_id_lookup(object_id)
   6   as
   7   select owner, object_name, rownum,
   8          object_type, created, last_ddl_time,
   9          timestamp, status
  10     from ( select * from dba_objects
  11            union all
  12            select * from dba_objects)
  13    where rownum <= 50000
  14   /
Table created.

ops$tkyte@ORA920> create table heap_table
   2   ( owner, object_name, object_id,
   3     object_type, created, last_ddl_time,
   4     timestamp, status,
   5     constraint heap_table_pk
   6       primary key(object_id) )
   7   as
   8   select owner, object_name, rownum,
   9          object_type, created, last_ddl_time,
  10          timestamp, status
  11     from ( select * from dba_objects
  12            union all
  13            select * from dba_objects)
  14    where rownum <= 50000
  15   /
Table created.
```

To compare the runtime characteristics of the two implementations, we'll query each and every record from both tables three times apiece. So, we'll do 150,000 lookups against each table in a loop:

```
ops$tkyte@ORA920> alter session set sql_trace=true;
Session altered.

ops$tkyte@ORA920> declare
  2         l_rec single_table_hash_cluster%rowtype;
  3  begin
  4      for iters in 1 .. 3
  5      loop
  6          for i in 1 .. 50000
  7          loop
  8              select * into l_rec
  9                from single_table_hash_cluster
 10               where object_id = i;
 11
 12              select * into l_rec
 13                from heap_table
 14               where object_id = i;
 15          end loop;
 16      end loop;
 17  end;
 18  /

PL/SQL procedure successfully completed.
```

When we look at the TKPROF report for these runs, we discover the following:

```
SELECT * from single_table_hash_cluster where object_id = :b1

call     count     cpu  elapsed disk    query current     rows
-------  ------  -----  ------- ----  ------- -------  -------
Parse         1   0.00     0.00    0        0       0        0
Execute  150000  13.60    14.01    0        2       0        0
Fetch    150000  12.93    12.64    0   189924       0   150000
-------  ------  -----  ------- ----  ------- -------  -------
total    300001  26.54    26.65    0   189926       0   150000

Rows     Row Source Operation
-------  -------------------------------------------------------
 150000  TABLE ACCESS HASH SINGLE_TABLE_HASH_CLUSTER

************************************************************
SELECT * from heap_table where object_id = :b1

call     count     cpu  elapsed disk    query current     rows
-------  ------  -----  ------- ----  ------- -------  -------
Parse         1   0.00     0.00    0        0       0        0
```

```
Execute 150000  16.36   17.86    0       0       0        0
Fetch   150000  11.02   11.05    0  450000       0   150000
------- ------  -----  ------- ---- ------- ------- -------
total   300001  27.38   28.91    0  450000       0   150000

Rows     Row Source Operation
-------  -----------------------------------------------------
 150000  TABLE ACCESS BY INDEX ROWID HEAP_TABLE
 150000   INDEX UNIQUE SCAN HEAP_TABLE_PK (object id 43139)
```

Note that the runtimes (CPU column) are more or less the same. If you ran this test over and over as I did, you would find the averages of the CPU times to be the same over time. The numbers of executes, parses, fetches, and rows are identical. These two tables gave the same output given the same inputs. The difference is all about I/O here. The QUERY column (consistent mode gets) values are very different.

The query against the single-table hash cluster did 42% of the logical I/Os that the conventional heap table performed. In this case, this did not show up in the runtimes (they appear equivalent) but as you've heard me say more than once in this book, "A latch is a lock, a lock is a serialization device, and serialization devices greatly inhibit concurrency and scalability." Anytime we can significantly reduce the amount of latching we perform, we will naturally increase our scalability and performance in a multiple-user environment. If instead of using SQL_TRACE and TKPROF, we used Runstats on the above test, we would find that the single-table hash cluster uses about 85% of the cache buffers chains latches (latches used to protect the buffer cache; we use fewer of them solely because we use the buffer cache less).

For applications that have read-only/mostly lookup tables, or those where the number of reads of a table by a key value is enormous as compared to the modifications, a single-table hash cluster can be the difference between simply performing and exceeding performance requirements.

# Clusters Wrap-Up

B*Tree clusters have their pros and cons. We've reviewed many of their advantages:

- Physical colocation of data

- Increased buffer cache efficiency

- Decreased logical I/Os

- Decreased need for indexes, as all tables share one cluster key index

However, B*Tree clusters do have some limitations. Along with their inability to do direct-path loading or partitioning, there are some general disadvantages:

- Correctly sizing clusters requires thought. Setting a SIZE value too large will waste space; setting a SIZE value too small can remove the main benefit of the cluster (physical clustering of data). In order to correct an incorrectly sized cluster, you would need to rebuild the cluster.

- Insertions into a cluster must be controlled or controllable, or else the clustering effect may deteriorate.

■ Clustered tables are slower to insert into than conventional tables, since the data has a location it must go into. A heap table can just add data wherever it pleases; it does not need to work hard to keep the data in some specific location. That does not mean that clustered tables are not appropriate for read/write applications. Consider the data dictionary of Oracle itself!

So, think about where you may be able to use these data structures. They can be used in a wide variety of applications, especially after you understand their benefits as well as their limitations. Many tables are never direct-path loaded or partitioned and do have controlled patterns of insertion. For these objects, consider a cluster.

# Index-Organized Tables (IOTs)

An IOT is basically a table stored in an index. It is similar in nature to a B*Tree cluster in that data is stored physically colocated by a key value, but it differs in the following ways:

■ There is a single data structure, a single index structure, whereas a B*Tree cluster has an index and a data segment.

■ The data is stored sorted by key, unlike a B*Tree cluster where the data is organized by key value, but the keys themselves are not stored sorted.

■ Sizing the IOT is somewhat easier than sizing a cluster. You do not need to estimate the maximum number of keys as with a hash cluster, and you have more flexibility in how you size the amount of data stored by key.

■ IOTs are very useful in a couple of implementation areas. One is as association tables— tables you use in a many-to-many relationship. The other is tables where physical colocation of data is important, but the order of insertion is unpredictable, or the data arrives in an order that makes it impossible for a cluster to maintain the data colocated over time.

## Use IOTs as a Space-Saving Alternative to Association Tables

Association tables generally are comprised of two columns or two keys and are used to relate two tables together. In the Oracle data dictionary, you could think of DBA_TAB_PRIVS as such an association object between DBA_USERS and DBA_OBJECTS. A single user may have one or more privileges on a given object; that given object may have one or more users that have privileges on it.

For association tables, normally you would set up a structure such as this:

```
create table association
( primary_key_table1,
  primary_key_table2,
  <possibly some columns pertaining to the relationship> );

create index association_idx1 on
association(primary_key_table1, primary_key_table2 );
```

```
create index association_idx2 on
association(primary_key_table2, primary_key_table1 );
```

So, you would have three structures: a table and two indexes. The indexes allow you to traverse either from TABLE1 to all related TABLE2 rows, or vice versa. In most implementations, the table itself is never even accessed; it is a redundant data structure that is considered a necessary evil, as it just consumes space. In some relatively rare cases, it contains additional data specific to the relationship, but this data is usually small in volume.

Using an IOT, we can get the same effect:

```
create table association
( primary_key_table1,
  primary_key_table2,
  <possibly some columns pertaining to the relationship>,
  primary key(primary_key_table1,primary_key_table2) )
organization index;

create index association_idx on
association(primary_key_table2);
```

We've removed the need for the table. Not only that, but if we need to retrieve the information pertaining to the relationship between two rows in TABLE1 and TABLE2, we've eliminated the TABLE ACCESS BY ROWID step. Note that the secondary index on the ASSOICATION table did not include both columns. This is a side effect of using an IOT the logical ROWID that is used for IOT's in the index structure and the value for primary_key_table1 is already there! We can see that with this small example:

```
ops$tkyte@ORA920> create table t
  2  ( a int,
  3    b int,
  4    primary key (a,b)
  5  )
  6  organization index;
Table created.

 ops$tkyte@ORA920> create index t_idx on t(b);
Index created.

ops$tkyte@ORA920> set autotrace traceonly explain
ops$tkyte@ORA920> select a, b from t where b = 55;

Execution Plan
----------------------------------------------------------
   0      SELECT STATEMENT Optimizer=CHOOSE (Cost=2 Card=1 Bytes=26)
   1    0   INDEX (RANGE SCAN) OF 'T_IDX' (NON-UNIQUE)
             (Cost=2 Card=1 Bytes=26)
```

Notice how there is no "TABLE ACCESS BY ROWID" step there. Even though column A is requested in the query, Oracle knows that it can get the value of column A from the logical ROWID in the index structure and hence does not go to the table to get it. Using this fact can save you much disk space in the creation of your secondary indexes on the IOT.

## Use IOTs to Colocate Randomly Inserted Data

In addition to being a space-saving device, by obviating the need for some redundant tables, IOTs excel in their ability to physically colocate related information for fast access. If you recall, one of the downsides to a cluster is that you need to have some control over the arrival of the data in order to optimize its physical colocation. IOTs do not suffer from this condition, because they will readjust themselves structurally in order to accommodate the data as it is inserted.

Consider an application that frequently retrieves a list of documents owned by a given user. In the real world, the user would not insert all of the documents he or she will ever own in a single session. This is a dynamic list of unpredictable size that will constantly be changing as the user adds and removes documents in the system. Therefore, in a traditional heap table, the rows that represent this user's documents would be scattered all over the place. Consider what would happen when you run a query such as this:

```
select * from document table where username = :bind_variable
```

Oracle would use an index to read many dozens of blocks from all over the table. If we used an IOT to physically cluster the data together, this would not happen. We can observe this behavior with a simple simulation and AUTOTRACE. For this example, we'll set up a pair of tables: one using an IOT and the other using a heap-based implementation.

```
ops$tkyte@ORA920> create table iot
  2  ( username        varchar2(30),
  3    document_name   varchar2(30),
  4    other_data      char(100),
  5    constraint iot_pk
  6    primary key (username,document_name)
  7  )
  8  organization index
  9  /
Table created.

ops$tkyte@ORA920> create table heap
  2  ( username        varchar2(30),
  3    document_name   varchar2(30),
  4    other_data      char(100),
  5    constraint heap_pk
  6    primary key (username,document_name)
  7  )
  8  /
Table created.
```

We use a CHAR(100) just to make the average width of a row in these tables about 130 bytes or so, since a CHAR(100) will always consume 100 characters of storage (it is a fixed-width datatype). So, the only difference between these two tables (besides their names) is the addition of the ORGANIZATION INDEX clause. That instructs Oracle to store the table data in an index segment instead of a table segment, so that all of the data for that table will be stored in an index structure.

Next, we populate these tables with some sample data. We construct a loop that adds 100 documents for each user in the ALL_USERS table. We do this in a fashion that emulates real life, in that the documents for a given user are added not all at once, but rather over time after many other documents have been added by other users.

```
ops$tkyte@ORA920> begin
  2        for i in 1 .. 100
  3        loop
  4            for x in ( select username
  5                            from all_users )
  6            loop
  7                insert into heap
  8                (username,document_name,other_data)
  9                values
 10                ( x.username, x.username || '_' || i, 'x' );
 11
 12                insert into iot
 13                (username,document_name,other_data)
 14                values
 15                ( x.username, x.username || '_' || i, 'x' );
 16            end loop;
 17        end loop;
 18        commit;
 19  end;
 20  /
PL/SQL procedure successfully completed.
```

And now we are ready for our performance comparison. Here, we will read all of the data from our table, user by user; that is, for USER1, we'll read out all of the rows that correspond to that user, and then for USER2, and so on. Additionally, we'll do this reading in two ways—one time using BULK COLLECT and the next using single-row fetches—just to see the difference that array processing can have on performance and scalability, and to show how significantly different this IOT can be from a heap table. Our benchmark routine is as follows:

```
ops$tkyte@ORA920> alter session set sql_trace=true;
Session altered.

ops$tkyte@ORA920> declare
  2        type array is table of varchar2(100);
  3        l_array1 array;
  4        l_array2 array;
  5        l_array3 array;
  6  begin
  7  for i in 1 .. 10
  8  loop
```

```
 9          for x in (select username from all_users)
10          loop
11              for y in ( select * from heap single_row
12                          where username = x.username )
13              loop
14                  null;
15              end loop;
16              for y in ( select * from iot single_row
17                          where username = x.username )
18              loop
19                  null;
20              end loop;
21              select * bulk collect
22                into l_array1, l_array2, l_array2
23                from heap bulk_collect
24               where username = x.username;
25              select * bulk collect
26                into l_array1, l_array2, l_array2
27                from iot bulk_collect
28               where username = x.username;
29          end loop;
30      end loop;
31      end;
32      /
PL/SQL procedure successfully completed.
```

The TKPROF report for the single-row fetches shows the following statistics:

```
select * from heap single_row where username = :b1

call     count    cpu elapsed disk   query current    rows
-------  ------  ----- ------- ----  ------- ------- -------
Parse        1   0.00    0.00     0        0       0       0
Execute    440   0.05    0.05     0        0       0       0
Fetch    44440   1.50    1.42     0    88886       0   44000
-------  ------  ----- ------- ----  ------- ------- -------
total    44881   1.56    1.48     0    88886       0   44000


Rows     Row Source Operation
-------  ------------------------------------------------
  44000  TABLE ACCESS BY INDEX ROWID HEAP
  44000   INDEX RANGE SCAN HEAP_PK (object id 43271)
*************************************************************
select * from iot single_row where username = :b1

call     count    cpu elapsed disk   query current    rows
-------  ------  ----- ------- ----  ------- ------- -------
Parse        1   0.00    0.00     0        0       0       0
Execute    440   0.07    0.05     0        0       0       0
Fetch    44440   1.11    0.99     0    44987       0   44000
```

```
------- ------ ----- ------- ---- ------- ------- -------
total    44881  1.18   1.04     0   44987       0   44000

Rows      Row Source Operation
-------   ---------------------------------------------------
  44000   INDEX RANGE SCAN IOT_PK (object id 43273)
```

The heap table, with its read-the-index-then-the-table approach, will do at least twice the I/O row by row by row. It must read the index block, and then read the table block. The IOT approach, on the other hand, simply reads the index and is finished. So, this is pretty good. Any day we can cut in half the number of I/Os our system must perform is a good day. Can it be even better? Yes, it can.

In Chapter 2, we used AUTOTRACE to demonstrate the effect that different array sizes (how many rows Oracle fetches in response to each fetch request) could have on an application. We saw that we can significantly reduce the I/O performed by a query if we fetch many rows at a time instead of fetching single rows. Here, we can really show the power of the IOT over the heap table in this regard. Reading further on in the TKPROF report we see this:

```
SELECT * from heap bulk_collect where username = :b1

call      count      cpu elapsed disk    query current    rows
-------  ------    ----- ------- ----  ------- ------- --------
Parse         1     0.00    0.00    0        0       0        0
Execute     440     0.06    0.05    0        0       0        0
Fetch       440     0.49    0.48    0    36100       0    44000
-------  ------    ----- ------- ----  ------- ------- --------
total       881     0.55    0.54    0    36100       0    44000

Rows      Row Source Operation
-------   ---------------------------------------------------
  44000   TABLE ACCESS BY INDEX ROWID HEAP
  44000    INDEX RANGE SCAN HEAP_PK (object id 43271)
*****************************************************************
SELECT * from iot bulk_collect where username = :b1

call      count      cpu elapsed disk    query current    rows
-------  ------    ----- ------- ----  ------- ------- -------
Parse         1     0.00    0.00    0        0       0        0
Execute     440     0.06    0.05    0        0       0        0
Fetch       440     0.24    0.24    0     2110       0    44000
-------  ------    ----- ------- ----  ------- ------- -------
total       881     0.31    0.30    0     2110       0    44000

Rows      Row Source Operation
-------   ---------------------------------------------------
  44000   INDEX RANGE SCAN IOT_PK (object id 43273)
```

The IOT using bulk fetches did less than 6% of the I/O of the query against the heap table using the same bulk collect. When running this test with Runstats instead of TKPROF, I discovered the heap table approach used *600% more latches*. These are some serious differences here!

## IOTs Wrap-Up

Much like clusters, IOTs are useful data structures for physically organizing your data on disk with the goal of improved access times. They have the same good attributes as clusters do:

- Physical colocation of data

- Increased buffer cache efficiency

- Decreased logical I/Os

- Decreased need for indexes; the table is the index

IOTs also have some advantages that clusters do not offer:

- The data is actually stored sorted by primary key, which may be of great benefit.

- Since an index is a fairly sophisticated data structure, it has the ability to move rows around (something a cluster cannot do), which allows it to better pack the related data together. The order of insertion, something to consider with clusters, it not as much of a factor with IOTs.

- They can be rebuilt (reorganized) online if the rare need to do this arises.

However, they do have some limitations. Along with the inability to do direct-path loading, there are some general disadvantages of using IOTs:

- As with clustered tables, IOT tables are slower to insert into than conventional tables, since the data has a location it must go into.

- You may need to consider the overflow segment. There are issues with very wide tables in an IOT structure. They are generally best suited for tall, "skinny" tables, but with some foresight, they can work with wide tables as well.

# External Tables

External tables are new with Oracle9i Release 1. They add to the growing list of ORGANIZATION clauses on tables. The ORGANIZATION EXTERNAL clause is used for a table whose data is stored outside the Oracle database.

External tables give us the ability to select from flat files, either delimited files or fixed-width positional files. You cannot modify these table types; you can just query them. They cannot be conventionally indexed, because the rows have no ROWIDs. Because you freely edit the files at anytime, moving the rows around, Oracle cannot index them in any fashion.

I recommend using external tables only for the loading and merging of data, not as a replacement for true database tables. If you find yourself querying external tables in an application, you are most likely misusing them. If you find yourself using them to load and reload data on an ongoing basis, you've found their purpose in life.

## Set Up External Tables

External tables rely on DIRECTORY objects in Oracle. You create a DIRECTORY object using a SQL DDL command such as this:

```
ops$tkyte@ORA920> create or replace directory data_dir as '/tmp/'
  2  /
Directory created.
```

This sets up a directory DATA_DIR that points to the /tmp/ directory in the file system.

The next step is to create a table that tells Oracle how to read this file:

```
ops$tkyte@ORA920> create table external_table
  2  (EMPNO NUMBER(4) ,
  3   ENAME VARCHAR2(10),
  4   JOB VARCHAR2(9),
  5   MGR NUMBER(4),
  6   HIREDATE DATE,
  7   SAL NUMBER(7, 2),
  8   COMM NUMBER(7, 2),
  9   DEPTNO NUMBER(2)
 10  )
 11  ORGANIZATION EXTERNAL
 12  ( type oracle_loader
 13    default directory data_dir
 14    access parameters
 15    ( fields terminated by ',' )
 16    location ('emp.dat')
 17  )
 18  /
Table created.
```

Most of this looks like a typical CREATE TABLE statement, until you get to the part in bold. This code should look familiar to anyone who uses SQLLDR, because it looks a bit like a control file used by that tool. In fact, if we compare the preceding listing to the equivalent SQLLDR control file, we see a lot of similarities:

```
LOAD DATA
INFILE /tmp/emp.dat
INTO TABLE emp
REPLACE
FIELDS TERMINATED BY ','
(empno,ename,job,mgr,hiredate,sal,comm,deptno)
```

We listed the column names, we have a FIELDS TERMINATED BY clause, and we have a location from which to read the data (INFILE)—all of the things an external table has.

The similarities to SQLLDR are not by chance. The relationship between SQLLDR and external tables is very close in Oracle9i—so close in fact that SQLLDR may be used as a front-end to external tables. What I mean by that is, if you have many existing control files for SQLLDR and would like to take advantage of external tables, you can do so easily using the EXTERNAL_TABLE= GENERATE_ONLY parameter to SQLLDR. It will convert a control file into a CREATE TABLE statement for you, easing the migration from SQLLDR to external tables. For example, suppose you have the following SQLLDR control file named T.CTL:

```
LOAD DATA
INFILE *
INTO TABLE emp
REPLACE
FIELDS TERMINATED BY '|'
( empno ,ename ,job ,mgr ,hiredate ,sal ,comm ,deptno)
```

You can run the following command:

```
$ sqlldr / t.ctl external_table=generate_only
SQL*Loader: Release 9.2.0.3.0 - Production on Fri Jul 4 12:42:35 2003
Copyright (c) 1982, 2002, Oracle Corporation.  All rights reserved.
```

When you edit the resulting T.LOG file, you'll discover in it this create table statement (I edited some columns out to make it small):

```
CREATE TABLE "SYS_SQLLDR_X_EXT_EMP"
(
  EMPNO NUMBER(4),
...
  DEPTNO NUMBER(2)
)
ORGANIZATION external
(
  TYPE oracle_loader
  DEFAULT DIRECTORY SYS_SQLLDR_XT_TMPDIR_00000
  ACCESS PARAMETERS
```

```
(
    RECORDS DELIMITED BY NEWLINE CHARACTERSET US7ASCII
    BADFILE 'SYS_SQLLDR_XT_TMPDIR_00000':'t.bad'
    LOGFILE 't.log_xt'
    READSIZE 1048576
    SKIP 7
    FIELDS TERMINATED BY "|" LDRTRIM
    REJECT ROWS WITH ALL NULL FIELDS
    (
        EMPNO CHAR(255) TERMINATED BY "|",
...
        DEPTNO CHAR(255) TERMINATED BY "|"
    )
)
    location
    (
        't.ctl'
    )
)REJECT LIMIT UNLIMITED
```

So, if you are ever stuck on the syntax for creating an external table, but you knew how to use SQLLDR to do it, or you have many control files to migrate to this new facility, this method is something to consider trying.

But, getting back to the original example, now, all we need is some data. In order to demonstrate this easily, we'll use a utility I have posted on the Internet at http://asktom.oracle.com/~tkyte/flat/index.html. There, I have three different data unloaders available for download: one that uses SQL*Plus, another that uses a Pro*C version, and a third using PL/SQL implementation. Each has its uses, but for this example, the easiest to use is the SQL*Plus version called `flat` (for flat file). Here, we'll unload the EMP table to /tmp/:

```
ops$tkyte@ORA920> host flat scott/tiger emp > /tmp/emp.dat
ops$tkyte@ORA920> host head /tmp/emp.dat
7369,SMITH,CLERK,7902,17-DEC-80,800,,20
7499,ALLEN,SALESMAN,7698,20-FEB-81,1600,300,30
7521,WARD,SALESMAN,7698,22-FEB-81,1250,500,30
...
```

As you can see, we have a simple delimited file from which to work. To use it, all we need do is this:

```
ops$tkyte@ORA920> select ename, job, hiredate
  2    from external_table
  3    /

ENAME      JOB       HIREDATE
---------- --------- ---------
SMITH      CLERK     17-DEC-80
ALLEN      SALESMAN  20-FEB-81
WARD       SALESMAN  22-FEB-81
...
```

```
MILLER      CLERK     23-JAN-82

14 rows selected.
```

Every time we execute this query, Oracle will open, read, and close that file in the operating system. None of the "blocks" are buffered in the conventional sense with an external table. Oracle always reads the data from the disk into the session space, bypassing the buffer cache. Since Oracle does not own this data, it must be read from the disk each time is it accessed. This can make interpreting a TKPROF or AUTOTRACE report against an external table a bit misleading, because the I/O for the external table (logical or physical) will not be accurate; it is different from normal Oracle block I/O.

So, very basically, that is all there is to get started with external tables. There is one other important note to beware of: The file to be read must be visible on the database server machine. It cannot be a file on your local PC client. It cannot be a file on an application server separate from the database machine. The database processes themselves must be able to see that file, open that file, and read that file. If they cannot, they will not be able to make use of it at all.

On Unix, this is somewhat easy to get around: You can simply use NFS mounts and make other file systems available to all processes on the database server. So, if you wanted a file that physically resides on your application server to be accessible on the database machine, you would export that file system from the application server and mount it on the database machine.

If you are using Windows shares, the rules are a bit different. Windows is primarily a single-user operating system. The file systems you see when you log in are not the file systems that every process on that machine can see. Each user has his or her own set of network drives that may or may not be visible to that user. Under Windows, this takes a bit of work to set up, to make it so the database server process can actually see a remote file system. For information about the necessary Windows-level setup for making a network drive visible to the user who runs the database itself, see Oracle Support Note 45172.1, available on http://metalink.oracle.com.

## Modify External Tables

You cannot use an UPDATE, an INSERT, or a DELETE statement on an external table. To modify external tables, you must use an operating system tool or a tool like UTL_FILE, which can write operating system files. However, as soon as data is added or modified in the operating system file, Oracle will see it immediately.

```
ops$tkyte@ORA920> host echo -
>'1234,KYTE,DBA/DEV,7782,23-JAN-2003,1300,,10' >> /tmp/emp.dat

ops$tkyte@ORA920> select ename, job, hiredate
  2    from external_table
  3    where ename = 'KYTE'
  4  /

ENAME      JOB       HIREDATE
---------- --------- ---------
KYTE       DBA/DEV   23-JAN-03
```

# Use External Tables for Direct-Path Loading

One of the main uses of SQLLDR over the years has been its high-speed direct-path load capability. Well, SQLLDR is no longer the only tool in our shed, because external tables do this quite nicely as well. You can use one of the following methods to perform direct-path loads:

- Script it on the command line with SQLLDR.

- Use an INSERT statement.

- Use a CREATE TABLE AS SELECT statement.

**NOTE**
*In the past, I was frequently asked how one could invoke SQLLDR, Oracle's loading tool, from a stored procedure or trigger. It was difficult at best, because you needed to set up a Java stored procedure or C-based external procedure in order to execute a host command and run the SQLLDR program. This is no longer the case. Now, in order to invoke SQLLDR, all you need to do is run a SELECT statement; SQLLDR has been burned into the Oracle database itself. In fact, it would be fair to say that running SQLLDR from the command line is old-fashioned. Using an INSERT INTO statement or CREATE TABLE AS SELECT or MERGE command to load the data transactionally in the database is the way to go.*

Let's set up a test with BIG_TABLE (ALL_OBJECTS copied repeatedly so that it has more than a million rows). We will use one of the data unloaders from http://asktom.oracle.com/~tkyte/flat/index.html to create a simple flat-file extract of these rows. Then we will direct-path load this data using all three methods. The SQLLDR control file looks like this:

```
LOAD DATA
INFILE big_table.dat
INTO TABLE big_table
truncate
FIELDS TERMINATED BY ','
trailing nullcols
(
owner ,object_name ,subobject_name ,object_id
,data_object_id ,object_type
,created date 'dd-mon-yyyy hh24:mi:ss'
,last_ddl_time date 'dd-mon-yyyy hh24:mi:ss'
,timestamp ,status ,temporary ,generated ,secondary
)
```

And here is the external table definition:

```
create table big_table_external
(  OWNER               VARCHAR2(30),  OBJECT_NAME         VARCHAR2(30),
   SUBOBJECT_NAME      VARCHAR2(30),  OBJECT_ID           NUMBER,
   DATA_OBJECT_ID      NUMBER,        OBJECT_TYPE         VARCHAR2(18),
   CREATED             DATE,          LAST_DDL_TIME       DATE,
   TIMESTAMP           VARCHAR2(19),  STATUS              VARCHAR2(7),
   TEMPORARY           VARCHAR2(1),   GENERATED           VARCHAR2(1),
   SECONDARY           VARCHAR2(1)
)
ORGANIZATION EXTERNAL
( type oracle_loader
  default directory data_dir
  access parameters
  (
    fields terminated by ','
    missing field values are null
    ( owner ,object_name ,subobject_name ,object_id ,data_object_id
      ,object_type,created date 'dd-mon-yyyy hh24:mi:ss'
      ,last_ddl_time date 'dd-mon-yyyy hh24:mi:ss'
      ,"TIMESTAMP" ,status ,temporary ,generated ,secondary
    )
  )
    location ('big_table.dat')
)
```

The results of repeated runs are shown in Table 7-1. (These results are from a NOARCHIVELOG mode database; if you are using an ARCHIVELOG mode database, make sure that BIG_TABLE is set to NOLOGGING to reproduce similar findings.)

| Method | CPU | Elapsed | Rows |
|---|---|---|---|
| SQLLDR direct=true | 29 | 42 | 1,833,792 |
| External table INSERT /*+APPEND*/ | 33 | 38 | 1,833,792 |
| External table CREATE TABLE AS SELECT | 32 | 37 | 1,833,792 |
| External table INSERT (conventional path) | 42 | 130 | 1,833,792 |
| SQLLDR (conventional path) | 50 | 410 | 1,833,792 |

**TABLE 7-1.** *Comparing direct-path load methods*

These results show that using an external table adds some nominal overhead compared with using SQLLDR when in direct-path mode. In conventional-path loads, external tables really start to shine. But also consider these advantages of external tables (long-time users of SQLLDR will recognize these limits):

- You can join an external table to another table during a load to do lookups directly in the load itself (less postprocessing).

- You can use any SQL predicate you can dream of to filter the data. The ability to filter the data in SQLLDR is somewhat primitive by comparison.

- You can do a direct-path load from a remote client without needing to telnet into the server itself.

- You can invoke SQLLDR functionality from within a stored procedure simply by using INSERT.

As you can see, the advantages and ease of using external tables over SQLLDR from the command line are compelling.

## Use External Tables for Parallel Direct-Path Loading

In the past, performing direct-path parallel loads using command-line SQLLDR was a bit of a pain. In order to accomplish this, you needed to script it all yourself. You decided the degree of parallelism, you split up the input files, you started N copies of SQLLDR in parallel, and you monitored them all. With external tables, this becomes as easy as this:

```
Alter table external_table parallel;
Create table T as select * from external_table;
```

That is it. If you are using parallel automatic tuning, Oracle will determine the degree of parallelism given the current system load, Oracle will split up the input files, and Oracle will start and monitor N parallel query slaves for you to process the load. This can be quite convenient for performing mass bulk loads of data.

## Use External Tables for Merging

The technique for merging described here is a combination of another new feature in Oracle9i Release 1 and later and external tables. Oracle9i Release 1 added the MERGE command to the SQL language. This is the ability to take two tables and merge them together by a common key. If a record exists in both tables, you can process it as an update. If a record exists in only the table you are merging from, you can insert it into the table you are merging into.

For example, suppose you have an existing table of employee information and another group gives you a file of updates. This file of updates contains both updates to existing records and data for new hires. In the past, you needed to process the changes something like this:

- Using SQLLDR, load the file into a staging table.
- For each record in the staging table, attempt to update the existing record.
- If no rows were updated, insert the record as new.

Not only is that a lot of code—a lot of procedural processing—it is definitely not the fastest way to perform this operation. Processing sets of data is best done a set at a time. Row-at-a-time procedural code is almost always slower than a single SQL statement doing the same thing.

Enter external tables and the MERGE command. As an example, we'll use the same EMP and EXTERNAL_TABLE as we did earlier in setting up external tables, except that we'll modify the existing EMP table data as follows:

```
ops$tkyte@ORA920> delete from emp where mod(empno,2) = 1
  2  /
4 rows deleted.

ops$tkyte@ORA920> update emp set sal = sal/2
  2  /
10 rows updated.
```

Here, we've removed four of the existing employees from our database and modified the salaries of the rest. Now, suppose that someone gives us that delimited file of employee information, which we place into /tmp/emp.dat. We've already set up the external table, so we are ready to reconcile what is in the flat file with what is in the database. To accomplish this, we simply do the following:

```
ops$tkyte@ORA920> merge into EMP e1
  2  using EXTERNAL_TABLE e2
  3  on ( e2.empno = e1.empno )
  4  when matched then
  5    update set e1.sal = e2.sal
  6  when not matched then
  7    insert (empno, ename, job, mgr, hiredate, sal, comm, deptno)
  8    values ( e2.empno, e2.ename, e2.job,
             e2.mgr, e2.hiredate, e2.sal, e2.comm, e2.deptno )
  9  /
14 rows merged.
```

And that is it. The file has been synchronized with the database table. For any record that existed both in the file as well as the database table, we updated the salary column in the database table from the file. Likewise, for any record that was in the file but was not found in the table, we inserted the record.

# Handle Errors with External Tables

External tables are a little lacking in handling rejected or bad records. SQLLDR suffered from the same problem. With SQLLDR, you more or less needed to manually inspect the log file to see if the load was successful.

With external tables, you can set up named log and bad files. By default, the log and bad files will be written to the same directory as the input file itself, but you are free to change this. You can also set up the name of a log or bad file so that it is in some well-known, named location. Here is an example:

```
ops$tkyte@ORA920> create table external_table
  2    (EMPNO NUMBER(4) ,
  3     ENAME VARCHAR2(10),
  4     JOB VARCHAR2(9),
  5     MGR NUMBER(4),
  6     HIREDATE DATE,
  7     SAL NUMBER(7, 2),
  8     COMM NUMBER(7, 2),
  9     DEPTNO NUMBER(2)
 10    )
 11    ORGANIZATION EXTERNAL
 12    ( type oracle_loader
 13      default directory data_dir
 14      access parameters
 15      (
 16        records delimited by newline
 17        badfile data_dir:emp_external_table
 18        fields terminated by ','
 19      )
 20      location ('emp.dat')
 21    )
 22    reject limit unlimited
 23    /

Table created.
```

Now, if some records in the input file EMP.DAT are invalid, instead of raising an error when we select from the external table, Oracle will write them to a bad file (emp_external_table.bad) in our directory. But how can we programmatically inspect these bad records and the log that is generated? Fortunately, that is easy to do by using yet another external table. Suppose we set up this external table:

```
ops$tkyte@ORA920> create table emp_external_table_bad
  2    ( text1 varchar2(4000) ,
```

```
 3     text2 varchar2(4000) ,
 4     text3 varchar2(4000)
 5  )
 6  organization external
 7  (type oracle_loader
 8   default directory data_dir
 9   access parameters
10   (
11     records delimited by newline
12     fields
13     missing field values are null
14     ( text1 position(1:4000),
15        text2 position(4001:8000),
16        text3 position(8001:12000)
17     )
18   )
19   location ('emp_external_table.bad')
20  )
21  /
```

This is just a table that can read any file without failing on a datatype error, as long as the lines in the file are less than 12,000 characters (simply add more fields if your input files are wider than 12,000 characters).

Let's add a row to our flat file to see how this works. Here, the record we add has yyy in the year portion of the date, so that record will be rejected:

```
ops$tkyte@ORA920> host echo '1234,KYTE,DBA/DEV,7782,23-JAN-yyy,1300,,10' >> /tmp/emp.dat

ops$tkyte@ORA920>
ops$tkyte@ORA920> select ename, job, hiredate
  2     from external_table
  3    where ename = 'KYTE'
  4  /
no rows selected
```

We can clearly see the rejected records via a simple query:

```
ops$tkyte@ORA920> select substr(text1,1,60) from emp_external_table_bad
  2  /

SUBSTR(TEXT1,1,60)
------------------------------------------------------------
1234,KYTE,DBA/DEV,7782,23-JAN-yyy,1300,,10
```

A COUNT(*) would tell us how many records were rejected. Another external table created on the log file associated with this external table would tell us why the record was rejected. You would need to go one step further to make this a repeatable procedure, however. There are two approaches:

- Capture the COUNT(*) from the bad file before you access the external table and make sure it is unchanged after you query it.

- Use UTL_FILE and reset the bad file—truncate it, in effect—by simply opening it for write and closing it.

In that fashion, you'll be able to tell if the bad records in the bad file were generated by you just recently or if they were left over from some older version of the file itself and are not meaningful.

# Indexing Techniques

Oracle has a wide variety of indexing techniques that you might consider for optimizing data access:

- **B*Tree**   The conventional, standard type of index that everyone uses.

- **Reverse-key index**   A B*Tree index where the bytes are reversed. This is used to randomly distribute modifications to an index structure over the entire structure that may otherwise happen to a single block with a monotonically increased value (like a sequence).

- **Descending index**   A B*Tree index where one or more of the fields is stored in descending sort order. For example, you can have an index on a table T(C1,C2 DESC,C3). The values for C1 and C3 in the index will be sorted in ascending fashion, whereas C2 will be sorted in descending order.

- **IOT**   A table stored in an index, as described earlier in the "Index-Organized Tables (IOTs)" section.

- **B*Tree cluster index**   An index that must be created to store data in a cluster, as described in the "Create Clusters" section earlier in the chapter.

- **Bitmap index**   An index in which a single index entry may point to many rows using a bitmap. Normally, in a B*Tree index, a single index entry points to a single row. With a bitmap index, a single index entry may point to many hundreds of rows or more.

- **Function-based index (FBI)**   An index on a complex calculation or a built-in or user-defined function. Instead of indexing ENAME in the EMP table, you could, for example, index UPPER(ENAME) to provide for fast, case-insensitive searches.

- **Domain index**   An index you could build yourself (if you feel you have a superior or data-specific indexing technique). Also, the developers at Oracle have created domain indexes on nonstructured datatypes such as text, video, audio, image, and spatial data.

For details about the basic Oracle index types, see the Oracle9i Release 2 *Concepts Guide*, Chapter 10, the "Indexes" section.

In this section, we'll look at using two index types: FBIs and domain indexes.

# Use FBIs—Think Outside the Box

FBIs were added to Oracle8i in version 8.1 of the database. They are currently available with all editions of Oracle in version 9iR2, but only with Enterprise and Personal editions in Oracle 9iR1 and before. FBIs give you the ability to index computed columns and use these indexes in a query. In a nutshell, this capability allows you to do the following:

- Have case-insensitive searches or sorts.

- Search on complex equations.

- Extend the SQL language efficiently by implementing your own functions and operators and then searching on them.

The nicest qualities of FBIs are that they are easy to implement and provide immediate, *transparent* value. They can be used to speed up existing applications without changing any of their logic or queries. It is not often that you can say such a thing about a database feature.

Here, we'll look at a couple of unique uses of FBIs. These are things that perhaps the inventors of this feature did not anticipate but are nonetheless not only possible but natural, once you start thinking about them.

"Thinking outside the box" is a popular saying. It means to not be confined to conventional wisdom, to tried-and-true methods—to go beyond where you've gone before. To think of new, unusual, creative solutions using the tools you have at your disposal. It is what the engineers did in Houston, Texas when Apollo 13 declared, "Houston, we have a problem." They spent time in a room with nothing more than the astronauts in space had and thought outside the box in order to solve the problem at hand.

Oracle has a lot of features and functionality. The documentation is very good at telling us how things work and what functions and features are available. But the documentation will never give us the creative solution to the particular problem we are facing. Coming up with that creative solution is our job: To put the disparate pieces together, in some unique, not necessarily anticipated fashion and to solve our technical problem in the simplest form possible. To that end, we will use two concrete examples that build on a pair of facts. These are the documented facts:

- A B*Tree index will never have an entirely NULL entry. If all of the columns in the index key are NULL, there will not be an entry in the B*Tree for that column. If you create an index on a million-row table using a column that is NULL for every row, that index will be empty.

- We have FBIs that can incorporate complex logic in them.

Using these two facts, we will set about to solve two common issues simply and elegantly. These problems are how to index selectively and how to achieve selective uniqueness.

## Index Selectively

Frequently, I hear questions like, "How can I index only some of the rows in a table?" and "Can I index a specific WHERE clause but not for all of the rows in the table?" Many times, this has to do with creating an index for a Y/N-type column—a processed flag, for example. You might have a table with a flag indicating whether a record has been processed, and the vast preponderance of records have Y as their value; only a few rows have an N to indicate that they are awaiting processing. You are looking for an index that will find the N records, without indexing the Y records.

What immediately pops into most people's heads at this point is, "Aha, this is a bitmap index we are looking for." They base that on what they've heard about bitmap indexes. A bitmap index is useful for indexing low-cardinality data, and what could be lower cardinality than just Y and N values? The problem is that these solutions are generally needed in a system that performs a lot of single-row updates to the indexed column in a transactional system. The column being indexed will be updated from N to Y, and many people are inserting into or updating this table concurrently. Those attributes preclude a bitmap index from even being considered. Bitmap indexes cannot be used in environments where the indexed value is modified frequently or the underlying table is concurrently modified by many sessions. So, some other solution must be found.

Here's where the FBI comes in handy. We have a requirement to index a subset of rows that satisfies some criteria. We do not want to index the remaining rows. We can index functions, and we know that entirely NULL entries are not made in B*Tree indexes. We can achieve our goal easily if we create an index like this:

```
Create index selective_index on table_name(
      Case when <some criteria is met> then 'Y'
      Else NULL
      End )
```

Let's walk through an example. We'll start by creating a table with many rows, all with a PROCESSED_FLAG column set to Y:

```
ops$tkyte@ORA920> create table t as
  2  select 'Y' processed_flag, a.* from all_objects a;
Table created.
```

Now, for programming simplicity, we'll create a view that will hide the complexity of our indexed column.

```
ops$tkyte@ORA920> create or replace view v
  2  as
  3  select t.*,
  4         case when processed_flag = 'N' then 'N'
  5                  else NULL
  6            end processed_flag_indexed
  7    from t;
View created.
```

This approach works well with most FBIs. Rather than have the developers or end users need to know the exact function to use, they just use a column in a view; that column has the function in it. Also, if the logic ever changes, you can simply re-create the index and update the view, and all the applications will be fixed immediately.

Now, we create the FBI using the same function:

```
ops$tkyte@ORA920> create index t_idx on
  2  t( case when processed_flag = 'N' then 'N'
```

```
   3          else NULL
   4     end );
Index created.
```

**NOTE**
*If you cannot (or do not want to) use CASE, DECODE works for most purposes. For example, instead of CASE, we could have indexed* `decode( processed_flag, 'N', 'N', NULL )` *instead.*

We'll use the ANALYZE INDEX VALIDATE STRUCTURE command to see how many rows are currently in the index:

```
ops$tkyte@ORA920> analyze index t_idx validate structure;
Index analyzed.

ops$tkyte@ORA920> select name, del_lf_rows, lf_rows, lf_blks
  2    from index_stats;
```

| NAME | DEL_LF_ROWS | LF_ROWS | LF_BLKS |
|------|-------------|---------|---------|
| T_IDX | 0 | 0 | 1 |

As you can see, it starts with nothing in the index: zero leaf rows (LF_ROWS) and no delete leaf row (DEL_LF_ROWS) entries.

Let's see what happens after we do an update operation, setting 100 rows to N:

```
ops$tkyte@ORA920> update t set processed_flag = 'N'
  2    where rownum <= 100;
100 rows updated.

ops$tkyte@ORA920> analyze index t_idx validate structure;
Index analyzed.

ops$tkyte@ORA920> select name, del_lf_rows, lf_rows, lf_blks
  2    from index_stats;
```

| NAME | DEL_LF_ROWS | LF_ROWS | LF_BLKS |
|------|-------------|---------|---------|
| T_IDX | 0 | 100 | 1 |

We can see the index has 100 entries. We know that the table has thousands of rows, but our index is very small and compact.

Now, since we must be using the cost-based optimizer (CBO) in order to use FBIs (and since we should be using the CBO for all things anyway), we'll analyze our structures.

```
ops$tkyte@ORA920> analyze table t compute statistics
  2  for table
  3  for all indexes
```

```
   4  for all indexed columns
   5  /
Table analyzed.
```

Then we'll simulate some processing to access the first unprocessed record, process it, and then update its flag. We'll do this two times, using AUTOTRACE the second time to see how efficient this is.

```
ops$tkyte@ORA920> column rowid new_val r

ops$tkyte@ORA920> select rowid, object_name
   2    from v
   3   where processed_flag_indexed = 'N'
   4     and rownum = 1;

ROWID               OBJECT_NAME
-----------------   ------------------------------
AAAKlgAAJAAAAI8AAA  /1005bd30_LnkdConstant

ops$tkyte@ORA920> update v
   2      set processed_flag = 'Y'
   3    where rowid = '&R';
old   3:   where rowid = '&R'
new   3:   where rowid = 'AAAKlgAAJAAAAI8AAA'
1 row updated.

ops$tkyte@ORA920> set autotrace on
ops$tkyte@ORA920> select rowid, object_name
   2    from v
   3   where processed_flag_indexed = 'N'
   4     and rownum = 1;

ROWID               OBJECT_NAME
-----------------   ------------------------------
AAAKlgAAJAAAAI8AAB  /10076b23_OraCustomDatumClosur


Execution Plan
----------------------------------------------------------
   0      SELECT STATEMENT Optimizer=CHOOSE (Cost=2 Card=1 Bytes=2700)
   1    0   COUNT (STOPKEY)
   2    1     TABLE ACCESS (BY INDEX ROWID) OF 'T' (Cost=2 Card=100
Bytes=2700)
   3    2       INDEX (RANGE SCAN) OF 'T_IDX' (NON-UNIQUE) (Cost=1 Card=100)

Statistics
----------------------------------------------------------
          0  recursive calls
          0  db block gets
          2  consistent gets
```

```
          0   physical reads
...
          1   rows processed
```

There are two consistent gets—two logical I/Os—one to read the very small index and one to read the table block. In reality, we would expect between two and three I/Os per query execution, depending on the number of index entries made over time.

Now, we'll just update this row, set it to processed, and check our index:

```
ops$tkyte@ORA920> update v
  2      set processed_flag = 'Y'
  3    where rowid = '&R';
old   3:    where rowid = '&R'
new   3:    where rowid = 'AAAKlgAAJAAAAI8AAB'
1 row updated.

ops$tkyte@ORA920> analyze index t_idx validate structure;
Index analyzed.

ops$tkyte@ORA920> select name, del_lf_rows, lf_rows, lf_blks
  2      from index_stats;

NAME                               DEL_LF_ROWS    LF_ROWS    LF_BLKS
------------------------------     -----------    -------    -------
T_IDX                                        2        100          1
```

We can see that there are still 100 entries in there; however, two of them are deleted, ready to be reused. Along comes another session and inserts some unprocessed data:

```
ops$tkyte@ORA920> insert into t
  2   select 'N' processed_flag, a.* from all_objects a
  3   where rownum <= 2;
2 rows created.

ops$tkyte@ORA920> analyze index t_idx validate structure;
Index analyzed.

ops$tkyte@ORA920> select name, del_lf_rows, lf_rows, lf_blks
  2      from index_stats;

NAME                               DEL_LF_ROWS    LF_ROWS    LF_BLKS
------------------------------     -----------    -------    -------
T_IDX                                        0        100          1
```

And the whole cycle begins again. Over time, this index will remain more or less at a steady state, with some deleted entries that will be reused by subsequent inserts. The index will stay small and will index only those rows that match our predicate encoded in the CASE statement (which can be quite complex).

By putting together two facts in a manner you will not see documented in the Oracle documentation set, we've solved a seemingly complex problem easily.

## Implement Selective Uniqueness

Another challenging problem is how to achieve "selective uniqueness." When a column in a table has a certain value, how can you make sure that other columns in that table are unique for that subset of rows?

> "I have a table project (`project_ID number primary key, teamid number, job varchar2(100), status varchar2(8)`). STATUS may have the values ACTIVE, meaning it is currently active, and INACTIVE, meaning it is archived. I was told to enforce a unique rule: the job has to be unique in the same TEAMID for the active projects. It means TEAMID and JOB have to be unique while STATUS=ACTIVE. What is the best way to do this?"

The question went on to suggest that a trigger of some sort or some procedural code might be the solution. Well, I had just used an FBI recently to solve something slightly different. Here, he was not trying to index a subset of rows. In fact, he did not want to index at all, but rather enforce a unique condition selectively: "This data must be unique when this condition is met." Okay, let's look at some useful facts:

- You can selectively index rows.

- Indexes can be unique and hence can be used to enforce uniqueness.

- Attempting to perform referential integrity on your own in a multiversioning, read-consistent database is a recipe for disaster.

Putting it together, all you need to do to solve this problem is uniquely index TEAMID, JOB *when* STATUS=ACTIVE.

An index to enforce a unique condition selectively might look something like this:

```
ops$tkyte@ORA920> create table project
  2  (project_ID number primary key,
  3   teamid number,
  4   job varchar2(100),
  5   status varchar2(20) check (status in ('ACTIVE', 'INACTIVE'))
  6  );
Table created.

ops$tkyte@ORA920> create UNIQUE index
  2  job_unique_in_teamid on project
  3  ( case when status = 'ACTIVE' then teamid else null end,
  4    case when status = 'ACTIVE' then job    else null end
  5  )
  6  /
Index created.
```

Now, when we try to insert a duplicate TEAMID/JOB pair in an active set of projects, we receive this error:

```
ops$tkyte@ORA920> insert into project(project_id,teamid,job,status)
  2  values( 1, 10, 'a', 'ACTIVE' );
1 row created.

ops$tkyte@ORA920> insert into project(project_id,teamid,job,status)
  2  values( 2, 10, 'a', 'ACTIVE' );
insert into project(project_id,teamid,job,status)
*
ERROR at line 1:
ORA-00001: unique constraint (OPS$TKYTE.JOB_UNIQUE_IN_TEAMID) violated
```

As soon as we retire (make inactive) that first row, the insertion of that second row goes through as expected:

```
ops$tkyte@ORA920> update project
  2     set status = 'INACTIVE'
  3     where project_id = 1
  4       and teamid = 10
  5       and status = 'ACTIVE';
1 row updated.

ops$tkyte@ORA920> insert into project(project_id,teamid,job,status)
  2  values( 2, 10, 'a', 'ACTIVE' );
1 row created.
```

We also have the nice effect that the index is only on active projects, so it is consuming as little space as possible. This implementation was possible only by thinking "outside the box" a bit.

**NOTE**
*If at all possible, uniqueness should be enforced via a UNIQUE constraint. Unique constraints can be used by the optimizer during query rewrites, whereas a simple unique index won't be used. Unique constraints add metadata to the data dictionary that may be used by many tools as well. However, due to the fact that a UNIQUE constraint will not accept a function like the one in this section, a unique index was our only course of action.*

## Use Domain Indexes

Application domain indexes are what Oracle calls *extensible indexing*. It is how you or I could create a custom index structure that works just like an index supplied by Oracle. When someone issues a CREATE INDEX statement using your index type, Oracle will run your code to generate the index. If someone analyzes the index to compute statistics on it, Oracle will execute your code to generate statistics in whatever format you care to store them in. When Oracle parses a query and develops a query plan that may make use of your index, Oracle will ask you how costly this function is to perform as it is evaluating the different plans. Application domain indexes, in short, give you the ability to implement a new index type that does not exist in the database yet.

I personally have not often found the need to build a new exotic type of index structure. I see this particular feature as being of use mostly to third-party solution providers that have innovative indexing techniques. However, you can do some interesting things, and we'll also take a quick look at how you can create indexes.

### Domain Indexes Can Implement Third-Party Indexing Techniques

Domain indexes allow some third-party company to create an index to use with your system. For example, if you inserted a fingerprint into the database via a BLOB type, some external software would be invoked to index this fingerprint data. It would store the point data related to the fingerprint in database tables, in clusters, or perhaps externally in flat files—wherever made the most sense. You would now be able to input a fingerprint into the database and find other fingerprints that matched it, just as easily as you select * from t where x between 1 and 2 using SQL.

Let's consider an example. Say you developed software that analyzed images stored in the database and produced information about the images, such as the colors found in them. You could use a domain index to create your own image index. As images were added to the database, your code would be invoked to extract the colors from the images and store them wherever you wanted to keep them. At query time, when the user asked for all blue images, Oracle would ask you to provide the answer from your index when appropriate.

The best example of this is Oracle's own text index. This index is used to provide keyword searching on large text items. Oracle Text introduces its own index type:

```
ops$tkyte@ORA8I.WORLD> create index myindex on mytable(docs)
2  indextype is ctxsys.context
3  /
Index created.
```

It also uses its own operators in the SQL language:

```
select * from mytable where contains( docs, 'some words' ) > 0;
```

It will even respond to commands such as the following:

```
ops$tkyte@ORA8I.WORLD> analyze index myindex compute statistics;
Index analyzed.
```

Oracle will participate with the optimizer at runtime to determine the relative cost of using a text index over some other index or a full scan. The interesting thing about all of this is that you or I could have developed this index. The implementation of the text index was done without inside kernel knowledge. It was implemented using the documented and exposed API for doing these sorts of things.

The Oracle database kernel is not aware of how the text index is stored (it's stored in many physical database tables per index created). Oracle is not aware of the processing that takes place when a new row is inserted. Oracle Text is really an application built on top of the database, but in a wholly integrated fashion. To you and me, it looks just like any other Oracle database kernel function, but it is not.

## Create Indexes

Knowing what is available as far as domain indexes go can prove very useful. If you need specialized information, it's possible that the database already stores that for you.

For example, Oracle has the ability to natively index point data—latitudes and longitudes in a simple sense—and provide spatial searches based on them, to be able to order data by them. It is a nontrivial problem in a relational database when you get down to it. Consider that latitude and longitude are two attributes. You want to sort all of the data in the database by distance from a given point. Well, you cannot sort by latitude and then longitude, nor can you do the opposite. You really need to sort by some derived, complex value. This is where spatial data comes into play. You can use spatial information to find all of the rows that are close to some point, sort them, and find the distance between the points represented by a pair of rows and so on.

The point I'm making here is not how to use spatial data. For that, you must read the documentation and spend a little while with the capability. Rather, my point is that the database contains many features and functions that are used to store and retrieve data quickly and efficiently. If you are aware of this functionality, you can use it.

"I have a function F_DIST written in PL/SQL to compute the distance between two points. When I call this from SQL in my query, I've discovered that it takes over one-half hour to execute. Now, if I "inline" the function—I do not use the PL/SQL call, but rather do the function inline using acos/sin and so in—it runs in about 15 seconds or so. My questions are 1) Why is the PL/SQL so much slower? and 2) Is there a way to speed this up more?"

This is an interesting question for two reasons. First, why did the PL/SQL function-based approach take so long, and second, why were they reinventing the wheel? After a little research (I got a hold of their data to play with), what we discovered was that with their data set, there were 612,296 invocations of the PL/SQL function F_DIST. Now, it took about 2,083 seconds to run this query on my system (about the same as theirs), meaning that we called that PL/SQL function 294 times a second. That is a context switch from the SQL engine to the PL/SQL engine 294 times every second. Each callout was taking at most 0.003 second, which by itself is very small but adds up when you do it 612,296 times! Anytime we can "inline" the code directly in SQL, we should, because it will almost certainly be faster than calling out to PL/SQL time and time again.

Now for the second part, reinventing the wheel and making it go faster. I don't like doing the first item, and I really enjoy it when the second item is easy to achieve. In this case, not only can we make it go faster, we can do it much easier. My solution was to augment the tables to have a spatial column, and then use that in the query. Here is the code we needed to add to their schema:

```
alter table b add
(geometry mdsys.sdo_geometry);

update b a
   set a.geometry =
     mdsys.sdo_geometry(2001,null,
          mdsys.sdo_point_type(a.longitude,
                              a.latitude,
```

```
                                    null),
            null, null)
      where latitude is not null;

      insert into user_sdo_geom_metadata
      values ('B','GEOMETRY',
         mdsys.sdo_dim_array(
            mdsys.sdo_dim_element
            ('X',-180,180,.00005),
            mdsys.sdo_dim_element
            ('Y',-90,90,.00005)), null);

      create index b_sidx on b(geometry)
      indextype is mdsys.spatial_index;
```

That is for table B in their example. For table C, we added a GEOMETRY column, registered it
with the USER_SDO_GEOM_METADATA table, and then created a spatial index on it as
well. Now, their query becomes simply:

```
      select substr(Z2.ZIPP, 1, 7) ZIP
        from A PT, B TA, C Z2
      where ( PT.REGION || PT.AREA ||
              PT.DISTRICT || PT.LOCATION) = :str
         and PT.LOCATION_ID = TA.LOCATION_ID
         AND MDSYS.LOCATOR_WITHIN_DISTANCE
           (Z2.AVG_GEOM, TA.GEOMETRY,
            'distance = '||:dist||', units=mile') = 'TRUE';
```

We found that same query runs in less than one second, versus more than 15 seconds using
straight SQL and one-half hour using PL/SQL called from SQL.

If I had a dollar for every time someone "invented" a text-indexing technique for indexing
documents in the database, I would be rich. If I had the money spent by their employers funding
the development, redevelopment, maintenance, bug fixing, and so on for these custom-developed
techniques, I would be perhaps the richest person alive.

What happens when these folks are shown that the functionality they painstakingly coded to
parse and keyword index documents already existed, was fully integrated with the optimizer, had
administrative ease of use (such as allowing rebuilding), and had many of the native database
features like partitioning and parallel processing? They are sometimes filled with amazement,
other times dismay, and many times, disbelief. In all cases, using native functionality would have
greatly improved development productivity, maintenance, and performance.

# Compression

We've discussed ways in which you can have Oracle physically organize your data for you—using
B*Tree clusters, hash clusters, IOTs, and the like. The last storage-related option we'll look at is

data compression. Oracle supports compression of both index structures (since Oracle8i Release 1) as well as database tables (since Oracle9i Release 2). The compression algorithm for both segment types is similar in that it relies on factoring out repetitive information and storing that repeating data once on a block, instead of once per occurrence on the block.

The compression of indexes and tables is a little different and can be used in different situations. For example, compressed indexes can be used on tables that undergo constant modifications, but table compression would not make sense in that case due to its implementation. We'll discuss index key compression and then table compression.

## Use Index Key Compression

Index key compression in Oracle allows you to factor out the repetitive leading edge of an index key and store the leading-edge values once per leaf block instead of once per row per leaf block.

Consider the database view DBA_OBJECTS. Suppose we copy that table and create an index on OWNER, OBJECT_TYPE, and OBJECT_NAME, to be able to quickly retrieve rows for a specific object owned by someone. Normally, the index would store values like this:

| User1,table,t1 | User1,table,t2 | User1,table,t3 | User1,table,t4 | User1,table,t5 |
| User1,table,t6 | User1,table,t7 | User1,index,i1 | User1,index,i2 | … and so on… |

Using index key compression, Oracle could instead store the values conceptually, like this:

| User1,table | T1 | T2 | T3 | T4 |
| T5 | T6 | User1,index | I1 | I2… |

In effect, Oracle could store significantly more data per index leaf block than an uncompressed index could store.

Before looking at an example, let's go over a couple of facts about compressed indexes. Here are some of their advantages:

- A compressed index consumes less disk space, so it provides some storage savings.

- A compressed index can reduce the amount of physical I/O your system performs.

- A compressed index increases the buffer cache efficiency. There are quite simply fewer blocks to cache. The index blocks are cached compressed as well as stored compressed.

And here are some of the disadvantages of compressed indexes:

- The compressed index puts more row entries per block, increasing contention on these already compact data structures even more. If before you were putting 200 rows per leaf block—200 possible rows people might update in concurrent sessions—you are now putting in about 400 rows.

- A compressed index requires slightly more CPU time to process at runtime because the structure is more complex. You may notice this during both insert and select operations.

Bear in mind these are simply considerations. It does not mean that there will be more contention. It does not mean that you will even notice the additional CPU time, if any, being used. They are things to watch out for and to test against as you implement this feature.

Let's take a look at this in action. We'll create the compressed and uncompressed indexes on this data and compare not only their size but their performance as well.

We start by creating a copy of DBA_OBJECTS, which we will quadruple in volume. That will mean that our index on (OWNER, OBJECT_TYPE, OBJECT_NAME) will point to about four rows per key value typically.

```
ops$tkyte@ORA920> create table t1
  2  as
  3  select * from dba_objects;
Table created.

ops$tkyte@ORA920> insert /*+ append */ into t1 select * from t1;
30975 rows created.

ops$tkyte@ORA920> commit;
Commit complete.

ops$tkyte@ORA920> insert /*+ append */ into t1 select * from t1;
61950 rows created.

ops$tkyte@ORA920> commit;
Commit complete.

ops$tkyte@ORA920> create index uncompressed_idx
  2  on t1( owner,object_type,object_name );
Index created.

ops$tkyte@ORA920> analyze table t1 compute statistics
  2  for table
  3  for all indexes
  4  for all indexed columns;
Table analyzed.
```

Now, since we cannot create another index on these same columns in this table, we'll copy the table again and index the same data, this time using index key compression on all three key values:

```
ops$tkyte@ORA920> create table t2
  2  as
  3  select * from t1;
Table created.

ops$tkyte@ORA920> create index compressed_idx
  2  on t2( owner,object_type,object_name )
  3  COMPRESS 3;
Index created.
```

```
ops$tkyte@ORA920> analyze table t2 compute statistics
  2   for table
  3   for all indexes
  4   for all indexed columns;
Table analyzed.
```

We are ready to measure the space differences between these two indexes. For this, we'll use the INDEX_STATS dynamic view. This view is populated with details about an index structure after an ANALYZE INDEX VALIDATE STRUCTURE statement. This view has, at most, one row at a time, so we'll copy the rows out as we validate the indexes.

```
ops$tkyte@ORA920> analyze index uncompressed_idx validate structure;
Index analyzed.

ops$tkyte@ORA920> create table index_stats_copy as select * from index_stats;
Table created.

ops$tkyte@ORA920> analyze index compressed_idx validate structure;
Index analyzed.

ops$tkyte@ORA920> insert into index_stats_copy select * from index_stats;
1 row created.
```

Now, we are ready to compare them. For a side-by-side comparison, we can use the following SQL:

```
select 'HEIGHT',
       max(decode(name,'UNCOMPRESSED_IDX',HEIGHT,null)),
       max(decode(name,'UNCOMPRESSED_IDX',to_number(null),HEIGHT))
  from index_stats_copy
 union all
select 'BLOCKS',
       max(decode(name,'UNCOMPRESSED_IDX',BLOCKS,null)),
       max(decode(name,'UNCOMPRESSED_IDX',to_number(null),BLOCKS))
  from index_stats_copy
 union all
...(query for each column)...
```

But, if you don't feel like typing that in, this bit of code generates it for you:

```
ops$tkyte@ORA920> variable x refcursor
ops$tkyte@ORA920> declare
  2       l_stmt long;
  3   begin
  4       for x in ( select '''' || column_name || '''' quoted,
  5                         column_name
  6                    from user_tab_columns
  7                   where table_name = 'INDEX_STATS_COPY'
  8                     and column_name not in
  9                         ('NAME','PARTITION_NAME') )
```

```
10      loop
11          l_stmt := l_stmt || ' select ' || x.quoted || ' name,
12                  max(decode(name,''UNCOMPRESSED_IDX'',' ||
13                  x.column_name || ',null)) uncompressed,
14                  max(decode(name,''UNCOMPRESSED_IDX'',
15                      to_number(null),' || x.column_name ||
16                      ')) compressed
17                  from index_stats_copy union all';
18      end loop;
19      l_stmt :=
20      'select name, uncompressed, compressed,
21              uncompressed-compressed diff,
22              decode(uncompressed,0,
23                  to_number(null),
24                  round(compressed/uncompressed*100,2)) pct
25          from ( ' ||
26            substr( l_stmt, 1,
27                    length(l_stmt)-length(' union all') ) ||
28              ') order by name';
29      open :x for l_stmt;
30  end;
31  /
```

PL/SQL procedure successfully completed.

```
ops$tkyte@ORA920> print x
```

| NAME | UNCOMPRESSED | COMPRESSED | DIFF | PCT |
|---|---|---|---|---|
| BLKS_GETS_PER_ACCESS | 5.50934125 | 5.50934125 | 0 | 100 |
| BLOCKS | 896 | 512 | 384 | 57.14 |
| BR_BLKS | 6 | 3 | 3 | 50 |
| BR_BLK_LEN | 8028 | 8028 | 0 | 100 |
| BR_ROWS | 841 | 379 | 462 | 45.07 |
| BR_ROWS_LEN | 37030 | 14367 | 22663 | 38.8 |
| BTREE_SPACE | 6780800 | 3061044 | 3719756 | 45.14 |
| DEL_LF_ROWS | 0 | 0 | 0 | |
| DEL_LF_ROWS_LEN | 0 | 0 | 0 | |
| DISTINCT_KEYS | 30831 | 30831 | 0 | 100 |
| HEIGHT | 3 | 3 | 0 | 100 |
| LF_BLKS | 842 | 380 | 462 | 45.13 |
| LF_BLK_LEN | 7996 | 7992 | 4 | 99.95 |
| LF_ROWS | 123900 | 123900 | 0 | 100 |
| LF_ROWS_LEN | 6021780 | 1362900 | 4658880 | 22.63 |
| MOST_REPEATED_KEY | 64 | 64 | 0 | 100 |
| OPT_CMPR_COUNT | 3 | 3 | 0 | 100 |
| OPT_CMPR_PCTSAVE | 54 | 0 | 54 | 0 |
| PCT_USED | 90 | 90 | 0 | 100 |
| PRE_ROWS | 0 | 30972 | -30972 | |
| PRE_ROWS_LEN | 0 | 1351112 | -1351112 | |

```
ROWS_PER_KEY          4.01868249 4.01868249         0         100
USED_SPACE               6058810    2728379   3330431      45.03
```

23 rows selected.

Now we have a side-by-side comparison of the uncompressed index and compressed index. First, observe that we achieved better than a 50% compression ratio. Ignore the BLOCKS value for a moment (that is space allocated to the segment but includes unused blocks as well). Looking at the BR_BLKS (branch blocks) and LF_BLKS (leaf blocks, where the actual index keys and ROWIDs are stored), we see that we have 50% of the branch blocks and 45% of the leaf blocks. The compressed index is consuming about half of the disk space. Another way to look at this is that every block in the compressed index contains twice the amount of data. Not only do we save disk space, but we also just doubled the size of our buffer cache. Also consider that Oracle reads blocks not rows; hence, anything that reduces the number of blocks Oracle must manage potentially "increases" the capacity of our buffer cache.

The other interesting thing to notice here is the OPT_CMPR_COUNT (optimal key compression length) and OPT_CMPR_PCTSAVE (percent savings in space if you compress) values. They estimated that if we used index key compression on the uncompressed index, we would save 54% in space—a value that is accurate, as shown by the actual compressed index. You can use these values to see if rebuilding an index with compression would be paid back with significant space savings.

The last items we'll consider here are the PRE_ROWS (prefix rows, or actual key values that were factored out) and the PRE_ROWS_LEN (length of these prefix rows) values. These numbers represent the number of unique prefix keys in the index. These represent the data that is factored out of the index structure and stored once per leaf block instead of once per row. Here, we find a value of 30,972. This is not surprising, since the number of rows in my DBA_OBJECTS table was 30,975 (you can see that by the first INSERT /*+ APPEND */ output shown earlier—the first doubling of the table added that many rows). That is just showing that apparently there are 30,972 unique (OWNER, OBJECT_TYPE, OBJECT_NAME) combinations in the table. The PRE_ROWS_LEN value shows these factored-out values take about 1.3MB of storage.

For the raw numbers, we can run a somewhat simple test that takes each key value and reads the entire row using that key. Bear in mind that each key value is in the index about four times, so we are actually fetching each key value out about four times, for 16 rows.

```
ops$tkyte@ORA920> alter session set sql_trace=true;
Session altered.

ops$tkyte@ORA920> begin
  2      for x in ( select * from t1 )
  3      loop
  4          for y in ( select *
  5                       from t1
  6                      where owner = x.owner
  7                        and object_name = x.object_name
  8                        and object_type = x.object_type )
  9          loop
 10              null;
 11          end loop;
```

```
12        end loop;
13        for x in ( select * from t2 )
14        loop
15            for y in ( select *
16                            from t2
17                          where owner = x.owner
18                            and object_name = x.object_name
19                            and object_type = x.object_type )
20            loop
21                null;
22            end loop;
23        end loop;
24  end;
25  /
PL/SQL procedure successfully completed.
```

The TKPROF report for this run shows the following statistics:

```
select * from t1
where owner = :b3 and object_name = :b2 and object_type = :b1

call       count      cpu elapsed disk   query current     rows
-------   ------  -------- ------- ----  ------- -------  -------
Parse          1     0.00    0.00    0        0       0        0
Execute   123900    16.54   17.42    0        0       0        0
Fetch     650828    39.69   41.09    0  1425552       0   526928
-------   ------  -------- ------- ----  ------- -------  -------
total     774729    56.24   58.52    0  1425552       0   526928

Rows     Row Source Operation
-------  ---------------------------------------------------
 526928  TABLE ACCESS BY INDEX ROWID T1
 526928   INDEX RANGE SCAN UNCOMPRESSED_IDX (object id 43577)
**************************************************************
select * from t2
where owner = :b3 and object_name = :b2 and object_type = :b1

call       count    cpu elapsed disk   query current     rows
-------   ------  ----- ------- ----  ------- -------  -------
Parse          1   0.00    0.00    0        0       0        0
Execute   123900  17.48   19.98    0        0       0        0
Fetch     650828  42.29   43.34    0  1425552       0   526928
-------   ------  ----- ------- ----  ------- -------  -------
total     774729  59.77   63.33    0  1425552       0   526928

Rows     Row Source Operation
-------  ---------------------------------------------------
 526928  TABLE ACCESS BY INDEX ROWID T2
 526928   INDEX RANGE SCAN COMPRESSED_IDX (object id 43579)
```

As you can see, the CPU times are more or less the same (yes, they vary by about 3 CPU seconds, but that is only a 5% variation, so they are more or less equivalent). If we were to run this again, the numbers may well be reversed. This is due to the fact that the 39.69 CPU seconds reported by the fetch phase for the first query is an aggregation of 650,828 discrete timed events. If some of the events took less time to execute than the granularity of the system clock, they would report 0; others may report 1 unit of time. (In fact, I did another couple of runs just to test that this is reproducible, and in one occurrence, I observed CPU times of 60.06 and 60.97 CPU seconds for the uncompressed versus compressed timings.)

The TKPROF report also shows that the amount of logical I/O performed by each was the same. This is not surprising, given that the height of both indexes was the same (as observed by the preceding INDEX_STATS output). Therefore, given any key entry, it would logically take the same amount of logical I/Os to get the leaf entry. In this case, it took two logical I/Os on average to get the leaf block and one more logical I/O to retrieve the table data itself.

I also ran these tests using the Runstats framework. The salient output showed that the latching differences between the two approaches was negligible. In the following, RUN1 is the uncompressed index and RUN2 is the compressed index attempt:

```
     RUN1          RUN2          DIFF RUN1_PCT_OF_RUN2
---------- ---------- ---------- ----------------
  3622897     3630132         7235             99.8
```

Additionally, the wall clock times were not significantly different either:

```
12058 hsecs
12467 hsecs
run 1 ran in 96.72% of the time
```

The uncompressed index was only 3% faster by the wall clock—an amount you most likely would not notice in the real world. Remember also that the wall clock time is easily influenced by external events. Our computers do more than one thing at a time, after all.

# Use Table Compression for Read-Only/Read-Mostly Tables

The ability to compress a table started in Oracle8i with IOTs. Since an IOT is really a special kind of index—one that supports index key compression—we could compress it using that technique.

True table-level compression for more general table types is new with Oracle9i Release 2. It is similar to index key compression in that it factors out repetitive information, but it differs in many ways. Table compression works on the aggregate-block level, not row by row as index key compression does; that is, when Oracle is building a database block, it is looking for repeating values across all columns and rows on that block. The values need not be on the leading edge of the row; they can be anywhere in the row.

The major difference between table and index compression is when each may be used. Index key compression works equally well on systems where the table is being modified frequently and on read-only or read-mostly systems. The index is maintained in its compressed state in both environments. However, table compression works well *only* in a read-only or read-mostly environment. It is not a feature you will use on your active transaction tables (although you can use it in your transactional systems, as you'll see). Table compression works only for bulk operations as well. A normal INSERT or UPDATE statement will not compress data. Instead, you need to use one of the following:

- CREATE TABLE AS SELECT
- INSERT /*+ APPEND */ (direct-path insert)
- SQLLDR direct=y (direct-path load)
- ALTER TABLE MOVE

Compressing a table does not prohibit you from using normal DML against it. It is just that the newly added or modified information will not be stored compressed. It would take a rebuild of that segment in order to compress it. So, table compression is most likely to be valuable in these situations:

- Large amounts of static reference information that is read-only or read-mostly
- Data warehousing environments where bulk operations are common
- Audit trail information stored in partitioned tables, where you can compress last month's auditing information at the beginning of a new month

Table compression should not be considered for most transactional tables where the data is heavily updated. There table compression would be defeated, as each update would tend to "decompress" the row(s).

Table compression in Oracle is achieved by factoring out repeating data found on a database block and creating a symbol table. It we started with a database block that looked like this (each cell in the table represents a row, the data is stored delimited in this conceptual depiction):

| | | |
|---|---|---|
| SCOTT,TABLE,EMP | SCOTT,TABLE,DEPT | SCOTT,TABLE,BONUS |
| SCOTT,INDEX,EMP_PK | SCOTT,INDEX,ENAME_IDX | SCOTT,INDEX,DEPT_PK |
| SCOTT,INDEX,EMP_DEPT | SCOTT,INDEX,DNAME_IDX | SCOTT,PROCEDURE,P1 |
| SCOTT,PROCEDURE,P2 | SCOTT,PROCEDURE,P3 | SCOTT,PROCEDURE,P4 |

A compressed block would conceptually look like this:

SCOTT=<A>,TABLE=<B>,
INDEX=<C>,PROCEDURE=<D>

| | | | |
|---|---|---|---|
| <A>,<B>,EMP | <A>,<B>,DEPT | <A>,<B>,BONUS | <A>,<C>,EMP_PK |
| <A>,<C>,ENAME_IDX | <A>,<C>,DEPT_PK | <A>,<C>,EMP_DEPT | <A>,<C>,DNAME_IDX |
| <A>,<D>,P1 | <A>,<D>,P2 | <A>,<D>,P3 | <A>,<D>,P4 |

Here, the repeating values of SCOTT, TABLE, INDEX, and PROCEDURE were factored out, stored once on the block in a symbol table, and replaced in the block with simple indexes into the symbol table. This can result in significant savings in space.

Consider this simple example where we store DBA_OBJECTS in an uncompressed and a compressed table. Note that the PCTFREE on the compressed table will be 0, so we'll use the same PCTFREE on the uncompressed table to be fair.

```
ops$tkyte@ORA920> create table uncompressed
  2  pctfree 0
  3  as
  4  select *
  5    from dba_objects
  6    order by owner, object_type, object_name;
Table created.

ops$tkyte@ORA920> analyze table uncompressed
  2  compute statistics
  3  for table;
Table analyzed.

ops$tkyte@ORA920> create table compressed
  2  COMPRESS
  3  as
  4  select *
  5    from uncompressed
  6    order by owner, object_type, object_name;
Table created.

ops$tkyte@ORA920> analyze table compressed
  2  compute statistics
  3  for table;
Table analyzed.

ops$tkyte@ORA920> select cblks comp_blks, uncblks uncomp_blks,
  2            round(cblks/uncblks*100,2) pct
  3    from (
  4  select max(decode(table_name,'COMPRESSED',blocks,null)) cblks,
  5    max(decode(table_name,'UNCOMPRESSED',blocks,null)) uncblks
  6    from user_tables
  7  where table_name in ( 'COMPRESSED', 'UNCOMPRESSED' )
  8          )
  9  /

COMP_BLKS UNCOMP_BLKS        PCT
---------- ----------- ----------
      217         395      54.94
```

This shows that we can store the same amount of information in 55% of the space. That is significant—we just cut our disk space needs in half for this table.

Notice that we put an ORDER BY on the CREATE TABLE COMPRESSED and ordered the table by data we knew to be compressible. We clumped together all of the SCOTT objects by type on the same blocks. This allows the compression routines to do their best job. Instead of storing SCOTT (or SYSTEM, or CTXSYS, or whatever) dozens or hundreds of times per block, we store it once. We also store TABLE and PACKAGE BODY once, and then point to them with a very small pointer.

You might think that is cheating; the data won't be sorted. I disagree. Table compression is useful only on read-only/read-mostly data. You have a great deal of control over the sorted order of that data. You load it into a warehouse, have an audit trail, or have reference information. All of this can be sorted. If your goal is to minimize disk use, you can achieve that.

Just for fun, let's see what happens if the data is somewhat randomly sorted:

```
ops$tkyte@ORA920> create table compressed
2   COMPRESS
3   as
  4   select *
  5     from uncompressed
6     order by dbms_random.random;
Table created.

ops$tkyte@ORA920> analyze table compressed
  2   compute statistics
  3   for table;
Table analyzed.

ops$tkyte@ORA920> select cblks comp_blks, uncblks uncomp_blks,
  2            round(cblks/uncblks*100,2) pct
  3     from (
  4   select max(decode(table_name,'COMPRESSED',blocks,null)) cblks,
  5     max(decode(table_name,'UNCOMPRESSED',blocks,null)) uncblks
  6     from user_tables
  7   where table_name in ( 'COMPRESSED', 'UNCOMPRESSED' )
  8            )
  9   /


COMP_BLKS UNCOMP_BLKS        PCT
---------- ----------- ----------
      287         395      72.66
```

Even if the data in this particular table arrives randomly, we achieve about a 25% reduction in space needed. Your mileage may vary on this; I observed numbers between 65% and 80% during repeated runs. The results depended on how the data ended up. Using the statistics in the USER_TAB_COLUMNS table for the UNCOMPRESSED table, I noticed that a particularly wide column TIMESTAMP had a lot of repetitive values and no NULL values:

```
ops$tkyte@ORA920> analyze table uncompressed compute statistics;
Table analyzed.

ops$tkyte@ORA920> select column_name, num_distinct, num_nulls, avg_col_len
  2   from user_tab_columns
  3   where table_name = 'UNCOMPRESSED'
  4   /
```

```
COLUMN_NAME      NUM_DISTINCT   NUM_NULLS  AVG_COL_LEN
---------------  ------------   ---------  -----------
OWNER                      37           0            5
OBJECT_NAME             19194           0           23
SUBOBJECT_NAME             46       30774            2
OBJECT_ID               30980           0            4
DATA_OBJECT_ID           2340       28603            2
OBJECT_TYPE                33           0            8
CREATED                  2143           0            7
LAST_DDL_TIME            2262           0            7
TIMESTAMP                2184           0           19
STATUS                      2           0            6
TEMPORARY                   2           0            1
GENERATED                   2           0            1
SECONDARY                   1           0            1

13 rows selected.
```

I rebuilt the compressed table sorting by TIMESTAMP this time, and the results were impressive:

```
ops$tkyte@ORA920> drop table compressed;
Table dropped.

ops$tkyte@ORA920> create table compressed
  2   COMPRESS
  3   as
  4   select *
  5     from uncompressed
  6    order by timestamp;
Table created.

ops$tkyte@ORA920> analyze table compressed
  2   compute statistics
  3    for table;
Table analyzed.

ops$tkyte@ORA920>
ops$tkyte@ORA920> select cblks comp_blks, uncblks uncomp_blks,
  2            round(cblks/uncblks*100,2) pct
  3      from (
  4    select max(decode(table_name,'COMPRESSED',blocks,null)) cblks,
  5      max(decode(table_name,'UNCOMPRESSED',blocks,null)) uncblks
  6      from user_tables
  7     where table_name in ( 'COMPRESSED', 'UNCOMPRESSED' )
  8            )
  9   /

 COMP_BLKS UNCOMP_BLKS        PCT
---------- -----------  ---------
       147         395      37.22
```

That table now takes one-third the space of the uncompressed version, due to factoring out that wide column and storing it once per block. This shows that a good understanding of the frequency of values in your data, the size of your data, and the ability to sort the data will allow you to achieve maximum compression, if that is your goal.

The examples in this section use different storage options to achieve different goals, and sometimes these goals are orthogonal to each other. For example, you might find that sorting by TIMESTAMP achieves maximum compression but you might also observe that people often query for all of the TABLES owned by some user. In that case, sorting by OWNER, OBJECT_TYPE would place the data people request in a query on the fewest number of blocks (all of the data for SCOTT's tables would tend to be collected on a small number of blocks, all colocated). So you have to make a trade-off here: Do you want to use as little of the disk as possible, but potentially spread SCOTT's objects over many blocks, or do you want to use a little more disk space, but have all of SCOTT's tables on the same blocks? There is no right or wrong answer. There is only the answer you come to after careful consideration of your goals and objectives—what you most want or need to have happen in your system.

Here are the three places where you might consider table compression:

- When you have large amounts of static reference information that is read-only or read-mostly
- In data warehousing environments where bulk operations are common
- For audit trail information stored in partitioned tables, where you can compress last month's auditing information at the beginning of a new month

### Compressed Tables for Static Information and Data Warehousing

If you have large amounts of static reference information already loaded into your database, you can use compressed tables as follows:

- Analyze the table to find the best sort columns to achieve maximum compression (assuming that is your goal).
- Use CREATE TABLE COPY_OF_TABLE *compress* AS SELECT with the requisite ORDER BY.
- Drop the old uncompressed table and rename this copy.

It you are in a data warehouse situation and are bulk-loading data, you can follow the same basic procedure. For example, you can use DBMS_STATS against external tables. If you are unsure of the frequencies in the data you are loading, you can use the same approach for your database tables. Using the BIG_TABLE_EXTERNAL table we used in the examples in the "External Tables" section earlier in the chapter, we can do the following:

```
ops$tkyte@ORA920> exec dbms_stats.gather_table_stats -
> ( user, 'BIG_TABLE_EXTERNAL' );
PL/SQL procedure successfully completed.

ops$tkyte@ORA920> select column_name, num_distinct, num_nulls, avg_col_len
  2  from user_tab_columns
  3  where table_name = 'BIG_TABLE_EXTERNAL'
```

```
  4   /

COLUMN_NAME                      NUM_DISTINCT  NUM_NULLS  AVG_COL_LEN
------------------------------   ------------  ---------  -----------
OWNER                                      28          0            6
OBJECT_NAME                             17130          0           24
SUBOBJECT_NAME                             31    1824766            2
OBJECT_ID                             1833792          0            6
DATA_OBJECT_ID                           1475    1737790            2
OBJECT_TYPE                                27          1            9
CREATED                                    13          0            8
LAST_DDL_TIME                              16          0            8
TIMESTAMP                             1833729         63            8
STATUS                                      2         63            6
TEMPORARY                                   2         63            2
GENERATED                                   2         63            2
SECONDARY                                   1         63            2

13 rows selected.
```

From that, we can deduce that maximum compression would be achieved by sorting on OBJECT_NAME. Because it has relatively few distinct values as compared to the number of rows in the table and the average row length is very wide, it would be the best candidate. We can load the table using this code:

```
ops$tkyte@ORA920> create table big_table_compressed
  2  COMPRESS
  3  as
  4  select * from big_table_external
  5  order by object_name;
Table created.
```

When I compared the sizes of a compressed versus uncompressed version of the same data, I found the compressed table used 4,831 blocks and the uncompressed version used 22,188— a 5-to-1 compression ratio!

### Compress Auditing or Transaction History

Suppose that you have a sliding window of data in a partitioned table. For example, you are keeping seven years of audit information online in your database. Every month, you take the oldest month of data and drop it, you add a new partition to the table to accommodate new data, and now you want to also compress the latest full month's worth of data. We'll take a look at how you could accomplish this step by step. We'll start with our partitioned AUDIT_TRAIL_TABLE:

```
ops$tkyte@ORA920> CREATE TABLE audit_trail_table
  2  ( timestamp date,
  3    username  varchar2(30),
  4    action    varchar2(30),
  5    object    varchar2(30),
```

```
  6    message    varchar2(80)
  7  )
  8  PARTITION BY RANGE (timestamp)
  9  ( PARTITION jan_2002 VALUES LESS THAN
 10    ( to_date('01-feb-2002','dd-mon-yyyy') ) ,
 11    PARTITION feb_2002 VALUES LESS THAN
 12    ( to_date('01-mar-2002','dd-mon-yyyy') ) ,
 13    PARTITION mar_2002 VALUES LESS THAN
 14    ( to_date('01-apr-2002','dd-mon-yyyy') ) ,
 15    PARTITION apr_2002 VALUES LESS THAN
 16    ( to_date('01-may-2002','dd-mon-yyyy') ) ,
...
 37    PARTITION mar_2003 VALUES LESS THAN
 38    ( to_date('01-apr-2003','dd-mon-yyyy') ) ,
 39    PARTITION the_rest VALUES LESS THAN
 40    ( maxvalue )
 41  )
 42  /
Table created.

ops$tkyte@ORA920> create index partitioned_idx_local
  2  on audit_trail_table(username)
  3  LOCAL
  4  /
Index created.
```

This table has a partition for each month's worth of data, dating back to January 2002 and up through the end of March 2003. Now, assume it is the beginning of April and we have a month's worth of audit information stored uncompressed in the MAR_2003 partition. We would like to do the following:

■ Get rid of the oldest data (slide that window of data to the right)

■ Add a new partition just for April 2003

■ Compress the data for March 2003, since we no longer will be adding to it (only querying it)

First, we'll generate some mock data for March 2003:

```
ops$tkyte@ORA920> insert into audit_trail_table
  2  select to_date( '01-mar-2003 ' ||
  3                    to_char(created,'hh24:mi:ss'),
  4                    'dd-mon-yyyy hh24:mi:ss' ) +
  5                    mod(rownum,31),
  6         owner,
  7         decode( mod(rownum,10), 0, 'INSERT',
  8               1, 'UPDATE', 2, 'DELETE', 'SELECT' ),
  9         object_name,
 10         object_name || ' ' || dbms_random.random
```

```
 11      from (select * from dba_objects
 12            UNION ALL
 13            select * from dba_objects
 14            UNION ALL
 15            select * from dba_objects
 16            UNION ALL
 17            select * from dba_objects)
 18   /
124072 rows created.

ops$tkyte@ORA920> analyze table audit_trail_table partition (mar_2003)
  2   compute statistics
  3   /
Table analyzed.

ops$tkyte@ORA920> select num_rows, blocks
  2     from user_tab_partitions
  3    where table_name = 'AUDIT_TRAIL_TABLE'
  4      and partition_name = 'MAR_2003'
  5   /

  NUM_ROWS     BLOCKS
---------- ----------
    124072       1440
```

Now, we'll use the column statistics to determine how we might want to sort this data to achieve our goal of maximum compression:

```
ops$tkyte@ORA920> select column_name, num_distinct, num_nulls, avg_col_len
  2     from USER_PART_COL_STATISTICS
  3    where table_name = 'AUDIT_TRAIL_TABLE'
  4      and partition_name = 'MAR_2003'
  5   /

COLUMN_NAM NUM_DISTINCT  NUM_NULLS AVG_COL_LEN
---------- ------------ ---------- -----------
TIMESTAMP         39763          0           7
USERNAME             37          0           5
ACTION                4          0           6
OBJECT            19199          0          23
MESSAGE          107394          0          34
```

We can see that MESSAGE is almost unique, but that OBJECT is not very selective and it is big. We decide to order by OBJECT and then USERNAME/ACTION based on this information. So, we'll create a table TEMP with the sorted, compressed data:

```
ops$tkyte@ORA920> drop table temp;
Table dropped.

ops$tkyte@ORA920> create table temp
```

```
  2   COMPRESS
  3   as
  4   select timestamp, username, action, object, message
  5     from audit_trail_table Partition(mar_2003)
  6     order by object, username, action
  7   /
Table created.
```

And we must index it, so it looks just like our partitioned table structurally:

```
ops$tkyte@ORA920> create index temp_idx on temp(username)
  2   /
Index created.

ops$tkyte@ORA920> analyze table temp
  2   compute statistics
  3   for table
  4   for all indexes
  5   for all indexed columns
  6   /
Table analyzed.
```

Now, we are ready to move data. We start by dropping the oldest partition, sliding the window to the right timewise.

```
ops$tkyte@ORA920> alter table audit_trail_table
  2   drop partition jan_2002;
Table altered.
```

Then we swap in our nicely compacted slice of data using the EXCHANGE PARTITION command.

```
ops$tkyte@ORA920> set timing on
ops$tkyte@ORA920> alter table audit_trail_table
  2   exchange partition mar_2003
  3   with table temp
  4   including indexes
  5   without validation
  6   /
Table altered.
Elapsed: 00:00:00.12
```

Note that this operation happens almost instantaneously. This is a simple DDL command that swaps names; the data isn't touched during this operation. Additionally, we can see the statistics are swapped as well:

```
ops$tkyte@ORA920> select blocks
  2     from user_tab_partitions
  3     where table_name = 'AUDIT_TRAIL_TABLE'
  4       and partition_name = 'MAR_2003'
```

```
      5   /

         BLOCKS
      ----------
           880
```

Instead of 1,440 blocks, we have 880, so the data is taking about 61% of the space it took originally.

All that is left now is to split the last partition at the end into a partition for April data and the rest.

```
ops$tkyte@ORA920> alter table audit_trail_table
  2    split partition the_rest
  3    at ( to_date('01-may-2003','dd-mon-yyyy') )
  4    into ( partition apr_2003, partition the_rest )
  5    /
Table altered.
```

Now, we are finished. It is interesting to note that March data is still modifiable here. We can insert, update, and delete that data. However, any rows we insert using a conventional INSERT or modify with an UPDATE will cause the affected data to be uncompressed. A table may consist of compressed blocks and uncompressed blocks. In fact, a single block may contain both compressed and uncompressed rows.

## Compression Wrap-Up

Compression is a powerful tool for saving disk space, although care must be taken to trade this off with other physical storage considerations. If the location of data is key, data must be clustered in order to give the best performance, and compression might not be the way to go. On the other hand, if you need to store massive amounts of read-only data, such as audit trail information and data warehouse tables, compression may be the tool you need. Care must be taken to have the data physically bulk-loaded in a sorted order to maximize your compression ratios. Fortunately, simple CREATE TABLE AS SELECT statements make this a straightforward proposition.

In the area of performance, compressed tables fair well. There is the small overhead of decompressing the block, similar to the overhead you find with index key compression. However, the reduced I/O, more efficient use of the buffer cache, reduced latching, and other benefits outweigh any perceived overhead. To view a demonstration of a compressed table versus an uncompressed table, visit http://asktom.oracle.com/~tkyte/compress.html.

# Summary

In this chapter, we covered many of the salient features of schema design. Unlike many other references on this topic, I didn't really go into data modeling or the normal forms. My goal was more pragmatic and more technical.

Many people confuse schema design with data modeling. To me, data modeling and schema design are related but separate events. One takes place before the other (data modeling and then physical schema design). The purity of the logical model is sometimes overcome by practical reality. For example, the people lookup example I used in this chapter is not something a logical data modeler would have come up with. Rather, the logical data model would have described the requirements, and the two-table people example would have been the physical, optimized realization of those requirements.

My fundamental schema principles are as follows:

- Let the database do your work. Use as many declarative statements as you can. Never implement procedurally what the database does declaratively.

- Always use the correct and most appropriate datatype. If you do not, you'll either be hating yourself over time if you need to maintain your own system, or the next people who need to do it will be using your name in vain for years to come.

- Optimize your database to efficiently and effectively answer your most frequently asked questions. I see many systems with pure logical models that stamped out a physical design—a physical design that looks nice on paper but doesn't respond very well in real life. Understand what will be asked of your system and design the system around that.

We looked at using various data structures in order to optimize access to data, paying the price at the time of insertion in order to optimize data retrieval. Remember that you generally insert a row of data once. You will query that data many times, so the price you pay during insertion will be repaid many times over, every time you retrieve the data. To design an efficient physical schema, you need to know what features and functions are available, how they work, and how to benchmark them under *your* conditions.

# CHAPTER
## 8

## Effective SQL

his was probably the hardest chapter of the book to write. That is not because the material is all that complex. It's because I know what people want, and I know what can be delivered. What people want is the ten-step process for tuning any query. What can be delivered is knowledge about how queries are processed, which you can use and apply as you develop queries.

If there were a ten-step, or even a million-step, process by which any query (or a large percentage of queries) could be tuned, we would write a program to do it. Sure, there are actually many programs that try to do this, such as Oracle Enterprise Manager with its tuning pack, SQL Navigator, and others. What they do is primarily recommend indexing schemes to tune a query, suggest materialized views, and offer to add hints to the query to try other access plans. They show you different query plans for the same statement and allow you to pick one. These tuning tools use a very limited set of rules that sometimes can suggest that index or set of indexes you really should have thought of during your design. They offer "rule of thumb" (what I generally call ROT, since the acronym and the word it maps to are so appropriate for each other) SQL optimizations. If these were universally applicable, the optimizer would do them routinely.

In fact, the CBO does tuning already. It rewrites our queries all the time. If there were an *N*-step process to tuning a query—to writing efficient SQL—the optimizer would incorporate it all, and we would not be having a discussion on this topic. It is like the search for the Holy Grail. Maybe someday the software will be sophisticated enough to take our SQL, understand the question being asked, and process the question rather than syntax.

This chapter will provide the foundation knowledge you need in order to begin thinking about how queries could be processed. Once you understand query processing, you can make the query do what you think might be best. Writing efficient SQL is no different from writing efficient C, Java, or even English. It takes an understanding of how things work and what is available. If you don't know some technique is available, you'll never be able to optimize to use it.

# What You Need to Write Efficient SQL

For every rule of thumb out there I've seen regarding writing efficient SQL, I've been able to come up with a slew of common (not esoteric) countercases to prove that rule of thumb is wrong as many times as it is right. I've talked to people who swear NOT IN is fatal, and you should never use it; instead, always use NOT EXISTS. Then I show them NOT IN running a query ten times faster than NOT EXISTS. I talk with people who feel NOT EXISTS is the worst construct on the planet; you must use NOT IN. Then I show them how NOT EXISTS can run many times faster than NOT IN.

Rather than following rules of thumb, writing efficient SQL requires the following:

- **Knowledge of the physical organization of what you're querying against**    That is, you should know the schema. (Refer to Chapter 7 of this book for information about designing an efficient schema.)

- **Knowledge of what the database is capable of doing**    For example, if you did not know about skip-scan indexes and what they do, you might look at a schema and say, "Aha, we are missing an index!" when, in fact, this is not true.

- **Knowledge of all of the intricacies of SQL**    You should be familiar with SQL, from the lowly WHERE clause up to analytics and pseudo columns. You should know what using a particular construct would do to your runtime processing.

■   **A solid understanding of the goal—what the question is**   Tuning a query or process is really hard (or impossible), unless you understand the question in the first place. For example, many people use outer joins in all queries, because they are afraid of losing a row. If the objects are related in a one-to-one mandatory fashion, they don't need an outer join at all. In many cases, the question derived from the query is much more confining than the real goal of the query.

In this chapter, we'll cover the topics of what the database is capable of doing in general, looking at many of the access paths and join operations available. We'll look at what SQL is capable of doing, but not by discussing the entire language, since that is a book in itself. Rather, we'll look at a couple of things that will whet you appetite, showing you how powerful this language can be—how much more than just SELECT, FROM, WHERE, and ORDER BY there is. Then we'll close up with a look at that most important topic: why understanding the *question* is more important than having a query at hand to tune. I hope that when you finish this chapter, you'll want to learn more about SQL and what it can do.

# Understand Access Paths

Access paths are the methods by which Oracle can get at our data. There are surprisingly few:

■   **The infamous full scan**   The access path people try to avoid (mistakenly) at all costs.

■   **Index accesses, of many types**   This is the path people are very comfortable with (mistakenly, in many cases).

■   **Directed access, by hash or ROWID**   Think of this as a GOTO statement in a 3GL language, but in a good way. This is the fastest way to a single row, in general.

There is no single best access path. If there were, Oracle would provide only that one. Each access path has its time and place. If you have fallen into the trap of tuning queries by looking for full scans and getting rid of them, I hope to change your mind. Each and every access path is useful under the right circumstances.

## Full Scans

Full scans are very much what their name implies. Oracle will read every block in a given segment that was used at some point or another. A full scan simply means to read all blocks sequentially. Here, Oracle will read from the beginning of a segment to the end, processing each block. Full scans are a very efficient method to read a lot of data in Oracle, since the database will employ a multiblock read. Since Oracle knows it is going to read each and every block in the segment, it will read many blocks at a time, not just a single block at a time.

One important item to keep in mind is that full scans are not evil. Many times, a full scan is by far the fastest method to get an answer. In Chapter 6, we looked at a concrete example where using indexes resulted in a one-hour execution, whereas using full scans resulted in a ten-second execution. As I've pointed out in earlier chapters, full scans (big bulk operations) can be incredibly efficient as opposed to using an index (which we are all taught is the fast way to the data), even though that idea seems to fly in the face of conventional wisdom.

"In your example, using nested loops has more buffer gets than, say, using a hash join. Okay, this translates into less latches and a better concurrent performance profile. Now, I'm trying to understand the reason. Suppose both tables are cached into the memory. Then we can ignore the random I/O versus sequential I/O difference. Is the nested-loop algorithm inherently "nonoptimal" compared to a hash join? What does the hash join do differently? It does put a hash table in front of the inner table. That's just extra work to me. Then it does the similar nested looping, which is only sugarcoated by the hash table probe. Specifically, Oracle probes the hash table, so that if there is no match, then the target table is not accessed. But an indexed nested loop does a similar probing of the join index! Why is a hash join considered more scalable?"

Think of it like this. Each consistent get takes CPU work. If you do something that takes 0.0001 CPU second once, it is really fast. Now, if you do it 100,000,000 times, it takes 10,000 CPU seconds!

For example, let's compare a nested loop row at a time process to a sort/merge bulk process. Suppose you have a room of boys and girls and you want to have a dance. You would like to have the kids paired up by size (tall girl, tall boy). That is your join condition. You could pick a girl, search for a boy about the same size, pair them up, and continue. This works well if you have about five boys and five girls. This is similar to a nested-loops join. You do some "looking around the room" to match everyone up.

Now, let's say you have 1,000 boys and 1,000 girls. It gets a little unwieldy now, because it takes quite a while to pair them up by picking one girl and then searching for a matching boy. Instead, you decide to have the boys sort themselves by height and then the girls. Now you pair them up quickly. That is similar to how a sort-merge join is processed in bulk. Do a sort of each set, and then merge it together. Now, the first method—pick a girl, find a boy, then output—gets the first couple on the dance floor really fast (it is like FIRST ROWS optimization), but it takes a long time to get all 1,000 couples out there. On the other hand, the second method keeps the dance floor empty during the sort, but when the rows start coming, they are flying out there, with very little work. You populate the dance floor with all of the couples very quickly.

Neither is less optimal—no more than an 18-wheeler is less optimal than a BMW. One is good for long hauls, and one is good for getting to work. You use different tools for different jobs. If you need the first row of a result set as soon as possible, a full scan and large bulk operations may be something you want to avoid. If you need to get the entire answer as soon as possible, full scans and large bulk operations may be the solution.

## Full Scans and Multiblock Read Counts

We've mentioned that full scans are performed by Oracle using multiblock I/O; that is, Oracle reads $N$ blocks at a time in a single I/O call, rather than one block at a time. We can see this multiblock read at work by using the 10046 trace event (the advanced way to enable SQL_TRACE) and watching wait events. We can also see the effect on performance you might experience with different values for the Oracle setting of DB_FILE_MULTIBLOCK_READ_COUNT.

We'll use our BIG_TABLE and full-scan it repeatedly using different multiblock read count values each time. Additionally, we'll flush our buffer cache for this object between each run to force a physical I/O on the data in question. To accomplish that, we can use an ALTER TABLESPACE statement and simply offline/online the tablespace that contains our data. That has the side effect of flushing the buffer cache of blocks for that tablespace.

**NOTE**
*Unless you have mounted your disks using* directio *(an option on many Unix systems) or are using raw partitions, the operating system will cache your data. Therefore, a physical I/O operation may not be a read from disk, but rather a read from the operating system file system buffer. That will affect the numbers you see in this example radically, because a read from the operating system file system buffer will complete much faster than a physical I/O operation.*

The procedure we'll use to automate this test is as follows:

1. Take offline the tablespace our BIG_TABLE is in (USERS, on my system), and then put it back online.

2. Set the session-level parameter DB_FILE_MULTIBLOCK_READ_COUNT to the value passed in.

3. Enable tracing with wait events and run a full scan of the BIG_TABLE using a uniquely identifiable query (so when we use TKPROF on the trace file, it will be clear which query used which value for the multiblock read count).

4. Turn off the trace event so our TKPROF report will have only relevant information in it.

    Here is the procedure:

```
ops$tkyte@ORA920> create or replace procedure
  2  full_scan_big_table( p_dbmrc in number )
  3  as
  4      l_cnt number;
  5  begin
  6      execute immediate
  7      'alter tablespace users offline';
  8
  9      execute immediate
 10      'alter tablespace users online';
 11
 12      execute immediate
 13      'alter session set
 14       db_file_multiblock_read_count=' || p_dbmrc;
 15
 16      execute immediate
```

```
         17        'alter session set events
         18         ''10046 trace name context forever, level 12''';
         19
         20        execute immediate
         21        'select /*+ FULL(bt_mbrc_' || p_dbmrc || ') */ count(*)
         22          from big_table.big_table bt_mbrc_' || p_dbmrc
         23          INTO l_cnt;
         24
         25        execute immediate
         26        'alter session set events
         27         ''10046 trace name context off''';
         28  end;
         29  /
         Procedure created.
```

Now, we are ready to test various values of the multiblock read count to see how many I/O requests to the operating system each query will perform. We will use this block of code:

```
ops$tkyte@ORA920> begin
    2        for i in 0..9
    3        loop
    4            full_scan_big_table( power(2,i) );
    5        end loop;
    6  end;
    7  /
Procedure created.
```

This simply calls our routine with multiblock read count values of 1, 2, 4, 8, 16, ... up to 512, using powers of 2.

After running TKPROF, we receive the following report for a DB_FILE_MULTIBLOCK _READ_COUNT of 16:

```
select /*+ FULL(bt_mbrc_16) */ count(*)
   from big_table.big_table bt_mbrc_16
```

| call | count | cpu | elapsed | disk | query | current | rows |
|------|-------|-----|---------|------|-------|---------|------|
| Parse | 1 | 0.00 | 0.00 | 0 | 0 | 0 | 0 |
| Execute | 1 | 0.00 | 0.00 | 0 | 0 | 0 | 0 |
| Fetch | 1 | **7.10** | **7.59** | 26535 | 27065 | 0 | 1 |
| total | 3 | **7.10** | **7.59** | 26535 | 27065 | 0 | 1 |

```
-------  ----------------------------------------------------------
      1  SORT AGGREGATE (cr=27065 r=26535 w=0 time=7590145 us)
1908096    TABLE ACCESS FULL BIG_TABLE
                  (cr=27065 r=26535 w=0 time=5075896 us)
```

Elapsed times include waiting on following events:
  Event waited on                    Times   Max. Wait   Total Waited

```
----------------------------  Waited  ----------  ------------
db file scattered read          1670      0.02         1.54
db file sequential read            3      0.00         0.00
```

For the ten queries I ran, the *only* variations in the TKPROF report were the text in bold, in two wait events: db file scattered read (a wait for multiblock I/O) and db file sequential read (a wait for single-block I/O). The interesting numbers are the times waited and the total waited statistics. Table 8-1 shows a summary of what I observed.

This test shows us a few interesting things:

■ There is a direct correlation between the number of times you wait and the number of blocks divided by the multiblock read count, up to a point. There is a 1:1 correlation at first, then 2:1, then 4:1, and so on, up to 128, where it remains 128:1 constantly.

■ More is not always better. Values above 16 for the multiblock read count actually appear to have significantly increased the service times on my particular system (your mileage will vary on this test). Every machine you run this on might return different results. For example, on another machine, the wait events were much larger and the best performance was observed at with the multiblock read count set to 128.

■ Single-block I/O is measured differently than multiblock I/O is measured. A multiblock read count of 1 removed waits for scattered reads but placed them squarely in the sequential read column.

| Multiblock Read Count | Scattered Read | | Sequential Read | |
|---|---|---|---|---|
| | Times Waited | Total Waited | Times Waited | Total Waited |
| 1 | 0 | 0 | 26,521 | 1.47 |
| 2 | 13,258 | 1.56 | 5 | 0 |
| 4 | 6,631 | 1.36 | 6 | 0 |
| 8 | 3,318 | 1.58 | 5 | 0 |
| 16 | 1,670 | 1.54 | 3 | 0 |
| 32 | 846 | 2.52 | 3 | 0 |
| 64 | 433 | 2.59 | 1 | 0 |
| 128 | 227 | 3.24 | 1 | 0 |
| 256 | 226 | 3.20 | 1 | 0 |
| 512 | 226 | 3.18 | 0 | 0 |

**TABLE 8-1.** *DB_FILE_MULTIBLOCK_READ_COUNT Value Effects*

The times-waited correlation with the multiblock read count is something that we could have anticipated, perhaps. It makes sense that if you read one block at a time, you'll wait for each block; if you read two blocks at a time, you'll have half the wait events, and so on. In this case, on a single-user system, the times did not change much, but we would expect some variation in a true multiuser environment, as people compete for this scarce resource (disk).

What we might not have anticipated is the cutoff at 128 we observed. Apparently, on my system, either the operating system or Oracle will not perform a read larger than 128 × 8KB (my block size), or 1MB. If you run this test yourself, you may discover a different breakpoint. Oracle is aware of this number and costs the query accordingly. In other words, Oracle does not believe that the cost to full-scan with a multiblock read count of 512 is less than 256 or 128. For example, I executed the following on my system:

```
set autotrace traceonly explain
alter session set db_file_multiblock_read_count = 1;
select /*+ FULL(b) */ count(*) from big_table.big_table b;
alter session set db_file_multiblock_read_count = 2;
select /*+ FULL(b) */ count(*) from big_table.big_table b;
alter session set db_file_multiblock_read_count = 4;
...
select /*+ FULL(b) */ count(*) from big_table.big_table b;
alter session set db_file_multiblock_read_count = 512;
select /*+ FULL(b) */ count(*) from big_table.big_table b;
set autotrace off
```

I observed these costs:

| DB_FILE MULTIBLOCK_READ _COUNT | Cost |
| --- | --- |
| 1 | 16,139 |
| 2 | 10,227 |
| 4 | 6,481 |
| 8 | 4,108 |
| 16 | 2,603 |
| 32 | 1,650 |
| 64 | 1,046 |
| 128 | 664 |
| 256 | 664 |
| 512 | 664 |

So, you can see that Oracle knew that 128 is the maximum—it costed the queries the same above that threshold. Note that this shows a "cheap" way to find the maximum reasonable value for DB_FILE_MULTIBLOCK_READ_COUNT on your system, without doing any I/O.

What we can take away from these observations—putting together the time waited by multiblock read count size and the cost of the queries—is that perhaps we don't want to set our multiblock read count above 16 on this particular system. For example, a setting of 32 would deflate the cost of doing a full scan, but it would actually be more expensive than doing the scan with a setting of 16 on this system (a Red Hat Linux system running on conventional, slow IDE drives). On another machine (running Sun Solaris on SCSI drives), my breakoff point was between 64 and 128 multiblock reads.

The multiblock read count threshold depends on your operating system and hardware. You will want to run this test many times, on as many different devices as you can, to get an overall view of what might be best on your system. Also, this points out the usefulness of gathering system statistics on your own machine (with Oracle9i Release 2 and later). Each machine will have its own unique fingerprint as far as performance profiles go.

## Full Scans and the High-Water Mark

The last item of note about a full scan is the fact that a full scan always reads all of the blocks "below the high-water mark" for a segment. Any block that, at some point, contained data will be scanned in a full scan. Consider this trivial example. We'll create a table, scan it, and observe the blocks scanned. Then we'll delete most of the rows in this table and do it again. Then we'll rebuild it and observe the results.

```
ops$tkyte@ORA920> create table t as select * from all_objects;
Table created.

ops$tkyte@ORA920> set autotrace on
ops$tkyte@ORA920> select count(*) from t;

  COUNT(*)
----------
     30545


Execution Plan
----------------------------------------------------------
   0      SELECT STATEMENT Optimizer=CHOOSE
   1    0   SORT (AGGREGATE)
   2    1     TABLE ACCESS (FULL) OF 'T'

Statistics
----------------------------------------------------------
...
       419  consistent gets
...

ops$tkyte@ORA920> set autotrace off

ops$tkyte@ORA920> delete from t where owner <> 'SCOTT';
30532 rows deleted.

ops$tkyte@ORA920> set autotrace on
ops$tkyte@ORA920> select count(*) from t;
```

```
    COUNT(*)
----------
          13

Statistics
----------------------------------------------------------
...
         419  consistent gets
```

Notice how Oracle did exactly the same number of consistent gets (logical I/Os). That is because each and every block under the high-water mark—all of the blocks that at some point contained data—must be inspected. They may or may not still have data on them. It is not possible to say until after we inspect them. Let's rebuild the table.

```
ops$tkyte@ORA920> set autotrace off
ops$tkyte@ORA920> alter table t move;
Table altered.

ops$tkyte@ORA920> set autotrace on
ops$tkyte@ORA920> select count(*) from t;

    COUNT(*)
----------
          13

Statistics
----------------------------------------------------------
...
           4  consistent gets
...
```

This removes all of those blocks. Now, there are only enough blocks below the high-water mark to actually hold the 13 rows of data.

This is something to consider if you have periodic purges of large amounts of information in a table that you full-scan occasionally (or frequently). You may want to use methods other than a simple DELETE, which does not lower the high-water mark, to perform your purge:

- Use partitioning. You can simply truncate or drop the partition with data to be purged. These acts lower the high-water mark or eliminate it altogether.

- Use CREATE TABLE TEMP AS SELECT <*data to keep*>, followed by DROP OLD_TABLE and RENAME TEMP; that is, copy the data to be retained instead of deleting the data to be purged.

## ROWID Access

ROWIDs in Oracle are physical addresses of data. A ROWID contains information about a row regarding the file, block, and row on the block. A rowid also contains other bits of data such as the relative file number and the OBJECT_ID. The supplied package DBMS_ROWID can be used to extract any of these pieces of information. If you have a ROWID, getting to the row is simple.

Oracle just reads that file/block and goes to the row on the block as directed by the ROWID. A ROWID is perhaps the fastest way to a particular row. However, using ROWIDs to get many thousands of rows will not be the fastest way in all cases. If you have thousands of rows to retrieve, a large bulk operation may be much more efficient.

Normally, ROWIDs are used to access a table after an index scan of some sort. That is, suppose that you issue a query such as this:

```
select * from table where indexed_column = value;
```

Oracle would scan the index on the indexed column, retrieve the ROWID of the row it points to, and then access the table by ROWID, doing a read of that specific file and block. There are other ways to use ROWIDs, however.

## ROWIDs to Speed Searches

The following is one of the most popular queries on one of my systems at work:

```
select *
   from wwc_people_people
 where ROWID in ( select row_id
                    from wwc_fast_people
                   where string like :bv
                     and ROWNUM < 101 )
 order by last_name;
```

That is a query that does a people search. Every night, we refresh a small warehouse table with all of the employee information. This is a very "fat" table, with many fields. Additionally, after the table is refreshed, we create another table.

```
insert /*+ append */ into wwc_fast_people
select ROWID row_id, upper(last_name)||'/'||
       upper(first_name) || ..<selected fields> string
   from wwc_people_people;
```

Here, we are storing the ROWIDs of a table in another table, building our own index structure for fast searching. We then use this table in a subquery, limiting the hits to some number of rows (100 in this example). Here, we simply traded a full scan of a big, fat table for a full scan of a much smaller, skinny table, using the skinny table like an index.

## ROWID Ranges

Another use of ROWID access involves ROWID ranges. In the section on analytics later in this chapter, we'll walk through an analytic query example that does something useful. It will produce ROWID ranges that cover a table. You can have that query return four ROWID pairs. Then the following would retrieve each and every row in the table at least once and at most once:

```
Select * from t where ROWID between :a1 and :a2
Union all select * from t where ROWID between :b1 and :b2
Union all select * from t where ROWID between :c1 and :c2
Union all select * from t where ROWID between :d1 and :d2
```

Interesting you say, but how is this useful? If you recall from the sections on parallel processing in Chapter 3, one of the ways in which you can speed up the processing of your batch operations is to parallelize your own code. Using ROWID ranges, you can parallelize any operations against a single table easily, just by running four copies of your stored procedure, each working against a different slice of the table. This is better than trying to use primary key ranges or some predicate, since it not only allows you to run more than one copy of your program (decreasing the total time to completion), but it also ensures that each copy works on data that is physically located together. The first copy of the program will not be contending with the second copy of the program for the same shared disk resources.

If you run a parallel query and look at the generated SQL, you'll discover that this is, in effect, how a parallel query works in Oracle: A single full scan of a table is broken into many ROWID range scans. This might not be as obvious in releases of Oracle after version 8.1.6.3, the queries you see in the shared pool now use a built in PX_GRANULE clause, but in prior releases, you would clearly see ROWID ranges. For example, in Oracle8i Release 8.1.5, a parallel full scan against a BIG_TABLE might look like:

```
SELECT /*+ PIV_SSF */ SYS_OP_MSR(COUNT(*))
FROM (SELECT /*+ NO_EXPAND ROWID(A2) */ 0
FROM "BIG_TABLE" A2
WHERE ROWID BETWEEN :B1 AND :B2) A1
```

But in Oracle8i 8.1.6.3 and later, you would see:

```
SELECT /*+ PIV_SSF */ SYS_OP_MSR(COUNT(*))
FROM (SELECT /*+ NO_EXPAND ROWID(A2) */ 0
FROM "BIG_TABLE" PX_GRANULE(0, BLOCK_RANGE, DYNAMIC)  A2) A1
```

Under the covers though, it is doing the equivalent of ROWID ranges.

# Index Scans

Index scans are perhaps the most familiar access path. You see them all of the time, as in this example:

```
scott@ORA920> select * from emp where empno = 1234;

Execution Plan
------------------------------------------------------------
SELECT STATEMENT Optimizer=CHOOSE (Cost=2 Card=1 Bytes=32)
  TABLE ACCESS (BY INDEX ROWID) OF 'EMP' (Cost=2 Card=1 Bytes=32)
    INDEX (UNIQUE SCAN) OF 'EMP_PK' (UNIQUE)
```

Here, we see a unique index scan of an index EMP_PK. This will, in effect, turn our key value of 1234 into a ROWID, and then that ROWID will be used to access that row directly in the table.

### B*Tree Structure

B*Tree, or what I call conventional, indexes are the most commonly used type of indexing structure in the database. They are similar in implementation to a binary search tree you might have learned about in a computer science course. Their goal is to minimize the amount of time Oracle spends searching for data. Loosely speaking, if you have an index on a number column, the structure might look as shown in Figure 8-1.

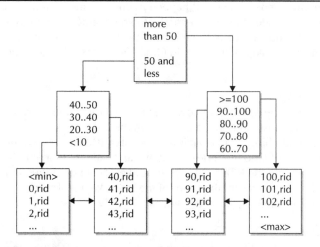

**FIGURE 8-1.**  *The structure of a B\*Tree index on a number column*

The lowest-level blocks in the tree, called *leaf nodes*, contain every indexed key and a ROWID (*rid* in the figure) that points to the row it is indexing. The interior blocks, above the leaf nodes, are known as branch blocks. They are used to navigate through the structure. For example, if we wanted to find the value 42 in the index, we would start at the top of the tree and go to the left. We would inspect that block and discover we needed to go to the block in the range less than 50 to 40. This block would be the leaf block and would point us to the rows that contained the number 42.

It is interesting to note that the leaf nodes of the index are actually a doubly linked list. Once we find out where to start in the leaf nodes—once we have found that first 42 value, in this example—doing an ordered scan (also known as an index-range scan) of values is easy. We don't need to navigate the structure anymore; we just go forward through the leaf nodes. That makes solving a predicate, such as the following, pretty simple:

```
where x between 20 and 30
```

Oracle finds the first index block that contains 20, and then just walks horizontally through the linked list of leaf nodes, until it finally hits a value that is greater than 30.

One of the properties of a B\*Tree is that all leaf blocks should be at the same level in the tree. This level is also known as the *height* of the index, meaning that all the nodes above the leaf nodes only point to lower, more specific nodes; entries in the leaf nodes point to specific ROWIDs, or a range of ROWIDs. Most B\*Tree indexes will have a height of 2 or 3, even for millions of records. This means that it will take, in general, two or three I/Os to find your key in the index.

In general, the B\*Tree is an excellent, general-purpose indexing mechanism that works well for large and small tables and experiences little, if any, degradation as the size of the underlying table grows.

There are two primary index scans that happen frequently: index-unique scans and index-range scans. Most people understand conceptually the mechanics of these types of index scans, so we'll take just a quick look at them here. Then we'll concentrate on the other types of index access plans: index-skip scans (new in Oracle9i), index full scans and fast-full scans, and index joins.

### Index-Unique Scans

With index-unique scans, the optimizer knows that in the index, the indexed columns are unique. There will be, *at most,* one row returned from the index lookup.

There really is no such thing as a nonunique index in a B*Tree. In a nonunique index, Oracle simply adds the row's ROWID to the index key to make it unique. In a unique index, as defined by you, Oracle does not add the ROWID to the index key. In a nonunique index, we will find the data is sorted by index key values (in the order of the index key) and then by ROWID. In a unique index, the data is sorted by the index key values only.

### Index-Range Scans

With index-range scans, the optimizer knows that zero, one, or more rows may be returned. There is no assurance that the index lookup will return at most one row.

It is interesting to note that an index-range scan may be performed in one of two directions. Normally, the index is read in ascending order, from low to high, but it may also be used backwards and read in descending order. Consider the following:

```
scott@ORA920> select empno
  2    from emp
  3    where empno < 5000
  4    order by empno desc
  5  /

Execution Plan
----------------------------------------------------------
   0      SELECT STATEMENT Optimizer=CHOOSE (Cost=2 Card=1 Bytes=3)
   1    0   INDEX (RANGE SCAN DESCENDING) OF 'EMP_PK' (UNIQUE)
            (Cost=1 Card=1 Bytes=3)
```

Here, Oracle recognized it could avoid the sort if it reads the index backwards.

There are other ways in which the database can use these indexes. Oracle can not only locate data by key or retrieve data sorted, but it can also find minimum and maximum values, as in this example:

```
scott@ORA920> select max(empno) from emp;
MAX(EMPNO)
----------
      7934


Execution Plan
----------------------------------------------------------
   0      SELECT STATEMENT Optimizer=CHOOSE (Cost=2 Card=1 Bytes=3)
   1    0   SORT (AGGREGATE)
```

```
     2    1       INDEX (FULL SCAN (MIN/MAX)) OF 'EMP_PK' (UNIQUE)
                  (Cost=2 Card=14 Bytes=42)
```

Here, the query plan seems to indicate a full scan of the index will take place; however, the MIN/MAX modifier indicates that the database knows to stop. It will not really full-scan the entire structure looking for the MAX(EMPNO). Instead, it will just start at the back of the index and read the last (highest) value.

### Index-Skip Scans

Normally, in order for an index to be used, the columns defined on the leading edge of the index would be referenced in the query. Consider this table and index:

```
create table t ( a, b, c, d, e, f, g );
create index t_idx on t(a,b,c);
```

Queries such as the following would, in general, use that index T_IDX in order to retrieve the rows from table T.

```
select * from t where a = :a;
select * from t where a = :a and b = :b;
select * from t where a = :a and b = :b and c = :c;
```

However, a query such as the following would not use the index:

```
select * from t where b = :b and c = :c;
```

In Oracle8i and before, the index T_IDX would not be a suitable candidate, although you could use an index hint to tell the database to full-scan the index structure—to find the row(s) with b = :b and c = :c, and then access table T.

```
ops$tkyte@ORA817DEV> create table t
  2   as
  3   select mod(ROWNUM,3) a, ROWNUM b, ROWNUM c, object_name d
  4      from all_objects;
Table created.

ops$tkyte@ORA817DEV> alter table t modify a not null;
Table altered.

ops$tkyte@ORA817DEV> create index t_idx on t(a,b,c);
Index created.

ops$tkyte@ORA817DEV> analyze table t compute statistics;
Table analyzed.

ops$tkyte@ORA817DEV> set autotrace traceonly explain
ops$tkyte@ORA817DEV> select * from t where b = 1 and c = 1;

Execution Plan
```

```
          ----------------------------------------------------------
             0          SELECT STATEMENT Optimizer=CHOOSE (Cost=5 Card=1 Bytes=35)
             1     0       TABLE ACCESS (FULL) OF 'T' (Cost=5 Card=1 Bytes=35)

ops$tkyte@ORA817DEV> select /*+ index( t t_idx ) */ * from t
  2  where b = 1 and c = 1;

Execution Plan
          ----------------------------------------------------------
             0          SELECT STATEMENT Optimizer=CHOOSE (Cost=95 Card=1 Bytes=35)
             1     0       TABLE ACCESS (BY INDEX ROWID) OF 'T' (Cost=95 Card=1 Bytes=35)
             2     1         INDEX (FULL SCAN) OF 'T_IDX' (NON-UNIQUE) (Cost=94 Card=1)

ops$tkyte@ORA817DEV> set autotrace off
```

In Oracle9i and later, however, this behavior is radically modified. Oracle9i implements the concept of an index-skip scan. It will be employed under the following conditions:

- You reference interior columns (B and C in our example) in the predicate.

- The optimizer knows the column(s) on the leading edge of the index has few discrete values (we used three values for A in the example).

When these conditions are true, the database will pretend the index is really *N* little index structures hidden inside one big one. In our example, it would be like three index structures: one where A = 0, another where A = 1, and a third where A = 2. The database will "skip around" in the index looking for B = 1 and C = 1 in each of these three virtual index structures. Running that same example in Oracle9i will result in the following query plan:

```
ops$tkyte@ORA920> set autotrace traceonly explain
ops$tkyte@ORA920> select * from t where b = 1 and c = 1;

Execution Plan
          ----------------------------------------------------------
             0          SELECT STATEMENT Optimizer=CHOOSE (Cost=5 Card=1 Bytes=33)
             1     0       TABLE ACCESS (BY INDEX ROWID) OF 'T' (Cost=5 Card=1 Bytes=33)
             2     1         INDEX (SKIP SCAN) OF 'T_IDX' (NON-UNIQUE) (Cost=4 Card=1)
```

So, this allows this index to be naturally used in more cases than before. In fact, this index could even be used to answer this query:

```
select * from t where c = 1;
```

Suppose that we modify the CREATE TABLE AS SELECT as follows:

```
ops$tkyte@ORA920> create table t
  2  as
  3  select mod(ROWNUM,3) a, mod(ROWNUM,3) b, ROWNUM c, object_name d
  4     from all_objects;
```

The query plan will again be an index-skip scan, since the leading edge of the index (A and B this time) is known to have few distinct values.

## Index Full Scans

An index full scan does not read every block in the index structure, contrary to what its name might imply and given our knowledge of what a full scan does. An index full scan processes all of the leaf blocks of an index, but only enough of the branch blocks to find the first leaf block.

If you refer back to Figure 8-1, you'll see that once you get to a leaf block in the index, the previous and next leaf blocks, in sorted order, are linked. That is, the leaf blocks are not only navigated by walking the branch blocks, but once you are on a leaf block, you can get to the next one simply by following a pointer. In fact, you can go backward or forward in the index structure using this doubly linked list.

So, an index full scan uses *single-block I/O* to read the index in order. It starts at the root block and branches down to the very first leaf block. Each of these blocks is read a single block at a time. Once you get to the first leaf block, you read each leaf block in order, a single block at a time.

One of the attributes of an index full scan is that it will read the data from the index *in sorted order, as it exists in the index structure.* So, an index full scan may be used to avoid a sort:

```
scott@ORA920> select empno, ename from emp order by empno;
14 rows selected.

Execution Plan
----------------------------------------------------------
   0      SELECT STATEMENT Optimizer=CHOOSE (Cost=2 Card=14 Bytes=112)
   1    0   TABLE ACCESS (BY INDEX ROWID) OF 'EMP' (Cost=2 Card=14 Bytes=112)
   2    1     INDEX (FULL SCAN) OF 'EMP_PK' (UNIQUE) (Cost=1 Card=14)
```

Here, we see the database is using the index in order to read the data sorted.

## Index Fast-Full Scans

An index fast-full scan differs significantly from an index full scan. An index fast-full scan has the following characteristics:

- It reads every block in the index structure, including all interior branch blocks.

- It employs multiblock reads, just like a table full scan does.

- It does not retrieve the data in sorted order.

In short, an index fast-full scan simply treats an index as if it were a skinnier version of the table itself. It reads the index data *N* blocks at a time, processes the data on leaf blocks, and ignores branch blocks when processing. It is able to read the entire index structure faster than an index full scan because it employs multiblock I/O.

Let's take the example we used in the section about full scans and modify these lines:

```
20      execute immediate
21      'select /*+ FULL(bt_mbrc_' || p_dbmrc || ') */ count(*)
```

```
22        from big_table.big_table bt_mbrc_' || p_dbmrc
23        INTO l_cnt;
```

We'll change them to the following:

```
20        execute immediate
21        'select count(*)
22        from big_table.big_table bt_mbrc_' || p_dbmrc
23        INTO l_cnt;
```

When we remove the FULL hint, the optimizer will change the plan from a full scan to this:

```
Rows       Row Source Operation
-------    ----------------------------------------------------
      1    SORT AGGREGATE (cr=4129 r=4117 w=0 time=5560153 us)
1908096      INDEX FAST FULL SCAN BIG_TABLE_PK
               (cr=4129 r=4117 w=0 time=3135411 us)(object id 31147
```

You can perform the same testing on the index fast-full scan we did on the full scan. You'll see analogous results in that the maximum read count will still be 128 and the optimum read size is 16 (or whatever you observe on your system).

So, the index fast-full scan is a high-speed method to use an index as a skinnier version of the table. It will be used, *in general*, when your query references only the indexed columns and a full scan of the table can be avoided by fast-full scanning this index instead. This is why it is sometimes advantageous to add what appears to be an unnecessary column to an index. An extra column or two at the end might be there not because you search by them, but rather, because you SELECT them in the select list. It should be noted that the index fast-full scan *cannot* be used in place of a sort, as the data is definitely not returned sorted from this type of index scan.

### Index Joins

An index join can be the path chosen to answer a query when multiple indexes exist on the table that contains all of the selected columns in the query (the table does not need to be accessed). Here, the optimizer will use some small number of indexes to perform the query, rather than accessing the table. It is most useful when you have a query of this form:

```
Select a, b, c
  From t
 Where a = :a
   And b = :b;
```

And there are indexes on A, B, and C (they could be concatenated indexes or indexes on individual columns). Suppose in the preceding example, we had an index on T(A) and T(B,C). The optimizer could choose to scan the index on T(A), scan the index on T(B,C), take the results, and join those subresults together by ROWID (remember the ROWID of the original source row is stored in the index), giving us the answer.

An example that you can observe for yourself can be constructed as follows. We'll copy the ALL_OBJECTS table, and index the OBJECT_ID column and the OWNER,OBJECT_TYPE columns:

```
ops$tkyte@ORA920> create table t
   2  as
   3  select * from all_objects;
Table created.

ops$tkyte@ORA920> create index t_idx1 on t(object_id);
Index created.

ops$tkyte@ORA920> create index t_idx2 on t(owner,object_type);
Index created.

ops$tkyte@ORA920> analyze table t
   2  compute statistics
   3  for table
   4  for all indexes
   5  for all indexed columns;
Table analyzed.
```

Now, when we run a query that needs the OBJECT_ID, OWNER, and OBJECT_TYPE columns, the database might perform an index join.

```
ops$tkyte@ORA920> set autotrace traceonly explain
ops$tkyte@ORA920> select object_id, owner, object_type
   2    from t
   3   where object_id between 100 and 2000
   4     and owner = 'SYS'
   5  /

Execution Plan
----------------------------------------------------------
   0      SELECT STATEMENT Optimizer=CHOOSE (Cost=9 Card=817 Bytes=13889)
   1    0   VIEW OF 'index$_join$_001' (Cost=9 Card=817 Bytes=13889)
   2    1     HASH JOIN
   3    2       INDEX (RANGE SCAN) OF 'T_IDX1' (NON-UNIQUE)
                 (Cost=10 Card=817 Bytes=13889)
   4    2       INDEX (RANGE SCAN) OF 'T_IDX2' (NON-UNIQUE)
                 (Cost=10 Card=817 Bytes=13889)
```

Here, the optimizer decided the best course of action would be to take these steps:

1. Read the T_IDX1 on T(OBJECT_ID) and find all of the OBJECT_ID/ROWIDs where the OBJECT_ID was between 100 and 2000.

2. Read the T_IDX2 on T(OWNER,OBJECT_TYPE) to find all column values and ROWIDs where OWNER = 'SYS'.

3. HASH JOIN those two subresults together to answer the query.

So, rather than picking one of the indexes, the database decided to use both indexes. That way, it could answer the query fully from the indexes and avoid accessing the table altogether.

We can see this is the optimal plan in this case when we use hints to have the optimizer just use one or the other index and compare the results with AUTOTRACE:

```
ops$tkyte@ORA920> set autotrace traceonly
ops$tkyte@ORA920> select object_id, owner, object_type
  2    from t
  3   where object_id between 100 and 2000
  4     and owner = 'SYS'
  5   /
1157 rows selected.

...
131  consistent gets

ops$tkyte@ORA920> select /*+ index( t t_idx1 ) */ object_id, owner, object_type
  2    from t
  3   where object_id between 100 and 2000
  4     and owner = 'SYS'
  5   /
1157 rows selected.


Execution Plan
----------------------------------------------------------
   0      SELECT STATEMENT Optimizer=CHOOSE (Cost=151 Card=817 Bytes=13889)
   1    0   TABLE ACCESS (BY INDEX ROWID) OF 'T' (Cost=151 Card=817 Bytes=13889)
   2    1     INDEX (RANGE SCAN) OF 'T_IDX1' (NON-UNIQUE) (Cost=6 Card=1846)


...
1777  consistent gets

ops$tkyte@ORA920> select /*+ index( t t_idx2 ) */ object_id, owner, object_type
  2    from t
  3   where object_id between 100 and 2000
  4     and owner = 'SYS'
  5   /
1157 rows selected.

Execution Plan
----------------------------------------------------------
   0      SELECT STATEMENT Optimizer=CHOOSE (Cost=48 Card=817 Bytes=13889)
   1    0   TABLE ACCESS (BY INDEX ROWID) OF 'T' (Cost=48 Card=817 Bytes=13889)
   2    1     INDEX (RANGE SCAN) OF 'T_IDX2' (NON-UNIQUE) (Cost=49 Card=13510)
...
667  consistent gets
```

Since the goal, *in general*, is to reduce logical I/O, the plan with the least amount of consistent gets wins here. Using the two indexes and turning our single-table query into what effectively amounts to a two-table join using indexes as tables is the superior plan.

## Cluster Scans

If you recall from Chapter 7, there are two types of cluster objects in Oracle:

- ■ **B\*Tree cluster**   There is a single cluster key index that is used to convert a cluster key into a database block address. All rows in the cluster with that key value will be found by starting on that block and walking the list of blocks that contain data for that key.

- ■ **Hash cluster**   There is no auxiliary index, rather the hash key itself is hashed to point to a database block address. All rows in the cluster that have a key that hash to that value will be found by starting on that block and walking the list of blocks that contain data for that key.

So, a cluster access is simply the process of taking either the B\*Tree key or hash key, getting the root database block address that contains this data, and then following the chained list of blocks connected to this root block. You can think of this list of blocks as if they were overflow blocks.

# Understand Joins

In this section, we'll look at the most common join techniques and the mechanics behind them. We'll start with the most famous and the most simple of all join techniques: the nested-loop join. Next, we'll move onto the more complex bulk or large join operations: hash joins and sort-merge joins. We'll also discuss the Cartesian join. After that, we'll look at a couple special kinds of joins, variations on a theme if you will: anti-joins and full outer joins.

**NOTE**
*There are other types of joins that are used in certain conditions. For example, the star transformation feature is available for data warehousing queries. The logic behind that particular technique is worthy of a chapter in itself. In fact, Oracle Corporation does a pretty good job of describing it in the* Data Warehousing Guide.

## Nested Loops

A nested-loop join is the workhorse join method of the database, perhaps the most common join technique.

### Natural Joins with Nested Loops

You'll recognize a query plan such as this:

```
scott@ORA920> select ename, dname
  2  from emp, dept
  3  where emp.deptno = dept.deptno
  4  /

Execution Plan
```

```
    ----------------------------------------------------------
    0       SELECT STATEMENT Optimizer=CHOOSE (Cost=4 Card=1909 Bytes=55361)
    1    0    NESTED LOOPS (Cost=4 Card=1909 Bytes=55361)
    2    1     TABLE ACCESS (FULL) OF 'EMP' (Cost=2 Card=14 Bytes=98)
    3    1     TABLE ACCESS (BY INDEX ROWID) OF 'DEPT' (Cost=2 Card=136 Bytes=2992)
    4    3      INDEX (UNIQUE SCAN) OF 'DEPT_PK' (UNIQUE)
```

This will be processed using the following pseudo code logic:

```
For x in ( select * from emp )
Loop
   Index lookup the ROWID for X.DEPTNO
   Select * from dept where ROWID = that ROWID
   Output joined record
End loop
```

It is sort of a brute force, logical approach to the problem. Pick one of the tables, iterate over its rows, and for each row, index-probe another table and find the matching rows.

This join technique is generally good at getting the first row back from a result set quickly. For example, with the sample query plan, we can get our first row back instantaneously. All the database needs to do is this:

1. Read the first block of the EMP table.

2. Take that first row and use its DEPTNO value.

3. Read the two or three index blocks that, at most, it takes to find that key value in the index.

4. Read the referenced block in the DEPT table.

So, in just four or five logical I/O operations, we can start getting data back in our client application.

## Outer Joins with Nested Loops

Nested loops can process a natural join, as in the previous example, or they can be used to process an outer join (we'll look at the special case of the full outer join separately in another section). Consider, for example, if we code the following:

```
scott@ORA920> alter session set optimizer_goal=first_rows;
Session altered.

scott@ORA920> select ename, dname
  2  from emp, dept
  3  where emp.deptno(+) = dept.deptno
  4  /


Execution Plan
----------------------------------------------------------
    0       SELECT STATEMENT Optimizer=FIRST_ROWS (Cost=43 Card=1909 Bytes=55361)
    1    0    NESTED LOOPS (OUTER) (Cost=43 Card=1909 Bytes=55361)
```

```
2    1      TABLE ACCESS (FULL) OF 'DEPT' (Cost=2 Card=409 Bytes=8998)
3    1      TABLE ACCESS (BY INDEX ROWID) OF 'EMP' (Cost=2 Card=5 Bytes=35)
4    3        INDEX (RANGE SCAN) OF 'EMP_DEPTNO_IDX' (NON-UNIQUE)
```

Notice here that the plan has flipped the join order, so that DEPT is now the "driving" table in the query. The pseudo code for processing this query is as follows:

```
For x in ( select * from DEPT )
Loop
    Found_record = FALSE
    For y in ( select * from EMP where EMP.deptno = X.deptno )
    Loop
        Found_record = TRUE;
        Output joined record
    End loop
    If (NOT found_record)
    Then
        OUTPUT a record anyway, with NULL values for EMP columns
    End if
End loop
```

That is the essence of an outer join: It will make up a record in the joined-to table and output every record from the driving table, regardless of whether there was a match. As you saw, the outer join forces a specific join order using nested loops. There is no way EMP can be used as the driving table in this plan; it must use the DEPT table.

Because using an outer join limits the options available to the optimizer, you should look at every query that uses an outer join and ask yourself if it is really necessary. You would be surprised how many times an outer join is used "just in case" it might be needed. If you do not need that outer join, you should remove it.

The nested-loop join technique is generally bad at getting the last row in a result set back quickly. Consider the example we used in Chapter 6, repeated briefly here:

```
select /*+ RULE */ t1.object_name, t2.object_name
  from t t1, t t2
 where t1.object_id = t2.object_id
   and t1.owner = 'WMSYS'
```

```
call       count    cpu  elapsed    disk      query cur      rows
-------  -------  ------  -------  -------  ---------- ----  -------
Parse          1   0.00     0.00        0           0    0        0
Execute        1   0.00     0.00        0           0    0        0
Fetch      35227 912.07  3440.70  1154555   121367981    0   528384
-------  -------  ------  -------  -------  ---------- ----  -------
total      35229 912.07  3440.70  1154555   121367981    0   528384
```

```
Execution Plan
----------------------------------------------------------
   0      SELECT STATEMENT Optimizer=HINT: RULE
   1    0   TABLE ACCESS (BY INDEX ROWID) OF 'T'
```

```
2    1        NESTED LOOPS
3    2          TABLE ACCESS (FULL) OF 'T'
4    2          INDEX (RANGE SCAN) OF 'T_IDX' (NON-UNIQUE)
```

Here, because of the sheer volume of data, using a nested-loop join is extremely inefficient. (You'll see in the next section how this query's performance improves when it uses a hash join.) If our goal were to run this query and just fetch the first ten rows for display, the nested-loop approach would be great. If we wanted to get the last row of data, however, it would take a very long time and a lot of logical I/Os—121,367,981 in this example—to get this result. This is because the time to iterate over hundreds of thousands of rows and perform hundreds of thousands of index lookups adds up. Even though each index-range scan is very fast, doing 100,000 of them takes considerable time. (For the full story behind this example, see http://asktom.oracle.com/~tkyte/lios.html.)

# Hash Joins

Before we get into the mechanics of the hash join, let's look at an example. Using the same query as in the previous section, without the RULE hint, and letting the optimizer choose our plan for us, we might find the following results:

```
select t1.object_name, t2.object_name
  from t t1, t t2
 where t1.object_id = t2.object_id
   and t1.owner = 'WMSYS'
```

| call | count | cpu | elapsed | disk | query | current | rows |
|------|-------|-----|---------|------|-------|---------|------|
| Parse | 1 | 0.00 | 0.00 | 0 | 0 | 0 | 0 |
| Execute | 1 | 0.00 | 0.00 | 0 | 0 | 0 | 0 |
| Fetch | 35227 | 5.63 | 9.32 | 23380 | 59350 | 0 | 528384 |
| total | 35229 | 5.63 | 9.33 | 23380 | 59350 | 0 | 528384 |

```
Rows     Row Source Operation
-------  ---------------------------------------------------
 528384  HASH JOIN
   8256    TABLE ACCESS FULL T
1833856    TABLE ACCESS FULL T
```

Yes, that is ten seconds, versus an hour using the nested-loop approach. And the amount of logical I/O is radically reduced, down to 0.04% (4/100 percent) of the nested-loop approach. How did this happen? It is all in how a hash join takes place.

## Hash Natural Joins

Under optimal conditions, Oracle will take the smaller of the two tables—in this example, it would take the results of t1.owner = 'WMSYS' after full-scanning T1—and create an in-memory hash table of this result. Since this table has only 8,256 rows (according to the TKPROF report shown here), this would have most likely been a pure RAM-based hash table. This hash table is not a hash cluster, but rather a more conventional hash table such as the hash tables used in Java or many 3GL languages as utilities/data structures. The join key—OBJECT_ID, in this case—was hashed to an index in the hash table. The hash table is an array and the row that went with that hash key was stored in that index entry.

So, Oracle now has an in-memory structure—an array—that it can access very quickly. If you get an OBJECT_ID value from T2 now, Oracle can hash it and index in memory the corresponding row from T1. Since this hash table is in our private memory, accessing this data structure does not incur the same latching activity that a normal logical I/O would. This is the major cause of our reduced logical I/Os here: Instead of constantly going to the buffer cache to get index blocks over and over, Oracle retrieved the 8,256 rows and hashed them in our private memory. This way, Oracle can access them at will, without needing to latch them. No one else has access to these rows, so protecting them with a latch is not necessary.

Once Oracle hashed the smaller table into memory, it full-scans the larger table—T2 in this example—then, for each row, it hashes the OBJECT_ID it retrieved, finds the matching rows (or not) in the hash table, and returns the joined image. The client application would need to wait for Oracle to full-scan T1 and hash it before getting the first row back, but then the remaining rows would start coming as fast or faster than we could receive them. It takes a while to get the first row, but getting all of the rows is as fast as possible.

The processing is a little different if the hash table being developed does not fit entirely in memory. In that case, Oracle will use TEMP space to hold portions (partitions) of the hash table and perhaps of the table that will be used to probe this hash table. When the hash area fills up and Oracle needs to use TEMP, it will find the largest partition within the hash table and write that out to TEMP. (Oracle actually uses a two-part hash table: there is a partition, or section, of the hash table a row belongs to and then a position in that partition.) Any new row retrieved that belongs to that on-disk partition will modify the on-disk image to contain it.

This process continues until the entire hash table is built, with part of it in memory and part of it on disk. Then Oracle begins reading from the other source. As before, the join key will be hashed in order to look up the other value. If the hashed value points to a row in memory, the join is completed and the row is returned from the join. If the row points to a hash partition on disk, Oracle will store this row in TEMP, using the same partitioning scheme it did for the original source data. So, when the first pass is done—all of the rows that could be joined to the in-memory hash table have been joined and some number of partitions remain in TEMP—each partition will be joined only to rows in the other corresponding partition. Oracle will then process each on-disk temporary partition one by one, reading them into memory and joining them, resulting in the final answer.

## Hash Outer Joins

So, now that we understand how a natural join works using hash joins—both in-memory and when some disk is required—we can look at how a hash outer join works. It is a little counterintuitive; at first, I thought the documentation was wrong. The Oracle documentation (the Oracle *Performance Guide*) states, "The outer table (whose rows are being preserved) is used to build the hash table, and the inner table is used to probe the hash table." That seemed backwards.

If I were to sit down and write the hash-join algorithm, I would have gone in the other direction. I would have hashed the table whose rows were *not* being preserved, and then read the table whose rows were being preserved, probing the hash table to see whether there was a row to join to. Oracle has chosen to do it the other way.

Consider a hash outer join such as this one:

```
scott@ORA920> select ename, dname
  2  from emp, dept
  3  where emp.deptno(+) = dept.deptno
  4  /

ENAME        DNAME
----------   --------------
SMITH        RESEARCH
ALLEN        SALES
...
FORD         RESEARCH
MILLER       ACCOUNTING
             OPERATIONS
15 rows selected.

Execution Plan
------------------------------------------------------------
   0      SELECT STATEMENT Optimizer=CHOOSE (Cost=5 Card=1909 Bytes=55361)
   1    0   HASH JOIN (OUTER) (Cost=5 Card=1909 Bytes=55361)
   2    1     TABLE ACCESS (FULL) OF 'DEPT' (Cost=2 Card=409 Bytes=8998)
   3    1     TABLE ACCESS (FULL) OF 'EMP' (Cost=2 Card=14 Bytes=98)
```

Here is how this is processed:

1. The DEPT table is scanned and hashed.

2. The EMP table is scanned and for each row.

3. The DEPT hash table is probed for matches. When a match is found, the row is output and the entry in the hash table is marked as matched to a row.

4. After the EMP table is exhausted, the DEPT hash table is gone over once again, and any rows that are not marked as matched are output with NULL values for the EMP columns.

Notice that the output of the previous query has SMITH, ALLEN, ..., FORD, MILLER in that order. Suppose you perform this query:

```
scott@ORA920> select ename
  2      from emp;

ENAME
----------
SMITH
ALLEN
...
FORD
MILLER
```

You will find that the hash outer join result set presents the rows in order of the EMP table, and then at the end of the result set are all of the unmatched rows from DEPT.

**NOTE**
*On your system, the rows may be in a different order. The results,
however, will be consistent on your machine. The order you see
them in the hash join will be the order you see them from a simple
full scan.*

In general, a hash join is excellent at joining two large sets or a small set with a large set. It is slow at getting the first row, because one of the sources must be hashed into memory (optimally), or memory and disk entirely, before the first row is returned. However, its performance in getting the remaining rows, especially when the hash table fits in memory, is excellent.

# Sort-Merge Joins

A sort-merge join is different from both a nested-loop and hash join in that there is no concept of a driving table, as there is in those methods. In a nutshell, a sort-merge join will sort input set 1, sort input set 2, and then merge the results.

Sort-merge joins are generally less efficient than hash joins, due to the fact that, in general, both input sets would need to be scanned and sorted. This is in contrast to hash joins, where only one input set is processed before data is output from the process. Sort-merge joins, in general, are useful in non-equijoin operations; that is, when the join condition is not an equality but a range comparison (for example, when the join operations are < or >=).

A sort-merge join might be used for a query to show every employee joined with every other employee who was hired on or after the day of hire for the first employee, like this:

```
scott@ORA920> explain plan for
  2  select a.ename, b.ename, a.hiredate, b.hiredate
  3    from emp a, emp b
  4   where a.hiredate <= b.hiredate
  5     and a.empno <> b.empno
  6  /
Explained.

scott@ORA920> @?/rdbms/admin/utlxpls
scott@ORA920> select plan_table_output from table(dbms_xplan.display);

PLAN_TABLE_OUTPUT
-----------------------------------------------------------------
```

| Id | Operation | Name | Rows | Bytes | Cost |
|-----|-------------------------|------|------|-------|------|
| 0 | SELECT STATEMENT | | 9 | 270 | 10 |
| 1 | MERGE JOIN | | 9 | 270 | 10 |
| 2 | SORT JOIN | | 14 | 210 | 5 |
| 3 | TABLE ACCESS FULL | EMP | 14 | 210 | 2 |
| * 4 | FILTER | | | | |
| * 5 | SORT JOIN | | | | |
| 6 | TABLE ACCESS FULL | EMP | 14 | 210 | 2 |

```
Predicate Information (identified by operation id):
```

```
    ----------------------------------------------------
    4 - filter("A"."EMPNO"<>"B"."EMPNO")
    5 - access("A"."HIREDATE"<="B"."HIREDATE")
        filter("A"."HIREDATE"<="B"."HIREDATE")
```

In this plan, EMP is read and sorted by HIREDATE (step 3). EMP is read again and sorted by HIREDATE (step 6). Then the sort-merge join takes place, applying the join condition A.HIREDATE <= B.HIREDATE. After that, the filter A.EMPNO <> B.EMPNO would be applied.

You would expect to see sort-merge joins only when performing non-equijoins, as in the example here. There are cases where the optimizer will choose to use a sort-merge join, however, if it sees an opportunity to bypass a sort for a GROUP BY or some other operation that it would need to do if hashing. As an example, we'll copy ALL_USERS and ALL_OBJECTS (just the structures) and lie to the optimizer, telling it ALL_USERS is very large and ALL_OBJECTS is modest in size, using DBMS_STATS.

```
ps$tkyte@ORA920> create table t1
    2  as
    3  select *
    4    from all_users
    5   where 1=0;
Table created.

ops$tkyte@ORA920> create index t1_username_idx on t1(username);
Index created.

ops$tkyte@ORA920> create table t2
    2  as
    3  select *
    4    from all_objects
    5   where 1=0;
Table created.

ops$tkyte@ORA920> exec dbms_stats.set_table_stats
    2  ( user, 'T1', numrows => 10000000, numblks => 1000000 );
PL/SQL procedure successfully completed.

ops$tkyte@ORA920> exec dbms_stats.set_table_stats
    2  ( user, 'T2', numrows => 10000, numblks => 1000 );
PL/SQL procedure successfully completed.

ops$tkyte@ORA920> set autotrace traceonly explain
ops$tkyte@ORA920> select t1.username, sum(t2.object_id)
    2    from t1, t2
    3   where t1.username = t2.owner (+)
    4   group by t1.username
    5  /

Execution Plan
----------------------------------------------------------
    0      SELECT STATEMENT Optimizer=CHOOSE
```

```
                    (Cost=158 Card=10000000 Bytes=470000000)
1    0    SORT (GROUP BY NOSORT) (Cost=158 Card=10000000 Bytes=470000000)
2    1      MERGE JOIN (OUTER) (Cost=158 Card=10000000 Bytes=470000000)
3    2        INDEX (FULL SCAN) OF 'T1_USERNAME_IDX' (NON-UNIQUE)
                (Cost=26 Card=10000000 Bytes=170000000)
4    2        SORT (JOIN) (Cost=155 Card=10000 Bytes=300000)
5    4          TABLE ACCESS (FULL) OF 'T2' (Cost=98 Card=10000 Bytes=300000)
```

Here, the optimizer sees it can read the index T1_USERNAME_IDX using an index full scan (which returns the data sorted by index key), sort this small table T2, and merge the two to do a GROUP BY NOSORT.

### NOTE
*GROUP BY does not always sort data. Even when sorting data, GROUP BY does a binary sort that may result in a different ordering of data than ORDER BY would return. The bottom line is that you should not rely on GROUP BY to sort data!*

This is more efficient in this case than hash-joining 10,000,000 rows with 10,000 rows and then sorting the resulting, at least, 10,000,000 rows (an outer join ensures there will be at least 10,000,000 rows, and there might be up to 10,010,000) to perform the GROUP BY operation.

## Cartesian Joins

A Cartesian join, also known as a Cartesian product, occurs whenever you have two tables referenced in a query that have no join conditions. In that case, every row in TABLE_A is joined to every row in TABLE_B. If TABLE_A has 100 rows and TABLE_B has 20 rows, the result set will contain 2,000 (100 × 20) rows.

Cartesian joins have a bad reputation, but for some queries, they are the only way to answer the question. The Oracle documentation includes statements such as, "Cartesian joins generally result from poorly written SQL." I say that if a query *needs* a Cartesian join, so be it. It is not poorly written SQL; rather, it is a requirement of the output.

"I have three tables in Oracle:

```
create table students
( registerNumber number constraint students_pk primary key,
  name varchar2(10) );

create table documentMaster
( documentId number constraint document_pk primary key,
  description varchar2(10) );

create table admission_docs
```

```
( registerNumber references students,
  documentId references documentMaster,
  dt date,
  constraint admission_pk primary key(registerNumber, documentId));
```

STUDENTS and DOCUMENTMASTER are master tables. ADMISSION_DOCS is a transaction table. Now for any particular student with a given REGISTERNUMBER, I need to output something like this:

```
Register    Name       Document      Submitted     Date
----------------------------------------------------------------
342         name       docname1      Yes           12/12/2002
342         name       docname2      Yes           13/12/2002
342         name       docname3      No
```

How can I do this?"

If you look at that result set, you will see that any given student record must be joined with *every* document record, and that result will be outer-joined to the ADMISSION_DOCS table in order to pick up the date, if available.

If you populate the preceding tables with some sample data:

```
insert into students
select object_id, object_name
  from all_objects;
```

That generated about 30,000 student records on my system. The next INSERT will generate five document master records:

```
insert into documentMaster
select ROWNUM, 'doc ' || ROWNUM
  from all_users
 where ROWNUM <= 5;
```

And then we'll generate three admission documents for each student, leaving the last two documents unentered to test our query results:

```
insert into admission_docs
select object_id, mod(ROWNUM,3)+1, created
  from all_objects, (select 1 from all_users where ROWNUM <= 3);
```

Lastly, we'll analyze all three tables:

```
analyze table students compute statistics
for table for all indexes for all indexed columns;
```

```
analyze table documentMaster compute statistics
for table for all indexes for all indexed columns;

analyze table admission_docs compute statistics
for table for all indexes for all indexed columns;
```

Now, a suitable query would be:

```
ops$tkyte@ORA920> set autotrace on
ops$tkyte@ORA920> variable bv number
ops$tkyte@ORA920> exec :bv := 1234
PL/SQL procedure successfully completed.

ops$tkyte@ORA920> select a.* , decode(b.dt,null,'No','Yes') submitted, b.dt
  2    from (
  3    select *
  4      from students, documentMaster
  5    where students.registerNumber = :bv
  6        ) a, admission_docs b
  7    where a.registerNumber = b.registerNumber(+)
  8      and a.documentId = b.documentId (+)
  9  /
```

```
Execution Plan
----------------------------------------------------------
   0      SELECT STATEMENT Optimizer=CHOOSE (Cost=9 Card=5 Bytes=375)
   1    0   NESTED LOOPS (OUTER) (Cost=9 Card=5 Bytes=375)
   2    1     VIEW (Cost=4 Card=5 Bytes=300)
   3    2       NESTED LOOPS (Cost=4 Card=5 Bytes=165)
   4    3         TABLE ACCESS (BY INDEX ROWID) OF 'STUDENTS'
                    (Cost=2 Card=1 Bytes=21)
   5    4           INDEX (UNIQUE SCAN) OF 'STUDENTS_PK' (UNIQUE)
                      (Cost=1 Card=29839)
   6    3         TABLE ACCESS (FULL) OF 'DOCUMENTMASTER' (Cost=2 Card=5 Bytes=60)
   7    1     TABLE ACCESS (BY INDEX ROWID) OF 'ADMISSION_DOCS'
                (Cost=1 Card=1 Bytes=15)
   8    7       INDEX (UNIQUE SCAN) OF 'ADMISSION_PK' (UNIQUE)
```

Here, there is an implicit Cartesian join at step 3 in the plan. EXPLAIN PLAN shows that the database will use an index-unique scan to find the single STUDENTS record, and then join that with each and every row in DOCUMENTMASTER. This result will then be joined to ADMISSION_DOCS using an outer join, so that each and every row from STUDENTS X DOCUMENTMASTER will be in the result set. We can also see this is a fairly efficient query. It uses a single-row lookup into STUDENTS, joined to five rows from DOCUMENTMASTER, and then an index probe for each of the five rows into the ADMISSION_DOCS table.

The optimizer itself will rewrite our queries to use Cartesian joins from time to time, even when we don't have a true Cartesian join in our query. For example, suppose we re-create the ADMISSION_DOCS table as follows:

```
create table admission_docs
( registerNumber references students,
  documentId references documentMaster,
  dt date,
  constraint admission_pk
  primary key(registerNumber, documentid, dt));
```

The change is to make the primary key all three columns now. Then we populate that table.

```
insert into admission_docs
select object_id, mod(ROWNUM,3)+1, created+object_id-ROWNUM
  from all_objects, (select 1 from all_users where ROWNUM <= 12);
```

This gives us about 12 rows per student in that table. Now, say we execute the following query to retrieve a specific document for a specific student.

```
ops$tkyte@ORA920> select *
  2    from documentMaster, admission_docs, students
  3   where documentMaster.documentId = :bv2
  4     and documentMaster.documentId = admission_docs.documentId
  5     and admission_docs.registerNumber = students.registerNumber
  6     and students.registerNumber = :bv
  7  /
no rows selected

Execution Plan
----------------------------------------------------------
   0      SELECT STATEMENT Optimizer=CHOOSE (Cost=4 Card=4 Bytes=184)
   1    0   NESTED LOOPS (Cost=4 Card=4 Bytes=184)
   2    1     NESTED LOOPS (Cost=3 Card=1 Bytes=33)
   3    2       TABLE ACCESS (BY INDEX ROWID) OF 'STUDENTS'
                  (Cost=2 Card=1 Bytes=21)
   4    3         INDEX (UNIQUE SCAN) OF 'STUDENTS_PK' (UNIQUE)
                    (Cost=1 Card=30567)
   5    2       TABLE ACCESS (BY INDEX ROWID) OF 'DOCUMENTMASTER'
                  (Cost=2 Card=1 Bytes=12)
   6    5         INDEX (UNIQUE SCAN) OF 'DOCUMENTS_PK' (UNIQUE)
   7    1     INDEX (RANGE SCAN) OF 'ADMISSION_PK' (UNIQUE)
                (Cost=2 Card=4 Bytes=52)
```

If you look at the predicate, it is clear that DOCUMENTMASTER is joined to ADMISSION_DOCS, which is then joined to STUDENTS. Looking at the query plan, however, we see that at step 2 in the plan, the database has chosen to once again join STUDENTS to DOCUMENTMASTER using a Cartesian join. The reason is that it is confident it will get one row from each of those tables, it can join them together resulting in one row, and it can use that resulting row's values to access ADMISSION_DOCS with more of its primary key columns. If it joined DOCUMENTMASTER to ADMISSION_DOCS by DOCUMENTID, it would get thousands of rows. If it joined ADMISSION_DOCS to STUDENTS by REGISTERNUMBER, it would get many records as well (a record for each document the student had on file). By Cartesian-joining STUDENTS to DOCUMENTS, it gets the fewest rows possible from ADMISSION_DOCS.

# Anti-Joins

This sounds interesting. An anti-join, what could that be? An anti-join is used to return rows from a table that are not present—not in some other row source. For example, consider this query:

```
select * from dept where deptno NOT IN ( select deptno from emp )
```

It might use an anti-join between DEPT and EMP and return only those rows in DEPT that didn't join to anything in EMP.

Another way to write that query would be like this:

```
select dept.*
  from dept, emp
 where dept.deptno = emp.deptno(+)
and emp.ROWID is null;
```

Here, we outer-join DEPT to EMP and keep only the rows where the EMP row did not exist.

Another way you might find this query written could be like this:

```
select *
   from dept
  where NOT EXISTS
     ( select null from emp where emp.deptno = dept.deptno );
```

An anti-join is generally the most efficient method of processing queries of this nature. I know many people believe that a NOT IN query is something to be avoided because it is a real performance issue. However with anti-joins and the CBO, NOT IN queries can be quite efficient. In order to see this, we'll set up two rather small tables, just about 10,000 rows apiece:

```
ops$tkyte@ORA920> create table t1 as select *
  2 from all_objects where ROWNUM <= 10000;
Table created.

ops$tkyte@ORA920> create table t2 as select *
  2 from all_objects where ROWNUM <= 9950;
Table created.

ops$tkyte@ORA920> create index t2_idx on t2(object_id);
Index created.
```

Now, we'll test the performance, using the deprecated RBO first, of the three techniques: using NOT IN, an outer join, and NOT EXISTS. The results are as follows:

```
select count(*) from t1 rbo
where object_id not in ( select object_id from t2 )
```

| call | count | cpu | elapsed | disk | query | current | rows |
|------|-------|-----|---------|------|-------|---------|------|

```
------- ------ ----- ------- ---- ------- ------- -------
total        4  16.66   18.86  134  735876       0       1

Rows      Row Source Operation
-------   --------------------------------------------------
    1     SORT AGGREGATE
   50      FILTER
10000       TABLE ACCESS FULL T1
 9950       TABLE ACCESS FULL T2
```

```
select count(*) from t1 rbo
 where NOT EXISTS (select null from t2 where t2.object_id = rbo.object_id )
```

```
call     count   cpu elapsed disk   query current    rows
-------  ------ ----- ------- ---- ------- ------- -------
total        4  0.13    0.18   22   20138       0       1

Rows      Row Source Operation
-------   --------------------------------------------------
    1     SORT AGGREGATE
   50      FILTER
10000       TABLE ACCESS FULL T1
 9950       INDEX RANGE SCAN T2_IDX (object id 44847)
```

```
select count(*) from t1, t2 rbo
 where t1.object_id = rbo.object_id(+) and rbo.object_id IS NULL
```

```
call     count   cpu elapsed disk   query current    rows
-------  ------ ----- ------- ---- ------- ------- -------
total        4  0.07    0.10    0   10161       0       1

Rows      Row Source Operation
-------   --------------------------------------------------
    1     SORT AGGREGATE
   50      FILTER
10000       NESTED LOOPS OUTER
10000        TABLE ACCESS FULL T1
 9950        INDEX RANGE SCAN T2_IDX (object id 44847)
```

As you can see, it would appear that the outer-join method is the way to go. Using the limited RBO, this may be the case. Overall, that technique, which simulates an anti-join, performed the best. After simply analyzing the tables, however, and running the same queries (I changed the table aliases from RBO to CBO in order to distinguish the queries), we find this:

```
select count(*) from t1 cbo
 where object_id not in ( select object_id from t2 )
```

```
call     count   cpu elapsed disk   query current    rows
-------  ------ ----- ------- ---- ------- ------- -------
total        4  0.03    0.32    0     161       0       1
```

```
Rows      Row Source Operation
-------   -------------------------------------------------------
     1    SORT AGGREGATE
    50    HASH JOIN ANTI
 10000      TABLE ACCESS FULL T1
  9950      INDEX FULL SCAN T2_IDX (object id 44847)
```

```
select count(*) from t1 cbo
 where NOT EXISTS (select null from t2 where t2.object_id = cbo.object_id )
```

| call | count | cpu | elapsed | disk | query | current | rows |
|------|-------|-----|---------|------|-------|---------|------|
| total | 4 | 0.13 | 0.16 | 0 | 20138 | 0 | 1 |

```
Rows      Row Source Operation
-------   -------------------------------------------------------
     1    SORT AGGREGATE
    50     FILTER
 10000      TABLE ACCESS FULL T1
  9950      INDEX RANGE SCAN T2_IDX (object id 44847)
```

```
select count(*) from t1, t2 cbo
 where t1.object_id = cbo.object_id(+) and cbo.object_id IS NULL
```

| call | count | cpu | elapsed | disk | query | current | rows |
|------|-------|-----|---------|------|-------|---------|------|
| total | 4 | 0.03 | 0.05 | 0 | 161 | 0 | 1 |

```
Rows      Row Source Operation
-------   -------------------------------------------------------
     1    SORT AGGREGATE
    50     FILTER
 10000      HASH JOIN OUTER
 10000        TABLE ACCESS FULL OBJ#(44845)
  9950        INDEX FULL SCAN OBJ#(44847) (object id 44847)
```

We see that the CBO, which has access to many more access paths than the RBO, is able to perform this query using an anti-join. And here, the logical I/Os (query) decrease dramatically, from more than 10,000 to 161. An anti-join can be a very efficient method by which to find rows in one source that are not in the other source. Also, as you can see, you do not need to code to get it. Instead, you can use the natural syntax of SQL, NOT IN, without fear.

An important factor to consider when trying this on your own schemas will be the NULL status of columns in the subquery. If you describe T2 in SQL*Plus, you will discover that OBJECT_ID is NOT NULL:

```
ops$tkyte@ORA920> desc t2;
 Name                             Null?    Type
 -------------------------------- -------- --------------------
 OWNER                            NOT NULL VARCHAR2(30)
 OBJECT_NAME                      NOT NULL VARCHAR2(30)
```

```
SUBOBJECT_NAME                          VARCHAR2(30)
OBJECT_ID                               NOT NULL NUMBER
```

What will happen if we allow OBJECT_ID to be NULL, however? Will that affect our query plan (and, hence our, performance)? Consider the following:

```
ops$tkyte@ORA920> alter table t2 modify object_id null;
Table altered.
```

Now, we run our NOT IN query.

```
select count(*)
from
 t1 cbo where object_id not in ( select object_id from t2 )
```

| call | count | cpu | elapsed | disk | query | current | rows |
|------|-------|-----|---------|------|-------|---------|------|
| Parse | 1 | 0.00 | 0.00 | 0 | 1 | 0 | 0 |
| Execute | 1 | 0.00 | 0.00 | 0 | 0 | 0 | 0 |
| Fetch | 2 | 17.67 | 20.36 | 134 | 737650 | 0 | 1 |
| total | 4 | 17.67 | 20.37 | 134 | 737651 | 0 | 1 |

```
Rows     Row Source Operation
-------  ---------------------------------------------------
      1  SORT AGGREGATE (cr=737650 r=134 w=0 time=20368980 us)
     50   FILTER  (cr=737650 r=134 w=0 time=20368825 us)
  10000    TABLE ACCESS FULL T1 (cr=138 r=134 w=0 time=93011 us)
   9950    TABLE ACCESS FULL T2 (cr=737512 r=0 w=0 time=20005383 us)
```

We discover we are back to the plan produced by the RBO! This is all because of a little NULL/NOT NULL constraint. We can no longer use an anti-join to execute this query. The reason is very simple: The queries we've been comparing—NOT IN versus NOT EXISTS, versus outer joins versus anti-joins—are not interchangeable queries if the subquery may return NULL. They return different answers!

Consider this simple query against the SCOTT/TIGER tables to find all employees who are not managers:

```
scott@ORA920> select ename from emp
  2 where empno not in (select mgr from emp);
no rows selected

scott@ORA920> select ename from emp
  2 where NOT EXISTS (select null from emp e2 where e2.mgr = emp.empno);

ENAME
----------
TURNER
WARD
```

```
MARTIN
ALLEN
MILLER
SMITH
ADAMS
JAMES
```
**8 rows selected.**

Many people assume that these queries should return the same answer, but the NULL values for MGR in EMP change the answer with the NOT IN query. Nothing is ever EQUAL to NULL, nor is anything NOT EQUAL to NULL; it is unknown. So, in a NOT IN situation, it quite simply is not known if your column is not in a set that contains NULLs! If your subquery can return a NULL value and it is used in a NOT IN, you may discover that you get zero rows back (after waiting a long time!). The solution for this is to restrict the rows in the subquery using the IS NOT NULL predicate:

```
select count(*)
from
 t1 cbo where object_id not in
( select object_id from t2 where OBJECT_ID IS NOT NULL )
```

| call | count | cpu | elapsed | disk | query | current | rows |
|------|-------|-----|---------|------|-------|---------|------|
| Parse | 1 | 0.00 | 0.09 | 0 | 2 | 0 | 0 |
| Execute | 1 | 0.00 | 0.00 | 0 | 0 | 0 | 0 |
| Fetch | 2 | 0.12 | 0.12 | 0 | 165 | 0 | 1 |
| total | 4 | 0.12 | 0.22 | 0 | 167 | 0 | 1 |

```
Rows     Row Source Operation
-------  ---------------------------------------------------
      1  SORT AGGREGATE (cr=165 r=0 w=0 time=129237 us)
     50   HASH JOIN ANTI (cr=165 r=0 w=0 time=129159 us)
  10000    TABLE ACCESS FULL OBJ#(51177) (cr=138 r=0 w=0 time=15395 us)
   9950    INDEX FAST FULL SCAN OBJ#(51179) (cr=27 r=0 w=0 time=15459
us)(object id 51179)
```

As you can see, we are back to the faster query plan. In fact, I would say a NOT IN subquery that could return a NULL and that doesn't have the IS NOT NULL predicate is probably a bug hiding in your code. It is unlikely you intended for zero rows to be returned in such an event!

## Full Outer Joins

Normally, an outer join of TABLE_A to TABLE_B would return every record in TABLE_A, and if it had a mate in TABLE_B, that would be returned as well. Every row in TABLE_A would be output, but some rows of TABLE_B might not appear in the result set.

A full outer join would return every row in TABLE_A, as well as every row in TABLE_B. The syntax for a full outer join is new with Oracle9i, but it is really a syntactic convenience; we have been able to produce full outer join result sets using conventional SQL.

Suppose we copy the SCOTT EMP and DEPT tables, but make it so that some EMP.DEPTNO values are not to be found in the DEPT table and vice versa.

```
ops$tkyte@ORA920> create table emp
  2   as
  3   select * from scott.emp;
Table created.

ops$tkyte@ORA920> update emp
  2      set deptno = 9
  3    where deptno = 10;
3 rows updated.

ops$tkyte@ORA920> create table dept
  2   as
  3   select *
  4     from scott.dept;
Table created.

ops$tkyte@ORA920> alter table emp add constraint emp_pk primary key(empno);
Table altered.

ops$tkyte@ORA920> alter table dept add constraint dept_pk primary key(deptno);
Table altered.

ops$tkyte@ORA920> analyze table emp compute statistics;
Table analyzed.

ops$tkyte@ORA920> analyze table dept compute statistics;
Table analyzed.
```

First, we'll start with a query that works in all releases and does all of the work of a full outer join. To accomplish this, we simply UNION ALL two queries. The first query will be a normal outer join of DEPT to EMP (all DEPT rows will be returned). The second query will be an anti-join from EMP to DEPT.

```
ops$tkyte@ORA920> set autotrace on explain

ops$tkyte@ORA920> select empno, ename, dept.deptno, dname
  2     from emp, dept
  3    where emp.deptno(+) = dept.deptno
  4    UNION ALL
  5   select empno, ename, emp.deptno, null
  6     from emp, dept
  7    where emp.deptno = dept.deptno(+)
  8      and dept.deptno is null
  9    order by 1, 2, 3, 4
 10   /

     EMPNO ENAME          DEPTNO DNAME
```

```
---------- ---------- ---------- --------------
     7369 SMITH               20 RESEARCH
     7499 ALLEN               30 SALES
...
     7902 FORD                20 RESEARCH
     7934 MILLER               9
                             10 ACCOUNTING
                             40 OPERATIONS
16 rows selected.


Execution Plan
----------------------------------------------------------
   0      SELECT STATEMENT Optimizer=CHOOSE (Cost=12 Card=28 Bytes=462)
   1    0   SORT (ORDER BY) (Cost=9 Card=28 Bytes=462)
   2    1    UNION-ALL
   3    2     HASH JOIN (OUTER) (Cost=5 Card=14 Bytes=294)
   4    3      TABLE ACCESS (FULL) OF 'DEPT' (Cost=2 Card=4 Bytes=44)
   5    3      TABLE ACCESS (FULL) OF 'EMP' (Cost=2 Card=14 Bytes=140)
   6    2     FILTER
   7    6      NESTED LOOPS (OUTER)
   8    7       TABLE ACCESS (FULL) OF 'EMP' (Cost=2 Card=14 Bytes=140)
   9    7       INDEX (UNIQUE SCAN) OF 'DEPT_PK' (UNIQUE)
```

In Oracle9i, we have syntax that greatly simplifies this query:

```
ops$tkyte@ORA920> select empno, ename, nvl(dept.deptno,emp.deptno), dname
  2    from emp FULL OUTER JOIN dept on ( emp.deptno = dept.deptno )
  3    order by 1, 2, 3, 4
  4    /

    EMPNO ENAME      NVL(DEPT.DEPTNO,EMP.DEPTNO) DNAME
---------- ---------- --------------------------- --------------
     7369 SMITH                               20 RESEARCH
     7499 ALLEN                               30 SALES
...
     7902 FORD                                20 RESEARCH
     7934 MILLER                               9
                                             10 ACCOUNTING
                                             40 OPERATIONS
16 rows selected.
```

But, it is important to note that it cannot greatly simplify the work performed by the database. If you look at the generated query plans for each query, you'll see many similarities. These two queries will have comparable runtime performance. A full outer join is a very expensive operation on large sets.

```
Execution Plan
----------------------------------------------------------
   0      SELECT STATEMENT Optimizer=CHOOSE (Cost=12 Card=15 Bytes=825)
   1    0   SORT (ORDER BY) (Cost=12 Card=15 Bytes=825)
```

```
2    1      VIEW (Cost=9 Card=15 Bytes=825)
3    2        UNION-ALL
4    3          NESTED LOOPS (OUTER) (Cost=4 Card=14 Bytes=294)
5    4            TABLE ACCESS (FULL) OF 'EMP' (Cost=2 Card=14 Bytes=140)
6    4            TABLE ACCESS (BY INDEX ROWID) OF 'DEPT'
                  (Cost=2 Card=1 Bytes=11)
7    6              INDEX (UNIQUE SCAN) OF 'DEPT_PK' (UNIQUE)
8    3          HASH JOIN (ANTI) (Cost=5 Card=1 Bytes=13)
9    8            TABLE ACCESS (FULL) OF 'DEPT' (Cost=2 Card=4 Bytes=44)
10   8            TABLE ACCESS (FULL) OF 'EMP' (Cost=2 Card=14 Bytes=28)
```

So, beware of the ease with which you can perform full outer joins now.

This concludes our discussion on joins and join techniques. We'll now take a look at what I call the physics of data—how the physical organization on disk can really impact your performance.

# Schema Matters (Physical)

We covered the topic of schema design in Chapter 7. Here, I'll revisit the subject to point out, via an example, the impact that physical storage—how the schema is physically implemented—can have on your runtime performance. It is not only how you ask the question (using SQL), it is how the data is organized physically. If the only types of database tables you use are heap tables (plain old tables) and the only indexing schemes you use are B*Tree indexes, there is a good chance you haven't given any thought to physical storage as a design and tuning tool.

Physical clustering of like data is an easy way to understand this. Suppose you have a process whereby you receive updates relating to some identifying key over time. Say, every hour you receive updates that list hostnames and load indicators on that host for the last hour. Or, you receive stock updates, consisting of a stock symbol plus price/volume, every night. Or, perhaps you receive personnel actions performed during the day to load into your data warehouse, keyed by employee number. The examples of this type of application are limitless. Your job is to load the information into the database, and others will query this information frequently (load once, query many).

Data of this nature generally has two distinguishing characteristics:

■ **People will ask questions relating to all records regarding a given key value.** For example, people will ask for the load statistics for hostname X over the last two days. Or they'll ask for the stock price of stock ticker A over the last five months. Or they'll ask for the history of employee 1234 for the last seven years. Wouldn't it be nice if all of the data for hostname X, stock ticker A, or employee 1234 were physically colocated together on disk? So, when you got the first row from disk for hostname X, you really got all of the rows for that key from disk?

■ **The data arrives out of this natural order.** For example, every hour you get 100 new rows to add to the table by hostname. If you just appended the data into a heap table, there would be 100 rows between every hostname *X* occurrence. They would not be located near each other, but rather spread out as far as possible. By not using a specialized structure to colocate the data, you are missing out on a huge opportunity to increase the efficiency of your system.

Let's simulate this. We'll assume we get 100 records for 100 hosts each hour and the records are about 80 characters each. We'll use these tables:

```
ops$tkyte@ORA920> create table hosts_heap
  2  ( hostname        varchar2(10),
  3    dt              date,
  4    load            number,
  5    other_stats     char(65),
  6    constraint hosts_heap_pk primary key(hostname,dt)
  7  )
  8  /
Table created.

ops$tkyte@ORA920> create table hosts_iot
  2  ( hostname        varchar2(10),
  3    dt              date,
  4    load            number,
  5    other_stats     char(65),
  6    constraint hosts_iot_pk primary key(hostname,dt)
  7  )
  8  organization index
  9  /
Table created.
```

And we'll load 100 hours of observations for 100 hosts into both of these tables and gather statistics.

```
ops$tkyte@ORA920> declare
  2      l_load number;
  3  begin
  4      for l_HOURS in 1 .. 100
  5      loop
  6          for l_HOSTS in 1 .. 100
  7          loop
  8              l_load := dbms_random.random;
  9              insert into hosts_heap
 10              (hostname,dt,load,other_stats)
 11              values
 12              ('hostnm' || l_hosts, sysdate-(100-l_hours)/24,
 13               l_load, 'x' );
 14              insert into hosts_iot
 15              (hostname,dt,load,other_stats)
 16              values
 17              ('hostnm' || l_hosts, sysdate-(100-l_hours)/24,
 18               l_load, 'x' );
 19          end loop;
 20          commit;
 21      end loop;
 22  end;
 23  /
```

```
PL/SQL procedure successfully completed.

ops$tkyte@ORA920> analyze table hosts_heap compute statistics;
Table analyzed.

ops$tkyte@ORA920> analyze table hosts_iot compute statistics;
Table analyzed.
```

Now, let's ask the question, "What was the average load for a given hostname over the last 100 hours?"

```
ops$tkyte@ORA920> set autotrace on
ops$tkyte@ORA920> select avg(load)
  2    from hosts_heap
  3   where hostname = 'hostnm50'
  4     and dt >= sysdate-100/24
  5  /

 AVG(LOAD)
----------
 128430102


Execution Plan
----------------------------------------------------------
   0      SELECT STATEMENT Optimizer=CHOOSE (Cost=2 Card=1 Bytes=22)
   1    0   SORT (AGGREGATE)
   2    1    TABLE ACCESS (BY INDEX ROWID) OF 'HOSTS_HEAP'
              (Cost=2 Card=5 Bytes=110)
   3    2     INDEX (RANGE SCAN) OF 'HOSTS_HEAP_PK' (UNIQUE) (Cost=2 Card=1)

Statistics
----------------------------------------------------------
        0   recursive calls
        0   db block gets
      102   consistent gets
...

ops$tkyte@ORA920> select avg(load)
  2    from hosts_iot
  3   where hostname = 'hostnm50'
  4     and dt >= sysdate-100/24
  5  /

 AVG(LOAD)
----------
 128430102

Execution Plan
----------------------------------------------------------
```

```
0       SELECT STATEMENT Optimizer=CHOOSE (Cost=2 Card=1 Bytes=22)
1   0     SORT (AGGREGATE)
2   1       INDEX (RANGE SCAN) OF 'HOSTS_IOT_PK' (UNIQUE)
                (Cost=2 Card=5 Bytes=110)

Statistics
----------------------------------------------------------
        0   recursive calls
        0   db block gets
        4   consistent gets
...
```

That is a large difference: 102 logical I/Os versus 4 logical I/Os. And the difference is because we used a physical structure that facilitated access to our data in the manner we actually use it.

As explained in the previous chapter, you should look for opportunities to use Oracle's various physical structures in your applications to gain an edge in performance and reduce your resource usage. These physical storage mechanisms are transparent to applications, meaning that the applications do not need to change their behavior to benefit from them.

# Really Know SQL

SQL is a very powerful language. You can do a lot with it. Consider this query for a minute:

```
ops$tkyte@ORA920> with players as
  2  ( select 'P'||ROWNUM username
  3      from all_objects
  4     where ROWNUM <= 8),
  5  weeks as
  6  ( select ROWNUM week
  7      from all_objects
  8     where ROWNUM <= 7 )
  9  select week,
 10         max(decode(rn,1,username,null)) u1,
 11         max(decode(rn,2,username,null)) u2,
 12         max(decode(rn,3,username,null)) u3,
 13         max(decode(rn,4,username,null)) u4,
 14         max(decode(rn,5,username,null)) u5,
 15         max(decode(rn,6,username,null)) u6,
 16         max(decode(rn,7,username,null)) u7,
 17         max(decode(rn,8,username,null)) u8
 18    from ( select username,
 19                  week,
 20                  row_number() over (partition by week order by rnd) rn
 21             from ( select username, week, dbms_random.random rnd
 22                      from players, weeks
 23                  )
 24         )
 25   group by week
 26  /
```

```
     WEEK U1 U2 U3 U4 U5 U6 U7 U8
---------- -- -- -- -- -- -- -- --
         1 P4 P1 P3 P6 P2 P8 P5 P7
         2 P3 P5 P4 P7 P8 P1 P6 P2
         3 P6 P7 P3 P2 P8 P4 P1 P5
         4 P8 P4 P6 P5 P1 P2 P3 P7
         5 P3 P8 P7 P4 P5 P6 P2 P1
         6 P3 P1 P6 P8 P5 P4 P7 P2
         7 P4 P8 P7 P1 P5 P2 P6 P3

7 rows selected.
```

Before you read on, try to figure out what this query is doing. It is a query I wrote in response to a request for a schedule for a golf tournament. The tournament was to last seven weeks and have eight participants. The objective was to randomly assign each of the eight players over a seven-week period to two groups of four.

This query sets up the schedule. It has seven rows for the seven weeks. If we consider U1 through U4 to be the first group and U5 through U8 the second group, we have our random assignments. Although many others might write procedural code for this type of application, my approach was to first consider whether I could do it in a query. I thought about what I needed in order to answer the question:

- I need seven weeks. That is the subquery WEEKS.

- I need eight players. That is the subquery PLAYERS.

- I need to have eight players by seven weeks. That is the Cartesian join on line 22.

- I need to randomly sort these eight players each week. That is the assignment of a random number on line 21.

- By week, I need to sort these eight players randomly to assign to one of two groups and pivot the data for display purposes. That is the goal of analytic function ROW_NUMBER() on line 20. It will assign, by week, the number 1, 2, 3, and so on to each player after sorting them randomly.

- Then I pivot. That is the MAX(DECODE()) construct.

And there I have the answer, simply by thinking in *sets* instead of attacking the problem procedurally.

The procedural approach seems to be the way most people will attempt to solve a problem like this, but when using the database, thinking in sets is important. Time and time again, we see that bulk operations are faster than single-row, procedural code. If you want to make that copy of data from your transactional system to the reporting system faster, you'll use a single SQL statement, not row-after-row-after-row processing. If you want to update a table using information in another table, you'll use a single UPDATE or MERGE statement, not row-by-row processing. The same is true with gathering data. If you need to create a summary and remove duplicates, you do not want to write procedural code to remove the duplicates; you want to let the query do the work for you.

"I am trying to tune a series of procedures. They all have the same pattern:

```
procedure p1(a1, a2) is
begin
  for c1 in (select * from table_name1 where col1 = a1 and col2 = a2)
  loop
    delete from table_name2 where c1.col1 = table_name2.col1;
    insert into table_name2 values(c1.col1, c1.col2, c1.col3,...);
  end loop;
end;
```

I have modified the procedure to use PL/SQL index by tables, but it only makes the procedures run three times longer. TABLE_NAME2 doesn't have any indexes in it, so DML on this table shouldn't have overhead related to indexes. I also tried to use parallel hints (PARALLEL and APPEND), but both also make processing time suffer. Do you have any suggestions that I could try? Please help!"

My answer was simple. They were doing a refresh. That process should have been simply:

```
delete from table_name2
where col1 in ( select col1
                  from table_name1
                where col1 = a1 and col2 = a2 );

insert into table_name2
select *
  from table_name1
 where col1 = a1 and col2 = a2;
```

This is true especially in light of the fact that TABLE_NAME2 didn't have any indexes on it! That implied a full scan for each and every DELETE statement in the procedural code. Not that full scans are evil, but if you do them often enough, they add up. The set-based approach using bulk functions will make a single pass, instead of a pass per row in TABLE_NAME1. It will generate the least amount of redo and undo data. It will run faster than procedural code.

For the rest of this section, we'll look at ways to make SQL perform efficiently—to work with sets and do as much as possible in a single statement. The idea is not to present every SQL feature and function you'll ever need, since that is what the Oracle documentation does. Here, I will expose you to some new ideas and different ways to look at things.

## The **ROWNUM** Pseudo Column

ROWNUM is a magic column in Oracle that gets many people into trouble. When you learn what it is and how it works, however, it can be very useful. I use it for three things:

- To tune queries
- To paginate through a query
- To perform top-*N* processing

We'll take a look at each of these uses, after we review how ROWNUM works.

### How **ROWNUM** Works

ROWNUM is a pseudo column (not a real column) that is available in a query. ROWNUM will be assigned the numbers 1, 2, 3, 4, … *N*, where *N* is the number of rows in the set ROWNUM is used with. A ROWNUM is not assigned to a row (this is a common misconception). A row in a table does not have a number. You cannot ask for row 5 from a table—there is no such thing.

Also confusing to most people is when ROWNUM is actually assigned. A ROWNUM is assigned to a row after it passes the predicate phase of the query but before any sorting or aggregation is done. Also, ROWNUM is incremented only after it is assigned. That last part is why the following query will never stand a chance of returning a row:

```
select * from t where ROWNUM > 1
```

Since ROWNUM > 1 is not true for the first row, ROWNUM does not advance to 2. Hence, ROWNUM never gets to be greater than 1. Consider a query with this structure:

```
Select …, ROWNUM
   From t
 Where <where clause>
 Group by <columns>
Having <having clause>
 Order by <columns>
```

Think of it as being processed in this order:

1. The FROM and WHERE clause go first.
2. ROWNUM is assigned and incremented to each output row from the FROM/WHERE.
3. SELECT is applied.
4. GROUP BY is applied.
5. HAVING is applied.
6. It is sorted.

That is why a query in the following form is almost certainly an error:

```
select * from emp where ROWNUM <= 5 order by sal desc;
```

The developers' intention was most likely to get the top-five paid people—a top-*N* query. What they will get is five random records (the first five we happen to hit), sorted by salary. The procedural pseudo code for this query is as follows:

```
ROWNUM = 1
For x in ( select * from emp )
Loop
    Exit when NOT(ROWNUM <= 5)
    OUTPUT record to temp
    ROWNUM = ROWNUM+1
End loop
SORT TEMP
```

It gets the first five records and then sorts them. A query with WHERE ROWNUM = 5 or WHERE ROWNUM > 5 doesn't make sense. This is because ROWNUM is assigned to a row during the predicate evaluation and gets incremented only after a row passes the WHERE clause.

Here is the correct version of this query:

```
select *
  from ( select * from emp order by sal desc )
 where ROWNUM <= 5;
```

This version will sort EMP by salary descending, and then give us the first five records (top-five records) we encounter. As we'll see in the top-*N* discussion coming up shortly, Oracle doesn't really sort the entire result set; it is smarter than that, but conceptually, that is what takes place.

## Tuning with **ROWNUM**

How can ROWNUM be used to tune queries? Part of the secret actually comes from how ROWNUM works. Consider the example in the previous section, which will "sort" EMP by salary descending and output the top-five records. Apparently, then, there is a way to change the natural ordering of operations. By using ORDER BY in the inline view, Oracle sorted, *and then* applied the WHERE ROWNUM <= 5 predicate. In fact, the Oracle documentation tells us that when an inline view (or just a view) contains things such as the following, the optimizer cannot merge the view:

- Set operators (UNION, UNION ALL, INTERSECT, and MINUS)
- A CONNECT BY clause
- ROWNUM pseudo columns
- Aggregate functions (AVG, COUNT, MAX, and so on) in the SELECT list

In some cases, Oracle can push predicates down into the inline view, achieving much the same as a view merge would, but none of those cases covers ROWNUM. What that means is that an inline view involving ROWNUM will be evaluated, or *materialized,* and then used in the rest of the query. That simple statement can have some profound effects, especially in the area of performance.

**Reduce Function Calls** The following example came from a real performance issue. The query as written took days to complete (we'll build the tables in a minute; we'll just look at the query for now).

```
select    a12.prc_chk_typ_desc  prc_chk_typ_desc,
          a11.prc_chk_dt  prc_chk_dt,
          a11.cmpt_loc_key  cmpt_loc_key,
          a11.prod_key  upc_prod_key,
          a11.loc_key  loc_key,
          max(f(a11.prod_key, a11.prc_chk_key, 'QTY', 'D', 1) ),
          max(f(a11.prod_key, a11.prc_chk_key, 'AMT', 'D',1) ),
          max(f(a11.prod_key, a11.prc_chk_key, 'CODE', 'D', 1) ),
          max(f(a11.prod_key, a11.prc_chk_key, 'PRC', 'D',1) )
   from   t1 a11,
          t2 a12
  where   a11.cmpt_loc_key = a12.cmpt_loc_key
    and   a11.loc_key = a12.loc_key
    and   a11.prc_chk_key = a12.prc_chk_key
 group by a12.prc_chk_typ_desc, a11.prc_chk_dt,
          a11.cmpt_loc_key, a11.prod_key, a11.loc_key;
```

If we simply change MAX into SUM in the query, it runs in minutes. The (false) conclusion is that MAX is broken. The real reason is that we are calling a PL/SQL function hundreds of millions of times with MAX and only hundreds of thousands of times with SUM. With MAX, the database calls F (...) hundreds of millions of times in order to process the data, never saving the result of F but invoking it repeatedly.

Consider how MAX is processed. It is almost like an ORDER BY. It may do many, many compare operations. SUM, on the other hand, keeps a running total. It doesn't need to do any compare operations, just an addition. MAX might compare a column many times (as a sort would), whereas SUM might process a column once.

So, how do we fix it? The answer is by using ROWNUM. Now, we'll set up a test:

```
ops$tkyte@ora920> create table t1
  2  ( prc_chk_key                number(9) not null,
  3    prod_key                   number(12) not null,
  4    cmpt_loc_key               number(5) not null,
  5    loc_key                    number(5) not null,
  6    prc_chk_dt                 date
  7  )
  8  /
table created.

ops$tkyte@ORA920> insert into t1 select 2, 3, 4, 5, sysdate
  2 from all_objects where ROWNUM <= 50;
50 rows created.

ops$tkyte@ora920> create table t2
  2  ( prc_chk_key                number(9) not null,
  3    prc_chk_typ_desc           varchar2(35) not null,
```

```
  4    cmpt_loc_key                      number(5),
  5    loc_key                           number(5) not null
  6  )
  7  /
table created.

ops$tkyte@ORA920> insert into t2 select 2, 'x', 4, 5
  2 from all_objects where ROWNUM <= 50;
50 rows created.
```

Next, we'll create a function F. This function will return a constant value, but it will increment a counter using DBMS_APPLICATION_INFO. This will permit us to count how many times F is called:

```
ops$tkyte@ORA920> CREATE OR REPLACE function F
  2    (v_prod_key       IN number default NULL,
  3     v_prc_chk_key  IN number default NULL,
  4     v_return  IN varchar2 default NULL,
  5     v_want_sr        IN varchar2 default NULL,
  6     v_version        IN number ) RETURN  varchar2
  7  as
  8  begin
  9      dbms_application_info.set_client_info
 10      (userenv('client_info')+1);
 11      return 'x';
 12  end;
 13  /
Function created.
```

Now, we are ready to test. We'll start by setting the CLIENT_INFO column in V$SESSION to zero and running our original query. Note that the use of a hint here is simply to achieve the same query plan as the original problem statement had. We have insufficient data to get a hash join, which is what we want, but adding sufficient data to make the database use a hash join makes the example run for days!

```
ops$tkyte@ORA920> exec dbms_application_info.set_client_info(0);
PL/SQL procedure successfully completed.

ops$tkyte@ora920> select             /*+ use_hash( a11, a12 ) */
  2            a12.prc_chk_typ_desc  prc_chk_typ_desc,
  3            a11.prc_chk_dt  prc_chk_dt,
  4            a11.cmpt_loc_key  cmpt_loc_key,
  5            a11.prod_key  upc_prod_key,
  6            a11.loc_key  loc_key,
  7            max(F(a11.PROD_KEY,a11.PRC_CHK_KEY, 'QTY', 'D', 1) ),
  8            max(F(a11.PROD_KEY, a11.PRC_CHK_KEY, 'AMT', 'D',1) ),
  9            max(F(a11.PROD_KEY, a11.PRC_CHK_KEY,'CODE','D', 1) ),
 10            max(F(a11.PROD_KEY, a11.PRC_CHK_KEY, 'PRC', 'D',1) )
 11    from      t1 a11,
 12              t2 a12
```

```
 13    where      a11.cmpt_loc_key = a12.cmpt_loc_key
 14      and   a11.loc_key = a12.loc_key
 15      and   a11.prc_chk_key = a12.prc_chk_key
 16    group by a12.prc_chk_typ_desc, a11.prc_chk_dt,
 17             a11.cmpt_loc_key, a11.prod_key, a11.loc_key;

Execution Plan
----------------------------------------------------------
   0      SELECT STATEMENT Optimizer=CHOOSE (Cost=8 Card=1 Bytes=119)
   1    0   SORT (GROUP BY) (Cost=8 Card=1 Bytes=119)
   2    1     HASH JOIN (Cost=5 Card=1 Bytes=119)
   3    2       TABLE ACCESS (FULL) OF 'T1' (Cost=2 Card=82 Bytes=5002)
   4    2       TABLE ACCESS (FULL) OF 'T2' (Cost=2 Card=82 Bytes=4756)

ops$tkyte@ORA920> set autotrace off
ops$tkyte@ORA920> select userenv('client_info' ) data from dual;

DATA
--------------------
10000
```

That shows we had 10,000 calls to F. That is really high given that we have 50 rows equijoined to 50 rows by a common key. If we doubled the data in this example to 100 rows, we would quadruple the calls to 40,000. Double it again to 200 rows, and Oracle would execute the function 160,000 times. At 200 rows, if the function took just 0.001 second to run and be called from SQL, you are looking at three minutes. Given that in the real world, the function was infinitely more complex than this and was measured in hundredths of seconds, we are talking days of processing time.

What happens if we write the query as follows?

```
ops$tkyte@ORA920> exec dbms_application_info.set_client_info(0);
PL/SQL procedure successfully completed.

ops$tkyte@ORA920> select /*+ USE_HASH( a11, a12 ) */
  2            a12.prc_chk_typ_desc  prc_chk_typ_desc,
  3            a11.prc_chk_dt  prc_chk_dt,
  4            a11.cmpt_loc_key  cmpt_loc_key,
  5            a11.prod_key  upc_prod_key,
  6            a11.loc_key  loc_key,
  7            max(a),
  8            max(b),
  9            max(c),
 10            max(d)
 11    from (select a11.*,
 12            F(a11.PROD_KEY, a11.PRC_CHK_KEY, 'QTY', 'D', 1 ) a,
 13            F(a11.PROD_KEY, a11.PRC_CHK_KEY, 'AMT', 'D',1 ) b,
 14            F(a11.PROD_KEY, a11.PRC_CHK_KEY, 'CODE', 'D', 1 ) c,
 15            F(a11.PROD_KEY, a11.PRC_CHK_KEY, 'PRC', 'D',1 ) d,
 16            ROWNUM r
 17          from t1 a11 ) a11,
```

```
18              T2 a12
19    where       a11.cmpt_loc_key = a12.cmpt_loc_key
20     and    a11.loc_key = a12.loc_key
21     and    a11.prc_chk_key = a12.prc_chk_key
22    group by a12.prc_chk_typ_desc, a11.prc_chk_dt,
23               a11.cmpt_loc_key, a11.prod_key, a11.loc_key;
```

The change is just an inline view that references ROWNUM. Here, Oracle must materialize that inline view in order to assign ROWNUM to the rows. Just as before, it needed to sort before assigning ROWNUM, and it goes the other way: It must assign ROWNUM permanently (in the context of this query) to the rows. At the same time, function F was evaluated in this temporary set and saved off to the side. We can see this in the query plan:

```
Execution Plan
----------------------------------------------------------
    0       SELECT STATEMENT Optimizer=CHOOSE (Cost=9 Card=1 Bytes=8127)
    1    0    SORT (GROUP BY) (Cost=9 Card=1 Bytes=8127)
    2    1      HASH JOIN (Cost=5 Card=1 Bytes=8127)
    3    2        TABLE ACCESS (FULL) OF 'T2' (Cost=2 Card=82 Bytes=4756)
    4    2        VIEW (Cost=2 Card=82 Bytes=661658)
    5    4          COUNT
    6    5            TABLE ACCESS (FULL) OF 'T1' (Cost=2 Card=82 Bytes=5002)
```

T1 was scanned, and turned into a view—it was materialized, and the results of that were used to hash-join to T2. Here is the net result:

```
ops$tkyte@ORA920> select userenv('client_info' ) data from dual;

DATA
--------------------
200
```

Now, we have 200 calls, rather than 10,000 calls. As you double the data, you double the calls. The number of calls is 100% predictable as well: NUMBER_OF_COLUMNS(4) * NUMBER_OF_ROWS_IN_T1(50) = 200. If you have 100 rows, you have 400 calls; for 200 rows, there are 800 calls; and so on. This query ran as efficiently using MAX as the original did using SUM.

**Join Queries**    Another use of ROWNUM comes into play when you have this conundrum: You run two queries, and each query by itself runs very fast, in a couple hundredths of a second. You need to join these two queries together. This takes a really long runtime. What to do? Well, you can use this same ROWNUM trick, as follows:

```
Select *
    From ( select ...., ROWNUM r1 from ... )  query1,
         ( select ..., ROWNUM r2 from ... ) query2
    Where join_condition...
```

You should find the runtime to be that of the two individual queries. Now, bear in mind, I generally see these sorts of issues in databases where something is *wrong*: Statistics are wrong or missing, or some setting is set totally inappropriately. For example, I used this technique on a system where a domain index was added to a table. That caused the CBO to be used as shown here:

```
ops$tkyte@ORA920> create table t ( x clob );
Table created.

ops$tkyte@ORA920> set autotrace traceonly explain
ops$tkyte@ORA920> select * from t;

Execution Plan
----------------------------------------------------------
   0      SELECT STATEMENT Optimizer=CHOOSE
   1    0    TABLE ACCESS (FULL) OF 'T'

ops$tkyte@ORA920> create index t_idx on t(x) indextype is ctxsys.context;
Index created.

ops$tkyte@ORA920> select * from t;

Execution Plan
----------------------------------------------------------
   0      SELECT STATEMENT Optimizer=CHOOSE (Cost=2 Card=82 Bytes=164164)
   1    0    TABLE ACCESS (FULL) OF 'T' (Cost=2 Card=82 Bytes=164164)
```

The developers had a text query that ran really fast. They also had a relational query that ran really fast. They put them together, and it ran really slowly. The reason is that they were using the CBO against unanalyzed tables. They did not realize that by putting a domain index on that table, every query that would hit it would use the CBO. The individual queries got lucky, but when they were run together, the optimizer (given its lack of information) made a bad decision. As a stopgap measure to make the query work, ROWNUM was very useful. However, they need to start analyzing tables. At that point, removal of the ROWNUM trick would probably allow the query to run even faster.

## Pagination with ROWNUM

Pagination is my all-time favorite use of ROWNUM and is the answer to the most frequently asked question I receive. Here we use ROWNUM to get rows *N* thru *M* of a result set. The general form of this is as follows:

```
Select *
  From ( select a.*, ROWNUM rnum
           From ( your_query_goes_here ) a
          Where ROWNUM <= :MAX_ROW_TO_FETCH )
 Where rnum  >= :MIN_ROW_TO_FETCH;
```

And many times, I add this:

```
Select *
  From ( select /*+ FIRST_ROWS */ a.*, ROWNUM rnum
           From ( your_query_goes_here ) a
```

```
               Where ROWNUM <= :MAX_ROW_TO_FETCH )
   Where rnum  >= :MIN_ROW_TO_FETCH;
```

This tells the optimizer, "Hey, we are interested in getting the first rows as fast as possible." The concept here is that end users at a browser have done a search and are waiting for the results. It is imperative to get them the first page (and second page and so on) as fast as possible.

Some people have been tempted to "simplify" this query down to this:

```
Select *
   From ( select /*+ FIRST_ROWS */ a.*, ROWNUM rnum
            From ( your_query_goes_here ) a )
   Where rnum between :MIN_ROW_TO_FETCH and :MAX_ROW_TO_FETCH;
```

But, as we'll see, that is not a good idea. In order to demonstrate this, we'll create a set of tables to use. Again, we'll copy and index ALL_OBJECTS and ALL_USERS, so we can use a nontrivial query for the demonstration.

```
ops$tkyte@ORA920> create table t1
   2  as
   3  select * from all_objects;
Table created.

ops$tkyte@ORA920> create table t2
   2  as
   3  select * from all_users;
Table created.

ops$tkyte@ORA920> alter table t2 add constraint
   2  t2_pk primary key(username);
Table altered.

ops$tkyte@ORA920> alter table t1 add constraint
   2  t1_pk primary key(object_id);
Table altered.
```

This next index will be added because our web site that displays this data will show it sorted by OWNER and OBJECT_TYPE. This index will facilitate our ability to page through the entire result set when the user does an unconstrained search (no WHERE clause). We would probably have other indexes as well, to facilitate other common searches.

```
ops$tkyte@ORA920> create index t1_sort_idx
   2  on t1(owner,object_type);
Index created.

ops$tkyte@ORA920> analyze table t1 compute statistics
   2  for table for all indexes
   3  for all indexed columns;
Table analyzed.

ops$tkyte@ORA920> analyze table t2 compute statistics
```

```
      2  for table for all indexes
      3  for all indexed columns;
Table analyzed.
```

And now we are ready to paginate. We'll set up our bind variables with the minimum and maximum rows to get:

```
ops$tkyte@ORA920> variable min_row number
ops$tkyte@ORA920> variable max_row number

ops$tkyte@ORA920> exec :min_row := 1; :max_row := 10;
PL/SQL procedure successfully completed.

ops$tkyte@ORA920> set autotrace on
ops$tkyte@ORA920> select *
      2    from ( select /*+ first_rows */ a.*, ROWNUM rnum
      3           from ( select t1.owner, t1.object_name,
                               t1.object_type, t2.user_id
      4                   from t1, t2
      5                  where t1.owner = t2.username
      6                  order by t1.owner, t1.object_type
      7                       ) A
      8                 where ROWNUM <= :max_row
      9         )
     10   where rnum >= :min_row
     11  /
```

| OWNER | OBJECT_NAME | OBJECT_TYP | USER_ID | RNUM |
|-------|-------------|------------|---------|------|
| A | EMP | TABLE | 294 | 1 |
| AQ | AQ$_OBJMSGS80_QTAB_I | INDEX | 270 | 2 |
| AQ | AQ$_OBJMSGS80_QTAB_T | INDEX | 270 | 3 |
| AQ | SYS_C006281 | INDEX | 270 | 4 |
| AQ | DEQUEUE_MSG | PROCEDURE | 270 | 5 |
| AQ | ENQUEUE_MSG | PROCEDURE | 270 | 6 |
| AQ | OBJMSGS80_QTAB | TABLE | 270 | 7 |
| AQ | MESSAGE_TYP | TYPE | 270 | 8 |
| AQ | AQ$OBJMSGS80_QTAB | VIEW | 270 | 9 |
| BIG_TABLE | DUMP_CSV | FUNCTION | 80 | 10 |

```
10 rows selected.


Execution Plan
-----------------------------------------------------------
      0      SELECT STATEMENT Optimizer=HINT: FIRST_ROWS
             (Cost=3166 Card=30577 Bytes=2170967)
      1    0   VIEW (Cost=3166 Card=30577 Bytes=2170967)
      2    1    COUNT (STOPKEY)
      3    2     VIEW (Cost=3166 Card=30577 Bytes=1773466)
```

```
4    3           NESTED LOOPS (Cost=3166 Card=30577 Bytes=1498273)
5    4              TABLE ACCESS (BY INDEX ROWID) OF 'T1'
                    (Cost=108 Card=30577 Bytes=917310)
6    5                INDEX (FULL SCAN) OF 'T1_SORT_IDX' (NON-UNIQUE)
                      (Cost=109 Card=30577)
7    4              TABLE ACCESS (BY INDEX ROWID) OF 'T2' (Cost=2 Card=1
Bytes=19)
8    7                INDEX (UNIQUE SCAN) OF 'T2_PK' (UNIQUE)


Statistics
----------------------------------------------------------
         0   recursive calls
         0   db block gets
        18   consistent gets
```

As you can see, the results are exactly the ten rows that we wanted, and we got them pretty fast. The COUNT (STOPKEY) portion of the plan is crucial here. It basically says, "This part of the plan will stop when we hit the count we need to get." That the query can be short-circuited like this is key; the first pages of the result set must come back quickly for this technique to work. If it takes five minutes to get the first row, this will not speed up that query—it will still take five minutes (you'll need to look at other techniques, such as a materialized view to search against, to correct that issue).

Now, if we ask for rows 5,000 to 5,010, we'll see it takes a tad more work.

```
ops$tkyte@ORA920> exec :min_row := 5000;  :max_row := 5010;
PL/SQL procedure successfully completed.

ops$tkyte@ORA920> /

OWNER      OBJECT_NAME                     OBJECT_TYP USER_ID  RNUM
---------  ------------------------------  ---------- -------  -----
SYS        /49854bf4_NodeFilter            JAVA CLASS       0   5000
SYS        /498c1db5_RuntimeRefErrorsText  JAVA CLASS       0   5001
SYS        /49938591_ErrorPosition         JAVA CLASS       0   5002
SYS        /49b3e168_OracleSavepoint       JAVA CLASS       0   5003
SYS        /49bea869_LoadJavaBeanInfo      JAVA CLASS       0   5004
SYS        /49cdec41_StyledEditorKit1      JAVA CLASS       0   5005
SYS        /49d2f4a7_ProfileGroupConnecte  JAVA CLASS       0   5006
SYS        /49d3c883_OraCustomizerErrorsT  JAVA CLASS       0   5007
SYS        /49d5c9c8_AbstractDocument2     JAVA CLASS       0   5008
SYS        /49db322c_LjUtilSorter          JAVA CLASS       0   5009
SYS        /49ea8f5e_URIResolver           JAVA CLASS       0   5010

11 rows selected.

Statistics
----------------------------------------------------------
         0   recursive calls
         0   db block gets
      5550   consistent gets
```

As you can see, it took 5,550 logical I/Os to get these rows. We needed to fetch over the first 4,999 rows in the server, ignore them, and return just the next ten rows. As you paged through this result set, you would find that getting to each page took a little more work than getting to the previous page.

As a closing on this topic, and as a nice lead-in to top-*N* query processing, I'll demonstrate why simplifying this query to use BETWEEN instead of two separate predicates to limit the rows is a bad idea. Consider the following:

```
ops$tkyte@ORA920> select *
  2    from ( select /*+ first_rows */ a.*, ROWNUM rnum
  3             from ( select t1.owner, t1.object_name,
                              t1.object_type, t2.user_id
  4                     from t1, t2
  5                     where t1.owner = t2.username
  6                     order by t1.owner, t1.object_type
  7                          ) A
  8              )
  9    where rnum between :min_row and :max_row
 10  /
```

```
OWNER      OBJECT_NAME                       OBJECT_TYP USER_ID RNUM
---------- --------------------------------- ---------- ------- -----
A          EMP                               TABLE          294     1
AQ         AQ$_OBJMSGS80_QTAB_I              INDEX          270     2
AQ         AQ$_OBJMSGS80_QTAB_T              INDEX          270     3
AQ         SYS_C006281                       INDEX          270     4
AQ         DEQUEUE_MSG                       PROCEDURE      270     5
AQ         ENQUEUE_MSG                       PROCEDURE      270     6
AQ         OBJMSGS80_QTAB                    TABLE          270     7
AQ         MESSAGE_TYP                       TYPE           270     8
AQ         AQ$OBJMSGS80_QTAB                VIEW           270     9
BIG_TABLE  DUMP_CSV                          FUNCTION        80    10

10 rows selected.


Execution Plan
----------------------------------------------------------
   0      SELECT STATEMENT Optimizer=HINT: FIRST_ROWS
          (Cost=3166 Card=30577 Bytes=2170967)
   1    0   FILTER
   2    1     VIEW (Cost=3166 Card=30577 Bytes=2170967)
   3    2       COUNT
   4    3         VIEW (Cost=3166 Card=30577 Bytes=1773466)
   5    4           NESTED LOOPS (Cost=3166 Card=30577 Bytes=1498273)
   6    5             TABLE ACCESS (BY INDEX ROWID) OF 'T1'
                      (Cost=108 Card=30577 Bytes=917310)
   7    6               INDEX (FULL SCAN) OF 'T1_SORT_IDX' (NON-UNIQUE)
                        (Cost=109 Card=30577)
   8    5             TABLE ACCESS (BY INDEX ROWID) OF 'T2'
```

```
                        (Cost=2 Card=1 Bytes=19)
    9     8                 INDEX (UNIQUE SCAN) OF 'T2_PK' (UNIQUE)


Statistics
-----------------------------------------------------------
          0   recursive calls
          0   db block gets
      18995   consistent gets
```

Notice how this particular query differs from the one shown at the beginning of this section. The COUNT is not followed by a STOPKEY. This query materialized the inline view:

```
    2     from ( select /*+ first_rows */ a.*, ROWNUM rnum
    3             from ( select t1.owner, t1.object_name,
                                 t1.object_type, t2.user_id
    4                     from t1, t2
    5                     where t1.owner = t2.username
    6                     order by t1.owner, t1.object_type
    7                              ) A
```

This is the same technique we used to our advantage with MAX(F(...)), in the section about tuning with ROWNUM. Here, however, it works against us. We know that we cannot push the predicates into an inline view that contains ROWNUM. By removing the where ROWNUM <= :max_row, we remove the ability for this query to stop early. Oracle built the entire result set for us, and then applied the where rnum between clause.

Now, we are ready to move to the last ROWNUM topic of using ROWNUM to efficiently process top-N queries.

## Top-N Query Processing with ROWNUM

In a top-N query, you are generally interested in taking some complex query, sorting it, and then retrieving just the first N rows (the top-N rows). ROWNUM has a top-N optimization (in Oracle9i Release 1 and later only) that facilitates this type of query. It can be used to avoid a massive sort of large sets. We'll discuss how it does this conceptually, and then look at an example.

Suppose you have a query in this form:

```
Select … From …. Where …. Order by columns
```

Assume this query returns a lot of data: thousands, or hundreds of thousands, of rows or even more. However, you are interested only in the top-N, say the top-10 or top-100. There are two ways to attack this:

- Have the client application open that query and fetch just the first N rows.

- Use that query as an inline view and use ROWNUM to limit the results, as in SELECT * FROM (*your_query_here*) WHERE ROWNUM <= N.

The second approach is by far superior to the first for two reasons. The lesser of the two reasons is that it requires less work by the client. The database will take care of limiting the result set. The most important reason is the special processing the database can do in order to give you just the top-N rows. Using the top-N query means you have given the database extra information.

You have told it, "I'm only interested in getting *N* rows; I'll never consider the rest." Now, that doesn't sound too earth-shattering until you think about sorting—how sorts work and what the server would need to do. Let's walk through the two approaches with a sample query.

```
select * from t order by unindexed_column;
```

Now, assume T is a big table, with more than one million records, and each record is "fat," say 100 or more bytes. Also assume that UNINDEXED_COLUMN is, as its name implies, a column that is not indexed. We are interested in getting just the first ten rows. Oracle would do the following:

1. Full-scan T.

2. Sort T by UNINDEXED_COLUMN. This is a full sort.

3. Presumably run out of sort area memory and need to swap temporary extents to disk.

4. Merge the temporary extents back to get the first ten records when they are requested.

5. Clean up (release) the temporary extents as we are finished with them.

Now, that is a lot of I/O. Oracle has most likely copied the entire table into TEMP and written it out, just to get the first ten rows.

Next, we'll look at what Oracle can do conceptually with a top-*N* query:

```
select *
  from (Select * from t order by unindexed_column)
 where ROWNUM < :N;
```

In this case, Oracle will take these steps:

1. Full-scan T, as before (we cannot avoid this step).

2. In an array of :*N* elements (presumably in memory this time), sort only :*N* rows.

The first *N* rows will populate this array of rows in sorted order. When the *N*+1 row is fetched, it will be compared to the last row in the array. If it would go into slot *N*+1 in the array, it gets thrown out. Otherwise, it is added, sorted to this array, and one of the existing rows is discarded. Our sort area holds *N* rows maximum, so instead of sorting one million rows, we sort *N* rows.

This seeming small detail of using an array concept and just sorting *N* rows can lead to huge gains in performance and resource usage. It takes a lot less RAM to sort ten rows than it does to sort one million rows (not to mention TEMP space usage!).

Using BIG_TABLE, we can run the following PL/SQL block to see that both approaches get the same results, but in radically different times:

```
big_table@ORA920> declare
  2      l_owner        dbms_sql.varchar2_table;
  3      l_object_name  dbms_sql.varchar2_table;
  4      l_object_type  dbms_sql.varchar2_table;
  5      l_created      dbms_sql.varchar2_table;
  6
  7      cursor c is
```

```
 8      select owner, object_name, object_type, created
 9        from big_table
10       order by created DESC;
11  begin
12      select owner, object_name, object_type, created
13        bulk collect into l_owner, l_object_name, l_object_type,
                            l_created
14        from ( select owner, object_name, object_type, created
15                 from big_table
16                 order by created DESC )
17       where ROWNUM <= 10;
18
19      open c;
20      fetch c bulk collect
21       into l_owner, l_object_name, l_object_type, l_created
22      limit 10;
23      close c;
24  end;
25  /
```

The top-N query has this execution profile:

```
select owner, object_name, object_type, created
    from ( select owner, object_name, object_type, created
             from big_table
             order by created DESC )
   where ROWNUM <= 10
```

| call | count | cpu | elapsed | disk | query | current | rows |
| --- | --- | --- | --- | --- | --- | --- | --- |
| Parse | 1 | 0.00 | 0.00 | 0 | 0 | 0 | 0 |
| Execute | 1 | 0.00 | 0.00 | 0 | 0 | 0 | 0 |
| Fetch | 1 | 8.98 | 9.53 | 26550 | 27065 | 0 | 10 |
| total | 3 | 8.98 | 9.53 | 26550 | 27065 | 0 | 10 |

```
Rows     Row Source Operation
-------  ---------------------------------------------------
     10  COUNT STOPKEY (cr=27065 r=26550 w=0 time=9537102 us)
     10   VIEW  (cr=27065 r=26550 w=0 time=9537065 us)
     10    SORT ORDER BY STOPKEY (cr=27065 r=26550 w=0 time=9537029 us)
1908096     TABLE ACCESS FULL BIG_TABLE
               (cr=27065 r=26550 w=0 time=5372534 us)
```

The "do-it-yourself" top-N query looks like this:

```
select owner, object_name, object_type, created
    from big_table
   order by created DESC
```

```
call       count     cpu elapsed    disk   query current    rows
-------   ------   ----- -------  -------  ------- -------  -------
Parse          1    0.00    0.00        0        0       0        0
Execute        2    0.00    0.00        0        0       0        0
Fetch          1   17.56   29.06    45303    27065     168       10
-------   ------   ----- -------  -------  ------- -------  -------
total          4   17.57   29.06    45303    27065     168       10

Rows     Row Source Operation
-------  -------------------------------------------------------
     10  SORT ORDER BY (cr=27065 r=45303 w=31780 time=29061743 us)
1908096    TABLE ACCESS FULL BIG_TABLE
           (cr=27065 r=26549 w=0 time=5445859 us)
```

Here, I used Oracle9i version 9.2.0.3 to show you the writes during the SORT ORDER BY step. I was on a single-user system with a generous PGA_AGGREGATE_TARGET (for a single user) of 250MB. That sort far exceeded my system's ability to do that in memory. The writes are all about swapping sort work areas out to TEMP. This is what accounts for the doubling of CPU time (sorting 1.9 million rows versus keeping the top-10 rows) and the tripling of runtime—reading and writing TEMP. Again, both versions do the same thing.

### ROWNUM Wrap-Up

I'll hazard a guess that many readers have a newfound respect for ROWNUM now. Now, you understand these aspects:

- How ROWNUM is assigned, so you can write bug-free queries that use it.

- How it affects the processing of your query, so you can use it to materialize a result set for performance, or to paginate a query on the Web.

- How it can reduce the work performed by your query, so that top-*N* queries that used to consume a lot of TEMP space now use none and return much faster.

With this knowledge, you'll be able to find many places to use ROWNUM.

## Scalar Subqueries

The scalar subquery is a neat capability in SQL that can provide the easiest way to get excellent performance from a query. Basically, since Oracle8i Release 1, you have been able to use a subquery that returns, at most, a single row and column anywhere you could use a character string literal before. You can code this:

```
Select 'Something'
  From dual
 Where 'a' = 'b'
```

So, you can also code this:

```
Select (select column from … where … )
  From dual
 Where (select column from … where … ) = (select … from …. )
```

I mainly use this capability for the following tasks:

■ Removing the need for outer joins

■ Aggregating information from multiple tables in a single query

■ Selectively selecting from a different table/row in a single query

We'll take a look at each of these uses in turn.

## Remove an Outer Join

When you remove an outer join, not only is the resulting query usually easier to read, but many times, the performance can be improved as well. The general idea is you have a query of this form:

```
Select …, outer_joined_to_table.column
   From some_table, outer_joined_to_table
 Where … = outer_joined_to_table(+)
```

You can code that as follows:

```
Select …, (select column from outer_joined_to_table where … )
   From some_table;
```

In many cases, there is a one-to-one relationship from the driving table to the table being outer-joined to, or an aggregate function is applied to the outer-joined-to column. For example, consider this query:

```
select a.username, count(*)
   from all_users a, all_objects b
 where a.username = b.owner (+)
 group by a.username;
```

Its results are equivalent to running this query:

```
    select a.username, (select count(*)
                          from all_objects b
                        where b.owner = a.username) cnt
      from all_users a
```

But somehow, the second query is more efficient. TKPROF shows us the efficiency, but this time, it lets us down. It isn't useful for seeing *why* this is more efficient.

```
select a.username, count(*)
   from all_users a, all_objects b
 where a.username = b.owner (+)
 group by a.username
```

| call | count | cpu | elapsed | disk | query | current | rows |
|------|-------|-----|---------|------|-------|---------|------|
| Parse | 1 | 0.00 | 0.00 | 0 | 0 | 0 | 0 |

```
Execute    1    0.00    0.00       0          0       0          0
Fetch      4    1.90    2.22       0     144615       0         44
-------  ------  -----  -------  -------  -------  -------  -------
total      6    1.90    2.22       0     144615       0         44

Rows     Row Source Operation
-------  -------------------------------------------------------
     44  SORT GROUP BY
  17924   MERGE JOIN OUTER
     44    SORT JOIN
     44     NESTED LOOPS
     44      NESTED LOOPS
     44       TABLE ACCESS FULL USER$
     44       TABLE ACCESS CLUSTER TS$
     44        INDEX UNIQUE SCAN I_TS# (object id 7)
     44      TABLE ACCESS CLUSTER TS$
     44       INDEX UNIQUE SCAN I_TS# (object id 7)
  17916    SORT JOIN
  30581     VIEW
  30581      FILTER
  31708       TABLE ACCESS BY INDEX ROWID OBJ$
  31787        NESTED LOOPS
     78         TABLE ACCESS FULL USER$
  31708         INDEX RANGE SCAN I_OBJ2 (object id 37)
   1035        TABLE ACCESS BY INDEX ROWID IND$
   1402         INDEX UNIQUE SCAN I_IND1 (object id 39)
      1        FIXED TABLE FULL X$KZSPR
      1        FIXED TABLE FULL X$KZSPR
      1        FIXED TABLE FULL X$KZSPR
      1        FIXED TABLE FULL X$KZSPR
      1        FIXED TABLE FULL X$KZSPR
      1        FIXED TABLE FULL X$KZSPR
      1        FIXED TABLE FULL X$KZSPR
      1        FIXED TABLE FULL X$KZSPR
      1        FIXED TABLE FULL X$KZSPR
```

Now, let's compare this to the second version:

```
select a.username, (select count(*)
                        from all_objects b
                      where b.owner = a.username) cnt
  from all_users a
```

| call | count | cpu | elapsed | disk | query | current | rows |
|------|-------|-----|---------|------|-------|---------|------|
| Parse | 1 | 0.00 | 0.00 | 0 | 0 | 0 | 0 |
| Execute | 1 | 0.00 | 0.00 | 0 | 0 | 0 | 0 |
| Fetch | 4 | 1.63 | 1.98 | 0 | 135594 | 0 | 44 |
| total | 6 | 1.63 | 1.98 | 0 | 135594 | 0 | 44 |

```
Rows      Row Source Operation
-------   --------------------------------------------------
     44   NESTED LOOPS
     44    NESTED LOOPS
     44     TABLE ACCESS FULL OBJ#(22)
     44     TABLE ACCESS CLUSTER OBJ#(16)
     44      INDEX UNIQUE SCAN OBJ#(7) (object id 7)
     44    TABLE ACCESS CLUSTER OBJ#(16)
     44     INDEX UNIQUE SCAN OBJ#(7) (object id 7)
```

We see it did less logical I/O, but all references to the ALL_OBJECTS part of the query are missing from the plan. In fact, it is not possible to see the plan for these scalar subqueries as of Oracle9i Release 2. This is unfortunate, and we can only hope that an upcoming version will show scalar subqueries.

What if you need more than one column from the related table? Suppose we needed not only the COUNT(*), but also the AVG(OBJECT_ID). We have four choices:

- Go back to the outer join.

- Use two scalar subqueries.

- Use a trick with a single scalar subquery.

- Use an object type.

Since the first option is pretty obvious, we won't demonstrate that. We will take a look at the other choices, and demonstrate why the third and fourth options may be worthwhile.

**Use Two Scalar Subqueries**     First, we'll look at using two scalar subqueries:

```
select a.username, (select count(*)
                       from all_objects b
                      where b.owner = a.username) cnt,
                    (select avg(object_id )
                       from all_objects b
                      where b.owner = a.username) avg
  from all_users a
```

```
call      count     cpu elapsed    disk   query current    rows
-------  ------   ----- -------  ------- ------- -------  -------
Parse         1    0.00    0.00        0       0       0        0
Execute       1    0.00    0.00        0       0       0        0
Fetch         4    3.18    3.25        0  271036       0       44
-------  ------   ----- -------  ------- ------- -------  -------
total         6    3.18    3.25        0  271036       0       44
```

That effectively doubled the work (look at the QUERY column and compare its values to the previous results). We can get back to where we were, however, just by using a small trick.

**Use a Single Scalar Subquery**    Instead of running two scalar subqueries, we will run one that will encode all of the data of interest in a single string. We can use SUBSTR then to pick off the fields we need and convert them to the appropriate types again.

```
select username,
       to_number( substr( data, 1, 10 ) ) cnt,
       to_number( substr( data, 11 ) ) avg
  from (
select a.username, (select to_char( count(*), 'fm0000000009' ) ||
                           avg(object_id)
                     from all_objects b
                    where b.owner = a.username) data
  from all_users a
     )
```

| call | count | cpu | elapsed | disk | query | current | rows |
|---------|-------|------|---------|------|--------|---------|------|
| Parse | 1 | 0.01 | 0.01 | 0 | 0 | 0 | 0 |
| Execute | 1 | 0.00 | 0.00 | 0 | 0 | 0 | 0 |
| Fetch | 4 | 1.66 | 1.73 | 0 | 135594 | 0 | 44 |
| total | 6 | 1.68 | 1.75 | 0 | 135594 | 0 | 44 |

So, in the inline view, we formatted the COUNT(*) in a ten-character wide, *fixed-width* field. The format modifier (FM) in the TO_CHAR format suppressed the leading space that a number would have, since we know the count will never be negative (so we do not need a sign). We then just concatenate on the AVG() we want. That does not need to be fixed width, since it is the last field. I prefer to use fixed-width fields in all cases because it makes the SUBSTR activity at the next level much easier to perform. The outer query then just must SUBSTR off the fields and use TO_NUMBER or TO_DATE, as appropriate, to convert the strings back to their native type. As you can see, in this case, it paid off to do this extra work.

One note of caution on this technique though: Beware of NULLs. On fields that allow NULLs, you will need to use NVL. For example, if COUNT(*) could have returned a NULL (in this case, it cannot), we would have coded this way:

```
nvl( to_char(count(*),'fm0000000009'), rpad( ' ', 10 ) )
```

That would have returned ten blanks, instead of concatenating in a NULL, which would have shifted the string over, destroying our results.

**Use an Object Type**    Lastly, we can use an object type to return a "scalar" value that is really a complex object type. We need to start by creating a scalar type to be returned by our subquery:

```
ops$tkyte@ORA920> create or replace type myScalarType as object
  2  ( cnt number, average number )
  3  /

Type created.
```

That maps to the two numbers we would like to return: the count and the average. Now, we can get the result using this query:

```
select username, a.data.cnt, a.data.average
   from (
select username, (select myScalarType( count(*), avg(object_id) )
                   from all_objects b
                  where b.owner = a.username ) data
   from all_users a
        ) A
```

| call | count | cpu | elapsed | disk | query | current | rows |
| --- | --- | --- | --- | --- | --- | --- | --- |
| Parse | 1 | 0.01 | 0.01 | 0 | 0 | 0 | 0 |
| Execute | 1 | 0.00 | 0.00 | 0 | 0 | 0 | 0 |
| Fetch | 4 | 1.56 | 1.63 | 0 | 135594 | 0 | 44 |
| total | 6 | 1.58 | 1.65 | 0 | 135594 | 0 | 44 |

Here, we get the same results without needing to encode the data using TO_CHAR and decode the data using SUBSTR and TO_NUMBER. Additionally, the presence of NULLs would not further complicate the query.

Using the object type is convenient to reduce the query complexity, but it does involve the extra step of creating that type, which some people are hesitant to do. So, while this technique is easier to use, I find most people will use the encode/decode technique rather than the object type approach. The performance characteristics are very similar with either technique.

## Aggregate from Multiple Tables

Suppose you are trying to generate a report that shows by username, the username, user ID, created date, number of tables they own, and the number of constraints they own for all users created within the last 50 days. This would be easy if ALL_OBJECTS had both TABLES and CONSTRAINTS, but it doesn't. You need to count rows in two different tables. If you just joined, you would end up with a Cartesian join, so that if a user owned six tables and had three constraints, you would get 18 rows.

I'll demonstrate two queries to retrieve this information: one with, and one without, scalar subqueries. Without scalar queries, there are many ways to achieve this. One technique is to use a Cartesian join. We could also use multiple levels of inline views and join ALL_USERS to ALL_CONSTRAINTS, aggregate that, and then join that to ALL_TABLES (or reverse the two) as well. We could join ALL_USERS to inline views that aggregate ALL_CONSTRAINTS and ALL_TABLES to the same level of detail. We'll compare the implementation of those last two methods to the scalar subquery here. The second inline view solution would look like this:

```
ops$tkyte@ORA920> select a.username, a.user_id, a.created,
  2              nvl(b.cons_cnt,0) cons, nvl(c.tables_cnt,0) tables
  3         from all_users a,
  4              (select owner, count(*) cons_cnt
  5                 from all_constraints
  6                group by owner) b,
  7              (select owner, count(*) tables_cnt
  8                 from all_tables
```

```
     9                     group by owner) c
    10   where a.username = b.owner(+)
    11     and a.username = c.owner(+)
    12     and a.created > sysdate-50
    13   /
```

| USERNAME | USER_ID | CREATED | CONS | TABLES |
|----------|---------|---------|------|--------|
| A | 511 | 04-JUL-03 | 3 | 1 |
| A1 | 396 | 20-JUN-03 | 0 | 1 |
| B | 512 | 04-JUL-03 | 3 | 1 |
| C | 470 | 21-JUN-03 | 0 | 0 |
| D | 471 | 21-JUN-03 | 0 | 1 |
| OPS$TKYTE | 513 | 05-JUL-03 | 17 | 6 |

```
6 rows selected.

Elapsed: 00:00:01.94
```

We had to use outer joins from ALL_USERS to the two inline views, otherwise we would lose rows for users that did not have any tables or had tables but no constraints. The performance of this query—about two seconds on my system—is not the best. Using scalar subqueries instead, we see a query that looks very similar, yet the performance characteristics are very different:

```
ops$tkyte@ORA920> select username, user_id, created,
     2          (select count(*)
     3             from all_constraints
     4            where owner = username) cons,
     5          (select count(*)
     6             from all_tables
     7            where owner = username) tables
     8     from all_users
     9    where all_users.created > sysdate-50
    10   /
```

| USERNAME | USER_ID | CREATED | CONS | TABLES |
|----------|---------|---------|------|--------|
| A | 511 | 04-JUL-03 | 3 | 1 |
| A1 | 396 | 20-JUN-03 | 0 | 1 |
| B | 512 | 04-JUL-03 | 3 | 1 |
| C | 470 | 21-JUN-03 | 0 | 0 |
| D | 471 | 21-JUN-03 | 0 | 1 |
| OPS$TKYTE | 513 | 05-JUL-03 | 17 | 6 |

```
6 rows selected.

Elapsed: 00:00:00.06
```

It is true that we can tune that first query. We can see that when using the inline views, Oracle is producing the aggregations for every user in the database and then outer joining these results to ALL_USERS. Most of our users are not in this report—only the recently created one—so we are computing aggregates for lots of data we are not going to use. Thus, we can manually push the predicate down into these inline views:

```
ops$tkyte@ORA920> select a.username, a.user_id, a.created,
  2          nvl(b.cons_cnt,0) cons, nvl(c.tables_cnt,0) tables
  3     from all_users a,
  4          (select all_constraints.owner, count(*) cons_cnt
  5             from all_constraints, all_users
  6            where all_users.created > sysdate-50
  7              and all_users.username = all_constraints.owner
  8            group by owner) b,
  9          (select all_tables.owner, count(*) tables_cnt
 10             from all_tables, all_users
 11            where all_users.created > sysdate-50
 12              and all_users.username = all_tables.owner
 13            group by owner) c
 14    where a.username = b.owner(+)
 15      and a.username = c.owner(+)
 16      and a.created > sysdate-50
 17   /
```

| USERNAME | USER_ID | CREATED | CONS | TABLES |
|----------|---------|---------|------|--------|
| A | 511 | 04-JUL-03 | 3 | 1 |
| A1 | 396 | 20-JUN-03 | 0 | 1 |
| B | 512 | 04-JUL-03 | 3 | 1 |
| C | 470 | 21-JUN-03 | 0 | 0 |
| D | 471 | 21-JUN-03 | 0 | 1 |
| OPS$TKYTE | 513 | 05-JUL-03 | 17 | 6 |

```
6 rows selected.

Elapsed: 00:00:00.10
```

Here, it is not just the performance boost you may achieve that makes the scalar subquery approach attractive, but also its simplicity.

## Select from Different Tables

Using scalar subqueries for selecting from different tables is one of the neater tricks by far. This is useful in two areas:

- Joining rows in a table/view to some set of other tables—using data in the query itself to pick the table to join to

- Looking up data in an INSERT statement or getting SQLLDR to do code conversions without needing to call PL/SQL

We'll demonstrate each in turn.

**Join Rows to a Set of Tables**   One of my core scripts is a script I call DBLS (for database `ls`, or database `dir` for Windows users). The query is as follows:

```
ops$tkyte@ORA920> select object_type, object_name,
  2             decode( status, 'INVALID', '*', '' ) status,
  3             decode( object_type,
  4             'TABLE', (select tablespace_name
  5                          from user_tables
  6                         where table_name = object_name),
  7             'TABLE PARTITION', (select tablespace_name
  8                                    from user_tab_partitions
  9                                   where partition_name =
                                                  subobject_name),
 10             'INDEX', (select tablespace_name
 11                          from user_indexes
 12                         where index_name = object_name),
 13             'INDEX PARTITION', (select tablespace_name
 14                                    from user_ind_partitions
 15                                   where partition_name =
                                                  subobject_name),
 16             'LOB', (select tablespace_name
 17                        from user_segments
 18                       where segment_name = object_name),
 19      null ) tablespace_name
 20    from user_objects a
 21   order by object_type, object_name
 22  /
```

This generates a report for the current schema of all of the objects, including their type and status. For many things that are segments (consume space), it reports the tablespace in which they reside. Now, you might wonder why I didn't just code the following:

```
select b.object_name, b.object_type,
       decode( b.status, 'INVALID', '*', '' ),
       a.tablespace_name
  from user_segments a, user_objects b
 where a.segment_name(+) = b.object_name
   and a.segment_type(+) = b.object_type;
```

It is more terse and seems like a better choice. AUTOTRACE will help to explain why it doesn't work as well.

```
ops$tkyte@ORA920> select object_type, object_name,
  2             decode( status, 'INVALID', '*', '' ) status,
  3             decode( object_type,
...
 21   order by object_type, object_name
 22  /

86 rows selected.
```

```
Statistics
----------------------------------------------------------
       820   consistent gets

ops$tkyte@ORA920> select b.object_name, b.object_type,
  2            decode( b.status, 'INVALID', '*', '' ),
  3                a.tablespace_name
  4     from user_segments a, user_objects b
  5     where a.segment_name(+) = b.object_name
  6       and a.segment_type(+) = b.object_type;

86 rows selected.

Statistics
----------------------------------------------------------
     12426   consistent gets
```

And the larger your schemas, the worse it gets. I discovered that if I did selective lookups to the less complex views using the DECODE row by row, the query would constantly perform in milliseconds, even on a large schema. Using USER_SEGMENTS, which is a very general-purpose view—sort of the kitchen sink of views—and outer-joining to that could be a killer in certain schemas, to the point where the script was useless since it would take so long to run.

This example shows a technique for joining each row in a result set with a different table. This is also useful when you have a design that uses a single field as a foreign key to N different tables. (Perhaps this is not a good idea, since you cannot use database-integrity constraints, but people do it.) In those cases, a construct such as this is key to pulling the data back together in a fairly efficient manner (in a single query).

**Perform Lookups**     Lastly, this scalar subquery technique is useful when used in conjunction with SQLLDR to perform lookups of data. Suppose you are given an input file where the fields are all specified using lookup codes, but you need to have the data decoded in your database tables. Rather than load the raw data into staging tables, performing joins, and inserting into the real tables, you can use a scalar subquery in the control files directly to load the data. For example, a control file could look like this:

```
LOAD DATA
INFILE *
INTO TABLE t
REPLACE
FIELDS TERMINATED BY '|'
(
username "(select username
           from all_users where user_id = :username)"
)
BEGINDATA
0
5
11
19
```

```
21
30
```

That would automatically convert the USER_ID in the data stream into the USERNAME by doing that lookup for you.

**NOTE**
*In Oracle8i, there is a product issue, whereby if you use this technique, you must also use* `rows=1` *on the SQLLDR command line. Otherwise, you will find the subquery is executed only once and will insert the same value over and over. There are patches that can be applied to various 8174 releases to correct this.*

## Analytics

Analytics are the coolest things to happen to SQL since the keyword SELECT was introduced. They make possible that which used to be impossible to do in SQL, or that was so inefficient to perform using straight SQL that we never would do it. Analytics bring to set-oriented SQL the ability to use array semantics to a degree on result sets.

We know we can compute values *in a row*, as in `select A + B from t`, for example. Analytics allow us to compute values *across rows*. This might not sound earth-shattering at first. Isn't that what aggregates do after all? `select sum(a) from t` computes values across rows, doesn't it? Yes, but analytics allow you to perform the same operation without grouping the rows. They allow you to compute those aggregates and then display them with the detail records. For example, you can run a query like this:

```
scott@ORA920> break on deptno skip 1
scott@ORA920> select deptno,
  2          ename,
  3          sal,
  4          sum(sal) over (partition by deptno order by sal) CumDeptTot,
  5          sum(sal) over (partition by deptno) SalByDept,
  6          sum(sal) over (order by deptno, sal) CumTot,
  7          sum(sal) over () TotSal
  8    from emp
  9   order by deptno, sal
 10   /
```

| DEPTNO | ENAME | SAL | CUMDEPTTOT | SALBYDEPT | CUMTOT | TOTSAL |
|---|---|---|---|---|---|---|
| 10 | MILLER | 1300 | 1300 | 8750 | 1300 | 29025 |
| | CLARK | 2450 | 3750 | 8750 | 3750 | 29025 |
| | KING | 5000 | 8750 | 8750 | 8750 | 29025 |
| 20 | SMITH | 800 | 800 | 10875 | 9550 | 29025 |
| | ADAMS | 1100 | 1900 | 10875 | 10650 | 29025 |
| | JONES | 2975 | 4875 | 10875 | 13625 | 29025 |
| | SCOTT | 3000 | 10875 | 10875 | 19625 | 29025 |

| | | | | | |
|---|---|---|---|---|---|
| | FORD | 3000 | 10875 | 10875 | 19625 | 29025 |
| 30 | JAMES | 950 | 950 | 9400 | 20575 | 29025 |
| | WARD | 1250 | 3450 | 9400 | 23075 | 29025 |
| | MARTIN | 1250 | 3450 | 9400 | 23075 | 29025 |
| | TURNER | 1500 | 4950 | 9400 | 24575 | 29025 |
| | ALLEN | 1600 | 6550 | 9400 | 26175 | 29025 |
| | BLAKE | 2850 | 9400 | 9400 | 29025 | 29025 |

```
14 rows selected.
```

Here we used:

- `sum(sal) over () TotSal` Computes a grand total. This is equivalent to `select sum(sal) from emp`, but that query would return only one row. Here, we get that `sum(sal)` associated with each detail row. We can easily compare each row in EMP to the grand total sum of SAL.

- `sum(sal) over (partition by deptno) SalByDept` Computes a department total. The SAL column was summed by department now. The individual EMP records could compare their salary to the total salary made in that department. The PARTITION keyword breaks up our result set into virtual partitions on which the analytic functions will be applied.

- `sum(sal) over (partition by deptno order by sal) CumDeptTot` Computes a running total within a department for the SAL column, in order of salaries from the smallest salary to the largest. Adding the ORDER BY clause changed the behavior of the analytic function. Instead of working on every row in the partition, it worked only on the current and prior rows in the partition after sorting by SAL.

- `sum(sal) over (order by deptno, sal) CumTot` Creates a running total of the SAL column after the data was sorted by DEPTNO and then SAL. Since our entire result set would be sorted this way, it becomes a running total for our result set.

The result set almost resembles a spreadsheet, doesn't it? You could sum across easily (that is obvious), but now you can sum up and down, do running totals, and perform other calculations. Analytics give you spreadsheet-like functionality in the SQL language.

In this section, I will demonstrate practical uses of analytic functions, not explain all of the intricacies of them. For details on using analytics, see the *Oracle Data Warehousing Guide*, the "SQL for Analysis in Data Warehouses" chapter (http://technet.oracle.com/docs/products/oracle9i/doc_library/release2/server.920/a96520/analysis.htm#1020, for the Oracle9i Release 2 documentation set, but there are versions for Oracle8i as well). Don't be misled by the fact that this information appears in a data warehouse document. Analytics apply to systems that generate reports, perform batch jobs, cleanse/validate data, and so on. In short, pretty much every system.

It is worth noting that in Oracle8i, analytics were a feature of the Personal and Enterprise Editions only; the Standard Edition did not support this functionality. However, starting with

Oracle9i Release 1, analytics are a base feature of Standard Edition as well, so every Oracle9i database has access to this functionality.

Now, we'll take a look at specific analytics use cases, and then close up with a rather large example, which will use analytics to help us "break a big table" into small chunks using ROWID ranges. These ROWID ranges may then be used as inputs into a PL/SQL routine that needs to process each row in a table but cannot be parallelized using parallel query. This is the "do-it-yourself" parallelism I described in Chapter 3.

## Find a Specific Row in a Partition

Frequently, I'm asked to help with problems like this:

- I need to find the record with the MAX END_DATE for every employee (their current record).

- I need to process the record with the MAX *COLUMN X* for every record in this table.

- I need the record that is closest to the average of the salary by department.

The general way to write this type of query used to be something along these lines:

```
select *
  from T T1
 where column = ( select max(column)
                    from T T2
                   where T2.KEY = T1.KEY)
```

For example, using our BIG_TABLE to find the last modified object by each OWNER, we might use this query:

```
big_table@ORA920> select *
  2  from big_table t1
  3  where last_ddl_time = (select max(last_ddl_time)
  4                           from big_table t2
  5                          where t2.owner = t1.owner )
  6  /
```

As you can see, we've used a correlated subquery in order to find the MAX(LAST_DDL_TIME) by owner, record by record. That means that correlated subquery *could* be evaluated once per row in the BIG_TABLE table. If there are very few records in BIG_TIME, this approach is doable; the performance will be sufficient. If there are tens of thousands or more records, however, the cumulative cost of executing that correlated subquery over and over would be large.

A better way to write that query might be as follows:

```
big_table@ORA920> select *
  2  from big_table t1, ( select owner, max(last_ddl_time) max_time
  3                         from big_table
  4                        group by owner ) t2
  5  where t1.owner = t2.owner
```

```
6       and t1.last_ddl_time = t2.last_ddl_time
7    /
```

In fact, the CBO may do that rewrite for us. Using the BIG_TABLE example we've been using so far, this was the case, and the query plans for both were the same. But that query still suffers from the fact that it would need to full-scan the BIG_TABLE table two times for us: once to compute the MAX LAST_DDL_TIME by owner and again to join that to BIG_TABLE to find the appropriate records to report.

We can instead query with analytic functions, as follows:

```
big_table@ORA920> select owner, last_ddl_time, object_name, object_type
2        from ( select t1.*,
3                        max(last_ddl_time) over (partition by owner) max_time
4                  from big_table t1
5                )
6    where last_ddl_time = max_time
7    /
```

This will make a single pass on the table and compute the maximum LAST_DDL_TIME as it is going along. Depending on various factors, such as the size of the table and the number of rows you expect to get back, this may be much more efficient than making two passes to achieve the same goal. A simple TKPROF comparison of the two shows the following:

```
select owner, last_ddl_time, object_name, object_type
  from big_table t1
 where last_ddl_time = (select max(last_ddl_time)
                          from big_table t2
                         where t2.owner = t1.owner )
```

| call | count | cpu | elapsed | disk | query | current | rows |
|---------|-------|-------|---------|-------|-------|---------|------|
| Parse | 1 | 0.00 | 0.00 | 0 | 0 | 0 | 0 |
| Execute | 1 | 0.00 | 0.00 | 0 | 0 | 0 | 0 |
| Fetch | 484 | 20.10 | 29.43 | 43590 | 44520 | 8 | 7233 |
| total | 486 | 20.10 | 29.43 | 43590 | 44520 | 8 | 7233 |

```
Rows     Row Source Operation
-------  ---------------------------------------------------------
   7233  HASH JOIN   (cr=44520 r=43590 w=0 time=29366146 us)
     28    VIEW   (cr=22002 r=21795 w=0 time=14710206 us)
     28     SORT GROUP BY (cr=22002 r=21795 w=0 time=14710075 us)
1833792      TABLE ACCESS FULL BIG_TABLE (cr=22002 r=21795 w=0 time=10315205 us)
1833792    TABLE ACCESS FULL BIG_TABLE (cr=22518 r=21795 w=0 time=6630213 us)

select owner, last_ddl_time, object_name, object_type
  from ( select t1.*,
               max(last_ddl_time) over (partition by owner) max_time
          from big_table t1
       )
```

```
where last_ddl_time = max_time

call     count       cpu    elapsed       disk      query    current       rows
-------  ------  --------  ---------  ---------  ---------  ---------     ------
Parse        1      0.00       0.00          0          0          0          0
Execute      1      0.00       0.00          0          0          0          0
Fetch      484     17.70      26.90      21790      22002          4       7233
-------  ------  --------  ---------  ---------  ---------  ---------     ------
total      486     17.70      26.90      21790      22002          4       7233

Rows       Row Source Operation
-------    ---------------------------------------------------
   7233    VIEW  (cr=22002 r=21790 w=0 time=26818267 us)
1833792     WINDOW SORT (cr=22002 r=21790 w=0 time=23798930 us)
1833792      TABLE ACCESS FULL BIG_TABLE (cr=22002 r=21790 w=0 time=10321786 us)
```

So, the next time you need to get the maximum row from within a group, consider using analytic functions.

## Top-N in a Group

Top-*N* in a group queries is an area where analytics shine. These queries allow you to get information like the top-three paid employees per department, or the top-scoring athletes by grade, or the top-revenue producing products by region. There isn't an efficient "straight SQL" solution, and coming up with inefficient ones is hard, if even possible.

Using analytics, you just need to make a choice as to what you mean by top-*N* per group. There are many ways to interpret this. Say someone asks you to report on the top-three paid people by department. This could be three rows per department, but it could also be some number of rows between one and infinity. What happens when the department has 50 people, all who make the same highest salary? Do you pick a random three? Do you show all 50? What is the correct answer? With analytics, you can get any of the answers you want; it is up to you to decide which one.

The functions we'll use for top-*N* processing and analytics are the following:

- ROW_NUMBER assigns a unique sequential number after sorting to every row in a partition.

- RANK assigns a ranking to each row in a partition. Rows with the same value get the same rank. The rankings can have gaps in them. For example, if two rows are ranked number 1, there will be no number 2. You cannot have a number 2 if there are two number 1s.

- DENSE_RANK, like RANK assigns a ranking to each row in a partition. Rows with the same value get the same rank. The rankings will be contiguous, without any gaps in the ranking.

We can see the difference between these three functions easily using the SCOTT/TIGER EMP table.

```
scott@ORA920> select deptno,
  2             ename,
```

```
3                   sal,
4             row_number() over (partition by deptno order by sal desc) rn,
5             rank() over (partition by deptno order by sal desc ) rank,
6             dense_rank() over ( partition by deptno order by sal desc ) dense_rank
7       from emp
8    order by deptno, sal DESC
9    /
```

| DEPTNO | ENAME | SAL | RN | RANK | DENSE_RANK |
|---|---|---|---|---|---|
| 10 | KING | 5000 | 1 | 1 | 1 |
| | CLARK | 2450 | 2 | 2 | 2 |
| | MILLER | 1300 | 3 | 3 | 3 |
| 20 | SCOTT | 3000 | 1 | 1 | 1 |
| | FORD | 3000 | 2 | 1 | 1 |
| | JONES | 2975 | 3 | 3 | 2 |
| | ADAMS | 1100 | 4 | 4 | 3 |
| | SMITH | 800 | 5 | 5 | 4 |
| 30 | BLAKE | 2850 | 1 | 1 | 1 |
| | ALLEN | 1600 | 2 | 2 | 2 |
| | TURNER | 1500 | 3 | 3 | 3 |
| | WARD | 1250 | 4 | 4 | 4 |
| | MARTIN | 1250 | 5 | 4 | 4 |
| | JAMES | 950 | 6 | 6 | 5 |

```
14 rows selected.
```

Notice in particular DEPTNO=20. There are two top-paid people: both SCOTT and FORD make $3,000 in that department. ROW_NUMBER assigned a 1 to SCOTT and a 2 to FORD arbitrarily. It could happen that FORD gets 1 and SCOTT gets 2 on your system. This is because they just happened to have sorted in that order here. When we use RANK and DENSE_RANK, however, both employees get the value 1. This makes sense. Since they both make the same amount, they are both 1 in that respect.

After that, however, RANK and DENSE_RANK diverge. A rank of 3 is assigned to the next record in that partition. JONES has a RANK of 3 but a DENSE_RANK of 2. This is the difference between RANK and DENSE_RANK. RANK says, "If there are two number 1 values, there cannot be a number 2. The next ranking must be 3 after that tie." In fact, if three people made $3,000, RANK would assign 4 to the next record in the partition; there would be no second or third ranks. Consider this example:

```
scott@ORA920> update emp set sal = 3000 where ename = 'JONES';
1 row updated.

scott@ORA920> select deptno,
  2             ename,
  3                   sal,
  4             row_number() over (partition by deptno order by sal desc) rn,
```

```
  5            rank() over (partition by deptno order by sal desc ) rank,
  6            dense_rank() over ( partition by deptno order by sal desc ) dense_rank
  7   from emp
  8 order by deptno, sal DESC
  9 /

    DEPTNO ENAME           SAL          RN        RANK DENSE_RANK
---------- ---------- ---------- ---------- ---------- ----------
...
        20 JONES          3000          1          1          1
           SCOTT          3000          2          1          1
           FORD           3000          3          1          1
           ADAMS          1100          4          4          2
           SMITH           800          5          5          3
...
scott@ORA920> rollback
  2 /

Rollback complete.
```

Now, getting the top three from each department is easy. Suppose we just wanted an arbitrary set of three rows for each department, a representation of the top-three salaried employees. In that case, we might use ROW_NUMBER like this:

```
scott@ORA920> select deptno, ename, sal, rn
  2    from (
  3   select deptno,
  4          ename,
  5          sal,
  6          row_number() over (partition by deptno order by sal desc) rn,
  7          rank() over (partition by deptno order by sal desc ) rank,
  8          dense_rank() over ( partition by deptno order by sal desc ) dense_rank
  9     from emp
 10          )
 11    where rn <= 3
 12    order by deptno, sal DESC
 13 /

    DEPTNO ENAME           SAL          RN
---------- ---------- ---------- ----------
        10 KING           5000          1
           CLARK          2450          2
           MILLER         1300          3

        20 SCOTT          3000          1
           FORD           3000          2
           JONES          2975          3
```

```
          30 BLAKE              2850           1
             ALLEN             1600           2
             TURNER            1500           3


9 rows selected.
```

Doing this example with RANK would give us the same results, due to this set of data. However, using DENSE_RANK, we get different results.

```
scott@ORA920> select deptno, ename, sal, dense_rank
  2    from (
  3   select deptno,
  4          ename,
  5          sal,
  6          row_number() over (partition by deptno order by sal desc) rn,
  7          rank() over (partition by deptno order by sal desc ) rank,
  8          dense_rank() over ( partition by deptno order by sal desc )
dense_rank
  9    from emp
 10          )
 11    where dense_rank <= 3
 12    order by deptno, sal DESC
 13   /

    DEPTNO ENAME             SAL DENSE_RANK
---------- ---------- ---------- ----------
        10 KING             5000          1
           CLARK            2450          2
           MILLER           1300          3

        20 SCOTT            3000          1
           FORD             3000          1
           JONES            2975          2
           ADAMS            1100          3

        30 BLAKE            2850          1
           ALLEN            1600          2
           TURNER           1500          3


10 rows selected.
```

Notice in Department 20 there are four rows, not three. We got the records of the employees making the top-three salaries. Most people might expect these results, but they might be surprised to see more than three records.

As you've seen here, you can use ROW_NUMBER, RANK, and DENSE_RANK to get the top-*N* result set you need.

If you can use ROWNUM for top-*N* query processing, you should. You use ROW_NUMBER() or its related functions RANK and DENSE_RANK only when you need to get the top-*N* rows in a partition. The reason is due to the ROWNUM optimization we discussed in the section, "Top-*N* Query Processing with ROWNUM." ROWNUM is uniquely suited to get the first "N" rows from a result set, and it can do so very efficiently as described. ROW_NUMBER() is, on the other hand, uniquely suited to get the first "N" rows of a group within a result set. It does not have the same characteristics of ROWNUM in that regard.

## Transposing (Pivoting)

Expanding on our problem in the previous section, suppose the requirement was to get the top-three salaries by department, with four columns: DEPTNO, SAL1, SAL2, and SAL3. How would we approach that? We need to use DENSE_RANK to assign 1, 2, 3, and so on to the salaries in each department (duplicate salaries receive the same dense rank). Then we can use a simple pivot with DECODE or CASE and group by DEPTNO.

First, we start with the query to assign the dense rank by DEPTNO to each salary.

```
scott@ORA920> select deptno, sal,
  2              dense_rank() over( partition by deptno order by sal desc)
dense_rank
  3    from emp
  4   /

    DEPTNO        SAL DENSE_RANK
---------- ---------- ----------
        10       5000          1
        10       2450          2
        10       1300          3
...
        30        950          5

14 rows selected.
```

Now, using an inline view, we'll begin to pivot. We want to have just a couple of rows per DEPTNO and the three columns filled in, like a matrix. Notice how it is a very sparse matrix, since each set of DEPTNOs will have only one value for SAL in each column (SAL1, SAL2, and SAL3). The remaining values will be NULLs. This is key to performing a pivot. We'll be able to use an aggregate later to remove the NULL values.

```
scott@ORA920> select deptno,
  2              decode( dense_rank, 1, sal ) sal1,
  3              decode( dense_rank, 2, sal ) sal2,
  4              decode( dense_rank, 3, sal ) sal3
  5    from (
  6   select deptno, sal,
  7              dense_rank() over( partition by deptno order by sal desc)
dense_rank
  8    from emp
  9         )
 10   where dense_rank <= 3
 11   /
```

| DEPTNO | SAL1 | SAL2 | SAL3 |
|--------|------|------|------|
| 10 | 5000 | | |
| 10 | | 2450 | |
| 10 | | | 1300 |
| 20 | 3000 | | |
| 20 | 3000 | | |
| 20 | | 2975 | |
| 20 | | | 1100 |
| 30 | 2850 | | |
| 30 | | 1600 | |
| 30 | | | 1500 |

```
10 rows selected.
```

Now, all that remains is to remove the NULLs. Remember that an aggregate function will ignore NULLs. So, we can simply use MAX (or MIN, SUM, or another aggregate function) to collapse the rows:

```
scott@ORA920> select deptno,
  2          max(decode( dense_rank, 1, sal )) sal1,
  3          max(decode( dense_rank, 2, sal )) sal2,
  4          max(decode( dense_rank, 3, sal )) sal3
  5     from (
  6   select deptno, sal,
  7          dense_rank() over( partition by deptno order by sal desc) dense_rank
  8     from emp
  9          )
 10    where dense_rank <= 3
 11    group by deptno
 12   /
```

| DEPTNO | SAL1 | SAL2 | SAL3 |
|--------|------|------|------|
| 10 | 5000 | 2450 | 1300 |
| 20 | 3000 | 2975 | 1100 |
| 30 | 2850 | 1600 | 1500 |

And there is our pivot, or transposition, of the data. Analytics such as ROW_NUMBER and DENSE_RANK lend themselves to pivoting quite easily.

## Prior Row/Next Row

Two other very popular analytic functions are LAG and LEAD. These magic functions allow you to look backwards (LAG) or forwards (LEAD) in a result set. In the past, this could be accomplished only by complex, inefficient self-joins. Now, it is as easy as using a simple function.

As an example, suppose we have a table like this (from an asktom.com question I received not too long ago):

```
port            activity           activity_date         area
-----           ----------         ---------------       ------
port1           load               10-aug-02             area1
port1           charg              15-sep-02             area1
port1           sendtorepair       10-feb-02             area1
```

We want to generate a report like this:

```
port1      from load      to charge        avg(days)
port1      from repair    to repaired      avg(days)
.
.

port2      from load      to charge        avg(days)
```

Basically, every row in this table needs to be "joined" to its next row, so we can see what activity is next and compute the days between activities.

For testing, we can set up a table with the following data:

```
ops$tkyte@ORA920> select * from t;

PORT   ACTIVITY          ACTIVITY_
-----  ---------------   ---------
port   load              10-AUG-02
port   charge            15-SEP-02
port   sendtorepair      10-FEB-03
port   repaired          22-FEB-03
port   load              10-MAR-03
port   charge            15-MAR-03
port2  load              11-AUG-02
port2  charge            17-SEP-02
port2  sendtorepair      13-FEB-03
port2  repaired          26-FEB-03
port2  load              15-MAR-03
port2  charge            21-MAR-03

12 rows selected.
```

We need to start with a query that takes each row, by port, and reports it with the data from the next row, as sorted by activity date.

```
ops$tkyte@ORA920> select port,
  2              activity,
  3              lead(activity)
  4                over (partition by port
  5                        order by activity_date) nxt_activity,
  6              activity_date,
  7              lead(activity_date)
```

```
 8                over (partition by port
 9                        order by activity_date) nxt_activity_date
10    from t
11  /
```

| PORT  | ACTIVITY    | NXT_ACTIVITY | ACTIVITY_  | NXT_ACTIV |
|-------|-------------|--------------|------------|-----------|
| port  | load        | charge       | 10-AUG-02  | 15-SEP-02 |
| port  | charge      | sendtorepair | 15-SEP-02  | 10-FEB-03 |
| port  | sendtorepair| repaired     | 10-FEB-03  | 22-FEB-03 |
| port  | repaired    | load         | 22-FEB-03  | 10-MAR-03 |
| port  | load        | charge       | 10-MAR-03  | 15-MAR-03 |
| port  | charge      |              | 15-MAR-03  |           |
| port2 | load        | charge       | 11-AUG-02  | 17-SEP-02 |
| port2 | charge      | sendtorepair | 17-SEP-02  | 13-FEB-03 |
| port2 | sendtorepair| repaired     | 13-FEB-03  | 26-FEB-03 |
| port2 | repaired    | load         | 26-FEB-03  | 15-MAR-03 |
| port2 | load        | charge       | 15-MAR-03  | 21-MAR-03 |
| port2 | charge      |              | 21-MAR-03  |           |

```
12 rows selected.
```

Notice how the LEAD function allows us to look forward in the result set, so that the first row with an ACTIVITY_DATE of 10-AUG-2002 has data from the *next* row in the result set, the record with ACTIVITY_DATE of 15-SEP-2002.

Let's look at the nonanalytic query that might achieve the same results:

```
ops$tkyte@ORA920> select port,
 2              activity,
 3              substr( data, 15 ) activity,
 4              activity_date,
 5              to_date( substr( data, 1, 14 ), 'yyyymmddhh24miss' )
 6      from (
 7   select port,
 8              activity,
 9              activity_date,
10              (select MIN(to_char(activity_date,'yyyymmddhh24miss'))||activity)
11                from t t2
12               where t2.port = t.port
13                 and t2.activity_date > t.activity_date ) data
14      from t
15              )
16  /
...
12 rows selected.
```

There are two issues with this approach. First, it is hard; we needed to use that encoding trick we learned about in the scalar subquery section. Second, its performance as the result set size increases is poor. It is a correlated subquery, one that will be executed for each row in the outer query. There are no bulk optimizations that can be done here, since the values for the join change for each row. This will be an expensive query to execute for more than a couple of rows. The LEAD function obviates those two issues, because it is easy to code and it is much more efficient than this self-join technique.

Now, moving onto producing the report, all we need to do is wrap our query in an inline view and a bit of math. We'll do this incrementally to see what happens. We'll start simply by computing the days between events:

```
ops$tkyte@ORA920> select port, activity, nxt_activity, activity_date,
nxt_activity_date,
  2           nxt_activity_date - activity_date days_between
  3     from (
  4   select port,
  5           activity,
  6           lead(activity)
  7             over (partition by port
  8                       order by activity_date) nxt_activity,
  9           activity_date,
 10           lead(activity_date)
 11             over (partition by port
 12                       order by activity_date) nxt_activity_date
 13     from t
 14          )
 15   /
```

| PORT  | ACTIVITY    | NXT_ACTIVITY | ACTIVITY_  | NXT_ACTIV  | DAYS_BETWEEN |
|-------|-------------|--------------|------------|------------|--------------|
| port  | load        | charge       | 10-AUG-02  | 15-SEP-02  | 36           |
| port  | charge      | sendtorepair | 15-SEP-02  | 10-FEB-03  | 148          |
| port  | sendtorepair| repaired     | 10-FEB-03  | 22-FEB-03  | 12           |
| port  | repaired    | load         | 22-FEB-03  | 10-MAR-03  | 16           |
| port  | load        | charge       | 10-MAR-03  | 15-MAR-03  | 5            |
| port  | charge      |              | 15-MAR-03  |            |              |
| port2 | load        | charge       | 11-AUG-02  | 17-SEP-02  | 37           |
| port2 | charge      | sendtorepair | 17-SEP-02  | 13-FEB-03  | 149          |
| port2 | sendtorepair| repaired     | 13-FEB-03  | 26-FEB-03  | 13           |
| port2 | repaired    | load         | 26-FEB-03  | 15-MAR-03  | 17           |
| port2 | load        | charge       | 15-MAR-03  | 21-MAR-03  | 6            |
| port2 | charge      |              | 21-MAR-03  |            |              |

```
12 rows selected.
```

Now, we need a very simple AVG and GROUP BY.

```
ops$tkyte@ORA920> select port, activity, nxt_activity,
  2           avg( nxt_activity_date - activity_date ) days_between
  3     from (
  4   select port,
  5           activity,
  6           lead(activity)
  7             over (partition by port
  8                       order by activity_date) nxt_activity,
```

```
 9              activity_date,
10              lead(activity_date)
11                over (partition by port
12                         order by activity_date) nxt_activity_date
13      from t
14           )
15    where nxt_activity is not null
16    group by port, activity, nxt_activity
17    order by 1, 2
18   /
```

```
PORT  ACTIVITY         NXT_ACTIVITY     DAYS_BETWEEN
----- ---------------- ---------------- ------------
port  charge           sendtorepair              148
port  load             charge                   20.5
port  repaired         load                       16
port  sendtorepair     repaired                   12
port2 charge           sendtorepair              149
port2 load             charge                   21.5
port2 repaired         load                       17
port2 sendtorepair     repaired                   13

8 rows selected.
```

And we have it. You can use this approach anytime you have time-oriented data and need to compare the current record to the prior record or next record. Also, LAG and LEAD can look further backwards or forwards in the result set; they are not limited to just the row preceding or following the current one.

## Parallelization

This final, complex example will show you the power of the analytics functions and walk through my thought processes when building a query. The problem we wish to solve is as follows:

- We have a large table.

- We process this table using PL/SQL row by row (employing bulk fetches, of course!).

- We have a large machine with many CPUs and a lot of disk space.

- We find our PL/SQL routine is not very scalable; it uses only a single CPU and doesn't make good use of the entire machine.

- A parallel query won't work because we have an inherently single-threaded process processing the rows.

Enter "do-it-yourself" parallelism. We want to break the table into *N* nonoverlapping chunks and start *N* copies of the PL/SQL routine running simultaneously. There are many ways we could do this, such as by using primary key ranges or by using the analytic functions (NTILE would be appropriate; it is useful for "binning" problems like this). But all of these would require either of the following:

- Reading every row via an index (primary key range). This would be very slow and inefficient, with a lot of single-block I/O.

■ Each of the *N* processes reading the entire table and ignoring the rows it is not tasked with processing. This incurs contention for the blocks on disk (everyone is reading them) and causes the PL/SQL routines to fetch *N*-1 times as much data as necessary.

We can avoid both of those issues using ROWID ranges. In fact, if you watch Oracle do a parallel query (monitoring the active SQL), you'll see that this is exactly how Oracle breaks up the problem. It assigns the parallel query slaves different ranges of a table to full-scan by ROWID ranges. All we need to do is assign different, nonoverlapping (yet covering) ROWID ranges to our PL/SQL routine, and we can achieve our own parallelism.

Our goal is to take the set of extents for a table using DBA_EXTENTS, break it up into *N* more or less equal-sized portions, and come up with ROWID ranges that cover that in a nonoverlapping fashion. We should be able to support objects that span datafiles. The output from this query will be something like this:

```
ops$tkyte@ORA920> @split BIG_TABLE_COPY 4
        GRP MIN_RID             MAX_RID
---------- ------------------  ------------------
          0 AAAMgQAAGAAAAAJAAA  AAAMgQAAGAAABaICcQ
          1 AAAMgQAAGAAABaJAAA  AAAMgQAANAAAA6ICcQ
          2 AAAMgQAANAAAA6JAAA  AAAMgQAAOAAAAgICcQ
          3 AAAMgQAAOAAAAgJAAA  AAAMgQAAOAAAB8IccQ
```

That script split the big table into four ROWID ranges (I used BIG_TABLE_COPY, as explained in a moment). We could now start four copies of a PL/SQL routine, each of which would execute this:

```
select * from big_table_copy where ROWID between l_lo_rid and l_hi_rid;
```

We would get a query plan much like this:

```
ops$tkyte@ORA920> select * from big_table_copy
  2 where ROWID between 'AAAMgQAAGAAAAAJAAA' and 'AAAMgQAAGAAABaICcQ';

Execution Plan
----------------------------------------------------------
   0      SELECT STATEMENT Optimizer=CHOOSE
          (Cost=2248 Card=4584 Bytes=412560)
   1    0   TABLE ACCESS (BY ROWID RANGE) OF 'BIG_TABLE_COPY'
          (Cost=2248 Card=4584 Bytes=412560)
```

This would read all of the records in that ROWID range, with minimal contention and greatest efficiency.

In order to test this, we can set up a tablespace, like this:

```
create tablespace demo datafile size 67174400, size 67174400, size 67174400
```

This is three 64MB + 64KB datafiles using system-allocated extents. We use this size so that when we copy over BIG_TABLE into this tablespace, it will more or less fill all three files evenly, giving us a nice spread of data over three files. That copy operation is what we do next:

```
create table big_table_copy TABLESPACE demo as select * from big_table;
analyze table big_table_copy compute statistics for table;
```

We need to analyze the table because the RBO is unaware of ROWID range query plans, and it would full-scan the table given ROWID pairs.

Now, we are ready to begin the development of our query. Our ultimate goal is to get $N$ rows where:

■ $N$ is the number of chunks we want to process.

■ Each row has a ROWID representing the lowest block ID in the lowest relative file in that chunk.

■ Each row has a ROWID representing the highest block ID in the highest relative file in that chunk.

■ Each chunk is ordered by relative file number and block ID. This is important because ROWIDs sort by file, then block, then row on the block. So, a ROWID with relative file 6 and block ID 1234 is less than a ROWID with relative file 7 and block ID 2.

My initial query started slowly, not achieving all of these goals. I built the final answer incrementally.

**Bin the Extents**     First, we need to just "bin" the extents, placing them into 1 of $N$ groups based on a cumulative size. So, if we have a table that is 100MB and we decide to process four chunks, we would like to see 25MB chunks. In order to achieve this, we need a running total of the size of the table after sorting the extents by file and within file by block, as well as the total size of the table.

If we integer-divide the running total by the total size/number of chunks, we'll get a grouping number assigned to each row. We have that 100MB table (total size), we know that 25MB = 100MB/4, and we have a running total of the size of the table. We can see that for any row where the running total size is less than 25, `trunc( running_total/25 )` = 0. As soon as we get to a running total over 25 but less than 50, `trunc(running_total/25)` = 1, and so on. This will place each extent into one of four groups. This initial query is as follows:

```
ops$tkyte@ORA920> select relative_fno,
  2             block_id,
  3             blocks,
  4             sum(blocks) over (order by relative_fno, block_id) cum_blocks,
  5             sum(blocks) over () tot_blocks,
  6      trunc( (sum(blocks) over (order by relative_fno, block_id)-0.01) /
  7                     (sum(blocks) over ()/&CHUNKS) ) grp
  8      from dba_extents
  9    where segment_name = '&TNAME'
 10      and owner = user
```

```
 11   order by relative_fno, block_id
 12  /
```

&TNAME is the table name, and &CHUNKS is the number of chunks we want to divide the table into. For my table, some of the results looked like this:

| RELATIVE_FNO | BLOCK_ID | BLOCKS | CUM_BLOCKS | TOT_BLOCKS | GRP |
|---|---|---|---|---|---|
| 6 | 9 | 128 | 128 | 23552 | 0 |
| 6 | 137 | 128 | 256 | 23552 | 0 |
| ... | | | | | |
| 6 | 3721 | 1024 | 4736 | 23552 | 0 |
| 6 | 4745 | 1024 | 5760 | 23552 | 0 |
| 6 | 5769 | 1024 | 6784 | 23552 | 1 |
| 6 | 6793 | 1024 | 7808 | 23552 | 1 |
| ... | | | | | |
| 13 | 2569 | 128 | 10496 | 23552 | 1 |
| 13 | 2697 | 1024 | 11520 | 23552 | 1 |
| 13 | 3721 | 1024 | 12544 | 23552 | 2 |
| 13 | 4745 | 1024 | 13568 | 23552 | 2 |
| ... | | | | | |
| 14 | 1801 | 128 | 17536 | 23552 | 2 |
| 14 | 1929 | 128 | 17664 | 23552 | 2 |
| 14 | 2057 | 128 | 17792 | 23552 | 3 |
| 14 | 2185 | 128 | 17920 | 23552 | 3 |
| ... | | | | | |
| 14 | 5897 | 1024 | 22528 | 23552 | 3 |
| 14 | 6921 | 1024 | 23552 | 23552 | 3 |

```
94 rows selected.
```

As you can see, the total blocks in this table as computed by SUM(BLOCKS) OVER() is 23,552. Therefore, we would expect about 5,888 blocks in each of the four chunks. This query got very close; for example, the first chunk contains 5,760 blocks. We'll never get to precisely 5,888, since we are constrained by extent sizes and such. Additionally, I purposely complicated this issue by using system-managed extents, so the extent sizes are different sizes. But, in general, we ended up with four groupings sorted by relative file number and block ID, and each of the four chunks had about the same number of blocks associated with it.

**Group the Data**    Now, for each group, we are interested in the relative file number/block ID for the lowest file and the highest relative file number/block ID. We can use FIRST_VALUE and LAST_VALUE analytics to pick off the first and last rows in each group after sorting. Additionally, we only care about distinct values—we expect *N* rows from this query, where *N* is the number of desired chunks. Just to check the math, we'll include the sum of blocks within each group to see how we did.

```
ops$tkyte@ORA920> select distinct grp,
  2             first_value(relative_fno) over
  3                (partition by grp order by relative_fno, block_id
```

```
  4                    rows between unbounded preceding
  5                              and unbounded following) lo_fno,
  6         first_value(block_id     ) over
  7            (partition by grp order by relative_fno, block_id
  8            rows between unbounded preceding
  9                     and unbounded following) lo_block,
 10         last_value(relative_fno) over
 11            (partition by grp order by relative_fno, block_id
 12            rows between unbounded preceding
 13                     and unbounded following) hi_fno,
 14         last_value(block_id+blocks-1) over
 15            (partition by grp order by relative_fno, block_id
 16            rows between unbounded preceding
 17                     and unbounded following) hi_block,
 18         sum(blocks) over (partition by grp) sum_blocks
 19    from (
 20  select relative_fno,
 21         block_id,
 22         blocks,
 23    trunc( (sum(blocks) over (order by relative_fno, block_id)-0.01) /
 24          (sum(blocks) over ()/&CHUNKS) ) grp
 25    from dba_extents
 26   where segment_name = '&TNAME'
 27     and owner = user
 28         )
 29  /
```

| GRP | LO_FNO | LO_BLOCK | HI_FNO | HI_BLOCK | SUM_BLOCKS |
|-----|--------|----------|--------|----------|------------|
| 0   | 6      | 9        | 6      | 5768     | 5760       |
| 1   | 6      | 5769     | 13     | 3720     | 5760       |
| 2   | 13     | 3721     | 14     | 2056     | 6144       |
| 3   | 14     | 2057     | 14     | 7944     | 5888       |

**NOTE**

*The rows UNBOUNDED PRECEDING and UNBOUNDED FOLLOWING set up a "window," To get the first and last values in the entire partition, we need to override the default window. To fully comprehend these "windows" and how to use them, read the "SQL for Analysis in Data Warehouses" chapter in the Oracle Data Warehousing Guide (http://technet.oracle.com/docs/products/oracle9i/doc_library/release2/server.920/a96520/analysis.htm#1020).*

Now, we are getting somewhere. We have the relative file number/block ID of the lowest block in group 0, as well as the highest. We can also spot-check and see that our binning did pretty well. We have close to 5,888 blocks in each chunk, achieving a fair split.

**Split into ROWID Ranges**    The last step is to take our query and wrap it in yet another inline view (in the following, replace ABOVE_QUERY_TEXT with the query from the previous section). We'll join that inline view to USER_OBJECTS to pick up the DATA_OBJECT_ID for our table, and then use DBMS_ROWID to generate ROWIDs from the DATA_OBJECT_ID, relative file number, data block ID, and row number. For the low block, we'll use a row number of 0 (row numbers on blocks are zero-based; the first row is in row number 0) and a row number of 10,000 for the high block (10,000 far exceeds the number of rows that will fit on any Oracle block). That will ensure that we start from the lowest row in the range and get the last row on the highest block.

```
ops$tkyte@ORA920> select grp,
  2           dbms_ROWID.ROWID_create
             ( 1, data_object_id, lo_fno, lo_block, 0 ) min_rid,
  3           dbms_ROWID.ROWID_create
             ( 1, data_object_id, hi_fno, hi_block, 10000 ) max_rid
  4      from ( ABOVE_QUERY_TEXT
...
 24           )
 25              ),
 26           (select data_object_id
 27              from user_objects
 28             where object_name = '&TNAME' )
 29  /


       GRP MIN_RID             MAX_RID
---------- ------------------- -------------------
         0 AAAMgQAAGAAAAAJAAA  AAAMgQAAGAAABaICcQ
         1 AAAMgQAAGAAABaJAAA  AAAMgQAANAAAA6ICcQ
         2 AAAMgQAANAAAA6JAAA  AAAMgQAAOAAAAgICcQ
         3 AAAMgQAAOAAAAgJAAA  AAAMgQAAOAAAB8IccQ
```

Now that we have the entire table split nicely into four ROWID ranges, we can easily parallelize our job using DBMS_JOB.

**Parallelizing**    We'll set up a JOB_TABLE with which to pass parameters to our job, as follows:

```
ops$tkyte@ORA920> create table job_table
  2  ( job_id int primary key,
  3    lo_rid ROWID,
  4    hi_rid ROWID,
  5    total_rows number )
  6  /

Table created.
```

Here, TOTAL_ROWS will be a column that our background job will update to let us know how many rows it got assigned to process. We can use this to see that every row will be covered.

Next, we'll create a routine that represents our job to parallelize. This would normally have your code in it—whatever you are doing "serially" now.

```
ops$tkyte@ORA920> create or replace
        procedure parallel_procedure( P_JOB in number )
  2  as
  3             l_job_table job_table%rowtype;
  4             l_cnt        number;
  5  begin
  6             select * into l_job_table from job_table where job_id = p_job;
  7
  8             select count(*)
  9               into l_cnt
 10               from big_table_copy
 11               where ROWID between l_job_table.lo_rid and l_job_table.hi_rid;
 12
 13             update job_table
 14                set total_rows = l_cnt
 15              where job_id = p_job;
 16
 17  end;
 18  /

Procedure created.
```

The emphasized code is where your processing would be normally. This sample job will get its parameters from the JOB_TABLE and process those rows (here, we just count them). Lastly, it will update its entry in the JOB_TABLE with the number of rows processed. We can sum them later. Then the parallel submission would be as follows:

```
ops$tkyte@ORA920> declare
  2             l_job number;
  3  begin
  4             for x in ( select * from job_view )
  5             loop
  6                     dbms_job.submit( l_job, 'parallel_procedure(JOB);' );
  7                     insert into job_table ( job_id, lo_rid, hi_rid )
  8                     values ( l_job, x.min_rid, x.max_rid );
  9             end loop;
 10             commit;
 11  end;
 12  /

PL/SQL procedure successfully completed.
```

Now, JOB_VIEW was simply a view created from our last query, the one that produced ROWID ranges for us. Anytime we select from that view, it will return four rows with four ROWID ranges. We simply loop over that view and submit a job. DBMS_JOB assigns a unique job ID, and we insert that job ID and the ROWID range into our JOB_TABLE. At the end, we commit so that the job queues will see those procedures and run them.

> **NOTE**
> *Make sure that JOB_QUEUE_PROCESSES, a system setting, is set*
> *sufficiently high enough to achieve your degree of parallelism.*

That's it. We can wait for the jobs to run, and then query the totals.

```
ops$tkyte@ORA920> select count(*) from big_table_copy;

  COUNT(*)
----------
   1833792

ops$tkyte@ORA920> select sum(total_rows) from job_table;

SUM(TOTAL_ROWS)
---------------
        1833792
```

Just to prove that the ROWID ranges totally covered the table, we can run this query:

```
select count(*)
   from
(select ROWID from big_table_copy where ROWID between X1 and Y1
 union
 select ROWID from big_table_copy where ROWID between X2 and Y2
 union
 select ROWID from big_table_copy where ROWID between X3 and Y3
 union
 select ROWID from big_table_copy where ROWID between X4 and Y4
)
```

This counted the number of distinct ROWIDs returned (since a UNION does a DISTINCT on the queries it unions together). We find the count of that query (replacing X*N* and Y*N* with ROWIDs) to be the same as the table.

## Analytics Wrap-Up

The goal of this section was to expose you to the immense power of analytics and to get you thinking about what you might be able to do with them yourself. We looked at just some of the more than 40 analytics we have at our disposal. Again, for details, read the "SQL for Analysis in Data Warehouses" chapter in the *Oracle Data Warehousing Guide* (http://technet.oracle.com/docs/ products/oracle9i/doc_library/release2/server.920/a96520/analysis.htm#1020). That information is crucial to fully understanding and exploiting the analytic functions!

Additionally, you saw a demonstration of do-it-yourself (DIY) parallelism. Just the other day, I used this technique to accomplish a bulk update that required Pro*C processing of the data. We had three-quarter billion records to process. Each record had three fields that needed to be sent through an extremely computation-expensive routine. When this routine was written in PL/SQL (not possible in SQL at all), we were able to do it in about 0.01 second. Contrast this to serial processing, which would take about $86 \times 3$ days (three calls per row). We did not have 258 days.

Additionally, even if we split it up in PL/SQL—did it in parallel 32 using the technique described in the previous section, it would take more than a week, and we didn't have that long.

Using C, we could execute this function in about 0.0002. So, we did a parallel 32 in Pro*C, with Pro*C bulk-fetching the data 100 rows at a time, calling the function 300 times and updating the data 100 rows at a time. It took about five hours to complete in that fashion. Instead of using DBMS_JOB and PL/SQL, we used Pro*C and shell scripts, but the concept was identical to the parallelization example you saw in the previous section. We fed ROWID ranges into the application and had it process its slice of the table.

# Don't Tune a Query

On the asktom web site, I am frequently presented with a long query or a block of code and the simple request to make it go faster. Others want to know how they can do a particular operation in a certain way, where they obviously want to make Oracle behave just like Sybase, Informix, DB2, or some other database. Many times, unless there is some obvious enhancement such as bulk processing, I cannot provide any help until I know what the goal is—what they are trying to achieve with the query.

## Understand the Question

When you look at a query, you see a set of requirements. You see joins, predicates, outer joins, and so on. But you need to understand the question being asked. I frequently see constructs like this:

```
Select *
  From t1, t2, t3
Where t1.c1 = t2.c1(+)
  And t2.c2 = t3.c2
  And <other predicates>
```

I immediately see something in that query that could be causing a performance issue. The developers have outer-joined to T2. However, later in the query, they use T2 as a constraining predicate AND T2.C2 = T3.C2. That tells me immediately that the outer join to T2 is there only to limit the optimizer's ability to optimize the query! The outer-join condition is not necessary. It serves only to remove many query plans from consideration by the optimizer, and chances are the plans that are being removed from consideration include their optimal plan! In short, I call that a *bug* in the query. The developers thought an outer join would be needed, but, in fact, it is not, since the predicate later in the query obviates its purpose.

More insidious, however, is this type of query:

```
Select *
  From t1, t2, t3
Where t1.c1 = t2.c1(+)
  And <other predicates>
```

Is that outer join necessary? If all you give me is a query to tune, I must assume that it is. So, I cannot simply remove the outer-join constraint. Before I could do that, I would need to understand your schema, and more important, the question you are trying to answer. It is for this reason that

I prefer to receive CREATE TABLE statements (along with the indexing strategy) and the requirements for the output in English (or other human language). In that fashion, I can effectively start from scratch and give you a tuned query. Working from your query without this information is quite difficult, and many opportunities could be lost due to artificial constraints placed on the query itself (that outer join, for example).

Consider a query in this form:

```
Select *
  From T
 Where X NOT IN ( select X from T2 )
```

And it turns out that T2 has a structure like this:

```
Create table T2 ( …, X INT, … );
```

X is NULLABLE. We know now that the subquery will be evaluated once per row in the outer query, probably via a full scan of T2 each time. The solution is to simply add the following to the subquery:

```
Select *
  From T
 Where X NOT IN ( select X from T2 and X is not null)
```

But hold on, can we? Are we allowed to? It materially changes the result set. We need the original requirements for this query—what is it supposed to return in the first place—in order to tune it. Furthermore, should we be adding the and X is not null and fixing this query? Or is the *data model in the database wrong*, and the correct action is alter table t2 modify x not null to correct the problem once and for all?

## A Proof-of-Concept Example

My co-workers and I did a proof of concept for a customer not too long ago. These developers were considering building a much larger database than they currently had. Given the amount of time it takes to process against their current modest-sized database, they were afraid they would not be able to scale up—the time to process a much larger database would be longer than they had. Enter the tuning challenge: Take the existing system and make recommendations about how to make it go faster. Given their time constraints, they would be able to provide just the code and scripts from the existing system. We would need to reverse-engineer it. We would have very limited knowledge of the real purpose behind each part of this system.

This was a ten-step extract/transform/load (ETL) procedure. It ran serially on a very large machine. The first step we undertook was to analyze the ten steps. From that, we determined that we could run as follows:

- Step 1, which fed step 2

- Step 2, which fed sets 3, 4, 5, 6, 7, and 8

- Steps 3, 4, 5, 6, 7, and 8 in parallel, concurrently (they were not dependent on each other)

- Step 9, which used the results of steps 3 through 8 and fed into step 10

- Step 10

That alone cut the processing time by half. The bulk of the work was done in steps 3 through 8. Simply by doing them concurrently—having six steps run in the time it took for the longest of the six to complete—we had accomplished our goal. But we were not finished yet.

There were many trivial inefficiencies in the code, such as this:

```
Delete from T;
Insert into T select …;
Select count(*) into l_cnt from T;
```

Code like that in an ETL process (especially since T was just a "scratch" staging table) should most certainly be as follows:

```
Truncate T;
Insert /*+ append */ into t select …
l_cnt := sql%rowcount;
```

Simple optimizations like that gave us an increase in performance on the order of two to three times. The DELETE statement was very expensive due to the amount of undo and redo data generated. The TRUNCATE statement was instantaneous. The INSERT statement was much more efficient on this work table with APPEND to bypass undo and redo (this table was put into NOLOGGING mode as well). Using the premise that the best way to make something faster is not to do it at all, we replaced the COUNT(*), which was simply there so someone could DBMS_OUTPUT.PUTLINE it, with a simple assignment. Rather than read the entire unindexed table just to count rows, we asked Oracle, "How many rows did you just put in there?" So far, so good. This was just applying our knowledge of Oracle (TRUNCATE, APPEND, SQL%ROWCOUNT, and so on) and common sense (run things concurrently on a big machine to take advantage of the horsepower you have). But we were not finished.

There was one step that really bothered me. I have a mantra:

- If you can do your processing in a single SQL statement, do it.

- If you cannot, use as little PL/SQL as possible.

- If PL/SQL cannot be used (functionality you need is not in the language), use as little Java in a stored procedure as you can.

   - If PL/SQL or Java won't work due to performance issues, using a bit of C (as I used in the DIY parallelism example earlier in this chapter) is the last choice.

I saw a lot of procedural code in the existing processes. We went looking for the lowest hanging fruit and found this snippet:

```
Insert into t ( c1, c2, .... )
Select c1, c2, ....
  From t1, t2, t3, t4, ....
  Where ....;
```

```
Loop
   Delete from t
    Where (c1,c2) in ( select c1, min(c2)
                         From t
                       Group by c1
                       Having count(1) > 1 );
    Exit when sql%rowcount = 0;
End loop;
```

The net effect of this process was to load the work table and then remove the duplicates. The INSERT itself didn't take too long, but the DELETE took on the order of an hour or more. It needed to generate a set of C1, MIN(C2) values, and then join that to T and delete the matches. If it found even a single match, it needed to repeat the entire process. Analyzing the process more closely, I listed the requirements:

- Remove rows with the OLDER C2 having the same C1.

- Additionally, if all of the rows for a given C1 have the same C2, these rows are to be removed as well.

The first point is fairly clear. It says that we desire a result set with a single row per C1 value. C1 is our "key." We would like the data associated with the row having the MAX(C2) value. That sounds just like our analytics example in the earier "Find a Specific Row in a Partition" section. C2 was a date field and the goal was to save the C1 record with the maximum C2 value.

The second point isn't so clear, but it was a side effect of their processing. Consider if the table T had two rows where C1 = 'X' and both rows had the same value for C2. Both rows would be deleted, because they would both be the MIN(C2) values for that table. Given that information, I developed the following SQL:

```
Insert into t ( c1, c2, .... )
   Select c1, c2, ......
     From
( Select c1, c2, .... ,
         Max(c2) OVER ( partition by c1 ) max_c2
         Count(*) OVER ( partition by c1, c2 ) cnt
            From t1, t2, t3, t4, ....
            Where .... )
   Where c2 = max_c2
     And cnt = 1;
```

That single INSERT statement, which ran in about the same time as their original INSERT statement, did all of the work. It inserted the data and "de-duplicated" it at the same time. *No procedural code was required or desired.* Here, analytic functions were used to compute the following:

- A COUNT of the number of rows by C1 and C2 (for example, if the values C1 = 'X', C2 = 01-JAN-2003 appeared twice, the COUNT(*) would be 2)

- The MAX value of C2 for a given C1 value

Then it was a simple matter of keeping the rows if, and only if, the C2 value was the MAX C2 value for that C1 occurrence and there was only one record in the set with that C1/C2 combination. I was pretty happy with the results. Using a little DIY parallelism, knowledge of Oracle, and advanced SQL techniques to remove as much procedural processing, we accomplished a night's work in about 20 to 30 minutes.

It was not until we presented the results and did the walk-through that we discovered something very interesting. The customers goals were never to do this:

■  Remove rows with the OLDER C2 having the same C1.

■  Additionally, if all of the rows for a given C1 have the same C2, these rows are to be removed as well.

That second point was wrong, they said. By pulling up the old code and pulling it apart, we were able to show that this is what the existing system actually did. What they really wanted was this:

■  Keep the newest C1 record. If multiple C1 records are the newest, keep any one of them.

Armed with that knowledge, we were able to simplify the query even further. The INSERT statement became simply:

```
Insert into t ( c1, c2, .... )
   Select c1, c2, ......
     From
( Select c1, c2, .... ,
         Row_number() OVER ( partition by c1 order by c2 DESC) rn
             From t1, t2, t3, t4, ....
             Where .... )
   Where rn = 1;
```

We just keep the first record (`row_number() = 1`) for a given C1 value after sorting by C2 descending (from big to small). We greatly improved the customer's system, and we also made them aware that they had a bug to fix in their system.

For this proof of concept, we felt that we could have made this go even faster if we had been given the requirements for the system in the first place. There were so many obvious things we could do. But how many nonobvious ones were still lurking out there? For example, was the ten-step process really necessary? Could it just as easily be a one-step process? What were the meanings of all of these things we were computing? Did the system *really* need them (going back to the best way to speed up something is to not do it)? We felt strongly that there was still room for improvement here, but it would take someone with a good knowledge of the database and the problem at hand. It is not that the database was slow, but rather that the original implementers asked it to do a lot of extra, unnecessary work. Our reading the code and figuring out what we thought was really necessary could only go so far. The question involved what we wanted to tune, not the already developed answer that would artificially limit us.

My point is that when someone asks you to tune a query, say, "But what is the question? Perhaps your query is wholly inappropriate in the first place." Start from the requirements, not from someone else's attempt at an answer.

# Overview of Other SQL Techniques

There are many other SQL techniques you can use to develop efficient SQL statements. Some of the many other techniques to consider include the following:

- **Materialized views**   Useful for pre-answering general classes of questions. Instead of everyone aggregating detail records all day long, you can do it once, up-front, for them.

- **Hierarchical queries**   Using CONNECT BY, START WITH, SYS_CONNECT_BY_PATH, and ORDER SIBLINGS BY. This technique is useful for processing hierarchical result sets resulting from self-referencing relations. The SCOTT.EMP table is the classic example. MGR in EMP is a foreign key to EMPNO in EMP. You can query a hierarchical tree using that table.

- **With subquery factoring**   For reusing an inline view in a single query.

- **Merge statements**   For incremental updates to a table where you must update existing records or insert new ones.

You will benefit from a quick read-through of the *SQL Reference* manual. Rather than just looking at all of the train-track diagrams showing the dry syntax of a statement, read the chapters on the following topics:

- Basic elements of SQL.

- Operators and how they work.

- Expressions. Here is where you'll learn about CURSOR expressions, scalar subqueries, CASE statements, and many more techniques. Unless you read this chapter, you may miss out on a large part of SQL.

- Conditions. Did you know SQL has ANY and SOME clauses? Do you know what they do? Have you ever used the keyword ESCAPE in SQL? Do you know what it does? How about LIKEC (that is not a typo—LIKEC, like with a C)? These and more techniques are covered in this chapter.

- Functions. This chapter has a rather inclusive list of all SQL functions, including the analytic functions.

- SQL queries and subqueries. This chapter covers the general classes of queries, hierarchical, sorting, joins, set operations (like INTERSECT and MINUS), and so on.

Another document of great use is the somewhat inappropriately named *Data Warehousing Guide* (http://technet.oracle.com/docs/products/oracle9i/doc_library/release2/server.920/a96520/toc.htm). Many of the concepts and constructs covered in that guide apply to day-to-day systems as well. For example, it includes information about analytic functions, advanced aggregations, partitioning, and the importance of integrity constraints (look at the difference a NOT NULL constraint can have!).

All you need to know is out there, waiting to be found in two documents: the *SQL Reference* manual and the *Data Warehousing Guide*.

# Summary

In this chapter, we've taken a look at developing efficient SQL statements. That can take place only once you have a full understanding of what is available: What access paths are out there, when they are useful, and how you can physically store data to improve access times. Having a good understanding of what the server is capable of doing, coupled with a knowledge of how you can help out—using IOTs or hash clusters, for example—will go a long way.

Additionally, an excellent working knowledge of what SQL has to offer—from simple things like ROWNUM to scalar subqueries to analytic functions—is crucial. If you did not know about analytic functions, for example, you might find yourself writing three or four queries to do the work of one.

As an example of tuning, I showed you what could happen if you don't know the goal of the system you are trying to improve. If you are given an inefficient process and told to tune it, but don't really understand its goals, you'll only be able to make incremental improvements. In order to really tune it, you must understand the system itself. Perhaps the thing you are asked to tune isn't even needed. That's the fastest you'll ever make it go—by not doing it. But only by understanding the requirements can you get there.

Unfortunately, the list of SQL techniques I didn't cover in this chapter is much longer than the list of what I did cover. The "Overview of Other SQL Techniques" section provides some direction on learning about these other techniques.

# CHAPTER
## 9

# Effective PL/SQL
# Programming

L/SQL is Oracle's procedural extension to SQL, and it is a true 3GL programming language. It was first introduced way back in version 6 of the database, giving us the ability to code "anonymous blocks" in our client applications and submit them for processing on the database. In Oracle6, there were no stored procedures, no packages, and no triggers. The ability to store PL/SQL in the database came with version 7 in 1992.

Today, PL/SQL is competent, mature, and full-featured, offering everything you expect to find in a 3GL programming language. In general, I find that PL/SQL is underused in Oracle applications and rarely exploited to its full potential. PL/SQL is often dismissed as a "legacy" language, to be avoided in favor of the current "hot" language (be it Java or whatever).

In this chapter, we'll look at why I think you should consider using PL/SQL in your applications. Then we'll cover some of the most important programming techniques that provide efficient, high-performance PL/SQL code.

# Why PL/SQL?

A question that I field frequently and that is a great lead-in for this first section is, "Since Oracle supports Java, PL/SQL, and C in the database, why would you use PL/SQL?"

It should speak volumes about PL/SQL's capabilities that entire products are written in the language. Here are a few examples:

■ Oracle's advanced replication was implemented in PL/SQL entirely in version 7.1.6 of the database. Over the years, parts of it have been internalized in C for the performance edge that language has. However, major portions of the replication functionality remain in PL/SQL.

■ Oracle's Application Suite (HR, Financial, ERP, and so on) was written in PL/SQL. Today, Java is being used as well for middle-tier GUI processing, but originally, the whole suite was in PL/SQL and currently almost all of the data processing still is.

■ Oracle's Workflow engine, which lives in the database, is written in PL/SQL.

■ The administrative interface to the database is written in PL/SQL. These include DBMS_STATS, UTL_OUTLN, and DBMS_RESOURCE_MANAGER, just to name a few.

Despite its proven power and versatility, many developers still tend to overlook the language. They work hard to implement a feature in a different language, when using PL/SQL would have been much quicker and more effective.

All you need to use PL/SQL is a good text editor and SQL*Plus. It is not very hard to get started with PL/SQL.

## PL/SQL Is the Most Efficient Language for Data Manipulation

If you are manipulating data, PL/SQL is quite simply the most productive language to use. Consider a simple routine to fetch data from the database and perform some process against it. The PL/SQL routine might look like this:

```
Create or replace procedure process_data( p_inputs in varchar2 )
As
Begin
   For x in ( select * from emp where ename like p_inputs )
   Loop
      Process( X );
   End loop
End;
```

Here, we can make the following observations:

- PL/SQL datatypes are SQL datatypes. There is no conversion between our programming language types and the database; they are the same.

- The tight coupling between the language and the database is visible in the ease with which we can commingle SQL and PL/SQL. Consider the line For  x  in  ( select ... ). The compiler knows how to define x, creates a record type for us implicitly, and does all of the work to get the data from the query into our implicitly defined record.

- We don't need to do things like open and close queries; they are taken care of for us.

- We are protected from many changes in the database. If we were to add or remove a column in the table, this procedure would remain unchanged. We would not need to revisit this piece of code at all.

Something you don't see, but that is there nevertheless, is the implicit cursor caching performed by PL/SQL. If we were to call that procedure 1,000 times with different inputs, we would discover that the SELECT statement is parsed *once* and executed 1,000 times. PL/SQL understands the importance of "parse once, execute many" for performance and scalability, and that approach is burned into the language itself.

Now, compare that with the equivalent Java/JDBC code:

```
static PreparedStatement pstmt = null;

public static void process_data( Connection conn, String inputs )
throws Exception
{
int    empno;
String ename;
String job;
int    mgr;
String hiredate;
int    sal;
int    comm;
int    deptno;

   if ( pstmt == null )
      pstmt = conn.prepareStatement
      ("select * from emp where ename like ? " );

   pstmt.setString( 1, inputs );
```

```
ResultSet rset = pstmt.executeQuery();

while( rset.next() )
{
    empno    = rset.getInt(1);
    ename    = rset.getString(2);
    job      = rset.getString(3);
    mgr      = rset.getInt(4);
    hiredate = rset.getString(5);
    sal      = rset.getInt(6);
    comm     = rset.getInt(7);
    deptno   = rset.getInt(8);
    // process( empno, ename, job, mgr, hiredate,
    // sal, comm, deptno );
}
rset.close();
}
```

None of the items on our previous list apply anymore:

- Java types are not SQL types and, in fact, we must take care to choose our Java types wisely. An Oracle NUMBER column can hold 38 digits. What Java type should we use in order to retrieve the NUMBER column and not lose precision or overflow it?

- There is no coupling between the SQL language and Java/JDBC. It is a totally procedural API. We must manually control everything procedurally.

- We are not protected from changes in the database. If we add, modify, or drop a column, our Java code will need to be revisited and changed.

- We must perform statement caching manually (the `PreparedStatement`, pstmt, in the example).

This is not a criticism of Java, or C for that matter (C is one of my favorite programming languages). The corresponding C code would look very similar to the example here in its verbosity, and it would have the same issues. These are great languages. It is just that if our goal is to process data, using a lot of SQL with a little bit of procedural work mixed in, PL/SQL is, by far, the most productive language to use, both in terms of speed and programmer productivity.

## PL/SQL Is Portable and Reusable

Here's my contention: PL/SQL is more portable and reusable than virtually any other language out there. Now, this raises a few eyebrows every time (probably yours are raised right now), so let me explain my logic.

Sure, Java and C are portable, reusable languages—within reason. However, Java is predominantly reusable by Java, and C is predominantly reusable by C. While it is possible for Java, C, and other languages to interoperate, to invoke each other, it is not natural. With PL/SQL, on the other hand, anything that can connect to the database in any way, shape, or form can invoke PL/SQL. It is true that technologies such as web services or CORBA allow the same for Java or C, but these technologies introduce their own extra levels of complexity at times. Of course, there is no reason your web service should not be written in PL/SQL! If your service is doing data manipulation, then writing it in PL/SQL might be the most efficient, secure way to do it.

The bottom line is that if you can connect to the database, you can use existing PL/SQL. If you look at the database itself, the predominant API to configure, adjust, and use the database is a PL/SQL-based API. Oracle uses it for replication, workflow, job scheduling, resource management planning, OLAP functionality, data mining, and so on. PL/SQL is the universal language you can use to talk to the database.

As with any language, however, you can write good code, you can write sufficient code, and you can write some of the worst, most miserably performing pieces of code humanly possible. PL/SQL is not magic. You can make all of the same mistakes in it you can make in many other languages. You can code infinite loops (but the database does allow you to set up resource profiles that would abort the offending code without bringing down the database). You can code logic errors. You can make many of the same errors you could in Java, C, Visual Basic, and the like. But you will find that many errors you might make in those languages are hard, if not impossible, to make in PL/SQL. Here are some examples:

- **Bind variable usage**   In PL/SQL, it is impossible to not use bind variables with static SQL. It is only possible to not use bind variables when you do dynamic SQL in PL/SQL, and even then, it is easier to code using bind variables than it is to code not using bind variables in PL/SQL. Many times, other languages make it not only possible, but easier to skip using bind variables. And, as you've learned in previous chapters, bind variable usage is key to database scalability and performance.

- **Parse once, execute many**   In PL/SQL, it is impossible to overparse a statement when using static SQL. You need to program using dynamic SQL in order to achieve this state (a state you do not want to be in). PL/SQL automatically caches statements for us transparently, providing its parse once, execute many capability. It is true that by using (or overusing) dynamic SQL, you can achieve the dubious goal of parsing as many times as you execute a statement, but done correctly, even dynamic SQL can parse once, execute many in PL/SQL.

- **SELECT ***   In PL/SQL it is safe to use SELECT *. It might not be the best approach as far as performance goes (it is always best to select only those columns you actually need). But in all other languages, SELECT * is something that you cannot afford to put into any programs at all! Simply re-creating a table with the columns defined in a different order, adding a column, or dropping a column will break your application (but not in PL/SQL; PL/SQL will fix itself when properly coded).

- **Database schema changes**   Suppose that your application modifies a COMMENTS column from VARCHAR2(80) to VARCHAR2(255). All existing applications that are not written in PL/SQL must be reprogrammed to accommodate this. Correctly written PL/SQL applications will not be affected.

- **I didn't know you were using that**   This error happens due to lack of dependency management tracking. Someone just didn't know you used a particular object and felt free to change it. With PL/SQL, the linkage between who uses what and where is stored right in the data dictionary! The opportunities to claim ignorance ("I didn't know") are very much reduced.

Not only is PL/SQL a more productive environment for creating data-oriented routines to be called from a variety of languages, it is a safer one as well. It is quite simply harder to make the most common programming mistakes in Oracle if you are using PL/SQL.

Now that we've gone over the reasons to use PL/SQL, the rest of this chapter is devoted to the ten most important things regarding PL/SQL programming/development. Some of it is general programming advice, such as write as little as you can. Other items are specific to the PL/SQL language itself, such as use %TYPE and %ROWTYPE. They are not in any specific order; they are all equally relevant.

> **NOTE**
> *A technique that is not listed here explicitly, but is sort of a theme of this book, is to benchmark. Use tools such as TKPROF, DBMS_PROFILER, and Runstats in order to evaluate how you are doing, how well your code is performing, and how different approaches to the same problem stack up against each other.*

# Write as Little as You Can

The goal is to write as little code as possible. In a relational database, procedural code should be used after you have proven that a set-based approach won't work. Many times, I see people writing procedural code that looks like this:

```
Begin
    For x in ( select * from table@remote_db )
    Loop
        Insert into table ( c1, c2, ... ) values ( x.c1, x.c2,... );
    End loop;
End;
```

There is no reason that code should not be written this way:

```
Insert into table (c1,c2,...) select c1,c2,.... From table@remote_db
```

The goal is to do it in SQL and to use PL/SQL only when SQL cannot possibly do it for you.

The other coding technique I see frequently looks like this:

```
For a in ( select * from t1 )
Loop
    For b in ( select * from t2 where t2.key = t1.key )
    Loop
        For c in ( select * from t3 where t3.key = t2.key )
        Loop
            ...
```

Here, the programmer didn't want to "burden" the database with a join, not realizing that approach is many times slower than this one:

```
For x in ( select *
                From t1, t2, t3
```

```
            Where t1.key=t2.key
               And t2.key=t3.key ) loop
```

As an example, suppose we had tables T1, T2, and T3 like this:

```
ops$tkyte@ORA920> create table t1
   2  ( a int primary key, y char(80) );
Table created.

ops$tkyte@ORA920> create table t2
   2  ( b int primary key, a references t1, y char(80) );
Table created.

ops$tkyte@ORA920> create index t2_a_idx on t2(a);
Index created.

ops$tkyte@ORA920> create table t3
   2  ( c int primary key, b references t2, y char(80) );
Table created.

ops$tkyte@ORA920> create index t3_b_idx on t3(b);
Index created.
```

So, we have a simple T1 -> T2 -> T3 set of tables. We use CHAR(80) just to give us an average row width that approximates what you will find in many tables. Now, we'll fill the tables.

```
ops$tkyte@ORA920> insert into t1
   2  select rownum, 'x'
   3    from all_objects
   4   where rownum <= 1000;
1000 rows created.
```

T1 has 1,000 primary key values 1 to 1,000. We'll load T2 with 5,000 primary key values 1 to 5,000 and five rows per foreign key value back to T1; that is, every row in T1 will match up with five rows in T2.

```
ops$tkyte@ORA920> insert into t2
   2  select rownum, mod(rownum,1000)+1, 'x'
   3    from all_objects
   4   where rownum <= 5000;
5000 rows created.
```

And lastly, in T3 we will place about 30,000 rows, so each row in T2 will match up with about six rows in T3.

```
ops$tkyte@ORA920> insert into t3
   2  select rownum, mod(rownum,5000)+1, 'x'
   3    from all_objects;
30583 rows created.
```

And then we analyze the tables. After that, we are ready to use Runstats to compare the two methods. Here is the code to let the database do its job:

```
ops$tkyte@ORA920> exec runstats_pkg.rs_start;

PL/SQL procedure successfully completed.

ops$tkyte@ORA920>
ops$tkyte@ORA920> begin
  2      for i in 1 .. 1000
  3      loop
  4          for x in ( select t1.a t1a, t1.y t1y,
  5                            t2.b t2b, t2.a t2a, t2.y t2y,
  6                            t3.c t3c, t3.b t3b, t3.y t3y
  7                       from t1, t2, t3
  8                      where t1.a = i
  9                        and t2.a (+) = t1.a
 10                        and t3.b (+) = t2.b )
 11          loop
 12                  null;
 13          end loop;
 14      end loop;
 15  end;
 16  /

PL/SQL procedure successfully completed.
```

Just to preclude the argument that the algorithms are not the same, because the second approach would retrieve data from T1 even it there were no children in T2, we used an outer join. The second, very procedural approach is as follows:

```
ops$tkyte@ORA920> exec runstats_pkg.rs_middle
PL/SQL procedure successfully completed.

ops$tkyte@ORA920> begin
  2      for i in 1 .. 1000
  3      loop
  4          for a in ( select t1.a, t1.y
  5                       from t1 where t1.a = i )
  6          loop
  7              for b in ( select t2.b, t2.a, t2.y
  8                           from t2 where t2.a = a.a )
  9              loop
 10                  for c in ( select t3.c, t3.b, t3.y
 11                               from t3 where t3.b = b.b )
 12                  loop
 13                          null;
 14                  end loop;
 15              end loop;
```

```
 16          end loop;
 17      end loop;
 18  end;
 19  /
PL/SQL procedure successfully completed.

 ops$tkyte@ORA920> exec runstats_pkg.rs_stop(1000);
Run1 ran in 196 hsecs
Run2 ran in 316 hsecs
run 1 ran in 62.03% of the time
```

As you can see, doing it in SQL is significantly faster by the wall clock in this example. Now, let's look at the latching report:

| Name | Run1 | Run2 | Diff |
|------|------|------|------|
| LATCH.cache buffers chains | 173,885 | 169,905 | -3,980 |
| STAT...buffer is not pinned co | 115,640 | 111,640 | -4,000 |
| STAT...no work - consistent re | 77,152 | 73,152 | -4,000 |
| STAT...consistent gets - exami | 5,003 | 9,005 | 4,002 |
| STAT...calls to get snapshot s | 1,001 | 7,001 | 6,000 |
| STAT...execute count | 1,005 | 7,005 | 6,000 |
| LATCH.shared pool | 1,085 | 7,148 | 6,063 |
| STAT...recursive calls | 32,580 | 44,584 | 12,004 |
| LATCH.library cache pin | 2,062 | 14,081 | 12,019 |
| LATCH.library cache | 2,116 | 14,164 | 12,048 |

We just did a ton of extra work in the second version. Our recursive SQL calls are way up (we ran more SQL), and the latching is high due to that. If we just look at the aggregate latching counts we see this:

```
Run1 latches total versus runs -- difference and pct
Run1        Run2        Diff        Pct
184,152     210,373     26,221      87.54%
```

We got away with about 15% less latching when we let the database do its job. That is significant. And these numbers only get better as the number of users increases or the size of the result sets goes up.

## Not Doing It Procedurally

You should always be looking at your procedural code and asking, "Is there a set-based way to do this?" Consider the example in Chapter 8, in which I was working on a proof of concept where I was given code similar to the following:

```
Insert into t ( c1, c2, .... )
   Select c1, c2, ....
     From t1, t2, t3, t4, ....
    Where ..join conditions..;
   Loop
```

```
      Delete from t
       Where (c1,c2) in ( select c1, min(c2)
                              From t
                          Group by c1
                          Having count(1) > 1 );
       Exit when sql%rowcount = 0;
    End loop;
```

This was the procedural logic. The loop was a "de-duplicate" loop. After reading the code and thinking about what the developers were doing, I expressed the requirements as such:

■ Remove rows with the older C2 having the same C1 value.

■ If all of the rows for a given C1 have the same C2, these rows are to be removed as well.

Realizing that the best way to speed up something is never to do it at all, I looked for ways to remove that "de-dup" loop. It took a long time for that loop (on the order of hours) to execute *once* and, unfortunately, if it found data to delete, it would do it all over again. I applied the requirements and realized that we needed the maximum C2 value for each C1 value, as well as the count of that C2 column for each C1 value. Then all we needed to do was keep the rows so that C2 was equal to that maximum C2 and the count was equal to 1. So, I modified the INSERT to read as follows:

```
Insert into t ( c1, c2, .... )
    Select c1, c2, ......
      From
( Select c1, c2, .... ,
          Max(c2) OVER ( partition by c1 ) max_c2,
          Count(*) OVER ( partition by c1, c2 ) cnt
              From t1, t2, t3, t4, ....
              Where .... )
    Where c2 = max_c2
      And cnt = 1;
```

And there it was: The equivalent logic rolled into a single INSERT INTO AS SELECT statement. By using analytic functions, I easily computed the maximum C2 value for each C1 group, as well as the count rows in each group. All I needed to do after getting those values was to determine the row where C2 = MAX_C2 (removing any of the "older rows") and keep that row if the COUNT(*) for that given C1, C2 pair was in fact 1.

That INSERT AS SELECT took the same amount of time to execute as the original INSERT. But since we never needed to do the "infinite loop" looking for data to delete, we shaved hours off the runtime of this process. This was accomplished by simply not doing something. Adding an APPEND hint to do a direct-path insert helped as well, but not nearly as much as removing the loop.

# Fit Your Code on the Screen

Here is a last bit of advice on writing as little as possible: When you are writing code, make sure your routines (methods, procedures, functions, or whatever you want to call them) fit on a screen. You should be able to see the logic from start to finish on your monitor. Buy the biggest monitor you can, and make the routines fit on your screen. This rule forces you to think modularly, so you break up the code into bite-sized snippets that are easily understood.

When someone comes to me with a routine that is 1,000 lines long, I send that person right back to break it up. I find I can get about 80 lines of code on my screen using the smallest readable font. Any procedural code, exclusive of SQL, longer than 80 lines gets broken up.

# Use Packages

If I had to pick the most important tip in this chapter, this would be it: Use packages, rather than stand-alone procedures or functions in *real code*. Packages are the only way to code in PL/SQL on a project of any scale.

## Advantages of Packages

Packages have these advantages over stand-alone procedures and functions:

- **They break the dependency chain.** Packages reduce or remove the effects of cascading invalidations.

- **They increase your namespace.** Normally, you can have only one procedure named P; now, you can have dozens of them. A single package can have many procedures. There will be one data dictionary object—the package—instead of a dictionary object per procedure/function.

- **They support overloading.** A single package can have the same named procedure in it many times, each of which takes a different set of inputs.

- **They support encapsulation.** In order to live up to my fit-on-a-screen rule, I write many small subroutines that are of no use outside the package itself. I hide these in the package, so they are not visible outside the package, and I am the only one who can see them.

- **They support session-persistent variables.** You can have variables that retain their values from call to call in the database.

- **They support elaboration or startup code.** A package can have a snippet of code that is executed the first time the package is referenced in a session, allowing you to have complex initialization code automatically executed.

- **They allow you to group related functionality together.** Grouping routines makes it obvious what pieces of code are to be used together.

The single most important reason to use packages is the fact that they break the dependency chain in the database. Let's take an in-depth look at how this works.

## Break the Dependency Chain

In the database, there is a highly sophisticated, built-in dependency mechanism. If you create a table, build a view on top of the table, have a procedure that uses the view, and have a function that uses the table, all of these objects will be tied together. Consider the following setup (in a schema that contains no other objects):

```
ops$tkyte@ORA920> create table t ( x int );
Table created.

ops$tkyte@ORA920> create view v as select * from t;
```

```
View created.

ops$tkyte@ORA920> create procedure p
  2  as
  3  begin
  4          for x in ( select * from v )
  5          loop
  6                  null;
  7          end loop;
  8  end;
  9  /
Procedure created.

ops$tkyte@ORA920> create function f return number
  2  as
  3          l_cnt number;
  4  begin
  5          select count(*) into l_cnt from t;
  6          return l_cnt;
  7  end;
  8  /
Function created.

ops$tkyte@ORA920> select name, type, referenced_name, referenced_type
  2    from user_dependencies
  3   where referenced_owner = user
  4   order by name
  5  /

NAME  TYPE              REFERENCED_NAME REFERENCED_TYPE
----- ----------------- --------------- -----------------
F     FUNCTION          T               TABLE
P     PROCEDURE         V               VIEW
V     VIEW              T               TABLE
```

Oracle has set up the dependencies between function F and table T, procedure P and view V, and view V and table T. If we check the status of all of these objects, we see this:

```
ops$tkyte@ORA920> select object_name, object_type, status
  2    from user_objects
  3  /

OBJECT_NAME                      OBJECT_TYPE        STATUS
-------------------------------- ------------------ -------
F                                FUNCTION           VALID
P                                PROCEDURE          VALID
T                                TABLE              VALID
V                                VIEW               VALID
```

The objects are currently valid—compiled and waiting to be executed. Let's see what happens if we modify table T.

```
ops$tkyte@ORA920> alter table t add y number
  2  /
Table altered.

ops$tkyte@ORA920> select object_name, object_type, status
  2     from user_objects
  3  /

OBJECT_NAME                      OBJECT_TYPE         STATUS
-------------------------------- ------------------- -------
F                                FUNCTION            INVALID
P                                PROCEDURE           INVALID
T                                TABLE               VALID
V                                VIEW                INVALID
```

These objects become invalid, because each of them must recompile now. The view must recompile in order to pick up the new column, and the procedure and function must recompile because they use the table and the view. Now, what if procedure P were used by dozens or hundreds of other routines in your system? They would also become invalid during this operation. Consider this example:

```
ops$tkyte@ORA920> create procedure p2
  2  as
  3  begin
  4         p;
  5  end;
  6  /
Procedure created.

ops$tkyte@ORA920> select name, type, referenced_name, referenced_type
  2     from user_dependencies
  3     where referenced_owner = user
  4     order by name
  5  /

NAME   TYPE              REFERENCED_NAME REFERENCED_TYPE
-----  ----------------- --------------- -----------------
F      FUNCTION          T               TABLE
P      PROCEDURE         V               VIEW
P2     PROCEDURE         P               PROCEDURE
V      VIEW              T               TABLE
```

Now, P2 is dependent on P. If we look at the status of the objects, we find this:

```
ops$tkyte@ORA920> select object_name, object_type, status
  2     from user_objects
  3  /

OBJECT_NAME                      OBJECT_TYPE         STATUS
-------------------------------- ------------------- -------
F                                FUNCTION            INVALID
P                                PROCEDURE           VALID
```

```
P2                                     PROCEDURE          VALID
T                                      TABLE              VALID
V                                      VIEW               VALID
```

Apparently, the simple compilation of P2 did a lot more work than just compile P2. It compiled P and V as well. In order to see if P2 was calling P in a valid manner, P needed to be compiled. In order for P to be compiled, V must be compiled as well (you can think of a view as "code" in the database).

Now, what happens if we add yet another column to T?

```
ops$tkyte@ORA920> alter table t add z number
  2  /
Table altered.

ops$tkyte@ORA920> select object_name, object_type, status
  2    from user_objects
  3  /

OBJECT_NAME                    OBJECT_TYPE        STATUS
------------------------------ ------------------ -------
F                              FUNCTION           INVALID
P                              PROCEDURE          INVALID
P2                             PROCEDURE          INVALID
T                              TABLE              VALID
V                              VIEW               INVALID
```

We can see that the invalidation of P also invalidated P2. So, if P were called by dozens of routines, and P2 were called by dozens of routines, we would have a lot of code that needed recompiling in our database.

Let's start over. This time, we'll use packages. We'll get rid of the stand-alone objects and create packaged procedures instead.

```
ops$tkyte@ORA920> drop procedure p;
Procedure dropped.

ops$tkyte@ORA920> drop procedure p2;
Procedure dropped.

ops$tkyte@ORA920> drop function f;
Function dropped.

ops$tkyte@ORA920> create package p1
  2  as
  3          procedure p;
  4  end;
  5  /
Package created.

ops$tkyte@ORA920> create package body p1
```

```
  2  as
  3  procedure p
  4  as
  5  begin
  6          for x in ( select * from v )
  7          loop
  8                  null;
  9          end loop;
 10  end;
 11  end p1;
 12  /
Package body created.

ops$tkyte@ORA920> create package p2
  2  as
  3          procedure p;
  4  end;
  5  /
Package created.

ops$tkyte@ORA920> create package body p2
  2  as
  3  procedure p
  4  as
  5  begin
  6          p1.p;
  7  end;
  8  end p2;
  9  /
Package body created.

ops$tkyte@ORA920> select name, type, referenced_name, referenced_type
  2    from user_dependencies
  3   where referenced_owner = user
  4   order by name
  5  /
```

| NAME | TYPE | REFERENCED_NAME | REFERENCED_TYPE |
| ----- | ------------------ | --------------- | ----------------- |
| P1 | PACKAGE BODY | V | VIEW |
| P1 | PACKAGE BODY | P1 | PACKAGE |
| P2 | PACKAGE BODY | P2 | PACKAGE |
| **P2** | **PACKAGE BODY** | **P1** | **PACKAGE** |
| V | VIEW | T | TABLE |

Notice here how the dependencies are set up. PACKAGE BODY P2 is dependent on PACKAGE P1, not the package body, but just the *package*, also known as the *specification* or *interface*. What that means is that the package body of P1 could become invalid and not affect anything else. Nothing is dependent on the package body of P1; things are dependent on the package specification.

Now, let's try modifying table T again.

```
ops$tkyte@ORA920> select object_name, object_type, status
  2     from user_objects
  3  /

OBJECT_NAME                       OBJECT_TYPE        STATUS
------------------------------    ----------------   -------
P1                                PACKAGE            VALID
P1                                PACKAGE BODY       VALID
P2                                PACKAGE            VALID
P2                                PACKAGE BODY       VALID
T                                 TABLE              VALID
V                                 VIEW               VALID
6 rows selected.

ops$tkyte@ORA920> alter table t add a number
  2  /
Table altered.

ops$tkyte@ORA920> select object_name, object_type, status
  2     from user_objects
  3  /

OBJECT_NAME                       OBJECT_TYPE        STATUS
------------------------------    ----------------   -------
P1                                PACKAGE            VALID
P1                                PACKAGE BODY       INVALID
P2                                PACKAGE            VALID
P2                                PACKAGE BODY       VALID
T                                 TABLE              VALID
V                                 VIEW               INVALID

6 rows selected.
```

This time, only the view and the package body of P1 become invalid. No longer does the procedure that calls P1.P become invalid, because we've broken the dependency chain. A change to our system does not cause all of our code to be invalidated and force our database to spend many cycles compiling code instead of running it!

As long as the specification—the interface to the package—does not change, the dependent code in the system will not become invalid. We can make localized changes without causing a mass recompilation of our system.

Just to show the nice side effect of this automated dependency mechanism in Oracle, let's run our code.

```
ops$tkyte@ORA920> exec p2.p
PL/SQL procedure successfully completed.

ops$tkyte@ORA920> select object_name, object_type, status
  2     from user_objects
```

```
3   /

OBJECT_NAME                      OBJECT_TYPE          STATUS
------------------------------   ------------------   -------
P1                               PACKAGE              VALID
P1                               PACKAGE BODY         VALID
P2                               PACKAGE              VALID
P2                               PACKAGE BODY         VALID
T                                TABLE                VALID
V                                VIEW                 VALID

6 rows selected.
```

This compiles all of the necessary objects transparently, which would happen with stand-alone procedures/functions as well; it is not reliant on the use of packages. It is just nice to know. You do not need to compile invalid objects by hand; they will take care of themselves.

## Packages Wrap-Up

To summarize here, for all production-quality code, you should use database packages. They provide the necessary programming constructs, such as encapsulation and namespace reduction, and they promote modular coding techniques. Most important, they break the dependency chain, making it so that changes to a database schema do not cause the entire schema, or even the database, to become invalid and require an expensive recompilation.

So, when are stand-alone procedures and functions acceptable? They work for stand-alone utilities that are never called by other code. The following are some of my tools:

- A SHOW_SPACE script that shows the space used by an object

- The PRINT_TABLE utility that prints result sets down the page in SQL*Plus

- My DUMP_CSV procedure (PL/SQL) that takes any query and creates a comma-separated-values file from it

Stand-alone functions and procedures are also acceptable for quick-and-dirty demonstrations of functionality or testing. However, for all "real code" in a system, packages are the only way to go.

# Use Static SQL

If you can achieve your goals using static SQL—even if you need to write a little more code—do it that way. Generic code using dynamic SQL is wonderful, but it will be less scalable, harder to debug and maintain, and slower running than the same code using static SQL.

## Advantages of Static SQL

The advantages of using static SQL over dynamic SQL in PL/SQL are many and profound. Consider some of these reasons to use static SQL:

- **Static SQL is checked at compile time.**   This way, you know that the procedure is valid and can execute. You might still have a bug in your code, but at least you know the SQL isn't the problem.

■ **PL/SQL will validate datatypes, sizes, and so on.** This means that you don't need to define records to fetch into or define tons of variables. You do less coding work, and the compiler does more work.

■ **The dependencies are set up and maintained in the data dictionary.** So, no one can claim "I didn't know you were using that."

■ **If the base objects change over time, your code fixes itself automatically.** If you add or remove columns or grants, you don't need to worry about your code. On the other hand, when you make these changes and are using dynamic SQL, you will need to inspect your code for correctness.

■ **Static SQL makes parse once, execute many a reality.** Dynamic SQL makes it easier to lose out on this benefit. This is especially true with the newer native dynamic SQL, where each and every execution of a statement is preceded by a parse call. With that version, you must work hard to achieve the parse once, execute many goal.

■ **Static SQL is faster.** Doing something with dynamic SQL in PL/SQL is slower than doing the same thing with static SQL.

The most important features of static SQL that we lose with dynamic SQL are dependency-tracking and performance-related issues surrounding parsing and overall execution speed.

## Look for Opportunities to Replace Dynamic SQL

People frequently use dynamic SQL where static SQL could be used instead. For example, suppose we want to write a small lookup routine that will return one of three columns. We might code that routine like this:

```
ops$tkyte@ORA920> create or replace function get_value_dyn
                ( p_empno in number, p_cname in varchar2 ) return varchar2
  2  as
  3      l_value  varchar2(4000);
  4  begin
  5      execute immediate
  6      'select ' || p_cname || ' from emp where empno = :x'
  7      into l_value
  8      using p_empno;
  9
 10      return l_value;
 11  end;
 12  /
Function created.
```

Instead, we could code this routine using static SQL, like this:

```
ops$tkyte@ORA920> create or replace function get_value_static
                ( p_empno in number, p_cname in varchar2 ) return varchar2
  2  as
  3      l_value  varchar2(4000);
  4  begin
```

```
 5          select decode( upper(p_cname),
 6                              'ENAME', ename,
 7                              'EMPNO', empno,
 8                              'HIREDATE', to_char(hiredate,'yyyymmddhh24miss'))
 9            into l_value
10            from emp
11           where empno = p_empno;
12
13          return l_value;
14   end;
15   /
Function created.
```

This version is not as generic as the dynamic SQL routine, so if we wanted to support additional columns over time, we would need to modify code. But a simple Runstats test might help convince you that it is well worth it. Here are the results when calling the dynamic function:

```
ops$tkyte@ORA920> exec runstats_pkg.rs_start;

PL/SQL procedure successfully completed.

ops$tkyte@ORA920>
ops$tkyte@ORA920> declare
  2            l_dummy varchar2(30);
  3  begin
  4      for i in 1 .. 500
  5      loop
  6          for x in ( select empno from emp )
  7          loop
  8              l_dummy := get_value_dyn(x.empno, 'ENAME' );
  9              l_dummy := get_value_dyn(x.empno, 'EMPNO' );
 10              l_dummy := get_value_dyn(x.empno, 'HIREDATE' );
 11          end loop;
 12      end loop;
 13  end;
 14  /

PL/SQL procedure successfully completed.
```

And here is what happens when we do it statically:

```
ops$tkyte@ORA920> exec runstats_pkg.rs_middle
PL/SQL procedure successfully completed.

ops$tkyte@ORA920> declare
  2            l_dummy varchar2(30);
  3  begin
  4      for i in 1 .. 500
  5      loop
  6          for x in ( select empno from emp )
  7          loop
```

```
 8                     l_dummy := get_value_static(x.empno, 'ENAME' );
 9                     l_dummy := get_value_static(x.empno, 'EMPNO' );
10                     l_dummy := get_value_static(x.empno, 'HIREDATE' );
11              end loop;
12        end loop;
13   end;
14   /
PL/SQL procedure successfully completed.

ops$tkyte@ORA920> exec runstats_pkg.rs_stop(1000);
Run1 ran in 1102 hsecs
Run2 ran in 703 hsecs
run 1 ran in 156.76% of the time
```

The static version is obviously faster by the wall clock. However, the more compelling reasons to use that version follow:

| Name | Run1 | Run2 | Diff |
|------|------|------|------|
| STAT...session cursor cache hi | 21,003 | 4 | -20,999 |
| STAT...opened cursors cumulati | 21,005 | 5 | -21,000 |
| STAT...parse count (total) | 21,005 | 5 | -21,000 |
| LATCH.shared pool | 63,565 | 21,566 | -41,999 |
| LATCH.library cache pin | 127,062 | 43,064 | -83,998 |
| LATCH.library cache | 127,087 | 43,088 | -83,999 |

Those are some really big differences. Look at the latching statistics here:

```
Run1 latches total versus runs -- difference and pct
Run1        Run2        Diff        Pct
463,431     253,318     -210,113    182.94%

PL/SQL procedure successfully completed.
```

This shows almost double the latching activity using dynamic SQL. Also notice the statistic for session cursor cache hits, which shows that we made heavy use of that feature. If session-cached cursors had been disabled on this system, the latching for the dynamic SQL would have been three times that of static SQL.

## Static SQL Wrap-Up

Yes, there are times when nothing else but dynamic SQL will do the job. But you should look for opportunities to remove dynamic SQL, especially if the dynamic SQL is there simply to save a couple lines of code. Consider this example:

```
If (condition1) then
    Update using predicate1
Elsif (condition2) then
    Update using predicate2
...
Elsif (conditionN) then
    update using predicateN
End if;
```

An alternative is to use this code:

```
L_stmt := 'update ...' || some_predicate;
Execute immediate l_stmt;
```

It would be worth having 40 to 60 lines of code (the first version) instead of 2 lines of code, *if this statement is executed repeatedly in a session.* The bottom line is to use common sense and be aware of the trade-offs.

Dynamic SQL is something you want to use when static SQL is no longer practical—when you would be writing hundreds of lines of code, not just 40 or so. Or, you will need to use dynamic SQL when no amount of static SQL will do.

When coding dynamic SQL, do not forget about the existing DBMS_SQL package in addition to native dynamic SQL. There are opportunities for scaling up with DBMS_SQL that are not available with native dynamic SQL. For example, with native dynamic SQL, every EXECUTE has a corresponding PARSE call to go along with it (as you can see from the Runstats example in the previous section). The additional parsing is the major cause of excessive latching. This can be removed by using the parse once, execute many rule.

DBMS_SQL, since it is a procedural API, allows Oracle to parse a statement once (such as an INSERT statement) and then execute it hundreds or thousands of times. So, if you know that your dynamic SQL statement will be executed many times but with different inputs, you would use DBMS_SQL. For example, with a dynamic-loader routine that accepts as inputs the table name and filename to load, the SQL INSERT will be constant; just the inputs will vary. If, on the other hand, you know your routine will rarely (if ever) execute the same dynamic SQL statement call after call, you would use native dynamic SQL.

# Bulk Processing

PL/SQL allows you to procedurally process data either a row at a time or a set of rows at a time. Most applications would benefit from processing the data using bulk, or array, operations. This is a feature of PL/SQL that allows you to fetch *N* rows at a time instead of one row at a time, to insert *N* rows at a time, instead of a single row at a time, and so on.

Bulk processing is one of those areas where you will make a trade-off between programming convenience and performance. It is easier to code a row at a time, but the resulting code will execute slower than it would using bulk processing. It is harder to code using bulk operations, but the resulting code will generally execute more rapidly that it would using row-at-a-time processing (as well as consume more memory, since you are caching an array of data).

## Use Bulk Processing When It Has Dramatic Effects

As an example, we'll compare processing the EMP table 14 rows at a time versus processing it a row at a time. Here is the version for row-at-a-time processing:

```
ops$tkyte@ORA920> exec runstats_pkg.rs_start;
PL/SQL procedure successfully completed.

ops$tkyte@ORA920> begin
  2      for i in 1 .. 5000
  3      loop
```

```
   4              for x in ( select ename, empno, hiredate from emp )
   5              loop
   6                  null;
   7              end loop;
   8       end loop;
   9   end;
  10   /
PL/SQL procedure successfully completed.
```

And here is the version that uses bulk processing:

```
ops$tkyte@ORA920> declare
   2       l_ename     dbms_sql.varchar2_table;
   3       l_empno     dbms_sql.number_table;
   4       l_hiredate  dbms_sql.date_table;
   5   begin
   6       for i in 1 .. 5000
   7       loop
   8           select ename, empno, hiredate
   9             bulk collect into l_ename, l_empno, l_hiredate
  10             from emp;
  11       end loop;
  12   end;
  13   /
PL/SQL procedure successfully completed.
```

Running Runstats to compare the versions shows the following:

```
ops$tkyte@ORA920> exec runstats_pkg.rs_stop(10000);
Run1 ran in 274 hsecs
Run2 ran in 132 hsecs
run 1 ran in 207.58% of the time
```

This shows that fetching our entire result set using BULK COLLECT in one SQL statement runs faster (about twice as fast in this case) than doing the same thing a single row at a time.

The response times you see will be a function of the amount of data you array-fetch, as well. More or less data in the result set will have a definite impact on the performance here. The more data you bulk-fetch, up to a point, the better relative performance you will see from the BULK COLLECT over time. For example, when I put 56 rows in EMP, the BULK COLLECT version was 380% better. When I put 1 row in EMP, both versions ran in the same amount of time. At some point, however, the BULK COLLECT will cease being more efficient, as the amount of RAM it consumes increases greatly. Where that point is varies, but I find a BULK COLLECT size of about 100 rows to be universally "good" in practice. Later, we'll look at using the LIMIT clause to control this.

Looking further in the Runstats report, we see some interesting numbers:

| Name | Run1 | Run2 | Diff |
|---|---|---|---|
| STAT...session logical reads | 80,522 | 15,525 | -64,997 |
| STAT...consistent gets | 80,003 | 15,004 | -64,999 |

```
STAT...buffer is not pinned co      70,000      5,000     -65,000
STAT...no work - consistent re      70,000      5,000     -65,000
STAT...table scan blocks gotte      70,000      5,000     -65,000
STAT...recursive calls              75,003      5,003     -70,000
LATCH.cache buffers chains         162,601     32,582    -130,019
```

Overall latching is reduced.

```
Run1 latches total versus runs -- difference and pct
Run1         Run2         Diff        Pct
188,736      58,658       -130,078    321.76%

PL/SQL procedure successfully completed.y
```

That is analogous to what we observed in SQL*Plus in Chapter 2, when we played with the ARRAYSIZE setting while using AUTOTRACE. The larger the array size, the fewer consistent gets we performed, and the better the performance and scalability. The same rules apply here, but the impact is not as transparent as just adjusting an ARRAYSIZE setting. Here, we needed to rewrite the code using PL/SQL table types or collections. We needed to declare variables to fetch into. We used more memory in our session. We can use V$MYSTAT, a dynamic performance view, to see the net effect on memory usage.

It is for these reasons that I recommend using bulk processing only where and when it would have the most dramatic effect. In the example shown here, it looks dramatic. But that is only because we did it 5,000 times for 14 rows. It would be worthwhile here, if you did that process many times. If you did that process once for 50 rows, you would discover they run in about the same amount of time and that the BULK COLLECT actually does more latching!

# Use Bulk Processing for ETL Operations

A predominant use of bulk processing is in ETL-type processes. ETL stands for extract, transform, and load and is a data warehousing term. Here is the structure of a typical ETL process:

```
For x in ( select * from ... )
Loop
    Process data
    Insert into table values (...);
End loop
```

If this cannot be turned into an INSERT AS SELECT statement (and I find that many operations like this can be), you can optimize this process using a BULK COPY.

We'll use the DBA_OBJECTS table in an example where we copy it a row at a time versus copying it *N* rows at a time. We'll pretend that inside the loop, there is some process taking place that is so complex we cannot possibly do it in SQL. The row-at-a-time procedure looks like this:

**NOTE**
*For the following procedures to compile successfully, you will need a direct GRANT on DBA_OBJECTS. Access via a role is not sufficient to compile an object in the database.*

```
ops$tkyte@ORA920> create table t1
  2   as
  3   select *
  4     from dba_objects
  5    where 1=0;
Table created.

ops$tkyte@ORA920> create or replace procedure row_at_a_time
  2   as
  3   begin
  4       for x in ( select * from dba_objects )
  5       loop
  6           insert into t1 (
  7           OWNER, OBJECT_NAME, SUBOBJECT_NAME,
  8           OBJECT_ID, DATA_OBJECT_ID, OBJECT_TYPE,
  9           CREATED, LAST_DDL_TIME, TIMESTAMP,
 10           STATUS, TEMPORARY, GENERATED, SECONDARY
 11           ) values (
 12           x.OWNER, x.OBJECT_NAME, x.SUBOBJECT_NAME,
 13           x.OBJECT_ID, x.DATA_OBJECT_ID, x.OBJECT_TYPE,
 14           x.CREATED, x.LAST_DDL_TIME, x.TIMESTAMP,
 15           x.STATUS, x.TEMPORARY, x.GENERATED, x.SECONDARY );
 16       end loop;
 17   end;
 18   /
Procedure created.
```

This is processing thousands of rows. The INSERT statement will be invoked thousands of times, as will the implied fetch in the loop. We would like to optimize this heavy-duty process. The corresponding bulk-processing code would be as follows:

```
ops$tkyte@ORA920> create table t2
  2   as
  3   select * .
  4     from dba_objects
  5    where 1=0;
Table created.

ops$tkyte@ORA920> create or replace procedure nrows_at_a_time
                                         ( p_array_size in number )
  2   as
  3       l_OWNER            dbms_sql.VARCHAR2_table;
  4       l_OBJECT_NAME      dbms_sql.VARCHAR2_table;
  5       l_SUBOBJECT_NAME   dbms_sql.VARCHAR2_table;
  6       l_OBJECT_ID        dbms_sql.NUMBER_table;
  7       l_DATA_OBJECT_ID   dbms_sql.NUMBER_table;
  8       l_OBJECT_TYPE      dbms_sql.VARCHAR2_table;
  9       l_CREATED          dbms_sql.DATE_table;
 10       l_LAST_DDL_TIME    dbms_sql.DATE_table;
 11       l_TIMESTAMP        dbms_sql.VARCHAR2_table;
 12       l_STATUS           dbms_sql.VARCHAR2_table;
```

```
13    l_TEMPORARY            dbms_sql.VARCHAR2_table;
14    l_GENERATED            dbms_sql.VARCHAR2_table;
15    l_SECONDARY            dbms_sql.VARCHAR2_table;
16    cursor c is select * from dba_objects;
17  begin
18      open c;
19      loop
20          fetch c bulk collect into
21          l_OWNER, l_OBJECT_NAME, l_SUBOBJECT_NAME,
22          l_OBJECT_ID, l_DATA_OBJECT_ID, l_OBJECT_TYPE,
23          l_CREATED, l_LAST_DDL_TIME, l_TIMESTAMP,
24          l_STATUS, l_TEMPORARY, l_GENERATED, l_SECONDARY
25          LIMIT p_array_size;
26
27          forall i in 1 .. l_owner.count
28              insert into t2 (
29              OWNER, OBJECT_NAME, SUBOBJECT_NAME,
30              OBJECT_ID, DATA_OBJECT_ID, OBJECT_TYPE,
31              CREATED, LAST_DDL_TIME, TIMESTAMP,
32              STATUS, TEMPORARY, GENERATED, SECONDARY
33              ) values (
34              l_OWNER(i), l_OBJECT_NAME(i), l_SUBOBJECT_NAME(i),
35              l_OBJECT_ID(i), l_DATA_OBJECT_ID(i), l_OBJECT_TYPE(i),
36              l_CREATED(i), l_LAST_DDL_TIME(i), l_TIMESTAMP(i),
37              l_STATUS(i), l_TEMPORARY(i), l_GENERATED(i), l_SECONDARY(i)
);
38          exit when c%notfound;
39      end loop;
40  end;
41  /
Procedure created.
```

This is significantly more code. Is it worth the effort? Yes, this is one of those few times where more code is better. In Oracle9iR2 you can code the preceding two routines in this fashion:

```
create or replace procedure row_at_a_time
as
begin
    for x in ( select * from dba_objects )
    loop
        insert into t1 values X;
    end loop;
end;
/

create or replace procedure nrows_at_a_time( p_array_size in number )
as
  type array is table of dba_objects%rowtype;
  l_data array;
  cursor c is select * from dba_objects;
```

```
begin
  open c;
  loop
     fetch c bulk collect into l_data LIMIT p_array_size;

     forall i in 1 .. l_data.count
         insert into t2 values l_data(i);

     exit when c%notfound;
  end loop;
end;
/
```

Here, we employed the new Oracle9iR2 capability to perform DML in PL/SQL using record types. There is still more code in the BULK code example, but not *significantly* more.

**NOTE**
*Again, consider whether a routine could be done as an INSERT SELECT instead. You would be surprised how often some complex procedural process can be implemented using SQL alone. Also, remember that you can use SQL to write SQL. I frequently use USER_TAB_COLUMNS to generate code for me. If the vast majority of the code is related to defining variables to hold the arrays of data, that would be easy to generate from USER_TAB_COLUMNS for really wide tables with a lot of columns.*

Now, we can use Runstats to compare the processing techniques.

```
ops$tkyte@ORA920> exec runstats_pkg.rs_start
PL/SQL procedure successfully completed.

ops$tkyte@ORA920> exec row_at_a_time;
PL/SQL procedure successfully completed.

ops$tkyte@ORA920> exec runstats_pkg.rs_middle
PL/SQL procedure successfully completed.

ops$tkyte@ORA920> exec nrows_at_a_time(100);
PL/SQL procedure successfully completed.

ops$tkyte@ORA920> exec runstats_pkg.rs_stop(5000)
Run1 ran in 1868 hsecs
Run2 ran in 179 hsecs
run 1 ran in 1043.58% of the time
```

The array-processing routine is, so far, an order of magnitude faster! Not only that, but look at the statistics/latching activity:

```
Name                            Run1        Run2
STAT...db block gets            37,124      5,869      -31,255
STAT...calls to get snapshot s  32,231        896      -31,335
STAT...redo entries             35,137      3,580      -31,557
LATCH.redo allocation           35,164      3,588      -31,576
STAT...execute count            32,123        364      -31,759
LATCH.shared pool               32,335        573      -31,762
STAT...consistent gets          69,004     25,529      -43,475
STAT...no work - consistent re  65,563     21,761      -43,802
STAT...buffer is pinned count    1,864     45,902       44,038
STAT...db block changes         68,239      5,375      -62,864
STAT...recursive calls          64,530      1,012      -63,518
LATCH.library cache             64,673      1,145      -63,528
LATCH.library cache pin         64,526        996      -63,530
STAT...session logical reads   106,128     31,398      -74,730
STAT...buffer is not pinned co 100,372     24,811      -75,561
LATCH.cache buffers chains     312,608     68,226     -244,382
STAT...redo size            11,532,084  3,691,620   -7,840,464
```

The bulk operation generated 7.5MB less redo data and did one-third the logical I/Os. In fact, every relevant statistic is decreased. Look at the aggregate latch differences:

```
Run1 latches total versus runs -- difference and pct
Run1        Run2        Diff        Pct
520,650     79,260      -441,390    656.89%
PL/SQL procedure successfully completed.
```

This shows a difference of more than 600%. So, if doing 100 rows at a time is good, doing 10,000 at a time would be really good, right? Let's try that. Here is what we accomplish when we do 100 rows at a time:

```
Loop
    Read 100 rows
    Write 100 rows -> putting data into redo log buffer which
                      Lgwr will start writing out
End loop, until no more data
```

So, every time we bulk-inserted 100 rows, we put data into the redo log buffer, and LGWR, the process responsible for writing such data out, starts writing in the background. Our 100 rows never flooded the redo log buffer; we just kept filling it up as LGWR wrote it out. Compare that with the results of doing it 10,000 rows at a time:

```
Loop
    Read 10,000 rows
    Write 10,000 rows -> flooding the redo log buffer, causing us
                         To WAIT while lgwr flushes the buffer
                         To disk
End loop, until no more data
```

We can see the wait times for the 100-row insert as reported by TKPROF:

```
Elapsed times include waiting on following events:
    Event waited on                Times    Max. Wait   Total Waited
    --------------------------      Waited   ----------  ------------
    db file sequential read           2         0.00         0.00
    log buffer space                  2         0.05         0.07
```

The 10,000-row insert test shows these wait times:

```
Elapsed times include waiting on following events:
    Event waited on                Times    Max. Wait   Total Waited
    --------------------------      Waited   ----------  ------------
    db file sequential read           2         0.00         0.00
    log buffer space                 16         0.29         0.68
```

Running these tests with TKPROF and the 10046 trace event shows that the first run with 100 rows at a time had very little in the way of waits on log buffer space. The run with 10,000 rows at a time had many more waits for this space. We could accommodate this by raising the log buffer size or by adjusting the array size we are using. Eventually, however, we run out of log buffer space, but we can still adjust the array size.

This is another excellent reason why the DBAs and developers need to work as a team (harking back to a point I made in Chapter 1 in this book). If the DBAs are unaware of and not participating in the approaches the developers are using, overall system performance will never be what it can be. (In this test, the DBA and developer were one in the same, so working together was not a problem.)

Lastly, in the following example, we'll see what happens when the objects we are inserting into are more "real world," in that they have pre-existing data and a couple of indexes. Continuing that same example, we'll add these indexes

```
create index t1_idx1 on t1(object_name);
create index t1_idx2 on t1(owner,object_type,object_name);
create index t1_idx3 on t1(object_id);

create index t2_idx1 on t2(object_name);
create index t2_idx2 on t2(owner,object_type,object_name);
create index t2_idx3 on t2(object_id);
```

and using Runstats once again, you will observe:

```
Run1 ran in 3019 hsecs
Run2 ran in 738 hsecs
run 1 ran in 409.08% of the time
```

The row-at-a-time method is once again significantly slower, further:

```
Name                            Run1         Run2         Diff
LATCH.simulator hash latch      24,879        6,481       -18,398
STAT...execute count            32,188          368       -31,820
STAT...calls to get snapshot s  33,322        1,474       -31,848
```

```
LATCH.shared pool                   32,604          680      -31,924
STAT...consistent gets              70,598       27,052      -43,546
STAT...no work - consistent re      65,711       21,769      -43,942
STAT...buffer is pinned count        1,887       46,031       44,144
STAT...recursive calls              64,754        1,018      -63,736
LATCH.library cache pin             64,894        1,110      -63,784
LATCH.library cache                 65,247        1,362      -63,885
STAT...buffer is not pinned co     100,613       24,850      -75,763
STAT...redo entries                137,154       35,215     -101,939
LATCH.redo allocation              137,289       35,286     -102,003
STAT...session pga memory                0      162,420      162,420
STAT...db block gets               265,724       67,191     -198,533
STAT...db block changes            273,710       69,004     -204,706
STAT...session logical reads       336,322       94,243     -242,079
LATCH.cache buffers chains       1,223,210      335,114     -888,096
STAT...redo size                44,656,988   24,186,116  -20,470,872
```

The row-at-a-time method uses significantly more resources. Look at the redo generation for example, here we shaved off 20 megabytes of redo, simply by bulk processing the data. Looking at the aggregate latching report, we observe:

```
Run1 latches total versus runs -- difference and pct
Run1         Run2        Diff       Pct
1,581,620    406,758  -1,174,862    388.84%
```

The latching is again way down as well. There is no question that bulk processing is the way to go here.

## Bulk Processing Wrap-Up

Bulk processing tends to be more code-intensive; however, the payback in throughput can be incredible. Bulk processing is *not* something I would suggest for each and every query in your system. Please don't run out and recode your entire system using BULK COLLECT. The ease with which you can code a simple cursor for loop far outweighs the nominal gain (and possibly even loss) in performance. Bulk processing is best suited for massive operations, as demonstrated here.

When you do bulk processing, you want to make sure to achieve a balance. This is a case where more is not always better. For example, in the bulk operation described in the previous section, when we used 10,000-row-at-a-time processing, the bulk operation is still much faster than row-at-a-time processing, but not as fast as 100-row-at-a-time processing, and it uses about 6MB more RAM. You'll want to always parameterize the array size so you can test different values. My starting point (and generally my ending point) is 100, but you may find larger values to be better. It depends on your data, how much memory your system has, and what else is going on in the system. If the array size is a parameter, you can always change it later.

# Returning Data

There is a rumor that Oracle does not support returning result sets from stored procedures. It does seem that every SQL Server programmer who uses Oracle has fallen into this trap. *PL/SQL can return result sets,* and it is no harder (or easier) to do than it is in other databases. It is just different. In Oracle you use a *ref cursor* (a pointer to a cursor). This is a feature that has been available with Oracle since version 7.2 of the database (introduced in 1995).

## Advantages of Ref Cursors

In general, using a ref cursor is the optimum method for returning results to clients. The reasons for this are as follows:

- **Ease of programming**   Every language can deal with a result set—a cursor.

- **Flexibility**   The client application can choose how many rows at a time to fetch. Rather than send back 10,000 items in an array, you send back a result set that the client can fetch from 10 items at a time.

- **Performance**   You do not need to have PL/SQL fetch the data from a cursor, fill up an array (allocating memory on the server), and send the array to the client (allocating memory on the client), making the client wait for the last row to be processed before getting the first row. Instead, a ref cursor will let you immediately return data to a client without doing any of that.

So, for reasons very similar to limiting the bulk collection size, you want to use ref cursors as opposed to PL/SQL table types or SQL collections to return result sets to client applications.

## Use Ref Cursors to Return Result Sets

As an example of where ref cursors are suitable, let's use a Java client that fetches data from a copy of ALL_OBJECTS. We will code this once using PL/SQL table types and once using ref cursors.

The following is the package specification for our example. It has an INDEX_BY routine that takes, as input, an OWNER name and returns, as output, three columns.

```
scott@ORA920> create table t
  2   as
  3   select * from all_objects;
Table created.

scott@ORA920> create or replace package demo_pkg
  2   as
  3       type varchar2_array is table of varchar2(30)
  4           index by binary_integer;
  5
  6       type rc is ref cursor;
  7
  8       procedure index_by( p_owner in varchar2,
  9                           p_object_name out varchar2_array,
 10                           p_object_type out varchar2_array,
 11                           p_timestamp out varchar2_array );
 12       procedure ref_cursor( p_owner in varchar2,
 13                             p_cursor in out rc );
 14   end;
 15   /
Package created.
```

You can see how this approach gets unwieldy for large (wider) result sets quickly. The ref cursor interface, on the other hand, simply takes as input the OWNER to search for and returns a single ref cursor that can select as many columns as you like.

Now, let's move onto the package bodies for the implementation.

```
scott@ORA920> create or replace package body demo_pkg
  2   as
  3
  4   procedure index_by( p_owner in varchar2,
  5                       p_object_name out varchar2_array,
  6                       p_object_type out varchar2_array,
  7                       p_timestamp out varchar2_array )
  8   is
  9   begin
 10      select object_name, object_type, timestamp
 11        bulk collect into
 12             p_object_name, p_object_type, p_timestamp
 13        from t
 14       where owner = p_owner;
 15   end;
 16
 17   procedure ref_cursor( p_owner in varchar2,
 18                         p_cursor in out rc )
 19   is
 20   begin
 21      open p_cursor for
 22      select object_name, object_type, timestamp
 23        from t
 24       where owner = p_owner;
 25   end;
 26   end;
 27   /
Package body created.
```

Here, the INDEX_BY routine uses BULK COLLECT to fetch all of the data. The REF_CURSOR routine simply does an OPEN.

The Java client for the INDEX_BY routine might look like the following. We'll start with a very simple timing routine that will print out elapsed times in milliseconds between calls.

```
import java.sql.*;
import java.util.Date;
import oracle.jdbc.driver.*;
import oracle.sql.*;

class indexby
{

static long start = new Date().getTime();
public static void showElapsed( String msg )
{
long end = new Date().getTime();

    System.out.println( msg + " " + (end - start) + " ms");
    start = end;
}
```

Every time we call that routine, it will print the elapsed time since the last time we called it, and then remember this new last time.

Next, let's look at the main routine. We begin by connecting to Oracle.

```java
public static void main(String args[])throws Exception
{
    DriverManager.registerDriver
    (new oracle.jdbc.driver.OracleDriver());

    Connection conn=DriverManager.getConnection
    ("jdbc:oracle:oci8:@ora920.us.oracle.com","scott", "tiger");

    showElapsed( "Connected, going to prepare" );
```

Then we prepare a call to the INDEX_BY routine in the DEMO_PKG. We will bind SYS to the first input, and then define the output PL/SQL index by tables, one by one.

```java
    OracleCallableStatement cstmt =
    (OracleCallableStatement)conn.prepareCall
    ( "begin demo_pkg.index_by(?,?,?,?); end;" );

    showElapsed( "Prepared, going to bind" );
    int maxl       = 15000;
    int elemSqlType = OracleTypes.VARCHAR;
    int elemMaxLen  = 30;

    cstmt.setString( 1, "SYS" );
    cstmt.registerIndexTableOutParameter
    ( 2, maxl, elemSqlType, elemMaxLen );
    cstmt.registerIndexTableOutParameter
    ( 3, maxl, elemSqlType, elemMaxLen );
    cstmt.registerIndexTableOutParameter
    ( 4, maxl, elemSqlType, elemMaxLen );
```

Notice that we are setting three elements: MAXL, which is the maximum number of "rows" we are prepared to deal with, the maximum size of our array; ELEMSQLTYPE, the datatype of each output array; and ELEMMAXLEN, the maximum width of each array element we anticipate.

Next, we execute the statement. After executing the statement, we retrieve the three arrays of data representing our result set.

```java
    showElapsed( "Bound, going to execute" );
    cstmt.execute();

    Datum[] object_name = cstmt.getOraclePlsqlIndexTable(2);
    Datum[] object_type = cstmt.getOraclePlsqlIndexTable(3);
    Datum[] timestamp    = cstmt.getOraclePlsqlIndexTable(4);
```

Then we simply access each one in turn to show how long it takes to go from the first row to the last row in this result set.

```
        showElapsed( "First Row "+object_name.length );
        String data;
        int i;
        for( i = 0; i < object_name.length; i++ )
        {
            data = object_name[i].stringValue();
            data = object_type[i].stringValue();
            data = timestamp[i].stringValue();
        }
        showElapsed( "Last Row "+i );
    }
}
```

The first time I ran this, I used 10,000 instead of 15,000 for MAXL (the maximum array length). Here is what I discovered:

```
$ java indexby
java.sql.SQLException: ORA-06513: PL/SQL:
        index for PL/SQL table out of range for host language array
ORA-06512: at line 1
```

I guessed wrong. The client undersized the array, so it received an error instead of data. Using this approach, the client needs to know the maximum number of rows as well as the maximum column width for each column. That is information you may not have at compile time.

Now we can look at the REFCUR class. The first half of this code is identical (except for the class name) to the INDEXBY class, up to the code immediately after the connect. We'll pick it up there, where we start by setting the row prefetch size (the array size). It defaults to 10 for JDBC, but I generally use 100.

```
        showElapsed( "Connected, going to prepare" );
        ((OracleConnection)conn).setDefaultRowPrefetch(100);
```

Now, we prepare and bind the statement just as with the PL/SQL tables, using the syntax for ref cursors instead of index by tables.

```
        OracleCallableStatement cstmt =
        (OracleCallableStatement)conn.prepareCall
        ( "begin demo_pkg.ref_cursor(?,?); end;" );

        showElapsed( "Prepared, going to bind" );
        cstmt.setString( 1, "SYS" );
        cstmt.registerOutParameter(2,OracleTypes.CURSOR);
```

Then we execute the statement and get the result set. Again, we print the time to get the first row and the last row after touching each column of every row in between.

```
        showElapsed( "Bound, going to execute" );
        cstmt.execute();
```

```
    ResultSet rset = (ResultSet)cstmt.getObject(2);

    if ( rset.next() )
        showElapsed("First Row");

    String data;
    int i;
    for( i = 1; rset.next(); i++ )
    {
        data = rset.getString(1);
        data = rset.getString(2);
        data = rset.getString(3);
    }

    showElapsed("Last Row "+i );
```

Table 9-1 provides a summary of the results of running these two versions.

Let's go a step further and add a table to the mix to keep statistics on the PGA and UGA memory use in the server.

```
scott@ORA920> create table stats ( which varchar2(30), uga number, pga number );
Table created.
```

And we'll add this SQL statement after the last showElapsed in each Java routine (replacing the indexby with ref_cursor in the other routine):

```
Statement stmt = conn.createStatement();
stmt.execute
( "insert into stats "+
  "select 'indexby',  "+
 "max(decode(a.name,'session uga memory max',b.value,null)) uga, "+
 "max(decode(a.name,'session pga memory max',b.value,null)) pga "+
    "from v$statname a, v$mystat b "+
    "where a.name like '%memory%max' "+
    "and a.statistic# = b.statistic# "   );
```

| Wait Time | INDEXBY | REFCUR | Difference |
|---|---|---|---|
| Time to first row | 825ms | 25ms | (800)ms |
| Time to last row | 1,375ms | 860ms | (515)ms |
| Total time to fetch all rows | 2,200ms | 885ms | (1,315)ms |

**TABLE 9-1.** *Comparing the PL/SQL table and reference cursor techniques for returning results*

We'll see that the INDEXBY approach consumes a large amount of memory as compared to the ref cursor approach.

```
scott@ORA920> select which, trunc(avg(uga)), trunc(avg(pga)), count(*)
  2  from stats
  3  group by which
  4  /
```

| WHICH | TRUNC(AVG(UGA)) | TRUNC(AVG(PGA)) | COUNT(*) |
|---|---|---|---|
| indexby | 76988 | 4266132 | 9 |
| ref_cursor | 76988 | 244793 | 9 |

This shows that over nine runs, the INDEXBY approach consumed 4.2MB of RAM on the server. The ref cursor approach used a rather small 244KB of RAM to accomplish the same thing.

# Use %TYPE and %ROWTYPE

PL/SQL makes it easy to ensure that the program variables you use in your code and the database datatypes you use in your tables stay totally in sync. Consider the examples of PL/SQL versus Java routines to process the contents of the EMP table in the "PL/SQL Is the Most Efficient Language for Data Manipulation" section earlier in this chapter. In PL/SQL, setting up variables to hold our rows was 100% transparent to us. Not only that, but if the database schema were altered by changing a datatype, increasing a length, or changing the name of a column, our PL/SQL code would have fixed itself (with the exception of the reference to ENAME in the predicate).

In the real world, however, coding is not always as easy as using simple FOR X IN (SELECT...) loops. You may have subroutines or need to define variables of your own. In those cases, you should strive to use %TYPE and %ROWTYPE whenever possible. Let's revisit that opening example:

```
Create or replace procedure process_data( p_inputs in varchar2 )
As
Begin
    For x in ( select * from emp where ename like p_inputs )
    Loop
        Process( X );
    End loop
End;
```

Note how we pass the record X to some routine PROCESS. What is the best way to define PROCESS? There are two ways we could do that: base the record types on a datatype or base the record types on a table. We'll take a look at each now.

## Base Record Types on a Table

Here is the package specification for the routine we'll use for this example:

```
ops$tkyte@ORA920> create or replace package demo_pkg
  2  as
  3      procedure process_data( p_inputs in varchar2 );
```

```
   4   end;
   5   /
Package created.
```

And the following is the package body:

```
ops$tkyte@ORA920> create or replace package body demo_pkg
   2   as
   3       type emp_rec is record
   4       ( EMPNO              NUMBER(4),
   5         ENAME              VARCHAR2(10),
   6         JOB                VARCHAR2(9),
   7         MGR                NUMBER(4),
   8         HIREDATE           DATE,
   9         SAL                NUMBER(7,2),
  10         COMM               NUMBER(7,2),
  11         DEPTNO             NUMBER(2)
  12       );
  13
```

Here, we start by defining a record type for out result set. We got this information from the data dictionary. It is an accurate representation of how our data looks right now using a copy of the SCOTT.EMP table.

Next, we'll set up two process procedures. The first will use my preferred method of defining a record. It is based on the EMP table itself.

```
  14       procedure process1( p_record in emp%rowtype )
  15       is
  16       begin
  17           null;
  18       end;
  19
```

The PROCESS1 procedure takes a record of EMP as input. We do not need to define this record, because the PL/SQL compiler does it based on the data dictionary itself.

And then we define an equivalent (for now) procedure based on the EMP_REC type we defined in the package body.

```
  20       procedure process2( p_record in emp_rec )
  21       is
  22       begin
  23           null;
  24       end;
  25
```

Now, we just need a PROCESS_DATA procedure that fetches the data and calls the process procedures. Here, we just copy the loops so that we can call PROCESS1 and then PROCESS2 independently:

```
26        procedure process_data( p_inputs in varchar2 )
27        is
28        begin
29            for x in (select * from emp where ename like p_inputs)
30            loop
31                process1(x);
32            end loop;
33
34            for x in (select * from emp where ename like p_inputs)
35            loop
36                process2(x);
37            end loop;
38        end;
39   end;
40   /
Package body created.
```

Now, both routines will execute successfully. We can see that clearly just by running the code against each and every record.

```
ops$tkyte@ORA920> exec demo_pkg.process_data( '%' );
PL/SQL procedure successfully completed.
```

But what happens if we make a small change to our application? Let's add a column to the EMP table.

```
ops$tkyte@ORA920> alter table emp add x number;
Table altered.

ops$tkyte@ORA920> alter package demo_pkg compile body;
Warning: Package Body altered with compilation errors.

ops$tkyte@ORA920> show errors package body demo_pkg
Errors for PACKAGE BODY DEMO_PKG:

LINE/COL ERROR
-------- -----------------------------------------------------------
36/13    PLS-00306: wrong number or types of arguments in call to
         'PROCESS2'
36/13    PL/SQL: Statement ignored
```

PROCESS2 now has a problem. In fact, anywhere we defined a record by hand is a potential problem after a modification such as a column addition. We need to go into the code and manually modify the record definition.

Let's get rid of that column and try some other minor change.

```
ops$tkyte@ORA920> alter table emp drop column x;
Table altered.

ops$tkyte@ORA920> alter package demo_pkg compile body;
```

```
Package body altered.

ops$tkyte@ORA920> show errors package body demo_pkg
No errors.

ops$tkyte@ORA920> alter table emp modify ename varchar2(11);
Table altered.

ops$tkyte@ORA920> update emp set ename = rpad( ename, 11, 'x' );
14 rows updated.
```

Here, we just increased the size of the ENAME column by one byte. Now the PL/SQL code *thinks* everything is okay. The code compiles, but we still get an error.

```
ops$tkyte@ORA920> exec demo_pkg.process_data( '%' );
BEGIN demo_pkg.process_data( '%' ); END;

*
ERROR at line 1:
ORA-06502: PL/SQL: numeric or value error: character string buffer too small
ORA-06512: at "OPS$TKYTE.DEMO_PKG", line 36
ORA-06512: at line 1
```

Line 36 is our call to PROCESS2. Apparently, the record structures were similar enough to compile, yet different enough that the data could not be moved from record to record. Here, we have a subtle, hard-to-find runtime bug introduced by a minor schema change. As more databases move from single-byte character sets such as US7ASCII or WE8ISO8859P1 to multibyte character sets such as UTF-8 or others, this error is becoming more common. A VARCHAR2(80) in a WE8ISO8859P1 will need to become a VARCHAR2(320) or the equivalent VARCHAR2(80 CHAR) in UTF8, because each character in UTF8 may take up to four bytes of storage! PL/SQL routines that used hard-coded VARCHAR2(*N*) sizes will suffer from massive amounts of ORA-06502 errors.

I never use this construct:

```
3        type emp_rec is record
4        ( EMPNO              NUMBER(4),
5          ENAME              VARCHAR2(10),
6          JOB                VARCHAR2(9), ...
```

In fact, I typically have to pull up the documentation for the syntax when I use it in examples (I did for this example!). I base all record types on either:

■ A table or view definition (*TABLE*%ROWTYPE)

■ A cursor (*CURSOR_NAME*%ROWTYPE)

For example, suppose in the preceding routine the query we needed to process was not a simple single table or it just selected some of the columns from the EMP table? Clearly, EMP%ROWTYPE would not work in those cases. There, we need to use an explicit cursor (which we can still process implicitly, losing no ease of use here) in order to be able to define our record type for us.

# Base Record Types on a Cursor

Consider this reimplementation of the body of DEMO_PKG. First, we'll start with our defining cursor.

```
ops$tkyte@ORA920> create or replace package body demo_pkg
  2  as
  3      cursor C1(p_inputs in varchar2)
  4      is
  5      select emp.ename, emp.hiredate, dept.dname
  6        from emp, dept
  7       where emp.deptno = dept.deptno
  8         and emp.ename like p_inputs;
```

This is a parameterized cursor. It will work just like the implicit cursor we used earlier in the FOR X IN ( SELECT...) construct. It defines a set of inputs and outputs based on whatever the data dictionary says that query should be returning.

Now, we can define our PROCESS routine simply as this:

```
  9
 10      procedure process( p_record in C1%rowtype )
 11      is
 12      begin
 13          null;
 14      end;
 15
```

PROCESS takes a record in the shape of *CURSOR_NAME*%ROWTYPE as input. If we were to modify EMP.ENAME in the database, the cursor would change its size and shape to reflect that. We are protected from the majority of changes we might make to a schema, such as changing datatypes or the physical size of a column. The calling routine would simply use the named cursor in the loop, as follows:

```
 16      procedure process_data( p_inputs in varchar2 )
 17      is
 18      begin
 19          for x in C1(p_inputs)
 20          loop
 21              process(x);
 22          end loop;
 23      end;
 24  end;
 25  /
Package body created.
```

A frequent question at this point is, "Well, fine, but what about dynamic SQL? I have a routine where I change the predicate frequently, what then?" There are two cases to consider:

■ **Using DBMS_SQL**  In this case, you won't be using a record at all, so there really isn't anything to talk about. You would use DBMS_SQL whenever the number and type of columns you are selecting are unknown at compile time (it is not possible to use native dynamic SQL if you do not know the number and types of the columns at compile time).

■ **Using native dynamic SQL** In this case, the number and types of columns in the query must be well-known at compile time. In fact, the SELECT list of your query does not change; only the base table or predicate changes (and if the base table changes, all of the base tables must have the same physical structures).

In the second case, I use a construct I call a *template cursor*. I simply create a cursor definition that selects what my dynamic query will be from the base tables, but I do not include a predicate.

Let's reimplement our PROCESS routine, but make it so that we can dynamically WHERE on either ENAME or JOB. Our new specification is as follows:

```
ops$tkyte@ORA920> create or replace package demo_pkg
  2  as
  3      procedure process_data( p_cname in varchar2,
  4                              p_inputs in varchar2 );
  5  end;
  6  /
Package created.
```

Here, we can pass in the name of the column we want to use for the LIKE operation.

Now, let's look at the package body. Here, we start with our TEMPLATE_CURSOR, which selects the relevant columns from the base tables. It does not involve any predicates or joins. We'll never actually use this cursor to retrieve data. We are just using it to get our record defined.

```
ops$tkyte@ORA920> create or replace package body demo_pkg
  2  as
  3      cursor TEMPLATE_cursor
  4      is
  5      select emp.ename, emp.hiredate, dept.dname
  6        from emp, dept;
  7
  8      type rc is ref cursor;
```

**NOTE**
*In Oracle9i you would not need to have line 8 in this example. You could just use the built-in type SYS_REFCURSOR. I've included the type definition here for backward compatibility.*

Here is the PROCESS routine, which is virtually unchanged from our previous implementation:

```
  9
 10      procedure process( p_record in template_cursor%rowtype )
 11      is
 12      begin
 13          null;
 14      end;
```

The actual PROCESS_DATA routine has the most changes from the original version, but that is to be expected. Now, it is doing dynamic SQL, not static SQL. But what is interesting to note is that even though we are using dynamic SQL, the package DEMO_PKG is related to the base tables EMP and DEPT. Our TEMPLATE_CURSOR does two things for us. Not only does it define our record (protecting us from changes in the schema), but it also sets up a dependency between our package and the base tables referenced in the FROM clause of the defining query. If those tables change, this package will automatically become invalid, recompile itself, and fix the TEMPLATE_CURSOR%ROWTYPE record for us. We have the advantages of dynamic SQL, but also the advantages of static SQL with regard to the dependency mechanism.

The PROCESS_DATA routine looks like this:

```
15
16      procedure process_data( p_cname in varchar2,
17                              p_inputs in varchar2 )
18      is
19          l_cursor rc;
20          l_rec    template_cursor%rowtype;
21      begin
22          open l_cursor
23          for
24          'select emp.ename, emp.hiredate, dept.dname
25            from emp, dept
26           where emp.deptno = dept.deptno
27             and emp.' || p_cname || ' like :x'
28           USING p_inputs;
29
30          loop
31              fetch l_cursor into l_rec;
32              exit when l_cursor%notfound;
33              process(l_rec);
34          end loop;
35          close l_cursor;
36      end;
37  end;
38  /
Package body created.
```

This routine dynamically opens the ref cursor, fetches the data into a record based on the template cursor, and processes that data via the PROCESS routine.

## Base Datatypes on a Column

The same advice about using types applies for simple scalar items as well as records. For example, consider the declaration of l_cname in the following:

```
ops$tkyte@ORA734> declare
2          l_cname varchar2(30);
3  begin
4          select column_name
5            into l_cname
6            from user_cons_columns
7           where constraint_name = 'CHECK_CONS'
```

```
    8                and position is null;
    9                dbms_output.put_line( l_cname );
   10  end;
   11  /
PL/SQL procedure successfully completed.
```

This worked fine in Oracle7.3 and earlier, since COLUMN_NAME was a VARCHAR2(30). However, in Oracle8 and later, it might result in this:

```
ops$tkyte@ORA817DEV> declare
    2               l_cname varchar2(30);
    3  begin
    4               select column_name
    5                 into l_cname
    6                 from user_cons_columns
    7                where constraint_name = 'CHECK_CONS'
    8                  and position is null;
    9
   10               dbms_output.put_line( l_cname );
   11  end;
   12  /
declare
*
ERROR at line 1:
ORA-06502: PL/SQL: numeric or value error: character string buffer too small
ORA-06512: at line 4
```

This happens because they changed the maximum length of the COLUMN_NAME attribute on us!

Instead, we should code the declaration as follows:

```
ops$tkyte@ORA817DEV> declare
    2               l_cname user_cons_columns.column_name%type;
    3  begin
    4               select column_name
    5                 into l_cname
    6                 from user_cons_columns
    7                where constraint_name = 'CHECK_CONS'
    8                  and position is null;
    9
   10               dbms_output.put_line( l_cname );
   11  end;
   12  /
"X"."LONG_NAME_HERE_LONG_NAME_HERE2"."LONG_NAME_HERE_LONG_NAME_HERE"
PL/SQL procedure successfully completed.
```

This will protect us from errors due to changes such as column name lengths. (This is the voice of experience talking—I don't know how many scripts I had that "went bad" due to the column names in USER_IND_COLUMNS and other dictionary fields changing over time.)

This is another reason why I really like using PL/SQL to work with data and then just have 3GL languages (like Java, C, or VB) call packaged procedures and functions to do the rest of the work, such as visualization of the data and interacting with the end user. If you stick with PL/SQL, many types of changes are automated for you.

# Using Invoker Rights

There are two ways stored PL/SQL can execute in Oracle:

- Using *definer rights*, which means the procedure runs SQL using the base privileges of the owner of the procedure

- Using *invoker rights*, which means the procedure will run SQL statements using the current privilege set of the invoking user

Prior to Oracle8i, all compiled stored objects were executed with the privileges and name resolution of the definer of the object. That meant that the set of privileges granted directly to the owner (definer) of the stored object were used at compile time to figure out which objects (tables and so on) to actually access and whether the definer had the necessary privileges to access them. This static, compile-time binding went as far as to limit the set of privileges to only the privileges granted to the definer directly (in other words, no roles were ever enabled during the compilation or execution of a stored procedure). Additionally, when anyone executed a definer rights routine, that routine would execute with the base set of privileges of the definer of the routine, not the invoker who executed the procedure.

Beginning in Oracle8i, we have a feature called invoker rights, which allows us to create procedures, packages, and functions that do not follow the rules for definer rights. We can now develop a stored procedure that executes with the privilege set of the invoker at runtime. This allows us to create a stored procedure that might execute properly and correctly for one user (who had access to all of the relevant objects) but not for another (who didn't have that access). This is because the access to the underlying objects is not defined at compile time (although the definer must have access to these objects, or at least to objects with those names, in order to compile the PL/SQL code), but rather at runtime. This runtime access is based on the privileges and roles of the current schema/user in effect.

**NOTE**
*Invoker rights are not available in the creation of views or triggers. Views and triggers are created with definer rights only. For detailed information on invoker and definer rights routines, see the Oracle9i Release 2* PL/SQL Users Guide and Reference, *Chapter 8, the section titled "Invoker Rights Versus Definer Rights."*

## Invoker Rights and Multiple Schemas

According to the Oracle documentation, invoker rights routines are especially useful in a situation where you have an application that uses multiple schemas. The goal is that USER1 would use USER1.TABLE and USER2 would use USER2.TABLE. I don't fully agree with this approach. I believe there should be one schema that holds all of the data. If you need the segregation of data for usability or security purposes, using fine-grained access control (FGAC) would be much more appropriate and scalable than using invoker rights. (For information about

FGAC, see Chapter 9 of the Oracle9i Release 2 *Security Overview*, the section titled "Virtual Private Database.")

There are several problems associated with using invoker rights routines in support of a multiple-schema installation:

- **You need to maintain the schemas.** You would need to keep *N* schemas in sync. A simple modification in one schema would need to be instantly performed in every schema simultaneously, or else the shared code would work for some people and not for others.

- **You lose the dependency mechanism.** The stored procedure is dependent on a single instance of some table, not on every instance of every table it might access.

- **You lose the reliability of stored code.** With PL/SQL and a definer rights routine, the code is validated—it has been security checked, datatypes are verified, and so on. You lose all of those sanity checks with invoker rights.

- **You flood the Oracle shared pool.** You will have *N* copies at least of each SQL statement, instead of the one statement that should be there.

- **You lose the primary benefits of PL/SQL.** You won't have PL/SQL's super-efficient caching and reuse of SQL statements, which really makes the shared pool work, or its tight coupling to the data structures in the database. The code no longer fixes itself in reaction to all schema changes, and its dependency tracking is defeated.

- **It is harder to develop and debug.** Different people executing the code will go against totally different data structures, making it impossible for you to have tested every path through the code. It's impossible for you to reproduce errors without being that user.

So, if you are tempted to use invoker rights routines to support a multiple-schema implementation, first look into FGAC to see if that would be the best approach.

## Criteria for Invoker Rights Routines

So, do I think invoker rights routines are useless? No, they are extremely useful in developing generic utilities. For example, I use a utility called DUMP_CSV, which is a PL/SQL routine. It takes any query as input and, using DBMS_SQL, will parse the query, execute it, and dynamically fetch the data row by row. It figures out the number of output columns at runtime and creates a flat file of the data. (See http://asktom.oracle.com/~tkyte/flat/index.html for this utility, as well as two others to unload data.)

In my DUMP_CSV utility, the code uses dynamic SQL, and the goal is for anyone to be able to unload their tables. Using a definer rights routine would be counterproductive, because the owner would need to have direct access to all tables and would need to verify that the invokers were allowed to access the tables they requested. This would be a lot of work, if you could do it at all (reimplement Oracle's security model).

For utilities like DUMP_CSV, using invoker rights routines makes sense because they meet the following criteria:

- The routine needs to run as caller. Running as the definer would incur significant security considerations.

■   It is infrequently invoked. It will not be used tens of times per second or even minute; it is a casual-use utility. Its ability to flood the shared pool with tons of statements is therefore limited.

■   It uses all dynamic SQL; it is not bound to a set of tables in the first place.

Before you consider writing a routine as an invoker rights routine, make sure it satisfies the first point in this list—the need to run as caller. Additionally, it must either be infrequently invoked or use all dynamic SQL anyway.

Another example of a routine that meets this requirements is my PRINT_TABLE utility, which prints output in SQL*Plus down the page, like this (see http://asktom.oracle.com/~tkyte/print_table/index.html for this utility):

```
ops$tkyte@ORA920> exec print_table( 'select * from dept' );
DEPTNO                         : 10
DNAME                          : ACCOUNTING
LOC                            : NEW YORK
-----------------
DEPTNO                         : 20
DNAME                          : RESEARCH
LOC                            : DALLAS
-----------------
DEPTNO                         : 30
DNAME                          : SALES
LOC                            : CHICAGO
-----------------
DEPTNO                         : 40
DNAME                          : OPERATIONS
LOC                            : BOSTON
-----------------
PL/SQL procedure successfully completed.
```

This utility must run as the invoker with roles enabled, or else every person would need to install their own copy of this routine and would not be able to use it against tables to which they had access via a role. Also, it is somewhat infrequently invoked. It is for casual ad-hoc use in SQL*Plus. You won't be using this in your high-end OLTP system. Finally, it uses only dynamic SQL. It doesn't know what the query is going to be until you pass it the query. It meets all of the criteria for an invoker rights routine. Running it as the definer would severely limit its usefulness (it would only print queries the owner of the procedure could run). On the other hand, you would not use an invoker rights routine for an application with the following characteristics:

■   You do not need a routine that runs as caller. There are other infinitely more effective methods (such as FGAC) that achieve this goal in a single schema.

■   The routine is frequently invoked. If these are the core APIs of your application, they are run all of the time.

■   The application uses static SQL. When you use an invoker rights routine, it isn't really static SQL; it does not have the same benefits as true static SQL in PL/SQL.

Invoker rights routines will number in the single digits, or maybe tens, in your database. They are not a good idea for large-scale implementations with hundreds of procedures.

# Make Your Lookups Work Efficiently

Suppose that we need to convert a code into a value, and we need to do it thousands of times (some data cleansing/loading process). Initially, our logic looks like this (in some language such as C, Java, or PL/SQL):

```
Loop over (select data from one_table )
    Select data from another_table where ...
    <maybe some processing here>
    Insert into a_third_table ( ... ) values ( ... );
End loop;
```

Here, we have a lot of procedural, row-at-a-time processing with lookups. We find that this is running much slower than we would like. We are processing tens or hundreds of rows per second and need to be doing it in the tens of thousands. How can we get from here to there?

The most common first approach to a solution for this problem is by replacing the SELECT DATA FROM ANOTHER_TABLE lookup with a procedural lookup, in code. The people following this path claim that SQL is slow and they need to help it out. In support of this claim, they'll have the benchmark that shows they can go 50% to 100% (or more) faster by using a lookup. The problem is that they should be able to get it at least 1,000% faster!

That SQL approaches are slower is a false claim (as we'll see). If we replace the procedural code with less, not more, procedural code, we'll see how fast this can really go. The less work we as developers or DBAs do, and the more we ask the database to do, the faster this process will go.

In order to test the various lookup techniques, I set up a new testing environment. The package I used is similar to Runstats, but it is able to compare and contrast *N* different approaches to a problem, rather than just two approaches.

> **NOTE**
> *Refer to the Appendix for the implementation of the package used to run the benchmarks discussed here. It is a general-purpose package to test the outcomes of* N *different alternative implementations. In this chapter, I present the results, rather than detailing the testing methodology.*

I tested different approaches, some of which are variations on a theme:

- **Single-row fetching, lookup via SQL**   This is the conventional approach and how most untuned code out there would perform this operation.

- **Single-row fetching, procedural lookup**   This is how most people fix the conventional approach when it is deemed too slow. This type of lookup provides an impressive 100% or more increase in throughput in many cases, but it falls far short of where you should be.

■ **Bulk processing**   This is where lookups get much faster. Rather than procedural row-at-a-time processing, you use sets, or collections. I tried five variations of this, all bulk-fetched and bulk-inserted but using different techniques to perform the lookups:

- ■ Use a SQL lookup against a conventional heap table in the INSERT statement, such as `insert into t ( c1, c2 ) values ( :some_value, (select value from lookup where key = :some_key ) );`.

- ■ Use a SQL lookup against a hash table.

- ■ Use a SQL lookup against an index-organized table (IOT).

- ■ Use a PL/SQL index by table in procedural code.

- ■ Use a PL/SQL lookup function in the SQL INSERT statement.

■ **Bulk processing of a more complex statement**   Rather than procedurally looking up a value row by row or using SQL in an INSERT statement to look up the data row by row, I used an outer join to do the lookup directly in the driving query itself. I compared three types of joins:

- ■ Hash cluster joins

- ■ Heap table joins

- ■ IOT joins

■ **Single-statement operations**   This approach provided the biggest bang for the buck by far. If you really desire speed and the least amount of resource usage, look into putting all of your procedural code into a single SQL statement, or as few statements as you can. I tested the same three table types but did the entire process in a single statement:

- ■ Hash cluster joins

- ■ Heap table joins

- ■ IOT joins

In order to set up for this test, I needed a lookup table of values. I decided to use a lookup that would convert one string into another string, rather than a simple number-to-string lookup. I used ALL_OBJECTS to generate a lookup table.

```
create table lookup_heap
( key_col  primary key,
  key_val
)
as
select object_name, max( owner||'_'||object_id )
  from all_objects
 group by object_name
/
```

On my system, that created about 18,000 unique values and can be used to convert an OBJECT_NAME value into the OWNER_OBJECT_ID value.

I created a single-table hash cluster and an IOT using the same information.

```
create cluster lookup_hash_cluster
( key_col varchar2(30) )
single table
hashkeys 20000
size 255
/
create table lookup_hash
( key_col, key_val )
cluster lookup_hash_cluster(key_col)
as
select * from lookup_heap;

create table lookup_iot
( key_col primary key, key_val )
as
select * from lookup_heap;
```

These are the three implementations we'll be considering. Lastly, we need the table we are going to populate ultimately. Here, I was interested in testing the efficiency of the lookup approaches, so I created a simple two-column table with a key column and a value column. We'll test inserting only those values into this table.

```
create table built_by_us as select * from lookup_heap where 1=0;
```

Now let's look at the different implementations.

**NOTE**
*I do not include all of the code for all of the routines here. I will just point out that a certain routine was used over and over, just by changing the table name from LOOKUP_HEAP to LOOKUP_HASH, for example.*

## Single-Row Fetching for Lookups

The first routine is the one most people typically start with: the row-at-a-time, look it up with a SELECT routine. Our logic here is we must load the BUILT_BY_US_TABLE from ALL_OBJECTS, performing a lookup to convert OBJECT_NAME into that other string we placed in our lookup table. So, we define a cursor and iterate row by row doing a SELECT INTO for each row to insert it.

```
create or replace procedure row_fetch_row_select
                            ( p_arraysize in number default 100 )
as
    l_key_col built_by_us.key_col%type;
    l_key_val built_by_us.key_val%type;
    cursor c is select object_name from all_objects;
begin
```

```
    open c;
    loop
        fetch c into l_key_col;
        exit when c%notfound;

        begin
           select key_val into l_key_val
              from lookup_heap
            where key_col = l_key_col;
        exception
            when no_data_found then l_key_val := null;
        end;

        insert into built_by_us ( key_col, key_val )
        values ( l_key_col, l_key_val );
    end loop;
    close c;
end;
/
```

This is very typical but also very slow, as we'll see. To make this faster, we might replace the code in bold with a simple lookup using procedural code. The bold code would be replaced with this code:

```
        begin
            l_key_val := lookup_pkg.g_lookup_tbl( l_key_col );
        exception
            when no_data_found then l_key_val := null;
        end;
```

Here, LOOKUP_PKG is a PL/SQL piece of code that loaded a PL/SQL index by table with values. Here is what that code might look like:

```
create or replace package lookup_pkg
as
    type array is table of lookup_heap.key_val%type
        index by lookup_heap.key_col%type;

    g_lookup_tbl array;

    function val( p_key in varchar2 ) return varchar2;
end;
/
```

I've created an ARRAY type that is a PL/SQL index by table whose key is a string and whose value is also a string. This is commonly referred to as an *associative array* in computer terms. It's an array whose index is a string, not a number. In this implementation, I've made the lookup table itself a global variable, G_LOOKUP_TBL, so that anyone may access its values directly. I've also provided a lookup function, VAL, that we'll implement in the package body. This function converts the key into the value from SQL statements.

The following is the package body, our implementation. Notice how it has elaboration, or *startup*, code. This ensures that anyone accessing the lookup table G_LOOKUP_TBL will actually find it populated with data. This startup code is executed automatically by Oracle the first time you reference this package in this session, allowing you to perform these sorts of complex initializations. I've highlighted this startup code in bold.

```
create or replace package body lookup_pkg
as

function val( p_key in varchar2 ) return varchar2
as
begin
    return g_lookup_tbl(p_key);
end;

begin
    for x in (select * from lookup_heap)
    loop
     g_lookup_tbl(x.key_col) := x.key_val;
    end loop;
end;
/
```

Now, before we get to the other implementations, we'll compare the performance of these two approaches using Runstats. After running both procedures, we get the following output:

```
2738 hsecs
1817 hsecs
run 1 ran in 150.69% of the time
```

Sure enough, we got at least a 50% increase in performance (this is where the myth, "SQL must be really slow, we need to write a lot of code to make it easier on that SQL language," comes into play). Additionally the statistics/latching report shows this:

```
NAME                            RUN1        RUN2        DIFF
-----------------------------   ----------  ----------  ----------
...
LATCH.cache buffers chains      466408      416511      -49897
LATCH.library cache pin         114120       57334      -56786
LATCH.library cache             115105       58110      -56995
STAT...consistent gets          200036      133915      -66121
STAT...session logical reads    230095      163894      -66201
STAT...consistent gets - exami   87769        2923      -84846
STAT...session pga memory max     65536     1966080     1900544
STAT...session uga memory max         0     2029384     2029384
STAT...session uga memory             0     2094848     2094848
STAT...session pga memory        -65536     2097152     2162688

84 rows selected.
```

And here are the total latching numbers:

```
     RUN1        RUN2        DIFF RUN1_PCT_OF_RUN2
---------- ---------- ---------- ----------------
    843752      645807    -197945           130.65
```

Obviously, the second method, even though it consumes significantly more RAM, would be the way to go—or would it?

Although the second method is better, it is far from optimal. I can get this 18-second process down to under two seconds, using less code. Let's look at a third approach mentioned: bulk processing.

## Bulk Processing for Lookups

The following routine uses array processing (BULK COLLECT, in PL/SQL terms). The code fetches *N* rows, processes them, and inserts *N* rows into the database using the scalar subquery to do the lookup.

```
create or replace procedure
array_fetch_heap_insert( p_arraysize in number default 100 )
as
    type array is table of all_objects.object_name%type
            index by binary_integer;
    l_key_col array;
    cursor c is select object_name from all_objects;
begin
    open c;
    loop
        fetch c bulk collect into l_key_col limit p_arraysize;

        forall i in 1 .. l_key_col.count
            insert into built_by_us ( key_col, key_val )
            values ( l_key_col(i),
                    (select key_val
                       from lookup_heap
                      where key_col = l_key_col(i))
                   );
        exit when c%notfound;
    end loop;
    close c;
end;
/
```

This is the template code for the conventional heap table approach. Notice the technique of putting a SELECT inside the VALUES clause of the INSERT statement. Alternatively, we could have put the scalar subquery in the cursor C itself—select object_name, (select ...) from all_objects—to the same effect. In fact, in Oracle8i, we would have used that approach and hidden that construct in a view, since PL/SQL did not have direct support for scalar subqueries in that version.

For two of the other implementations, I just changed LOOKUP_HEAP to LOOKUP_HASH or LOOKUP_IOT to use the other structures. I also implemented this routine using the PLSQL LOOKUP_PKG shown in the previous section. In order to use the PL/SQL function LOOKUP_PKG.VAL, the FORALL statement was converted to this:

```
forall i in 1 .. l_key_col.count
    insert into built_by_us ( key_col, key_val )
    values ( l_key_col(i), lookup_pkg.val( l_key_col(i) ) );
```

The function was used in place of the scalar subquery.

To use the PL/SQL lookup table directly involved a tad more coding changes. I rewrote the main loop as follows:

```
loop
    fetch c bulk collect into l_key_col limit p_arraysize;

    for i in 1 .. l_key_col.count
    loop
    begin
        l_key_val(i) := lookup_pkg.g_lookup_tbl(l_key_col(i));
    exception
        when no_data_found then l_key_val(i) := null;
    end;
    end loop;

    forall i in 1 .. l_key_col.count
        insert into built_by_us ( key_col, key_val )
        values ( l_key_col(i), l_key_val(i) );
    exit when c%notfound;
end loop;
```

Here, we fetched *N* rows, performed *N* lookups, and then bulk inserted *N* rows.

Using the same techniques we've used with Runstats to capture the session statistics and latches statistics before and after each run, I found the results of the seven (the first two single-row implementations and the five new bulk ones) different implementations to be as shown in Table 9-2.

Looking at the CPU and elapsed times, we see more than an order-of-magnitude increase in performance by writing less code. The use of a single-table hash cluster or an IOT to do our lookup paid off hugely here. We go from over 27 seconds down to about 2. Much of that is due to the reduced execute count (the number of statements executed), but you can also see the efficiencies gained using bulk processing in the amount of redo generated. We drop from a high of almost 7MB of redo data generated by the single-row processing down to about 1.3MB. The logical I/O is dramatically reduced as well using bulk processing.

When we compare these techniques, we should be looking for what is the most efficient, yet still easy to code, implement, and maintain. Using an IOT or a single-table hash cluster meets those criteria. Using the PL/SQL lookup table or function results in comparable runtimes, but these techniques use more RAM than the hash table and IOT approaches, and you need to type in more code. More code means the technique is less maintainable, has more bugs, and requires

| | Row Fetch | | | | Array Fetch | | |
|---|---|---|---|---|---|---|---|
| Statistic | Row Select | Row Lookup | Heap Table Insert | Hash Table Insert | IOT Insert | PL/SQL Index by Table Lookup | PL/SQL Function Called in Insert |
| CPU used by this session | 2,160 | 1,611 | 195 | 189 | 189 | 231 | 256 |
| Elapsed time | 2,710 | 1,865 | 255 | 234 | 223 | 248 | 348 |
| Execute count | 49,933 | 24,988 | 137 | 137 | 137 | 138 | 138 |
| Redo size | 6,915,040 | 6,915,316 | 1,360,000 | 1,359,560 | 1,359,492 | 1,365,000 | 1,359,492 |
| Session logical reads | 211,879 | 155,791 | 164,378 | 113,752 | 155,159 | 99,066 | 99,075 |
| PGA memory max | 1,310,720 | 1,966,080 | 1,310,720 | 1,310,720 | 1,310,720 | 2,028,000 | 2,011,572 |
| UGA memory max | 0 | 1,963,920 | 0 | 0 | 0 | 1,963,920 | 1,963,920 |

**TABLE 9-2.** *Comparing Lookup Approaches*

longer development cycles. I would go for the hash table or IOT approach, if this is where I had to stop. But I would be tempted not to stop here. I would go one step further.

## Single-Statement Operations for Lookups

As I pointed out in the "Write as Little as You Can" section earlier in this chapter, SQL is very powerful, and many times procedural logic can be scrapped and implemented using set processing. Take a look at the following code. Is there some processing here that precludes set-based processing?

```
    ...
    loop
        fetch c bulk collect into l_key_col limit p_arraysize;

        some_process_takes_place;
```

```
        forall i in 1 .. l_key_col.count
            insert into built_by_us ( key_col, key_val )
            values ( l_key_col(i),
                     (select key_val
                      from lookup_hash
                      where key_col = l_key_col(i))
                   );
        exit when c%notfound;
    end loop;
  ...
```

As in at least half of the cases I observe, there is no reason not to use set-based processing. The procedural code should be replaced with the use of a DECODE or CASE statement. The lookups should be replaced with joins.

With this in mind, I tested four more lookup routines that are similar in nature. They actually are just SQL statements. The first one uses the PL/SQL lookup function.

```
insert into built_by_us
select object_name, lookup_pkg.val(object_name)
  from all_objects;
```

The remaining insert operations are identical, with the exception of the table names. Here is the insert for the hash table:

```
insert into built_by_us
select object_name, key_val
  from all_objects, lookup_hash
 where all_objects.object_name = lookup_hash.key_col(+);
```

Just replace HASH with HEAP or IOT to derive the remaining statements.

Table 9-3 shows the statistics collected by comparing those four insert operations. For comparison, I've included the hash table insert method. As you can see, removing procedural code further reduced the resources needed to perform this particular operation. And these techniques require very little code, so there is little to debug, maintain, or develop in the first place.

# Lookup Wrap-Up

Be aware that calling PL/SQL from SQL comes with a price, one that is generally avoidable. Rather than implementing a lookup in PL/SQL and calling it from SQL, just do the work directly in SQL. You'll get the best overall performance and most efficient usage of memory.

If you find yourself doing a lot of single-row processing with lookups (as we all do at one time or another) realize the following:

■ Procedural lookups can help you go 50% to 100% faster.

■ Bulk processing will start you off in the order-of-magnitude increase in performance.

■ Doing it in a single SQL statement will not only reduce the code you must write, it will be among the fastest ways to do it in most cases.

| Statistic | Hash Table Insert | Single SQL Hash | Single SQL PL/SQL | Single SQL Heap | Single SQL IOT |
|---|---|---|---|---|---|
| CPU used by this session | 189 | 175 | 316 | 190 | 185 |
| Elapsed time | 234 | 200 | 330 | 265 | 201 |
| Execute count | 137 | 40 | 41 | 40 | 40 |
| Redo size | 1,359,560 | 1,472,680 | 1,472,556 | 1,475,720 | 1,472,492 |
| Session logical reads | 113,752 | 118,403 | 98,979 | 136,819 | 136,814 |
| Session PGA memory max | 1,310,720 | 1,310,720 | 1,966,080 | 1,310,720 | 1,310,720 |
| Session UGA memory max | 0 | 0 | 1,963,920 | 0 | 0 |

**TABLE 9-3.**   *Comparing Single-Statement Lookup Techniques*

# Be Careful with Autonomous Transactions

Autonomous transactions, a feature of Oracle8i Release 1 and later, allow you to create a new "transaction within a transaction," independent of its parent transaction. Using an autonomous transaction, you can suspend the currently executing transaction, start a new one, do some work, and commit or roll back—all without affecting the currently executing transaction state. Autonomous transactions provide a new method of controlling transactions in PL/SQL. (For details on autonomous transactions, refer to the Oracle9i Release 2 *PL/SQL Users Guide and Reference*, Chapter 6, the section titled "Doing Independent Units of Work with Autonomous Transactions.")

## Criteria for Autonomous Transactions

Efficient PL/SQL is PL/SQL that works correctly. Here is the short list of when autonomous transactions are appropriate:

- **To provide for auditing that cannot be rolled back**   You would like to audit failed as well as successful attempts to modify information. Your trigger must be able to insert an audit trail record and commit that insert, without committing the surrounding transaction that invoked the trigger.

As you can see, this is a really short list. In the past, I've listed other reasons: to perform DDL in triggers, to write to the database from a SELECT statement, and to develop more modular code. However, using DBMS_JOB to schedule the trigger's DDL to execute after the transaction commits is a much better method than using autonomous transactions. There are many cases where an autonomous transaction goes wrong, and the DDL executes but the surrounding transaction that initiated the DDL rolls back. This leads to dangling database objects and bugs in the application. Using an autonomous transaction to write to the database from a SELECT statement (really just a case of auditing) is no longer necessary in Oracle9i because you can use DBMS_FGA (Fine Grained Auditing) for this type of processing. Finally, developing more modular code is just a variation on the auditing theme. Transaction control should be done by only the client application.

In virtually all cases of using autonomous transactions that I've observed, it is a misguided attempt to avoid a mutating table constraint. Although an autonomous transaction can be used to avoid getting the "ORA-04091 table is mutating" message, its usage almost always compromises data integrity.

**NOTE**
*If you search for pragma autonomous_transaction on http:// asktom.oracle.com, you'll see many questions where the answer begins with something like, "Also, to use an autonomous transaction to get around a mutating table sounds very, very, very suspicious to me. I would question a) the need, and b) the results. I've seen far too many people use this as the way to get around 'mutating tables,' only to totally miss the point. They are not able to enforce the business rules they believe they are enforcing, so data integrity is out the window. And you'll see that I use autonomous transactions a lot to show what happens in a multiuser environment without having to open two sessions as well (so, maybe there are two reasons for using them!).*

Now, we'll look at a small example to demonstrate why autonomous transactions should be viewed with some amount of suspicion, unless they are obviously being used for auditing. In general, however, they may only be the beginning of a new set of logic problems.

## Autonomous Transactions Can Impact Data Integrity

Let's say we want to enforce a rule that the average salary of all employees cannot be less than half of the maximum salary for anyone in their department. We might start with a procedure and trigger what looks like this:

```
ops$tkyte@ORA920> create or replace
  2  procedure sal_check( p_deptno in number )
  3  is
  4          avg_sal number;
  5          max_sal number;
  6  begin
  7          select avg(sal), max(sal)
  8            into avg_sal, max_sal
  9            from emp
 10         where deptno = p_deptno;
 11
 12          if ( max_sal/2 > avg_sal )
 13          then
```

```
14                         raise_application_error(-20001,'Rule violated');
15             end if;
16   end;
17   /
Procedure created.

ops$tkyte@ORA920> create or replace trigger sal_trigger
  2   after insert or update or delete on emp
  3   for each row
  4   begin
  5             if (inserting or updating) then
  6                     sal_check(:new.deptno);
  7             end if;
  8
  9             if (updating or deleting) then
 10                     sal_check(:old.deptno);
 11             end if;
 12   end;
 13   /
Trigger created.

ops$tkyte@ORA920>
ops$tkyte@ORA920> update emp set sal = sal*1.1;
update emp set sal = sal*1.1
       *
ERROR at line 1:
ORA-04091: table TKYTE.EMP is mutating, trigger/function may not see it
ORA-06512: at "TKYTE.SAL_CHECK", line 6
ORA-06512: at "TKYTE.SAL_TRIGGER", line 3
ORA-04088: error during execution of trigger 'TKYTE.SAL_TRIGGER'
```

That didn't work too well. We hit the mutating table error right away, because we quite simply cannot read the table we are in the process of modifying. So, we apply an autonomous transaction to our procedure to avoid the mutating table error.

```
ops$tkyte@ORA920> create or replace
  2   procedure sal_check( p_deptno in number )
  3   is
  4             pragma autonomous_transaction;
  5             avg_sal number;
  6             max_sal number;
  7   begin
```

And sure enough, it appears to have fixed the problem.

```
ops$tkyte@ORA920> update emp set sal = sal*1.1;
14 rows updated.

ops$tkyte@ORA920> commit;
Commit complete.
```

But, upon closer inspection, we find that we have a fatal flaw in our design. During testing, we find that something like this could easily happen:

```
ops$tkyte@ORA920> update emp set sal = 99999.99 where ename = 'WARD';
1 row updated.

ops$tkyte@ORA920> commit;
Commit complete.

ops$tkyte@ORA920> exec sal_check(30);
BEGIN sal_check(30); END;

*
ERROR at line 1:
ORA-20001: Rule violated
ORA-06512: at "TKYTE.SAL_CHECK", line 14
ORA-06512: at line 1
```

We updated WARD with a very high salary. WARD works in Department 30. His salary is now much higher than half of the average salary in that department. The trigger did not detect that. However, after the fact, running the same code the trigger would run, we see that the rule was violated. Why did this happen? The reason is that our autonomous transaction cannot see any of the changes we are making. Hence, the update of the salary to a large amount appears okay because the procedure is validating the table as it existed *before* our update began! It would be the next unlucky end user who would trigger this violation (as we artificially forced it by running the SAL_CHECK procedure).

Anytime you use an autonomous transaction to avoid a mutating table, you must make sure that you are doing the right thing. Every trigger that uses an autonomous transaction should be verified for correctness.

# Choose Whether to Use Implicit or Explicit Cursors

There are two basic types of cursors in PL/SQL:

- **Implicit cursor**   With this type of cursor, PL/SQL does most of the work for you. You don't have to open close, declare, or fetch from an implicit cursor.

- **Explicit cursor**   With this type of cursor, you do all of the work. You must open, close, fetch, and control an explicit cursor completely.

There is a myth that explicit cursors are superior in performance and usability to implicit cursors. However, the truth is that equivalent implicit cursors are faster and much easier to code. Does that mean you'll never use an explicit cursor? No, you only need to look at the "Make Your Lookups Work Efficiently" section earlier in this chapter to see a case where explicit cursors are necessary: When you are performing large bulk operations. Explicit cursors are also necessary when you are using dynamic SQL and fetching more than a single row. Here, you do not have a choice. There is no way to dynamically process an implicit cursor. So, when processing dynamic SQL using ref cursors, you will be using explicit cursors.

Here, we will look at two cases where implicit cursors should be used:

■ Single-row selects, when you are retrieving at most a single row from a query

■ Result sets, when you are retrieving a limited number of rows (ten rows at most)

We'll take a look at using both types of cursors for these tasks.

## Use Implicit Cursors for Single-Row Selections

Suppose that we have a query that will return, at most, one row but may return less than one row. We can code this:

```
Select <columns> INTO <variables>
  From <tables> ...
```

Or we can code this:

```
...
Is
    Cursor c is select <columns> from <tables> ...
    ...
Begin
    Open c;
    Fetch c into <variables>;
    Close c;
    ...
```

Which should we use? *Without exception,* we should use SELECT INTO, for the following reasons:

■ It is less code (less chance for bugs) and easier to read.

■ It runs faster (more efficient).

■ It makes our code safer (more bug-free).

In order to fully emulate the entire functionality of a SELECT INTO, we must code this:

```
...
Is
    Cursor c is select <columns> from <tables> ...
    ...
Begin
    Open c;
    Fetch c into <variables>;
    If ( c%notfound )
    Then
        Raise NO_DATA_FOUND;
    End if;
    Fetch c into <variables>;
```

```
If ( c%found )
Then
   Raise TOO_MANY_ROWS;
End if;
Close c;
...
```

The semantics of a SELECT INTO are such that the query must return *at least one row and, at most, one row.* The explicit cursor makes you code that yourself.

Can you spot the bugs in the following code? This code is designed to report by department the department number, name, and the name of the most highly paid person in that department:

```
ops$tkyte@ORA920> declare
  2        l_dname   dept.dname%type;
  3        l_deptno  dept.deptno%type;
  4        l_ename   emp.ename%type;
  5
  6        cursor c1
  7        is
  8        select deptno, dname
  9          from dept
 10         order by deptno;
 11
 12        cursor c2( p_deptno in number )
 13        is
 14        select ename
 15          from emp
 16         where deptno = p_deptno
 17           and sal = (select max(sal)
 18                        from emp
 19                       where deptno = p_deptno);
 20  begin
 21      open c1;
 22      loop
 23          fetch c1 into l_deptno, l_dname;
 24          exit when c1%notfound;
 25          open c2(l_deptno);
 26          fetch c2 into l_ename;
 27          close c2;
 28          dbms_output.put_line
              ( l_deptno || ', ' || l_dname || ', ' || l_ename );
 29      end loop;
 30      close c1;
 31  end;
 32  /
```

The two bugs are that it erroneously reports an employee name for Department 40 and erroneously forgets to tell us there are two people that make the most in Department 20. The output is as follows:

```
10, ACCOUNTING, KING
20, RESEARCH, SCOTT
30, SALES, BLAKE
40, OPERATIONS, BLAKE

PL/SQL procedure successfully completed.
```

Those are bugs that might go undetected for a long time, leading to other erroneous decisions. At the very least, they make you look bad when discovered; at worst, they lead to other data-integrity issues.

Let's see what happens when we rewrite the code to use implicit cursors.

```
ops$tkyte@ORA920> declare
  2      l_ename   emp.ename%type;
  3  begin
  4      for x in (select deptno, dname from dept order by deptno)
  5      loop
  6          select ename into l_ename
  7            from emp
  8           where deptno = x.deptno
  9             and sal = (select max(sal)
 10                          from emp
 11                         where deptno = x.deptno);
 12          dbms_output.put_line
 13          ( x.deptno || ', ' || x.dname || ', ' || l_ename );
 14      end loop;
 15  end;
 16  /
10, ACCOUNTING, KING
declare
*
ERROR at line 1:
ORA-01422: exact fetch returns more than requested number of rows
ORA-06512: at line 6
```

Immediately, this is telling us, "That query you expected a single row from returned two (or more)." We have a choice to make here now:

- We can report the first one back only. We would add and rownum = 1 to the query to indicate that was our intention.

- We can report all of the highest paid people.

Let's say we want to report just the first occurrence. We'll add the WHERE clause and restart.

```
ops$tkyte@ORA920> declare
  2      l_ename   emp.ename%type;
  3  begin
...
```

```
  9                and sal = (select max(sal)
 10                              from emp
 11                            where deptno = x.deptno)
 12                    and rownum = 1;
 13            dbms_output.put_line
...
 17   /
10, ACCOUNTING, KING
20, RESEARCH, SCOTT
30, SALES, BLAKE
declare
*
ERROR at line 1:
ORA-01403: no data found
ORA-06512: at line 6
```

Now, Oracle is telling us that for some DEPTNO, there is no data to be found. The first query using explicit cursors found data didn't it? How could this be? The fact is that the explicit cursor did not find any data, but we didn't check. The SELECT INTO won't permit that; it makes us handle this case by throwing an exception. Here is our solution for that:

```
ops$tkyte@ORA920> declare
  2      l_ename   emp.ename%type;
  3  begin
  4      for x in (select deptno, dname from dept order by deptno)
  5      loop
  6         begin
  7            select ename into l_ename
  8              from emp
  9             where deptno = x.deptno
 10               and sal = (select max(sal)
 11                             from emp
 12                           where deptno = x.deptno)
 13               and rownum = 1;
 14          exception when no_data_found
 15          then
 16              l_ename := '(none)';
 17          end;
 18          dbms_output.put_line
 19             ( x.deptno || ', ' || x.dname || ', ' || l_ename );
 20      end loop;
 21  end;
 22  /
10, ACCOUNTING, KING
20, RESEARCH, SCOTT
30, SALES, BLAKE
40, OPERATIONS, (none)

PL/SQL procedure successfully completed.
```

Now, we have a debugged, safe report. It gets the right answer and takes a lot less code as well. But how does it perform?

Let's compare the performance of a SELECT INTO with that of an OPEN/FETCH/*TEST*/ FETCH/CLOSE. To set up this test, we'll create a table to look up from:

```
ops$tkyte@ORA920> create table t ( object_id primary key, object_name )
  2  organization index
  3  as
  4  select object_id, object_name from all_objects;

Table created.
```

Next, we'll set up two procedures to run against it.

```
ops$tkyte@ORA920> create or replace procedure explicit
  2  as
  3      l_object_name t.object_name%type;
  4      l_dummy       t.object_name%type;
  5
  6      cursor c( l_object_id in number )
  7      is
  8      select object_name
  9        from t
 10       where object_id = l_object_id;
 11  begin
 12      for i in 1 .. 30000
 13      loop
 14          open c(i);
 15          fetch c into l_object_name;
 16          if ( c%notfound )
 17          then
 18              l_object_name := null;
 19          end if;
 20          fetch c into l_dummy;
 21          if ( c%found )
 22          then
 23              raise too_many_rows;
 24          end if;
 25          close c;
 26      end loop;
 27  end;
 28  /
Procedure created.
```

This uses explicit cursors and simply iterates from 1 to 30,000 looking up object names. It must look for the NOTFOUND condition and set the object name to NULL if found (to avoid leaving garbage in the variable it is fetching into). It must look for and raise an error if too many rows are found, indicating logical data-integrity issues.

Now, let's code the same thing using a SELECT INTO.

```
ops$tkyte@ORA920> create or replace procedure implicit
  2   as
  3       l_object_name t.object_name%type;
  4   begin
  5       for i in 1 .. 30000
  6       loop
  7       begin
  8           select object_name into l_object_name
  9             from t
 10            where object_id = i;
 11       exception
 12         when no_data_found then
 13               l_object_name := null;
 14       end;
 15           end loop;
 16   end;
 17   /
Procedure created.
```

Notice that there is a lot less code in the second implementation. After running this test with Runstats, we discover the following:

```
ops$tkyte@ORA920> exec runStats_pkg.rs_start
PL/SQL procedure successfully completed.

ops$tkyte@ORA920> exec implicit
PL/SQL procedure successfully completed.

ops$tkyte@ORA920> exec runStats_pkg.rs_middle
PL/SQL procedure successfully completed.

ops$tkyte@ORA920> exec explicit
PL/SQL procedure successfully completed.

ops$tkyte@ORA920> exec runStats_pkg.rs_stop
Run1 ran in 419 hsecs
Run2 ran in 546 hsecs
run 1 ran in 76.74% of the time
PL/SQL procedure successfully completed.
```

This shows that the SELECT INTO is more efficient in its processing. It is the all-around winner. It is faster and results in code that is more bulletproof out of the box. I would much rather my code fails at some point with NO_DATA_FOUND or TOO_MANY_ROWS than have it succeed in such a case. Here, succeeding would actually be a bug and would either result in my application reporting back incorrect information or not detecting a logical integrity issue that exists in my database. It is interesting to note that even if we remove all of the "extra" code in the explicit routine on the supposition that you didn't care if there was no data found, or more than one row to be found, the implicit cursor still performs better. So, changing the explicit routine to be:

```
ops$tkyte@ORA920> create or replace procedure explicit
  2   as
  3       l_object_name t.object_name%type;
  4       l_dummy        t.object_name%type;
  5
  6       cursor c( l_object_id in number )
  7       is
  8       select object_name
  9         from t
 10        where object_id = l_object_id;
 11   begin
 12       for i in 1 .. 30000
 13       loop
 14           open c(i);
 15           fetch c into l_object_name;
 16           close c;
 17       end loop;
 18   end;
 19   /

Procedure created.
```

And re-executing the runstats process, I observed:

```
ops$tkyte@ORA920> exec runStats_pkg.rs_stop
Run1 ran in 423 hsecs
Run2 ran in 481 hsecs
run 1 ran in 87.94% of the time
```

So, in every case, the SELECT INTO is faster and easier to code.

## Use Implicit Cursors for Result Sets with a Limited Number of Rows

Suppose that we have a query that returns some small number of rows, less than 100. Rather than use an explicit cursor, we can simply code that like this:

```
For x in ( select ... from ... where ... )
Loop
    Process...
End loop;
```

This form lets PL/SQL set up the record, handle the opening and closing of the cursor, and, in short, do a lot of work for us. The implicit cursor performs at least as well as, and in most cases better than, the explicit cursor (with similar performance characteristics to the SELECT INTO example in the previous section). Here, the major efficiency is gained in programmer productivity.

Consider these two equivalent pieces of code:

```
ops$tkyte@ORA920> create or replace procedure explicit
  2   as
  3       l_rec   dept%rowtype;
  4
  5       cursor c
  6       is
  7       select * from dept;
  8   begin
  9       open c;
 10       loop
 11           fetch c into l_rec;
 12           exit when c%notfound;
 13       end loop;
 14       close c;
 15   end;
 16   /
Procedure created.

ops$tkyte@ORA920> create or replace procedure implicit
  2   as
  3   begin
  4       for x in ( select * from dept )
  5       loop
  6           null;
  7       end loop;
  8   end;
  9   /
Procedure created.
```

They are identical in functionality, but one of them is much easier to code and will be much easier to maintain. The implicit cursor code is not only shorter, but it also stands less chance of having bugs in it. The scope of the cursor is fixed inside the loop, so there is no chance of accidentally leaving it open, forgetting to check the cursor attributes to see if we even fetched any data. It doesn't contain any infinite loops (what happens if you forget line 12 in the explicit cursor procedure?).

Runstats shows that these two pieces of code are more or less equivalent in their performance.

```
ops$tkyte@ORA920> declare
...
 10       for i in 1 .. 10000
 11       loop
 12           explicit;
 13       end loop;
...
 20       for i in 1 .. 10000
```

```
21      loop
22          implicit;
23      end loop;
...
33  /
393 hsecs
376 hsecs
run 1 ran in 104.52% of the time
```

PL/SQL procedure successfully completed

It is true that there are efficiencies that could be gained by using BULK COLLECT here, but on such a small number of rows, you will find the differences to be marginal. The implicit cursor is preferable for ease of programming.

However, explicit cursors definitely come into play when your result sets are very large, as demonstrated in the "Make Your Lookups Work Efficiently" section earlier in this chapter. When you're dealing with hundreds or thousands of records, bulk-collecting is the only way to go. There, the additional code is well worth the results.

## Implicit/Explicit Cursors Wrap-Up

In summary, if you are fetching a single row, you should use an implicit cursor with SELECT INTO. You not only gain performance, but you also get the extra layer of code that PL/SQL automatically adds to the SELECT INTO processing that helps protect you from missing data or data that somehow has more rows than you expected.

If you are processing tens of rows, implicit cursor FOR loops are excellent for their programming ease, reduced code, and fewer chances for you to make a mistake. For tens of rows, the programming ease of use outweighs other considerations. On the other hand, it you are retrieving hundreds of rows or more, explicit cursors with the BULK COLLECT clause would be the way to go (assuming you cannot skip the procedural code altogether and just do the work in a single SQL statement).

Finally, if you need to do dynamic SQL, you cannot use implicit cursor techniques; you must explicitly manage the cursor yourself.

# Summary

In this chapter, we explored the PL/SQL language. It is *the* language to use when manipulating data in the database. That is what PL/SQL excels at. There is, quite simply, no other language so expressive yet tightly coupled to SQL structures. Using PL/SQL is not only more efficient from a physical machine utilization perspective, it is also immensely more efficient as a programming language. You will find you can write database-specific code faster, with fewer chances for bugs, using PL/SQL than you can with other languages.

We discussed the portability of PL/SQL as well. PL/SQL was not designed to be portable across databases, but rather across operating systems and languages. I do not know of a commercially viable programming language that cannot invoke PL/SQL (anything that can connect to Oracle can do that). PL/SQL is implemented consistently on every platform Oracle is on—from a Macintosh, to Linux, to Unix, to a mainframe, to Windows. Its portability is unquestioned. When I develop in PL/SQL on one platform, I have a very high degree of confidence that it will work on all platforms consistently.

In this chapter, we also looked at ten important things to consider when developing in PL/SQL. The topics ranged from writing as little code as you can, to using packages instead of stand-alone procedures and functions, to using static SQL whenever possible. You saw examples of these uses, so you can decide for yourself when and where the advice applies to you. As usual, there are no "one-size-fits-all" rules. Features should be applied in the appropriate circumstances. For example, you saw that using dynamic SQL to save a few lines of code may not be worth it in terms of performance; however, there are times when dynamic SQL is the only way to accomplish your goal. So, you will need to weigh the costs and benefits associated with dynamic SQL and use it appropriately.

# CHAPTER
## 10

## So, You Had an Accident

t is inevitable that, one day, everything will go wrong. The end users are lined up waiting for you to arrive at work, your inbox is full of new mail, and the light on your phone is blinking from the messages waiting for you. The system is really slow, or the system is very broken. Whatever is wrong is very wrong, and it must be corrected immediately or sooner. What do you do now?

This is my short list of things to do:

- Find out what's different.

- Change one thing at a time.

- Have a sound reason for changing that one thing.

- Be able to unchange things.

- Build a test case.

This chapter goes into detail about each of these actions. You should read this *before* an accident occurs, because, in most cases, you need information that predates the accident in order to be out of trouble as quickly as possible.

# Find Out What's Different

When a production system goes bad overnight, *something* changed. When you upgrade from Oracle8i to Oracle9i and the system seems slower, you need to see what changed (besides the obvious database version). The only way to find out what is different is to know what was happening in the past. Maintaining a history of past performance is the single most important thing you can do to facilitate this.

For example, suppose you had a Statspack report from when things were "good" and compared it to when things were "bad." You discovered that the redo size per transaction had gone from 3KB to 3MB, and your major wait event was now log file sync. That would be a clear indication of where to start looking: You need to find out why you are generating so much more redo than before. It doesn't tell you why it changed, but it does get you on the path to discovery. Without that piece of information—that you used to generate 3KB of redo data and now you generate 3MB—you would be shooting in the dark trying to figure out what is different.

Another case of where things shift (and is frequently the culprit) is a change in a query plan. Suppose you have automated the gathering of statistics on your system so every night a job gathers statistics on some or all segments. One day you come in and the system is slow. You suspect it might be a bad query plan or a set of bad plans, but nothing changed since yesterday *except* for some statistics. Now how can you identify which plans actually changed? In Oracle9iR1 and up, it is quite easy. In the V$ tables, Oracle is storing query plans as well as a hash of the query plan itself. If we keep a historical record of this information, we can easily identify both new and modified query plans.

There are many ways to maintain this history. Statspack is an excellent "low-bandwidth" method. It is very nonintrusive, and many other tools can use the information it collects. Oracle Enterprise Manager (OEM) with its diagnostic pack is another choice. There are also many third-party tools available.

What I'll demonstrate here is the basic capability you would want to have in place in order to identify new or modified query plans. We'll basically "snapshot" the V$SQL table allowing us to maintain a history of

- The first 1,000 characters of the SQL query
- The hash for that query
- The hash of the query plan itself

If we have that information, we can, at any time, ask for a report of any SQL in the shared pool that either was not present in our snapshot (it is a new query) or is in our snapshot but has a query plan different from what we've seen in the past. We'll start with this table:

```
create table plan_hashes
( sql_text            varchar2(1000),
  hash_value          number,
  plan_hash_value     number,
  constraint plan_hashes_pk
  primary key(hash_value,sql_text,plan_hash_value)
)
organization index;
```

We'll seed that table with our current shared pool contents. The only types of statements we are interested in tracking are the DML operations of SELECT, INSERT, UPDATE, DELETE, and MERGE. The in clause in the following query ensures we capture only those statement types. Additionally, we are not entirely interested in recursive SQL, although you could certainly track that. We remove that from consideration by using the predicate on the parsing schema and user IDs. The insert would be

```
insert into plan_hashes( sql_text, hash_value, plan_hash_value )
select distinct sql_text,
       hash_value,
       plan_hash_value
  from v$sql
 where command_type in (
 /* DELETE */ 7,    /* INSERT */ 2,
 /* MERGE  */ 189,  /* SELECT */ 3,
 /* UPDATE */ 6 )
   and parsing_user_id <> 0
   and parsing_schema_id <> 0;
```

That captured our "current as is" state. It is important to do this when things are running smoothly because this is the baseline we need to compare against. To see this in action, we'll create a small simulation. We'll start by copying the SCOTT.EMP and SCOTT.DEPT tables into our schema:

```
create table emp
as
```

```
select * from scott.emp;

alter table emp
add constraint emp_pk
primary key(empno);

create table dept
as
select * from scott.dept;

alter table dept
add constraint dept_pk
primary key(deptno);
```

And then executing a simple query against it:

```
select ename, dname
  from emp, dept
 where emp.deptno = dept.deptno;
```

Now, since we did not analyze that table yet, we will be using the rule-based optimizer (RBO) during the optimization of that query. The RBO will definitely use the indexes and perform a nested loops join. On my system, the plan was actually:

```
Execution Plan
----------------------------------------------------------
   0        SELECT STATEMENT Optimizer=CHOOSE
   1     0   NESTED LOOPS
   2     1    TABLE ACCESS (FULL) OF 'EMP'
   3     1    TABLE ACCESS (BY INDEX ROWID) OF 'DEPT'
   4     3      INDEX (UNIQUE SCAN) OF 'DEPT_PK' (UNIQUE)
```

Now, suppose our system was running smoothly and we created that baseline (so the preceding query is, in fact, in the baseline). Now, someone decides to analyze the tables and the next day the system is running slow. It is time to find out what changed. Fortunately, we can do that easily with the previous information by executing this query:

```
ops$tkyte@ORA920LAP> select distinct sql_text,
  2              hash_value,
  3              plan_hash_value,
  4              decode( (select 1
  5                         from plan_hashes
  6                        where plan_hashes.hash_value = v$sql.hash_value
  7                          and plan_hashes.sql_text = v$sql.sql_text
  8                          and rownum = 1), 1, 'Changed', 'New' ) status
  9     from v$sql
 10    where (sql_text, hash_value, plan_hash_value)
 11   not in (select sql_text, hash_value, plan_hash_value
 12                 from plan_hashes)
 13      and command_type in (
```

```
14    /* DELETE */ 7,     /* INSERT */ 2,
15    /* MERGE  */ 189,   /* SELECT */ 3,
16    /* UPDATE */ 6 )
17      and parsing_user_id <> 0
18      and parsing_schema_id <> 0
19  /
```

```
SQL_TEXT                             HASH_VALUE PLAN_HASH_VALUE STATUS
------------------------------------ ---------- --------------- -------
select ename, dname   from emp, dept  wh 1380487067    615168685 Changed
ere emp.deptno = dept.deptno
```

We'll have a complete report of every query in the shared pool that is either new or has a plan different from what we've seen in the past. We can now quickly look at those queries to see if they are the problem (a Statspack top SQL report might help us there) and can zero in on correcting whatever went wrong with them.

On the other hand, suppose you come to work and everything is running fine. You'll want to periodically refresh this baseline snapshot either by truncating this table and reloading, or by just adding all of the new and modified plans. This insert will add all of those new or modified statements into this table:

```
insert into plan_hashes( sql_text, hash_value, plan_hash_value )
select distinct sql_text,
       hash_value,
       plan_hash_value
  from v$sql
 where (sql_text, hash_value, plan_hash_value)
not in (select sql_text, hash_value, plan_hash_value
          from plan_hashes)
   and command_type in (
 /* DELETE */ 7,     /* INSERT */ 2,
 /* MERGE  */ 189,   /* SELECT */ 3,
 /* UPDATE */ 6 )
   and parsing_user_id <> 0
   and parsing_schema_id <> 0
/
```

Alternatively, you can achieve the same goal using Statspack and collecting snapshots at a sufficiently high level (level 6 or above).

# Start Collecting History Today

No matter which method you use, start collecting data now, before an accident occurs. Without this history, you have only one choice, and that is to tune the entire system from top to bottom. You cannot isolate what is different, so everything must be suspect.

If you use Statspack or a similar tool for the first time only when faced with a performance issue, that will definitely slow down your ability to respond to a sudden change in your system. When you look at the Statspack report that represents only what the system looks like when it is having a problem, you need to investigate everything and anything. That query that is doing 10,000 logical I/Os and is executed frequently, is it the culprit? It is hard to say, since it may have been doing 10,000 logical I/Os frequently from the first day it was introduced into the system. If you can tune it, that is all well and good, but it most likely won't fix the problem you are having since it was not the cause.

If you cannot find out what changed, doing the root-cause analysis to find out why you have a problem (and so you can prevent it from happening again), becomes a job for a detective.

## Detective Work

To help a customer fix a broken system, my co-workers and I were asked to perform a root-cause analysis. The client wanted to know what went wrong. This was very difficult to achieve because we had no history, no baseline for comparison. The database owners had made many changes to their system, and the system broke.

We fixed the system, but only by tuning the entire thing. We were unable to back out of the changes they made, rather we needed to tune what they ended up with. After spending a lot of time looking at the system, fixing this and that, gathering statistics over there, tweaking a query here, we had the system performing at acceptable levels (it was a very large system, with dozens of separate applications running on it). What we didn't know was if the system was running *as it used to*. Sure, the system was running acceptably fast, but was it doing the same things it did before the problems arose? If not, determining the root cause was something of a guessing game.

Our hypothesis was put together by a series of facts, which when pieced together, sounded plausible. These are some of the facts we had:

- The system had been running Oracle7.3.

- They used ANALYZE TABLE <*TABLE NAME*> COMPUTE STATISTICS or ESTIMATE STATISTICS to gather statistics when using Oracle7.3. This gathered statistics for the table and all indexes, and gathered histograms for all columns as well.

- They upgraded to Oracle 8.1.7 six months ago.

- Upon upgrading, they started using DBMS_STATS to gather statistics. They decided to use DBMS_STATS with a METHOD_OPT parameter of NULL and CASCADE of TRUE. The METHOD_OPT parameter specifies how, and for what, statistics will be gathered for the table. Someone discovered this ran faster than the default setting of METHOD_OPT. However, what they didn't know is that they were now gathering only table and index statistics, not histograms. The histograms were left over from the last time they used ANALYZE. Additionally, the AVG_ROW_LEN was no longer being calculated by DBMS_STATS because of this parameter value, but the old value persisted in the data dictionary; that is, it was not defaulted but kept its old stale value.

- Performance was deemed to be getting worse over time. The DBAs and developers were told to make things go faster, to tune this system. They developed a list of 16 things to change. One of the items was to reorganize some tables using ALTER TABLE MOVE, another was to move files around in the file system, and so on. They implemented all 16 changes simultaneously on the production machine. The next day, the system broke.

Our root-cause analysis came to this conclusion: It was the table reorganizations that caused the problems. When they moved the table, they lost both the column-level histograms and the AVG_ROW_LEN statistics (although these were out of date, they were still representative of the existing data). They then ran the DBMS_STATS GATHER_TABLE_STATS routine as they had been doing since their 8.1.7 upgrade. The AVG_ROW_LEN was set to 100 (its default value) for all tables they analyzed using this method, and no histograms were computed for any of the tables. The query plans for most all of the queries against these objects changed dramatically. We could show empirically that the plans did change, and they changed for the worse with the "bad" statistics.

By simply gathering statistics at the same level they used to before the upgrade, the queries performed much better. In some cases, the queries went from running in many minutes with millions of logical I/Os to executing in seconds with hundreds or tens of logical I/Os.

We can only be pretty sure that this was the root cause here, and it took us quite a while to come to this conclusion. So many things had changed that it was impossible for us to pinpoint the exact cause with 100% certainty. In the heat of trying to fix the problem, many queries were hinted by the developers (the statistics needed to be fixed, but they took the route of hinting, because they were in panic mode). Processes were changed, and procedures were recoded. Parameters were altered, changing the memory and other settings for the database. Files were moved around. The system administrators had the storage vendor in, and he tweaked their system. At the end of the day, all we could do is put together a logical-sounding story to explain what happened.

If only we had the history of how this system used to perform, with the top SQL, for example. Then we could have discovered that the top SQL in the poorly performing system was totally different. It would have given us a place to start looking. We could have asked directly, "What is different about these tables?" We would have discovered they were the ones reorganized. We might have been able to find the root cause much more rapidly and corrected the system sooner, using fewer people. As it was, it took more than a couple of hours (it took a couple of days) to get the system back to acceptable levels.

# Change One Thing at a Time

Change one thing, or as few things as possible, at a time. Consider the example in the previous section. There were developers adding hints in one place, hardware vendors changing things at another level, DBAs changing parameters, and consultants each doing their own thing—all simultaneously. So, what change actually fixed (or just as important, which change broke) something? It is very hard to say, especially if three things were changed by three different groups at the same time, without knowledge of what the others were doing.

When you are in this "fix it and fix it now" mode, you need a plan—a set of steps to be taken one by one. You have a large complex system, with many people sticking their fingers into it. You may never solve the problem if you have five teams working independently. That is not to say you should send four of the teams home, rather that you should make one team responsible for implementing all of the changes, or coordinating them at the very least. Consider what happens if simultaneously:

- The developers implement hints.
- The DBAs gather fresh, more detailed statistics.
- The storage vendor changes settings and moves the disks around, redistributing the workload.
- A process is disabled temporarily.

And the system starts running better. What fixed it? Can you remove those hints (you really want to)? If you do, and that was what fixed the system, it will be broken again. Was it that process you disabled? Maybe it was the storage-related changes, and it had nothing to do with the hints or the statistics. Now, you have a system that will have legacy hints in it and will collect more statistics than you will ever use. You have code that is harder to maintain, and a system that is doing more work than it needs to do. And this is because you don't know which of the four changes fixed the problem.

This is doubly true for implementing tuning ideas when things are still running okay. Take that customer from the previous section again. The developers and DBAs came up with 16 independent ideas and implemented them all at once without testing them. That was a certain recipe for disaster.

# Have a Sound Reason for Changing that One Thing

As I advised back in Chapter 1, don't do something because "everyone knows you should." Conventional wisdom is wrong as often as it is right. Using the example in the "Detective Work" section, the developers' reasoning for performing the ALTER TABLE MOVE on many tables was because "everyone knows that if you reorganize a table, it always performs better." They did not identify these tables as being an issue. They did not do the move for any one of a host of valid reasons such as the following:

- Many rows in the table were migrated, and the table fetch continued row statistic was large.

- The table was full-scanned frequently, and the way the table was used had pushed the segment high-water mark higher than it needed to be for the volume of data. The current high-water mark for the table was very "high."

- The cluster factor on a key index could be significantly decreased if the table were rebuilt in a certain sorted order.

They rebuilt the tables because it might accomplish something. They were right, it did accomplish something, but not the desired thing. They were looking for a magic silver bullet, a `fast=true` setting, and they ended up making things really bad.

You must *identify* the cause of poor performance. Only then can you apply the correct remedy.

## Have a Goal

Before you undertake a change or perform some maintenance operation, be ready to state a goal, the reason why you are doing such a thing. Then collect metrics that can be used to substantiate your reasons. For example, you might analyze a table and list the chained rows to verify the table has a large percentage of migrated rows. Use Statspack or some other tool to collect statistics showing that you constantly encounter table fetch continued row conditions. Then perform a reorganization.

Afterwards, you can analyze the table to check that the rows are no longer chained. If they still are, you might question why you did this operation. If they are not, you should also be able to observe decreased table fetch continued row counts in a Statspack report. If not, then you just worked on the wrong table.

# Validate Your Hypothesis

Having an idea of how you might fix something—a hypothesis—is good. But the first thing you need to do after developing a hypothesis is set up some sort of test to validate it.

"We have a big customer table, which is referenced by many other tables. The table's primary key is NUMBER(12). However, the foreign key columns of some of the tables that are referencing this customer table were defined as NUMBER. (Seen as NUMBER(38) in data dictionary.) This datatype difference causes a data conversion during the checking of the foreign keys and thus a performance loss. In order to prevent it, we tried to alter the NUMBER columns to be the same type as our customer table's primary key—NUMBER(12). Since Oracle doesn't allow us to do this unless the column values are NULL, we had to insert them with their ROWIDs to a temporary table, setting them to NULL, altering the column to NUMBER(12), and populating the original values from the temporary table again. This is a very slow process. We couldn't even see its end after eight hours of working, and we had to stop it. The total size of the tables we have to alter is about 220 million rows. We are running all DML in parallel and NOLOGGING mode. We are creating the temporary table by CREATE AS SELECT. My question is, could you please offer us a faster way of doing this operation?"

Fortunately, there was a very easy answer to their question: Don't do this conversion. The datatype differences are *not* the cause of any performance issues. In fact, you may discover that the system runs slower if you make this change!

The developers came up with a hypothesis: The datatypes are not the same and this must be causing a performance issue. Where they went wrong here was in not validating the hypothesis. They did not, in a test environment, benchmark to see if this modification would make any material *positive* change in performance.

After running a benchmark test, I found that performing a reorganization to introduce the foreign key datatype of NUMBER(12) would be an utter waste of time. Even worse, since it involved making massive changes using UPDATE statements, it would do nothing more than negatively impact performance across the board.

For example, setting up a benchmark to test whether datatype differences are impacting performance is very straightforward. We can test a couple of things against a parent/child table where the scale of the NUMBER type is identical versus the case where the child table's NUMBER column is unconstrained. We can evaluate the following operations:

- Bulk inserts of many rows into the child table
- Single-row inserts into the child table

- Bulk updates against the child table's foreign key
- Single-row updates against the child table's foreign key
- Bulk deletes against the parent table employing ON DELETE CASCADE logic
- Single-row deletes against the child table

These represent many normal operations against this parent/child set of tables. The schema we will use for the benchmark is as follows:

```
/* set up parent child WITHOUT constrained type...*/
create table p1 ( x number(12) primary key);
create table c1 ( x number references p1  on delete cascade);
create index c1_idx on c1(x);

/* set up parent child WITH constrained type... */
create table p2 ( x number(12) primary key);
create table c2 ( x number(12) references p2 on delete cascade );
create index c2_idx on c2(x);
/* created some parent data... */
insert into p1 select rownum from all_objects;
insert into p2 select rownum from all_objects;
commit;
```

In my database, that creates about 30,000 rows in the two parent tables.

To test a bulk insert, we perform the following operations, once on P1/C1 and again on P2/C2:

```
insert into c1 select * from p1;
commit;
insert into c2 select * from p2;
commit;
```

Then we run a block of PL/SQL code to test single-row insertions:

```
begin
    for x in ( select * from p1 )
    loop
        for i in 1 .. 5
        loop
            insert into c1 values ( x.x );
        end loop;
        commit;
    end loop;
end;
```

We also perform this operation for P2/C2. Next, we perform the bulk-update operations, and then the single-row updates, repeating the code block for the single-row updates for P2/C2.

```
update c1 set x = x+1 where x < 5000;
commit;
update c2 set x = x+1 where x < 5000;
commit;

begin
    for x in ( select * from c1 where x between 5000 and 10000)
    loop
        update c1 set x = x+1 where x = x.x;
    end loop;
    commit;
end;
/
```

And finally, we perform bulk deletes—deleting every other row in a single statement, followed by single-row deletes to remove the remaining data.

```
delete from p1 where mod(x,2) = 0;
commit;
delete from p2 where mod(x,2) = 0;
commit;

begin
    for x in ( select * from p1 )
    loop
        delete from p1 where x = x.x;
    end loop;
end;
/
commit;
```

I performed all of these operations with SQL_TRACE = TRUE enabled. Table 10-1 shows the difference between the two examples.

| Operation | CPU Time in Seconds for C1 with NUMBER | CPU Time in Seconds for C2 with NUMBER(12) |
|---|---|---|
| Bulk insert | 0.80 | 0.79 |
| Single-row inserts | 78.21 | 80.12 |
| Bulk update | 0.36 | 0.41 |
| Single-row updates | 89.15 | 90.30 |
| Bulk delete | 7.15 | 6.92 |
| Single-row deletes | 12.44 | 12.74 |

**TABLE 10-1.** *Comparing CPU Times for Matched and Unmatched Datatypes*

Interestingly, in most cases, the unconstrained number was marginally faster (stress *marginally*). In fact, I would say it was a tie—there was no significant difference between the two implementations.

A simple, small benchmark can show conclusively whether what you propose to do will have the effect you desire on your system. You need to identify the cause of your performance issues, develop a solution, test or benchmark that solution, and then inflict it on the production system. Never be in the position of guessing.

# Be Able to Unchange Things

Being able to reverse a change requires two preparations:

- You need to keep a clear record of exactly what has been changed in the system.

- You must have a plan to revert the system back to the way it was.

Once again, using the example in the "Detective Work" section earlier in the chapter, one of the problems we ran into was that the developers and DBAs changed so many things in so many ways that they could no longer enumerate exactly what changed. They knew they moved some files around, changed the disk layouts, but they weren't really sure of what went where (or why). Some of the information was in the alert log, but the lower-level changes, those outside the database, were not logged. Also, moves of objects via the ALTER TABLE MOVE were not recorded. So, we knew only that a lot of stuff was moved, we didn't know exactly what and how.

The other necessity is to have a plan. If you make some change, such as moving files around, make sure you can move them back. If you move a table, make sure the new table is the same as the old table (for example, the level of statistics are the same). Understand what the change will do and how you can revert back to the original implementation.

The only way to prove you can revert a change is to actually revert the change. For this, you need a test environment (as discussed in Chapter 1). That implies you've made the change in the test environment and you reverted it. Additionally, it means that you had the opportunity to *test* the impact of the change before exposing it to your users. Making a horrible mistake in the test environment is okay. Maybe a co-worker will laugh at you, but no harm done. If you make that horrible mistake in your production environment, no one will be laughing.

So, if you have a plan to upgrade—to apply a patch to the system, upgrade the application software, or upgrade the database—make sure that you know how to downgrade, to revert back, as well.

# Build a Test Case

Suppose that the system is failing, but not because of some massive performance issue; rather, you are getting an internal Oracle error, or something is not working as you believe it should. Now is the time to build a test case.

## Test Case Requirements

Your test case needs to have the following characteristics:

- It reproduces the error clearly.

- It is self-contained (you do not need your entire system to run it).

- It is small. It contains nothing extra—no bells and whistles. This is crucial: it needs to be as small as possible.

- It should run with the minimum set of privileges possible, to further reduce the problem.

This test case will demonstrate concisely what the problem is. This is the first thing Oracle support technicians, or anyone who is asked to diagnose the issue, will request.

The smaller this test case can be, the better. My goal, whenever possible, is to get a test case that fits on a screen, meaning in a text editor, so I can see the entire thing. The smaller the example, the less chance you have a bug in that example. That point is particularly important, so we'll look at some examples.

## Keep Your Test Cases as Small as Possible

I was working with a customer on a large Pro*C application. The developers claimed that Pro*C would run only so long, and then the application would fail in an Oracle routine with a segmentation fault. Since this was a very large application, we needed to cut down on the test case size. It was literally hundreds of source code files, it took over an hour to compile and build, and the supporting database needed to run it was huge.

The Oracle support technicians struggled with this one. Just getting an environment whereby they could compile the code was hard. Pinpointing the error was going to be even harder. So, we set about to create a smaller test case while they were attempting to reproduce the error with the monolithic code.

What we discovered while developing the test case was that the C code developed by the customer was riddled with string overwrites (buffer overflows). Virtually every source code file we inspected had suspect code in it. We introduced a bounds checker into their system by compiling their code with a third-party library that looks for buffer overwrites and invalid memory accesses. Then we removed all of the string overwrites.

The support technicians were still struggling to set up the test environment, but that was all right. The removal of the overwrites had a nice side effect: The code no longer crashed. The Pro*C application could run for as long as they wanted to run it, without errors. As it turned out, the string overwrites were corrupting memory elsewhere and that was causing the segmentation fault in the Oracle routines.

Many times, during the development of a test case, I find a bug in my developed code that was causing the erroneous behavior. On the other hand, you may actually find a bug. In these cases, having the smallest, most concise test case possible for Oracle support is still necessary. If the example is too large to understand, or has many dependencies on your system, it will never be reproducible.

Recently, I was working with developers on some code for the next release of the database (after Oracle9i Release 2). They had some PL/SQL code that worked fine in Oracle9i but was failing with an "LPX-00271: invalid character" error in the newer version. The test case they had encompassed a couple hundred lines of code with many dependencies. This error was being raised in a piece of code I worked on, so I was asked to look into it.

My first goal was to reproduce the issue with as little code as humanly possible. There was a lot of stuff going on in the code before it got to my layer, so I just recorded the inputs being sent to me and worked on stripping away the entire layer. After doing that, the problem still existed. That was a good thing, for if the problem disappeared at that point, I would need to layer code back in until I reproduced it (or found the underlying cause).

So, now I had a smaller test case, but one that was still sizable. I went to work removing even more code. My goal was to get a test case that fit on a screen. What I discovered was the routine they were invoking did some dynamic SQL calls (dynamically ran a PL/SQL block), and it was this block that was raising the error. I removed yet another layer of code and was now able to reproduce the error by simply running the block of PL/SQL code dynamically in SQL*Plus. All I needed to do to reproduce was this:

```
SQL> begin some_procedure; End;
  2  /
PL/SQL Procedure successfully completed

SQL> exec execute immediate 'begin some_procedure end;'
ORA-xxxxx...
```

If I ran the block of code, it worked fine. If I dynamically executed the same block of code, it failed. Clearly now, this was a bug. But in order to really get the test case right, I needed to isolate what in SOME_PROCEDURE was going wrong. SOME_PROCEDURE was still a fairly large chunk of code with many dependencies. I whittled it down to just four lines of code in the end.

I now had the perfect test case. It was small. It was concise. It was complete. Anyone could simply run this code, with no other setup, and clearly reproduce the issue. Filing this bug was easy. The developers had everything they needed in order to attack and fix the problem. I proved that our developed code was not the cause, by removing all of it, and removing all of the dependencies to our system. I gave them something that demonstrated the problem clearly. They could take that small example and, immediately and without any large setup, reproduce the issue on their own machines.

By making your test cases as small as possible, you can save many hours, if not days, of repeated requests for information while trying to diagnose issues. In this book, you've seen dozens of test cases that fit on a page or two and clearly demonstrate a single concept. Test cases for problems in the database should be done using the same model. Imagine if I only presented the results and not the code that led up to the results? You would not be able to reproduce my findings, or you might question the findings altogether.

# Summary

The most crucial information you need when you have an accident is historical facts of what used to be. Without that information, you are stuck with looking at the entire system—every component is suspect, and you must look at everything. It is as if you had no prior knowledge of the system.

Many of the concepts we discussed in Chapter 1 found their way into this chapter as well. For example, I reiterated that you should have a sound reason for changing something. In order to have a sound reason, you need to be very confident that the change you are going to make provides benefits. We looked at a case whereby a hypothesis was proven wrong using a simple, straightforward, small benchmark of the current implementation and the proposed change. From that ten-minute exercise, we discovered the massive change would not result in any benefits and would seriously impact the system.

We talked about taking a steady, measured approach to the problem. Never change many things simultaneously. That would be like trying to tune a system by concurrently fine-tuning the application's SQL, tuning the database, and tuning the operating system. That, in general, is a study in frustration. For the database instance to be tuned, you need a stable set of applications. In order to fine-tune the operating system, you need a stable set of processing. If you tune the operating system before making large changes to the database or applications, you may find yourself back at the drawing board doing it over again. Incremental change, one thing at a time, after taking into consideration the effects of prior changes, is the way to go.

Lastly, we looked at building a test case. Whether you are hitting a bug in the database or just trying to prove a point, a small, simple, concise, yet complete test case is necessary. It is much easier to see where a problem is if you strip away as much irrelevant material as possible. When your test case is simple, stand-alone, and consistent, it will be taken much more seriously and can be used to solve the problem. Besides, many times, you'll discover either a workaround or the issue in your own code during the development of such a test case.

# APPENDIX

## Setting Up and
## Some Scripts

n this appendix you will find two things:

1.  A setup script for the BIG_TABLE used in many of the examples in this book.

2.  A series of scripts I use every day and have used heavily during the course of writing this book.

The BIG_TABLE setup script is one I use whenever I get a new "test database" to generate a table with lots of rows to test with. The SCOTT/TIGER EMP and DEPT only go so far after all. You have seen this table used throughout the book, here you will see how I generate it.

After that, I have four scripts that I use frequently along with detailed explanations of exactly what they do, how they do it, and how to use them. I hope you find them as useful as I do.

# Setting Up BIG_TABLE

For examples throughout this book, I use a table called BIG_TABLE. Depending on which system I use, this table has between one record and four million records and varies in size from 200MB to 800MB. In all cases, the table structures are the same.

To create BIG_TABLE, I wrote a script that does the following:

1.  Creates an empty table based on ALL_OBJECTS. This dictionary view is used to populate the BIG_TABLE.

2.  Makes this table NOLOGGING. This is optional. I did it for performance. Using NOLOGGING mode for a test table is safe; you won't use it in a production system, so features like Oracle Data Guard will not be enabled.

3.  Populates the table by seeding it with the contents of ALL_OBJECTS and then iteratively inserting into itself, approximately doubling its size on each iteration.

4.  Creates a primary key constraint on the table.

5.  Gathers statistics.

6.  Displays the number of rows in the table.

To build the BIG_TABLE table, you can run the following script at the SQL*Plus prompt and pass in the number of rows you want in the table. The script will stop when it hits that number of rows.

```
create table big_table
as
select rownum id, a.*
  from all_objects a
 where 1=0
/
alter table big_table nologging;
```

```
declare
    l_cnt number;
    l_rows number := &1;
begin
    insert /*+ append */
    into big_table
    select rownum, a.*
      from all_objects a;

    l_cnt := sql%rowcount;

    commit;

    while (l_cnt < l_rows)
    loop
        insert /*+ APPEND */ into big_table
        select rownum+l_cnt,
                OWNER, OBJECT_NAME, SUBOBJECT_NAME,
                OBJECT_ID, DATA_OBJECT_ID,
                OBJECT_TYPE, CREATED, LAST_DDL_TIME,
                TIMESTAMP, STATUS, TEMPORARY,
                GENERATED, SECONDARY
          from big_table
         where rownum <= l_rows-l_cnt;
        l_cnt := l_cnt + sql%rowcount;
        commit;
    end loop;
end;
/

alter table big_table add constraint
big_table_pk primary key(id)
/

begin
   dbms_stats.gather_table_stats
   ( ownname    => user,
     tabname    => 'BIG_TABLE',
     method_opt => 'for all indexed columns',
     cascade    => TRUE );
end;
/
select count(*) from big_table;
```

I gathered baseline statistics on the table and the index associated with the primary key. Additionally, I gathered histograms on the indexed column, something I typically do. Histograms may be gathered on other columns as well, but for this table, it just isn't necessary. Also, occasionally in this book, you will find there are indexes on other columns, depending on the example. I simply add or drop indexes as needed, using the following script:

```
create index big_table_owner_idx
on big_table(owner)
COMPUTE STATISTICS;
```

For example, in Chapter 6, I used that index when querying the BIG_TABLE with, and without, a /*+ RULE */ hint.

# Frequently Used Scripts

This section presents scripts I use frequently but are not included in the book's chapters:

- **PRINT_TABLE**   Prints a result set down the page, rather than across the page, in SQL*Plus. This utility is handy for people who use a character-mode terminal frequently.

- **SHOW_SPACE**   Prints a detailed report of the space used by an object.

- **COLS_AS_ROWS**   Performs a column-by-column comparison of two rows. This utility is handy for finding the differences between two rows.

- **GEN_DATA**   Generates random data into a database table. It uses the built-in DBMS_RANDOM package to generate strings, numbers, and the like.

These scripts may not be mentioned by name in this book, but I use them daily. Other scripts that I use are presented in the book's chapters, so they are not repeated here. For example, Runstats is shown in Chapter 2.

## PRINT_TABLE

Printing the results of a query down the page, instead of across, is handy when result sets would otherwise wrap to the next line and become unreadable. For example, your results might look something like this:

```
ops$tkyte@ORA920> select * from user_objects where object_name = 'EMP';

OBJECT_NAME                          SUBOBJECT_NAME                    OBJECT_ID
------------------------------------ ------------------------------- ----------
DATA_OBJECT_ID OBJECT_TYPE           CREATED   LAST_DDL_
-------------- ------------------    --------- ---------
TIMESTAMP            STATUS   T G S
-------------------- ------- - - -
EMP                                                                        53737
         53737 TABLE                 29-JUN-03 29-JUN-03
2003-06-29:11:35:25 VALID     N N N
```

With PRINT_TABLE, you can get output that is easier to read, like this:

```
ops$tkyte@ORA920> begin
  2      print_table( 'select * from
  3                     user_objects where object_name = ''EMP'' ' );
  4   end;
  5   /
OBJECT_NAME                    : EMP
SUBOBJECT_NAME                 :
OBJECT_ID                      : 53737
DATA_OBJECT_ID                 : 53737
OBJECT_TYPE                    : TABLE
CREATED                        : 29-jun-2003 11:35:25
LAST_DDL_TIME                  : 29-jun-2003 11:35:25
TIMESTAMP                      : 2003-06-29:11:35:25
STATUS                         : VALID
TEMPORARY                      : N
GENERATED                      : N
SECONDARY                      : N
-----------------
PL/SQL procedure successfully completed.
```

When querying the data dictionary, or just printing a really wide row or two, this utility is indispensable.

The commented code is as follows:

```
create or replace
procedure print_table
( p_query in varchar2,
  p_date_fmt in varchar2 default 'dd-mon-yyyy hh24:mi:ss' )

-- This utility is designed to be installed ONCE in a database and used
-- by all.  Also, it is nice to have roles enabled so that queries by
-- DBAs who use a role to gain access to the DBA_* views still work.
-- That is the purpose of AUTHID CURRENT_USER.
AUTHID CURRENT_USER
is
    l_theCursor     integer default dbms_sql.open_cursor;
    l_columnValue   varchar2(4000);
    l_status        integer;
    l_descTbl       dbms_sql.desc_tab;
    l_colCnt        number;
    l_cs            varchar2(255);
    l_date_fmt      varchar2(255);

    -- Small inline procedure to restore the session's state.
    -- We may have modified the cursor sharing and nls date format
    -- session variables. This just restores them.
    procedure restore
    is
```

```
    begin
        if ( upper(l_cs) not in ( 'FORCE','SIMILAR' ))
        then
            execute immediate
            'alter session set cursor_sharing=exact';
        end if;
        if ( p_date_fmt is not null )
        then
            execute immediate
                'alter session set nls_date_format=''' || l_date_fmt || '''';
        end if;
        dbms_sql.close_cursor(l_theCursor);
    end restore;
begin
    -- I like to see the dates print out with times, by default. The
    -- format mask I use includes that.  In order to be "friendly"
    -- we save the current session's date format and then use
    -- the one with the date and time.  Passing in NULL will cause
    -- this routine just to use the current date format.
    if ( p_date_fmt is not null )
    then
        select sys_context( 'userenv', 'nls_date_format' )
          into l_date_fmt
          from dual;
        execute immediate
        'alter session set nls_date_format=''' || p_date_fmt || '''';
    end if;

    -- To be bind variable friendly on ad-hoc queries, we
    -- look to see if cursor sharing is already set to FORCE or
    -- similar. If not, set it to force so when we parse literals
    -- are replaced with binds.
    if ( dbms_utility.get_parameter_value
        ( 'cursor_sharing', l_status, l_cs ) = 1 )
    then
        if ( upper(l_cs) not in ('FORCE','SIMILAR'))
        then
            execute immediate
            'alter session set cursor_sharing=force';
        end if;
    end if;

    -- Parse and describe the query sent to us.  We need
    -- to know the number of columns and their names.
    dbms_sql.parse( l_theCursor,  p_query, dbms_sql.native );
    dbms_sql.describe_columns
    ( l_theCursor, l_colCnt, l_descTbl );
```

```
    -- Define all columns to be cast to varchar2s. We
    -- are just printing them out.
    for i in 1 .. l_colCnt loop
        dbms_sql.define_column
        (l_theCursor, i, l_columnValue, 4000);
    end loop;

    -- Execute the query, so we can fetch.
    l_status := dbms_sql.execute(l_theCursor);

    -- Loop and print out each column on a separate line.
    -- Bear in mind that dbms_output prints only 255 characters/line
    -- so we'll see only the first 200 characters by my design...
    while ( dbms_sql.fetch_rows(l_theCursor) > 0 )
    loop
        for i in 1 .. l_colCnt loop
            dbms_sql.column_value
            ( l_theCursor, i, l_columnValue );
            dbms_output.put_line
            ( rpad( l_descTbl(i).col_name, 30 )
              || ': ' ||
              substr( l_columnValue, 1, 200 ) );
        end loop;
        dbms_output.put_line( '-----------------' );
    end loop;

    -- Now, restore the session state, no matter what.
    restore;
exception
    when others then
        restore;
        raise;
end;
/
```

It should be noted that for columns larger than 4000 characters (rows with longs/clobs for example), you may encounter:

```
BEGIN print_table('select * from T'); END;

*
ERROR at line 1:
ORA-22921: length of input buffer is smaller than amount requested
ORA-06512: at "OPS$TKYTE.PRINT_TABLE", line 104
ORA-06512: at line 1
```

This utility does not work well with those columns.

## SHOW_SPACE

The SHOW_SPACE routine prints detailed space utilization information for database segments. Here is the interface to it:

```
ops$tkyte@ORA920> desc show_space
PROCEDURE show_space
 Argument Name                    Type                    In/Out Default?
 -------------------------------- ----------------------- ------ --------
 P_SEGNAME                        VARCHAR2                IN
 P_OWNER                          VARCHAR2                IN     DEFAULT
 P_TYPE                           VARCHAR2                IN     DEFAULT
 P_PARTITION                      VARCHAR2                IN     DEFAULT
```

The arguments are as follows:

P_SEGNAME       Name of the segment—the table or index name, for example.

P_OWNER       Defaults to the current user, but you can use this routine to look at some other schema.

P_TYPE       Defaults to TABLE and represents the type of object you are looking at. For example, `select distinct segment_type from dba_segments` lists valid segment types.

P_PARTITION       Name of the partition when you show the space for a partitioned object. SHOW_SPACE shows space for only a partition at a time.

The output of this routine looks like the following when the segment resides in an Automatic Segment Space Management (ASSM) tablespace:

```
big_table@ORA920> exec show_space( 'BIG_TABLE' );
Unformatted Blocks ....................          9
FS1 Blocks (0-25)  ....................          0
FS2 Blocks (25-50) ....................          0
FS3 Blocks (50-75) ....................          1
FS4 Blocks (75-100)....................          0
Full Blocks        ....................     21,794
Total Blocks...........................     22,192
Total Bytes............................ 181,796,864
Total MBytes...........................        173
Unused Blocks..........................          0
Unused Bytes...........................          0
Last Used Ext FileId...................          9
Last Used Ext BlockId..................     54,280
Last Used Block........................         88
PL/SQL procedure successfully completed.
```

The items reported are as follows:

| | |
|---|---|
| Unformatted Blocks | The portion of the number of blocks that are allocated to the table and below the high-water mark but which have not been used. Add unformatted and unused blocks to get a total count of blocks allocated to the table but never used to hold data in an ASSM object. |
| FS1 Blocks–FS4 Blocks | Formatted blocks with data. The ranges of numbers after their name represent the "fullness" of each block. For example, (0–25) is the count of blocks that are between 0 and 25% full. |
| Full Blocks | The number of blocks that are so full, that they are no longer candidates for future inserts. |
| Total Blocks, Total Bytes, Total Mbytes | The total number allocated to the segment measured in database blocks, bytes, and megabytes. |
| Unused Blocks, Unused Bytes | Represents a portion of the amount of space never used. These are blocks allocated to the segment but are currently above the high-water mark of the segment. |
| Last Used Ext FileId | The ID of the file that contains the last data extent. |
| Last Used Ext BlockId | The block ID of the beginning of the last extent; the block ID within the last-used file. |
| Last Used Block | The offset of the last block used in the last extent. |

When you use SHOW_SPACE to look at objects in user space managed tablespaces, the output resembles this:

```
ops$tkyte@ORA920> exec show_space( 'BIG_TABLE' );
Free Blocks.............................            0
Total Blocks............................       27,648
Total Bytes.............................  226,492,416
Total MBytes............................          216
Unused Blocks...........................          389
Unused Bytes............................    3,186,688
Last Used Ext FileId....................            6
Last Used Ext BlockId...................       26,633
Last Used Block.........................          635

PL/SQL procedure successfully completed.
```

The only difference is the Free Blocks item at the beginning of the report. This is a count of the blocks in the first freelist group of the segment. My script reports *only* on this freelist group. You would need to modify the script to accommodate multiple freelist groups.

The commented code follows. This utility is a simple layer on top of the DBMS_SPACE API in the database.

```
create or replace procedure show_space
( p_segname in varchar2,
  p_owner    in varchar2 default user,
  p_type     in varchar2 default 'TABLE',
  p_partition in varchar2 default NULL )
-- This procedure uses AUTHID CURRENT USER so it can query DBA_*
-- views using privileges from a ROLE and so it can be installed
-- once per database, instead of once per user who wanted to use it.
AUTHID CURRENT_USER
as
    l_free_blks                number;
    l_total_blocks             number;
    l_total_bytes              number;
    l_unused_blocks            number;
    l_unused_bytes             number;
    l_LastUsedExtFileId        number;
    l_LastUsedExtBlockId       number;
    l_LAST_USED_BLOCK          number;
    l_segment_space_mgmt       varchar2(255);
    l_unformatted_blocks number;
    l_unformatted_bytes number;
    l_fs1_blocks number; l_fs1_bytes number;
    l_fs2_blocks number; l_fs2_bytes number;
    l_fs3_blocks number; l_fs3_bytes number;
    l_fs4_blocks number; l_fs4_bytes number;
    l_full_blocks number; l_full_bytes number;

    -- Inline procedure to print out numbers nicely formatted
    -- with a simple label.
    procedure p( p_label in varchar2, p_num in number )
    is
    begin
        dbms_output.put_line( rpad(p_label,40,'.') ||
                            to_char(p_num,'999,999,999,999') );
    end;
begin
    -- This query is executed dynamically in order to allow this procedure
    -- to be created by a user who has access to DBA_SEGMENTS/TABLESPACES
    -- via a role as is customary.
    -- NOTE: at runtime, the invoker MUST have access to these two
    -- views!
    -- This query determines if the object is an ASSM object or not.
    begin
        execute immediate
            'select ts.segment_space_management
               from dba_segments seg, dba_tablespaces ts
              where seg.segment_name       = :p_segname
```

```
                and (:p_partition is null or
                    seg.partition_name = :p_partition)
                and seg.owner = :p_owner
                and seg.tablespace_name = ts.tablespace_name'
             into l_segment_space_mgmt
           using p_segname, p_partition, p_partition, p_owner;
    exception
       when too_many_rows then
          dbms_output.put_line
          ( 'This must be a partitioned table, use p_partition => ');
          return;
    end;


    -- If the object is in an ASSM tablespace, we must use this API
    -- call to get space information; else we use the FREE_BLOCKS
    -- API for the user managed segments.
    if l_segment_space_mgmt = 'AUTO'
    then
      dbms_space.space_usage
      ( p_owner, p_segname, p_type, l_unformatted_blocks,
        l_unformatted_bytes, l_fs1_blocks, l_fs1_bytes,
        l_fs2_blocks, l_fs2_bytes, l_fs3_blocks, l_fs3_bytes,
        l_fs4_blocks, l_fs4_bytes, l_full_blocks, l_full_bytes, p_partition);

      p( 'Unformatted Blocks ', l_unformatted_blocks );
      p( 'FS1 Blocks (0-25)  ', l_fs1_blocks );
      p( 'FS2 Blocks (25-50) ', l_fs2_blocks );
      p( 'FS3 Blocks (50-75) ', l_fs3_blocks );
      p( 'FS4 Blocks (75-100)', l_fs4_blocks );
      p( 'Full Blocks        ', l_full_blocks );
    else
      dbms_space.free_blocks(
         segment_owner     => p_owner,
         segment_name      => p_segname,
         segment_type      => p_type,
         freelist_group_id => 0,
         free_blks         => l_free_blks);

      p( 'Free Blocks', l_free_blks );
    end if;

    -- And then the unused space API call to get the rest of the
    -- information.
    dbms_space.unused_space
    ( segment_owner      => p_owner,
      segment_name       => p_segname,
      segment_type       => p_type,
      partition_name     => p_partition,
      total_blocks       => l_total_blocks,
```

```
    total_bytes          => l_total_bytes,
    unused_blocks        => l_unused_blocks,
    unused_bytes         => l_unused_bytes,
    LAST_USED_EXTENT_FILE_ID => l_LastUsedExtFileId,
    LAST_USED_EXTENT_BLOCK_ID => l_LastUsedExtBlockId,
    LAST_USED_BLOCK => l_LAST_USED_BLOCK );

    p( 'Total Blocks', l_total_blocks );
    p( 'Total Bytes', l_total_bytes );
    p( 'Total MBytes', trunc(l_total_bytes/1024/1024) );
    p( 'Unused Blocks', l_unused_blocks );
    p( 'Unused Bytes', l_unused_bytes );
    p( 'Last Used Ext FileId', l_LastUsedExtFileId );
    p( 'Last Used Ext BlockId', l_LastUsedExtBlockId );
    p( 'Last Used Block', l_LAST_USED_BLOCK );
end;
/
```

# COLS_AS_ROWS

COLS_AS_ROWS is a utility I use to compare two rows that have the same columns, column by column. For example, I might compare one row in USER_OBJECTS with another row in USER_OBJECTS and report what is different about them. It is similar to my PRINT_TABLE utility, but instead of just printing a result set, it returns a result set that SQL can manipulate further.

### A COLS_AS_ROWS Example

An example of where I used this recently was to answer this question:

"Can anyone shed any light on why analyze table tab compute statistics for table for all indexes for all indexed columns; might give different results from exec dbms_stats.gather_schema_stats(ownname => 'schema',cascade => true);?"

My response was to say those two commands are very different at the histogram level. The DBMS_STATS.GATHER_SCHEMA_STATS routine uses FOR ALL COLUMNS SIZE 1 by default, so the histograms collected will be very different for each command. I set up a small test case to prove this. I created two users, A and B, and gave them privileges to create tables. Then I ran the following in each schema:

```
connect a/a
create table t as select * from all_users;
create unique index t_idx1 on t(username);
create index t_idx2 on t(created);
analyze table t compute statistics
for table
for all indexed columns
for all indexes;

connect b/b
create table t as select * from all_users;
create unique index t_idx1 on t(username);
```

```
create index t_idx2 on t(created);
exec dbms_stats.gather_schema_stats( user, cascade=>true);
```

I wanted to compare the data in DBA_TABLES for the row where TABLE_NAME = 'T' and OWNER = 'A' with the row where OWNER = 'B'. Using COLS_AS_ROWS, I was able to turn those single-row queries into result sets that included the column name as a column and the value as a column. For example, here are the statistics for table A.T using COLS_AS_ROWS:

```
ops$tkyte@ORA920> select *
  2    from table( cols_as_rows( 'select *
  3                                  from dba_tables
  4                                 where table_name = ''T''
  5                                   and owner = ''A'' ' ) )
  6  /

        RNUM CNAME                            VAL
  ---------- ----------------------------    ----------
           1 OWNER                            A
           1 TABLE_NAME                       T
           1 TABLESPACE_NAME                  USERS
           1 CLUSTER_NAME
...
           1 DEPENDENCIES                     DISABLED
           1 COMPRESSION                      DISABLED

47 rows selected.
```

Now, I do a join to see the differences between any two rows in DBA_TABLES, for example:

```
ops$tkyte@ORA920> select a.rnum, a.cname, a.val t1, b.val   t2
  2    from table( cols_as_rows( 'select *
  3                                  from dba_tables
  4                                 where table_name = ''T''
  5                                   and owner = ''A'' ' ) ) a,
  6         table( cols_as_rows( 'select *
  7                                  from dba_tables
  8                                 where table_name = ''T''
  9                                   and owner = ''B'' ' ) ) b
 10    where a.rnum = b.rnum
 11      and a.cname = b.cname
 12      and ( a.val <> b.val or
 13       ((a.val is null or b.val is null) and a.val||b.val is not null))
 14  /

        RNUM CNAME                            T1          T2
  ---------- ----------------------------    ----------  ----------
           1 AVG_ROW_LEN                      20          17
           1 AVG_SPACE                        7141        0
           1 EMPTY_BLOCKS                     4           0
```

```
     1 GLOBAL_STATS                         NO          YES
     1 OWNER                                A           B
```

ANALYZE and DBMS_STATS get AVG_ROW_LEN a little differently, but this is not significant. Also, ANALYZE gets some statistics, such as AVG_SPACE, EMPTY_BLOCKS, and CHAIN_CNT, which DBMS_STATS skips. The optimizer doesn't use those values, and DBMS_STATS gets only optimizer-related statistics. The point here is that I can easily see the differences between the statistics for user A's table versus user B's table at a glance.

Continuing on, I can see the differences for the index on the table as well using the same technique:

```
ops$tkyte@ORA920> select a.rnum, a.cname, a.val t1, b.val   t2
     2    from table( cols_as_rows
     3              ( 'select ''A.''||index_name nm, dba_indexes.*
     4                   from dba_indexes
     5                  where index_name like ''T_IDX_''
     6                    and owner = ''A''
     7                  order by index_name' ) ) a,
     8         table( cols_as_rows
     9              ( 'select ''B.''||index_name nm, dba_indexes.*
    10                   from dba_indexes
    11                  where index_name like ''T_IDX_''
    12                    and owner = ''B''
    13                  order by index_name' ) ) b
    14   where a.rnum = b.rnum
    15     and a.cname = b.cname
    16     and ( a.val <> b.val or
    17        ((a.val is null or b.val is null) and a.val||b.val is not null) )
    18  /

      RNUM CNAME                            T1          T2
---------- ------------------------------ ---------- ----------
         1 GLOBAL_STATS                     NO          YES
         1 NM                               A.T_IDX1    B.T_IDX1
         1 OWNER                            A           B
         1 TABLE_OWNER                      A           B
         2 GLOBAL_STATS                     NO          YES
         2 NM                               A.T_IDX2    B.T_IDX2
         2 OWNER                            A           B
         2 TABLE_OWNER                      A           B

8 rows selected.
```

Now, since there were two rows to compare, I added a column, NM in this case, to show the name of each index in the output. When RNUM = 1, I am comparing A.T_IDX1 with B.T_IDX1, and so on. This shows that the index statistics were effectively the same in this case; there were no material differences between the two numerically. The GLOBAL_STATS setting is not significant, since this test is not dealing with partitioned objects.

Just to finish up this example, here is the histogram information:

```
ops$tkyte@ORA920> select column_name, owner, count(*)
  2     from dba_tab_histograms
  3   where owner in ( 'A', 'B' )
  4   group by column_name, owner
  5   order by column_name, owner
  6   /

COLUMN_NAM OWNER                                    COUNT(*)
---------- ------------------------------------- ----------
CREATED    A                                           29
CREATED    B                                            2
USERNAME   A                                            2
USERNAME   B                                            2
USER_ID    B                                            2
```

As you can see, histograms will be very different here due to the default of SIZE 1 used by DBMS_STATS. The CREATED column in schema A has 29 entries in DBA_TAB_HISTOGRAMS, whereas the same object in B's schema has only two entries. Not only that, but DBMS_STATS analyzed all of the columns in the table, not just the indexed columns.

Just to be complete, I reanalyzed B's schema using a DBMS_STATS invocation that more closely mimics the ANALYZE command used:

```
ops$tkyte@ORA920> connect b/b
b@ORA920> begin
  2       dbms_stats.delete_schema_stats( user );
  3       dbms_stats.gather_schema_stats
  4       ( user,
  5         method_opt => 'for all indexed columns',
  6             cascade => true
  7       );
  8   end;
  9   /
PL/SQL procedure successfully completed.
```

And then I compared them:

```
ops$tkyte@ORA920> connect /
ops$tkyte@ORA920> select a.rnum, a.cname, a.val t1, b.val  t2
  2     from table( cols_as_rows( 'select *
  3                                  from dba_tables
  4                                 where table_name = ''T''
  5                                   and owner = ''A'' ' ) ) a,
  6          table( cols_as_rows( 'select *
  7                                  from dba_tables
  8                                 where table_name = ''T''
  9                                   and owner = ''B'' ' ) ) b
```

```
10    where a.rnum = b.rnum
11      and a.cname = b.cname
12      and ( a.val <> b.val or
13        ((a.val is null or b.val is null) and a.val||b.val is not null))
14   /
```

| RNUM | CNAME | T1 | T2 |
|------|-------|----|----|
| 1 | AVG_ROW_LEN | 20 | 100 |
| 1 | AVG_SPACE | 7003 | 0 |
| 1 | EMPTY_BLOCKS | 4 | 0 |
| 1 | GLOBAL_STATS | NO | YES |
| 1 | OWNER | A | B |

Here, note that DBMS_STATS is using the default AVG_ROW_LEN of 100. That is a side effect of DBMS_STATS. Unless you analyze *all columns,* it does not compute this statistic and defaults it.

The index statistics were identical in this example, regardless of the analysis method. However, the histograms are still different:

```
ops$tkyte@ORA920> select column_name, owner, count(*)
  2    from dba_tab_histograms
  3    where owner in ( 'A', 'B' )
  4    group by column_name, owner
  5    order by column_name, owner
  6   /
```

| COLUMN_NAM | OWNER | COUNT(*) |
|------------|-------|----------|
| CREATED | A | 37 |
| CREATED | B | 37 |
| USERNAME | A | 2 |
| USERNAME | B | 47 |

As you can see, the same sets of columns had histograms generated, but in a slightly different fashion. DBMS_STATS generated histograms at a more granular level of detail than ANALYZE did.

## COLS_AS_ROWS in Oracle9i

Now, that you've seen what COLS_AS_ROWS does, we'll look at how it works. It is a smaller, more compact version of PRINT_TABLE implemented as a pipelined function (I'll show how to do this in Oracle8i in the next section).

To begin, I use a collection type that the COLS_AS_ROWS function will return. Think of this like a view—it is the structure of the result set the function is sending back. In this case, it has three values: the row number in the result set (RNUM), the column name (CNAME), and the value of that column (VAL):

```
create or replace type myScalarType as object
( rnum number, cname varchar2(30), val varchar2(4000) )
/
```

```
create or replace type myTableType as table of myScalarType
/
```

And then it has a function that takes a query to execute as its input. This function will dynamically execute the query and output a row per column in it. For example, if the query result set would return 10 rows and had 5 columns, COLS_AS_ROWS would return 50 rows. The commented code is as follows:

```
create or replace
function cols_as_rows( p_query in varchar2 ) return myTableType
-- This function is designed to be installed ONCE per database, and
-- it is nice to have ROLES active for the dynamic sql, hence the
-- AUTHID CURRENT_USER.
AUTHID CURRENT_USER
-- This function is a pipelined function, meaning that it'll send
-- rows back to the client before getting the last row itself.
-- In 8i, we cannot do this.
PIPELINED
as
    l_theCursor     integer default dbms_sql.open_cursor;
    l_columnValue   varchar2(4000);
    l_status        integer;
    l_colCnt        number default 0;
    l_descTbl       dbms_sql.desc_tab;
    l_rnum          number := 1;
begin
    -- Parse, describe and define the query.  Note, unlike print_table,
    -- I am not altering the session in this routine.  The
    -- caller would use TO_CHAR() on dates to format and if they
    -- want, they would set cursor_sharing.  This routine would
    -- be called rather infrequently. I did not see the need
    -- to set cursor sharing therefore.
    dbms_sql.parse( l_theCursor, p_query, dbms_sql.native );
    dbms_sql.describe_columns( l_theCursor, l_colCnt, l_descTbl );
    for i in 1 .. l_colCnt loop
        dbms_sql.define_column( l_theCursor, i, l_columnValue, 4000 );
    end loop;

    -- Now, execute the query and fetch the rows.  Iterate over
    -- the columns and "pipe" each column out as a separate row
    -- in the loop.  Increment the row counter after each
    -- dbms_sql row.
    l_status := dbms_sql.execute(l_theCursor);
    while ( dbms_sql.fetch_rows(l_theCursor) > 0 )
    loop
        for i in 1 .. l_colCnt
        loop
            dbms_sql.column_value( l_theCursor, i, l_columnValue );
            pipe row
            (myScalarType( l_rnum, l_descTbl(i).col_name, l_columnValue ));
```

```
        end loop;
        l_rnum := l_rnum+1;
    end loop;

    -- Clean up and return...
    dbms_sql.close_cursor(l_theCursor);
    return;
end cols_as_rows;
/
```

And that is it. You are now ready to use it:

```
ops$tkyte@ORA920> select *
  2      from TABLE( cols_as_rows('select *
  3                                  from emp
  4                                 where rownum = 1') );

      RNUM CNAME                            VAL
---------- ------------------------------ ----------
         1 EMPNO                          7369
         1 ENAME                          SMITH
         1 JOB                            CLERK
         1 MGR                            7902
         1 HIREDATE                       17-DEC-80
         1 SAL                            800
         1 COMM
         1 DEPTNO                         20

8 rows selected.
```

## COLS_AS_ROWS in Oracle8i

In Oracle8i, the COLS_AS_ROWS implementation is a little different. The types are the same as in the Oracle9i version, but the code cannot be pipelined. In Oracle8i, I fill up a collection variable and then return it at the end. The code, with modifications highlighted, is as follows:

```
create or replace function
cols_as_rows8i( p_query in varchar2 ) return myTableType
authid current_user
as
    l_theCursor     integer default dbms_sql.open_cursor;
    l_columnValue   varchar2(4000);
    l_status        integer;
    l_colCnt        number default 0;
    l_descTbl       dbms_sql.desc_tab;
    l_data          myTableType := myTableType();
    l_rnum          number := 1;
begin
    dbms_sql.parse( l_theCursor,  p_query, dbms_sql.native );
    dbms_sql.describe_columns( l_theCursor, l_colCnt, l_descTbl );
```

```
    for i in 1 .. l_colCnt loop
        dbms_sql.define_column( l_theCursor, i, l_columnValue, 4000 );
    end loop;
    l_status := dbms_sql.execute(l_theCursor);
    while ( dbms_sql.fetch_rows(l_theCursor) > 0 )
    loop
        for i in 1 .. l_colCnt
        loop
            dbms_sql.column_value( l_theCursor, i, l_columnValue );
            l_data.extend;
            l_data(l_data.count) :=
              myScalarType( l_rnum, l_descTbl(i).col_name, l_columnValue );
        end loop;
        l_rnum := l_rnum+1;
    end loop;

    dbms_sql.close_cursor(l_theCursor);
    return l_data;
end cols_as_rows8i;
/
```

That's it. Now, in Oracle8i, you are ready to query:

```
ops$tkyte@ORA920> select *
  2      from TABLE( cast( cols_as_rows8i('select *
  3                                          from emp
  4                                         where rownum = 1')
  5                  as myTableType ) );

      RNUM CNAME                             VAL
---------- ------------------------------ ----------
         1 EMPNO                          7369
         1 ENAME                          SMITH
         1 JOB                            CLERK
         1 MGR                            7902
         1 HIREDATE                       17-DEC-80
         1 SAL                            800
         1 COMM
         1 DEPTNO                         20

8 rows selected.
```

Note that in Oracle8i you need to use the CAST .. AS *typename* syntax when using a PL/SQL function as a table source.

# GEN_DATA

When benchmarking two approaches to a problem or testing ideas, I frequently need to fill a table with data—just a bunch of random data values. For this, I use GEN_DATA, a small PL/SQL routine that uses DBMS_RANDOM to generate test data. To use it, I simply pass it a table name and the desired number of rows, like this:

```
ops$tkyte@ORA920> create table t ( x number(5,2), y date, z varchar2(10) );
Table created.

 ops$tkyte@ORA920> exec gen_data( 'T', 5 );
PL/SQL procedure successfully completed.

ops$tkyte@ORA920> select * from t;

          X Y             Z
---------- --------- ----------
     769.32 01-NOV-03 EobYtSewY
     217.99 09-OCT-05 qBPAhTKsw
     388.15 10-DEC-03 ITD
     412.96 24-MAR-06 NPVmAOIcJ
     600.64 17-AUG-04 zDcL

ops$tkyte@ORA920>
```

GEN_DATA builds an INSERT INTO SELECT statement that invokes DBMS_RANDOM for each column and uses ALL_OBJECTS to query from (to generate rows). Here is the commented code for GEN_DATA:

```
create or replace
procedure gen_data( p_tname in varchar2, p_records in number )
-- This routine is designed to be installed ONCE per database, hence
-- the CURRENT_USER AUTHORIZATION.
AUTHID CURRENT_USER
as
    l_insert long;
    l_rows   number default 0;
begin
    -- dbms_random can be very cpu intensive. I use dbms_application_info
    -- to instrument this routine, so I can monitor how far along it is
    -- from another session.  Every bulk insert will update v$session for us.
    dbms_application_info.set_client_info( 'gen_data ' || p_tname );

    -- The beginning of our insert into statement.  Using a direct path
    -- insert, if you alter your table to be nologging in an archive
    -- log mode database, it'll generate no redo (assuming the table
    -- is not indexed).
    l_insert := 'insert /*+ append */ into ' || p_tname ||
                ' select ';

    -- Now, we build the rest of our insert.  We select the datatype
    -- and size of each column.  MAXVAL is used for numbers only. Using
```

```
        -- the precision defined for the column, we determine the maximum number
        -- that we can stuff in there.
        for x in
        ( select data_type, data_length,
      nvl(rpad( '9',data_precision,'9')/power(10,data_scale),9999999999) maxval
            from user_tab_columns
           where table_name = upper(p_tname)
           order by column_id )
        loop
            -- If number, generate a number in the range 1 .. maxval.
            if ( x.data_type in ('NUMBER', 'FLOAT' ))
            then
                l_insert := l_insert ||
                            'dbms_random.value(1,' || x.maxval || '),';

            -- If a date/timestamp type, add some random number to sysdate.
            elsif ( x.data_type = 'DATE' or x.data_type like 'TIMESTAMP%' )
            then
                l_insert := l_insert ||
                    'sysdate+dbms_random.value(1,1000),';

            -- If a string, generate a random string between 1 and data length.
            -- bytes in length
            else
                l_insert := l_insert || 'dbms_random.string(''A'',
                    trunc(dbms_random.value(1,'|| x.data_length || '))),';
            end if;
        end loop;
        l_insert := rtrim(l_insert,',') ||
                    ' from all_objects where rownum <= :n';

    -- Now, we just execute the insert into as many times as needed
    -- in order to put L_ROWS rows in the table.  Since we are direct path
    -- loading, we must commit after each insert. In this case, since
    -- we are generating test data, it is OK from a transactional perspective.
    -- And since this operation should generate little redo in all cases,
    -- it will not affect our performance as well.
    loop
        execute immediate l_insert using p_records - l_rows;
        l_rows := l_rows + sql%rowcount;
        commit;
        dbms_application_info.set_module
        ( l_rows || ' rows of ' || p_records, '' );
        exit when ( l_rows >= p_records );
    end loop;
end;
/
```

# Index

# J

Java and VB, using bind variables with, 273–279
JDeveloper (and debugging), 156–160
Joining queries, 495–496
Joins, 465–484
   anti-joins, 477–481
   ask Tom, 473
   Cartesian, 473–477
   full outer, 481–484
   hash, 468–471
   index, 462–464
   natural, 465–466
   nested loops, 465–468
   outer, 466–468
   setting HASH_JOIN-ENABLED to control hash, 326
   sort-merge, 471–473
Joins, hash, 468–471
   hash natural joins, 468–469
   hash outer joins, 469–471
Joins, removing outer, 505–509
   object types, 508–509
   using single scalar subqueries, 508
   using two scalar subqueries, 507

# K

Keys, primary and foreign, 24

# L

Labs, don't test in dust-free, 33–34
LMT caveats, 221–226
   autoextend datafiles, 225
   legacy storage clauses, 225–226
   system-managed LMT allocation from files, 222–225
   uniformly sized extents, 221–222
LMTs (locally managed tablespaces), 216–226
   caveats, 221–226

obsolescence of DMTs, 216–217
   system-managed LMTs and objects, 217–219
   uniform extent sizes and objects, 220
Loading
   using external tables for direct-path, 409–411
   using external tables for parallel direct-path, 411
Lookup tables, read-only, 394–397
Lookups
   bulk processing for, 593–595
   single-row fetching for, 590–593
   single-statement operations for, 595–596
Lookups, making them work efficiently, 588–597
   bulk processing for lookups, 593–595
   single-row fetching for lookups, 590–593
   single-statement operations for lookups, 595–596
Loops, nested, 465–468

# M

Marks, full scans and high-water, 453–454
Memory, controlling PGA, 355–358
Merging, using external tables for, 411–412
Metrics, collect and log, 41–42
Middle tier checking, 26–28
   it's more secure, 28
   it's database independence, 28
   it's faster, 27
   it's more flexible, 27–28
Models
   designing data, 37–40
   don't use generic data, 34–37
Modes
   ALL_ROWS, 341–348
   choosing, 338–340
   FIRST-ROWS, 341–348
   RULE, 341

# Q

# T

## U

## V

## W

# INTERNATIONAL CONTACT INFORMATION

**AUSTRALIA**
McGraw-Hill Book Company
Australia Pty. Ltd.
TEL +61-2-9900-1800
FAX +61-2-9878-8881
http://www.mcgraw-hill.com.au
books-it_sydney@mcgraw-hill.com

**CANADA**
McGraw-Hill Ryerson Ltd.
TEL +905-430-5000
FAX +905-430-5020
http://www.mcgraw-hill.ca

**GREECE, MIDDLE EAST, & AFRICA**
**(Excluding South Africa)**
McGraw-Hill Hellas
TEL +30-210-6560-990
TEL +30-210-6560-993
TEL +30-210-6560-994
FAX +30-210-6545-525

**MEXICO (Also serving Latin America)**
McGraw-Hill Interamericana Editores
S.A. de C.V.
TEL +525-1500-5108
FAX +525-117-1589
http://www.mcgraw-hill.com.mx
carlos_ruiz@mcgraw-hill.com

**SINGAPORE (Serving Asia)**
McGraw-Hill Book Company
TEL +65-6863-1580
FAX +65-6862-3354
http://www.mcgraw-hill.com.sg
mghasia@mcgraw-hill.com

**SOUTH AFRICA**
McGraw-Hill South Africa
TEL +27-11-622-7512
FAX +27-11-622-9045
robyn_swanepoel@mcgraw-hill.com

**SPAIN**
McGraw-Hill/
Interamericana de España, S.A.U.
TEL +34-91-180-3000
FAX +34-91-372-8513
http://www.mcgraw-hill.es
professional@mcgraw-hill.es

**UNITED KINGDOM, NORTHERN,**
**EASTERN, & CENTRAL EUROPE**
McGraw-Hill Education Europe
TEL +44-1-628-502500
FAX +44-1-628-770224
http://www.mcgraw-hill.co.uk
emea_queries@mcgraw-hill.com

**ALL OTHER INQUIRIES Contact:**
McGraw-Hill/Osborne
TEL +1-510-420-7700
FAX +1-510-420-7703
http://www.osborne.com
omg_international@mcgraw-hill.com

# Sound Off!

Visit us at **www.osborne.com/bookregistration** and let us know what you thought of this book. While you're online you'll have the opportunity to register for newsletters and special offers from McGraw-Hill/Osborne.

## *We want to hear from you!*

# Sneak Peek

Visit us today at **www.betabooks.com** and see what's coming from McGraw-Hill/Osborne tomorrow!

Based on the successful software paradigm, Bet@Books™ allows computing professionals to view partial and sometimes complete text versions of selected titles online. Bet@Books™ viewing is free, invites comments and feedback, and allows you to "test drive" books in progress on the subjects that interest you the most.

# GET YOUR FREE SUBSCRIPTION
# TO ORACLE MAGAZINE

*Oracle Magazine* is essential gear for today's information technology professionals. Stay informed and increase your productivity with every issue of *Oracle Magazine*. Inside each free bimonthly issue you'll get:

- Up-to-date information on Oracle Database, E-Business Suite applications, Web development, and database technology and business trends
- Third-party news and announcements
- Technical articles on Oracle Products and operating environments
- Development and administration tips
- Real-world customer stories

IF THERE ARE OTHER ORACLE USERS AT YOUR LOCATION WHO WOULD LIKE TO RECEIVE THEIR OWN SUBSCRIPTION TO ORACLE MAGAZINE, PLEASE PHOTOCOPY THIS FORM AND PASS IT ALONG.

## Three easy ways to subscribe:

### ① Web
Visit our Web site at www.oracle.com/oraclemagazine. You'll find a subscription form there, plus much more!

### ② Fax
Complete the questionnaire on the back of this card and fax the questionnaire side only to +1.847.647.9735.

### ③ Mail
Complete the questionnaire on the back of this card and mail it to P.O. Box 1263, Skokie, IL 60076-8263

**Oracle Publishing**

○ Yes, please send me a FREE subscription to *Oracle Magazine* ○ NO

To receive a free subscription to *Oracle Magazine*, you must fill out the entire card, sign it, and date it (incomplete cards cannot be processed or acknowledged). You can also fax your application to +1.847.647.9735.

Or subscribe at our Web site at www.oracle.com/oraclemagazine/

○ From time to time, Oracle Publishing allows our partners exclusive access to our e-mail addresses for special promotions and announcements. To be included in this program, please check this box.

○ Oracle Publishing allows sharing of our mailing list with selected third parties. If you prefer your mailing address not to be included in this program, please check here. If at any time you would like to be removed from this mailing list, please contact Customer Service at +1.847.647.9630 or send an e-mail to oracle@halldata.com.

signature (required)

X

date

name                                                    title

company                                                 e-mail address

street/p.o. box

city/state/zip or postal code                           telephone

country                                                 fax

YOU MUST ANSWER ALL NINE QUESTIONS BELOW

**① WHAT IS THE PRIMARY BUSINESS ACTIVITY OF YOUR FIRM AT THIS LOCATION?** (check one only)

- ☐ 01 Application Service Provider
- ☐ 02 Communications
- ☐ 03 Consulting, Training
- ☐ 04 Data Processing
- ☐ 05 Education
- ☐ 06 Engineering
- ☐ 07 Financial Services
- ☐ 08 Government (federal, local, state, other)
- ☐ 09 Government (military)
- ☐ 10 Health Care
- ☐ 11 Manufacturing (aerospace, defense)
- ☐ 12 Manufacturing (computer hardware)
- ☐ 13 Manufacturing (noncomputer)
- ☐ 14 Research & Development
- ☐ 15 Retailing, Wholesaling, Distribution
- ☐ 16 Software Development
- ☐ 17 Systems Integration, VAR, VAD, OEM
- ☐ 18 Transportation
- ☐ 19 Utilities (electric, gas, sanitation)
- ☐ 98 Other Business and Services

**② WHICH OF THE FOLLOWING BEST DESCRIBES YOUR PRIMARY JOB FUNCTION?** (check one only)

Corporate Management/Staff
- ☐ 01 Executive Management (President, Chair, CEO, CFO, Owner, Partner, Principal)
- ☐ 02 Finance/Administrative Management (VP/Director/ Manager/Controller, Purchasing, Administration)
- ☐ 03 Sales/Marketing Management (VP/Director/Manager)
- ☐ 04 Computer Systems/Operations Management (CIO/VP/Director/ Manager MIS, Operations)

IS/IT Staff
- ☐ 05 Systems Development/ Programming Management
- ☐ 06 Systems Development/ Programming Staff
- ☐ 07 Consulting
- ☐ 08 DBA/Systems Administrator
- ☐ 09 Education/Training
- ☐ 10 Technical Support Director/Manager
- ☐ 11 Other Technical Management/Staff
- ☐ 98 Other

**③ WHAT IS YOUR CURRENT PRIMARY OPERATING PLATFORM?** (select all that apply)

- ☐ 01 Digital Equipment UNIX
- ☐ 02 Digital Equipment VAX VMS
- ☐ 03 HP UNIX
- ☐ 04 IBM AIX

- ☐ 05 IBM UNIX
- ☐ 06 Java
- ☐ 07 Linux
- ☐ 08 Macintosh
- ☐ 09 MS-DOS
- ☐ 10 MVS
- ☐ 11 NetWare
- ☐ 12 Network Computing
- ☐ 13 OpenVMS
- ☐ 14 SCO UNIX
- ☐ 15 Sequent DYNIX/ptx
- ☐ 16 Sun Solaris/SunOS
- ☐ 17 SVR4
- ☐ 18 UnixWare
- ☐ 19 Windows
- ☐ 20 Windows NT
- ☐ 21 Other UNIX
- ☐ 98 Other
- 99 ☐ None of the above

**④ DO YOU EVALUATE, SPECIFY, RECOMMEND, OR AUTHORIZE THE PURCHASE OF ANY OF THE FOLLOWING?** (check all that apply)

- ☐ 01 Hardware
- ☐ 02 Software
- ☐ 03 Application Development Tools
- ☐ 04 Database Products
- ☐ 05 Internet or Intranet Products
- 99 ☐ None of the above

**⑤ IN YOUR JOB, DO YOU USE OR PLAN TO PURCHASE ANY OF THE FOLLOWING PRODUCTS?** (check all that apply)

Software
- ☐ 01 Business Graphics
- ☐ 02 CAD/CAE/CAM
- ☐ 03 CASE
- ☐ 04 Communications
- ☐ 05 Database Management
- ☐ 06 File Management
- ☐ 07 Finance
- ☐ 08 Java
- ☐ 09 Materials Resource Planning
- ☐ 10 Multimedia Authoring
- ☐ 11 Networking
- ☐ 12 Office Automation
- ☐ 13 Order Entry/Inventory Control
- ☐ 14 Programming
- ☐ 15 Project Management
- ☐ 16 Scientific and Engineering
- ☐ 17 Spreadsheets
- ☐ 18 Systems Management
- ☐ 19 Workflow

Hardware
- ☐ 20 Macintosh
- ☐ 21 Mainframe
- ☐ 22 Massively Parallel Processing

- ☐ 23 Minicomputer
- ☐ 24 PC
- ☐ 25 Network Computer
- ☐ 26 Symmetric Multiprocessing
- ☐ 27 Workstation

Peripherals
- ☐ 28 Bridges/Routers/Hubs/Gateways
- ☐ 29 CD-ROM Drives
- ☐ 30 Disk Drives/Subsystems
- ☐ 31 Modems
- ☐ 32 Tape Drives/Subsystems
- ☐ 33 Video Boards/Multimedia

Services
- ☐ 34 Application Service Provider
- ☐ 35 Consulting
- ☐ 36 Education/Training
- ☐ 37 Maintenance
- ☐ 38 Online Database Services
- ☐ 39 Support
- ☐ 40 Technology-Based Training
- ☐ 98 Other
- 99 ☐ None of the above

**⑥ WHAT ORACLE PRODUCTS ARE IN USE AT YOUR SITE?** (check all that apply)

Software
- ☐ 01 Oracle9i
- ☐ 02 Oracle9i Lite
- ☐ 03 Oracle8
- ☐ 04 Oracle8i
- ☐ 05 Oracle8i Lite
- ☐ 06 Oracle7
- ☐ 07 Oracle9i Application Server
- ☐ 08 Oracle9i Application Server Wireless
- ☐ 09 Oracle Data Mart Suites
- ☐ 10 Oracle Internet Commerce Server
- ☐ 11 Oracle interMedia
- ☐ 12 Oracle Lite
- ☐ 13 Oracle Payment Server
- ☐ 14 Oracle Video Server
- ☐ 15 Oracle Rdb

Tools
- ☐ 16 Oracle Darwin
- ☐ 17 Oracle Designer
- ☐ 18 Oracle Developer
- ☐ 19 Oracle Discoverer
- ☐ 20 Oracle Express
- ☐ 21 Oracle JDeveloper
- ☐ 22 Oracle Reports
- ☐ 23 Oracle Portal
- ☐ 24 Oracle Warehouse Builder
- ☐ 25 Oracle Workflow

Oracle E-Business Suite
- ☐ 26 Oracle Advanced Planning/Scheduling
- ☐ 27 Oracle Business Intelligence
- ☐ 28 Oracle E-Commerce
- ☐ 29 Oracle Exchange
- ☐ 30 Oracle Financials

- ☐ 31 Oracle Human Resources
- ☐ 32 Oracle Interaction Center
- ☐ 33 Oracle Internet Procurement
- ☐ 34 Oracle Manufacturing
- ☐ 35 Oracle Marketing
- ☐ 36 Oracle Order Management
- ☐ 37 Oracle Professional Services Automation
- ☐ 38 Oracle Projects
- ☐ 39 Oracle Sales
- ☐ 40 Oracle Service
- ☐ 41 Oracle Small Business Suite
- ☐ 42 Oracle Supply Chain Management
- ☐ 43 Oracle Travel Management
- ☐ 44 Oracle Treasury

Oracle Services
- ☐ 45 Oracle.com Online Services
- ☐ 46 Oracle Consulting
- ☐ 47 Oracle Education
- ☐ 48 Oracle Support
- ☐ 98 ther
- 99 ☐ None of the above

**⑦ WHAT OTHER DATABASE PRODUCTS ARE IN USE AT YOUR SITE?** (check all that apply)

- ☐ 01 Access ☐ 08 Microsoft Access
- ☐ 02 Baan ☐ 09 Microsoft SQL Server
- ☐ 03 dbase ☐ 10 PeopleSoft
- ☐ 04 Gupta ☐ 11 Progress
- ☐ 05 BM DB2 ☐ 12 SAP
- ☐ 06 Informix ☐ 13 Sybase
- ☐ 07 Ingres ☐ 14 VSAM
- ☐ 98 Other
- 99 ☐ None of the above

**⑧ DURING THE NEXT 12 MONTHS, HOW MUCH DO YOU ANTICIPATE YOUR ORGANIZATION WILL SPEND ON COMPUTER HARDWARE, SOFTWARE, PERIPHERALS, AND SERVICES FOR YOUR LOCATION?** (check only one)

- ☐ 01 Less than $10,000
- ☐ 02 $10,000 to $49,999
- ☐ 03 $50,000 to $99,999
- ☐ 04 $100,000 to $499,999
- ☐ 05 $500,000 to $999,999
- ☐ 06 $1,000,000 and over

**⑨ WHAT IS YOUR COMPANY'S YEARLY SALES REVENUE?** (please choose one)

- ☐ 01 $500, 000, 000 and above
- ☐ 02 $100, 000, 000 to $500, 000, 000
- ☐ 03 $50, 000, 000 to $100, 000, 000
- ☐ 04 $5, 000, 000 to $50, 000, 000
- ☐ 05 $1, 000, 000 to $5, 000, 000

123101